THE LOST LIFE OF EVA BRAUN

Angela Lambert

St. Martin's Press ⚓ New York

Also by Angela Lambert

Unquiet Souls: The Indian Summer of the British Aristocracy
(Macmillan, London and New York, 1984)
1939: The Last Season of Peace
(Weidenfeld & Nicolson, London, 1989)
A Rather English Marriage
(Hamish Hamilton, London, 1992)

to my well-beloved German relatives:

my grandfather
Wilhelm (Willy) Schröder
(8 February 1877–1959)

and my great-aunt
Elizabeth (Lidy) Neubert
(1895–12 July 1981)

who spent the war in Hamburg, and endured

www.stmartins.com

Library of Congress Cataloging-in-Publication Data

Lambert, Angela.
    The lost life of Eva Braun / Angela Lambert.—1st U.S. ed.
      p. cm.
    Includes bibliographical references and index.
    ISBN-13: 978-0-312-36654-4
    ISBN-10: 0-312-36654-X
    1. Braun, Eva. 2. Spouses of heads of state—Germany—Biography. I. Title.

DD247.B66 L46 2007
943.086092—dc22
[B]

                                                        2006051160

First published in the United Kingdom by Century, an imprint of
The Random House Group Limited

First U.S. Edition: January 2007

10 9 8 7 6 5 4 3 2 1

Contents

Introduction   ix

PART 1 NEVER SUCH INNOCENCE AGAIN
1 The First Strange and Fatal Interview   3
2 Eva's Family   16
3 Eva, Goethe, Schubert and Bambi   26
4 Tedious Lessons and Rebellious Games   35
5 Hitler's Childhood   55

PART 2 ADOLF TO FÜHRER, SCHOOLGIRL TO MISTRESS
6 Eva Becomes Fräulein Braun, Hitler Becomes *Führer*   71
7 Bavaria, the German Idyll   91
8 Geli and Hitler and Eva   100
9 Dying to Be with Hitler   125
10 Diary of a Desperate Woman   148
11 The Photograph Albums and Home Movies   161

PART 3 MISTRESS-IN-WAITING
12 Eva Leaves Home   177
13 Mistress   191
14 1936 – Germany on Display: The Olympics   211

PART 4 THE BEST YEARS: IDLING AT THE BERGHOF
15 The Women on the Berg   225
16 Three, Three, the Rivals . . .   235

17 1937–9 – Eva at the Berghof: 'A Golden Cage' 253
18 1938–9 – The Last Summers of Peace 271

PART 5 THE WAR YEARS
19 1939 – War Approaches 281
20 Waiting for Hitler to Win the War 298
21 Eva, Gretl and Fegelein 311
22 1941–3 – What Could Eva Have Known? 323
23 . . . What Could Eva Have Done? 340
24 What Hitler Did 358

PART 6 CULMINATION
25 February 1944–January 1945 – Eva
at the Berghof with Gertraud 371
26 The Stauffenberg Plot and its Consequences 390
27 In the Bunker 401
28 Hitler's Last Stand 433
29 Frau Hitler for Thirty-six Hours 451

Aftermath 460
Acknowledgements 467
Select Bibliography 470
Appendix A 476
Index 477

Introduction

More than seven hundred biographies have been written about Adolf Hitler but this life of Eva Braun, his devoted mistress, is only the second in English and the first by someone of her own gender. Hitherto, the known facts of her life would hardly have filled a chapter. Yet the thirty-three years between her birth and death spanned momentous, murderous times during which she was closer to the *Führer* than any other woman. He in turn remained faithful to her throughout their relationship. She has almost been ignored by male historians, or dismissed as brainless, shallow and flighty. Hitler's associates thought Eva vulgar and insignificant. Their wives barely tolerated her. Nobody from their inner circle of friends and hangers-on bothered to record her in any detail and no one else knew of her existence. She was such an elusive figure that as late as June 1944 the British secret service still thought she was one of Hitler's secretaries.[1]

Inevitably, Adolf Hitler figures large in this book, *and* Eva Braun lets us glimpse a dictator through the eyes of someone who loved him. Through his relationship with her one begins to discern the private man; a secret Hitler who was afraid of intimacy with women and dreaded fatherhood, Hitler the soppy dog-lover, a man who loved the popular songs of the day as well as the operas of Wagner, who watched

---

1. see *Operation Foxley: The Plan to Kill Hitler*: Introduction by Mark Seaman, pubd 1998 by PRO: "*Gästehaus Hoher Göll* in woods behind the Berghof – accommodates Frl Eva (Evi) Braun, Hitler's secretary, and press chief Dr Dietrich, as well as *aides-de-camp* and less important guests."

trashy films and, for all his public adulation, still craved flattery and cosseting and cosy evenings at the Berghof. Eva realised that even dictators need home comforts and made it her job to provide them. And, she truly, single-mindedly, loved him.

I began this book in a state of comparative ignorance about the Third Reich and the events of World War Two. In the fifties, English schoolgirls were taught little military history beyond the reassuring fact that we always won. Questioning my mother was no help; she would close up and change the subject. When I embarked on this book, therefore, I turned to the latest, finest interpreters of that period, Michael Burleigh and Ian Kershaw, reading and annotating their books with care and admiration. I then read Gitta Sereny, an inspired chronicler not only of Albert Speer but the Germany of his time. By the time I had finished it, my 'Hitler and Eva library' extended across several shelves but those first three were my main guides and I owe them a beginner's thanks for enlightening me. They gave me a perspective on Eva and her contemporaries and the times in which she lived.

An accident of timing brought that ordinary girl, caught in the spotlight by her connection with Hitler, oddly close to me. Eva Braun came into the world on February 6, 1912. My German mother, Edith Schröder, was born a short month later, on March 5, 1912. Thanks to her, German was my first language: literally, my mother-tongue.

This account of Eva's life is larded with stories of my mother's parallel childhood. Her memories made the life I was trying to reconstruct, six decades after Eva's death, spring into focus. Both girls came from middle class families with no sons but three daughters; each was the middle child. Their older sisters had the same name: Ilse. As children they fell asleep to the same fairy tales and lullabies and learned to read and write from the same books. They studied the same school texts and – judging by family snapshots – wore the same clothes. In their teens and twenties Fräulein Braun and Fräulein Schröder would have heard the same popular songs – '*Schläger*' as they were called – (meaning, literally, hits); songs such as – for those who remember them too – *Heimat deine Sterne; Vergiss mein Nicht*[2] and – my mother's favourite – *Schau mich bitte nicht so an: Please Don't Look at Me Like That,* to the tune of *La Vie en Rose.* My mother hummed and sang them while I was growing up. She and Eva also shared a passion for

2. the titles translate as: *Home to Your Star* and *Don't Forget Me.*

films and film stars and the names of those whom Eva admired stirred long-forgotten echoes of the stars my mother had raved about, starting in childhood with Grock, the famously sad clown, and moving on in adolescence to the singers Zarah Leander, Lotte Lenya and the iconic Marlene Dietrich.

This biography was enormously helped by those coincidences.[3] The events that shaped Eva's girlhood also shaped my mother's. Nice *bürgerliche* (middle class) German girls who were twelve in 1924, seventeen in 1929, or twenty-one in 1933, had a great deal in common – but unlike millions of their contemporaries, neither Eva nor Edith ever joined the Nazi Party.

For a proper understanding of Eva and my mother and those who grew up with them, I began by studying the times in which they lived. Around them surged vast choruses of marching soldiers, stadiums full of gymnasts forming the Nazi insignia, farmhands and schoolgirls shining with health and fervour, factory workers and slave labourers working round the clock to turn out fighter planes, tanks, antiaircraft guns, uniforms, boots – never enough boots – for the glory of *Führer* and Fatherland. But behind these displays of blondness, vigour and patriotism, seen not as individuals or even dots but a dark mass, spreading like a bloodstain, were those judged unworthy to live and bear children in the Thousand Year Reich: the mentally and physically handicapped, homosexuals, gypsies and, in their millions, the Jews of Europe, all of whom the wholesome efficient Germans were being taught to hate and kill without scruple.

Nerin Gun,[4] a Turkish/American journalist, published a biography of Eva Braun in 1968, at a time when many of her family and friends

---

3. A further tiny coincidence cropped up when I was halfway through writing this book. Browsing a Web site selling Eva memorabilia, I found her silver propelling pencil on offer (for $350). It was identical to the one my mother used for fifty years.

4. A former free-lance journalist and writer working for Swiss newspapers and the Turkish press service in Berlin. For his reports to the world about the Warsaw ghetto and predictions of the defeat of the German armies in Russia, he was arrested by the Nazis and sent to eleven prisons and three concentrations camps, ending at Dachau. One of only two foreign correspondents accredited to Berlin to have been put into a concentration camp solely because of his journalistic activities, he was still at Dachau when it was liberated on April 29, 1945, by American troops of the U.S. Seventh Army.

were still alive.[5] He used his investigative skills as a newspaper reporter to track down some of the people who had been close to Eva and persuaded them to talk about her at length. Gun himself and all his informants are now dead but I have drawn on a few of his anecdotes, although the indignation of Eva's family at the way he "trivialised" her life suggests that his accuracy cannot be relied on. His book is anecdotal rather than authoritative, cites few dates, has not a single footnote and no bibliographical references, so nothing he asserts can be verified.[6] Even the jacket photograph has been doctored. It made little impact and is now hardly to be found outside the rare or neo-Nazi books section of Internet booksellers.

David Irving knew Nerin Gun and described him as 'my good friend' – which, given Irving's notoriety as a Holocaust denier[7], may be signif-

5. This biography, entitled *Hitler's Mistress: Eva Braun*, was published in 1968. It has long been out of print and I have not been able to trace the author's research papers or interview transcripts. David Irving described Gun, now dead, as 'my good friend.' Irving lost a libel action in April 2000 that he had brought against the historian Deborah Lipstadt, for asserting that he [Irving] had knowingly lied in his academic and historical writing. At the end the judge, Mr Justice Gray, called him "a liar, a distorter of historical evidence, an anti-Semitic racist and a 'Holocaust-denier'." Eva Braun's family greeted Gun's book with indignation and dismay, as described by her cousin GW in an e-mail to the author dated February 19, 2004: "As to Nerin Gun, when I visited my cousin Ilse in Munich in October 1978, she told me about the interview with him. She was highly indignant about it. My uncle [Alois Winbauer] had already sent her the book, which, he pointed out, was untrustworthy and sensationalised. My uncle had himself been a journalist and had reported on the Nuremberg Trials." "*Zu Nerin Gun: als ich meine Cousine Ilse im Oktober 78 in München besucht habe, hat sie mir von dem Interview mit Gun erzählt. Sie war höchst indigniert über ihn und schon vorher hat mir mein Onkel das Buch geschickt mit dem Hinweis, dass er unglaubwürdig und sensationslüstern an das Buch heran gegangen ist. Mein Onkel ist selbst Journalist gewesen, hat auch über die Nürnberger Prozesse berichtet.*"
6. I contacted Nerin Gun's publishers in case they had any information about his interview notes, but was told: "What old files we did have got lost in the floods of 1993."
7. In April 2000 Irving lost a libel action in the British High Court that he had brought against historian Deborah Lipstadt for asserting that he had knowingly lied in his academic and historical writing. At the end the judge, Mr Justice Gray, called Irving "a liar, a distorter of historical evidence, an anti-Semitic racist and a Holocaust denier." The case, apart from proving the bias that had long been asserted against him, almost bankrupted Irving and destroyed his claims to be a reliable historian of the Third Reich. He is currently imprisoned in Austria for entering that country illegally, in order to attend neo-Nazi meetings.

icant. When I contacted him in the hope that he might know the whereabouts of Gun's original interview notes, he invited me to his London apartment to discuss the matter, saying "I could be very helpful to you."

Arrogant and defiant, Irving made no attempt to hide his contempt for me (a woman, lacking proper academic credentials[8]) and also for Eva Braun herself. In spite of this he helped me to gain access to Eva's original hand-written diary and suggested that I trawl the back catalogues of a Munich auction house specialising in Third Reich memorabilia in my search for crucial evidence that she never joined the Nazi Party.

When it came to discovering new sources of information about her, beyond a handful of official dates and addresses, I had to dig deep for evidence – both written and oral – from the few remaining people who had known her. My most valuable informant was her younger cousin, Gertraud Weisker, who had spent time alone with Eva (along with a score of servants and security guards) at the Berghof in July 1944, when she (Gertraud) was twenty. I met her fifty years later, thanks to the generosity of filmmaker Marion Milne, who had just completed the award-winning documentary *Adolf and Eva*[9], in which Frau Weisker was interviewed.

On April 2, 2001, I flew to Frankfurt and in the small village of Eppelheim, near Heidelberg, I met Frau Weisker. Although in her late seventies she was full of energy, warmly hospitable and, since she had kept the family connection secret for more than fifty years, her memories were crystal clear. Her parents had been resolutely anti-Nazi (Red Cross records verified that her father had secretly worked against the party) and Gertraud was adamant that her own views had never changed. She hated Hitler. 'It has weighed on me all my life,' she said, 'that my beloved cousin sacrificed her life to a mass murderer.'[10]

On that first occasion Frau Weisker and I talked for several hours and I gained a vivid impression of the young woman, her cousin, who had lived in Hitler's shadow. My interest in Eva Braun dates from that

8. a degree from Oxford in Philosophy, Politics and Economics rather than History, let alone Third Reich history.
9. first shown on ITV, April 29, 2001.
10. Gertraud Weisker to the author, August 25, 2005: '*Es bedrückt mich doch ein Leben lang, dass meine-Lieblingscousine ihr Leben einem Massenmörder geopfert hat.*'

day. We met several more times and Frau Weisker showed me her private family albums with photographs of a smiling Eva, the figure beside her scissored out. Most German Catholics had opposed the Nazis and the Braun family were deeply ashamed of Eva's link with him. In a reversal of the usual procedure – pictures of Eva with him were censored and they were never photographed together in public – her mother had literally cut Hitler out of the picture.

When Fräulein Braun first met the *Führer* she was seventeen and fresh from her convent school, attractive but not beautiful, not by any means stupid but limited by the tastes of her class and age; quite unsuited to bear the weight of history. Because she was Hitler's mistress, people tend to assume she must have been a dedicated Nazi and a racist. In researching this book my main purpose was to discover whether this was true. She had started life as a decent, well-brought-up Catholic girl with a strong moral sense and like the rest of her family, she was not anti-Semitic. For Hitler's sake Eva gave up everything that might have fulfilled her in life . . . marriage, motherhood, her own home, the pride and approval of her parents . . . to become the unacknowledged shadow behind Hitler's public acclaim and eventual downfall. In April 1945, as the Russian army advanced through the rubble of Berlin, she committed suicide with him in the bunker. By then she had been his mistress for fourteen years, yet hardly a soul in the outside world knew her name or her face. Hitler had kept her out of the public eye so successfully that she lived and died anonymously.

Did she make these sacrifices for the man himself or because she shared his ideology? I was baffled by her sheer ordinariness and by the difficulty of solving the riddle: who was she? So little is known about her that she remained an enigma, both at the time and today – an enigma that I wanted to explore. Did she (and by extension all German women, including my mother) share Hitler's and the Nazi Party's guilt for the atrocities of the Second World War, above all for the slaughter of millions of Jews and others that has come to be known as the Holocaust?[11] Were those acts of mass murder the crime of a whole nation, or did they result from the racism of a short-lived

---

11. In the minds of many people 'the Holocaust' has come to signify the mass murder of Europe's Jews, but I use it in this book to include the genocide of millions more people deemed by the Nazis 'unfit to live' . . . all the racial (Roma or Gypsy), ethnic (Poles, chiefly, religious: Roman Catholic and Jehovah's Witness) and political minorities, as well as the mentally handicapped and homosexuals.

political party whose followers turned its leader's ideology into heaps of corpses?

My mother was a product of her time. She always refused to discuss the fate of the Jewish schoolfriends in Hamburg with whom she had played in the days when it was still an easy-going, liberal port. On a rare occasion when she was already over eighty and becoming forgetful, I asked – knowing it could be my last chance – what had become of them. My mother said:

> "They were from rich families . . . so, when the war came . . . they went away . . . on holiday."
> "And did you see them again?"
> "No. They never came back. Being Jewish they could afford not to, you see."

My mother loved reminiscing about what were, for her, the happy, innocent days of her childhood and youth. Those stories, which I heard over and over again as I grew up, overlap seamlessly with Eva's. I wish now that I had questioned more and listened better.

PART 1
NEVER SUCH INNOCENCE AGAIN

Chapter One

The First Strange and Fatal Interview

Schellingstrasse runs from west to east through the heart of Munich, parallel with the grand trio of art galleries known collectively as the Pinakothek. It's a main artery of Schwabing, a district whose atmosphere combines London's Bloomsbury and Soho, the bookish and the raffish.[1] The German word *Schellen* (as in Schellingstrasse) can mean anything from a jack of diamonds to the jingling of bells, a Turkish crescent, a Chinese pavilion or a fool's cap – images that epitomise the maverick, playful nature of the street. Prosaically, it is more likely to have been named after Friedrich Schelling,[2] the nineteenth-century German philosopher. Today it is lined with bars (more beer than wine, this being Munich), book shops (with well-thumbed textbooks set out on trays on the pavement), cafés (providing free newspapers for their patrons), restaurants and tatty second-hand clothes shops. These cater to a hard-up bohemian crowd, mainly students from the surrounding university faculties. Eva Braun, between the ages of seventeen and twenty-five, spent more of her life in this street than anywhere else, not because she was having fun or studying but because she was working as apprentice and counter assistant at Photo Hoffmann; a

1. Ernst 'Putzi' Hanfstängl, of whom much more will be heard later, called it 'the Montparnasse of Munich' (*Unheard Witness*, p. 31).
2. Christiane Gehron points out that Friedrich Schelling was the *Wunderkind* of German idealism. Born 27 January 1775, Leonberg, near Stuttgart, Württemberg; died 20 August 1854, Bad Ragaz, Switzerland. Philosopher and educator, a major figure of German idealism, in the post-Kantian development in German philosophy. Ennobled by the addition of *von* to his name in 1806. (Source: www.britannica.com/eb/article?tocld=9066105).

flourishing camera supply shop and photographic studio that occupied the ground floor and basement of number 50.[3] Today there is no sign, plaque or indication to the casual passer-by that here, in October 1929, Eva Braun came face to face with Adolf Hitler for the first time.

Heinrich Hoffmann, who owned the shop, had been quick to spot Hitler's potential as a political leader and iconic figure and shrewdly secured the job of his official photographer as early as 1922, when the rabble-rousing orator from the NSDAP (*National Sozialistische Deutsche Arbeiterpartei*, or National Socialist German Workers' Party, soon shortened to Nazi Party) scarcely seemed worth recording. Over the next two decades Hoffmann took two and a half million photographs of the *Führer*, providing a comprehensive history of the man and the Reich.[4] He also took a commission on each picture sold, making him a millionaire within the decade and a multimillionaire ten years later. Host and parasite served one another's purpose. Each was invaluable to the other and Hoffmann knew it, and jealously guarded his privileged position.

Eva had been keen on photography ever since she was given her first camera at the age of about thirteen. Four years later she had progressed from out-of-focus pictures of grinning schoolfriends to more ambitious back-lit shots of the family posed on the balcony. She took pictures of herself (always her favourite subject) in front of the mirror in fancy-dress costume or her latest party frock. Her father hoped to encourage this small talent and Eva was sure that learning to be a photographer would be more exciting than life as a secretary in some dreary office. Photo Hoffmann was ideally placed at the centre of student and artistic life, being a few tram stops or, if she could get up in time, a brisk twenty minutes' walk from the family flat. All this appealed to her, though it fell short of her secret ambitions.

When little Eva Braun applied for a job in Hoffmann's shop, he liked her face and her vivacity. On this slender basis, she was hired. She started

3. Shortly after she started work there the business and shop moved to nearby Amalienstrasse, but Eva continued to frequent Schellingstrasse because it remained the hub of Hitler's Party and leisure activities.
4. Much of it is now in the Hoffmann Picture Archive (Bildarchiv Hoffmann) at Munich's Bayerische StaatsBibliothek.

at the beginning of October 1929[5] as a junior assistant and apprentice in the studio and darkroom next door. Her duties included serving behind the counter, typing invoices, filing, learning how to process film and print photographs in the studio, running errands and occasionally modelling for her employer – never, of course, other than fully clothed.

On that momentous October evening in 1929, Eva had only been working in the shop for two or three weeks when Hitler arrived from the Braun Haus – the Nazi Party headquarters further up Schellingstrasse – to select photographs from a recent sitting. He was the first politician to grasp the importance of projecting the right image, and he scrutinised every print. Self-conscious about his bulbous nose and unusually large nostrils (the moustache was intended to obscure them), he retained absolute control over his image, deciding how he should be presented to the German people and censoring any photograph that showed him in an unflattering light. The best would be issued as official portraits.

Hitler turned up at Hoffmann's discreetly, at closing time. When he entered the shop Eva was not in the least intimidated by the stranger towards whom her employer was being unusually genial and ingratiating. She was a well-brought-up girl who had been taught manners by her parents and her convent school so she was polite to Hitler although she hadn't the least idea who he was. That evening, it seems, she told her sister Ilse what happened next:

> I had climbed up a ladder to reach the files that were kept on the top shelves of the cupboard. At that moment the boss came in, accompanied by a man of a certain age with a funny moustache, a light-coloured English-style overcoat[6] and a big felt hat in his hand. They both sat down on the other side of the room,

5. Eva's uncle, Alois Winbauer, claims that Gretl also worked for Hoffmann (see *Eva Braun's Familiengeschichte*, p.10. (This private account by Dr Alois Winbauer, written in 1976 at the request of his niece, Gertraud Weisker, has never before been published.). If he is right, she can't have started at the same time as Eva since she would only have been fourteen. Heinrich Hoffmann, in his memoir, *Hitler Was My Friend*, says on p. 160, 'Gretl was also one of my employees' but does not say when, or in what capacity she worked for him. Winbauer was writing more than forty years after the event so he may have been mistaken; nobody else mentions Gretl being in the shop.
6. Hitler invariably wore a belted, fawn Burberry raincoat at this stage of his career, like a private eye in a thirties film.

opposite me. I tried to squint in their direction and sensed that this character was looking at my legs. That very day I had shortened my skirt and I felt slightly embarrassed because I wasn't sure that I had got the hem even.[7]

She climbed down from the ladder and Hoffmann presented her fulsomely as: 'Our good little Fräulein Eva . . .' before introducing their visitor as 'Herr Wolf' – Hitler's preferred alias, part of the blackly romantic imagery he liked to create around himself.

It was part of Eva's job at Photo Hoffmann to develop and print, enlarge and make copies of, among others, Hitler's publicity photographs. She spent hours under the ruby-red light of the studio

---

7. From Nerin E. Gun, Hitler's Mistress: Eva Braun (Meredith Press, New York 1968). Gun was a former freelance journalist and writer working for Swiss newspapers and the Turkish press service in Berlin. For his reports to the world about the Warsaw ghetto and predictions of the defeat of the German armies in Russia, he was arrested by the Nazis and sent to eleven prisons and three concentration camps, ending at Dachau. One of only two foreign correspondents accredited to Berlin to have been put into a concentration camp solely because of his journalistic activities, he was still at Dachau when it was liberated on 29 April 1945 by American troops of the US seventh army. Gun's biography, published in 1968, has long been out of print and I have not been able to trace the author's research papers or interview transcripts. His publishers tell me that any notes or original notes they might have held from his research for the biography of Eva were destroyed by a flood at their premises in 1993. Eva Braun's family greeted Gun's book with indignation and dismay, as described by her cousin Gertrude Weisker in an email to the author dated 19 February 2004: 'As to Nerin Gun, when I visited my cousin Ilse in Munich in October 1978, she told me about the interview with him. She was highly indignant about it. My uncle (Alois Winbauer) had already sent her the book, which, he pointed out, was untrustworthy and sensationalised. My uncle had himself been a journalist and had reported on the Nuremburg trails. 'Zu Nerin Gun: als ich meine Cousine Ilse im Oktober 78 in München besucht habe, hat sie mir von dem Interview mit Gun erzählt. Sie war höchst indigniert über ihn und schon vorher hat mir mein Onkel das Buch geschickt mit dem Hinweis, dass er unglaubwürdig und sensationslüstern an das Buch heran gegangen ist. Mein Onkel ist selbst Journalist gewesen, hat auch über die Nürnberger Prozesse berichtet.' David Irving knew Nerin Gun, now dead, and described him as 'my good friend'. Irving lost a libel action in April 2000 that he had brought against the historian Deborah Lipstadt, for asserting that he [Irving] had knowingly lied in his academic and historical writing. At the end the judge, Mr Justice Gray, called him 'a liar, a distorter of historical evidence, an anti-Semitic racist and a "Holocaust-denier"'.

darkroom, poring over strong-smelling chemicals, swirling them round the developing tank, watching the white sheets of photographic paper darken and coalesce into the glowering face of Adolf Hitler. His stern, unsmiling gaze and the subliminal message it conveyed were to be imprinted on the mind of every German. Eva's task, bent over the tank and counting down the seconds until the image was correctly developed, and one endlessly repeated, would over time stamp his features on her consciousness like a watermark.

Heinrich Hoffmann later described Eva Braun as she was then:

In spite of her nineteen years[8] she had a somewhat naive and childish air. Of medium height, she was greatly preoccupied with her slim and elegant figure. Her round face and blue eyes, framed by darkish blonde hair, made a picture that could only be described as pretty – an impersonal, chocolate-box type of prettiness. [. . .] She had not yet aspired to lipstick and painted fingernails.

Her younger cousin Gertraud Weisker, source of many personal insights about Eva, said:

She had dreamed of an artistic career, either as a photographer or in the cinema. She was twelve years older than me and as a child I hero-worshipped her. She was not vain, but conscious of the effect her 'dreamy beauty' had on others. Even in those days she was vivacious and feminine; already dedicated to her appearance. She was interested in clothes and fashion, mad about sport, and she liked to take pictures. That was her world. [. . .] When she met Hitler she was a very healthy young girl, full of life and curiosity. She was sporty – she bicycled to the nearby lakes and like me and my parents, climbed the mountains, sleeping in little huts . . . She was simply a very nice young girl.[9]

Her new employer needs a proper introduction. He had been the only other person present at Adolf and Eva's original meeting – which he would have encouraged – and he remained a figure of lasting importance to both for the rest of their lives.

8. In October 1929 Eva was in fact seventeen and a half years old.
9. Gertraud Weisker in conversation with the author, 2 April 2001, at her house in Eppelheim, Bavaria.

One of the first men to join the newly founded NSDAP, or Nazi Party, in 1920, Heinrich Hoffmann was four years older than Hitler. His father had been court photographer to Prince Regent Luitpold and King Ludwig III and young Heinrich had worked in the family shop as a boy. In 1908 he opened his own premises at 33 Schellingstrasse, later expanding into the larger shop at number 50. During the First World War he had served as an official cameraman in the Bavarian army. He met Adolf Hitler in 1919 when Hitler was thirty and the two men took to each other at once. It was the start of a lifelong friendship.

Heinrich Hoffmann, though generous and convivial, was a chancer, a fixer, a manipulator, quick to exploit a person or a situation to his own advantage. When their relationship began he was already well established and prosperous, unlike Hitler who hadn't enjoyed home comforts for years. From 1920 onwards the unkempt and as yet little known Adolf was a constant visitor to Hoffmann's house, enjoying the lavish hospitality of his beautiful first wife Lelly and playing with their two small children, Henriette, or 'Henny', and Heinrich, or 'Heini'. The family home in the smart Munich suburb of Bogenhausen became a haven, a place where he could relax, enjoy home-baked cakes and talk about art and music – subjects on which both men considered themselves experts. Soon Hitler was spending so much time at the Hoffmann villa that it had become almost his second home.

Even in those early days Hoffmann hadn't been exactly abstemious and, after Lelly's death in 1928, his behaviour degenerated from wit and gusto into drunken boorishness. Yet he remained one of Hitler's closest and most trusted colleagues; one hesitates to use the word 'friend' only because it's doubtful that Hitler was capable of having a real friend. His pictures of the *Führer* sold in their tens of thousands, postcards by the million. Hoffmann expertly boosted his subject's appeal with heroic poses and artful lighting, transforming his mentor into the last and greatest of the Teutonic Knights. Through his lens, in his studio, he created the mythical, long-awaited leader destined to lead Germany into a glorious thousand-year future.

In 1929, when Adolf Hitler first met guileless young Eva Braun, he was already well known in Munich as the orator and driving force behind the NSDAP. His face should have been familiar to her from Hoffmann's pictures as well as newspapers and posters, but Eva didn't recognise him. Despite having grown up in the city that was the birth-place and epicentre of the Nazi Party, Eva's knowledge of politics was scant and her interest nil. Her family mistrusted and disliked the Nazis, who in turn despised Christianity for its Judaic roots. If Hitler's name were ever mentioned in Eva's home, her father Fritz Braun would no doubt have dismissed him outright. At their first meeting it was beyond Eva's – beyond anyone's – imagination to picture the genocide. Hitler would initiate, even if she'd read *Mein Kampf*,[10] which she certainly hadn't. Her convent sermons had evoked the Devil and all his works with sadistic hellfire imagery that presaged the gas ovens of Auschwitz, but in 1929 no one yet suspected what was to come, except the handful of men close to Hitler whose dream, like his, went beyond anti-Semitism to the complete annihilation of the Jews. Now, in the light of what we have learned about the Holocaust, about the decade between 1935 and 1945, we cannot see him without the retrospective contempt of history, but at the time Hitler made a very different impression. Already a charismatic public figure, he could be equally charismatic in private.

It may be anathema to those who regard him as the incarnation of evil but the truth is that the German *Führer* was far from being overtly sinister or repellent, let alone an absurd little fellow with a black cow's lick over his forehead and a toothbrush moustache, as portrayed by Charlie Chaplin in *The Great Dictator*. Quite the reverse. Hitler was a most attractive man, particularly when talking to impressionable young women, whom he liked to charm. Everyone agreed that his gaze, through eyes as blue as forget-me-nots, was mesmerising.[11] Like all extremely powerful men, especially politicians, Hitler projected a force field that was impossible to resist. Seen through the eyes of a gullible girl, fresh from the convent and meeting him for the first time, he would have radiated magnetism. Gitta Sereny, whose books castigate the evils of the Nazi régime, told me: 'As far as his looks were concerned, I met him once, in Berlin in 1940, and was actually surprised at how nice-looking he was. He wasn't ugly. He was well-groomed, extremely clean and always smelled freshly of soap, although he did have halitosis, which he

10. *Mein Kampf* (*My Struggle*) was the book, written in prison and later in Hitler's retreat in Bavaria between 1923 and 1926, that gave a (far from accurate) picture of his life until he was thirty and set out his political ambitions and ideology. To anyone reading between the lines his anti-Semitism was obvious, though not so the extremes to which it would finally lead.
11. Cf Herbert Döring, manager at the Berghof: 'Just the look in his eyes . . . he could really bore through you with that stare. It rendered anyone powerless.' Interview with Marion Milne.

fought with constant tooth-cleaning.'[12] She stressed the uncomfortable truth:

> Power is very attractive, you know. It's a huge sexual come-on. And of course Hitler had considerable charm. He had far, far more intelligence than most people want to admit. He was an extremely intelligent man who was a monster. He liked to be surrounded by women, he enjoyed chit-chat, hand-kissing and all that and was incredibly charming to those close to him.

This, not a monster, was the so-called 'Herr Wolf' whom Eva encountered. Seen through the eyes of a gullible girl, fresh from her convent and meeting him for the first time, he would have radiated magnetism.

Yet quite why a giddy seventeen-year-old should have been so powerfully drawn to a man much older than herself remains a mystery. When an ignorant girl meets any man who takes an interest in her she's bound to be flattered, but there was more to it than that. The histrionic explanation would be that he was Eva's destiny, as he was Germany's destiny. Their relationship is worth investigating because his treatment of this one young woman – first enthralling, then dominating and finally destroying her – reflects in microcosm the way he also seduced and destroyed the German people.

The Hoffmanns' comfortable house in Schnorrstrasse was five minutes' walk from the shop and conveniently close to the party's headquarters. It was here that Hitler met like-minded friends including Ernst Röhm and Bernhardt Stempfle, men who crucially helped to shape his political philosophy, and they would become overexcited and garrulous over beer and cigars (except for Hitler, who detested smoking and alcohol), projecting visions of a glorious Nazi future that as yet only a few thousand converts believed in. Hoffmann, by providing this Nazi 'salon', the seedbed of its racist ideology, was a formative influence.

At other times it was simply a place where the *Führer*, who had been effectively homeless since his mid-teens, could relax and feel at ease in, a family home. 'After lunch at the restaurant Osteria Bavaria,' Albert Speer remembered later,

12. Conversation with the author, London, 5 August 2003.

he would go on to his next destination: the home of his photographer in Munich-Bogenhausen. In good weather coffee would be served in the Hoffmanns' little garden. Surrounded by the gardens of other villas, it was hardly more than 2000 feet square. Hitler tried to resist the cake but finally consented, with many compliments to Frau Hoffmann, to have some put on his plate. If the sun were shining brightly, the *Führer* and Reichs Chancellor might even take off his coat and lie down on the grass in shirt-sleeves. At the Hoffmanns he felt at home.[13]

Hitler called their daughter Henny, who was exactly a year younger than Eva, '*mein Sonnenschein*' (my sunshine) and he became so fond of her that at one stage her father even hoped the two might marry; but this was an ambition too far. Hitler wasn't looking for a relationship let alone marriage, not with little Henny and even less with some 'alpha-female', as brainy as she was beautiful. He was not ready to marry, now or ever, for reasons that not even Hoffmann guessed.

When she came on the scene, Eva Braun was dismissed by Hitler's friends and acolytes as a feather-brained nonentity. They would have preferred the *Führer* to consort with someone more sophisticated, elegant, polished; they failed to grasp that it was precisely her lack of these qualities that suited him. Even so, Hitler might never have picked her out had she not single-mindedly pursued him over the next two years, aided by the machinations of Hoffmann, who contrived to bring her to his notice as often as possible. Herbert Döring, who had known both men since the 1920s, recalled:

'My wife and Hitler's sister[14] always said after the war that in the ordinary course of events Hitler and Eva Braun would never have come together. But Hoffmann was so cunning in the way he continued to present the girl as if on a silver platter, presented her like this to Hitler. He kept holding her out until Hitler took the bait.'[15]

13. Speer, *Inside the Third Reich*, p. 81.
14. Döring's wife Anna was Hitler's cook and Angela Raubal, Hitler's half-sister, his housekeeper in Munich – though Döring could be referring to the full sister, Paula.
15. Unpublished transcript of an interview with Herbert Döring in Munich, recorded winter 2000/2001, for the television documentary *Adolf and Eva*, 3BMTV.

Hitler's sex drive seems never to have been strong, judging by his long periods of celibacy, but when he did feel sexually attracted it was invariably to girls half his age – sixteen was not too young, twenty almost too old. Heinrich Hoffmann's daughter Henriette recalled encountering him in her nightdress when she was only twelve (this would have been around 1924, when Hitler was a frequent visitor to the Hoffmanns' house) and he asked if he might kiss her. She responded with a horrified 'No!' and he did not insist. In the autumn of 1926, when he was thirty-seven, he had a brief flirtation with a sixteen-year-old, Maria ('Mimi') Reiter, whom he had met in Berchtesgaden. They got as far as kissing in a forest glade but the encounter was fleeting and Hitler did not pursue it. For Maria it was serious enough for her to have considered it a prelude to marriage and to prompt a bungled suicide attempt.[16] Until he was forty, Hitler's only other girlfriend, according to Anna Winter who later became his housekeeper in Munich, was a charming teenager called Ada Klein who, realising that Hitler would never marry her, sensibly went off and married someone else.[17] Like his father, Adolf preferred girls who were virgin, malleable and unthreatening, but in his own case the reason must have had a lot to do with the fact that he remained a virgin for so long. A woman who was sexually experienced would have posed too much of a threat. With the possible exception of Winifred Wagner, doyenne of the Wagner family, the *Führer* never risked being challenged by a relationship with a woman of his own age. Even Winifred was eight years his

16. Kershaw, *Hitler, 1889–1936: Hubris.* It is not easy for a young woman to survive being close to a dictator, or even a genius. Nadezhda Alliluyeva, Stalin's much younger wife, committed suicide in 1932, thirteen years after meeting him. Modigliani's mistress, Jeanne Hébuterne, was nine months pregnant when she killed herself in January 1920, two days after his death from TB. So eventually did Picasso's widow, Jacqueline. Powerful men are hard to live with – or without.

Gertraud Weisker drew my attention to other parallels between Hitler and Stalin. On 8 July 2005 she wrote: 'Both loved their mothers and were loved by them with equal ardour. Throughout her life Stalin's mother made jam for her beloved son. (!)' '*Es gibt eine Ähnlichkeit zwischen Hitler und Stalin. Beide lieben ihre Mütter und werden von ihnen ebenso heiß geliebt. Stalins Mutter hat zeit ihres Lebens Marmelade für ihren lieben Sohn gekocht.*'

17. Musmanno Collection, Vol. XII, Gumberg Library, Duquesne University, Pittsburgh, PA. This assertion is suspect, since Ada Klein is not mentioned in any major biography of Hitler, or in the memoirs of his close friends.

junior, although her matronly figure and severe hairstyle made her seem older.[18]

Heinrich Hoffmann described – no doubt with the help of hindsight – the first impression Eva Braun had made on Hitler, without mentioning his own role as go-between: 'Sweet. Pretty in a sweet way. Blonde. Next time Hitler saw her, he gave her some tickets to the theatre. Finally he invited her to go and see him . . . in Munich, in his apartment. Somebody had to be present – a chaperone. He was very cautious in those things at that time.'[19] Later on he wrote in his memoirs:

> Hitler knew all my employees and it was among them that he first made the acquaintance of Eva Braun, with whom he sometimes chatted in a normal, quite inconsequential manner; occasionally he would come out of his shell a little and pay her the sort of little compliment he was so fond of paying women. Neither I myself nor any of my employees noticed that he paid her any particular attention. But not so Eva; she told her all her friends that Hitler was wildly in love with her and that she would [. . .] marry him.[20]

In spite of photographs taken in beer halls or nightclubs showing her cuddling up to some strapping, smirking youth it seems that the romantic cliché was true: when she met Adolf Hitler, Eva Braun met her destiny.

Her cousin Gertraud recalled, 'If you look at some of those old films of the female Hitler Youth,[21] pigtails were the thing. They were supposed to be natural and unspoilt. We were told that German women don't smoke, don't drink, don't wear make-up. But Eva never fitted that stereotype.'[22] Fritz Braun, as well as the dictates of the Nazi Party, disapproved of cosmetics, but this merely obliged Eva to apply lipstick, rouge

---

18. She was also a good three inches taller than Hitler while Unity Mitford was even taller, and the *Führer* disliked women who towered over him. Eva was 5 foot 3, which was just right for Hitler's 5 foot 7 inches.
19. Musmanno Collection, Vol. XI, interrogation of Heinrich Hoffmann, Nuremberg, 19 July 1948 – one of more than two hundred interviews conducted by Rear Admiral, later Judge, Michael Angelo Musmanno.
20. Hoffmann, *Hitler Was My Friend*, p. 160. This was one of a number of books by Hoffmann that boasted about his close acquaintance with the *Führer* and served as a vehicle for photographs of him.
21. *Bund Deutscher Mädel* (BDM), or League of German Girls – the female equivalent of the Hitler Youth.
22. Quoted in Knopp, *Hitler's Women*, p. 10.

and scent when she arrived at the evening's entertainment – cinema, opera, club or party – and rub them off again in the Ladies before going home. Hitler may have advocated the scrubbed milkmaid look but he was seldom personally attracted by such women. Eva contrived to flout her father's strictures. She adored make-up and used it all her life, regardless of his or Hitler's views. Despite their joint attempts to break her into submission, they never entirely succeeded.

> My mother Edith Schröder, always known as Ditha (pronounced 'Deeta'), was another healthy, hearty, sporty girl whose idea of fun was being rowed round Hamburg's Lake Alster in a hired boat by a boyfriend or taking vigorous, day-long walks in the countryside, swimming in summer, skating and shrieking on the city's ice-rinks in winter. Her attitude to her own looks was the very opposite of Eva's. Make-up never interested her, which was just as well since her father would not have tolerated it. Her girlhood photographs show her as an Ingrid Bergman type, although her features were coarser, her expressions less subtle, and she lacked Bergman's touching beauty. The only make-up she ever used (much later in life) was a dark, ruby-red lipstick, applied to her mouth with a curious dabbing gesture, dot dot dot . . . With a fluffy powder puff she would pat rose-pink powder on to her nose and cheeks, leaving tiny specks embedded in the pores.[23]

Eva's cousin Gertraud is convinced that 'One reason for starting the relationship with Hitler while she was still in her teens was that Eva wanted to get away from her father and family.'[24] Girls who escape from a bullying father are often attracted to authoritarian men, only to realise that they have gone from the frying pan into a far hotter fire. The rigidity with which her father controlled her had unconsciously prepared Eva for Hitler. At seventeen, she had already been kicking against authority – religious and paternal – for years. She could not have chosen a more compulsively controlling man to love than Adolf Hitler.

23. I remember an encounter with my grandfather – who was born in Berlin, 4 February 1877 – in 1957, when he hadn't seen me for three years. I was seventeen and had just left school. As we entered his room he exclaimed: 'Oh, she's become a beauty!' – adding disappointingly, 'Oh no she hasn't, *sie hat sich geschminkt* [she's painted her face].'
24. Gertraud Weisker in conversation with the author, 2 April 2001.

Chapter Two

Eva's Family

On the night of 6 February 1912, the night Eva Braun was born in Munich, it was raining; a cold wintry drizzle. While the midwife helped Fanny (Franziska) through the rigours of a long birth, her husband Fritz waited impatiently in the next room. He already had a three-year-old daughter and was very much hoping for a son.[1] His mother-in-law, Josefa Kronburger, who was with him, was sure the baby would be a boy although in fact girls tended to predominate on her side of the family; she herself had five daughters. If the child struggling into the world were to be male his parents had decided to call him Rudolf, after the Habsburg Crown Prince who died in a suicide pact with his mistress at Mayerling – an ill-omened choice, one might have thought. Why call a baby after a deluded prince who had killed himself? However, the infant who slid into the midwife's hands at 2.22 a.m. was a strapping girl. She weighed 5½ kilos – 12 pounds – and her parents called her Eva (the first in the family to bear the name) Anna (after one of her Kronburger aunts) Paula (after another). Eva Anna Paula Braun: a good, solid, humdrum name. Judging by her first photograph, she was an exceptionally ugly baby.

The Brauns had married in July 1908 when Fritz was twenty-nine and his bride six years younger. They were both hard-working citizens – the German adverb is *fleissig*, which has overtones of industry, probity and respectability. Eva's mother, Franziska née Kronburger – always known as Fanny – came from an exceptionally devout Roman Catholic family. (One of her sisters, Anni, later became a nun in

---

1. Gertraud Weisker in conversation with the author, 2 April 2001.

Eichstätt.²) They were all so deeply grounded in the Catholic Church that Fanny could not imagine abandoning her faith. Fritz, who had been raised in the pious but more tolerant Lutheran Church, was prepared to allow their children to be brought up as Roman Catholics but did not himself convert. Like any German husband of the time, he took it for granted that he would rule the household in every respect, but he did concede on the matter of religion. Fanny's Catholicism, reinforced by her mother and her four sisters, rather than Fritz's Lutheran obduracy, was to have a lifelong effect on their children. Eva Anna Paula Braun was baptised into the Roman Catholic Church when she was a few weeks old, with aunt Paula as her godmother.

Eva's parents had grown up in a pre-First World War Germany with a rich, handmade culture and a class-ridden social structure dominated by the nobility, the military and the clergy. That was still, just, the society she was born into – so utterly different from the one that replaced it twenty years later that it's hard to believe such a way of life existed less than a century ago. In 1912 the recently unified Germany³ was an empire ruled by Kaiser Wilhelm II whose government was rapidly rearming, strengthening the navy and forcing its rival, Britain, to do likewise. It was a rigid, hierarchical, uneasy set-up. The old belief in God and the ruling aristocracy had been shaken by the murderous exploits of the anarchists at the turn of the century and further undermined by early portents of revolution in Russia. Yet tolerance of minorities was still the norm; Jews were not overtly singled out for persecution or prejudice and the province of Bavaria was stable, prosperous and cultured: as good a place as any in Germany to start life.

Fritz Braun came from nearby Schwabia,⁴ a province north-west

2. Although Gertraud Weisker is my main source of information about the Braun family, many details and names from Eva's time in Beilngries are taken from an article by Josef Riedl, editor, *Donaukurier*, 2–3 October 2004, kindly sent to me by the town's deputy mayor, Herr Anton Grad.

3. Kaiser Wilhelm was crowned Emperor of all Germany in the Hall of Mirrors at Versailles in 1871.

4. Schwabia is the old name for the land, people and culture of a large part of south-western Germany. The Black Forest borders its western edge, the Alps the south, the Bavarian Highlands are on the east and Frankish Germans to the north. It was ruled by a variety of medieval kings, the strongest emerging as ruler of Württemberg. At the time of the Protestant Reformation in the 1520s Württemberg became a Protestant kingdom, lasting until 1871 when it was incorporated into the German Reich. Schwabia or Württemberg is a hilly and forested area with valleys of vineyards, orchards and wheatfields. Its main cities are Stuttgart and Ulm.

of Bavaria. Its people are known for their thrift and craftsmanship, qualities which Fritz had in abundance. As a young man he was frugal, even abstemious, with a sense of civic duty and a leaning towards the past, which always seems a simpler time, most at ease within a hierarchy where he knew his place and others knew theirs. His parents were prosperous furniture manufacturers from Stuttgart who had hoped their son would follow them into the business. Fritz's twin brother had emigrated to South America as a young man; his sister Johanna lived in Stuttgart and had no children. Fritz was evidently a contrary character, even in youth, and he aspired to be an architect, not a furniture salesman. Realising that it was beyond him (Hitler had the same ambition and it was beyond him, too) he chose instead to become a teacher. This decision may have led to tension between him and his parents since as soon as he obtained his diploma he left home and took a teaching job in Württemberg before moving to Munich to teach in a *Fachhochschule*, a higher technical school. A few years later he met, courted, and married Fanny Kronburger.

Their three daughters were born in 1909 (Ilse), 1912 (Eva) and 1915 (Gretl). As they grew from babies into toddlers and then into sturdy little girls, they seldom saw their paternal grandparents. Stuttgart was a big city 137 miles north-west of Munich, while Fanny's parents lived in a lush countryside of rolling hills and valleys, nearer, more thrilling and healthier for children than the town. Perhaps because Beilngries, where Fanny's parents lived, was more accessible, or because a wife's attachment to her mother becomes stronger once she is a mother herself, or simply because Fritz was not on particularly good terms with his parents, whose shop would in any case have precluded them from taking long summer breaks – whatever the reason, the Braun family[5] spent every summer with their Kronburger grandparents.

When Eva was born her older sister, Ilse, was nearly three. A third daughter, Margarethe, known all her life as Gretl, completed the family. Fritz Braun had evidently given up hope of a son. The two youngest were very close, as close as twins, and Ilse, despite being older and cleverer, resented her exclusion from their private, giggling gang of two.

5. Winbauer, *Eva Braun's Familiengeschichte*, p. 3 (translated by the author). 'It was an unwritten but strong and lasting family bond that came about as a result of school summer holidays spent in Beilngries, that idyllic little town in the Altmühl River valley.'

Nevertheless, in an era when many children were still expected to address their parents formally: '*Herr Vater*' and '*Frau Mutter*' – as Fanny herself had done – the Braun family was loving and demonstrative and the young parents generous in the amount of time they spent with their children. Fritz's sternness was mitigated by the indulgent Fanny, which was just as well since Eva was stubborn to the point of mulish obstinacy. A well-worn family anecdote has it that on one occasion her mother, exasperated at her daughter's refusal to give way in some trivial argument, plunged her head into a basin of cold water. It made no difference. Once Eva had made up her mind nothing would persuade her to budge.

Fanny was an ideal mother – happy and funny, pleasure-loving, easy-going, equable. When not earning extra money making clothes or, later on, taking in lodgers, she worked hard to keep her family clean, well fed and, as far as possible, contented. She had inherited an interest in the arts from her father and shared his taste for the finer things of life, traits that she handed on to her own daughters.[6] Their cousin Gertraud remembers that she and the girls were always laughing at jokes together. 'She was a joyful and happy mother.' Fanny had trained as a dressmaker and the family photograph albums are full of pictures of her three girls showing off the dresses she made for them. Fritz acquired a handsome tabby cat whom the family named *Schnurrlei der Kater*, meaning, more or less, Purrer the tom cat, and in several early pictures Eva is clutching him tightly; *too* tightly.

Eva's maternal grandfather, Franz-Paul Kronburger, was a towering figure in all their lives despite his small stature. Born in 1858, the son of a butcher, he was the eldest of nineteen children, eleven of whom survived into adulthood. All eight of his brothers went on to practise a profession. Franz-Paul himself chose to become a vet, earning the title Herr Doktor Veterinär Kronburger and privileged to use the additional honorific *Kaiser– und Königlicher Veterinärrat*[7] (Imperial District Veterinarian). Every year, in honour of the Kaiser's birthday, he would wear the court regalia to which this entitled him, topped by a preposterous ceremonial hat called a *Picklhauber* – a sort of civilian helmet

---

6. *Wer War Eva Braun?*, p. 8. In about 1998, more than fifty years after the events she described, Gertraud Weisker wrote a long descriptive account of her memories of cousin Eva called *Wer War Eva Braun?* (*Who Was Eva Braun?*). It has never before been published.

7. Imperial and Royal Veterinary doctor.

– and carry an épée. Franz-Paul made a good marriage. His wife Josefa, seven years older, came from a well-known line of watchmakers. Her brother Alois Winbauer[8] had been one of the imperial jewellers to Emperor Franz Joseph of Austria at a time when royal connections conferred real prestige. Josefa Winbauer was thirty before she married – on the verge of being an old maid, by the standards of the time – and must have been grateful to Franz-Paul for making her his wife. But she had no reason to feel in any way inferior to her husband.

Herr Doktor Veterinär Kronburger would probably have liked to found a dynasty himself, perhaps five or six sturdy sons – one to follow in his footsteps as a vet; the others, if they were clever and hard working, maybe a doctor or lawyer or chemist, the one who was better with his hands than his brain might be apprenticed to a watchmaker and, as for the youngest, he'd defer to his wife and let the boy enter the Church – but his plans were frustrated by the arrival of five daughters, one after another, born in the space of nine years: Josefa (also nicknamed 'Pepi'), Franziska ('Fanny'), Anni, Paula and Bertha. (The sixth and last child had been the longed-for boy, Franz, but he died suddenly of unknown causes when he was eighteen months old.) Franz-Paul had no alternative but to rule over a household of six women. Not that the girls were oppressed, even less so his wife. Josefa was a gentle woman of strong character and a devout Roman Catholic. She was a formidable housewife and organiser who, with only a couple of village girls to help her, welcomed the entire family to Beilngries at least twice a year. Eva's younger cousins, Gertraud and aunt Bertha's son Willy, as well as her uncle Alois (the only child of Josefa's brother, born in 1896, he was sixteen years older than Eva)[9] *and* all their parents, spent every Easter, Christmas and summer holiday here. The Kronburgers' big old house had eight or ten bedrooms and the veterinary practice on the ground floor was always full of people and animals, coming and going in various stages of injury, sickness or pain, which appealed to Eva's love of animals as well as drama. There was a kitchen garden where hens pecked and squabbled, reluctant rabbits who could be prised out of their cages to be stroked, and a stream nearby for paddling and fishing.

8. Father of 'young' Alois whose unpublished family recollections *Eva Braun's Familiengeschichte* provided much material for this chapter.
9. He was born in 1896 and died 17 October 1983 (source: his niece, Gertraud Weisker).

Alois fondly remembered his aunt Josefa:

> She was carved from a more yielding wood . . . being a gentle, kind and profoundly religious woman, forever anxious about her daughters. Her temperament balanced and compensated for the harshness of her husband's, maintaining peace and harmony in their household. She mediated between his authoritarian nature and her girls, all of whom possessed emerging and distinct wills of their own. She had a warm heart, a sense of humour that could smooth over conflict and an instinct for the things that really mattered in life. Thanks to all this she created a loving family home and a welcoming place for guests.[10]

Well into her sixties and even seventies, *Oma* (Granny) Kronburger continued to preside over at least four families as well as her own unmarried daughters and – most demanding of all – her husband. She was adored by everyone for her goodness and hospitality. She died in 1927, having bequeathed her generous nature to her daughters and her distinctive beaked nose to two of them (including Fanny) and one granddaughter (Ilse).

Franz-Paul played an active and vital part in his daughters' upbringing though he always maintained a certain distance, making the girls use the respectful '*Sie*' to their parents, rather than the familiar '*Du*'. He believed passionately in the importance of education and taught his five girls Latin and Greek – not subjects offered in the average girls' school,[11] let alone in a place like Beilngries, the little Bavarian town where he and his wife lived and brought up their daughters in the big house at Hauptstrasse 1. Their knowledge of the classics was quite exceptional for the time. 'My grandfather Kronburger was very advanced in his view on the education of women,' said Gertraud Weisker, 'and insisted that all his daughters learned a skill that would lead to a profession, so that they could support themselves if necessary.'[12]

Franz-Paul was the most powerful figure in his five daughters' lives and

---

10. Winbauer, *Eva Braun's Familiengeschichte*, p. 6 (translated by the author).
11. Weisker, *Wer War Eva Braun?*, p. 8 (translated by the author). 'The poor education his daughters received in the convent school was a thorn in his flesh and he went to a good deal of trouble to make up for its deficiencies, taking it upon himself to teach them Latin and Greek, with moderate success.'
12. Gertraud Weisker in conversation with the author, 25 March 2004.

quite possibly those of his granddaughters as well, an old-fashioned autocrat dedicated to the service of the Kaiser as well as of his peasant customers. No matter how the political climate changed during his lifetime – and he didn't die until 1933, the year Hitler became Chancellor – he never abandoned the precepts of an orderly society governed by an ascending ladder of rights and duties, nor ever doubted that he was close to the topmost rung. Whether or not this was really the case, he was a forceful presence in Beilngries, feared for his temper and his importance to the farmers, respected for his skill in treating their animals. It made no difference that the Herr Doktor Veterinär became, as he grew older, domineering and not a little eccentric, parading in brightly coloured, old-fashioned clothes and growing a huge red beard. This did nothing to undermine the esteem in which he was held.

On Sunday outings with his family Franz-Paul Kronburger would assume an imperious expression, a billowing green *loden* cape and a traditional Bavarian hat. He was the first person for miles around to own a car – one of the earliest Maybach models – of which he was enormously proud, though he prudently kept a landau and a horse-drawn cart in reserve.[13] Alois, his nephew by marriage, remembered a cumbersome, awkward vehicle, 'a great box with two lamps and a stentorian hooter attached', big enough to take the entire family on outings round the countryside and on professional visits to the surrounding villages. He has left a charming account[14] of the family's motoring expeditions:

> Those who travelled in his car risked life and limb and no family outing was ever an unadulterated pleasure. On a trip up the mountain the snorting, struggling vehicle frequently refused to proceed, so that instead of enjoying the beauties of the Altmühl valley, we passengers were forced to get out and heave it back to life. [. . .] No journey began without a racket and few ended without a breakdown. These proud expeditions very often finished in a lamentable homecoming, the stately vehicle being towed back by a couple of oxen, its owner's pride in its achievements reduced to a steady stream of curses aimed at the 'shitmobile'.

13. *Eva Braun's Familiengeschichte*, pp. 3–4 (translated by the author).
14. Ibid., p. 4.

Franz-Paul could be kindly as well as irascible. He took Alois fishing (his second passion, after the car). Together the two men – Alois in his early twenties, his uncle in his sixties – hooked fat trout in a private stream belonging to Plankstetten, the local monastery, a favour the vet repaid by inoculating their 120 pigs free of charge. 'Uncle Franz taught me how to fish, not with much patience but with great thoroughness, thereby presenting me with a gift that gave me more pleasure than anything I'd known in my life so far, and perhaps ever.' In the absence of a son of his own, it must have given his uncle pleasure, too. In addition to the use of their trout stream he himself had exclusive rights to a 4-kilometre stretch of the Altmühl, said to be the best fishing river in the whole of Bavaria.[15]

Fanny's sister Bertha, his older cousin (by four years), was Alois's first love. 'She was the object of my first schoolboy passion; she nurtured it gently and my heart started pounding the moment I boarded the train in Geiselhöring for my summer holiday.' Long afterwards Alois confessed that he used to carry secret billets-doux between Fanny and the local chemist, her admirer and sweetheart, while her father slept after lunch. Alois's reward would be a bag of liquorice. Secrecy was needed because Franz-Paul would have thought such a romance was beneath any daughter of his.

Fritz Braun – dour and frustrated in his dreams and ambitions – may unconsciously have modelled himself on his father-in-law. He too tried to impose a rule of iron on the females he felt were ranged against him. His job as a teacher of crafts and technical studies was respectable enough but as a youth he had aimed far higher. Now, he was forced to teach in order to support his family. The relationship between him and Fanny gradually came to resemble that between her parents, as did their opposite attitudes towards their daughters. At weekends, absenting himself from the household, he would often go fishing, alone or with his father-in-law. He belonged to a group of volunteers called

15. Weisker, *Wer War Eva Braun?*, p. 7. 'In every spare moment he [i.e. Fritz Braun, Eva's father] went fishing in the Altmühl River, where my grandfather had fishing rights. He was also a member of a mountain watch team on the Wendelstein and spent many hours, summer and winter, looking for injured climbers on the mountain. He and my father had an excellent relationship, being united in their disapproval of the Nazis. Whether this isolation was chosen by him or enforced by his wife I don't know, nor if whatever it was that he did justified the departure of his daughters.'

the *Bergwacht* who went out on the mountains in search of climbers lost or overwhelmed by avalanches. These pursuits monopolised his spare time, summer and winter, widening the gap between him and his wife.

Today the former Kronburger home is barely recognisable. It used to be on the outskirts of the town but Beilngries has grown since then and the old house has been absorbed into the centre and now serves as premises for Ströbl, a business selling classy household accessories – designer kitchen utensils, bowls, vases – the sort of thing people are given as wedding or leaving presents. It is surrounded by small shops – one of which sells lottery tickets – and street signs, all tending to obscure its splendid four-square dimensions.[16] The twin green and gold spires of the main church, the *Stadtpfarrkirche*, dating back to the sixteenth century, are visible in the background. The area is, of course, Roman Catholic: 90 per cent of Beilngries residents are of that faith today.[17] The present Pope, Benedict XVI, was born in nearby Markt am Inn and practised his ministry as Archbishop of Munich in Ruhpolding, another little local town. Catholicism of the most conservative kind is deeply rooted in this part of Germany. For that and many other reasons, Eva would still feel at home here. Little seems to have changed in its rural surroundings – the wide, wooded Altmühl valley remains an agricultural Utopia of rolling fields (many growing long-stemmed hops trained up tall triangular staves) and dark forest, bypassed nowadays by the autobahns racing from north to south between Nuremberg and Munich.

Beilngries is not the sort of ostentatiously picturesque place to which tourists flock, yet it dates from the fifteenth century and has nine square, ancient towers and many old half-timbered buildings as well as many beautiful Baroque houses. There are statues of the Virgin Mary, gilded signs bearing the names of inns and hanging baskets of flowers everywhere. It would be hard to imagine a more wholesome holiday retreat and Eva cherished its memory all her life, not least because her grandfather was one of its most prominent citizens.

16. The deputy mayor of Beilngries, Herr Anton Grad, by e-mail to the author, 27 October 2004: 'The house that belonged to Eva Braun's grandparents is still standing, though other houses have grown up around it and nowadays it functions as premises for a business.'
17. Source: Anton Grad.

In June 1914, when Eva was two and a half, Archduke Ferdinand, the heir to the Austro-Hungarian throne, and his wife were assassinated by a Serbian nationalist. This spark ignited the tinderbox of the Balkans and almost before the summer was over, war had broken out. It was, a modern historian has said, a 'march of fools' – long, purposeless and deadly.

A few hundred miles away in Munich, Eva and her sisters were hardly touched by the slaughter of their fellow Germans. Towards the end of the war food became restricted and, in a remark that entered the family's anecdotal memory, Eva said you could only tell that your bread was buttered if it shone under the light. But the fighting never bled across on to German soil, air raids were a thing of the future, the proud and beautiful city of Munich remained undamaged and life for the Braun children and their mother continued much as usual, except that the head of the household wasn't there.

Chapter Three

Eva, Goethe, Schubert and Bambi

The mind of every German child is crammed with music and song, legends, folklore and fairy stories, a carnival[1] of the tawdry and the epic, freaks and fairies, wolves and Easter bunnies, the savage and the saccharine. They are first met in the nursery, through haunting melodies and verses whose underlying theme is often violence. The forest, swirling with fog and darkness, populated by wolves, dwarves, witches and satanic figures all looking out for small children to waylay – these provide a wonderful insight into the German soul and justify dwelling on them at some length. Many songs and stories dated from long before unification,[2] when Germany was still made up of dozens of separate princely states. If one thing linked them and defined the national character it was the glory of German music and poetry and the sadistic terror of the nursery stories traditionally told to children not yet able to read for themselves.

1. The twenty-four-part German TV series *Heimat*, a masterpiece directed by Edgar Reitz and first shown in 1984, culminated in a scene that reunited all the characters in a fairground, bobbing and swaying on carousels or strolling past the fair's attractions. Fairs have always had a particular resonance in the German collective unconscious.
2. When the North German Confederation was formed in 1867, it had twenty-one members – two kingdoms, four grand duchies and seven principalities, as well as three Free and Hanseatic Cities, including Hamburg, my mother's birthplace. The former Kingdom of Hannover, the Electorate of Hesse, the Duchy of Nassau, the Free City of Frankfurt and the Landgraviate of Hesse-Homburg were annexed by Prussia. Four other states on the losing side of the Seven Weeks' War did not become members of the North German Confederation, but would join the German Empire in 1871. http://home.att.net/~david.danner/militaria/states.htm

Children's songs – lullabies, nursery rhymes, playground jingles – are the most enduring of all oral traditions. Repeated over and over again at an age when every sense is magnified and every impression new, they are wedged in the unconscious forever. A generation later they re-emerge exactly as they were first heard in the days before the child could speak or sing. Fanny Braun and her daughters' earliest memories were of the old, old songs by Goethe, Heine or Schiller, set to music by Schubert and Brahms. One of the most famous, *Schlafe, mein Prinzchen, schlaf ein*, is often attributed to Mozart but probably goes back to well before the eighteenth century. Its exact provenance is unknown – like that of most oral memories – but every German mother crooned it to her baby in its cradle, calming its fear of being alone: *Schlafe, mein Prinzchen, schlaf ein*[3] . . . and the tired princeling's eyes would begin to close. No doubt Josefa Kronburger sang it to her daughters and they to theirs, including Eva. My mother, in her throbbing contralto voice, would sing me to sleep exactly as her mother had sung to her. Even now, as the tune rises tinnily from the Internet on my computer, it conjures up that ready-for-bed sleepiness. Another equally tender lullaby, set to a lilting melody by Brahms, is *Guten Abend, gute Nacht*. These are only two out of hundreds, many now forgotten.

As the infant grew older and livelier, so did the songs.

> *Hup, hup, hup,*
> *Go on horsey, gallop!*
> *Over sticks and over stones*
> *Mind you don't break all your bones!*[4]

3. which translates as:
Sleep, little prince, go to sleep!
Schlafe, mein Prinzchen, schlaf ein,
Es ruh'n Schäfchen und Vögelein
Garten und Wiesen verstummt
Auch nicht ein Bienchen mehr summt
Luna mit silbernen Schein
Kucket den Fenster herein,
Schlafe beim silbernem Schein
Schlafe, mein Prinzchen, schlaf ein
Schlaf ein, schlaf ein . . .
(Trad./J. Johns/Chappell)
http://www.nanamouskouri.de/schlafem.htm
4. *Hop! Hop! Hop!*
Pferdchen lauf Gallopp!

Every German child was perched on its father's hard knees and jogged up and down to this one, mesmerised by his looming mouth and big teeth. The rhythm started at a gentle trot, working up to a fast, jolting gallop until, overcome with terror or excitement, the toddler Eva or infant Gretl began to laugh or howl. *Fuchs, Du hast die Gans gestohlen* was another country song:

> *Mr Fox you've stolen the goose*
> *Bring him right back here!*
> *Or the farmer will let loose*
> *His trusty fusilier!*

The peasant farmer springs to life, flintlock in hand. These play songs were rooted in the world from which they sprang. The galloping tune refers to a time when everyone travelled on horseback, which, in 1912, was the very recent past. As a country vet, Eva's grandfather ministered to surrounding farms where all but the poorest farmers had a horse and every housewife raised hens and geese. Rural life was hardly a generation away. Today the songs have little relevance to reality but when Fanny sang them she was singing about a way of life she had known as a child.

The intertwining of words and tunes is all the more evocative when it's subliminal. From time to time I find myself remembering Heine's poem *Lorelei*, a mariners' fable about the treacherous Rhine maidens, singing it in my mind, under my breath, or even – when happily, mightily, pissed – out loud. These songs carry an emotional charge that has little to do with their artless words. When my mother felt depressed she would intone *Meine Ruh ist hin*[5] or sing Goethe's *Heidenröslein*. It begins 'Sah ein Knab' ein Röslein stehn' – A boy admires a rose and threatens to pick it. The rose warns him, if you do I'll prick you, but the boy breaks it off defiantly and is pricked. The simple ditty in a minor key is far more sinister than the words and cheery tune suggest. Read

5. *Meine Ruh ist hin,*
Mein Herz ist schwer;
Ich finde sie nimmer
Und nimmermehr.
I have no peace / My heart is sore / I'll never find it / Never more.

with an adult sensibility, it is about the loss of sexual innocence: literally, about being deflowered.

When young Ditha Helps (as she became in June 1936 when, aged twenty-four, she married my father, John Helps) felt *Heimweh* (homesick) during the lonely war years – trapped in hostile England and condemned by her German accent to be stigmatised as the enemy – she would console herself by singing *Der Erlkönig*. The *Erl-King* is a poem by Goethe set to music by Schubert about a sick boy clasped in the arms of his father who, though he gallops like the wind, cannot outrun Death. It was a melancholy but potent link with her mother and sisters, trapped in Hamburg; bombed, battered and half-starved by the forces of the country to which she now officially belonged. She had seen her mother for the last time in Hamburg in 1939 but could only stay for three days because war was imminent. (Did she realise this? Didn't my *father*? How extraordinarily naive they must both have been.) My mother was far from simple-minded but, like Eva, she was remarkably ignorant about politics. When it came to the outbreak of war my mother hardly knew whose side she was on, only that she didn't want anyone she loved to die.

My mother was no intellectual but all her life she was sustained by the poems she had learned as a child. She knew them by heart and could recite line after sonorous line of Goethe's *Der König in Thule* or Schiller's *Der Taucher*.

Had German children fully understood the words they might have wondered why their bedtime songs were so often about pain and cruelty, the remorselessness of fate; and why the beckoning, beguiling Rhine maidens and the Erl-King's daughters were calling humans to a cold world underwater or to the hereafter. Like the fairground – which hid pain and cruelty behind a garish exterior – outward appearances were deceptive. Sentimentality and brutality are two extremes of a single impulse: the need to control, the desire for power over someone else, whether achieved by deceptively soft-voiced manipulation or morbid and sadistic force. These innocent poems embody traits that were grounded in the German character, instilling at an early age a fatalistic acceptance of suffering and death; the sense that these, too, are part of the human condition, along with the birdies and the princeling.

The Braun parents certainly read *Grimm's Fairy Tales* to their daughters – all German parents did – although they are among the grimmest stories ever told,[6] conjuring up a world of dark forests, dank caves and cold stone castles where pain and terror, strength and weakness, power and vulnerability, intermingle. For Eva, this backdrop was no Gothic fantasy. Half her life would be set amid forests and cold castles and it would end in a dank cave. *Hänsel und Gretel* is about two children abandoned by their stepmother because she cannot feed them: the classic theme of rejection, hunger and poverty. Such tales had their roots deep in a very old European culture as well as recent German history, drawn from a remorseless world where witch trials were normal, witch burning a public spectacle and only the toughest survived.[7]

The final collection of two hundred tales (*Grimm's Märchen*) became the single best-known and most influential book in the German language. It must have tapped some very deep springs. Assembled and published in the early 1800s, the stories reflect the experience of generations of peasants whose lives were hard, arbitrary and pitiless. If national characteristics can be deduced by analysing the themes and archetypes of folklore and fairy tales,[8] the Brothers Grimm, Jacob and Wilhelm, offered German children a harsh prospect. Wolf packs marauded through Europe's wild places until as recently as the early twentieth century. The very word 'wolf' evoked fears that were by no

6. It is the novelist A.S. Byatt's view, and that of many literary anthropologists, that these fairy tales are the purest expression of the German psyche or collective unconscious. Byatt believes that the German nature is more profoundly expressed in its fairy tales than in any other art form. (See also her article in the *Guardian*, 4 January 2004.) 'The Grimms' preface to volume two of the first edition of the *Children's Stories and Household Tales* [. . .] supports their claims for the Germanness of the tales. German perception of German folklore is bound up with the Germanic sense of the all-importance of the surrounding "Wald" the forest [. . .] The Grimms thought, among other things, that they were recovering a German mythology and a German attitude to life. They saw themselves as asserting what was German against the French occupying forces of the Napoleonic empire. The allied occupying forces in Germany after the Second World War tried to ban the Grimms because it was felt that their *bloodthirstiness, gleeful violence, heartlessness and brutality had helped to form the violent nature of the Third Reich* [my italics].'
7. Lyndal Roper's *Witch Craze* goes into great detail about these old stories and their roots in history or myth. As a formative influence on the German psyche their importance cannot be overestimated.
8. See Jack Zipes, *The Trials and Tribulations of Little Red Riding Hood* (Routledge, 1993) and Robert Darnton, *The Great Cat Massacre* (London: Allen Lane, 1984; New York; Basic Books, 1984).

means exaggerated or foolish, and the feral wolf remained an object of terror in folklore and in many European forests. 'Wolf' was a thoroughly Freudian pseudonym for Hitler to have selected. By calling himself 'Mr Wolf', he may have plumbed his unconscious more deeply than he knew. If he wanted to epitomise his vision of Germany, 'Herr Adler' – 'Mr Eagle' – would have been more apt, but he planned to master his followers rather than let them soar.

In these bedtime stories, small boys and girls are despatched on ordeals from which they return – if at all – to parents who seem almost disappointed by their survival. Their trials are described with sadistic relish. Little Red Riding Hood in her bright red bonnet – a beacon to any passing predator – is sent through the dark forest by her mother to deliver her granny's lunch. A wolf lurking among the pine trees thinks: 'What a tender young creature! What a nice plump mouthful!', an observation unlikely to usher tender, plump children into dreamless sleep. *Hänsel und Gretel* features a gruesome female ogre; *Walpurgisnacht* celebrates the night when witches fly through the night on broomsticks as the Devil's outriders, a scene recreated in Goethe's *Faust*. These atavistic horrors resonated through German children's unconscious minds and would haunt their imagination for life. They may also have prepared them for atrocious acts.

The first present I can remember getting from *Opa*, my German grandfather, was a copy in German of *Andersen's Fairy Tales*. It sits on my bookshelf to this day, the jacket disintegrating, the much-thumbed pages foxed. In retrospect it's interesting – if almost certainly accidental – that he chose to give me the more benign Danish stories of Hans Christian Andersen rather than those of his grim German equivalent. Andersen's stories are not exactly happy or optimistic – *The Little Mermaid* is positively sadistic – but they deal with the subjects children love best – romantic quests and magical tasks, disguise and revelation, innocence battling against evil[9] – whereas Grimm deals with real horror and cruelty towards vulnerable children. Written by my grandfather in pencil on the flyleaf of the book are the words: '*To my well-beloved granddaughter, Christmas 1949*', an inscription whose brevity and affection move me

9. See article on Hans Christian Andersen by Judith Mackrell in the *Guardian*, 1 November 2004.

almost to tears. I don't think my parents ever called me 'well-beloved'. I knew my grandfather loved me; we had recognised one another as kindred spirits the day we first met in Hamburg in 1947, a few weeks before my seventh birthday. *Opa* was unlike anyone else in the family. Unconventional, bookish, with an anarchic wit, he was largely self-educated, self-made and fiercely individual. I hoped I'd grow up to be like *Opa*, and he hoped so too.

Other books read aloud by Eva's parents, if the girls weren't already reading for themselves, had the same half-teasing, half-horrifying quality. The bizarre *Struwwelpeter* – subtitled 'Happy Tales and Funny Pictures' – is in a class of its own.[10] It is a humorous (to Germans, at any rate) set of verses by a writer called Dr Heinrich Hoffmann (no relation to Hitler's photographer) who practised in Frankfurt as a 'medical man of the lunatic asylum' – presumably an early psychotherapist. He wrote *Struwwelpeter* in December 1844 as a Christmas present for his small son, in the belief that 'A story, invented on the spur of the moment [. . .] and humorously related, will calm the little antagonist [he is speaking here of calming a child, not a lunatic], dry his tears, and allow the medical man to do his duty. [. . .] The book was bound, put under the Christmas tree, and the effect on the boy was just what I expected.'[11]

Struwwelpeter describes in doggerel a number of gruesome punishments meted out to naughty children, guilty of doing the sort of things all children do. A girl who plays with matches burns to a heap of ash, a thumb-sucker has his thumbs cut off with a huge pair of scissors and a boy who doesn't like soup starves to death. Parallels with the future hardly need stressing. The book satisfies every child's fascination with the grotesque, eccentric, hideous or mad as well as licensing its own fantasies of sadism and destruction. Whatever the reason, it was read to shreds in every German household. The Braun sisters, along with my mother and hers, might have deduced that they were not growing up into a kind or forgiving world.

Eva and Hitler both loved *Max und Moritz*, a book in cartoons and verse about two rampaging small boys by Wilhelm Busch, a south

10. The nearest English equivalent is Hilaire Belloc's gentler – and much funnier – *Cautionary Tales*.
11. www.shockheadedpeter.com/struww.html

German painter, cartoonist and poet.[12] At first glance the tales seem to be sanctimonious pegs on which to hang moral lessons but this was only a device to make them acceptable to parents. In fact they cele-brate the joyous power of a couple of naughty boys to cause mayhem.[13] Wilhelm Busch's verses delighted the Braun children and so did his drawings of fat peasant women in aprons and clogs, raging futilely when they discover that their precious hens have been plucked and hung up by their beaks on the washing line; or old men in nightcaps whose plump feather beds have been stuffed with maybugs. Eva must have laughed; my mother and I did, too. The discomfiture of the pompous and elderly *is* funny.

As they grew older, Eva and her sisters read Johanna Spyri's *Heidi*, a saccharine story about an orphan girl living on a mountainside with her grandfather, set in a Swiss village very much like the ones they knew in the Bavarian Alps, and *Bambi* by Felix Salten, an Austrian-Jewish writer.[14] This book follows a fawn from birth as it learns about the harshness of nature and the threat from man: exactly the sort of sentimental story that would appeal to Eva. It is a paean to the law of the wild, the survival of the fittest, but it can also be seen as a political allegory on the treatment of Jews in Europe. At any rate, the Nazis thought so. In 1936 they banned it.[15]

In her teens, Eva became addicted to Wild West adventure stories by a popular German author called Karl May. (They were Hitler's favourites, too, when he was a boy.) More surprisingly, she was a great

12. This horribly convincing pair – rude, scruffy and cruel to animals – origin-ated when *Fliegende Blätter*, (Falling Leaves), a popular German satirical maga-zine founded in Munich in 1848, commissioned Busch to draw some caricatures. They went down so well that he began to add humorous verses, which eventu-ally led to the *Max und Moritz* books.
13. Both these books are available in English or German from Verlag J. F. Schreiber, Postfach 10 03 25, 73703 Esslingen, Austria, or in English from www.reclam.de.
14. Felix Salten had arrived in Austria as an infant in 1870 during Vienna's Jewish renaissance and had to flee for his life after the Nazi *Anschluss* of March 1938. *Bambi: A Life in the Woods*, his second book, published in 1923, was hugely popular.
15. Walt Disney made *Bambi* into an animated film which opened in Britain and the United States in 1942. My mother took me to see it when I was seven or eight and we wept together over the death of Bambi's mother. The original book has been overshadowed by Disney's film version, yet despite its ingratiating sentimentality it retains Salten's focus on the primitive beauty of nature and the harshness of man, so much so that the U.S. National Rifleman Association, the powerful NRA, protested at its depiction of hunters as cruel predators (www.elliemik.com/salten.html).

admirer of Oscar Wilde, and with her growing predilection for melo-drama and flirtation she probably fancied herself as Salomé beguiling the evil Herod. *Salome*'s decadent setting, its underlying theme of control through pleasure, luxury and cruelty, foreshadowed her own future experience. As happens with all impressionable children, the rich, suggestive words of the songs she heard and the books she read were buried deep. For the rest of her life they would fertilise her imag-ination and influence the way she interpreted and responded to people – most of all, to Mr Wolf.

Chapter Four

Tedious Lessons and Rebellious Games

When the Great War was over everybody swore it had been the war to end all wars. There would never be another. It ended better for Franziska and her children than for many German families – Fritz returned, physically undamaged though with deep mental scars that soon undermined the harmony of the Braun family. He had been called up as a reserve officer in the Bavarian army and came back a lieutenant. For his wife and the girls, the war years had passed in safety and only moderate hardship; for him they had meant fear, cold and disillusionment. Sickened by what he had seen – the pointless blood and carnage – his angry mood reflected that of Germany, its military ambitions crushed, its empire humiliated. But Fritz had been fortunate, surviving the Flanders front more or less intact. In 1919 he came home looking forward to domestic harmony and a lifetime of peace. Peace of a kind was what he found, but a costly, jagged peace imposed by the punitive Treaty of Versailles on a sullen and resentful people.

The war had left two and a half million fighting men dead, four million wounded and a shattered and demoralised Germany. The old order collapsed and in November 1918 Kaiser Wilhelm II, last of the Hohenzollern dynasty,[1] abdicated. Germany was proclaimed a republic

---

1. The royal family of Prussia from 1701 to 1918 and the imperial family of Germany from 1871 to 1918, the Hohenzollerns claimed descent from one of Charlemagne's generals. William II, the last Hohenzollern emperor, reigned from 1888 to 1918. The Habsburgs ruled in Austria until 1918 when Emperor-King Charles went into exile. Bavaria's last king, Ludwig III, ruled from 1913 to 1918. The war put an end to them all, their dynasties, courts, uniforms, titles and empty magnificence.

but the decline continued. The war created a generation of spinsters who, lacking a role as wives and mothers, went into the workforce. A great many unemployed men were deeply hostile towards these women, whom they regarded as having taken their jobs. Their world had changed, and the new order challenged their masculinity. Under such pressures society, and families, cracked from side to side.

Struggling to provide for his family, Fritz Braun grew increasingly moody and inaccessible. Fanny may have been too wrapped up in the girls to coax him out of his depression or let him unburden his experiences and he resented her failure to put him at the centre of her life, or to acknowledge his wartime ordeal. His face, as is clear from the family photographs, acquired a new rigour, with narrow eyes and a thin mouth twisted sideways. By the time he was forty in 1919 he had lost most of his hair and become a tough, bullet-headed authority figure who thought his three little daughters had been spoiled by their mother's benevolent régime. The strong marriage, welcoming children and *Gemütlichkeit*[2] he so missed had let him down.[3] His family had evidently managed perfectly well without him and seemed almost to resent his return. He failed to realise that, like most combatants, he had changed. In November 1918 Ilse was nine and Gretl only just beyond the toddler stage but, young as they were, they already resisted his authority. Of the three, Eva had changed the most. She was used to people responding to her charm and prettiness and wanted to please her father but nothing could shake his black gloom. Accustomed to stringent discipline, he tried to tame her bouncy self-confidence. The overcrowded, ebullient flat in Isabellastrasse became a quieter, sterner place when *Vati* was around.

In the years that followed, Fritz returned to his old job as a teacher of crafts and technical studies. More important, he became a dedicated Bavarian patriot, forever harking back to the imperial past. Preoccupied by the illegal *Freikorps Oberland* – a 'shadow army' that aimed to undermine the Treaty of Versailles – he joined the *Bayerischer Heimat- und Königsbund*[4], withdrew from family life and spent most of his spare time closeted in his room with his newspaper, his pipe, his

2. Cosiness, home comforts, homeliness.
3. Most of these family details are taken from Winbauer, *Eva Braun's Familiengeschichte*. I am most grateful to Frau Weisker for letting me see and quote from it.
4. The Bavarian League for King and Homeland, a patriotic group founded in 1921.

beer and his cat. There he remained, morose and silent, while his wife and daughters raged cheerfully on the other side of the closed door.

Some time in 1919, Eva's youthful uncle Alois Winbauer began his studies at Munich University.[5] The kind-hearted and cash-strapped Fanny Braun suggested he should be their lodger, evening meal thrown in. Nearly sixty years later he recalled her deliciously crunchy fried potatoes. He describes Eva, who would have been about seven, as an unusually pretty child, good-tempered, cheerful, and affectionate. Already she showed signs of being gifted and intelligent, with a quick grasp of anything new. School, her uncle Alois thought, gave her no problems at all. She took its trials and tribulations in her stride, though she became impatient if an exercise wasn't to her liking. Although Ilse was cleverer and more studious, Eva's charm gave her an unfair advantage. She already lived through her senses and emotions, rather than the rational world of knowledge and logic: 'a combination,' notes Alois, wise after the event, 'that would determine the tragedy of her life.'

Experts in child psychology tend to classify the middle child in a family as the lucky one. The confrontations with her parents suggest that Eva was more secure than her introverted older sister Ilse – intellectual, determined, distanced (the German word is *apart*), as her cousin would later describe her – or clinging little Gretl. Eva was a show-off, a performer, a leader and instigator. At school she seemed to have grasped the secret of popularity (be pretty, funny and capricious) and she lorded it over her sisters at home. Despite the ructions, she was obviously a much-loved child. Both Alois and Gertraud, members of the family on the Kronburger side, sensed that Eva was her mother's favourite. They shared a love of clothes and fashion and Fanny dreamed that Eva might one day open her own couture salon in Berlin. Her father spotted early on that Eva was remarkably talented at all kinds of sport and would often take her with him on skiing expeditions, leaving the other two girls at home.

Nevertheless, Herta Ostermayr, a schoolfellow who would become Eva's lifelong friend, believed that Eva was sometimes deeply unhappy at home. Yet despite the fractious, competitive relationship with her father,

---

5. Alois Winbauer, born in 1896 and thus sixteen years older than Eva, married young and had two children, but his wife died early. He went on to become a journalist and was editor-in-chief for the *Neue Mannheimer Zeitung* from 1933 until 1945. He became editor-in-chief for the *Heidelberger Tageblatt* after the war.

her childhood doesn't sound unhappy. One senses a vigorous, even fierce family where Fritz ruled and Fanny ran the household and did her dress-making, while acting as diplomat, role model and referee. The girls laughed, sulked, experimented with moods, opinions, clothes and, in Eva's case, tantrums. Nobody in the Braun family was dull. There's no evidence that any of the three girls ever suffered abuse or emotional neglect, which is not to say that Eva must therefore have been happy.

Barely a hundred miles away in Vienna, Freud was psychoanalysing unhappy women oppressed by the men in their family, but Fritz Braun thought Freud the Devil's disciple and would have dismissed the notion that the models of behaviour and control imposed on small children dominate the rest of their lives. From a psychoanalytical point of view it may well be true that Fritz Braun's treatment of his strong-minded middle daughter set the pattern that fixated her on control-ling men whose approval she craved. A child feels love and hate towards its parents, never entirely one or the other.

Fritz Braun, 'Vati', or, when he was annoyed with her, 'Papa', remained a nineteenth-century patriarch who insisted on strict obedience and it seems that, like many disciplinarians, he seethed with inner furies. The rebellious Eva, in failing to be as docile as he required, infuriated him. Reckless, defiant and physically daring, she bore the brunt of her father's aspirations as well as his disapproval. In a family circle consisting almost entirely of women Eva unconsciously took on the role of the much-hoped for son. Her mother used to say, 'Fritz wanted our second child to be a boy. Well, now he's got one!'[6] There was a good deal of confrontation but no suggestion that Fritz Braun beat any of his girls. Ilse Braun recalled later, 'The three of us were brought up in a very Catholic atmosphere and had to obey without question. We could argue as much as we liked but in the end our father would always say, "As long as you sit at my table you'll do what I want. Later on you can do what *you* like."'[7]

Boredom was not a problem for the Braun daughters. In those pre-television days, families were closer and more dependent on one another for their amusements. On dark winter evenings they would sit round

6. Jean-Michel Charlier and Jacques de Launay, *Eva Hitler, née Braun* (Paris: Editions de la Table Ronde, 1978), p. 10. Translated into German as *Eva Hitler, geb. Braun, Die führenden Frauen des Dritten Reiches* (Essen: Magnus Verlag, 1978).
7. Ibid.

the table playing games – not cards, at least not yet (in later life Eva became quite a keen bridge player), but competitive board games like Ludo, known in German by the wonderful slang name of *Mensch, Ärgere Dich Nicht!* which translates into modern idiom as '*Hey Man, Don't Get Mad!*'. It's a game for four players whose object, by throwing dice and avoiding being sent back to base, is to race four coloured pawns round the board and get them home before anyone else. Like all the best games, it encourages players to sabotage their opponents, and tempers flare across the board. My mother played it with her sisters when she was a child and so did I – every evening, if possible. Today's children, heads bent over solitary computer games, don't know what they're missing. '*Mensch, Ärgere Dich Nicht!*' is a wonderful way of acting out family tensions. No doubt Eva flounced and stamped and pouted and won, if necessary by cheating, as long as she got away with it.

When the girls played on their own they would cut round the outlines of paper dolls printed on stiff card, whose sexless bodies were concealed by modest vests and pantaloons. Small tabs protruding from the edges of their clothes were bent round behind their backs so that the dolls could be dressed up in eighteenth-century court costume – also cut out of the book – or modern fashions. Their feet could be bent forwards to make them stand upright, only they never did, keeling over on to their vain little faces. Little girls loved them and they survived as popular toys for girls until well into the 1970s. Simpler still were glossy coloured paper cutouts called *Oblaten* printed with fairies, angels, puppies and kittens, blossom and roses – anything a child could stick in a scrapbook or use to decorate a letter. There were colouring books and sliding wooden boxes of coloured pencils manufactured by Staedtler or Faber-Castell, arranged in graduating shades – a dozen, two dozen, or as many as seventy-two different coloured pencils. Eva and her sisters, Ditha and hers, rattled kaleidoscopes and peered down them at the glowing shapes inside that tumbled and reassembled in ever-shifting patterns. There were sets of wooden cubes for smaller children with a fairy tale illustrated on each face that, when put together properly, made up a scene from, say, *Red Riding Hood*. If turned over in one solid block it would reveal Hansel and Gretel magically intact on the underside, but one cube always dropped out, whereupon the remaining ones fell apart between your fingers.

After that, for older children, came impossible five-hundred-piece wooden jigsaws of seascapes (all waves and sky), improving maps to teach children the national borders, capital cities and rivers of Europe, or famous scenes from history. The girls' favourite toy was a large dolls' house that Fritz Braun himself had built, working secretly for months, making floors, walls and furniture. He was practised with his hands but scaling down his carpentry skills to miniature proportions must have been a labour of love. Fanny filled the tiny rooms with handmade rugs and curtains, cushions and bedspreads, doll-sized pots and pans and crockery. It was never too early to learn to take pride in a nice home.

When they were small the girls wore dresses and aprons with frills, large floppy bows on top of well-brushed hair and long white socks or stockings with shiny buttoned-up shoes. (I have a picture of my mother in almost identical clothes to those Eva wears in a Braun family photograph.) Clothes were decorative, not practical, trousers for girls unthinkable. They looked like large dolls until they were fifteen, underlining their role as playthings for Papa, helpmeets for *Mutti*. Fanny was keen to teach her daughters the history of costume and get them interested in clothes. It mattered that a young woman should be well-turned-out, smart and well-groomed. From early childhood Eva adored dressing up in exotic costumes. The family album has pictures of Eva aged six with a frilly cabbage leaf instead of a bow in her hair; Eva aged ten in fairy costume, Eva aged fifteen blacked up to look like Al Jolson – not to mention Eva with kitten; Eva with squirrel; Eva sitting on a large dappled cow; Eva on skis and skates – always laughing and showing off for the camera.

In the first decades of the twentieth century the nearest most children ever came to pictures on a screen was in the form of stereoscopic slides. The slides were in fact a pair of images, almost but not quite identical, printed on celluloid and framed in a cardboard rectangle. This slotted into a viewer, clumsier than yesterday's slide viewers and double the width. If you held this gadget – known as a stereoscope – to your eyes and lined it up correctly, the scene sprang to life with magical three-dimensional immediacy. Such stereoscopic images might have been the origin of Eva's lifelong passion for photography. The same three-dimensional viewers were also used to show erotica: arch, teasing, and, by today's standards, blithely innocent. The Braun girls were unlikely to have seen moving pictures (pioneered by Edison from 1891, the Lumière brothers from 1895), except perhaps at fairgrounds where people paid to watch jumpy black and white melodramas with handwritten white subtitles. However primitive they would seem today, these were thrilling: real people, moving and gesticulating on a flat screen.

Christmas has a special glow in everyone's memories. My mother left no more than half a dozen pages of her own recollections, but these included a paragraph about her childhood Christmases. Here it is, exactly as she wrote it when she was well into her fifties. After thirty years as an English wife she still hadn't quite got the hang of her adopted language, written or spoken, and she never lost the German profligacy with commas:

> The highlights of my childhood were our birthdays, and Christmases. My dear mother always bought lovely presents, and in the morning of my birthday, for breakfast, she put lovely different flowers, where I sat. For Christmas, we had a special little silver bell, our 'Weihnachtsglocke' and on Christmas Eve, 'Heiligabend' we always received our presents. While my mother got the Weihnachtszimmer (Christmas room) ready, my father and sisters waited anxiously, for the bell to ring, so, while we were waiting, we sang lots of lovely German Christmas carols, and suddenly, we heard the dainty tone of the bell, and all rushed into the living room, where the Tannenbaum (Christmas tree) was greeting us, beautifully decorated and with lots of real candles. The Weihnachtstisch (Christmas table) was laden with presents, and we all were full of joy and Christmas spirit.

(The word 'Christmas' appears eight times in that 139-word paragraph. In my mother's mind the very word was enough to trigger feelings of family love and warmly sentimental memories.)

The highlight of a child's year was the Christmas Fair, held in every German town during the four Advent weeks leading up to Christmas. In the centre of the main square stood a resinous pine tree perhaps 40 feet tall, the *Weihnachtsbaum*, hung with fine silver strips of *Lametta* that shimmered with every breath of wind. Coloured lights powered by hissing gas cylinders were looped between stalls decorated with branches of pine and fir cones, red-berried holly and mistletoe. The sweaty smell of frying onions and sizzling sausages, the spicy aroma of fat ginger biscuits called *Lebkuchen*, of sweet toffee apples, hot punch or *Glühwein* and coffee; the hanging rows of biscuits decorated with coloured icing and shaped like stars or Christmas trees; the sweet sound of carol singers: real ones, not CDs blasting out from loudspeakers; a band oompahing on gleaming brass trumpets; St Nikolaus in his cape and fur-lined hood, who only brought presents for *good* children (*they* knew they hadn't always been good but did *he* know?) – every sense was stirred and many a child howled because the excitement was more than it could bear. My mother remembered the freak shows best, the booth at the Hamburg Christmas Fair that had fascinated her when she was small. This was just after the end of the First World War and it seems likely that some of the freaks exhibited ('The Man With No Legs' or even 'The Man Without a Face') were war casualties trying to supplement inadequate army pensions by exhibiting their disfigurements, amputations and deformities. They were further evidence of a morbid German preoccupation with the maimed, the grotesque and the cruel. The link to Hitler's euthanasia programme two decades later is complex but that fascination and disgust with handicap may help to explain the acquiescence of ordinary, 'decent' Germans in the euthanasia of people 'unfit to live'; the first step along the line that ultimately led to the Nazi extermination camps.[8]

8. Burleigh, *The Third Reich: A New History*. In 1933 the Nazis introduced the Law for the Prevention of Hereditarily Diseased Progeny with effect from 1 January 1934. It included eight allegedly hereditary illnesses including mental illness, retardation, physical deformity, epilepsy, blindness, deafness and severe alcoholism. It also permitted the sterilisation of chronic alcoholics. Forced sterilisation began in January 1934 and in the next ten years an estimated 300,000 to 400,000 people were sterilised. In 1935 the law was strengthened to include eugenic abortion up to the sixth month. (. . .) In August 1939 doctors and nurses were told to inform a Reich committee set up to register serious hereditary and congenital illnesses, of cases of Down's syndrome, micro- and hydrocephaly, absence of a limb or spastic paralysis. Some 6,000 infants and children up to sixteen years old were subsequently killed. In October 1939, Hitler initialled a decree that empowered physicians to grant a 'mercy death', really murder, to patients considered incurable. The code name for this was Operation T4, or Aktion T-4. Its stated aim was 'to create bedspace for anticipated military casualties'. T4 reached its target of seventy thousand victims, making savings of nearly 900,000 Reichsmarks over ten years (documentation in Holocaust Museum, Washington DC). Starting in Dachau, gas chambers disguised as showers murdered the victims who were wheeled to crematoria. These were experimental prototypes of those built in extermination camps in Poland. Between 1941 and 1945 T4 organised euthanasia centres which murdered concentration camp inmates in Germany and Austria, Jews and Gentiles, who could no longer work. During the war the T4 perpetrators were told to halt the mass gassing of mental patients. In future they would be killed by starvation or lethal medication in a number of asylums, which would be easier to conceal than their removal. SS units in Poland and the Soviet Union simply shot mentally and physically handicapped people in Nazi-occupied conquered territory. In all, about 250,000 mentally and physically handicapped people met their deaths under this false 'euthanasia' programme.

The flu epidemic that swept Europe in 1919 cost as many lives as the Black Death six hundred years earlier,[9] shattering families and adding to the general sense of random catastrophe. And then came inflation. By 1918 the Deutschmark had fallen to a quarter of its pre-war value, playing havoc with people's savings. Decent people were plunged into poverty and many committed suicide. A burgeoning black market in which only spivs and swindlers flourished undermined former standards of probity. Thrifty, honest people used to efficient administration and civic incorruptibility lost faith in the government. There was 'a "moratorium on morality" in personal conduct, it being both necessary and legitimate to get along by any means, no matter how underhand'.[10] At the same time inflation worsened and by 1923 a barter economy had developed in which profiteers thrived. One of the most drastic consequences of this economic chaos was that it greatly heightened the perception of Jews as financially manipulative parasites, making those who had suffered under hyperinflation all the more open to anti-Semitism.

Fanny's niece Gertraud remembers her surprise on visiting the Braun household (this must have been many years later, however) and finding that Fritz had his own study/bedroom and ate there at mealtimes, rather than at the dining table with everyone else. When he was at home he would retreat to this room and sit playing with his cat, assembling a radio or planning lessons, marking homework and reading. 'They [i.e. Fritz and Fanny] didn't understand each other,' Gertraud surmised, 'and as far as I remember they never shared a bedroom. It was not a close marriage. But in those days families were surrounded by taboos and these things were not discussed. It was kept secret.'[11] The tensions escalated into ugly rows which the children, cramped in the small flat in Isabellastrasse, could not have failed to overhear. As so often happens, Fanny had chosen a man whose character in many ways mirrored her father's – rigid and authoritarian, self-centred and humourless, expecting his wife to defer to him in everything (the same could be said of many German husbands at the time). In due course their daughter Eva would repeat exactly this pattern.

9. Including that of my mother's younger sister Hilde, who died during the epidemic aged three and a half.
10. Burleigh, *The Third Reich: A New History*, pp. 29–30.
11. Interview with Gertraud Weisker, 24 March 2004.

On 2 February 1919 (four days before Eva's seventh birthday) a seismic, almost unthinkable event shook the Braun family. Fritz and Fanny formally separated.[12] He the stern Protestant head of the family and she the devout Catholic abandoned their most deeply held principles to go their different ways. It's not known what precipitated the separation although the parents obviously had opposite temperaments. Fritz's behaviour later in life (in his seventies he was said to have had a mistress in Berlin) suggests that, despite his upright manner and the strong moral expectations he imposed on his daughters, he was not always the most faithful of husbands. If an affair, or perhaps a French *mam'selle* left behind in Flanders, *had* come to light Fanny would have found this hard to accept. She was far from being a puritan – she loved good food, good clothes and good company – but she was too proud to have tolerated infidelity. Fritz had gradually cut himself off from the rest of the family: but was this his own choice or was it forced upon him? Even if he chose it, Gertraud wondered, was that a good enough reason for his wife to leave, taking the three girls with her?[13]

For the time being, Fritz went on living in the family flat and continued to teach while Fanny took her daughters, now ten, seven and four, back to her parents in Beilngries to try and work things out. Although Fanny's mother, the devoutly Catholic Josefa, deeply disapproved of the separation, she listened to the girls' prayers every night and tried to advise her daughter by day, perhaps with examples and anecdotes from her own marriage.

Eventually it was decided that Eva should go to the local Catholic day school, no doubt the one her mother and four aunts had attended

12. Author's note: I remain unconvinced that this was a divorce rather than a temporary but legal separation. Given her family background, it is hard to believe that Fanny would have divorced her husband only to remarry him less than two years later. But Gertraud Weisker wrote to me in an e-mail dated 26 May 2004: 'It is hard to know what to make of the document I saw in the Munich Amtsgericht [county court] but I am absolutely certain that I have copied the details in the original document correctly and am also correct in interpreting "*Heirat-Scheidung*" as meaning divorce rather than separation and "*Wiederheirat*" as remarriage.' [*Ich kann aus dem Dokument des Amtsgerichtes München schwer alles heraus lesen. Bin aber doch sicher, dass ich Dir die richtigen Angaben für Heirat-Scheidung und Wiederheirat gemacht habe.*] If her reading is correct, they divorced on 3 April 1921 in Munich and remarried on 16 November 1922.
13. Taken from Weisker, *Wer War Eva Braun?* (translated by the author).

when they were small.[14] She was left on her own with her grandparents while Fanny returned to Munich with the other two girls and moved back into the flat. Eva's new school was a *Volksschule*, an elementary school, and according to Herr Max Künzel – the *Kreisheimatpfleger*, or archivist, of Beilngries – Eva was there for a few months at most. The school records from that period have been preserved in the city archive but there is no report for Eva Braun and for some reason her name does not appear in the school register. Yet a former mayor of Beilngries, the late Max Walthierer, together with the late brewery owner Franz Schattenhofer and Maria Krauss of Beilngries (who was still alive in 2004, aged ninety-two) all remembered being at school with her in 1920–21. Maria Krauss recalled, 'Eva was a friendly classmate, and me and my sister liked playing with her. She was a "townie", with a page-boy haircut and white socks, but she quickly made friends with "us country children".'[15] 'These friendships lasted till the death of Frau Hitler,' says Wolfgang Brand, a doctor in Beilngries whose family were friendly with the Brauns and Kronburgers over several decades.

Judging by photographs from that time the school seems to have been affiliated to an old-fashioned orphanage, though it must also have accepted children from better-off families. A formal school photograph from about 1920, preserved in the photographic library at Munich's Staatsbibliothek, shows Eva with a group of pupils in the care of a nun. Another photograph from one of Eva's private albums, captioned

---

14. Gertraud Weisker's e-mail of 26 May 2004 to the author attempts further to clarify the situation: 'All I remember clearly is a photograph taken at the time when Eva was staying with her grandparents and going to the school in Beilngries. She is about seven or eight years old with a huge bow in her hair, so it must have been around 1919/1920. Fanny was on her own then and it seems very likely that she had sent Eva to stay with the grandparents, as she was the youngest one of school age. Ilse had already come through the difficult years [*aus dem Gröbsten heraus*] and Gretl, being only about three or four years old, would definitely have stayed with her mother.' In German, her e-mail reads: '*Das kann nur 1919–1920 gewesen sein, sie etwa 7–8 Jahre mit einer riesigen Schleife im Haar. Damals war Fanny allein erziehend und es liegt nahe, dass sie Eva als die kleinste schulpflichtige zu den Großeltern gegeben hat. Ilse war bereits aus dem Gröbsten raus und Gretl sicher bei der Mutter, denn sie war ja erst 3–4 Jahre alt.* Is it possible that Gertraud – who was not yet born when these events took place – is mistaken? It is hard to believe that two such morally entrenched parents should have made the decision to divorce, only to get back together again within less than a couple of years.

15. From Josef Riedl, editor, *Donaukurier*, 2–3 October 2004.

'*In der Klosterschule an Beilngries*' (the convent school at Beilngries) shows a line-up of the unlucky orphans. Forty years earlier, similar pictures recorded the unkempt, half-starved street children who were brought to Dr Barnardo's in London in the 1880s. Those battered, defeated little girls convey the same air of unutterable misery. Eva cannot have been happy there, nor entirely happy living with her grandparents. Summer holidays in the country were one thing; being forced to leave her parents, her friends and her familiar routine at the age of seven was quite another.

'These were troubled times for Munich, where the Braun family lived, shortly after the First World War,' explained Max Künzel. 'That might be the reason why they sent Eva to stay with her grandparents in Beilngries and attend the *Volksschule*.' His guess is backed up by Wolfgang Brand who remembered that Fanny had had to sublet rooms to keep the family out of debt. It's not known where Fritz went: given the shortage of money he may simply have slept on a bed in his study.

Eva and my mother grew up in similar respectable *bürgerliche* (middle-class) families, albeit at opposite ends of Germany – Eva down south in Bavaria and my mother far to the north, in Hamburg. By a curious coincidence, in 1924, when my mother was a girl of twelve, her parents also separated a few years after the Brauns, only they never got together again. This early sundering of what, to their daughters, had been an indissoluble family unit goes a long way to explain why both Eva and my mother regarded marriage as the greatest good. It makes clear why Eva longed more than anything else to be a wife and felt a failure when she could not coax Hitler into marriage. It also explains why my mother stayed married to my father, a typically laconic, undemonstrative Englishman who was sent away, aged eight, to a minor public school. After their first fifteen years together he fulfilled her need for security but could never supply the fun, praise and drama she craved.

Divorce was extremely rare in Germany in the twenties, despite a raffish minority culture based on the decadent nightclubs of Berlin between the wars. Such decadence was confined to a very few. The permanence of marriage, deeply inculcated by Church and state, was taken so much for granted and its premature termination such a disgrace that her parents' divorce caused my mother lifelong shame. I was in my fifties and had myself been divorced for nearly thirty years before she spoke about it and it was for her a terrible, humiliating confession. For the first time I understood why she had differentiated so cruelly between her parents, worshipping her stout, sentimental mother and often neglecting her father. She never forgave him for leaving when she was at her most impressionable and defenceless. If the parallel holds good, Eva never forgave *her* father either.

The effect of these upheavals on the three girls can only be guessed at; but that it could have happened at all, at a time when separation and divorce were virtually unknown in Germany, proves that something went very wrong between husband and wife. The whole event was completely buried for more than eighty years until Gertraud, researching the family history, came across the legal certificates in the Munich city archives – to her utter astonishment. It was the first time in her life she'd known anything about it. The truth behind this puzzling sequence of events remains obscure, but in 1922 the Braun parents resumed living together in the apartment in Isabellastrasse. They were officially reunited – possibly even remarried in a civil ceremony – on 16 November 1922.[16] After this, Fritz and Fanny Braun stayed married, apparently contentedly enough, for more than forty years.[17]

In Munich during the winter when the temperature dropped below freezing the Braun family would skate on the municipal ice-rinks, swooping and circling under the bright lights. Eva was an expert skater – photographs show her gliding confidently on one leg, the other held high in the air. Fanny Braun had been a ski champion in her teens and the family sometimes went skiing in the Bavarian Alps. At weekends, once the girls were old enough, they all went to operettas together or to the cinema, implanting in Eva a life-long passion for artistic kitsch – romantic music and slushy or swashbuckling films. They had a piano at home and Eva took – and must have enjoyed, or she'd never have stuck at them – piano lessons. Her mother had a beautiful singing voice and both sets of sisters – the Brauns and my mother's,

16. Verified by legal documents researched and copied in the Munich city archives by Gertraud Weisker.
17. They are buried in the same grave in the cemetery of St George's Church, a peaceful spot on a hillside just outside Ruhpolding, the village to which they retreated after the war to spend the rest of their lives in blessed anonymity. Their red marble tombstone bears only their names and dates, inscribed in gold: FRITZ BRAUN, Studienrat [teacher], 17.9.1879–22.1.1964, followed by FRANZISKA BRAUN 12.12.1885–13.1.1976.

the Schröders[18] – were almost the last generation to gather round the piano and sing for pleasure. It's hard to imagine, in these days of electronic sound-surround, how often and how unselfconsciously people used to sing. Walking, working, with their friends or their children, women sang as naturally as they spoke. The wind-up gramophone had become a major cultural influence and thanks to huge sales of 78 rpm records and sheet music everyone knew the words to the popular songs of the day and even arias, especially those from light opera.

Eva and my mother Ditha were taught to say their prayers, respect and obey their parents, their teachers and indeed any grown-up. In the 1920s families were organised for the benefit and according to the rules of adults and, unless the family could afford servants, girls were expected to help in the kitchen and with the daily round of housework. Boys, of course, were not – treatment of the sexes was sharply differentiated. They were reared to be manly, brave, laconic, studious and gallant to women. It was 'manly' not to show emotion and while the occasional maternal embrace might be accepted they would never hug or kiss their fathers but shake hands, or, if they were in the armed services, salute. Girls were expected to be affectionate, silly and overexcitable, scared of mice, spiders, insects. Vanity was indulged: most parents believed it was more useful in life to be pretty than clever.

Modesty between the sexes was strictly preserved. Hygiene was a priority but although the whole family would use one bathroom, children never saw their parents naked, nor would boys and girls take baths together. The cult of a sound mind in a chaste and healthy body was supreme. Both sexes were encouraged to take vigorous exercise at home and school, preferably in the open air, better still in the cold. People slept with their windows open even on freezing nights and every morning, my mother remembered, she had to leap out of bed, throw her arms wide and fill her lungs with fresh air. '*Tief atmen!*' her father would instruct – breathe deeply! '*Tief atmen, zwölf mal . . . eins, zwei, drei . . . langsam, Schätzchen . . . vier, fünf, sechs . . .*'[19] Thirty years later she made me do the same, so firmly had the habit been instilled.

18. My mother describes in her own, very brief, memories of her childhood, how 'My mother liked playing the piano and also the zither and I often sang while she played'.
19. 'Breathe deeply, twelve times . . . one, two, three . . . slowly, my treasure . . . four, five, six . . .'

In 1925 when Eva was thirteen and the family reunited they moved to a more spacious flat a few streets away in Schwabing-West, on the third floor of an apartment building several blocks north of Munich's shopping centre. Hohenzollernstrasse 93/III would have been quite a good address in the twenties, though the taint of bohemianism lingered. Around the turn of the century, particularly during the Art Deco years, Schwabing had been famous for a generation of reckless avant-garde youth – artists, poets and jazz musicians, uninhibitedly pursuing free art, verse, dancing and love. The area once dominated by elaborate *Art Nouveau* or *Jugendstil* apartment buildings was flattened by Allied bombs and much of it has now been rebuilt with duller modern replacements. The Braun family flat survived however and, with the wartime bomb damage repaired, is once again part of a well-maintained, desirable block whose windows look out on to Hohenzollernplatz, a pleasant small square with a few trees and swings for children to play on. The ground floor is now a chemist, Spitzweg-Apotheke (in Eva's day it was a bakery).[20]

In 1924, having completed four years at the *Volksschule*, Eva Braun – now twelve – was sent to a girls' Catholic *Lyzeum* in Munich, within easy walking distance in Tengstrasse, a few streets away.[21] This was unusual at the time – only one in twenty-five girls attended an academic-based senior school (rather than a school teaching domestic skills) and only 9 per cent of those went to a *Lyzeum*, which paved the way to higher education.[22] The decision must reflect her mother's liberal upbringing in a family of girls who had all been trained for a profession, as well as Fritz's inclination, as a teacher, to value the benefits of a good education. The new school suited Eva. At the *Lyzeum* – unlike the gloomy convent school in Beilngries – she was the centre of attention. The atmosphere was lively and open minded, the teachers were liberal and thought highly of her. Vivacious, outgoing, definitely a leader; curious and quick thinking, she was a promising pupil with a good mind.

But she could not, or *would* not, concentrate. 'Every nonsense in the classroom originated with her,' said her teacher, Fräulein von Heidenaber, who recalled: 'Eva was the trouble-maker of the class but

20. Winbauer, *Eva Braun's Familiengeschichte*. The present owners, understandably, are not keen on callers, above all when they turn up unannounced.
21. There is some confusion about Eva's secondary schooling. Both her uncle Alois and cousin Gertraud remember her attending the Ursuline Institute at Nymphenburg; yet Eva's photograph album with her school pictures is clearly captioned '*Lyzeum*'. Perhaps she went to both.
22. Jill Stephenson, *Women in Nazi Society* (London: Croom Helm, 1975), p. 14.

she was intelligent and quick to seize the essential aspects of a subject, and she was capable of independent thought.'[23] If she'd been prepared to take her work more seriously, Eva Braun could have done well at her lessons and got good reports. She did not. As far as she was concerned, being popular was far more important.

Soon she was seeking approval from boys as well as girls. By the time she was fifteen Eva had puppy fat and thick legs but she knew already that promise is all. She was a blatant flirt, copying the gestures of her favourite film stars, their wise-cracking retorts, their tantalising blend of bravado and coyness. To boys, all this, combined with her vivacity and *Lebenslust* – love of life – was hugely appealing. Early photograph albums show her at parties making eyes at a number of clean-shaven, clean-limbed, grinning young men, but these displays of teenage daring are curiously sexless. She was testing her effect on boys but that was all. Other snapshots show her on a motorbike belonging to the big brother of her best friend, Herta Ostermayr, with another schoolfriend, all three leaning forward like racers, giggling at the camera. In one picture Eva clasps her hands coquettishly round her knees, smiling invitingly over her bare shoulder. She was, to use the affectionate German word for a teenager, a typical *Backfisch*.

By the mid-1920s Fritz Braun had already begun to fret about his older daughters' marriage prospects. His main concern was to guard their virginity, this being his first obligation to their future husbands. It is impossible to exaggerate the importance that German parents of the time placed on their daughters' chastity. Their religious and social background demanded it, above all for Catholics. An unmarried girl who had lost her virginity was a reproach to her father and a disgrace to the whole family. Protecting Ilse was easy: she was a late developer, shy with boys, but Eva was an exception and a challenge from the very beginning. Her adolescence was spent confronting her father, fighting for the right to be herself. He never seems to have grasped that she was more than a silly schoolgirl interested only in the pursuit of pleasure. Behind the self-obsessed exterior, the show-off who played up to attention and applause, was someone less obvious and more interesting. Thanks to her mother's insistence on church and Mass and catechism she went through a phase of extreme religious fervour, according to her uncle Alois: 'Her deep religious commitment could be a source of great embarrassment to her father. Sometimes when

23. Quoted in Gun, *Eva Braun: Hitler's Mistress*, p. 21.

she was out walking with him she would meet one of her Divinity teachers and hail him with the words, "The Lord be praised" and Fritz, though not exactly shocked, would shake his head in disapproval.'[24] Later, although she ceased to be a practising Catholic or a regular church-goer, she never ceased to be aware that life demanded moral decisions and it mattered which path one took.

According to Henriette Hoffmann, Fritz Braun was ambitious for his daughters and determined that they should work hard and get good school results, more to qualify them for a well-educated husband than as the first step towards successful careers of their own. Eva could have been top of the class like her conscientious sister Ilse, but she refused to apply herself. To her father's fury, Eva's reports from the *Lyzeum* didn't improve. They continued to praise her intelligence while deploring her idleness. Geography and history, grammar and mathematics, the future of Germany, its politics, leaders, slogans, inflation – none of these interested her. Despite this refusal to concentrate on studying, she left school having got a diploma with several credits, proving that she had enough intelligence to compensate. According to cousin Gertraud,[25] none of the three Braun daughters took *Abitur* (the German equivalent of today's A levels) – which was surprising, given their parents' respect for academic achievement. This meant they all left school without the option of university and had to go straight into work.

In 1928 Eva assumed she would start earning her living, since she was now sixteen and a half and her high school education was complete. Her parents, however, decided that her behaviour needed to be tamed, her manners and social graces improved if she were ever to find a respectable job, let alone make a respectable marriage. It would do her good to spend a couple of years in a convent/finishing school that would give their wayward girl some social graces, including good table manners. (Later in life Eva would judge her guests' social adroitness by how cleanly they could fillet a trout, lifting away the backbone to leave two boneless slices of fish.)[26] More important, Fanny hoped it would deepen Eva's religious sense and add a veneer of culture. Eva would be forced to leave home, leave her friends and her social life, the noisy, exuberant hangouts where she was known and welcomed, to be incarcerated for

24. Winbauer, *Eva Braun's Familiengeschichte*, p. 9.
25. In an interview with the author, 25 March 2004.
26. Gertraud Weisker in conversation with the author, March 2004.

two years with *nuns*. She raged and wept and sulked in her room but her parents were adamant.

It's likely that, behind the histrionics, she felt rejected. During those years when her father left the family, Eva had been the only daughter to be banished from Munich to Beilngries. She was only seven or eight at the time, but girls of that age brood and reason things out.

By 1928 Ilse was almost twenty, a 'goody-goody' who never came in for criticism; Gretl, at thirteen, was still the baby of the family, adored by all for her sweet ways. Fritz Braun's discontent was chiefly directed at Eva, who bore the brunt of the tensions that may have seethed below an outwardly calm domestic surface. Did her craving for public admiration reflect her sense of being unwanted at home? She was always more confrontational towards her father than the other two, but he often criticised her unfairly. She was a good Catholic girl; she didn't smoke or drink; she'd worked, if not hard, at any rate hard enough at school; as she saw it, she'd done nothing worse than giggle and gossip with her girlfriends and flirt with gauche teenage boys. Now they were going to send her away again.

The convent her parents selected, the Convent of the English Sisters, or *Kloster der Englischen Schwestern*, was in the small town of Simbach, 120 kilometres north-east of Munich, right on the border with Austria. It's not clear where Fritz Braun found the money to pay for an expensive boarding school, but Herr Doktor Veterinär Kronburger may have helped. Eva's photograph albums contain only one picture dating from her time there. In the annual class photograph, a score of stolid, miserable looking girls, hair scraped back into tight plaits, wearing unflattering uniforms, stare unsmilingly into the camera, victims of the Sisters' determination to suppress any trace of sexuality and high spirits. The food at the *Kloster* was doughy and sweet and Eva gained weight – 5 kilos – which bloated her pretty face and thickened her body and legs. One of the nuns recalled many years later that Eva had had no close friends during her time at the convent – unimaginable, for someone so gregarious. Angry, lonely and bored, there would have been nothing to entertain her even if she had managed to get out occasionally.

Simbach is a small provincial town, its importance deriving from its position on the River Inn, directly on the border, opposite the small town of Braunau am Inn – Hitler's birthplace – in Austria. The convent was on the German side. The bridge spanning the border and the river is barely half a mile from where Eva was incarcerated, while on the Austrian side it leads straight into the main street of Braunau. Simbach boasts some five Bavarian Baroque buildings – but then Eva grew up amid those – and much elaborate Catholic art in its churches, but for a teenager bent on fun it must have been a depressing prospect.

The two towns were conservative and smug, reflecting the values of Alois Hitler, the portly customs official who had used the prestige of his office to lord it over his subordinates, his family and, crucially, his son twenty-five years earlier.

The convent now serves as a care home, still run by the English Sisters, steering the fretful souls of the old and sick towards a pious death. Inside, the fine early nineteenth-century building has been completely refurbished to comply with modern standards but it retains the depressing air of a closed, authoritarian institution. Small, narrow doors open into small, narrow rooms along small, narrow corridors. Nuns in white wimples and black robes glide in and out. No one there remembers Eva – the nuns who taught her would be well over a hundred by now – and the convent's records, including her school reports, have gone missing or been destroyed. The present Mother Superior confirmed that Eva had been a pupil, if only briefly, adding 'We still get lots of enquiries', but offered no further information. Fräulein Braun clearly remains something of an embarrassment to the Sisters.

The institutional atmosphere I sensed when I visited it in August 2004 can't have been very different in Eva's day. Hating the convent and its smiling, hard-line nuns, she fretted and fumed under the strict régime and threatened murder and mayhem if she were forced to stay on, swearing she'd run away to Vienna. Defying her parents, she flatly refused a second year – and she got her way. After only nine months Eva left the convent, not in 1930, as her parents had intended but a year earlier, in July 1929. For a second time she failed to sit *Abitur*, leaving with only a 'certificate of secondary education': not because she was stupid – far from it – but because, as before, she would not take her schoolwork seriously. The final report from the convent was disparaging: 'Your daughter is intelligent and ambitious . . . yet she was not interested in the curriculum and thought that the regulations were unduly restrictive.' Between the disapproving words glimmers the quicksilver ghost of a teenager chafing against 'restrictive regulations' and impatient to embark on Life. But note that at the Lyzeum she had been considered 'capable of independent thought' and 'ambitious'. Sister Marie-Magdalena told an interviewer, 'Eva was ambitious and intelligent and had a pretty voice. She excelled as a performer in amateur theatricals. She regularly attended the religious services.'[27] (Did she have any choice?) One thing the convent *had* achieved. It conducted annual gynaecological examinations of all its pupils, which confirmed that at seventeen and a half Eva was a guaranteed virgin.

The two-hour train back to Munich left from Simbach railway station. It is one of the very few remaining places that looks today exactly as it did when Eva passed through. Its size comes as a shock: for such a small town, the station is huge. To one side of the rails, on the left, are broad sidings, now rarely used. In front of them stretches a 200-metre line of low redbrick warehouses which look out through iron-barred windows to where the incoming goods trains unloaded their contents for inspection by customs and excise. To the right is an imposing station building dating from the 1870s, with tall arched doorways opening on to a dozen high-ceilinged rooms, dusty and half-abandoned. The size and former elegance of these rooms is heightened by peeling doors and rusty window frames, evocative of a time when everyone travelled by train. Even the railway track still has wooden sleepers. Standing on the platform one sees exactly what Eva saw as she waited to be transported back to Munich: the one-storey buildings on the left, the railway lines converging as they stretch into the distance. With her suitcase beside her, school, convent and nuns behind her, the future ahead, Eva Braun was free at last.

27. Gun, *Eva Braun: Hitler's Mistress*, p. 22.

Chapter Five

Hitler's Childhood

After leaving the convent in July 1929, Eva was quick to shed her schoolgirl self. She was seventeen and a half when she returned home; a round-faced, plump adolescent, not startlingly pretty but precociously aware of her looks and sex appeal. Her idea of fun was chatting, listening to the latest popular music, watching the latest films and seizing every opportunity to whip up a party in the cafés, beer gardens and clubs of Munich. She had always been an outrageous tease and a flirt and made no secret of her growing interest in the opposite sex, although she was already used to the company of teenage boys. Fritz Braun's job as a teacher had provided her with ample opportunity to tag along when he took his pupils hiking or skiing, in the days before *Hitler Jugend* monopolised all youthful open-air activities. In group photographs recording these occasions Eva lolls in the centre, laughing, her hand on one young man's shoulder or another's knee, revelling in the attention. If her father had suspected anything improper he would certainly not have let her join these all-male trips,[1] but, as the convent

1. This enthusiasm for tough physical exercise was not confined to Fritz, or Germany. Baden-Powell's best-selling *Scouting for Boys* – a title whose *double entendre* is certainly unconscious – reflects the same insistence on teenage self-control, though its dire warnings and cold showers suggest the old soldier knew *something* was going on among his decent, healthy chaps; something beyond even his control. He would have been appalled to learn that it was often instigated by the wise old wolf Akela, as the Scouts' Pack Leader was known. (A story circulated about Baden-Powell and a fellow soldier at the end of the Boer War, discussing what they would do when they got back to England. Baden-Powell described his plan to assemble groups of young boys, dress them in shorts and go for long hikes, naked bathes and so on. 'You could get ten years for that,' said his friend.)

must have informed him, he had no reason to worry. His daughter was still virgo intacta.

Had she been prepared to concentrate she could have trained for a career, but Eva revelled in her first few months of adolescent freedom. Much against her parents' wishes, she had had enough of studying. Spontaneous and uninhibited, she couldn't wait to get away from her father's disapproval of nearly everything she did. Her older sister Ilse, now twenty, was still living under his roof even though, working as a receptionist in a Jewish doctor's surgery, she earned good money and could afford to rent or share an apartment. But Fritz Braun, like most fathers at the time, expected his daughters to live with their parents until they married. He took for granted his right to ensure that his daughters were 'good girls', by which he meant obedient and faithful to their husbands, domesticated, virtuous and devout. The quiet and serious Ilse might accept this but freewheeling, exuberant Eva chafed under his régime. She would have liked to be an actress or film star; or if that was impossible, a champion skater – anything, as long as she was an object of public admiration. Her father had other ideas. He made her do a brief shorthand/typing course, then despatched her to work in a doctor's surgery. Eva hated both. Spotting an advertisement for an apprentice/assistant to start in Hoffmann's photography shop she – or more probably her father – replied, explaining that she had finished her education, done a short commercial course, worked briefly as a receptionist but was more interested in photography, for which she showed some fledgling aptitude. She might well be a suitable candidate for the post. She was, and Hoffmann hired her.

When she first encountered Hitler, Eva was still very much an innocent but Hitler liked his women young, naive and compliant and would have regarded the twenty-three-year age difference as ideal. She fitted perfectly his need for a relationship in which he could dictate the rules. He used to say, 'There's nothing better than training a young thing [*sich ein junges Ding zu erziehen*]. A girl of eighteen or twenty is as impressionable as a piece of wax. It should be possible for a man . . . to stamp his imprint upon her. That's all the woman asks for, by the way.'[2] In the Germany of the late 1920s he could even have been right. Eva – artless, lively and eager to please – was ideal 'wax' for Hitler to mould. One can't know what Eva thought about the age gap except that, as Hitler was only ten years younger than her father, she

2. *Hitler's Table Talk, 1941–1944.*

must have regarded him as 'an older man' though not necessarily as a father figure. In spite of this she fell in love with him on sight. Fifteen years later she would tell him in a letter: 'From our first meeting I swore to follow you anywhere – even unto death. I live only for your love.' The fact that she was so powerfully drawn to him had nothing to do with Hitler's fame as a politician: Eva, who knew the words and the steps to every current popular song and dance and could gossip about the stars of every current film, was blissfully ignorant on the subject of politics. Politics were men's business.

Apart from her malleability, which Eva shared with most young women of her age, what did Hitler see in her? She was *familiar*. She came from the same part of the world as he did and her Bavarian manners and Munich accent would have appealed to him from the start. She was not dim but not brilliant either; pretty but not beautiful; lively but not hysterical. She didn't threaten him. She wanted only to please. No one in his inner circle could understand why he was interested in her, though they were all sure they knew exactly why she was interested in him, yet her attraction for Hitler makes perfect sense in the light of his earliest years; above all, his relationships with his parents. He never divulged the shameful details, even to his oldest and closest Nazi colleagues; indeed, he took pains to obscure them. *Mein Kampf* paints a glamourised but largely fictional version of his home life and the anecdotes that he loved repeating to his friends were designed to cast him in a good light and make him seem destined for *Führer*dom. They had little to do with the truth. If the childhood of young Adolf evokes a certain sympathy, it is sympathy for the battered child.

Adolf Hitler was born in 1889 before Freud's ideas, in particular his theory of the Oedipus complex, revolutionised attitudes towards child-rearing. Children were hardly thought of as separate, sentient beings but as little savages needing to be tamed. Boys were unruly cubs to be cuffed or thrashed into obedience. The admonition 'Spare the rod and spoil the child' made perfect sense to most parents. He grew up at a time when beating male children was normal, almost justified; a man was master in his own household. The domestic microcosm, with its emphasis on the superiority of the strong over the weak, was replicated in millions of families between millions of fathers and sons. This hierarchical use of force pointed the way towards Hitler's later use of power. As *Führer* he had at his disposal vast destructive forces in the form of slavishly obedient collaborators. Violence and contempt often grow out of humiliation and there was plenty of that in his youth.[3] The American child psychiatrist Alice Miller pointed out:

. . . a connection between the systematic cruelty of the pedagogical advice to parents in Germany a century ago and the systematic cruelty of Hitler's executioners forty years later. Numerous widely-read tracts counselled that the new-born child should be forced from the very first day to obey and to refrain from crying. One of Dr Daniel Gottlieb Schreber's convictions [Schreber was the Benjamin Spock or Penelope Leach of his time] was that when babies cry they should be made to desist by the use of spanking. The rigorous obedi-ence training undergone in earliest infancy stunted the development of such human capacities as compassion and pity for the sufferings of others.[4]

3. James Gilligan is a leading psychotherapist who has studied some of the most violent members of America's prison population. He has likened the motives behind their collective acts of atrocity to those of the Nazis: 'Hitler's writings constitute one long chronicle of complaints about the shame and humiliation to which both he, in his youth, and the German-speaking peoples after World War One had been subjected – all of which he managed to blame mostly on the Jews, for whom it is hard to say which he feels more strongly, envy or hate. Envy, like jealousy, is a form of shame . . . to feel envious of someone is to feel inferior to that person.'

Shame is a crucial factor in detonating violence. Neither individuals nor coun-tries can endure it for long. Gilligan continues: 'By the time of the depression on the crest of which Hitler rode to power in 1933 the group who supported him most strongly at the polls were the lower middle class. The members of this group felt in danger of losing their capital and suffering a loss of social and economic status, a degradation, by becoming part of the humiliated, inferior, poverty-stricken lower class . . . and were eager for revenge – for a way of re-establishing their status or sense of power – which Hitler and his Nazi Party promised them in abundance. *Downward social mobility, unemployment and homelessness are among the most potent stimuli of shame and a key to the politics of violence* [my italics].' Gilligan believes the Jews were singled out because they were identified with wealth. Great families like the Rothschilds seemed to threaten the economic status of the lower middle class while another group of Jews led by Marx – the Bolsheviks – threatened them by giving power and encouragement to the prole-tariat. James Gilligan, *Violence: Reflections on a National Epidemic* (New York: Vintage Books, 1997), p. 67.

4. Alice Miller, *The Childhood Trauma*, from a lecture given in New York on 22 October 1998.

Leaving aside the sadistic advice of paediatricians, what genes swam in the stagnant pool from which came the warped phenomenon of Adolf Hitler?

In June 1837, in a remote and poverty-stricken corner of Austria between the Danube and the Bohemian border, to be precise in the village of Strones, a maid-servant called Maria Schicklgruber gave birth at the age of forty-two to an illegitimate son. He was, remarkably, her first child and she had him baptised Alois. This unclaimed boy, whose birth certificate recorded him as 'son of a man unknown', would, fifty-two years later, be the father of Adolf Hitler. Local gossip had it that he was the son of an itinerant miller called Johann Georg Hiedler. Five years later, when she was forty-seven, Maria married Hiedler, who never bothered to legitimise his son (assuming Alois *was* his son); afterwards she handed her only child into the care of her husband's younger brother, a farmer called Johann Nepomuk Hiedler (who sometimes spelled his surname Hüttler[5]). The truth about Alois's paternity remains uncertain but illegitimacy was common and he used the surname Schicklgruber until he was nearly forty. Any rumours of Jewish blood can with certainty be discounted[6] and it's more than likely that one of the brothers, Johann Georg or Johann Nepomuk, was the father of Alois Schicklgruber.

Hitler's father grew up to be a womaniser; the sort of man whom gossipy neighbours describe as 'a randy old goat'. A petty official, strict and pedantic at work, he was respected in the community but at home

5. Ian Kershaw notes several variants: Hiedler, Hietler, Hutler and Hitler – all based on the word for 'smallholder'. Kershaw, *Hitler, 1889–1936: Hubris*, p. 7.
6. Biographers and rumourmongers have sometimes claimed that Hitler's father was Maria's illegitimate son by her Jewish employer, a man called Frankenberger, and that this event, assumed to have been a rape, was at the root of Adolf's visceral hatred for Jews. A detailed check of the town records by Nikolaus Preradovic, a historian at Graz University, proved this to have been quite impossible since not one single Jew had lived in the locality, or indeed the entire province, at the time. (*Der Spiegel*, number 24, 12 June 1957.) Simon Wiesenthal's research came up with the same result. (*Der Spiegel*, letter to the editor, 7 August 1967.) From the early nineteenth century until one hundred years later, Germany's Jews were concentrated overwhelmingly in big cities, particularly Berlin, Frankfurt and Hamburg. The likelihood of a Jewish family in a small border town like Graz is remote. 'Frankenberger' may have been a mythical figure. It also remains unexplained why, if he existed at all, he should allegedly have paid Maria for the support of her son until the age of fourteen.

he was an unstable tyrant, a mean and violent drunk who beat his wife and son for no more reason than a bellyful of beer. To be fair, he must also have been ambitious and diligent, since he rose as high in the Austrian Finance Office as his humble origins allowed. He became a customs officer, justifiably proud of his rank, his career evidently not impeded by his greed for women – the younger, the better. In spite of this, Alois's first marriage was to a woman fourteen years older than himself called Anna Glassl, whom he may well have married for her money, as hard-up young men often did. She died ten years later without having borne him children (she was fifty when they married so from the start it was highly unlikely). He also had a teenage mistress, Franziska Matzelsberger – Fanni – twenty-four years younger than him, and fathered a son by her to whom he gave his own Christian name, Alois. His first wife's death obliged him to marry Franziska in 1883 when she was already pregnant with their second child, a girl named Angela. He decided at the same time to legitimise their little son, Alois. One bastard in the family was not going to pass on the stigma to another.

Being a figure of substance in the community, each time he found himself widowed Alois Hitler had to make an honest woman of the girl he had seduced in the meantime. Ever since she was sixteen Klara Pölzl had been the family's maidservant, cook and, inevitably, Alois's mistress. (It seems to have been something of a Hitler family tradition to take in young female relatives as maidservants and seduce them.) When Fanni died in 1884 she was swiftly followed as third wife by Klara, by this time in her mid-twenties, twenty-three years Alois's junior. They married in January 1885 when Klara too was already pregnant. Like her new husband, she came from the tiny village of Spittal in the Waldviertal, a poor corner of Austria devoted mainly to subsistence farming. Knowledge of eugenics at that time was slight, despite the biblical list prohibiting intermarriage. The roots, branches and twigs of this family tree are not easy to follow but what is important is that the marriage of Adolf Hitler's parents was deeply entwined in the genealogical pool of the Spittal community from which they both came, many of whose offspring were mentally or physically handicapped. Klara's mother had been Johanna Hiedler before she married, so *her* father must have been one of the two Johanns who probably fathered Alois. Klara was all too closely related to her husband, being his second cousin and the daughter of his half-sister, which would make her his niece. She innocently addressed her husband as 'Uncle

Alois'. The troubled ancestry of the inbred Schicklgrubers may not have bothered the village but it was to be a source of deep disquiet to its most famous son and forty years hence would profoundly influence the course of Eva's future.

Over the next four years Klara bore her husband two sons, Gustav and Otto, and a daughter, Ida, all three of whom died young. On 20 April 1889, in the small Austrian town of Braunau am Inn, across the river from Simbach in Bavaria, a third son was born and named Adolf. Three years earlier his father had changed his name from Schicklgruber to Hitler, which meant that the new baby's surname was Hitler – fortunately for him – rather than Schicklgruber.[7] This was almost his only piece of luck. In most other respects the future *Führer* started life at a disadvantage, being born into a family whose combination of interbreeding and poverty was made worse by ignorance, brutishness and the absence of anyone – teacher, priest, grandparent – who might have noticed that Adolf Hitler was an unusually clever and impressionable child and, in the light of this, intervene to protect him.

The one exception was his mother. Klara Hitler was twenty-nine when her son Adolf came into the world. She had already borne her virile fifty-two-year-old husband three children in quick succession as well as acting as stepmother to Alois and Angela, the older pair from his second marriage. She was a hard-working, dutiful wife, loyal and faithful to the self-important customs official old enough to be her father, and well aware that he had married her to maintain the necessary façade of respectability by legitimising her unborn child. Marriage to a well-placed customs official would have been regarded as highly advantageous for a lowly servant girl. In return for this she was expected to look after his motherless children as well as her own surviving two, Adolf and his younger brother Edmund. And, of course, to share Alois's bed. In 1896 Klara bore him the last of their six children – a daughter, Paula. Paula was slightly mentally handicapped[8] and throughout his adult life her brother Adolf was careful to keep her at a distance.

It is not easy, given today's attitudes to romantic love, to believe that Klara ever loved her bullying husband. Love, in a poor rural community 120 years ago, had very different connotations and little to do with romance. It meant duty, stoicism, constant hard work, piety but, above

---

7. *Heil* Schicklgruber?
8. The American psychiatrist Walter C. Langer, in the brutal jargon of the 1940s, described her as 'a high-grade moron'. How did he know?

all, it conferred the status of marriage; in return for which a wife offered absolute obedience to her lord and master. Those attitudes were slow to change. My German mother, who married almost exactly fifty years later, addressed my father as 'Lord and Master' for the first dozen years of their marriage. It was not altogether a joke – she also meant it.

Wives obeyed not only their husbands but also the Church. Klara was a devout Roman Catholic who attended Mass regularly and encouraged Adolf to serve as an altar boy in the church at Braunau where he had been baptised. In the section about his childhood in *Mein Kampf* he wrote: 'At Lambach I had an excellent opportunity to intoxicate myself with the solemn splendour of the brilliant church festivals.'[9] This indoctrination went deeper than he cared to admit. A month after his fifteenth birthday (unusually late, for a Catholic) Adolf Hitler was confirmed in Linz. To the end of his life he never repudiated his faith, although this didn't stop him persecuting and murdering millions of his co-believers.

Young women had to conform to the unspoken but sacrosanct rules imposed by their elders. In the late nineteenth century, in a primitive farming community, women were looked on as child-bearing drudges, hardly more valuable than a high-yielding milk cow or fertile sow. Husband, priest and frowning village matriarchs all exploited their power, but in Klara's case her husband Alois was the heaviest oppressor. She lived in fear of his beatings although, as was expected of her, she endured them without complaint. Her sensitive and observant little son witnessed and heard her ill-treatment but could do nothing to prevent it.[10] As Adolf got bigger he too began to suffer at the hands of his father. According to Angela, the half-sister from the second marriage who lived with them, he 'got his sound thrashing every day', which can only have increased his fear and hatred of his father. Years later he told one of his secretaries, 'After reading one day in Karl May [author of his favourite adventure stories] that the brave man gives no sign of being in pain, I made up my mind not to let out any sound next time I was beaten. And when the moment came I counted every blow. My mother thought I'd gone mad when I proudly told her, "Father hit me thirty-two times".' In compensation his mother poured all her love and hopes into the only one of her four sons to reach his teens.

9. Adolf Hitler, *Mein Kampf*, translated by Ralf Manheim (London: Hutchinson, 1969), p. 5.
10. Christa Schröder, *Er War Mein Chef* (Munich: Langen Müller, 1985), p. 63. He also repeated this story of thirty-two strokes to his housekeeper, Anna Winter; see Maser, *Hitler*, p. 208.

The relationship between mother and son was exceptionally close. By 1844, when Adolf was five, Klara had already lost two small sons and was perhaps overprotective towards the only one to survive. Adolf, who inherited her extraordinarily piercing pale blue eyes, believed he took after her in character as well, though it is hard to reconcile this with the description of her as 'submissive, retiring, quiet . . . saddened and careworn'.[11] Their relationship developed into an intense bond, almost a *folie à deux*, and all his life she remained his model of perfect wife- and motherhood, with weighty consequences for a whole gener-ation of German wives and mothers. Convinced that a woman's sole destiny was to bear and rear children and maintain a frugal and spot-less household,[12] the young Hitler – like most of his contemporaries – grew up with a narrow view of how men and women should order their relationships.

In November 1898 Alois, now sixty-one and on the verge of retire-ment, moved his family to Leonding, a village on the outskirts of Linz, a sleepy provincial town of some sixty thousand inhabitants. Young Adolf was nine at the time, but for the rest of his life he regarded Linz as his home town. The same year, in 1898, the time came for him to leave the primary school run by Benedictines at the Lambach monastery, where he had found the work easy, and go on to a more demanding *Realschule* (a secondary school concentrating on contemporary rather than classical subjects) in Linz. He was not happy there. He resented discipline, the teachers didn't like him and his work deteriorated. So did relations with his father.

Adolf, about to enter his teens, was repelled by Alois's coarse behav-iour and excessive eating and drinking, although to most Bavarians they signified no more than convivial high spirits and a hearty appetite. His own tastes were positively ascetic. As a boy and later as a man, his only self-indulgence seems to have been a lifelong passion for rich cream cakes. A vegetarian throughout his adult life, he rarely drank alcohol and never smoked; never swam or danced, let alone joined in

11. Kershaw *Hitler, 1889–1936: Hubris*, p. 12.
12. In this, Hitler was backed by the German Civil Code of 1900, which decreed that a husband had the right in law to choose where to live, the names and reli-gion of the children of a marriage, and the nature and length of their education. The wife was 'entitled and obliged' to conduct the family household and also obliged to work in her husband's business, if appropriate. The Roman Catholic Church, which ordained the children should be brought up in their mother's faith, was evidently permitted to override this law.

male-bonding outbursts of thigh-slapping, beer-swilling gluttony and lechery like his father. It may have been a relief to the family when Alois Hitler died suddenly of a heart attack at the local inn in 1903, aged sixty-five. By then Adolf was fourteen and his only surviving full sibling,[13] the handicapped Paula, was seven. The half-sister from his father's second marriage, Angela, now twenty, had married Leo Raubal (another tax official) in September that year and left home. The remaining family – Klara and her two surviving children, as well as her sister Johanna Pölzl, a bad-tempered hunchback who had inherited a bit of money – now looked forward to a quiet life supported by Alois's generous state pension.

In June 1905 Klara sold the family house in Leonding and, helped by a contribution from Johanna, they all moved into a small flat in the centre of Linz. For a short time Adolf continued to study, though no more attentively than before. He was a highly intelligent boy – all his teachers agreed on that – but arrogant and lethargic. He couldn't be bothered to work or concentrate and thought he knew it all anyway. Not that he was distracted by the stirrings of adolescent sexuality; a former classmate insisted: 'Out of the question. Adolf was never interested in girls.'[14] He spent a year at a senior school – having presumably been expelled from the Benedictine school – and in September 1905, now sixteen, ended his education with a distinctly unsatisfactory report and no diploma. Undeterred, he set about spending as much of his father's legacy as he could cajole from his mother, since his own share would not come to him until his twenty-fourth birthday in 1913.[15] His profligacy may have been an act of angry revenge or perhaps the first of many attempts to hide his *petit bourgeois* background. This skinny teenage youth strolled through Linz wearing a silk-lined overcoat and black kid gloves, carried an ivory-tipped cane, had no job and earned no money but went to the opera night after night, dressed like a Parisian dandy and indulging his new-found passion for Wagner. He must have looked absurd but he was determined to reinvent himself in the classless role of artist and aesthete.

13. His younger brother Edmund had died of measles in 1900, aged six. Three other siblings – Otto and Ida, just babies at the time, and Gustav aged two and a half – died in the space of three weeks in the hard winter of 1887–8, before Adolf was born.
14. Franz Jetzinger, *Hitler's Youth* (London, 1958).
15. See Kershaw, *Hitler, 1889–1936: Hubris*, p. 68. When Hitler did finally receive his legacy it amounted to 820 kronen, a sizeable sum that he soon squandered.

Before long the provincial confines of Linz were too narrow for him. He travelled to Vienna, visited its theatres and art galleries, sketched and read compulsively. He was an oddity, a loner, living in a fantasy world. His face already had its lifelong pallor, his hair was glossy black, he was gaunt, timid, afraid of women. Even as a boy Hitler had avoided and disliked girls and as a youth he had an almost phobic horror of prostitutes.[16] As he got older he put up elaborate barriers against physical intimacy with any female. This may partly be explained by the fact that he had an undescended testicle[17] and, while this need not have affected his potency, it would not have been something he cared to expose unless he was very sure a woman would not ridicule him; and perhaps not even then.[18] His celibacy also reflected a belief that sex was a primitive impulse, necessary to create children but otherwise carnal, shameful, and to be suppressed as far as possible.[19] Eva, an uninhibited child of nature, would have a lot to overcome.

In January 1907, hearing that his mother Klara was about to be operated on for breast cancer, Adolf came home from Vienna. Slow to grasp that she was seriously, terminally ill, he left Linz in September and returned to sit the entrance examination to the Academy of Fine Arts. He was failed because of his inability to draw. The Director kindly suggested he might consider studying architecture, though he could not offer him a place. Hitler took this to mean that he could be a great architect – a dream he cherished for the rest of his life. He was so self-absorbed that not until his mother could no longer leave her bed did he realise how close she was to death. He hurried back to Linz and for the remaining weeks of her life he cared for her tenderly. On 21 December 1907 she died, aged forty-seven. Dr Bloch, the Jewish doctor who had been attending her, said he had 'never witnessed

16. This alone casts doubt on the allegations that he suffered from syphilis and, forty years later, the absence of venereal disease was confirmed by his personal physician, Dr Theodore Morell.
17. As every marching soldier knew, 'Hitler has only got one ball . . .' The fact is medically attested in Lev Bezymenski, *The Death of Adolf Hitler: Unknown Documents from Soviet Archives* (New York: Harcourt, Brace, 1968), p. 49. In a gruesome account of the autopsy on Hitler's charred corpse carried out in Berlin on 8 May 1945 the investigating doctor reported: 'The left testicle could not be found either in the scrotum or on the spermatic cord inside the inguinal canal, nor in the small pelvis.' But how did the *soldiers* know?
18. More details of Hitler's physical abnormalities can be found in Chapter 13.
19. This was the view of his only friend at the time, a young musician called August Kubizek; see Kershaw, *Hitler, 1889–1936; Hubris*, pp. 45–60.

a closer attachment . . . and . . . never seen a boy so completely bereft'. Adolf was eighteen and from then on, for the rest of his life, he carried his mother's photograph in his breast pocket.

On 4 June 1908, six months after the death of her stepmother, Adolf's half-sister Angela Raubal gave birth to her second child, a daughter whom she named Angela Maria.[20] Two years later, in 1910, her husband Leo died, leaving his 27 year-old widow to bring up three children on her own as well as caring for Hitler's handicapped sister Paula. Frau Raubal had only her widow's pension and a small legacy from her father on which to support this family of five and her three children spent most of their childhood in poverty. Adolf, idling away his life in Vienna, offered no help and refused to share responsibility for Paula.

In 1908 Hitler was nineteen, orphaned, unqualified, unemployed, unattached, an outcast from the bourgeois world. Angry and frustrated, his hands and pockets were empty but his mind was filled with towering ambition and grandiose ideas. He was certain he had enough talent, perhaps even genius, to be a painter or architect. Several years later, in a highly coloured version of his years in Vienna, he wrote to his intellectual mentor, Dietrich Eckart:[21] 'I studied the history of art, of civilisation and of architecture as much as my means allowed and also took an interest in political problems. Though I came from a fairly cosmopolitan family, the school of harsh reality turned me into an anti-Semite within barely a year.'[22] *'Fairly cosmopolitan family'* . . . ? Eckart was rabidly anti-Semitic and Adolf may have been trying to ingratiate himself with his important new friend, for it seems that during the Vienna years he had a number of Jewish acquaintances. His extreme racial bigotry developed gradually, rather than in the space of a single year, but in its crudest, most brutal form, that time in Vienna laid its foundations, imbuing Hitler with the beginnings of a pathological hatred of the people he secretly envied for their culture, influence and wealth – the Jews.

Hitler's only close friend in those days was a contemporary called August – 'Gustl' – Kubizek, who also came from Linz. Kubizek recalled

20. They are my Christian names, too.
21. Poet, playwright and translator of *Peer Gynt*, philosopher and journalist, Dietrich Eckart (1868–1923) was the only intellectual among Hitler's early companions. Intensely anti-Semitic, he was one of the first members of the Nazi Party, a believer in the occult and acknowledged by Hitler as joint creator of National Socialism.
22. Maser, *Hitler's Letters and Notes*, p. 107.

years later: 'Books were his whole world . . . he read prodigiously and with the help of his extraordinary memory, stored up an amount of knowledge far above the normal standard of a twenty-year old – but he avoided any factual discussion about it.'[23] The two young men shared lodgings for a while and Kubizek claimed '. . . Unlike most adolescents [Hitler] did not indulge in frequent masturbation . . . adhering in all matters to the rigid code which he prescribed both for himself and for the future state.' Their Munich landlord, Joseph Popp, was able to keep an eye on his lodger although Herr Adolf had his own private entrance. He claimed that Hitler never took a girl up to his room or made assignations with the kind of woman with whom he might have been sexually intimate. German historian Werner Maser interviewed the former landlord in 1966 and reported: 'Neither Herr Popp nor his wife can recall ever having seen Hitler in the company of a woman or having heard him refer to a girlfriend.'[24]

In the course of the next four years Adolf sank through the strata of Viennese society until he reached the very bottom, lodging in a squalid working men's hostel, almost friendless and often penniless, though he did stay in touch with Kubizek, who remains the only reliable witness to the years in Vienna. The army would have offered a way out: at least he would have had regular meals and something to occupy him. By law he should have registered for military service in 1909 but for three years he failed to do so. In May 1913 he reached the age of twenty-four, which entitled him to the long-delayed inheritance of 820 kronen from his father. With the authorities at his heels, he left Vienna and went to Munich, but the Austrian police caught up with him in January 1914. Hitler was summoned, arrested, but found medically unfit to fight. However, in August 1914, as soon as war was declared, he volunteered for the Bavarian army and was accepted into the 16th Bavarian Reserve Infantry Regiment with the rank of corporal. He never earned promotion but served with some distinction as a messenger on the Western Front and won the Iron Cross First and Second Class. His regiment took part in the Battle of Ypres, after which only six hundred men out of three thousand survived. He left the army in 1918, coarsened and brutalised by war and by what he had seen of death on a huge scale, more alienated and intolerant than ever.

23. August Kubizek, *Young Hitler: The Story of our Friendship* (Graz, 1953; Maidstone Press, 1973), pp. 134–7.
24. Maser, *Hitler*, p. 196 (told to him by Joseph and Elizabeth Popp in May 1966).

The age gap between Hitler and Eva is highlighted by the fact that in 1918 he was a war veteran and she a bossy little girl of six, quite unaffected by the war, playing with her dolls, her kitten and her little sister Gretl. The Brauns had been lucky – nobody in their immediate family circle died in the conflict.

My mother, also six, could remember her aunt (my great-aunt, the much-loved *Tante* Lidy) and her efforts to find two of her brothers posted 'missing, presumed dead'. Lidy's mother would send her, a young woman in her early twenties, to the *Hauptbahnhof*, Hamburg's main station, every time a troop train returned bringing soldiers home from the Front. Lidy had to stand at the barrier holding up a photograph of the missing pair, calling out vainly 'Has anyone seen my brothers? Please have a look – does anyone recognise them? I am sorry, *gnädige Frau*, it will only take a moment . . . please?' On all sides, haggard soldiers embraced their wives, mothers and sisters, ignoring her. Each time Lidy returned from this ordeal to tell her weeping mother that no one had recognised the two young men. They never came home and their bodies were never found. Two more brothers – August and Julius – died in the war, but their graves were never visited. Twenty years ago, in the bleak flatlands of northern France, I looked for my dead great-uncles in the German war cemeteries, often on the other side of the road opposite the British ones. Each British grave was marked by a stone cross, many bearing the words 'A soldier known only unto God'. The German double crosses were made of iron. I went from one to another searching for the name NEUBERT but there were too many graves and I never found it. Four young men had vanished into the gunfire, smoke and mud of the Great War, leaving no trace.

The humiliating aftermath of the First World War, when the victors imposed towering reparations on Germany as well as emasculating it by reducing its armed forces to a fraction of their pre-war strength, inspired Hitler with the mission to create a new Germany out of carnage and defeat. For Fritz Braun it intensified his determination to hold on to the remnants of the old, dignified, disciplined Germany in which he had grown up and ardently believed.

PART 2
ADOLF TO *FÜHRER*, SCHOOLGIRL TO MISTRESS

Chapter Six

Eva Becomes Fräulein Braun, Hitler Becomes *Führer*

Not a great deal had changed in the relationship between the sexes since the end of the nineteenth century, despite anarchists, bohemians and a war in which women had shown themselves capable of working in factories and offices or nursing the most horribly wounded soldiers. This, if anything, hardened male attitudes rather than inclining them towards greater equality. Men would rather wield power over women, guide and control them, and most wives took that authority for granted: *Vati* made the rules and *Mutti* supported him. Who could blame them for wanting to rear fit, law-abiding, civic-minded young people, keen to work hard and play hard, imbued with high principles and obedient to the rules of hierarchy and order? A dutiful daughter did as her parents, above all her father, told her.

It was crucial to the damaged self-esteem of a whole generation of men crippled and unmanned by their country's defeat in the First World War that a wife deferred to her husband. They needed proof of their authority as civilians in private life and, since the family circle was often the only arena in which they had any authority at all, many became quite tyrannical. These controlling attitudes were not only prompted by the war or, later, the Nazi Party; they also reflected those of their parents and grandparents. The rigours and instability of post-war life led to a generation of conformist young people ripe for the Nazi diktat. One result was the emergence in the twenties of a small and isolated group of German feminists, the BDF, or *Bund Deutscher Frauenvereine*,[1] but its membership was tiny and chiefly confined to

---

1. The BDF – *Bund Deutscher Frauenvereine* – the most powerful German feminist organisation, interested mainly in the affairs of professional, vocational and

71

women whom the war had denied the chance of marriage, so their influence was negligible. Most feminists opposed the Nazi Party but they greatly underestimated its threat, although it portrayed the women's movement as a sign of decadence. They were soon rendered powerless. In May 1933 the BDF dissolved itself and by 1936 the Party had banned all such groups.

To describe the role of women in the Nazi scheme and the background against which Eva reached adulthood it is necessary to jump ahead, beyond the immediate chronology of Eva's life. For her and my mother, Ditha Schröder, the accident of being born in 1912 had meant that as adolescents they escaped the worst of Nazi indoctrination, though no one could avoid it entirely. Between the late twenties and early thirties the power of the party grew rapidly, especially among students and young people. One of my daughters once asked my mother outright if she had ever been a member of a Nazi youth group and was told that my grandfather had forbidden her to join. In fact she had already reached the upper age limit for membership by the time the *Bund Deutscher Mädel* (League of German Girls), or BDM, was founded in 1932. This would have debarred both Eva and Ditha who, at twenty, were considered adults.

In the early Nazi years membership of a patriotic organisation was merely desirable but in 1933 after they came to power it became compulsory between the ages of ten and twenty. Girls born a few years after Eva were moulded by the BDM from their early teens into the Nazis' concept of the ideal woman – healthy, hard working, biddable and, above all, fertile. These teenage *Mädel* often wore their hair in two plaits, sometimes wound round their ears in 'Schnecken' (snails) like headphones – not a flattering style for an energetic schoolgirl. They projected innocence rather than sexuality, vigour rather than brains, blooming good health rather than intellectual curiosity. The *Bund*'s activities were much like the Girl Guides', aiming to instil efficiency, resourcefulness and self-sacrifice, the defining characteristics of the New German Woman. Its members were taught that their destiny was to marry, serve their husband and bear children for the Fatherland. Just that, nothing

clerical working women. Most were spinsters and thus out of touch with German wives and mothers. For more details see a discussion in Jill Stephenson, *Women in Nazi Society* (London: Croom Helm, 1975).

else.[2] When they reached the age of eighteen they could enlist in a senior organisation whose name translates as 'Belief and Beauty'. By this time, they had been indoctrinated to believe, as one German woman recalled sixty years later, that 'We were the best – and most competent – and the best-looking people in the world – and the Jews were the exact opposite.'[3] Another insisted, 'We didn't know about anything . . . we didn't! We thought what we were being trained to believe was *true*,' but the next woman riposted drily, '*We knew*.'

As the party gained ever-increasing power it began to monopolise every spare moment in young people's lives, until it challenged the influence of parents and was taking more and more responsibility for training adolescents in their duty to the Fatherland. Schoolchildren who belonged to a youth group enjoyed regular sessions of sport, gymnastics and synchronised exercises as well as camping weekends and free holidays. Anyone who refused to join was suspect – an outcast, a loner – so much so that in the end almost everyone took part. There was some truth in the joke current at the time, that, with a father in the SA (*Sturmabteilung*, or Brownshirts[4]), mother a member of the NSF (*National Sozialisten Frauen*, or Nazi women), a son in the HJ and a daughter in the BDM, the family only crossed paths at a Nuremberg Rally.[5] By the mid-thirties half the nation's youth had joined an organisation run by the party, designed to weld the next generation of Germans into a coherent whole, ready to carry out Hitler's will. Nazi propaganda worked most insidiously and effectively upon the young[6] and both sexes were taught 'racial awareness'. (It goes without saying that Jews and the children of other despised minorities were not allowed to belong to any youth group.) This was the background against which

2. In this the *Bund Deutscher Mädel* resembled the health advice given to teenagers funded by George W. Bush's government, one of which – puzzlingly named *Why Know* – said: 'Women gauge their happiness and judge their success by their relationships. Men's happiness and success hinge on their accomplishments.' Quoted in an article by Gary Younge in the *Guardian*, 3 December 2004.
3. Quoted in the TV documentary *Hitler's Children*, shown on Channel Four, 30 July 2005, directed and produced by Daniel Fromm for ZDF.
4. The SA (the *Sturmabteilung*, or Brownshirts), founded in 1921 under Ernst Röhm, originally as *Schutz und Sport Abteilung*.
5. Burleigh *The Third Reich: A New History*, p. 234.
6. Adapted from Melissa Müller's Introduction to Junge, *Until the Final Hour*, pp. 17–20.

Eva and Ditha grew into adulthood. It does not excuse their lack of interest in the fate of the Jews but it may go some way to explain it.

Hitler Jugend, the boys' movement, was brilliantly structured to transform boys into 'good' Nazi men and – according to the long-term plan of Hitler and the Youth leader, Baldur von Schirach – prepare them ultimately to be slaughtered by the Allied and Soviet armies.[7] In 1938, membership of Hitler Youth was made compulsory for all German boys between fourteen and eighteen. The organisation was a recruiting ground for Nazi Party paramilitary groups, with the *Schutzstaffel* (SS) taking a specially keen interest. Several corps of Hitler Youth also existed to train boys to become officers in the *Wehrmacht* (the army). All members of *Hitler Jugend* wore a semi-military uniform, observed a strict hierarchy, were drilled, taught to handle weapons and encouraged to be ruthlessly aggressive. 'You are destined,' Hitler told them, 'to be warriors for Greater Germany.' Few realised how literally he meant it. By the end of 1936 membership of Hitler Youth had reached five and a half million: trained and disciplined youths who would fight and die – and kill – for Hitler.

These various groups came together for huge annual rallies at which thousands marched, shouted *Sieg Heil!* and sang patriotic songs, whipping up near-hysterical worship of Hitler and von Schirach. 'He [Hitler] was our idol. He was a demi-god. I'd have died for him,' said one old man, remembering those heady days.[8] They sang songs which seem absurd now but were deadly serious then:

> We are the Happy Hitler Youth,
> We do not need the virtues of the church
> for it is our Führer Adolf Hitler
> who stands at our side.[9]

'These songs,' confessed cartoonist and writer Tomi Ungerer, who grew up during the Nazi years, '. . . these songs work like a drug. [. . .] If you're brought up by the Nazis then the songs stay twenty, thirty years

7. By 1933, the year Hitler and the Nazis came to power, joint membership of the two organisations was 3.5 million – and growing fast. By 1938 the *Bund Deutscher Mädel* alone had 3.5 million members.
8. From the documentary *Hitler's Children* shown on Channel 4, 23 July 2005.
9. Adam Lebor and Roger Boyes, *Seduced by Hitler: The Choice of a Nation and the Ethics of Survival* (Naperville, IL, 2001), p. 120.

in your brain.'[10] He added that in spite of all that had happened, whenever he feels down he sings these songs that he learned as a boy, in spite of their banal and ridiculous words.

Eva and my mother Ditha, on the other hand, would have been singing the popular songs of the day, '*Schlagers*' as they were called (it means, literally, hits) with romantic lyrics about true love and faithlessness. My mother's favourite was *Schau mich bitte nicht so an* – 'Please Don't Look at Me Like That' – to the tune of *La Vie en Rose*. They both had a passion for films and film stars and many of the ones Eva admired were those I later heard my mother talk about – Grock, the famous 'sad clown', singers Zarah Leander – Swedish by origin, German by choice – Sari Barabbas and many others whose names I have now forgotten; Lotte Lenya, her gravelly voice the perfect vehicle for the songs of Bertolt Brecht and her husband, composer Kurt Weill; and of course Marlene Dietrich, whose plangent version of *Lili Marleen* made it the defining song of the Second World War for both German and English audiences – the divine Dietrich who, when not portraying glamorous women, could be sexier than any man in a slender dinner jacket and trousers. Eva's perceptions of glamour and allure were shaped by these stars; my mother preferred more 'natural' beauties such as Ingrid Bergman or Magda Schneider. When Zarah Leander said 'Ninety per cent of the songs I sing are about love. That's because ninety per cent of people think love is more important than politics . . .'[11] she expressed Eva's lifelong belief. Surprisingly, Eva also loved Kurt Weill's songs, in particular the 'Cannon Song'[12] – '*Soldaten Wohnen / auf den Kanonen – Soldiers spend their lives on cannons*'.

In most respects Eva Braun and Ditha Schröder were like any other young women of their age and time, full of energy and frustration, devoted to and yet resentful of the older generation who stifled their freedom of choice; devoted because, despite occasional tantrums or sulks, they lived in a *gemütlicher Kreis* – a cosy circle – and still enjoyed

10. Ibid., p. 102.
11. Knopp, *Hitler's Women*, p. 206.
12. The *Kanonen Lied* from *Die Dreigroschenoper* – *The Threepenny Opera* – Act 1, Scene 2, by Kurt Weill and Bertolt Brecht, adapted from *The Beggar's Opera* by John Gray. It was written in 1928 and first performed in Berlin at the Theater am Schiffbauerdamm on 31 August 1928. It was a huge public success and remains popular to this day.

sporty weekends and family holidays together. Much more important were the good times they had with their friends, going to the cinema, sharing a consuming interest in film stars, movie magazines, actresses and singers.[13] A fixation upon one particular star was known as a '*Schwärmerei*' – an infatuation, like a schoolgirl's 'crush' or 'pash' – and Eva swooned over publicity photographs and postcards of John Gilbert, Garbo's silent film partner, a remote idol whose bloodless features seemed carved from ivory. The social lives of young girls in the Germany of the 1930s were not so very different from those of the hectic young women in today's 'girly' soaps and chick-lit except that their alcohol intake rarely amounted to more than a glass or two of beer, the use of drugs was unknown and few slept with the men they loved. Virginity was the bait, marriage their aim, and they chivvied one another towards it with advice and enthusiasm.

Not that the Brauns prevented their daughters from having fun. Munich was a great city for parties and no opportunity was missed. The *Oktoberfest* (the annual Beer Festival) along with Christmas, New Year's Eve and the the start of Lent, were all marked by exuberant public celebrations. Everyone wore fancy dress or evening clothes and cafés and beer halls all over the city throbbed with laughter, toasts, accordion music or jazz and dancing. Eva was only playing at being outrageous: she was in search of pleasure, not erotic experience. It was the same for the young men – girls were for fun rather than sex. However provocative she seemed, Eva remained '*ein braves Mädchen*' – a good girl – who enjoyed trying out her sex appeal but would not give up her virginity lightly.

When Adolf Hitler returned to Munich after the war he was thirty, an age at which a man should have some achievements to show for his first adult decade. Throughout his twenties he had been dismissed as a no-hoper, destined to sink to the lowest level of society. At best he might become a minor clerk or petty bureaucrat like his father, marry, father a couple of brow-beaten children and stumble towards an unremarked death. Excluding the war years, he had scarcely earned an honest *Pfennig* in his life but subsisted on charity, which in practice meant scrounging

13. Eva herself, seven decades later, became a mini obsession with punk rockers and even had a band named after her, not forgetting '(I Never Loved) Eva Braun' by the Boomtown Rats – a great song. (Information from Sadakat Kadri, with many thanks.)

off his female relatives until they had nothing left to give, whereupon he lost interest in them. He seemed a nonentity without a future. His record was dismal: failed artist, aspiring but completely untrained architect, decorated (Iron Cross, First and Second Class) but non-commissioned and now a demobbed soldier. Unemployed and drifting, Hitler needed some outlet that would enable him to expound his ever more fanatical anti-Semitism. He was also keen to recapture the sense of belonging to a like-minded group that he had experienced in the army. In September 1919 he began to attend meetings of a tiny nationalist group, the newly founded German Workers' Party, or DAP. (It became the NSDAP, or *Nationalsozialistische Deutsche Arbeiterpartei,* later known by the less cumbersome title of the Nazi Party.) Shortly afterwards he applied to join and was allotted membership number 555, although the size of the party was less impressive than this implied since, to swell its ranks, numbering started at 501. Its latest member was homeless, friendless, arrogant, idle, largely self-educated and more ignorant than he would ever admit – but despite these shortcomings he harboured grandiose ambitions. Against all the odds, he was right. Although even he may not have realised it yet, this nobody had a genius for oratory.

He made his first political speech in July 1919 to an audience of returning prisoners of war. Afterwards a witness called him 'A born people's orator, who with his fanaticism and common touch knows how to appeal to an audience'.[14] On 16 October 1919 he addressed 111 fellow members at the NSDAP's first public meeting and later wrote: 'I could speak! The people in the small room were electrified . . . I had found my vocation.'[15] It came as a blinding revelation that he had the power to move people to attention, to anger, resolve and passionate conviction; and having been moved – out of their seats, to their feet, hands above their heads, applauding wildly, faces glistening with tears or sweat or emotion – they would follow wherever and do whatever he told them. By mid-November at the next meeting his audience had swelled to more than seven hundred and a police report acknowledged his extraordinary talent as an orator. Hitler was thirty and launched at last upon his political destiny.

He was already a hard-core anti-Semite, convinced that the Jews,

14. E. Deuerlein, 'Hitler's Eintritt in die Politik und die Reichswehr', *Vierteljahreshefte für Zeitigeschichte,* vol. vii (1959).
15. Adolf Hitler, *Mein Kampf* (London: Hutchinson, 1969), pp. 322–3.

in their supposed desire to emasculate Germany, were engaged in an economic conspiracy whose aim was world domination. His creed was apocalyptic and paranoid. Hitler was conscious that this was a large part of his appeal to poor workers and the unemployed who suffered most from galloping inflation. He adopted 'Germany Awake!' as the Nazi slogan, often followed by *'Jude Verrecke!'* (literally, Jews Croak).[16] He saw history as a struggle between two hostile forces, the Jew and the Aryan: the latter a heroic, almost god-like figure. Although this was not yet made explicit, in his distorted mind this confrontation (he wrote in September 1919) necessitated 'the removal of the Jews altogether'.[17] These ideas spread rapidly, not only among louts but in the minds of people who regarded themselves as, and perhaps in many respects were, 'ordinary, decent Germans'. In July 1921, at the age of thirty-two and at his own suggestion, he became leader of the renamed Nazi Party, now three thousand strong. After this Hitler was increasingly referred to as *der Führer* in imitation of his Italian counterpart, Benito Mussolini, who had assumed the title *Il Duce*.

He began to hone his oratorical skills at ever larger meetings. 'In front of an audience Hitler was transformed from a windless flag into a billowing banner calling to arms.'[18] His favourite theme was comparing the altruistic, idealised Aryan hero to the egotistical and sinister Jew. From a mishmash of Wagnerian legend, Teutonic myth, pan-German politics, idealistic socialism and pseudo-scientific theories about the genetic superiority of Nordic bloodlines, Hitler evoked an Ice Age, an Iron Age, helmets, shields, warriors, heroes with fair, blue-eyed consorts; a proud, implacable people buried in the collective memory, awaiting the leader's return. He had grasped the importance of words and names that evoked a heroic past and adopted the wolf as his symbol – hence the 'Mr Wolf' alias. (His wartime operations HQ in the disputed eastern part of Poland, close to the Russian border, was called the Wolf's Lair and his mountain-top retreat in Bavaria the Eagle's Nest.) The swastika and the eagle – two very ancient emblems – represented the Nazi Party and the Third Reich; the swastika being a symbol from far back in Indo-European history; the eagle, like the wolf, suggesting strength, power and freedom. From their earliest beginnings the Nazis

16. Kershaw *Hitler, 1889–1936: Hubris*, p. 124–5; 146–153.
17. Ibid., p. 124. Kershaw refers to the original typed letter, dated 16 September 1919, addressed to Hitler's superior, Captain Mayr.
18. Burleigh, *The Third Reich: A New History*, p. 100.

established a powerful iconography, setting the black swastika inside a white circle in the centre of a red flag and using the same jagged black, white and red for their posters.[19] Hitler knew instinctively that if he wanted to conjure strong feelings of nationalism he had to evoke Germany's history and, building on its mythology, promise an equally triumphant future.

His new-found command of rhetoric was not the only reason for the sudden change in Hitler's fortunes. As he got older, his looks improved. The starveling's face hardened and matured, to be replaced by a broad forehead, square jaw and resolute expression. He developed a firm, manly handshake and exploited his mesmerising light blue eyes with his habit of staring into and *through* the eyes of every man he met – the magnetic stare of a practised manipulator or magician – until they were compelled to acknowledge his dominance by looking away first.[20] It was a trick he only used with men; towards women he was always fulsomely courteous.

By 1923 the *Führer* projected a flare path of confidence and idealism that attracted a growing tide of supporters far beyond the initial ranks of former soldiers, now swelled by the common-or-garden riffraff from the streets. From his time in the gutter he had learned that simplistic stereotypes appealed to a not overbright audience of men reduced to watching with baffled fury as their puny wages or army pensions were devoured by inflation. He promised an inspiring future for all who were disillusioned and dispossessed; a future that would liberate Germany from the shame of defeat in the First World War and solve its desperate economic problems. This was politics pitched at a level his audience could understand. The mob element in the Nazi Party was solidly united behind its pulse-quickening demagogue. In five formative years from 1919 to 1924 the one-time nonentity became a contagious force for evil.

19. Ibid., p. 129. It is interesting that the nascent Communist Party in the USSR chose very similar colours and iconography, with the hammer and sickle replacing the swastika and, even more than Stalin himself, the worker holding aloft the Red Flag being the figurehead that pointed to the future.
20. The aristocratic and courageous lawyer Claus von Stauffenberg was a notable exception. As always on encountering a new face, Hitler endeavoured to stare von Stauffenberg down but he remained unintimidated, his eyes locking and holding the *Führer*'s. For the first time in the experience of those present, Hitler gave way. Von Stauffenberg commented afterwards 'The man is a magician. He almost hypnotised *me!*'

These were years of unprecedented inflation. By the end of 1922 prices had risen from ten to a hundred times their pre-war level, but as wages and salaries rose at the same rate it hardly seemed to matter. By the following year inflation had reached unsustainable levels. Small change vanished – what use was it, when a tankard of beer cost a million Reichsmarks: the equivalent of 25 cents?[21] A few statistics will show how fast inflation took hold. In August 1922 a loaf of bread cost RM (Reichsmarks) 8.20. By October it was RM12.25 and by December that same year, RM150. In June 1923 it had risen to RM1600 and by August to RM35,000 – from RM8.20 to RM35,000 in one year. Other basic foodstuffs rose similarly, sometimes more steeply. A litre of milk went from RM14.60 in August 1922 to RM47,000 a year later.[22] In Munich, as elsewhere, prices became ruinous. The Braun family were short of food like everyone else but their diet was supplemented by eggs and fresh vegetables from Josefa Kronburger's kitchen garden. My grandfather, trying to provide for his young family in Hamburg, suffered much more. He used to show me million mark banknotes overstamped in black with the words ZEHN MILLION, ten million – and still worthless. It took a wheelbarrow full of notes, he told me, to buy a half kilo loaf of black bread and by the time you left the shop the price had risen again. In August 1923, one US dollar was worth a million Reichsmarks. By September, a million marks had no value any more; the minimum

21. In December 1918 there were nearly RM8 to the dollar; by November 1921 RM263 = $1; by July 1922 RM493 = $1; in October 1922 RM3,000 = $1; and between January and November 1923 the price rose from RM17,100 to RM353,000, after which it soared into a billion, then multi-billion Reichsmark stratosphere, at which point money lost all meaning.
22. Information taken from the exhibition *Munich During the Third Reich* displayed at Munich City Museum, March 2005. Further prices of foodstuffs, given in Reichsmarks:

1/2 kilo of:	Bread	Potatoes	Pork	Butter	Cheese	Sugar	One egg	Milk (1 litre).
Aug. 1922	8.20	5.50	60.40	120.00	77.00	22.00	7.40	14.60
Oct. 1922	12.25	5.80	167.70	450.00	237.00	42.00	17.50	50.00
Dec. 1922	150.00	8.50	390.00	20000.00	750.00	220.00	46.00	202.00
Feb. 1923	550.00	45.00	2920.00	590.00	2500.00	500.00	130.00	548.00
June 1923	1600.00	200.00	8250.00	13,600.00	6,500.00	1750.00	660.00	1140.00
Sept. 1923	35,000.00	57,000.00	234,000.00	750,000.00	210,000.00	163,000.00	14,000.00	47,000.00

From November 1923 all prices had to be reckoned in millions of Reichsmarks. Source: *Handbook of Statistics for Munich*, 1928.

unit of usefulness was a milliard.[23] 'No one quite knew how it happened. Rubbing our eyes, we followed its progress like some astonishing natural phenomenon . . . Suddenly, looking around, we discovered that this phenomenon had devastated the fabric of our daily lives.'[24] October 1923 was the climactic month: a billion Reichsmarks to the dollar. Madness! Why bother to print notes any more? Paper currency no longer had credibility or value and the Reichsbank stopped printing money. People reverted to barter, or went hungry. Many died of starvation, collapsing shrivelled and helpless on park benches or on the streets. This was the social and economic situation that Hitler inherited.

A year earlier, in late 1922, Hitler had met the ideal person to introduce him to the high society whose acceptance he craved and the Party needed; a man who was well-born, well-connected, cultivated and, above all, *rich*. His name was Ernst Hanfstängl[25] but he was always known as 'Putzi'.[26] Hitler's new patron could hardly have been less conventional, a most unlikely supporter for Hitler and the infant Nazi Party. He was a giant of 6 foot 4 inches with a jaw like a shovel and a shock of thick wiry hair. An art dealer, pianist and connoisseur, his German father had founded the dealership in the United States and made a lot of money out of it. His mother was American, one of the Sedgwicks of Boston, quite a distinguished family, and her son had been brought up in that city and educated at Harvard between 1905 and 1909. He had come to Germany in 1921 to expand the family business there.

Putzi heard Hitler speak for the first time in November 1922, at the Kindl Keller beer hall in Munich, when he was thirty-five – two years older than Hitler – and was completely overwhelmed. His memoirs devote a full five pages to the impact this hitherto unknown young orator made on the cosmopolitan Hanfstängl. His initial impression was that Hitler looked like a waiter in a railway

23. A milliard = one thousand million; a billion = one hundred million.
24. Sebastian Haffner, *Defying Hitler* (London: Weidenfeld & Nicolson, 2002), p. 44.
25. Ernst F. Sedgwick Hanfstängl ('Putzi'), 1887–1975 had a very beautiful young blonde wife, Helene, whom Hitler idolised. In the early years of his career, theirs and Hoffmann's were the only private circles in which Hitler felt at ease. Putzi was a good pianist whose playing often relaxed Hitler and calmed his overwrought nerves. See Ernst Hanfstängl, *Hitler: The Missing Years*, Introduction by Brian Connell (New York: Little, Brown, 1994).
26. 'Putzi' is a Bavarian diminutive meaning 'little fellow' given to Ernst when he was two by his peasant nurse.

buffet but he changed his mind when he heard him speak.

> He had a command of voice, phrase and effect which has never
> been equalled . . . used his hands and arms in gestures, of which
> he had an expressive and extensive repertoire . . . He attacked
> the Jews, Communists and Socialists . . . these enemies of the
> people, he declared, would one day be *beiseitigt* – literally 'side-
> lined' though he really meant removed or done away with.[27]
> The hubbub and chattering [of the audience] had stopped and
> they were drinking in every word. [At the end] they responded
> with a final outburst of frenzied cheering, hand-clapping and a
> cannonade of table-pounding. It had been a masterly perfor-
> mance. I was really impressed beyond measure by Hitler.

When the audience had dispersed, Hanfstängl went up to the platform.

> 'Herr Hitler . . . I can only say I have been most impressed . . .
> I would very much like to talk to you.'
> 'Why, yes, of course,' Hitler said. He made a very pleasant
> impression, modest and friendly. So we shook hands again and I
> went home.[28]

This acquaintance was Hitler's entrée to the real circles of power
in Munich – the influential upper middle classes. If his intellectual
mentor was Dietrich Eckart (and that of the fledgling NSDAP), poet,
philosopher and political thinker, his social patron was this new admirer
and friend, Hanfstängl. Interrogated by Norman Birkett in 1937,[29]
Putzi claimed to have had such influence over the leader of the up
and coming NSDAP that, he later told a British court of enquiry,
'Hitler was like putty in my hands.'[30] (Hitler was never putty in anyone's

27. The literal translation is 'set aside'.
28. Hanfstängl, *Unheard Witness*, pp. 34–8.
29. Putzi forfeited Hitler's confidence and fled Germany in 1935 for England,
where he was interned as an enemy alien. His case came up before an advisory
committee chaired by Sir Norman (later Lord) Birkett and he was offered his
freedom in return for helping the British with anti-German propaganda, an offer
he refused. In 1941 he was deported to Canada, where his offer to help the
Americans was accepted and Putzi was released to 'act as political and psychological warfare adviser to President Roosevelt'. This, at any rate, is the story he
relates in *Unheard Witness*, pp. 308–11.
30. Appendix to Hanfstängl's memoirs, p. 412.

hands but, shrewdly, he must have flattered Putzi by letting him think so.) Putzi never ceased to be impressed by the *Führer*'s ability to arouse his listeners – and himself:

> His reaction to an audience was the counterpart of sexual excitement. He became suffused like a cock's comb or the wattles of a turkey, and it was only in this condition that he became formidable and irresistible. [. . .] The last eight to ten minutes of a speech resembled an orgasm of words. He found relaxation only in the atmosphere which corresponded to his own psyche, in the erotic crescendos of Wagner's music. [. . .] He possessed to a remarkable degree the gift of all great demagogues, that of reducing complicated issues to fiery catch-phrases.

Social background and 'good blood' mattered very much in Germany in the 1920s and 1930s. The nobility was regarded as a superior class and treated with obsequious deference. The upper middle class was superior to the middle class, which was superior to the lower middle class, and they were all superior to the workers, whether factory or farm, who took this precedence for granted except when it came to Jews, to whom the lowest class, along with most upper-class and *bürgerliche* Germans, felt superior.

Hitler, with his peasant background, could hardly have come from more undesirable stock. There were many skeletons in his cupboard – drunkenness, inbreeding and quite possibly incest. Johanna Pölzl, his aunt on his mother's side, was hunch-backed and 'simple', possibly schizophrenic. His first cousin Edward was also a hunchback. One of his brothers was described as an imbecile, though since he died in infancy it's not clear who made the diagnosis or on what basis. Many of his relations were dead and couldn't reveal his secrets, except his younger sister Paula – 'not quite right in the head', people might say, twisting one finger significantly against their temple – but Paula was never around for public scrutiny.[31] Throughout her adult life he kept her out of sight and made her change her surname to his own preferred alibi, 'Wolf', in semi-concealment of their

---

31. She cannot have been too severely mentally handicapped, however, since at one time she worked as a secretary for a group of doctors in a military hospital; but as always, she kept her identity a secret.

relationship.[32] Pictures of her (there are few) show a plain, short, square-faced woman with a nose like her brother's; otherwise there is little resemblance.[33] Her hair was black like his, but thick and wavy. She looks innocuous enough, and must have been, for she told an interviewer after the war that every time she passed a church, she went in and said a prayer for her brother. Only his half-sister Angela Raubal, whose brood of three seemed perfectly sane, would be evidence that Hitler had relatives. No risk from *that* branch of the family, anyway.

Eva's Kronburger ancestors on the other hand, coming from a rural village but with links to Vienna and imperial patronage, were never in any doubt about their social position and had no reason to be ashamed of it. Her Braun grandparents were people of good standing in their local Stuttgart community. They lived in a solid house with handsome furniture; their children had professional careers. No need for false modesty there either.

Hitler's new patron Putzi Hanfstängl and his glamorous young wife Helene introduced their electrifying but raw and mannerless protégé to Munich high society. Thanks to them he met people whose patronage and contributions would win the street-fighting Nazi Party much-needed supporters, new respectability and an injection of funds. But first, his manners and his clothes had to be changed to confer the right kind of social veneer. This real-life Eliza Doolittle needed to be disguised in order to mingle plausibly with the upper classes.

Crucially for Hitler, Putzi gave him the entrée to the homes of two wealthy Munich hostesses, Elsa Bruckmann and Helene Bechstein. The besotted Frau Bruckmann soon took it upon herself to make him *salonfähig* – fit for polite society – teaching him how to kiss a lady's hand, how to arrive and greet and take his leave with charm and modesty; how to bone a trout, eat an artichoke or a lobster.[34] She

32. During much of the Third Reich period she lived under the name Paula Wolf, incognito, as her brother wished, although every year Hitler would send her a ticket to the Nuremberg Rally. In March 1941, Hitler was staying at the Imperial Hotel in Vienna and it was here that Paula met him for the last time. Until the last weeks of the war, Paula Hitler lived in Vienna where she was interviewed by US intelligence officers in May 1945. Reluctant to talk she said tearfully, 'Please remember, he was my brother.' After the war she never married but lived near Hamburg (other sources say in Berchtesgaden). She died in 1960 and was buried in the Bergfriedhof cemetery.
33. Paula however did look very much like her half sister, Frau Raubal (née Hitler) with the same stocky build and dark colouring.
34. Large, *Where Ghosts Walked*, pp. 152ff.

modified his ingratiating manner and extreme deference towards his social superiors. Quite bowled over by their latest discovery, these two rich women competed to replace his cheap blue serge suit with tailored suits and well-cut dinner jackets, hats and handmade patent leather shoes, elegant clothes that Hitler had no scruples about accepting. So successfully did they turn their ugly duckling into a swan that one old lady recalled, 'He had mastered the five different types of hand-kissing and knew exactly which level was appropriate!'[35]

Some of his new admirers tried to match-make, introducing the newly eligible Hitler to suitable young women. Frau Bechstein even wanted him to marry her daughter, Lotte,[36] but when it came to emotional let alone sexual relationships, Hitler remained aloof.[37] Putzi diagnosed him as 'a barren hero', adding, 'From the time I knew him [late 1922] I do not suppose he had orthodox sexual relations with any woman. He was probably incapable of a normal reaction to their physical proximity.' Putzi's erotic imagination was vivid but in this case he was on the wrong track.

The reason Hitler wanted nothing to do with marriageable young women was that, like many people trying to climb out of their class, he was afraid of being exposed. But there was another, more persuasive reason. He could never forget that he carried in his genes a secret that ran counter to the very basis of Nazi racial ideology. As a child he had not been aware of the significance of his siblings' handicaps but once he grasped their implications, those flawed and incestuous genes became

---

35. Anecdote told to the author by Stephen Wright (a personal friend); March 2003.
36. Large, *Where Ghosts Walked*, p. 151.
37. Putzi Hanfstängl always claimed that Hitler was impotent. See Ernst Hanfstängl, *Hitler: The Missing Years* (London: Eyre and Spottiswood, 1957), pp. 122–4.
38. Suspicions grew, however, after he became *Führer*. Painstaking research by Dr Timothy Ryback and Florian Beierl of the Obersalzberg-Institut e.V in Berchtesgaden has revealed that on 6 October 1940, as part of the euthanasia programme, Adolf Hitler's second cousin on his father's side, Aloisia Veit, a forty-nine-year-old schizophrenic who suffered from depression and is described in official documents as an 'abnormal personality', was gassed to death at Hartheim castle, near Linz. It is not known whether Hitler was aware of her condition or her death. They were tenuously linked, Aloisia – the name alone is significant – being the great-granddaughter of the sister of Adolf Hitler's paternal grandfather and thus from the Schicklgruber side of the family. In 1944 a Gestapo report described the Schicklgrubers – to whom Hitler was linked through both his parents – as 'idiotic progeny'. Much later, it was proved right and Aloisia V. was discovered to be only one of several cases of physical or mental disability in Hitler's family, as revealed by the Obersalzberg Institute.

Adolf Hitler's deepest dread.[38] Throughout his life he refused to be lured into marriage. The risk of fathering imperfect children was too great.

Hitler may not have been prepared to marry their daughters but he was happy to exploit his benefactors. They and their friends swelled NSDAP funds, persuaded people like themselves to join the party, created a broader class profile for the Nazis and made his apocalyptic warnings seem much more convincing. Most new members belonged to Church committees, business, dining or sporting clubs, anchoring the coarse and inexperienced party with solid citizens who added an air of respectability to the flotsam and jetsam. Within two or three years the Nazi Party was recruiting landowners, schoolmasters and professional people; solid conservative types who joined to protect their threatened way of life, its traditional family and religious values. At the same time Hitler was shrewd enough not to abandon his earliest disciples. He continued to meet them over tea and cakes in his favourite cafés – Café Heck and Café Weichand – and hector them in Munich's rowdy beer halls. Hermann Göring dismissed them as 'a bunch of beer-swillers and rucksackers with a limited, provincial horizon'[39] and so they were, very often, but they came from the same background as Hitler and he felt more at ease with them than in the scented drawing rooms of the ladies Bruckmann and Bechstein.

Another source of intellectually respectable Nazis was Bernhardt Stempfle, a professor at Munich University whom Hitler met through Heinrich Hoffmann. Stempfle edited a newspaper – little more than a racist tract – called the *Miesbacher Anzeiger* – *Miesbach Reporter* – and his students provided valuable support.[40] Their boisterous adulation inflated Hitler's sense of himself as a messianic figure.

His early fantasies finally coming true, Hitler set about building the party into a political juggernaut. The disaffected mob was at his feet and although the middle-of-the-road bourgeoisie viewed their thuggish antics with contempt, Hitler knew that leading the party involved tolerating – if not secretly encouraging – the street demonstrations that gave the mob element its thrill. They *needed* riots and violent outbreaks of racism. They would much rather beat up Jews and political opponents than get on with the serious business of recruiting members and raising funds. Nazi youth organisations combined discipline with delinquency but, while the party might turn a blind eye,

38. Large, *Where Ghosts Walked*, p. 154.
39. Ibid., p. 105.

Hitler needed to protect his image. By 1923 the authorities were beginning to be alarmed by Nazi militancy and the speed at which the movement was growing;[41] its rough ways with opponents and the spectacular intensity of its public meetings.[42] This had become the seamy underside to the newly sanitised Hitler.

By late 1923 the *Führer* and his cronies were convinced that the Weimar Republic was about to collapse. The moment had come to take advantage of public anger: the NSDAP must act, publicly and decisively. In their overenthusiasm they failed to plan their tactics in detail, moved too fast and misjudged the moment. An over-ambitious and premature putsch, or coup, against the Bavarian government on 8–9 November 1923, lasting for several hours and involving three thousand men and much street violence, was put down, not before the SA had searched out numbers of Jews, arrested, beaten and narrowly been prevented from killing them. The first victims of the Holocaust were already being persecuted before the eyes of Munich's citizens.

For the first time the world of politics began to impinge on Eva and her family. The Beer Hall Putsch took place not far from where they lived. The worst of the violence was cornered and concentrated in Residenzstrasse, near Odeonsplatz, only streets away from the Brauns' modest apartment, then in Isabellastrasse. The family – like many upright Munich residents – crowded at their windows in the late afternoon of 9 November, watching as panicky figures in the street below fled from the shooting that ended the abortive rebellion. All this only increased the contempt felt by high-principled *Vater* Braun for the Nazi Party, its leader and his boorish followers. No doubt the events were discussed around that evening's supper of *Kalte Platte* – a few precious slices of cold meat, sausage and cheese sent from Beilngries, such luxuries having become unobtainable in Munich – eaten with pumpernickel. Eva would only have been eleven at the time but was no doubt furious at missing the drama. Guns! Shooting! Just like a gunfight in a cowboy story by Karl May.

The Beer Hall Putsch of November 1923 cost nearly a score of lives: fourteen Nazis – later to be glorified as martyrs for the party – four policemen and an unlucky passing waiter. The rioters dispersed as fast as possible. Hitler was wounded though hardly heroically – he

41. By 1923 membership had reached some 45,000 (source: Burleigh, *The Third Reich: A New History*).
42. Burleigh, *The Third Reich: A New History*, p. 93.

fell and dislocated his shoulder while making his escape from the Odeonsplatz where the violence was worst. He was hustled to safety by his closest collaborators and took refuge with his new friend Putzi and his wife in their house at Uffing on the Staffelsee, thirty-five miles outside Munich.

Police found Hitler lurking in the Hanfstängls' attic and in February 1924, he and some of his henchmen appeared in court accused of high treason. Heinrich Hoffmann recorded the trial with a camera hidden under his coat. Hitler was found guilty of conspiring to foment rebellion against the Bavarian state and sentenced to five years in Landsberg prison, along with forty other members of the Nazi Party. This sentence was later shortened to nine months. In prison he was given privileged treatment with extra visits and special food. In the eyes of his increasingly fanatical followers, the fact that he was in gaol only increased his charisma.

His widowed half-sister, Angela Raubal, whom he hadn't seen for several years, came to visit him with her three children, making the journey from Vienna to the prison on 17 June 1924. It was a kind and conciliatory gesture. She must have pictured him depressed, lonely and hungry. In fact her half-brother was housed in some comfort in a large, sunny room. Adolf Hitler evidently felt some affection for her since he had taken the trouble to keep in touch occasionally after the death of her husband in 1910, though once he had left Vienna for Munich they had seldom, if ever, met.

In 1919 Frau Raubal had managed to find work, cooking – the only skill she possessed – in the kitchen of a hostel for Jewish students in Vienna, which meant she had to learn to prepare kosher food. The Raubal family had a regular source of income at last. The job kept her away from her three children all day but since the oldest, Leo, was now twelve, her elder daughter Geli eleven and their quiet sister Elfriede nine, they were able to look after themselves after school. Their aunt Paula would be at home, not that simple, easy-going *Tante* Paula was much use. The Raubal children's teenage years during the Weimar era (1919–33) of national disintegration were hard but thanks to the hostel kitchen they never went short of food. Leo grew strong on kosher leftovers and Geli became positively buxom.

His nine months in gaol enabled Hitler to reflect more deeply. As with many political agitators, his cell provided him with a fresh opportunity and he later described that enforced detention as 'my university at state expense'. Here for the first time his ideas seethed and fermented into the sour brew of Nazism.[43] He read widely and dictated Part 1 of *Mein Kampf*[44] – a poisonous concoction of racism, myth, obsession and political philosophy – to Rudolf Hess, his slavish follower, and Emil Maurice, the chauffeur imprisoned with him. When he left Landsberg prison nine months later, in December 1924, Hoffmann was there again to record the event. A condition of his early release prohibited Hitler from speaking in most German states so once he was free he focused on consolidating his grip on the Nazi Party and its paramilitary army. No rivals for the leadership had emerged during his incarceration and the *Führer* felt he had gained 'a self-confidence and belief that simply could not be shaken'. As the unchallenged head of a fast-growing Nazi Party with a newly honed ideology to fire his speeches, the time had come to reinvent himself as a noble, flint-eyed patriot pointing the way forward for Germany, leaving behind the image of a hard man leading a mob of bigoted roughnecks.

By the end of the twenties the Nazis' paid-up sympathisers had risen from a mere two thousand in 1920 to 180,000. These ardent followers were snared not by reason, not discipline, not even conviction but by the uncanny ability of the party's orators to use the subliminal power of emotion. The galvanising force of the irrational was their secret weapon. The NSDAP was close to the people of the street and had an intuitive ability to discern and embody their unspoken longings, personal and patriotic, using huge rallies to hypnotise their members with the black magic of Hitler's oratory. Dreams and emotions first; *then* reason, brain, statistics, facts, politics. There they are in the films of Leni Riefenstahl or in propaganda photographs, jostling to get closer to Hitler, waving, smiling, laughing, weeping, arms upthrust, filled with healthy German joy.

---

43. '*Mein Kampf* as an historical force [. . .] did not amount to much. It was not for some time a commercial success. People did not become Nazis by reading *Mein Kampf*; they bought it – and sometimes read it – because they had already become Nazis. In 1928 its sales were just over 3,000. In 1932, after the remarkable Nazi success in the elections of 1930, they rose to 90,000. By 1940 six million copies had been sold. By then it was an established practice that every bride and bridegroom were given a copy at their marriage.' Robert Birley, *Spectator*, 20 April 1985.
44. Sold in the late twenties and early thirties for the absurdly low price of RM2.85 for the two volumes, *Mein Kampf* earned Hitler millions in royalties, formed the basis of his personal fortune and made him the richest author in Germany. He said that after his death his money should go into beautifying the city of Linz for the benefit of the German people.

Hitler's nine months in prison had not been too uncomfortable but he wouldn't have wanted to repeat the experience. The solution was to lie low at times when the havoc wreaked by Nazi hooligans became greater than Germany's enfeebled rulers were prepared to tolerate. What he needed was a bolt hole. For that he chose Bavaria.

Chapter Seven

Bavaria, the German Idyll

Bavaria was Eva's homeland. Her nature responded to the physical challenge as well as to the beauty of mountains and pines, winter and summer panoramas, ice-cold lakes and shimmering green meadows, while her spirit was uplifted by the crucifix beside every path and in every shop and kitchen. Religious devotion in this southern corner of Germany is part of people's daily lives. Bavarians greet and take leave of one another with the words '*Grüss Gott!*' – 'God's greeting!' (It must have needed a good deal of practice to replace that with '*Sieg Heil!*'.) She had spent two of the formative years between seven and nine, when a child's mind is at its most impressionable, staying with her grandparents in Beilngries while her parents sorted out their marriage and throughout her childhood the family spent holidays there. Later, as a young woman, Eva often wore the local costume – a flowered dirndl dress with an apron skirt, worn over a crisp white blouse with a deep décolleté, precisely the uniform that a sexist male would dream up for a compliant female – the apron signifying readiness for kitchen or nursery tasks, the flowered dress feminine prettiness, the white blouse hygiene and laundry skills and the décolleté a fecund availability. The whole ensemble conveyed childlike innocence and submission, exactly what Hitler required from women. One might think that, given her fashion sense, Eva only wore this get-up under protest but apparently not. According to her cousin Gertraud she loved it.

Although she grew up in Munich her albums contain almost no photographs of the Braun family in the city. Most are set against a mountain backdrop and show wayside picnics, skiing trips, expeditions to lakes and waterfalls, flower-filled meadows; Eva reclining, sunbathing, posing; trout fishing or sitting on a cow, Eva's athletic prowess on skis or skates or in walking boots. The lilting Bavarian accent, warmed by diminutives and endearments, came naturally to her. The toy villages of chalets and log piles, clanking cows and grazing goats, were familiar and reassuring. This was home – *Heimat* – with the deep emotional resonance that word carries for Germans. Here, in the setting of her childhood memories, Eva felt happy.

Hitler was not Bavarian nor even German by birth. He had revoked his Austrian citizenship in August 1925 but astonishingly for someone who aspired to lead and reinvigorate Germany, he then remained state-less for seven years. He didn't adopt German nationality until February 1932, just in time to be eligible for the German Chancellorship. But he too felt at ease in Bavaria and this shared southern connection formed a strong bond between him and Eva. The fact that her convent had been barely a kilometre away from Braunau, the town where he was born and where his father had been a customs official, was deeply significant. Hitler's childhood had not been happy and his memories were mixed but he liked the people of Bavaria, their voices, manners and temperament and felt at ease with them as with no other Germans. Unconsciously, he would have recognised in Eva something that instantly appealed to him.

It was natural, therefore, that during the ruffian years of the emerging Nazi Party, when Hitler needed a quiet retreat, he should turn to Bavaria. He found his bolt hole in a mountainside hamlet of fifty houses called Obersalzberg, high above the picturesque town of Berchtesgaden, a fashionable resort for wealthy Müncheners. Bavaria invites, almost compels, people, to commune with nature, tramp the forest paths and inhale the tough, clean air, as if physical exercise were not only good for their health but good for their *German-ness*. Communing with nature, communing with the past – it came to the same thing. Physical exercise was a moral imperative; laziness was degenerate, a waste of a vigorous body. People walked briskly and purposefully, swinging their arms and breathing deeply. Dawdling along with slumped shoulders and bent head was unGerman; it showed a lack of self-respect.

We have forgotten how much people used to walk – chiefly to get from A to B, from home to school, to church, the butcher or baker's shops, the station – before cars were universal. They also

walked for pleasure. Nowadays the young are far more likely to exercise in city gyms but seventy years ago indoor gyms were mainly for
boxers and people preferred synchronised open-air gymnastics or
day-long bicycling, their limbs buffed to a muscular glow by wind
and weather. But mostly they walked: merrily, in groups, singing as
they went.

Although he liked to project a sturdy woodsman image, Hitler was
not a great walker. He liked more passive pursuits such as talking,
reading or going to the opera. One of the few people he was prepared
to listen to was Dietrich Eckart, whose anti-Semitic philosophy he so
much admired. Hitler became his devoted acolyte. He had visited
Berchtesgaden with him for the first time in the winter of 1922, undeterred by the fact that by this stage in his life Eckart was an alcoholic.
(Many of Hitler's friends were heavy drinkers and, unusually for a
teetotaller, he didn't seem to mind.)

Eckart had become a father figure to him while, to his guide and
master, Hitler's fanaticism marked him out as the man destined to put
his extreme racist and nationalist ideology into practice.[1] In
Obersalzberg the two men, along with Rudolf Hess, held long late-
night discussions that formulated and refined the policies underlying
Nazi thinking so as to make them palatable and attractive to a wide
public. Even after Eckart's early death in December 1923[2] the *Führer*
continued to find this Alpine retreat so congenial that he often went
back there to enjoy the beauty of the mountains, unwind from stress
and focus his mind. He rented a small chalet where he wrote the
second part of *Mein Kampf*. This became known in Nazi mythology as
the *Kampfhäusl* – a Bavarian diminutive that could be translated as
Little House of Struggle, or Combat Cottage. The landscape and traditions of his adopted home in Bavaria played a large part in shaping
Hitler's perception of Germany's destiny as set out in *Mein Kampf*.
That, and the proximity of Braunau and Linz, where he had spent
some of his teenage years, were his main reasons for choosing
Obersalzberg as the greenhouse for his political flowering as well as

1. Together the two men wrote a pamphlet entitled *Der Bolshevismus von Moses
bis Lenin – Bolshevism from Moses to Lenin –* setting out their mad theory that
Jews were the secret power behind revolutionary subversion which had always
sought to undermine the rest of mankind's natural instinct towards progress. It
was published in Munich in 1923.
2. He was buried in Berchtesgaden.

his home when he was off-duty. Here he felt safe and protected among like-minded people.

Bavaria has much in common with Austria, Switzerland and the provinces set in the Alps and Dolomites of northern Italy. The observance of law and order, good citizenship, cleanliness, energy, tradition, church attendance are valued. Bavarians embodied *good* people. This well-ordered province in the south-eastern corner of Germany suited Hitler's chill, authoritarian nature while at the same time pandering to his love of the epic. He admired anything that was on a grand scale – history, art, opera, buildings, rhetoric. Bavaria seemed to nurture and sustain his vision of himself as the *Führer* who would preside over all this – and eventually over all Germany – the superhuman leader, the *Übermensch* foretold by Nietzsche.

Hitler was also inspired by Bavarian mythology and folk memory. The seven peaks of the Wachensberg range bordering Königssee, the lake below Obersalzberg, were called the King and Queen and their five daughters, harking back to the old legends of witches, devils and saints that not only gullible peasants but even Hitler half believed. Crags, cliffs and valleys were a recurring theme in German art for hundreds of years and these archetypal landscapes, primitive and sublime, are embedded in the German unconscious.[3] Peaks and pines form the background to Matthias Grünewald's tortured, almost sadistic fifteenth-century altarpieces and recur in the visionary paintings of Altdorfer (who was Bavarian), the woodcuts of Albrecht Dürer (from Nuremberg), and paintings and portraits by Lucas Cranach, who also worked in Bavaria. These artists, with their microscopic depictions of pain and piety, reflect a very Bavarian sensibility. In the nineteenth century, mountain panoramas were painted in the Romantic idiom by Caspar David Friedrich but this time, instead of saints and soldiers, his pictures show brooding, solitary figures silhouetted against dawn skies or golden sunsets. The same jagged rocks recur as the backdrop to many of Wagner's operas, in which heroes from Nordic mythology

---

3. Isaiah Berlin, in a letter to Elizabeth Bowen in 1936, wrote about his dislike of sublime landscapes: 'Very high mountains, very low valleys, angry torrents, pure & snowy peaks etc. The sublime in nature directly connects with Nazi heroes, T.E. Lawrence . . . bully boy etc & moral bullying. This in its turn leads to reactionary romanticism, the Germans, chivalry & the beauty of danger.' See p. 191, Henry Hardy (ed.), *Flourishing: Letters from Isaiah Berlin 1928–1946* (London: Chatto & Windus, 2004; Pimlico, 2005).

with iron names like Siegfried, Brünnhilde, Wotan and Fricka engage in the battle between good and evil, the fair against the dark. In literature, too: Goethe's *Faust* is populated by a bat-like swarm of witches, devils and supernatural beings at the beck and call of Mephistopheles, the fallen angel lamenting his banishment from heaven to whom the scholar Faust sells his soul in return for infinite knowledge.

Bavaria's mountains and toy-like villages touched something superstitious and childish in Hitler, a side of his nature that had been arrested rather than outgrown after his mother's early death. He was sentimental about children and dogs, yet also fascinated by cruelty. As a child, the young Adolf must have heard stories about witch-hunts (real, historical events), harking back in the collective memory to late medieval times when this province in southern Germany persecuted, tried, found guilty and hanged more witches than all the other states.[4] The portrayal of old women as hideous and malevolent crones, like the gleeful caricatures of Jews or the handicapped as hook-nosed, secretive, grimacing or malformed, fostered the subliminal belief that anyone not conforming to an idealised Aryan norm deserved to be ostracised by pure-blooded Germans. Blondness appeals to racists, Nazis in particular, although it is no more than a genetic trait developed in climates that get little exposure to the sun. The Viennese-Jewish writer and journalist Joseph Roth, an astute and prophetic observer, wrote in an article for a Berlin newspaper in 1924: 'You see them at railway stations, the blooming, wheat-blonde girls, born to be mothers but turning into political Furies.'[5] Blondness defined what it meant to be Aryan and perhaps there *is* something specially clean and appealing about young blonde women. Nazi propaganda encouraged the entire German nation to think so.

Such were the stereotypes and panoramas that inspired Hitler's vision of Germany and enabled him to seduce the *Volk* with his own rabid anti-Semitism. Nobody, at this stage, could have anticipated how far he would go to put it into practice.

---

4. Roper, *Witch Craze*.

5. The quotation is taken from Joseph Roth, *What I Saw: Reports from Berlin, 1920–1933*, translated from the German and with an Introduction by Michael Hofmann (New York: Norton, 2003). Joseph Roth, 1894–1939, born in Austro-Hungary, moved to Vienna, then Berlin (1920–25), then to Paris as correspondent for the *Frankfurter Zeitung* for whom he wrote a column known then – and now – as a *feuilleton*.

In the summer of 1948[6] my parents, with my younger sister and me, drove down the autobahn in our Volkswagen (we had an early version of the people's car, the 1946 model with a divided rear window) for a holiday in Garmisch-Partenkirchen, a village on the lower slopes of the Zugspitze mountain. It was as far away as possible from Nordenei, the North Sea resort where my mother had spent many weekends when she was young, swimming in sharp, cold sea water, swishing through the marram grass at the edge of the beach and singing round the camp fire as the summer dusk declined into night. The 1920s and 1930s were the heyday of *Wanderlieder* – songs to whose energetic rhythms everyone strode along – an activity my mother tried vainly to recreate with us. She talked a lot about the *Wandervögel*, a pre-Nazi organisation for young people based on nothing more political than the pleasures of walking and singing. Poor Ditha longed for those carefree times, which to her carried no stigma, no Nazi undertones, but were simply the happiest days of her youth. She tried to recapture these *Wanderungen* with her dawdling, reluctant family but my father and I hated walking and my sister was too small to be brisk. At Garmisch-Partenkirchen we were all made to go on long healthy walks up the mountainside and chivvied up ever-steeper slopes through pine forests whose dappled shadows cooled our path. I was out of breath, my legs ached from all that strenuous walking and my fringe kept flopping over my steamed-up glasses but, looking back, it feels like happiness.

The village of Obersalzberg overlooked the valley of the River Ach and from the heights above his chalet Hitler could, on a clear day, see all the way to Salzburg, 30 kilometres to the north. Nuremberg, soon to provide a vast auditorium for triumphal party rallies, was a few

---

6. We lived in Germany from 1946 to 1950. My father was working for the CCG (Control Commission of Germany), charged with restoring Germany's shattered infrastructure. My mother, my sister and I travelled from London by boat and train to join him in January 1947, arriving at Hamburg *Hauptbahnhof* to a freezing, bitter winter. British families were billeted in 'the Streits', a hastily refurbished hotel. In late 1947 we moved to a home of our own in a spa town called Bad Salzuflen, designated for the use of CCG personnel, where we lived for three years in a rustic, *gemütliches* little house.

hours' drive away and Bayreuth, where Wagner's operas were staged in accordance with the Master's vision, half a day's drive. Hitler's passion for Wagner, awakened long ago when he was a youth in Linz and indulged at every opportunity since, was intensified in September 1923 when the composer's English daughter-in-law Winifred Wagner invited him to stay. Winifred was a devoted follower of the Nazi Party and she gave Hitler the admiration he craved as well as the illusion of being intimate with a distinguished family – though her husband, Siegfried, thought him 'a fraud and an upstart'.[7]

By 1927 Hitler was overworked and exhausted. The sales of *Mein Kampf* were beginning to run into millions and he was rich enough to rent somewhere more suitable to his position as leader of the Nazi Party. He found the ideal chalet in Obersalzberg, larger than the *Kampfhäusl* though still quite modest. On 15 October 1928 he took out a lease, renting it for £400 a month in today's money. Originally called Haus Wachenfeld, this was the acorn from which the mighty Berghof grew. Within less than a decade it would be Germany's second centre of government, the playground of the Nazi Party and its top dogs. The chalet, which had a wide terrace overlooking a stupendous view, was the right size for Hitler and offered privacy and security, fresh air and a cosy atmosphere. Albert Speer, soon to be Hitler's favourite architect and most cherished collaborator, visited it in the early days. He recorded with a faint patrician curl of the lip:

> Hitler's small, pleasant wooden house had a wide overhanging roof and modest interior: a dining room, a small living room and three bedrooms. The furniture was bogus old-German peasant style and gave the house a comfortable petit-bourgeois look. A brass canary cage, a cactus and a rubber plant intensified this impression. There were swastikas on knick-knacks and pillows embroidered by admiring women.[8]

Haus Wachenfeld was described in (of all places) an article in *Homes and Gardens* dated November 1938 – two years after Hitler had occupied the Rhineland, six months after the *Anschluss* of Austria and only a week before *Kristallnacht*, the notorious 'Night of Broken Glass'. The

---

7. Kershaw, *Hitler, 1889–1936: Hubris*, p. 189.
8. Speer, *Inside the Third Reich*, pp. 86–7.

article, headlined 'Hitler's Mountain Home', is a breathless, three-page tour of the chalet written in the fulsome style of a visit to a minor celebrity's lovely home in today's fan magazines. Ignatius Phayre, the pseudonymous author (whose real name was William George Fitzgerald), told his readers:

> It is over 12 years since Herr Hitler fixed on the site of his one and only home. The colour scheme throughout this bright, airy chalet is light jade green. The *Führer* is his own decorator, designer and furnisher, as well as architect . . . [Hitler] has a passion for cut flowers in his home. He delights in the society of brilliant foreigners, especially painters, musicians and singers. As host, he is a droll *raconteur* . . .

The article was illustrated with several photographs taken by Heinrich Hoffmann. *Homes and Gardens* had got them from the Nazis' press office and they were years out of date,[9] but whatever made the phrase 'droll *raconteur*'?

Having found somewhere to live, the next thing Hitler needed was someone to look after him. Although they had not been close for more than fifteen years, he wrote to his widowed half-sister, Angela Raubal, suggesting she should become his cook/housekeeper, adding that her children were welcome too. At first sight it was a sensible solution. He could trust his half-sister to be discreet. He may even have felt faintly guilty about the years during which he had neglected her and her children and felt he should make amends, although Frau Raubal had never looked for help from her wastrel of a half-brother. Employing her at Haus Wachenfeld, he must have thought, would make her life easier while at the same time securing home comforts for himself. Two problems solved. The invitation could also have had something to do with the fact that Frau Raubal specialised in the rich, sugary cakes he remembered from his childhood. Henriette, the daughter of his official photographer, Heinrich Hoffmann, wrote: 'She was a kindly, sympathetic woman, an expert in cooking Austrian specialities. She could make feather-light puff pastry, plum cakes with cinnamon, spongy poppyseed *strudel* and fragrant vanilla pancakes – all the irresistible things her brother loved eating.'[10]

9. *Guardian*, 3 November 2003, 'At Home with the Führer' by Simon Waldman, Guardian Unlimited © Guardian Newspapers Limited 2003.
10. Henriette von Schirach, *Frauen um Hitler* (Munich: Herbig, 1983), p. 49.

The invitation was accepted. Frau Raubal left her job in Vienna and moved to Obersalzberg in March 1927, bringing only her younger daughter Elfriede. Their arrival gave Hitler a taste of family life for the first time since his early teens, with his half-sister taking care of his practical needs and Elfriede a shy, unobtrusive presence: he scarcely noticed her mute figure fetching and carrying, tidying up after him and opening the door to visitors. The older girl, his niece Angela Maria – known since childhood as Geli[11] to distinguish her from her mother – did not join them but stayed on in Vienna, planning to follow when her *Abitur* or final school exams were over. She had been to Munich once before, in 1925, on a school outing with her teacher and sixteen-year-old classmates. On that occasion she had written to her uncle in advance saying she would like to visit him, but he replied that he couldn't spare the time. Instead, one of his aides took her sightseeing. It might even have been Emil Maurice, Hitler's chauffeur, who was soon to play a crucial part in her life.

Geli was a strong-minded girl who went her own way with style and élan, indifferent to the opinions of her classmates and teachers. She was very bright or she worked very hard; either way she passed her *Abitur*, the first person in her family ever to do so. In July 1927 her uncle himself went to Berchtesgaden station to fetch her from the train. If she remembered him at all, it was as a skinny, dishevelled chap forever spouting politics. He probably expected a shy, pigtailed school-girl. They must both have had quite a shock.

11. Pronounced with a hard 'g', as in *gaily*.

Chapter Eight
Geli and Hitler and Eva

During the extra two years she had spent studying for her *Abitur* Geli had grown from a teenager into a buxom and self-assured young woman. She and her uncle shared two unhealthily close relatives (hot-tempered Alois was both Hitler's father and Geli's grandfather and of course Geli's mother Angela was the *Führer*'s half-sister) but judging by photographs she didn't resemble him at all. He was pallid, she olive-skinned; his eyes were light blue, hers dark brown; he had fine straight hair, hers was thick and curly. Nor were their characters similar. She was animated, defiant and pleasure-loving, and her interest in the opposite sex already suggested a healthy sex drive. Hitler was austere, inhibited and controlling. Yet beneath the surface both uncle and niece were highly emotional, liable to fits of temper or depression, mood swings and sulks. Neither knew this – nor anything else much – about the other. Their relationship was founded on a host of false assumptions. She thought he would provide her with money and status and let her get on with her life; while Hitler, from the moment he met his niece again in July 1927, planned to mould her into a model of young womanhood, an exemplary Miss Deutschland.

With Geli he could play the role of mentor and protector, guide and confidant. Hitler decided that his niece was gifted and should study further. His own lack of education – no matter that it was largely his fault – irked him. He was willing to pay for her continued education – surprisingly, for someone who believed that women's preserve was wife- and motherhood. Geli thought of becoming a doctor and in October she moved into a guesthouse, Pension Klein, and enrolled as a medical student at Munich University. She didn't persist with medicine for very long. Then she decided she'd rather be a singer, so her uncle paid for singing lessons. He would turn up early to collect her and sit outside the practice room listening as she struggled with arias. She soon abandoned that idea, too. After nearly two decades of poverty, a tough upbringing, the absence of a father (he had died when she was two) or any other guiding male presence, she was not disposed to defer to a man and had no desire to grind through years of hard slog to earn a professional qualification. She wanted to have fun. Freed from the constricting routine of school, she could hardly wait to practise her skills on the opposite sex.

At nineteen, Geli Raubal possessed enormous charm. She was never classically good-looking yet it was said that men would sometimes stop in the street, staring after her, electrified by her sheer physical exuberance. Others saw a dumpy little nobody with thick legs. The same contradiction is clear from her photographs. In studio portraits by Hoffmann her fat cheeks and square jaw reveal all too clearly the stolid housewife she could easily have become.[1] In others, especially snapshots catching her in an unguarded moment, she sparkles with vitality and sex appeal. One picture taken at Haus Wachenfeld shows her wearing a student's cap tipped at a rakish angle with an oversized tweed jacket and trousers, anticipating the film *Annie Hall* by four decades. Hands thrust in her pockets, hips jutting forward, cigarette drooping between her lips (Hitler hated women to smoke) she grins wickedly, defying every bourgeois convention. Geli would not easily knuckle under to one man. She may, consciously or not, have been copying the ambiguous sexuality of Marlene Dietrich, wholly female, tantalisingly masculine, playing with androgyny. Other photographs show Geli yanking up her bathing suit to flaunt plump, naked thighs or pulling her skirt well above her knees while pretending to show off the tame jackdaw perched on her lap; or lolling about at picnics, clowning, showing her white teeth, laughing openly at the camera. Geli scorned glamour. Original to the point of eccentricity, she was the Sally Bowles type: quirky and magnetic. If she had been able to sing, even a little, she might have made a great cabaret artist.

Geli's effect upon Hitler was remarkable. His avuncular concern soon became a fiercely possessive passion and they were both drawn into a relationship that overwhelmed them with its emotional intensity. In a disturbing echo of his mother Klara, who had called her husband 'Onkel Alois' – Uncle Alois – Geli teasingly called him 'Onk'

---

1. But as his daughter Henriette wrote: 'Geli's charm couldn't be photographed. It wasn't present in any of the pictures that my father took of her.'

Alf' – Uncle Adolf. She too was part of the dysfunctional Hitler clan stemming from a small peasant community, its roots deeply inter-twined. Once again incest tiptoed round the Hitler family.

'Onk' Alf' quickly ceased to be the hovering, protective uncle and became the hovering, jealous lover. Soon she was accompanying him to social events in the role of consort, a quite exceptional privilege and one seldom granted to any other woman. Baldur von Schirach, a member of his inner circle, recorded his first impression of Geli:

> Hitler was suddenly standing amongst us, and I have rarely seen him looking so happy. And in his tone of voice there was a mixture of pride and tenderness as he introduced 'My niece, Fräulein Raubal.'
>
> The girl at Hitler's side was of medium size, well developed, had dark, rather wavy hair, and lively brown eyes. A flush of embarrassment reddened the round face as she entered the room with him, and sensed the surprise caused by his appearance. I too stared at her for a long time, not because she was pretty to look at but because it was simply astonishing to see a young girl at Hitler's side when he appeared at a large gathering of people.[2]

Hitler's old friend Putzi Hanfstängl described Geli as 'an empty-headed little slut without either brains or character' but Putzi was notoriously malicious and in due course he would use much the same words about Eva. His descriptions are not reliable. Contrast his contempt with Hoffmann's fulsome admiration for Geli: '. . . a lovely and confident young woman who, with her artless and carefree manner, captivated everyone. Geli Raubal was an enchantress . . . She succeeded, by her mere presence, in putting everybody into the best of good spirits; each and every one of us was devoted to her.'[3]

There were plenty of reasons for Hitler to be attracted to his niece, despite the fact that she was the exact opposite of the young women he usually fancied. She reminded him of his youth in Linz and Vienna, in the days when he had aspired to the same sort of unconventional, electrifying personality. Her headstrong self-confidence was a large part of her appeal but for her uncle it also posed a threat. Within a few weeks Hitler was no longer content for her to live at Obersalzberg,

2. Baldur von Schirach, *Ich glaubte an Hitler* (Hamburg, 1967).
3. Hoffmann, *Hitler Was My Friend*, p. 148.

which meant he saw her chiefly at weekends, but wanted to have her near him in Munich all the time. His obsession with Geli's virginity made him unreasonably demanding. He justified his possessiveness, Hoffmann reported, by claiming that his niece needed guidance:

> You know, Hoffmann, I'm so concerned about Geli's future that I feel I have to watch over her. I love Geli and could marry her, but you know what my viewpoint is. I want to remain single. So I retain the right to exert an influence on her circle of friends until such time as she finds the right man. What Geli sees as compulsion is simply prudence. I want to stop her from falling into the hands of someone unsuitable.[4]

If this report is accurate, Hitler was deceiving himself. Putzi Hanfstängl once noticed him making 'moon-calf' eyes at Geli when he thought no one was looking. 'We saw her on one occasion with Hitler at the Residenz theatre . . . they were standing in one of the side galleries during an interval, with Hitler mooning at her, thinking he was unobserved, but as soon as he saw me he switched his face to the Napoleonic look.'[5]

Even if Adolf Hitler was not considering marriage to Geli, his friends noticed the erotic charge between them. They could not know that it was fatally impeded by what was then called 'bad blood' due to inbreeding in Strones, the village of his father's birth. Hitler, who advocated the use of eugenic murder to create a race of perfect human beings, nursed a lifelong fear that his genes carried the stigma of mental and physical deformity. In that case it was more than likely that Geli's did too, doubling the risk. Marrying her was out of the question, parenthood unthinkable.[6]

Yet Hitler was in love for the first time in his life; bafflingly, inconveniently, passionately in love. Geli's feelings were harder to read. She flaunted her power over him but resisted his attempts to limit her freedom. Hitler was up against someone he could not dominate – not by giving her orders or presents, not even by locking her up. Despite

---

4. Baldur von Schirach, *Ich glaubte an Hitler* (Hamburg, 1967).
5. Hanfstängl, *Unheard Witness*, pp. 171–2.
6. If they had produced a child, it would have had the same grandfather and great-grandfather in Alois Schicklgruber-Hitler and possibly also the same grandfather, great-grandfather and great great-grandfather in Johann Nepomuk Hüttler.

himself, Hitler was fascinated by this 'wild child' and infuriated by her resistance. She needed to be free, to have fun, to flirt and dance and go to the cinema, to smoke and drink and meet a handsome sexy youth and marry him. All these pursuits he prevented. He took her with him everywhere: to meals at the Osteria Bavaria, to the opera and to the countryside for picnics. At weekends, if he was not away on Party business or speaking engagements, they usually went to Obersalzberg, though her mother's presence must have inhibited sexual activity, let alone consummation, since in those days Haus Wachenfeld was a small chalet. Could Angela Raubal have been unaware of Hitler's passion for her daughter or did she turn a blind eye, in the hope that Geli would one day stand beside him as First Lady of Germany?

On 5 August 1928, a year after coming to Haus Wachenfeld, Geli moved to lodgings next door to Hitler's Munich base at 43 Thierschstrasse, a few steps from the River Isar in the part of the city called Isartor, well away from the bohemian temptations of Schwabing, with its smoky cafés full of hungry, argumentative students. It meant her uncle could keep an eye on her, but he never forgot that others were keeping an eye on *him*. Hitler was the heartbeat of the Nazi Party, creator and spokesman of its ideology, revered by men and adored by women. He dared not risk a scandal, least of all with his niece. Despite the highly coloured rumours over the last eight years that had linked him with a number of glamorous, elegant or famous women, he was almost certainly still a virgin. His growing popularity and prominence enforced discretion in public. There was gossip enough as it was and political opponents were already making capital out of Geli's constant presence. At meals she always sat beside him and was the only person allowed to interrupt him. She would break into one of his monologues with an impatient remark, tell a joke or a funny story, to which Hitler would listen indulgently, delighted that she amused the company – above all, himself. He had little sense of humour (though some said he was a good mimic) but he did like people who made him laugh. Geli's unconventional jokes scandalised him yet she was permitted to break his rules: that women should not draw attention to themselves in male company, and should never be vulgar. Geli, shamelessly, broke both.

Despite the indulgence he showed her among his inner circle, Geli was beginning to chafe under her uncle's control. By 1929 the *Führer* was increasingly preoccupied with politics. He travelled all over Germany making inflammatory speeches, leaving Geli on her own. However important and generous he might be, he was no fun. He didn't like jazz, 'hot' or otherwise, or syncopated music and dancing or indeed anything modern, yet he wouldn't let her spend time with her friends (who did). Heinrich Hoffmann described an occasion when Geli begged to be allowed to attend one of Munich's big social events, the Shrovetide Ball. At first Hitler refused, saying it was his duty to protect her. Eventually he gave in, on condition she was escorted by two of his friends (Hoffmann and Max Amann, both twice her age), that he vetted her dress, and that she left by 11 p.m.: the hour at which any decent ball is just beginning to swing. Geli spent the evening bored and self-conscious in a dowdy evening gown that completely obscured her splendid bosom. She was home before midnight, seething. Hoffmann said afterwards, 'It seemed simply intolerable to this child of nature that he should want to monitor her every step and that she shouldn't be allowed to speak to anyone without his knowledge.'[7]

Hoffmann's daughter Henriette, now seventeen and an occasional member of the circle round the table at the Osteria, was an acute and reliable observer of Hitler's relationships. She recalled, 'There was nothing she [Geli] wanted less than to be watched over. She was ready for new adventures, hungry for new experiences.'[8] Her father came to the same conclusion: 'This rigid supervision of her every step, this prohibition against making the acquaintance of any men or indulging in any normal social intercourse without Hitler's knowledge were intolerable to a character which was as free as nature itself.'[9] Poor, fettered Geli longed to go out unchaperoned or take the train to Vienna to meet her old school-friends (and keep other, riskier, assignations). At the same time, well aware of the adulation he inspired, Geli was reluctant to surrender her role as Hitler's favourite. She enjoyed having power over this powerful man and exercised it as much as she dared. He was adoring and enraged by turns, but as time went on the risk she posed to his public image became greater than he could tolerate.

Hitler had suppressed his sex drive for so long – even avoiding mastur-bation in adolescence, if his friend Kubizek is to be believed – that he must have worried about his untried sexuality.[10] Was he potent? Had

7. Hoffmann, *Hitler Was My Friend*, p. 7.
8. Henriette von Schirach, *Frauen um Hitler* (Munich: Herbig, 1983), p. 49.
9. Hoffmann, *Hitler Was My Friend*, p. 151.
10. 'It can be said with near certainty that by the time he left Vienna at the age of 24, Hitler had had no sexual experience.' Kershaw, *Hitler, 1889–1936; Hubris.* 'None of his liaisons had been more than superficial. No deep feelings were ever stirred.' Ibid., p. 352.

he ever been? Geli was half his age and sexually naive when he first brought her to Obersalzberg but her physical instincts, uncomplicated by scruples, demanded their natural expression. Two years was a long time to wait, too long, and the delay damaged their relationship. When it was eventually consummated – if ever, and no one can be sure of this, though it seems more than likely – she was about twenty-one to his forty, by which time he would have waited for more than twenty years, the whole of his adult life, for the experience of making love to a woman. Hitler was right in thinking that when he was absent his niece would make a play for any attractive male. Unable to defer her needs any longer, Geli had taken other partners, and his desire, too long postponed, curdled into neurosis and pathological jealousy.

It may seem impossible that after two years during which they had seen one another almost daily, Hitler and Geli were not yet lovers. But if the relationship were to take on a sexual dimension they needed privacy, and this may be what drove Hitler to look for a larger, more secure home than his cramped quarters in Isartor. In December 1929 (a few weeks after first meeting Eva Braun) he took possession of a nine-roomed apartment at 16 Prinzregentenplatz, a prosperous middle-class residential quarter in central Munich. Funded and furnished by the party, the apartment[11] occupied the entire second floor of the building and was far more modern and spacious than anywhere he had lived before. He employed a couple, Herr and Frau Winter, to look after his domestic needs while Frau Raubal, Geli's mother, remained in Obersalzberg as housekeeper.

> The flat in no way differed from the home of a well-placed solid bourgeois. There was wicker furniture, brightly-patterned curtains and in the dressing room a full-length mirror and wall lights. Soft carpets everywhere. Also a study and library for Hitler. Two rooms had been knocked together to make a single spacious living room . . . Hitler liked large rooms.[12]

Hitler cultivated the myth of his own frugality and while it's true that his tastes were modest, he allowed his financial manager, Martin Bormann, full rein in the management of his affairs. Bormann eventually bought the entire Prinzregentenplatz block for Hitler out of party

11. The building still exists but the apartment itself is now a police station.
12. Junge, *Until the Final Hour*, p. 112.

funds, as well as seeing to the ever-growing royalties from *Mein Kampf*. Bormann made sure that the *Führer* was not poor.

Two months later Geli moved in, taking over a bedroom and bathroom at the end of his corridor. It was a reckless step that was bound to come to light eventually but Hitler must have thought it was the only way to keep a closer watch on her. Now he could monitor where she went, whom she met and when she came home, under the observant eyes of her bodyguards who were effectively spies for him.

Exactly when uncle and niece first slept together and exactly how it happened remains pure guesswork. The secrets of other people's sex lives are the most secret of all and single men in positions of power always attract speculation. Hitler's supposedly bizarre sexual tastes were the subject of excited but unprovable theories but there is no reliable evidence whatsoever that the rumours were true. Putzi Hanfstängl, confidently omniscient, wrote in his memoirs:

> From watching Hitler and talking to those near him I had formed the firm conviction that he was impotent, the repressed, mastur-bating type . . . He had hated his father, a stupid, petty, brutal, small-time provincial customs inspector, and adored his mother. Once he got his clothes off he was absolutely useless . . . the barren hero, I suppose you might call him [No evidence offered or confidences cited]. An impotent man with tremendous nervous energy, Hitler had to release this tension somehow . . . His eroti-cism was purely operatic, never operative. He was in turn sadist and masochist [again, no evidence adduced], and in the sexual half-light of his life he never found physical release . . . In due course he did become identified with various women and *the case of his niece Geli Raubal to my mind was a turning point of the most sinister nature* [my italics].[13]

Hanfstängl imputes several perverse practices to Hitler, ascribing his passion for Geli to her willingness to cooperate with his warped desires, adding coyly: 'I only got the story at third hand. It was not the sort of thing you could expect a young woman to talk about.' The third-hand informant is not named.[14]

13. Hanfstängl, *Unheard Witness*, pp. 129–30.
14. Ibid., pp. 169–70.

This analysis of Hitler's sexuality is typically exaggerated.[15] Once he had fallen from favour, Putzi became unduly dismissive of his former protégé's motives and character but in the decade after 1923 he did spend more time with Hitler than almost anyone else except Hoffmann and his opinion has to be taken into account, although his dislike of Geli is obvious in every word of his memoirs. The only time he relaxes his venom comes in a double-edged comment, when he saw Hitler walking beside Geli carrying a whip: 'Whips as well, I thought, and really felt sorry for the girl.'[16] In fact Hitler often held a whip, to impress women and to control his dogs, Wolf, Prinz, or Bella or Blondi.

The American psychiatrist Dr Walter C. Langer, commissioned in 1943 by the US intelligence service to draw up a psychological report on Hitler, concluded that he was possibly a sexual masochist though definitely not impotent or homosexual, but Langer was working with limited information, some of which later proved to be wrong.

There has been endless speculation about Hitler's erotic tastes, particularly in relation to his niece, with confident pronouncements disguised as character analysis. Every historian rewrites Hitler in his own image. The 'proof' in most cases is thin and largely speculative, telling more about the author than the subject. Otto Strasser, a middle-ranking henchman on the left wing of the Nazi Party, hinted at nasty sexual practices but his testimony was tainted by a desire for revenge. In June 1934 Hitler would order the execution of his older brother Gregor during the Night of the Long Knives (a purge of anyone suspected of not giving the *Führer* their full support) and after this Otto was always looking for ways to blacken his name.[17] Others who

15. Ian Kershaw, whose biography of Hitler, *Hitler, 1889–1936; Hubris*, entitles him to be regarded as the foremost authority, writes (p. 352), 'Whatever the basis of the rumours [i.e. about Hitler's sexuality and relations with women] – often malicious, exaggerated, or invented – none of his liaisons, it seems, had been more than superficial. No deep feelings were ever stirred . . . It was different with Geli. Whatever the exact nature of the relationship – *and all accounts are based heavily upon guesswork and hearsay* [my italics] – it seems certain that Hitler . . . became emotionally dependent on a woman. Whether his involvement with Geli was explicitly sexual cannot be known beyond doubt . . . *But lurid stories of alleged deviant practices put about by Otto Strasser ought to be viewed as the fanciful anti-Hitler propaganda of an outright political enemy* [my italics].'
16. Hanfstängl, *Unheard Witness*, p. 172.
17. See Kershaw's footnote in *Hitler, 1889–1936: Hubris* on p. 704: 'Otto Strasser in *Hitler und Ich* hinted strongly at perverted sexual practices inflicted by Hitler on his niece. In an interview with the American OSS on 13 May 1943 he was explicit, but his account is unreliable and speculative.'

were closer to Hitler – his manservant, the housekeeper who cleaned the bedrooms, and Albert Speer, an intimate of both Hitler and Eva – dismissed all these highly coloured allegations and claimed that Hitler's sexuality was perfectly normal.

Did Hitler make Geli perform acts that repelled her? Was he avoiding intercourse for fear of incest but satisfying himself in other ways? Was he, as posthumous psychoanalysts have suggested, anally obsessive and did he find pleasure in coprophilia? Or were '*Onk*' Alf' and his niece enjoying the sort of sex life that is the stuff of advice columns in today's teenage magazines – oral and perhaps anal sex – but in the thirties was regarded as depraved if not actually illegal? Titillating speculation has sold many books but the truth remains unknown and always will.

At first, in the months after October 1929 when Eva Braun first met Hitler, there was no rivalry between her and Geli Raubal. Eva appealed to him – her youth, her prettiness, her obvious *Schwärmerei* (infatuation) – but she was a very small star circling the outer edges of his orbit, along with several others. Hitler liked to go backstage after a performance of opera or ballet and dazzle the cast with his expertise. (He was genuinely knowledgeable about Wagner's operas but ill-informed and biased about anyone else's.) In the days before Geli monopolised him he used to pick out one or two members of the chorus to join him for supper, after which he might invite one back to his flat; but his chauffeur, waiting patiently outside, always ferried the girl home after an hour or so. Those who divulged what went on never had anything more colourful to report than a certain amount of mild fondling and a good deal of hand stroking. Later, after he had become entirely obsessed by his niece, his 'Princess' (as he called her), these minor excursions stopped. By 1929 Hitler had good reason to believe he was on the verge of power. The Nazi movement had grown to a million members. He already dominated the party; soon it could be all Germany. He was not about to risk this even for the niece he worshipped, let alone for the sake of a little pigeon from the chorus or an adoring shop girl. A scandal or pregnancy at this stage would be catastrophic and Hitler took very good care to avoid both.

Yet Eva gradually began to stand out from the other orbiting starlets. Her chief appeal for Hitler lay in her joyous nature and her undisguised love for him. She had the gift of lightening the atmosphere, infecting others with her gaiety, being funny and inconsequential and naive while Geli, two years older and much more critical, was becoming sullen and confrontational. At the same time Eva was not afraid to push herself forward, manoeuvring for a few moments alone with Hitler. Soon she was telling her friends she would make him fall in love with her. 'Hitler says he's a hardened bachelor but he has his Achilles heel,' she boasted, 'and you'll see: he'll marry me!'[18] Her cousin Gertraud comments: 'Her will was already very strong and beneath a gauche exterior her determination to inveigle her way into Hitler's life was *absolute*. If she didn't know about Geli at the very beginning, Hoffmann would soon have told her.'[19] Eva risked pursuing him openly, not realising how much this evidence of her devotion endeared her to Hitler. Eva's straightforward hero-worship was a relief after Geli's melodrama; the scenes, the tantrums, the shouting and sulking. He might be idolised by the party but he craved uncritical love from a woman and he didn't get it from Geli, whose affections – not that Hitler knew this yet – were focused elsewhere.

That Hitler seduced Eva while he was involved with Geli seems somewhat unlikely, though it is possible. He had little time, or need, for another sexual entanglement; the relationship with his niece was quite demanding enough. He saw 'little Fräulein Braun' regularly since she was still in the shop, working by day at Photo Hoffmann, dealing with dull customers and their trivial demands or developing photographs downstairs in the darkroom before returning to have supper with the family. She consoled herself by reflecting that when Hitler turned up at the shop he made a point of talking to her; brought her small gifts and even took her to the opera occasionally, until even her cynical boss had to admit that he seemed to take *some* interest in her. 'He's like that with all my employees,' Hoffmann boasted to Eva. She knew it wasn't true. Her cousin Gertraud later surmised:

> He was attracted by this cheerful, uncomplicated young creature, still below the age of sexual consent (legally, that was twenty-one). He was the kind of man who would have liked the thought of keeping her secret and whenever it looked as though she might become inconvenient he simply avoided her. Surrounded as he was by the most beautiful women from the worlds of the cinema and high society, Hitler hardly bothered about her.[20]

18. Gun, *Hitler's Mistress; Eva Braun*, p. 59.
19. Gertraud Weisker in conversation with the author, March 2004.
20. Ibid.

Gertraud was only seven or eight at the time so she can't have seen any of this at first hand, though much later she did become one of Eva's confidantes. For the time being Hitler's immediate cronies paid Eva Braun little or no attention and to the public, she – like Geli – remained unknown.

How unusual were these two young women, who had inveigled themselves into Hitler's circle and were tolerated by his garrulous, self-important friends? Perhaps the chief surprise is that they were both brought up to be well-behaved middle-class girls, treading well-mapped social paths towards the altar and the cradle, at a time when the young women more usually found in the company of older men were raffish figures from the world of the theatre or nightclub; performers or hostesses known to be 'easy', compliant and – if a scandal should arise – tainted by already dubious reputations. Munich was not like the Berlin or Hamburg documented by George Grosz and Christopher Isherwood, cities whose night life was decadent, where even 'nice' girls might take to drugs and alcohol and ride in fast cars with dangerous young men. The schoolfriends with whom Eva had grown up, and with whom she might have been expected to spend most of her free time, would have been mildly shocked by her unmaidenly behaviour in consorting publicly with older men. Her parents, had they known, would have been appalled. At this stage they did not know and by the time they found out there was no going back.

When Eva watched Hitler with Geli she could hardly fail to have been jealous – love and jealousy go hand in hand, especially in girls of seventeen. Her mother Fanny, questioned after the war,[21] said: 'I think she knew Geli because she often talked about her but I never saw the two of them together and I don't know whether they met often.' Geli, born in 1908, was four years older than Eva, at a stage in life when four years makes a real difference. Geli seemed grown up and sophisticated, way beyond her own experience, but, most crucial of all, Hitler loved her: that was obvious. Yet Eva must have been encouraged when she began to be included in his evenings at the opera, even if it did mean that, like the rest of his circle, she was forced to sit through hours of Wagner and look attentive as the *Führer* extolled the Teutonic virtues of Siegfried. In 1930, several months

21. Musmanno Collection, Vol. IV, interview with Eva's parents at their home in Ruhpolding, 4 September 1945, taken from files held in the Musmanno Collection.

after they had met, she acquired a further privilege. Hitler invited her to join him for supper at the Osteria Bavaria at 62 Schellingstrasse, 50 yards down the street from Hoffmann's studio.

The *Führer* was a man of fixed habits. Once he decided he liked a place he would patronise it for decades. Café Heck in the Hofgarten and Café Neumaier were two favourites and the Carlton Teeraum on the Briennerstrasse another, but he liked Osteria Bavaria best of all for its hearty food and *gemütliche* atmosphere. After a day formulating policy and tactics at the Braun Haus, the NSDAP headquarters in Schellingstrasse, or checking on the *Völkischer Beobachter*, the party's propaganda sheet, the offices of which were another hundred yards along, it was handy and welcoming. He admitted, 'I can no longer bear solitude. What I like best is to dine with a pretty woman. And rather than be left at home by myself, I'd go and dine at the Osteria.'[22]

Throughout the late twenties and 1930s, whenever he was in Munich, the *Führer* would come several times a week to this apparently ordinary restaurant.[23] Owned by a Bavarian, Ernst Deutelmoser, the Osteria Bavaria was founded in 1890 and had always been a favourite among Munich's artistic community. A large recess to the right of the entrance had a wide doorway across which a curtain could be drawn for privacy, enabling Hitler and his crew to roister unobserved without being interrupted by overenthusiastic supporters, though his impassioned monologues on the usual topics – art, architecture and Germany's destiny – would have been perfectly audible to other diners. As a teetotaller and vegetarian, he appreciated the restaurant's cooking, in particular a dish of oven-baked cauliflower cheese, while its kitchen specialised in sweet cakes and pastries. Eva was to spend many long evenings there, trying not to look bored as Hitler held forth to his party cronies – the usual suspects: Hoffmann, Himmler, von Schirach, Bormann and Hess. At least when two or three pretty young women were in attendance the conversations were not solely about politics, out of consideration for them. Affairs of state were never discussed in female company.

After the war the restaurant's close association with Hitler forced it to change its name and nature. The Osteria Bavaria was taken over by a north Italian couple, the Salvatoris, and renamed Osteria Italiana,

22. *Hitler's Table Talk, 1941–1944*, night of 10/11 March 1942, p. 360.
23. Stefano de Michaelis, *Osteria Italiana* (Munich: Heinrich Hugendubel, 1998), pp. 12–15.

though apart from the addition of a few pasta dishes the cuisine didn't change much. It has lasted for more than a century, a good deal longer than the Thousand Year Reich, and continues to draw a varied clientele including neo-Nazi groupies and the curious of all nationalities.

I lunched there in August 2003[24] and the Osteria seemed to have altered little in seventy years. It is dark, intimate, with low ceilings from which cast-iron circles supporting yellowing parchment lamp-shades are suspended. The panelled walls are decorated with Bavarian-style motifs and there is a coat of arms over the door leading to Hitler's former sanctum. Banquettes line the walls on which hang rustic scenes of nineteenth-century peasants in traditional costume. I chose a corner table by the entrance, possibly the very one at which Unity Mitford had stationed herself, hoping to catch Hitler's eye. Outside, the cheerful student population of Schwabing went about its business unconcerned, preferring to patronise a café called *Schall und Rauch* – Noise and Smoke or, more vividly, Din and Fug. After lunch I strolled back up Schellingstrasse and stopped outside number 50, Hoffmann's former studio, now a shop selling cheap Asian fabrics and furniture of the sort that students like and can afford. Carved in stone over the next-door entrance to a dental surgery is one of the icons of the Third Reich: a battered eagle with outspread wings indicating that in the early twenties the Nazis had their headquarters here. A swastika that used to signal the entrance has been erased. The eagle may have survived because, blurred with age, it's barely noticeable. As thor-oughly as it can, Munich has obliterated all Nazi connections from the years 1920 to 1945, yet in spite of its attempt to deny those shameful years, faint, insistent traces linger.[25]

Hitler spent hours with his crowd in his favourite *Lokalen* (local joints) where everyone except him ate and drank heartily. Jolly Heinrich

24. Telephone number for bookings: [00 49] 089 272 0717 or e-mail www.osteria.de – reservations recommended but not essential. The website, though boasting of a history that dates back to 1890, makes no mention whatsoever of its most famous patron – Adolf Hitler.

25. The city may be coming round to accepting its ineradicable history. In 2004 the city museum mounted an exhibition of documents and memorabilia from the Third Reich. On the day I went it was sparsely attended but the exhibits were detailed and there was no attempt to cover up the truth of what had really happened.

Hoffmann in particular was already too fond of alcohol; Göring already had a gargantuan appetite. After the death of Hoffmann's first wife Lelly in 1928 he had become even more of 'a drinker and raconteur, the court jester of Hitler's inner circle'.[26] Hitler excused his drinking by saying that Lelly's death had hit him hard. It was tacitly accepted that these informal gatherings were private and off the record. Hitler and Hoffmann both fancied themselves as art connoisseurs and would hold forth on the merits of their favourite German painters, the type who depicted jolly monks holding frothing tankards of beer or cheerful, bosomy young wives going about their simple tasks. The other pictures Hitler liked best verged on pornography – vigorous images of muscle-bound, homoerotic young men posing as noble workers for the Fatherland, often strikingly similar to the Soviet Realism school of art featuring farmers and factory workers wielding hammer or sickle. The *Führer*, his pronouncements becoming more emphatic as the meal progressed, swore that 'German realism' outranked and would one day outsell Rembrandt. As Chancellor, he would insist that Germany's municipal galleries displayed this noble proletarian art.

Hoffmann knew a bit about art and Putzi Hanfstängl a great deal but Hitler was ignorant – Putzi once mocked him behind his back for having mistaken Caravaggio's *St Matthew* for a Michelangelo – and like most art philistines he possessed natural bad taste.[27] He ridiculed all innovatory modern art as the work of degenerates and charlatans, banning everything except the stuff he approved, which had about as much aesthetic value as recruiting posters for *Hitler Jugend*. Equally,

26. As he was described by Julius Streicher's younger son, Elmar. Streicher was a founder member of the German Socialist Party. Fanatically anti-Semitic, he established the newspaper *Der Stürmer* to further his obscene views. Although he was a bully and a troublemaker, Hitler remained loyal to him, as he did to nearly all his early associates, even expressing his gratitude to Streicher in *Mein Kampf*.

27. Adolf Ziegler, president of the Reich Chamber for the Visual Arts, ingratiated himself with Hitler by painting Geli's portrait. His favourite genre was recumbent nudes of 'startling verisimilitude', which won him the mocking accolade 'official pubic hair painter to the Reich' (Large, *Where Ghosts Walked*, p. 264). Ziegler painted a triptych of four nudes entitled *Four Elements* which hung above a peasant-style brick fireplace in the living room of the *Führer's* apartment in Munich, the four compliant naked ladies gazing mistily down at a deep-cushioned sofa and four armchairs. Only the rampant unicorn is missing; otherwise they could be the sisters of the fair-skinned nudes adorning the former palaces of Saddam Hussein. (*Four Elements* is shown in vol. 2 issue 10, 1938, p. 295 of *Die Kunst im Dritten Reich, 1937–1945*, the official art magazine of the Third Reich that first appeared in 1937.)

he despised contemporary drama, ballet and music, which he thought decadent. So much for the pretensions to connoisseurship.

Heinrich Hoffmann underestimated 'little Fräulein Braun' and throughout her life he continued to treat her as a junior employee. He quite failed to grasp the significance of her entry to the inner circle:

> To him [i.e. Hitler] she was just an attractive little thing in whom, in spite of her inconsequential and feather-brained outlook – or perhaps just because of it – he found the type of relaxation and repose he sought. Frequently when he intended coming to see us he would say, 'Ask that little Eva Braun of yours to come along too – she amuses me.' On other occasions he would say, 'I think I'll pop in and see little Eva for half an hour; give her a ring like a good chap and ask her if I may'; and very often, indulging in his favourite relaxation, we would all go on a picnic together to one of the beauty spots in which the surroundings of Munich abound . . . He gave her gifts in abundance: but they were flowers, chocolates, trinkets of modest value and the trivialities of the ordinary gallantry in which he delighted.[28]

But Eva was not as 'inconsequential and feather-brained' as Hoffmann assumed. She pursued Hitler with subtlety and persistence, noticing what pleased him and moulding herself into his ideal woman. She knew it would take time but she was eighteen – she had time. Geli must have realised how determined Eva was to insinuate herself into Hitler's life and may even have begun to feel slightly insecure. One of her bodyguards, Wilhelm Stocker, claimed, 'Geli worried that there might be another woman in Hitler's life because she mentioned to me several times that her uncle didn't seem to be as interested in her as he once was'.[29]

For some time now Geli herself had not been faithful. She had met Emil Maurice, Hitler's chauffeur and bodyguard, as long ago as 1926 at a party function in Weimar, when she would have been a school-girl of eighteen and he, at twenty-nine, was already attached to Hitler's

28. Hoffmann, *Hitler Was My Friend*, p. 161.
29. This claim is said to have came from Wilhelm Stocker himself, interview with Ronald Hayman, author of *Hitler and Geli* (London: Bloomsbury, 1998).

staff. When she moved to Munich in 1927 she saw him almost daily, since he drove Hitler everywhere and would take the *Führer* and Geli on excursions to the surrounding countryside. This proximity soon led to a serious affair and the two became secretly engaged. When Hitler found out he fell into such a violent rage that Maurice was afraid the *Führer* was going to shoot him. Hitler persuaded Geli to test the strength of her feelings by waiting two years before marrying. Geli objected fiercely but not even she could sway Hitler once his mind was made up. In a letter to Maurice written on 24 December 1928 she said:

> Uncle Adolf is insisting that we should wait two years. Think of it, Emil, two whole years of only being able to kiss each other now and then and always having Uncle Adolf in charge. I can only give you my love and be unconditionally faithful to you. I love you so infinitely much. Uncle Adolf insists that I should go on with my studies.

She knew she could never wait two years. Despite his promise, Hitler began putting pressure on her to break the engagement and Geli seems to have capitulated. For Christmas 1929 she gave her fiancé a studio portrait of herself taken by Hoffmann; it is a particularly flattering picture showing her back-lit, haloed in light and swathed in a white fur stole, smiling enticingly.[30] Below it she wrote '*My Beloved Emil – In Memory – From Your Geli*'. The affair was over.

Emil Maurice was given a job as head of Hitler's bodyguard at public meetings, so ensuring that he was rarely in Munich, and replaced as chauffeur by Julius Schreck (who died in 1936) and then by Erich Kempka. Hitler never dismissed him altogether from his service, despite the business with Geli, and Maurice repaid him with unquestioning loyalty. He was responsible for killing the Munich University professor Bernhardt Stempfle, an early intellectual influence on Hitler, allegedly because Stempfle talked too openly about the *Führer's* relationship with his niece.

Geli became yet more reckless in her search for other relationships, offering herself – rumour had it – to attractive students whom she picked up in cafés. One would like to know more about Geli's lovers,

30. The photograph is reproduced in the Hermann-Historica catalogue and was sold at Auction 47 on 15 October 2004, Lots 2023–4, for an estimated €3,500. This price, and the competitive interest it reflects, is an indication of the rising value of Nazi memorabilia.

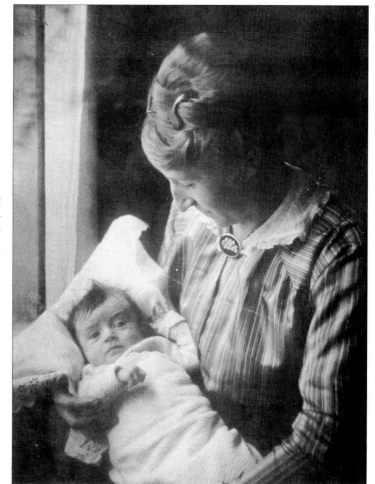

Eva Braun – *not* a pretty baby – in the arms of her mother, Franziska (Fanny) Braun, February 1912. (NARA)

Eva is about a year old in this portrait; her sister Ilse would have been four. It is captioned in Eva's handwriting 'Ich und Ilse' – me and Ilse. She forgot the family cat, *Schnurrer* (the purrer). (NARA)

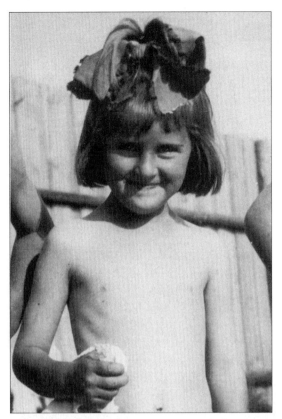

Eva aged five or six at the beach, wearing a cabbage leaf on her head. Already she was learning to play to the camera. (NARA)

Eva (fourth from right, front row) smiling wickedly. Hers is almost the only cheerful face in this group of miserable-looking children. She captioned it 'In der Klosterschule an Beilngries' – 'In the convent school at Beilngries' so it must have been taken at the time of her parents' separation in 1919, when Eva was seven. (By kind permission of Karl Westermeier, Beilngries)

a's maternal grandmother,
sefa Kronburger, *née* Winbauer,
eds the chickens in her back
rden in 1925, watched by her
ughter Antonia ('Anni'). (NARA)

This picture of Eva with an
Alsatian dog is undated but
she looks in her early teens
so it would have been taken
in the mid-1920s, after her
parents' reconciliation. (NARA)

Eva in her teens, sitting on the floor of the Braun family's flat at 93 Hohenzollernstrasse, displaying the new kitten – and her legs. (NARA)

Eva as a young teenager, artfully posed on her bed at home, possibly reading a book. (NARA)

Eva has captioned this picture 'Im Geschäft 1930' – 'in the shop'. If the date is correct, it would have been taken soon after she met Hitler for the first time and shows that she could already look sultry, even at 18. (NARA)

ne of a series by Hoffmann showing Eva in the office at Amalienstrasse in Munich. It is undated
id the hairstyle is not flattering (she is attempting the currently fashionable shingled bob). (NARA)

Heinrich Hoffmann's photographic shop, to which he moved his premises from
Schellingstrasse soon after Eva was hired. Appointed official photographer as early
as 1922, Hoffmann transformed Hitler's sallow face and lumpy features into those of a
charismatic leader. This window display shows several portraits of the *Führer*.
Hoffmann's exclusive copyright of such photographs earned him a fortune. (NARA)

These crucial photos from Eva's album are captioned in her handwriting 'Berchtesgaden 1931'.
They prove she first visited Hitler's private retreat at Obersalzberg as early as 1931. His adored
niece Geli died on 18 September, so the visit took place within months if not weeks of her
suicide. The wintry weather suggests they could have been taken in November or December.
The man with a bowed head, wearing a light raincoat and trilby, is probably Hitler himself.
It shows the Berghof – still called Haus Wachenfeld in 1931 – before the work of
enlargement began. (NARA)

Hitler often presented this brooding portrait to visitors, along with signed copies of *Mein Kampf*. The signature in the left-hand corner is Hoffmann's. Such memorabilia are ardently sought by Third Reich collectors and change hands for many thousand euros. (This sold for 12,500 in 2004.) (Hermann Historica)

This statuesque nude by Ivo Saliger, dated 1941, personifies the buxom yet modest woman – and style of painting – that Hitler liked best. He believed 'Aryan realism' would in time outrank and outprice the Renaissance masters. In 2004 this example sold for 5,000. (Hermann Historica)

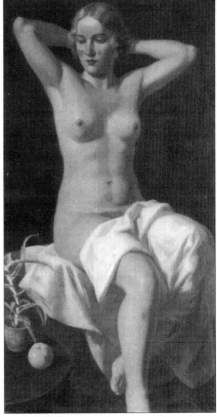

Hitler's niece, Geli Raubal, photographed by Hoffmann in September 1929. She had lived with the *Führer* since 1927, the object of his incestuous passion, but this picture was a Christmas gift for her secret lover Emil Maurice, Hitler's chauffeur. Hitler forced the pair to separate for two years and the photograph is inscribed in her handwriting, '*Meinen lieben Emil, zur Erinnerungen, von Deiner Geli*' – 'My dearest Emil, remember me, your Geli.' (Sold for 3,500) (Hermann Historica)

Eva and her flirtatious younger sister Gretl looked so alike that in photographs they are almost indistinguishable but Gretl had wider, darker eyes and a heart-shaped face. This picture shows her cheek-to-cheek with a personable young man. (NARA)

Eva bicycles through the gates of the little house in a discreet Munich suburb given to her by Hitler in late 1935, as a private retreat where he could safely visit her. (Bavarian State Library, Munich)

Within a year she had also been allocated a suite next to Hitler's in the refurbished and renamed Berghof. This corner of her bedroom shows a smart modern dressing table on which stand cosmetics, three different mirrors and a portrait of Hitler. (NARA)

These pictures were taken by Eva and captioned "*1936 – the new 'Berghof'*". The first photograph shows work in progress, enlarging and rebuilding 'Haus Wachenfeld', the modest chalet that became Hitler's country house and Germany's second centre of government. Much of his social life and that of his henchmen and their families was enacted on its huge terrace. (NARA)

A corner of Eva Braun's living room,
showing her favourite portrait of Hitler painted
by Theodor Bohnenberger, which hung in the
place of honour. (NARA)

At the opposite end of the room
stood her desk; above it another picture
of Hitler. Eva was a great letter-writer
but unfortunately very few of her letters
have survived. The large, soft, inviting
sofa on which Eva and Hitler relaxed.
Behind it, a telephone (her number was
unlisted) and a few books. (NARA)

Hitler and his beloved Alsatian bitch, Blondi, in identical poses, peering over the wooden railings that surrounded the Teehaus and overlooked a wonderful view. (NARA)

Hitler greets Eva with a stiff little bow; she sketches a curtsey for him. For the first ten years together their demeanour in front of others remained impeccably formal. (NARA)

The body language here is expressive. Neither looks at ease, let alone intimate. Hitler stands with arms crossed, almost leaning backwards; her pose is deferential, her legs awkward as a child's, and the space between them seems unnecessarily wide. She wears the Bavarian costume – a dirndl dress – that he preferred. (NARA)

va and her mother Franziska
(Fanny). This portrait must
have been taken after 1938,
when her parents had been
persuaded to tolerate Eva's
relationship with Hitler;
although as good Catholics,
in their eyes it remained
sinful. (NARA)

Eva and Hitler taking tea
at the Bavarian resort of
Garmisch-Partenkirchen, some
time in the 1930s. The hand
obtruding on the left shows
that other people were present,
which makes their close
proximity and relaxed manner
unusual. (Bavarian State
Library, Munich)

When Hitler was away, Eva's life was monotonous. She was always in search of pleasure, stimulus – and a chance to show off her figure. Here she clowns in a swimsuit. (Bavarian State Library, Munich)

Same again, sunbathing in a different swimsuit. (Bavarian State Library, Munich)

And again, this time on the terrace at the Berghof. In photographs like these – and there are scores – her flat stomach proves that Eva was never pregnant. (NARA)

To keep herself fit and fill the many hours when Hitler wasn't there, Eva practised gymnastics until her body was honed and toned to perfection. (NARA)

More of the same ... a sequence photographed and also filmed at a small private beach on the Königssee near Berchtesgaden, her favourite spot for relaxation. (NARA)

The fun and laughter are becoming strained and artificial; the eyes and mouth too exaggeratedly round to be spontaneous. By now – the late thirties – the terrace and the mountains were all too familiar. (Bavarian State Library, Munich)

serious or casual, but she knew she was watched and that in being unfaithful to Hitler she took her life – and theirs – in her hands, which was reason enough to be discreet. Nonetheless, her behaviour made her the subject of gossip. Wilhelm Stocker told an interviewer:

> Many times when Hitler was away for several days at a political rally or tending to party matters in Berlin or elsewhere, Geli would associate with other men. I liked the girl myself so I never told anyone what she did or where she went on these free nights. Hitler would have been furious if he had known that she was out with such men as a violin player from Augsburg or a ski instructor from Innsbruck . . . She was a girl who needed attention and needed it often. And she definitely wanted to remain Hitler's favourite girlfriend.

Hitler suspected what was going on and his jealousy became – not paranoid, since it was entirely justified – but a source of anguish to him and bitter resentment to her.

Hitler's chalet above Berchtesgaden remained exclusively Geli's domain, if only because her mother was its housekeeper. Eva was barred from visiting. She retaliated by slipping loving notes into Hitler's pocket, although she knew Geli might find them. She did. Erich Kempka's second wife[31] told a questioner in 1948, 'Geli knew something was "going on" between Hitler and Eva and that made her desperate, after being told he must live only for his people.'[32]

Henriette Hoffmann, who knew both Eva and Geli, once remarked: 'Geli was opera; Eva was operetta.' She wasn't referring to their musical tastes, which in the case of all three girls inclined towards popular music or light opera rather than the grand baritone variety. Henny meant that Geli was a tragic heroine and Eva just a pretty prattler in a little operetta by the Viennese Franz Lehár. But did Geli really live her life on a grander and deeper scale than Eva, with a greater capacity for joy and suffering?

31. According to Herbert Döring (not always a reliable witness) his first wife was Gerda Christian, née Daranowski, the most beautiful of Hitler's long-serving secretaries, but they divorced after several years of marriage.
32. Musmanno Collection, Vol. VII, interview with Erich Kempka, Munich, 19 August 1948.

In many ways their relationships with Hitler were similar. Had he been anyone else, these would have been little more than a crush on an older man, a rite-of-passage melodrama, banal and soon forgotten. Both girls met him when they were very young, straight from school, with little or no previous experience of a romantic relationship; each slept with him only after a lengthy procrastination, probably of more than two years. Eva, and Geli too, for all her defiant refusal to conform, had been brought up to believe in love and marriage. The narrative had been familiar since childhood . . . Cinderella is rescued from the ashy fireplace . . . goes to the palace ball . . . drops her shoe . . . the Prince searches for the tiny foot it fits; and flash! the moment of mutual recognition. Except that Hitler was no handsome prince but Bluebeard.

Both girls defied their families to pursue the affair and it was the greatest misfortune of their lives to become embroiled with him when they lacked the emotional intelligence or maturity to realise that they had no place in his larger world, nor was there any hope of him marrying them. Adolescents in love for the first time, they simply refused to believe that Germany would always be his first priority or that being *Führer* left no time for a wife, let alone children. They should have known better. Hitler was fond of saying,

> For me, marriage would have been a disaster. Misunderstanding is bound to arise between husband and wife when the husband cannot give his wife all the time she feels entitled to demand. One must understand this demandingness. A woman who loves her husband lives only for his sake . . . The man on the other hand is a slave to his thoughts. The idea of his duties rules him . . . The wife does not only complain of her husband's absence; she resents his being preoccupied. The bad side of marriage is that it creates rights. *That's why it's better to have a mistress. The burden is lightened and everything is placed on the level of a gift* [my italics].[33]

To compensate, he was generous to both girls. Geli could be demanding, but Eva's motives were not materialistic; for years she wouldn't accept money from him, not even her taxi fare home, which impressed Hitler a great deal. He often cited it to friends as proof that she wasn't interested in his wealth or his power as *Führer*.

33. *Hitler's Table Talk, 1941–1944*, pp. 245–6.

Both young women were more intelligent than they were given credit for, only one chose to hide and the other to flaunt it. Eva was not a 'goose', as some of Hitler's cronies called her, or a silly cow – *'ein blöde Kuh'* – while Geli, though she had no inclination for academic work, was certainly no fool. They knew Hitler couldn't bear clever women, least of all those who tried to argue with him. He preferred silly girls who laughed easily and took his mind off weightier business. As he said: 'Intelligence in a woman is not an essential thing. My mother, for example, would have cut a poor figure in the society of our cultivated women. She lived strictly for her husband and children. They were her entire universe. But she gave a son to Germany.'[34]

In their different ways both were the type described as 'a man's woman'. Eva, with her shapely figure and fine legs, was more conventionally beautiful but Geli was surely sexier. Julius Schaub, who was to be Hitler's adjutant for twenty years, described her as 'A brown-eyed brunette, 5 foot 6 tall, well-built with a blooming appearance, animal spirits and a pleasing voice. She was an open character, always ready for a joke . . . extraordinarily self-possessed.' 'Well-built' . . . 'blooming' . . . 'animal' . . . 'open' . . . the implication is clear: Geli was not a one-man woman like Eva – nowadays she'd be damned as 'fun-loving'. In the course of their affair she defied Hitler by choosing her own lovers, something Eva never did. Eva has often been wrongly dismissed as a 'bimbo' but no one ever questioned her fidelity.

But perhaps in the end the main difference between Eva and Geli was the intensity with which Hitler loved Geli. She was never in any doubt of '*Onk*' Alf's' passion while only very late in their relationship did Eva realise how important she was to him. Both suffered intense emotional crises on his account and attempted suicide more than once, this being the only way to compel his attention and concern. Both were utterly excluded from Hitler's political life although to everyone's astonishment he allowed himself to be photographed in public with Geli, a privilege only very rarely granted to Eva and then unwittingly. Scraps of evidence suggest that the two young women resented one another but if they did it can only have

---

34. Ibid., night of 10/11 March 1942, p. 359. (Note that Hitler describes his mother without making specific reference to the humble peasant background from which she – and he himself – came.)

been because of their rivalry; otherwise they would probably have got on splendidly.

With so much in common, why should one be characterised as opera and the other mere operetta? If Henny was thinking of their characters, Geli was apparently the more intense, with a powerful love of life's pleasures and a mind of her own, unwilling to subjugate herself to anyone. Compared with her, Eva seems a typically helpless little woman. Yet, as we shall see, she had greater emotional depths than anyone gave her credit for and despite her superficial bubbliness she suffered periods of profound depression that she concealed from everyone, above all Hitler. She was not only cleverer but also tougher than she seemed: it was no easy feat to bring herself to his notice, to become chief among the many other women clamouring for his attention.

Hitler's involvement with Geli was, after his love for his mother, the deepest emotional relationship of his life and the only one he could not control. She may have been infatuated by him and his importance at the beginning, but as time went on his company no longer made her happy; instead it became an intolerable burden. For her, the pressure of being loved by him was greater, though not necessarily any greater than the pressure for Eva of *not* being loved by him. Obsessional or unrequited love: which is harder to endure? Geli's attempt to assert her independence against the man who would soon threaten half Europe was a struggle she was bound to lose. She was fighting the feminist battle at a time when assertive women were unheard of. The extent of that battle and her courage and persistence as she struggled to win it make her seem a more serious character, better suited to grand opera, but Eva's ordeals honed her into a brave, strong and generous woman. In the end, being Hitler's partner – whether for four years or thirteen – entitles both young women to be called tragic heroines.

Four years after she had come to Obersalzberg to join her mother at Hitler's suggestion, Geli finally accepted that her uncle would never marry her, never give her children, never make her Germany's First Lady, and knew that by staying with him she was sacrificing her youth and her prospects of falling in love, marrying some ordinary, anonymous young man and, maybe, being happy.

By the summer of 1931 she was said to have a new lover, variously described as a Jewish violinist in Vienna, a Jewish artist in Linz or some other nameless attractive chap. She was also said to be pregnant. Who this lover was and whether he even existed is mere gossip. In September Hitler gave her permission to go to Vienna for a few days while he was away campaigning for the municipal elections in Hamburg. Hours before he set off there was a violent row. The maid – washing up in the kitchen, several rooms away – *thought* she heard the words 'I can shoot myself'. As Hitler was leaving and about to get into his car he was heard to shout at Geli: 'For the last time, no!' An unfinished letter was found on Geli's desk, ending in mid-sentence: 'When I come to Vienna – I hope very soon – we'll drive to Semmering [a resort outside the city] an . . .' – and there the letter broke off. It reads as if written to a lover but might equally have been addressed to one of her former schoolfriends. Anna Winter, the housekeeper at the Prinzregentenplatz flat, later claimed that Geli had come across a note in Hitler's pocket earlier in the day which she angrily tore up. Retrieved from her wastepaper basket and pieced together, it read: 'Thank you again for the wonderful invitation to the theatre. It was a memorable evening. I am most grateful to you for your kindness. I am counting the hours until I may have the joy of another meeting. Yours, Eva.'[35] They are the words of a besotted teenager but hardly enough reason to spark a major row between Geli and Hitler. Yet on 18 September 1931 *something* drove her to despair.[36]

Some people claim she was murdered by Himmler because she was threatening to blackmail Hitler, though it seems extraordinarily improbable that he could have ordered the death of the girl he worshipped.

35. Quoted in Gun, *Eva Braun: Hitler's Mistress*, p. 27. The original – being in shreds – disappeared long ago. He must have based it on Frau Winter's verbal evidence.
36. Putzi Hanfstängl claims that in the autumn of 1937 he was visited in London by a woman called Brigid Hitler, the estranged wife of Angela Raubal's brother Alois, who would have been Geli's uncle and Hitler's half-brother. This woman Brigid – who certainly did exist, and had a son, Patrick Hitler – apparently told Putzi that 'the family knew very well that the cause of Geli's suicide was the fact that she was pregnant by a young Jewish art teacher from Linz whom she had met in 1928 and wanted to marry'. He goes on, 'With her [i.e. Geli's] death the way was open for his final development into a demon, with his sex life deteriorating again into a sort of bi-sexual narcissus-like vanity, with Eva Braun little more than a vague domestic adjunct.' For someone who never saw inside Hitler's bedroom, Putzi claims to know a great deal about what went on behind its door. Hanfstängl, *Unheard Witness*, p. 176.

A more plausible explanation is that she shot herself with Hitler's pistol, a Walther 6.35 that he kept in his unlocked desk drawer. Her body was not found until the following morning. She had bled to death from a bullet wound close to the heart. She was twenty-three years and four months old when she died.

Henny Hoffmann, perhaps the only person who reported on the two relationships compassionately and impartially, said afterwards of Geli: 'He fenced her life so tightly, confined her in such a narrow space, that she saw no other way out. Finally she hated her uncle, she really wanted to kill him. She couldn't do that. So she killed herself, to hurt him deeply enough to disturb him. She knew that nothing else would wound him so badly.'[37] Her last words on the subject were: 'After Geli's death, much changed in our lives. Picnics didn't happen. Nobody talked about Geli, it was as if she'd never existed. Her room was closed, the clothes remained in the wardrobe.'[38] There they stayed, the bedroom an untouched shrine, for the rest of Hitler's life.

Was it really suicide? Did her uncle have her killed or was Geli's a frustrated life that ended in a self-inflicted, operatic death? The facts remain contradictory and inconclusive, especially since the Bavarian Minister for Justice refused a post-mortem, which meant there could be no official forensic examination of the body to quash the rumours that buzzed like flies around her corpse. Geli's body was hurriedly taken to Vienna for burial:[39] she had indeed got there 'very soon', though not in the way she would have predicted. The event triggered a huge scandal and a 'feeding frenzy' in the newspapers,[40] especially the Socialist *Münchener Post* and

37. Henriette von Schirach, *Frauen um Hitler* (Munich: Herbig, 1983), pp. 73–5, 79–80.

38. Ibid., p. 48.

39. Her grave is in Vienna, Zentralfriedhof. It is now unmarked, but according to Geoff Walden's contribution on the web it is/was Group 23E, Row 2, Plot number 73, her death date given as 18.09.31. Her body was exhumed in 1946 and reburied. Source: gwalden1864@earthlink.net or www.findagrave.com

40. One Munich newspaper printed a number of sensational details, none confirmed by the autopsy: 'On Saturday 19 September it was reported that Fräulein Geli had been found shot in the flat with Hitler's gun in her hand. The dead woman's nose was broken, and there were other serious injuries on the body. From a letter to a female friend living in Vienna, it is clear that Fräulein Geli had the firm intention of going to Vienna. The letter was never posted. The mother of the girl, a half-sister of Herr Hitler, lives in Berchtesgaden; she was summoned to Munich.'

the gutter press[41] – so much so that Hitler was obliged to issue a statement denying that he had engineered Geli's death.[42] The news would
certainly have reached my mother in Hamburg. Ditha was twenty by then
and, given her love of gossip and interest in the peccadilloes of great men,
she must have speculated about the truth behind the denials. Was it
possible that the *Führer* had murdered his own niece?

In the following days and weeks Hitler seemed utterly devastated.
Heinrich Hoffmann, meeting him next day, said 'He looked like a
broken man', and even Putzi Hanfstängl, who had despised Geli,
admitted that Hitler was 'prostrate with grief'. Herbert Döring, later
to be manager at the Berghof, remembered Anna Winter saying: 'Hitler
was at his wits' end. He really wanted to kill himself, to commit suicide.
He locked himself in Haus Wachenfeld, in Geli's room, would not eat,
wanted to kill himself: the loaded pistol was lying on the table.' [. . .]
'My wife,' Döring went on to claim, 'tempted him to eat by bringing
him light meals and after eight days she took the pistol away and saved
his life.'[43] The *Führer* sank into mourning and melancholy, from which
he was forced to emerge within days. The juggernaut of politics was

41. Even respectable papers hinted at dark motives for her death. The *Münchener
Post* reported Geli's death (20 September 1931) in a story that read: 'In a flat on
Prinzregentenplatz a 23-year-old music student, a niece of Hitler's, has shot herself.
For two years the girl had been living in a furnished room in a flat on the same
floor as that on which Hitler's flat was situated. What drove the student to kill
herself is unknown. She was Angela Raubal, the daughter of Hitler's half-sister. On
Friday 18 September there was once again a violent quarrel between Herr Hitler
and his niece. What was the reason? The vivacious 23-year-old music student, Geli,
wanted to go to Vienna, she wanted to become engaged. Hitler was strongly opposed
to this. The two of them had recurrent disagreements about it. After a violent scene,
Hitler left his flat on the second floor of 16 Prinzregentenplatz.'
Hitler was compelled to issue a statement which the paper printed:
42.1. It is untrue that I had either 'recurrent disagreements' or 'a violent quarrel'
with my niece Angela Raubal on Friday 18 September or previously. 2. It is
untrue that I was 'strongly opposed' to my niece's travelling to Vienna. The
truth is that I was never against the trip my niece had planned to Vienna. 3.
It is untrue that my niece wanted to become engaged in Vienna or that I had
some objection to my niece's engagement. [Statement published in the
Münchener Post, 20 September 1931.]
43. Interview with Herbert Döring, 2000, 3BMTV. Several people, including Putzi
Hanfstängl and Heinrich Hoffmann, claimed to have prevented Hitler from
shooting himself in the aftermath of Geli's death. One thing on which they all
agree that he was in a state of extreme grief.

rolling on and he was in the driving seat. Yet the impact of the relationship with Geli and the sense of helplessness, of being overwhelmed by passionate love, had revealed emotions he would not risk experiencing twice. That year his Christmas cards were edged in black. He told Winifred Wagner, 'This has been a very sad time. I will have to come to terms with this great loneliness.'[44]

44. Brigitte Hamann, *Winifred Wagner: A life at the Heart of Hitler's Bayreuth* (London: Granta Books, 2005), p. 165.

Chapter Nine

Dying to Be with Hitler

At the time of Geli's death in September 1931 Eva was almost twenty; popular, full of energy and thoroughly frustrated. She resented being treated like a teenager by her parents. She was earning her own living and had reached the age when, rather than going home to a family supper every night, she would have preferred to spend the evenings having fun with her friends in cafés, nightclubs or at the cinema, although if she stayed out too late this often meant she had to spend the night at Herta Ostermayr's house (luckily Herta's parents were rich and their house was large) or even on a bench in Hoffmann's shop. Eva had a full life but, despite the superficial frivolity, she remained obsessed with Hitler. She had been well aware of the relationship with his niece – half Munich knew about that – but she continued to pursue him, slipping loving notes into his trenchcoat pocket when he came to Hoffmann's, as he often did.

Hitler's grief over the death of his niece was genuine but his fidelity to her memory was short lived. Eva's persistence and her obvious devotion were flattering. He responded by inviting her to the Troubadour – a favourite café but one he frequented less often than the Osteria – and soon after that to the opera. Within weeks – in December 1931, as a caption in Eva's photograph album triumphantly records – he had taken her with him to Haus Wachenfeld for the first time, a privilege never granted while Geli was alive. In case she only went there once, Eva grabbed the opportunity for a number of covert snapshots, including one of Hitler looking like a private eye, his hat tipped over his face and the collar of his beige raincoat turned up. Another picture showed a view of the house taken from the snow-covered meadow below.

Eva probably lost her virginity to him then or very soon afterwards,[1] two years after their first meeting in October 1929, although there can be no proof that they went to bed together, let alone when and where. Henriette Hoffmann was convinced it happened within weeks of Geli's death, which would date their first lovemaking to late 1931 or early 1932. Eva was physically mature and though she may have been apprehensive she was far from reluctant. Presumably they found one another sexually compatible or the relationship would have ended there, but not a word of evidence from either of them – not a note or a love letter – survives to confirm this. At the beginning, Hitler might have been moved by Eva's willingness to surrender her youth and virginity or perhaps stimulated by the novelty of a different partner. At this stage of their relationship he would have been at his most sexually active. Young flesh is ravishing, especially to an older man. Had Eva been more experienced she would quickly have realised that his libido was at best low. If she confided in anyone it would have been her sister Gretl, to whom she was always closest, but Gretl was only sixteen, too young for sexual revelations, while her dearest friend Herta Ostermayr was not yet married, so she would have been no better informed.

If Hitler had become used to regular sex with Geli, he was probably grateful for the solace Eva offered, not least her absolute discretion. Staff at the Prinzregentenplatz apartment in Munich too were trustworthy and loyal, although the *Führer* used to give Anna Winter theatre tickets to make sure she was out of the way when he wanted to spend an evening alone with Eva, Henriette reported. Afterwards Eva would make her own way home or, as time went on, be driven home in Hitler's distinctive Mercedes and dropped off a street away from her own front door, in case her father were looking out for her.

Putzi Hanfstängl wrote condescendingly after meeting her for the first time:

> There is an entry in my guest-book dated 1 January 1933 signed in our Pienzenauerstrasse house by half a dozen of Hitler's close friends, Hitler himself – and Eva Braun. They had all come for coffee after a performance of *Meistersinger* at the Hof Theatre . . . She was a pleasing-looking blonde, the slightly helpless type who appears to need protection, well-built, with blue eyes and a

1. His housekeeper at Prinzregenplatz, Anni Winter, told Werner Maser in 1969 that Eva's deflowering happened early in 1932.

modest, diffident manner. I had seen her working behind the counter at Heinrich Hoffmann's shop some months earlier. She was friendly and personable and eager to please. We had no sense that evening that she was there in any particular capacity but rather as a friend of one of the other girls in order to make up the party.[2]

Nobody in Hitler's circle guessed that Eva was anything more than a passing fancy, a distraction from his grief over Geli's death. Hermann Göring tried hard at about this time – the early 1930s – to introduce Hitler to suitable young women. One in particular was a vivacious blonde called Gretl Slezak whose father, Leo, was a famous opera singer. 'She was probably about twenty-seven or twenty-eight at the time but she was a professional *ingénue* and asked the most delightfully asinine questions.' Hitler seemed rather taken with her and escorted her home but when Putzi asked her what had gone on she looked up at the ceiling and 'just shrugged'. Perhaps she was *too* asinine, or maybe he was genuinely taken with Eva.

Eva's uncle Alois described their early relationship in his private memoir of the Braun family. He could have heard about it from his cousin Fanny, who might have picked up hints from Gretl or one of Eva's friends.

Everything changed in September 1931, when Angela Raubal [Geli] was found dead in Hitler's nine-room flat. [. . .] It is clear that Hitler was deeply affected by the death of his niece; he astonished people with his outbursts of self-reproach and for a long time he avoided contact both with the public and with his friends. [. . .] By 1932 Hitler was paying more and more visits to Hoffmann's house and it became obvious to all that he was courting Eva. But it was important to 'keep up appearances' and when he took Eva on excursions around Munich they were always accompanied by two female secretaries. Still, everyone in his circle and in the Hoffmann household knew about it, though Eva's parents – Fritz and Fanny – were kept in the dark. She took care to conceal her relationship from them. Her father was, as she knew, very far from being a Nazi, quite the opposite: he was a Bavarian patriot and royalist.[3]

2. Hanfstängl, *Unheard Witness*, p. 204.
3. Winbauer, *Eva Braun's Familiengeschichte*, pp. 8–9 (translated by Christiane Gehron).

One clue to their growing intimacy is a series of photographs taken between November 1931 and the spring of 1932 showing them side by side. Hitler even let himself be photographed with Eva on an official tour of Herrenchiemsee, one of the very few times in fourteen years he knowingly let himself be pictured with her in public. Even when he was surrounded by friends he knew and trusted, Hitler always made sure that they were separated by several other people, to deflect suspicion. In thousands of Hoffmann's photographs and miles of Eva's home movies she hardly ever touches him except on meeting. He doesn't smile at her but leans back, arms defensively folded, leaving plenty of space between them. Döring recalled this awkwardness: 'He had all kinds of other things on his mind, you can see that in the photographs, if you analyse the faces. Hitler is not looking happy and gazing at her lovingly; on the contrary, he's looking away stubbornly, in a trance-like state.'[4]

Among members of Hitler's tight little circle there was endless speculation. Many people tried to give the impression that they alone were privy to the real nature of Hitler's sexual relations with Eva. Heinrich Hoffmann wrote in a memoir of Hitler:

Eva moved into his house, became the constant companion of his leisure hours and to the best of my knowledge, that was all there was to it. That Eva became his mistress some time or other before the end is certain but when, neither I nor anyone else can say. Not at any time was there any perceptible change in his attitude towards her which might have pointed to the assumption of more intimate relations between them.[5]

Common sense points overwhelmingly to the conclusion that, at least for the first ten years, their relationship was based on sex. If a young woman starts getting regular visits and presents from an older man, the general assumption is that she has become his mistress. If he has no other 'constant companion' and she, despite her charm and ebullience, no other recognised suitor or boyfriend, the general assumption is that she is his mistress. If in due course she is allotted a bedroom next to his, starts turning up in elegant and expensive outfits, is accepted

4. Herbert Döring interviewed 2001 for *Adolf and Eva*, 3BMTV, roll 15.08.27.
5. Hoffmann, *Hitler Was My Friend*, pp. 162–3.

by his friends (whether or not they approve of her) and treated by the domestic staff as head of his household, the general assumption would be that she is indeed his mistress. Theories can be constructed and anecdotes or opinions cited that seek to demonstrate that Hitler was impotent, masochistic or homosexual, and that Eva died a virgin, but if the contrary looks overwhelmingly more probable, then the contrary is probably true.

Eva began to realise that the role she aspired to as Hitler's consort would not be easy, given his emotional turmoil and insistence on secrecy. Their burgeoning relationship was known only to the domestic staff and a few close friends. Anna Winter remembered Hitler being very affectionate to Eva when they were alone together, and very concerned about her health: 'He used to lecture her on smoking, telling her the bad effects of nicotine, yet Eva chain-smoked' – behind Hitler's back, it's true, but as often as possible, and so did her sister Gretl. Yet Albert Speer noted: 'He hid her from everybody except his most intimate circle [. . .] denied her any social standing and constantly humiliated her. It was a painful thing to see.' Marriage, as Hitler often told her and said to others in her presence, was out of the question.[6] If he needed unconditional love there were always the Alsatians, Blondi and Prinz.

Eva's uncle Alois has left a sharp analysis of Hitler's character that helps to explain his reluctance to acknowledge her openly:

The demands of political leadership detained Hitler in Berlin, while Eva stayed behind in Hoffmann's studio in Munich. Fritz and Fanny were deeply rooted in a strict tradition of family life that left very little room for the cultivation of the joys of youth. Hitler came back to Munich remarkably often [. . .] for clandestine assignations with Eva but as *Führer* he could not risk going beyond these occasional meetings: Hitler was in all respects the very model of a conventional philistine *bourgeois* [*Spiessbürger*]. [. . .] If the *Führer* had decided to commit himself openly to one woman and make room in his life for some personal happiness, the nation would certainly not have objected. But Hitler himself would have regarded it as an act of self-betrayal which would be unthinkable in view of his public position and

---

6. Ibid., Chapter 4, for his full statement.

national eminence. Of course these considerations did not mean much to Eva. Having finally been awakened, she didn't want to be the friend and confidante of Chancellor Hitler: she wanted to be the mistress of Hitler the man. But for Hitler that was impossible. He was twenty-three years older than Eva and this constituted a barrier – not to an emotional bond but to a genuine life partnership; and he believed he had been called by fate – *providence*, as he called it – to guide mankind as a whole.[7]

Right up to the end of 1932, by which time the affair had been going on for a year, Eva's parents still knew nothing about it. At weekends she sometimes went with Hitler on excursions to the countryside around Munich and occasionally to Haus Wachenfeld. All this had to be kept from her father. Meanwhile she continued to work at Hoffmann's photo shop, a lowly apprentice earning a pittance, and to spend most evenings at home with her family.

In due course, inevitably, her parents began to suspect. Her easy-going mother Fanny, once she realised that what had seemed a temporary infatuation was looking serious, said dismissively, 'She'll drop him soon enough when she meets a younger man.'[8] She tried to moderate her husband's anger but Fritz despised Hitler's racist slogans and his bigoted followers and was mortified by the apparent seduction of his daughter. To Fritz Braun, steeped in Lutheran tradition and ethics, Nazism represented an assault on his fundamental values. It made no difference to him that his daughter had been chosen by one of the most powerful men in Germany. Her father made Eva feel miserably guilty by his fierce opposition to her liaison. Much of his anger may well have been based on wounded pride and the offence to his paternal duty. His daughters were his *property* until they married, when they would become their husbands' property, but until then he had an obligation to preserve their virtue. Now he could no longer deliver a virgin Eva to her future husband. The best solution was for Hitler – since he had seduced her – to make amends by marrying her; but Hitler had made it clear that she could never hope to be his wife. A

7. Winbauer, *Eva Braun's Familiengeschichte*, p. 13 (translated by Christiane Gehron).
8. Weisker, *Wer War Eva Braun?*.

secretary wrote down a telling remark made in an unguarded moment: 'I asked him once why he'd never married. His answer was puzzling: "I wouldn't be a good father and I think it's irresponsible to produce a family if I couldn't devote enough time to my wife. In any case I don't want children of my own. I've noticed that the offspring of geniuses often have a very hard time."'[9] He could hardly tell Eva the real reason, the unexploded secret of his imperfect genes. Well, argued Fritz Braun, if that were the case and marriage impossible, she must leave him.

Gertraud Weisker has nothing to say about this period since she was only nine or ten at the time, so the best evidence of how the family viewed her affair – based no doubt on many earnest discussions – comes, again, from Alois Winbauer:

> Hitler's dreams weren't centred on the young girl in Munich but on his self-elected task and his own glory. Certainly he didn't want to have to sacrifice his affair with Eva to this dream since he needed it as proof of his own humanity, but [. . .] he wanted the two strands of his life – the private and the political – to be kept firmly apart. Eva had nothing to do with his political life; the affair with her must remain a private oasis. This attitude could only lead to friction. Not that Eva had any political ambitions – she had not the least interest in politics and the great events of the time were nothing to her but background rumblings, affecting her only insofar as they impinged on her emotional life. She wanted to be with the man she felt her fate was bound up with, even if he did happen to be the *Führer* and Reichs Chancellor. But he held court in Berlin and she was in Munich, depressed and bored. His phone calls, sometimes almost daily and at other times just once a week, were not enough for her. A serious crisis was about to overwhelm this young girl who had spun such romantic dreams when she fantasised about her affair with Hitler. She was still a secretary at Hoffmann's studio and still lived with her parents, having to hide the truth about her connection with Hitler and cope with her doubts and longings alone. Having come to the affair with Hitler with so many romantic ideals, the young girl sank into a deep crisis.[10]

9. Junge, *Bis Zur Letzten Stunde*, p. 92 (translated from the original German edition by the author).
10. Winbauer, *Eva Braun's Familiengeschichte*, pp. 13–14 (translated by the author).

Few people suspected how deeply Eva Braun, a privileged young woman with abundant energy and beauty and many friends, was suffering. If her parents (preoccupied with their daughter's loss of virginity and their own humiliation) were aware of it they showed only indifference. Alois Winbauer remembers them saying that in 1933 Eva became 'distraught, unapproachable and irritable during Hitler's first year as Chancellor'. She could not have confided her feelings to her younger sister, Gretl, now eighteen but still a fragile figure, incapable of making up her own mind about anything. Eva could not burden this little clinging vine by admitting to the despair she felt. She could have told Ilse, a stronger character, but relations between the two were never close and sometimes downright hostile. Ilse would not have offered much comfort. As time went on the nightly recriminations undermined the love Eva had always felt for her parents. Determined not to give up her lover, riven by two sets of obligations and attachments and two incompatible choices, she was the focus of a tug-of-war between the two men who dominated her life, both in their different ways immensely powerful. The strain became intolerable. She grew more and more convinced that there was only one way out.

Suicide, the ultimate gesture of despair,[11] pervades Hitler's life, drawing him and those around him towards a self-inflicted death. He himself came close to suicide on several occasions: at the time of the Beer Hall Putsch in 1923; after Geli's death in 1931 and again after the Strasser crisis in 1932. Henriette von Schirach, Hoffman's daughter, was by now married to the Hitler Youth leader, Baldur von Schirach, which meant she had less time to spend with Eva. Henry said, 'I believe there are certain people who attract death and Hitler was very definitely one of them.'[12] Too many of those he enthralled were enthralled by the notion of suicide as well. It is remarkable how many women close to him attempted or committed suicide. As we have seen, sixteen-year-old Mimi Reiter was the first, in 1926. Then Geli, in 1931. On 1 October 1937 the actress and morphine addict

11. In a study of *Tristan and Isolde* Roger Scruton suggests: 'By accepting death through an act of sacrifice we transcend death and raise ourselves above the mortal condition.' Roger Scruton, *Death-Devoted Heart: Sex and the Sacred in Wagner's Tristan and Isolde* (Oxford: Oxford University Press, 2004).
12. Henriette von Schirach, *Frauen um Hitler* (Munich: Herbig, 1983), p. 226. Henny was nineteen when she married Baldur von Schirach in 1932.

Renate Müller, who claimed a number of amorous encounters with Hitler, was looking out of her window when a car pulled up outside and four SS officers got out. She panicked, jumped, and was killed. Another version of this story suggests that Fräulein Muller was thrown out by the Gestapo, after being charged with having a Jewish lover. Suicide has not been proved as the cause of her death, but it looks quite likely that she wanted to kill herself. Unity Mitford certainly intended to die on 3 September 1939, the day Britain declared war on Germany, though the bullet she fired into her temple took eight years to finish her off. Inge Ley, the blonde, beautiful and unhappy wife of Dr Robert Ley, leader of the German Labour Front, committed suicide on 10 December 1942 by jumping from a Berlin hotel window, allegedly after writing Hitler a letter that affected him deeply. (It has been said that she killed herself in despair because the war was being lost, but in 1942 this was far from clear.) This list of suicides does not begin to take into account the scores, perhaps hundreds of thousands of Jews, Bolsheviks, homosexuals, Catholics, Roma (gypsies) and others who chose to kill themselves rather than wait for the tramp of feet on the stairs and the thump of the thugs at the door.

Assassination rather than suicide was a perpetual threat in Hitler's life. German politics in the 1920s and 1930s had a distinctly violent side, with rival gangs battling in the streets and frequently assassinating their opponents. There were 376 political murders between 1919 and 1922 alone, by men whom the war had inured to violence. From his earliest days as leader of the Nazi Party, Hitler had been aware of the risk and the need to ensure his personal safety. His paranoia, the dictator's occupational hazard, was often justified. SS bodyguards formed an all but impenetrable shield but, even so, there were at least forty-six significant plots or attempts on his life, almost two a year, between 1921 and 1945.[13] In 1933 alone – the year he became Chancellor and his ambition was fully revealed – there were ten.[14] He himself said: 'Not a soul could cope with an assassin who, for idealistic reasons, was prepared quite ruthlessly to hazard his own life in the execution of his object. I quite understand why 90 per cent of the historic assassinations have been successful.'[15]

13. P. Hoffmann, *Hitler's Personal Security* (London: Macmillan, 1979), pp. 268–9.
14. See *Operation Foxley: The Plan to Kill Hitler*, Introduction by Mark Seaman.
15. The term wasn't yet in use, but Hitler gives here the precise reason why suicide bombers often succeed.

Prompted perhaps by Geli's example, Eva began to contemplate suicide as the only way to make Hitler take her seriously. Paradoxically, it would only succeed if she survived, yet it must be meant in earnest. He would be unmoved by 'a cry for help'. Throughout October 1932 the *Führer* was heavily committed to speaking engagements all over Germany in preparation for the forthcoming general election on 6 November. Its outcome was not looking good for the NSDAP and Hitler exhausted himself in the campaign to raise popular support and increase the party's vote. For two months he was hardly ever in Munich. In four crucial weeks he addressed crowds in sixty different cities, travelling between them in a new Junkers Ju-52 made available to him by the Lufthansa company thanks to the machinations of Göring, himself a former First World War pilot. On 1 November alone he made rousing speeches in four separate locations and was due to speak in Berlin the following day.

But on 1 November 1932, Hallowe'en night, Eva Braun tried to kill herself. The rest of the family had gone out for the evening but she had stayed at home, probably hoping to be able to take a phone call from Hitler in private. He didn't ring. She waited until midnight, the hour when the Devil consorts with his witches, then took her father's First World War pistol from his bedside drawer and aimed at her jugular. She missed the vein and was found in the nick of time by Ilse, who had returned home early. A doctor whose discretion could be relied on was called and he drove her to hospital where urgent intervention prevented her from bleeding to death. Hitler believed this bungled suicide attempt was real enough: it's too risky to fire a gun at one's neck simply as a threat. He interrupted his campaigning and rushed to her bedside with a large bouquet of flowers. To his immense relief, Eva survived. Coming barely two years after Geli's suicide, her desperate action evoked a rare sense of guilt. He *had* neglected her, conceding a few palpitating hours followed by endless afternoons when he knew she was waiting for him to telephone, or making appointments at Hoffmann's house for which he failed to turn up without bothering to let her know. This realisation, and no doubt the fear of a scandal, persuaded him to visit her more regularly from then on and to be less offhand and dismissive.

Alois Winbauer believed[16] that after the near-disaster of her

16. Winbauer, *Eva Braun's Familiengeschichte*.

attempted suicide, Hitler didn't only make concessions; he really began to love her. In the private family memoir he claims: '[while] the unsophisticated and malleable Eva Braun saw in Adolf Hitler, not perhaps her ideal romantic figure, but the epitome of the man her destiny demanded.'[17] He goes on: 'The turning point came early in 1933: Hitler openly declared his affection. The new German Chancellor and self-proclaimed leader of the nation confessed on 6 February – her birthday – to this daughter of a teacher in a Munich technical college that she was his heart's choice. Eva was moved and thrilled by this confession.'[18] That sounds far-fetched. Looking at the *Führer*'s hectic schedule it's hard to see when the newly appointed Chancellor could have found time to travel back to Munich from Berlin to declare love for Eva, though he did manage to squeeze in an interview with the *Daily Mail*. Even so, since uncle Alois doesn't explicitly say they met, Hitler might have telephoned her – it was, after all, her twenty-first. He, or someone following his instructions, arranged to have a set of tourmalines (light green semi-precious stones) delivered to her on the day – a necklace, ring and earrings – as well as the usual giant bouquet. The jewels went well with Eva's fair colouring and a matching set would have been elegant without seeming extravagant. Her birthday in 1932 had been ignored. By 1933 things were different.

Just over a year after Geli's death, the *Führer* seemed to have found her successor. Eva became an accepted and frequent visitor at Obersalzberg. No doubt out of consideration for Frau Raubal (who can't have been overjoyed to see her daughter so quickly supplanted) she was not installed in rooms near Hitler's in the main house but was forced to lodge with his secretaries in the nearby Platterhof. Their lovemaking must have been hurried and clandestine, which perhaps made it all the more exciting.

Alois's interpretation of Hitler's actions may have helped Eva's parents to accept the inevitable. Perhaps they told themselves, 'He

17. Ibid., p. 11. This sentence is at least as obscure in the original German. It reads: '*Eva Braun, das unverbildete, leicht beeinflussbare Mädchen entdeckte Adolf Hitler auch nicht als den Idealmann ihres Herzens, aber als Auszeichnung und Aufforderung persönlichen Schicksals.*'
18. Ibid. In the original, Winbauer writes: '*Die grosse Wende brachte der Beginn des Jahres 1933: Hitler bekannte Eva offen seine Zuneigung. Der neue Kanzler des Deutschen Reiches und selbsternannter Führer der Nation gestand an ihren Geburtstag, am 6 Februar der Tochter des Münchner Gewehrbeschullehrers, dass sie die Erwählte seines Herzens sei und Eva nahm dieses Geständnis gerührt und beglückt auf.*'

really loves our daughter but isn't (yet) in a position to marry her. We must be realistic and worldly since opposition has become futile.' The flowery assertion that 'Eva was his heart's choice' is supported by a comment in her diary three years later, in May 1935: '*He* [Hitler] *has so often told me he is madly in love with me.*' Telling young girls you love them madly is a well-known seducer's ploy but there must have been more to it than that, otherwise why single *her* out when so many young beauties clamoured for his attention? Hitler was only fond of Eva in a very limited way and she would never come first in his life, but if he were physically and sexually beguiled by her he might well, in moments of passion, have translated this into words of love. Men do.

Whatever *her* reasons for loving him, they had nothing to do with greed. In time she learned to covet beautiful clothes and shoes but she never hankered after – or was given – expensive jewellery. In photographs she is almost always wearing the same modest watch and bangle. 'Hitler was never generous with personal gifts for Eva. He had always been a mediocre philistine and he regarded flowers and cheap tokens as perfectly sufficient tokens of his friendship. The diamond necklaces and tiaras that featured in stories of Eva after the war were – like so much else – pure inventions of cheap, salacious journalism,'[19] sniffed Alois. What mattered to Eva was that she had broken away from the circling starlets to take the leading role as Hitler's sole mistress. Over the last two years she had made herself indispensable in subtle ways: giving him pleasure, making him laugh, bringing him the gossip and voices of the young from the streets and cafés of Munich. She was the person he turned to when he needed solace. Having grown used to her he had neither the time nor the inclination to look for anyone else. According to an adjutant, Fritz Wiedemann, one of the earliest Nazi supporters, the *Führer* once commented that being a bachelor had its uses, adding casually, 'and as for love, I keep a girl for myself in Munich'. Eva's perspective was quite different. Four years had passed since their first meeting and she hoped she was on the way to becoming his wife.

In January 1933 Hitler had achieved national power as Reichs Chancellor. Thomas Mann noted in his diary that he had witnessed a revolution of a kind never seen before: 'without underlying ideas, against ideas, against everything nobler, better, decent, against freedom,

19. Ibid., p. 20.

truth and justice.' Nevertheless his appointment was greeted with rapture by many, and not just the Nazis. Manfred von Schröder, an intelligent and sophisticated private banker from Hamburg, said – still with traces of the pride and joy he had felt seven decades earlier – '1933 seemed the beginning of a new and wonderful period. It had the feeling of a fresh start.'[20]

Now that the *Führer* was based in Berlin, his official duties multiplying and his plans for the Nazi Party maturing fast, Eva was forced to become the woman whose name was never spoken and who did not exist. Hitler wanted to make her disappear altogether. In today's world of total disclosure nothing is hidden and the most intimate sexual and financial matters are public property. It would be impossible for such a relationship to remain secret. Back in the deferential thirties German women had no difficulty in believing that their *Führer* was celibate and dedicated to Germany. 'I am married to Germany,' he would say. 'He is waiting for me,' they thought.[21] This enabled them to indulge in erotic (or touchingly domestic) fantasies. Tens of thousands wrote to him, sometimes in the most explicit detail. Thousands more waited outside his house in Obersalzberg. Women in crowds would shout, '*Mein Führer* I would like to have a child by you!' and become hysterical, rushing forward to try and get close enough to embrace and kiss him, until they had to be dragged away by his bodyguards. Given this adulation and his belief that after Geli he would never let himself be embroiled with one woman again, Eva's 'capture' of Hitler – though far from complete – seems quite an achievement, demonstrating her pride, strength of will and subtlety in handling Hitler, himself the arch manipulator.

Manfred von Schröder may have seen it as a new beginning but Hitler's sudden rise to power astonished many Germans. It was based

---

20. Cited on p. 7, *The Anatomy of Fascism* by Robert O. Paxton, published by Alfred A. Knopf, New York, 2004. Quoted on *Inside the Nazi State*, a TV documentary by Laurence Rees broadcast on UKTV History Channel, 24 August 2005.

21. Hitler received hundreds of letters a week from adoring, deluded women, many using the most extravagant language. 'Darling can I come to you soon? Do you doubt my love? Today I had such a strong longing for you,' wrote Eva K., a German housewife, on 20 July 1940. Quoted in Adam Lebor and Roger Boyes, *Surviving Hitler: Choices, Corruption and Compromise in the Third Reich* (London; Simon & Schuster, 2000), p. 75. Another woman wrote, not untypically, 'You are looking for a woman and I need a man,' ibid., p. 51.

chiefly on the calamitous economic situation, caused by the Great Depression that followed the American stock market crash of October 1929. By the end of 1932 the Nazi Party had nearly one and a half million members but Germany had six million men unemployed. Discontent was muttering and rumbling. It was a pivotal moment – the country might have swung left or right. The Nazis had lost thirty-four Reichstag seats and two million votes in the November 1932 elections but Communism was a growing force: its vote had risen to six million. The New Year saw a panicky flurry of meetings in an attempt to resolve this inflammable situation. Hitler was offered the Vice-Chancellorship; refused. It was offered again, along with a coalition government; again refused. Angry letters were exchanged; Hitler called upon the government to resign; refused. On 30 January 1933 the Prime Minister capitulated and Hitler was appointed Chancellor by the ageing President Hindenburg. The announcement was followed by a huge, ecstatic torchlight procession through Berlin. Hitler, standing at a window of the Reichs Chancellery, was acclaimed by a vast crowd.

From the day he became Chancellor the relentless march towards racial terror began. In February 1933 freedoms of speech, assembly, press and other basic rights were suspended. In the March 1933 general election the Nazis got 52 per cent of the vote, giving them 340 of the 547 Reichstag seats. Within days of coming to power Hitler declared a one-day boycott of all Jewish shops – testing the water, as it were, of German anti-Semitism, waiting to see whether there would be protests or general acquiescence. The boycott took place on 1 April 1933 and was supported – wrote Goebbels in his diary – 'with exemplary discipline. [. . .] A huge moral victory for Germany: we have shown everyone abroad that we can call on the whole nation for action without the least excesses.'[22] It was true. Nobody could have failed to be aware of the boycott – throughout Germany whole streets ceased trading – yet most people remained passive. Hitler moved fast and ruthlessly to impose his will on the German people and suppress even the possibility of revolt. There was no official opposition since the Reichstag seldom met and no longer debated. *Der Führer* was the sole speaker. In July 1933, when the Nazis became the only legal party, opposition became illegal. The rule of law was replaced by arbitrary police terror. Compassion, humility or love of one's neighbour were dismissed as weakness by the Nazi élite and

22. Sereny, *Albert Speer: His Battle with Truth*, p. 170.

racial fanaticism, led and enforced by the SS, began to break down the front door that had always protected people in their own homes. Children spied on their parents, parents on their neighbours, customers on shopkeepers – nobody could feel safe anywhere. In March 1933, seven weeks after Hitler became Chancellor, the first concentration camp[23] opened at Dachau, not far from Munich.

In March 2005 I went to Dachau. It was a bitterly cold day but despite the weather some twenty English-speaking tourists had assembled for a five-hour guided tour. As we left the coach the chatter subsided and people became solemn, as though about to enter a religious sanctuary. Snow prettified the single-storey camp buildings, already cleaned up for visitors, into a soft Impressionist village. The camp is vast, organised around a central grass assembly area the size of two playing fields. On here at dawn, winter or summer, the inmates lined up in thin pyjamas and felt slippers for roll call. This lasted an hour and they had to maintain a preordained stance throughout – feet together, arms by their sides, looking straight ahead, no eye contact. Before the day had properly begun they were already frozen. We who had come to remember, to mourn, or to see for ourselves were bundled up in coats, scarves, woolly hats and snow boots – and we were still cold.

As the first camp to be built, Dachau was the prototype for all subsequent concentration camps in its layout and its unforgiving rules and discipline. Some of the early guards may have found it hard at first to treat their prisoners as 'non-humans' but they soon got the hang of it. Local people (the camp is a few kilometres from Munich and on the outskirts of the village of Dachau, formerly an artists' colony) were told it was a camp for 'political dissidents' – troublemakers, political opponents and enemies of the new Reich. Few bothered to follow

23. It is important to make a distinction between *concentration* camps – which were initially designed as hard-labour camps for Jews, Bolsheviks, gypsies, homosexuals, the handicapped and other racial 'undesirables', but degenerated into killing camps because so many of the inmates were starved to death – and *extermination* camps, which didn't come into existence until 1942/3 and were specifically designed to kill in vast numbers, with only the healthiest Jews retained to be worked to death in a matter of weeks. Of the latter, Auschwitz was responsible for the most deaths.

up their disquiet after that. As for Eva, the significance of the camp, had she known about it, would have been incompatible with her love for Hitler: the truth was unthinkable. The people of Dachau shut their eyes and ears for a decade, but they could no longer deny its existence when the stench of putrefaction from thousands of unburied corpses assailed their noses; yet still, apparently, no one protested.

In April 1933 the Nazis organised a boycott of Jewish businesses. Elegant women complained that with the disappearance of Jewish dress designers, German fashion lost its chic. Ironically, the wives of Hitler's leading associates, Magda Goebbels and Emmy Göring, took no notice and continued to buy their clothes from Jewish dressmakers and retailers until official decrees promoting complete Aryanisation in the late 1930s made it impossible.

Jews were excluded from all government employment, including teaching. The list of racial undesirables grew. In July 1933 a new law provided for the forced sterilisation of handicapped persons, Roma, black Germans and those of mixed race ('mulattos', as they were called).[24] In case anyone should be made uneasy by these measures – and many were – the propaganda machine trumpeted Hitler and the National Socialist Party for fulfilling the promise to provide new hope, new jobs and new pride to Germany. In September 1933, seven hundred unemployed men from a Frankfurt labour exchange were told they would join three hundred thousand others in building the new autobahns. They were driven to the site where, in a symbolic gesture of camaraderie, Hitler shovelled the first two cubic metres. The spot where he dug until sweat dripped from his brow had to be fenced off to prevent workers taking away handfuls of the soil as precious relics.[25]

The following year, July 1934, in an audacious move legally sanctioned under a retroactive Law Concerning Measures for the Defence of the State, the so-called 'Führer principle' was enacted. According

24. From January 1934 onwards the Nazis introduced a compulsory sterilisation programme in order to 'improve' Germany's racial stock. Those considered racially unfit were barred from having children. Doctors (half of the Third Reich's doctors belonged to the Nazi Party) decided men and women would be sterilised on the basis of feeble mindedness, anti-social behaviour, drunkenness, promiscuity and idleness. By the start of the war 320,000 people had been sterilised. The Nazis planned to sterilise anywhere between 5 and 30 per cent of the population. Source: M. Burleigh and W. Wipperman, *The Racial State: Germany 1933–45* (Cambridge; Cambridge University Press, 1993).
25. Burleigh, *The Third Reich: A New History*, p. 240.

to this he alone embodied the nation's will and his wish became paramount. A month later, after the death of Hindenburg, Hitler was proclaimed '*Führer* of the German Reich', to whom, as head of state and supreme commander of the armed forces, all officers had to take an oath of loyalty. Eighteen months after becoming Chancellor almost by default, the man Hindenburg and his ministers thought they could keep under their control had become a one-party dictator. Debate, consensus and reason were replaced by adulation, reinforced by huge rallies at which Hitler and his ministers were greeted with carefully choreographed mass acclaim. The SS and Gestapo obeyed Hitler's wish rather than that of the law, and his wishes were soon made clear. In October 1934 homosexuals throughout Germany were arrested. The following March, military conscription was introduced. In April thousands of Jehovah's Witnesses were arrested and in September more anti-Jewish racial and citizenship laws were issued. For those who could distinguish these portents through a camouflage of Nazi propaganda, the genocide was looming, overshadowing the promise of sunlit autobahns and fertile harvests.

The years between 1932 and 1935, before Eva was established as *maîtresse en titre*, continued to be years of uncertainty, yet judging by her photographs she never allowed the strain to show. She entertained, posed sweetly on the terrace of Haus Wachenfeld, twirled and pirouetted as if she had not a care in the world. The façade was so convincing that she was dismissed as shallow and frivolous, although the surviving pages of her diary reveal aching despair and unhappiness.[26] Few people knew she was subject to black moods that at times amounted to severe depression. This was a tendency that Hitler shared. The unstable Schicklgruber temperament manifested itself in outbursts of rage or maudlin sentimentality which his secretaries described as 'almost schizophrenic',[27] his moods swinging between the extraordinary kindness and consideration he displayed towards them to outbursts of uncontrollable rage witnessed by the men on his staff. But while Hitler might indulge himself, Eva could not let her moods affect her outward gaiety – he would not have tolerated a long-faced Eva. Her job, the job of

26. There is a fuller text from Eva's handwritten diary in Chapter 10, 'Diary of a Desperate Woman'.
27. Traudl Junge was aware of Hitler's notorious fits of temper, though she claimed never to have witnessed them.

all mistresses, was to bring some fun into his life; help him relax from his arduous duties. She was there to love and cosset him and must always be available to prove it.

His official duties continued to keep Hitler and Eva apart. While he revelled in mass adulation, she was stuck as an anonymous shop girl, under the thumb of her controlling father. Hitler had forbidden her to talk about him to *anyone* and this forced her to confide in her diary that her private misery became unbearable. On 28 May 1935 she wrote him a letter pleading for – what? A visit, some proof of affection, a dog at least, to provide devotion and loyalty? She would not have dared to write what she really wanted to say: *Make up your mind – either love me, or leave me alone!* Later on, at the end of a long and tortured day Eva was at her wits' end and the diary more incoherent than usual. '*I have just sent him the crucial letter. Question: will he attach any importance to it? We'll see. If I don't get an answer before this evening, I'll take 25 pills and gently fall asleep into another world.*' She waited for a reply, her mood becoming bleaker, powerless to force a response: '*God, I am afraid he won't give me his answer today. If only somebody would help me – it is all so terribly depressing.*' Her family were out somewhere, enjoying themselves. Alone in their flat (she must have organised this, which shows how little her parents knew of her emotional state) Eva recorded her final thoughts: '*Perhaps my letter reached him at an inopportune moment. Perhaps I should not have written. I have made up my mind to take 35 pills this time, and it will be "dead certain". If only he would at least get someone to call.*' Still no answer. It was late and she knew that when Hitler was in Munich he liked to spend evenings relaxing with his friends. Having waited all day in a state of escalating suspense and misery, Eva became more and more desperate. Finally, having heard nothing, she swallowed twenty tablets of Vanodorm, a powerful sedative – enough, she believed, to kill her.

After this episode, which would probably have been fatal had not Ilse found her again, this time in a coma, Hitler said, 'In future I must worry about her more' – '*Ich muss mich mehr über sie kümmern.*'[28] The second suicide attempt forced him to put their relationship on a proper footing but for Eva it had been a dangerous tactic. Next time he might not believe it was genuine, or she might not survive.

A few days later, Heinrich Hoffmann – whose memoirs are always self-serving – claims to have arranged a meeting between the two at

28. Gertraud Weisker in conversation with the author, 2001.

his house. Hitler watched, genuinely shocked, as Eva – wan and frail – slowly descended the stairs towards him.[29] The last thing he needed was another furore like the one that had loomed after Geli's death. He'd managed to hush that up and keep the details out of the newspapers – though he could not suppress a good deal of undesirable speculation – but that had been back in 1931, two years before he became Chancellor. Now that he was Germany's leader, another young woman's suicide attempt would provoke some very awkward questions. At the very least it was bound to undermine his image as the celibate *Führer*. It was a turning point for the relationship. He asked Anna Winter, 'What shall I do now? I cannot have a scandal.'[30] If Eva's suicide attempt had been designed to focus Hitler's attention, it worked.[31]

By this time, mid 1935, Hitler had known Eva for exactly six years. She seemed to suit him physically and, even more important, she was discreet. He was used to her and genuinely fond of her, though he concealed his feelings from everyone – including, probably, himself. He liked her younger sister Gretl (who always came to the Berghof with Eva) and the Braun family were respectable – *anständig* was the crucial word – *decent* people. The *Führer* enjoyed feeling like a ladies' man, a seducer, virile, potent and irresistible, even if he didn't take advantage of the opportunities he created. (Albert Speer noticed, 'With pretty women he was, oddly enough, quite physical. He was always linking arms with them, or cupping their elbows.'[32]) There was no other plausible challenger for the role of mistress, although rumours flickered round more obvious candidates like Leni Riefenstahl, the dazzling actress and film director, and Unity Mitford, the Aryan giant who had recently entered his circle protesting passionate love for him. Only Eva was shrewd enough to realise that Hitler didn't hanker after beauty, wit or class, though he liked to spend an evening in their company. The attribute he prized most was *Gemütlichkeit*: cosiness, the familiar and welcoming domesticity that greeted him the moment he walked through the door. *Gemütlichkeit* was exactly what Eva offered. 'A woman must be a cute, cuddly, naive little thing – tender, sweet

29. Cited in Christa Schröder, *Er War Mein Chef* (Munich: Langen Müller, 1985), p. 164.
30. Musmanno Collection, Vol. XII.
31. David Irving believes this second suicide was a joke, so that Eva and her friends could laugh at the distraught Hitler's reaction. Such an interpretation says more about Irving than it does about Eva Braun.
32. Sereny, *Albert Speer: His Battle with Truth*, p. 110.

and dim.'[33] Eva was all those, though a good deal less dim than she allowed him to think.

Within three months Eva, along with her sister Gretl – now twenty-three and twenty years old respectively – had left home in August 1935 and at Hitler's suggestion (and at his expense) moved into a temporary, rented flat overlooking the River Isar at 42 Wiedenmayerstrasse in Munich,[34] close to the Englische Garten, arranged and paid for by Heinrich Hoffmann on the *Führer*'s instructions. They never returned to live with their parents again. The break must have been painful for Fanny and humiliating for Fritz, whose daughters had flouted his authority and escaped his control. He was not a subtle man and he had never treated Eva with sensitivity and affection. Instead of condemning her love for Hitler he should have asked himself why she had fallen for a man who was anathema to him. His self-respect would not let him admit that a more authoritarian, dominant male had taken possession of his favourite child, proving Fritz Braun the weaker of the two.

Yet he was not entirely powerless. Hitler's change of heart may have been prompted in part by a letter from Eva's father, though it's not certain if the letter ever reached Hitler. Henriette von Schirach – though no longer a close friend of Eva's since her marriage – tells an oddly convincing anecdote about Fritz Braun's attempt to intercede with Hitler on behalf of his daughter. It happened in September 1935, soon after the second suicide attempt. In Henny's version:[35]

Herr Braun knew that on his way from Munich to Obersalzberg Hitler would stop at a certain inn [the Lambacher Hof] and planned to accost him there and tell him that the safety, the good name and the future of his daughter were threatened if she continued to live with him at the Berghof. Later Hitler described this conversation as 'the most unpleasant in his life'. But the outcome was favourable. Hitler bought Eva a little house in Wasserburgerstrasse and gave her a monthly sum that

33. 'Eine Frau muss ein niedliches, molliges, Tschapperl sein: weich, süss und dumm,' Quoted in Maser, *Hitler*, p. 79.
34. Source: Eva Braun's official death certificate, dated 29.4.45 Berlin, a fascimile of which was shown to the author by Gertraud Weisker, 25 March 2004.
35. Henriette von Schirach, *Frauen um Hitler* (Munich: Herbig, 1983), p. 28.

guaranteed her enough to live on. But he made it absolutely clear to Herr Braun that marriage was out of the question. And so, paradoxically, Eva became Hitler's accepted mistress. She no longer had to pretend to keep him a secret from her family but it was understood that she would not have children. Hitler wanted no personal claims on him, least of all those of a wife.

The truth of this story is both reinforced and questioned by a different version in the Musmanno Collection, from a compilation of interviews with surviving members of the Hitler circle recorded by Michael Musmanno. Speaking under oath, Fritz Braun denied that any such incident had occurred. He would never have put himself in a grotesque situation by broaching the subject and in any case, he said, he knew better than to show such audacity to the all-powerful Hitler. Fanny too assured Musmanno, off the record, that it was 'ridiculous'. Yet Fritz Braun *did* write a letter to Hitler which Nerin Gun quotes in full.[36] Alois Winbauer also vouches for its accuracy. Its mixture of deference, formality and fatherly concern is touching and Fritz Braun's awkward denial does not necessarily disprove the letter's authenticity:

Munich

7 September 1935

Your Excellency,

I find myself in the extremely unpleasant position of having to importune you with a problem of a private nature, in other words, of having to explain to you my distress as a paterfamilias. You, the *Führer* of the German nation, who are confronted by other and certainly much greater cares. But since the family is the smallest but also the most vital of the social cells, a cell that enables an honest and well-organised state to develop, I think that this step is to some extent justified, and I would therefore ask you to help me.

My family is at the moment divided, for my two daughters Eva and Gretl have moved into an apartment that you have put at their disposal and I, as head of the family, was presented with

36. Gun, *Eva Braun: Hitler's Mistress*, p. 101.

it as an accomplished fact. Naturally, I have always greatly reproached Eva when she came home long after normal office closing hours. I believe that a young girl who is working intensely for eight hours a day needs to relax in the family circle in the evening in order to remain in good health. I know that I am thereby defending a point of view that, alas, seems old-fashioned. The parents' supervision of the children and the children's obligation to live at home until such time as they get married is nonetheless an inviolable principle. This is my code of honour. Quite apart from this, I miss my daughters enormously.

I should therefore be very grateful, your Excellency, if you would grant me your comprehension and your help, and I conclude this letter with a plea that you will not encourage this thirst for liberty in my daughter Eva, despite the fact that she is over twenty-one. Please advise her to return to the bosom of the family.

Yours very respectfully,

Fritz Braun

Alois Winbauer comments, 'The letter is very revealing about Fritz's relationship with his daughter. He emerges as a conventional patriarch and a man of principle, racked with anxiety about a child who has escaped from his control and deeply offended by the callousness with which she has been lured from the family and its traditions, leaving him completely powerless as a father.'[37]

Apparently, Herr Braun chose not to entrust the letter to the post but asked Hoffmann to pass it on to Hitler personally. Hoffmann, not wishing to kill his golden goose, passed it on to Eva instead and she, according to Nerin Gun, 'tore the letter into a thousand pieces'. Fanny Braun told him that she had written a similar letter, but never received a reply.

Whatever the fate of the parental letters, Hitler had come to realise that accepting Eva as his unofficial mistress would solve a lot of problems. He needed the cosseting that a husband gets from a wife but without the encumbrance of marriage. Over the past six years Eva had proved loyal, faithful, charming to look at but not chillingly beautiful, cheerful and lively without being brilliant, and – this was essential – utterly uninterested in politics. She would never ask awkward

37. Winbauer, *Eva Braun's Familiengeschichte*, p. 16.

questions; never interfere when he gloated over his grandiose visions for the future with Albert Speer, his young architect; she would happily leave his 'fixer', *Reichsleiter* Martin Bormann, to get on with running Obersalzberg. If Eva were to become extravagant in her desire for clothes and shoes and all the feminine trappings, Bormann would take care of that. He would instruct Bormann to pay her a monthly allowance and deal with her bills.

Hitler bowed to the inevitable and – insisting on a total blackout of her name, her face and her existence – accepted that the time had come to install Fräulein Braun as his recognised companion and mistress: recognised, that is, by the friends and people closest to him. He might as well have thrown her to the wolves.

Chapter Ten

Diary of a Desperate Woman

In thousands of photographs and hours of home movies Eva presents herself as she wanted to be seen: a golden girl, laughing, spinning, giddy. Very few people knew the darker side of her life and character and she went to great lengths to hide it. She only told the truth in her diary.[1] It differed from the photographs and home movies in being entirely private. Never intended to be seen by her friends, let alone posterity, it was by Eva, *for* Eva. Here she could drop the façade of gaiety and tell the truth.

Eva Braun's diary is completely at odds with history's disparaging

---

1. This early, authentic diary for the period 6 February to 28 May 1935 can be found in Old German script with a rough English translation in typescript, at the National Archives II, College Park, Maryland, near Washington DC, catalogued under Foreign Service Posts of the Department of State (RG 84) [CIVILIAN AGENCY RECORDS – Department of State and Foreign Affairs Records] NARA 841.4 Public Records location: Eva Braun's Diary 350/57/25/06 1946. A photostat can be more easily seen in Box 6 820.02 [photostat] location: 350/68/19/07.

David Irving is expert at tracking down manuscripts pertaining to Hitler and the Third Reich, although the use he makes of them is highly questionable and his standing as a historian was destroyed when, in April 2000, he sued historian Deborah Lipstadt for libelling him by calling him 'a Holocaust denier' in her book *Denying the Holocaust: The Growing Assault on Truth and Memory* (New York: Tree Press, *1993*), and lost. Irving is of the opinion that these few pages from Eva Braun's genuine diary as well as her intimate correspondence with Hitler were acquired by the CIC team of Colonel Robert A. Gutierrez, based in Stuttgart-Backnang in the summer of 1945. After a brief sifting by Frau Ursula Göhler on their behalf, these papers have not been seen since. Gutierrez was the CIC interrogator who tracked it down after prolonged and repeated sessions with two German agents, Konrad and Spacil, Fegelein's underlings, into whose hands it fell. These dubious characters had been given the version of her. It explodes with the passionately scrawled thoughts, fantasies and terrors of a young woman quite unlike the featherweight portrayed by male historians. She is revealed as a tormented figure, emotionally starved by her lover's neglect and driven half insane by her need for him. At a pivotal moment in her life, having given herself mind and body to Hitler, he gave so little in return that she wondered if her life was worth living. It never crossed her mind to leave him but in the course of the four months the diary spans she gradually became convinced that the only way out was to kill herself. When at the end of May 1935 she tried to commit suicide for the second time, Ilse – as we have seen – summoned a doctor, who got Eva to hospital, where her life was saved. Afterwards, catching sight of the diary on her bedside table, Ilse hid and may later have destroyed it, except for the final twenty-two pages covering the time between Eva's lonely twenty-third birthday on 6 February and 28 May 1935, the day she planned to kill herself. Why Ilse kept these pages – whether to protect their parents from knowing the real reason in case Eva died, as a source of future blackmail (unlikely), or evidence to produce at an inquest – is not known; but in due course she returned them to her sister.[2]

task of restoring a trunk containing Hitler's and Eva's private letters, some foreign currency, her jewellery and the diary to Gretl née Braun, Fegelein's wife. However it was lost track of (had they sold it?) on its journey from the bunker to Gretl in Munich and somehow ended up in the hands of their interrogator, Colonel Gutierrez. Irving goes on: 'I visited Gutierrez twice in New Mexico. He subsequently released Eva Braun's wedding dress and silver flatware (which he admitted having retained) to my research colleague Willi Korte, but he has not conceded an inch over the missing papers and diaries.' The letters were glimpsed by one or two people before they disappeared, but no notes were made of their contents. Gutierrez, the last person known to have them in his possession, died in 2002 or 2003 – elusive to the last. Before his death he said: 'These letters will never be released. They show Hitler as a human being, and that would not be right.' This information is taken from the introduction to the new edition of David Irving's book *Hitler's War, 1942–1945* (London: MacMillan, 1989). It can also be found on www.fpp.co.uk/Hitler/Gutierrez/, part of a website hosted by Irving. Further evidence can be found at http://www.codoh.com/irving/irvhitmar.html. Both are © Dr David Irving.
2. A decade later, just before the end of her life, Eva sent instructions to both her sisters, Ilse and Gretl, to destroy the diary. Instead, for some reason, according to Werner Maser (*Hitler's Letters and Notes*), who was told this personally by Ilse Braun in 1973, they handed the diary (perhaps much augmented by then with later entries) to the mother of an SS officer for safekeeping. It was later discovered by the Americans and taken to the USA. This version overlaps, but does not conflict with Irving's sleuthing (above).

Why should Eva have kept a diary in the first place? Most people don't, but of those who do, many are young girls in a state of emotional chaos. Gitta Sereny, biographer of Albert Speer and a leading authority on the Third Reich, says simply, 'She was just the sort of girl to keep a diary.'[3] She was at the age when many young women need an outlet for their private thoughts, especially if they are unable to confide in anyone – and Hitler insisted on total secrecy. Her parents, who finally learned about the affair in 1934, were unapproachable. To them the subject was taboo. Eva had girlfriends, but it's hard to imagine today how privately discreet people were in the thirties. They did not talk about their sex lives or bandy about their emotional problems. 'There was more respect between people in those days,' her cousin Gertraud explained, 'however great their intimacy.'[4] The secrets of Eva's connection with the greatest and most powerful man in Germany were a heavy burden. She had plenty of reasons to keep a diary.

Its scant two thousand words (which I have read both in German and in an English translation) portrayed an Eva one would not otherwise have suspected, but a translation, even a good one (and, in the case of the diary, most are bad) is as different from the original as a postcard from the actual painting it depicts, and even the best facsimile lacks the sense of direct contact between author and reader. If I wanted to understand the real Eva rather than the multiple versions of herself that she presented to her family, her friends, and, above all to Hitler, it was necessary to study it with almost forensic thoroughness. That meant getting access to the original. Unlike photographs or film, which remain the same no matter how often they are duplicated from the original negatives, a diary is a unique, handmade object. I was impatient to see this numinous relic, breathe its pages, examine the nuances of her handwriting. I needed to hold – albeit in gloved hands – the very book on which her hand had pressed exactly seventy years before, searching her writing for clues until I was finally convinced that the diary was the real thing.

In March 2005 I travelled to Washington for a second time with the express purpose of getting my hands on the diary. It is guarded assiduously by officials at NARA, the National Archives and Records Administration, America's national and military archive. Below the building known as Archives II in College Park, Maryland, are vast catacombs of storage space: two million cubic feet of shelving.

3. Gitta Sereny in an interview with the author, March 2003.
4. Gertraud Weisker interviewed by the author at home, 24 March 2004.

Here, in the bowels of this concrete fortress, the diary is stowed in a torn brown envelope, only to be seen by the most persistent researchers and then only with the express permission of two senior archivists. It is only available to those who know where to look and whom to ask. In 2004 I had spent a week at College Park trawling for material on Eva Braun and no one bothered to inform me that NARA held her diary in that very building. Persistent researchers, who will need much patience, *may* be granted access. It did not prove easy.

My mentor was John Taylor, an eighty-four-year-old archivist who has been at NARA for sixty years and knows the secrets of the archives like the veins on the back of his hand. Their labyrinthine grid is not organised logically like, say, the dear familiar Dewey system. *This* system, to the novice, is rocket science. Mr Taylor, however, understands how it works; the classifications, cross headings and box numbers which must otherwise be located by scrolling through miles of microfilm to track down the necessary code before submitting a request on a pink slip with up to five different sets of identifying numbers. Having got this far, the slip must be taken to another room, presented to a bevy of desk clerks (Time Out/Time In/initials/date) and signed for. Once that has been achieved, the process of retrieving the desired documents is dazzlingly swift and efficient. *Except* in the case of Eva's diary, when the hopeful seeker is impeded in the quest for Sleeping Beauty by a dense thicket of bureaucracy and security.

I arrived at NARA at 9.30 on a snowy Monday in March 2005 but although I had signalled my purpose well in advance it was not until Friday that week, the day before I was booked on an unalterable flight back to London, that Mr Taylor beckoned with a conspiratorial whisper: *'Follow me!'* A numbered and timed top security badge round my neck, signed for, dated, Time Out duly listed, I followed him through doors that could only be opened with a special smart card, into an empty office where, in the presence of another senior archivist, I was handed a plain brown envelope and a pair of white cotton gloves. Under the watchful eyes of the archivists I pulled on the gloves and settled down to read Eva's diary.

Inside the envelope was a book roughly nine inches square, bound in grubby cream leather that had darkened over the years, with a broken padlock. The key had disappeared long ago. Twenty-two pages of heavy, unlined cream paper had been roughly torn out and loosely reinserted. The remaining pages were blank. I opened it at the beginning and found myself confronting one last obstacle. The diary was not written in Eva's usual curving hand but in the spiky Old German script that had been in use since medieval times; not at all like the one she used in captions for the photograph albums and hard, at first impossible, to decipher. The script was swift and unhesitating, an educated and intelligent hand, but as different from ordinary German writing as Cyrillic.[5]

> Luckily I had learned to read Old German as a child. During the late forties, when we were living in Germany, I sometimes went to stay with my great-aunts *Tante* Lidy and *Tante* Anni in their cramped Hamburg flat. They would let me rummage through their papers, many of which were written in this outdated hand, and with a child's facility for language and symbol I quickly got the knack of it. Books were printed in a similar font and if I wanted to read what remained of *Tante* Lidy's collection of children's stories I had to master that as well. I would sit hunched in a corner, reading happily, until suppertime. The three of us gathered at a round table under a low-wattage bulb made dimmer by a fringed lampshade, eating heavy but delicious stews that contained little more than crumbly boiled potatoes in gravy. Lidy and Anni were very poor, like most Germans after the war. At bedtime *Tante* Lidy would tell me stories in her calm, low, velvety voice. It still rings in my ears; the most beautiful speaking voice, I think, that I have ever heard.[6]

5. A useful guide to this handwriting can be found on the Internet at www.familysearch.org/Eng/Search/Rg/Guide/Germany17.asp#handwriting

6. *Tante* Lidy, the last and the youngest of my mother's Neubert aunts – *her* mother's sisters – died on 12 July 1981 in Hamburg aged eighty-six and, after a life caring for other people, alone. It saddens me very much to think that *Tante* Lidy died all alone. I, her great-niece, was then forty-one and I would have travelled to Hamburg to be with her had I known how ill she was. But either she never told my mother or my mother never told me. My mother Ditha wrote a brief recollection immediately after her death in which for once every flowery adjective is justified: *Tante* Lidy *was* a marvel; more full of goodness than anyone I have ever known. Here is what my mother said about her, adorned with the usual confetti of commas: 'I am deeply sad at heart, because with my dear Lidy's passing, I feel that the last link of my family is closed. I don't quite know, how to put into words, what a wonderful, most loving, sweet and kind person Lidy was, in fact, to me she is unique, and I shall honour her memory till the rest of my life, and, I have said this often about people, who have passed on, but for Lidy it is the most meaning and deserved wish: may all the trumpets in heaven greet her, when she arrives there.' This continues for several paragraphs, ending: 'Wherever you are now, darling Lidy, may you be reunited with all your loved ones, and may you never be lonely again.'

The diary was written in 1935 and quite possibly continued later but 1935 is the only year from which extracts survive.[7] It is not filled in methodically, day following day in orderly succession – that was not Eva's style. She seems to have used it as a safety valve when Hitler's coolness and unpredictability became more than she could bear. Slight as it is, the diary offers a biopsy of her emotional state, showing the effect Hitler had on her; how he gradually undermined her ebullient self-assurance as well as her mental stability. She never knew when she would see him next and this uncertainty kept her in perpetual suspense.

The first entry, dated '11.II.35', reassured me at once that the diary was no fake. (It also, poignantly, reminded me of my mother. She formed her numerals *exactly* as Eva did. They must have been taught from the same copybook.) This is without any doubt at all the *only* account of her inner life by Eva Braun herself.[8] The diary spans 113 days and consists of a dozen irregular entries. It is written in pencil and the thickness of the strokes and size of the letters – the more agitated she gets the larger they become – are a guide to her state of mind. Small, sharp writing denotes calm. Its legibility deteriorates with her emotional state. As she spirals out of control, the words grow

7. It is not certain by what circuitous route the diary reached the labyrinthine stacks of NARA but Gitta Sereny thinks it is possible that Eva may have continued to write in a different diary and given it for safekeeping to Luis Trenker, a film director. He was very attractive and a terrific skier as well as a film-maker: it is just feasible that she would give him her diary, possibly because she was afraid it might be read by others. If Trenker ever had a continuation of it, written after May 1935 – which is extremely doubtful – that subsequent diary is now lost.
8. Other diaries also purport to have been written by Eva Braun but they are *all* forgeries. A half-plausible fake was published after the war but was soon shown to have been plagiarised from memoirs written decades earlier by a certain Countess Irma Larisch-Wallersee, inserting a few necessary changes of name to make it accommodate Eva's life. In addition, this forgery was sexed up to become more titillating, with several mildly pornographic episodes along the lines of 'How he loves me to wear my chamois leather underwear!' (On the contrary, Hitler the great animal lover would have been appalled.) It continues to be republished from time to time, cf Alan Bartlett's recent edition, which called itself *The Diary of Eva Braun* and was published by Spectrum International in 2000, but only the most gullible – and prurient – could mistake it for the real thing. It is inaccurate in every respect, particularly in his colourful re-creations of their supposed sex life together, which are prurient rather than erotic, let alone pornographic.

wilder and the pencil is blunted by her vehemence. Yet her fluent style clearly demonstrates that she was more than able to express herself. It contains few crossings out, nor did she resort to underlining or exclamation marks for emphasis. Eva knew what she wanted to say and her thoughts boiled over on to the page.

By early 1935 Adolf Hitler had been Chancellor for two years. He was forced to spend a great deal of time in Berlin, preoccupied with affairs of state, meetings with ingratiating or hostile foreign delegates and the infighting of his Rottweiler-like ministers, forever seeking favour and promotion. When he did come back to Munich at weekends he often met up with old comrades rather than Eva. Weeks might pass without her seeing him, with hardly a word. A brief meeting would revive her joyous optimism. Then silence.

Eva had been the *Führer*'s mistress for at least three years. They were occasionally alone together, presumably in his flat since it would have been too risky for him to visit her at her parents' place: '*Yesterday he came quite unexpectedly, and we had a delightful evening.*' (18 February.) She describes that time as '*entzückend*' – charming, delightful – rather than passionate. Perhaps that's what she offered: delicious evenings of giggly, innocent, playful sex, Eva playing Bridie O'Murphy to his Louis XV. If so, it must have been a hard role for her, though she describes those hours as '*wunderbare schöne Stunde*' – wonderful times. (4 March.)

A series of photographs dated by Eva 16 March 1935 shows her with a party including Hitler at the Zugspitze, a popular mountain resort near Berchtesgaden. But on that day, the 16th, after issuing a proclamation that announced the reintroduction of conscription, Hitler was in Berlin reviewing his troops. Eva was notoriously slapdash with her picture captions and the date must be wrong – it's much more likely to have been 1934, at a time when Hitler was in Munich. Had it been 1935 she would surely have mentioned it in her diary.

At other times when she saw Hitler he might treat her with indifference or even ignore her completely. On 1 April 1935 she wrote: '*Yesterday he invited us* ["us" meant her and Gretl] *to dinner at the Vier Jahreszeiten* [Four Seasons Hotel]. *I sat near him for three hours and could not exchange a single word. By way of goodbye he handed me, as he has done before, an envelope with money in it. It would have been much nicer if he had enclosed a greeting or a loving word. I would have been so pleased if he had.*' Albert Speer, who was also there, recorded that she blushed deeply. Eva later confided that the envelope had contained money, and that this had happened before. (That Hitler paid her anything is significant. It proves that he felt he owed her some support.) Speer was furious at Hitler's lack of tact: 'I felt horribly embarrassed for her.'[9] After three years as mistress of the *Führer* Eva's very existence was wiped out, her name never spoken, her face never seen, her love nullified by his callous neglect. Speer commented: 'He hid her from everybody except his most intimate circle but at that point, even there, denied her any social standing *and constantly humiliated her* [my italics].' The relationship Hitler offered was the reverse of everything she needed. '*The weather is so wonderful, and I, the mistress* [the noun she uses in the original is '*die Geliebte*', meaning the beloved, which often carries a specifically sexual implication] *of the greatest man in Germany and in the world, am sitting here and gazing at the sun through a window. How can he be so crass as to leave me here, nodding at strangers?*' (10 May.) That entry ends: '*It is a pity it is spring.*'

A woman who could write that was no 'silly goose' or 'stupid cow' but articulate, capable of deep feeling and the ability to express it. The voice in the diary is not that of a whining shop girl lacking education or intelligence, as her detractors claimed. The day after her birthday she comments ironically, '*my whole office resembles a flower shop and smells like a cemetery chapel*'. (7 February.) A less sensitive woman might have boasted about the magnificent flowers she'd been sent. Eva realised that, delivered by Frau Schaub (wife of Hitler's adjutant and presumably in the know) they signified no more than a casual order tossed to an underling. She saw through the floral ostentation to the emptiness of the display.

What does the diary reveal about her character? She was generous, both to her family and to Hitler. For her birthday she had planned an excursion with her mother and sisters to the Harz mountains, north of Munich. '*I should have had a wonderful time, for it is always most enjoyable when other people are enjoying themselves, too. But nothing came of it.*' (6 February.) Perhaps she cancelled the trip in the hope that Hitler would surprise her on her birthday. If so, she was disappointed. Second, unusually for the mistress of a rich and powerful man, her material expectations were modest. When Hitler finally turned up empty-handed five days later she wrote, '*He's just been to see me, but*

9. Sereny, *Albert Speer: His Battle with Truth*, p. 192.

no sign of a dog[10] or a chest of drawers. He didn't even ask me what I wanted for my birthday. So I bought some jewellery for myself. A necklace, earrings, and a matching ring for 50 marks. All very pretty, and I hope he likes it,' adding with unexpected tartness, 'If he doesn't, then he should choose something for me himself.' (11 February.) A woman whose highest hopes are for a dog or a chest of drawers and who consoles herself with a handful of cheap jewellery cannot be called mercenary. Nor was she ambitious for power or status. She never aspired to be First Lady of Germany – she wanted the man, not the *Führer*. Third, in spite of everything she was an optimist. She rarely indulged in self-pity but always tried to look on the bright side, making an effort not to wallow in her darkest moods. She was without question faithful: no other man's name is ever mentioned in the diary and there is no hint of a 'suitor in waiting'. Not once did she consider trying to live an ordinary life with an ordinary man who would marry her and give her children. Last, and crucially, she was discreet. She must have kept the diary locked and hidden away but even so she never uses Hitler's name. She invariably refers to him as '*Er*' – 'He' – and only once alludes to his prominence.

Eva Braun suffered from jealousy, the cancer of love. She was too young to see that his blowing hot and cold left her in a constant state of insecurity. The banal but obvious truth – that Hitler was genuinely preoccupied with affairs of state and too busy to spend time with her – didn't cross her mind, though she tried to make allowances: '*After all, it is quite obvious that he is not really interested in me when he has so much to do in politics,*' (16 March) or '*So he has had a head full of politics all this time, but surely he needs to relax a little.*' (28 May.) Like all women insecure about their lover, she worried endlessly in case he succumbed to one of the women crowding around him, most of whom would have been delighted to be his mistress. Some of the diary entries are almost insane with jealousy yet the next day she could laugh at herself: ('*That was just my mad imagination.*') (16 March.) When someone she considered a serious contender entered his orbit, however, the jealousy became unbearable. '*Ich zerbreche mit Wahnsinn*' she wrote on 4 March 1935: 'I'm cracking up.'

---

10. Hitler refused to give her a dachshund because, according to Werner Maser, *Hitler's Letters and Notes*, p. 371, he thought the breed was independent and disobedient – two qualities he could not stand in dogs or humans. He hated her cat, Peter, because it went its own way.

It would have been hard for her if she'd got word of the private lunch Hitler gave six weeks later for Sir Oswald Mosley and his prospective sister-in-law Unity Mitford, along with Winifred Wagner, his long-standing and fanatically loyal admirer. Hitler was overimpressed by the fact that Unity was English and upper class, though not quite as upper as he thought. Unity Valkyrie Mitford was the Hon. Miss Mitford since her father, Lord Redesdale, was only a baron. The most 'upper' thing about her was her height: at 6 foot she was exceptionally tall. Their relationship was based on misguided mutual admiration and never grounded in reality, but Eva was not to know this. She knew that a powerful and charismatic leader like Hitler would always be surrounded by predatory women – hadn't she been one herself? He did nothing to allay her fears, while the Hoffmanns, who persisted in seeing her as Fräulein Braun, their little shop assistant, fed her doubts: '*As Frau Hoffmann so affectionately and tactlessly informed me, he has now found a replacement for me. She is called Valkyrie, and that's what she looks like, including her legs. He likes measurements of this kind, but if she is really like that, he will soon make her thin with vexation,*' Eva noted on 10 May. Even though she was writing for herself, she managed to make her jealousy and spite funny. '*Including her legs*' was justified, coming from a young woman who by sheer self-discipline had reduced her own stocky legs to elegant slimness. Her main concern was for Hitler's happiness: '*If Frau Hoffmann's information is correct. I think it is terrible that he should say nothing to me about it* [implying that they had an established relationship which gave her some right to expect fidelity, or at least disclosure]. *After all, he should know me well enough to realise that I would never put anything in his way if he suddenly discovered his heart belonged to someone else.*' This generosity contrasts starkly with her fear of his indifference: '*What happens to me is no concern of his.*' On 10 May she also wrote: '*Maybe it is another woman, not the Valkyrie . . . But there are so many other women.*' Beset by rumours, gossip and malice, it was hard for Eva to believe she was the only woman he was sleeping with and the only one he came close to loving, and Hitler did little to reassure her. Having been the victim of acute jealousy himself during his time with Geli, he knew what a torment it is. A few words would have put Eva's mind at rest. He never spoke them.

She was seldom on her own with him. Sometimes they went on outings to the country together but these were rare and they were always accompanied by other people. Throughout April 1935 it was difficult for practical reasons to spend time alone together. Hitler's flat was being decorated and while this was going on he was based in a hotel, so they had to meet at the Hoffmanns' round the corner from the Osteria – in the company of both Heinrich and his new wife, Erna. Three months of this reduced the twenty-three-year old Eva to despair, however hard she tried to look on the bright side. Her thoughts seesawed between life and death but she struggled to remain cheerful: 'What is important is not to give up hope.' (6 February.) She reminded herself, 'In the past everything turned out well, and it will be the same this time.' (16 March.) She made excuses for him, reassuring herself that basically, everything was all right. 'I should have learned to be patient by now.' In the depths of misery, she did her utmost to hang on to her sense of humour and innate optimism and this particular entry, having started in a frenzy, ends quite calmly, her mood and her handwriting back under control.

Six weeks later optimism was getting harder to sustain. 'I am in great trouble, very great trouble. I keep on saying to myself, like Coué,[11] "I am getting better and better", but it is no use.' (29 April.) She owed money – she doesn't say how much or to whom – but her debts were such that she needed to sell one or two of her dresses and even her precious camera. It didn't occur to her to ask Hitler to bail her out. She was trapped in the photo shop by her continuing need to earn, however monotonous the job. By mid-1935 she had been working almost six years for Hoffmann – too long. And she was living at home, at odds with her father, forced to write her diary in secret and hide it from everyone.

Her mood darkened: 'I'm only going to wait until June 3rd, when three months will be up since our last meeting.' (10 May.) Since they had seen one another on 31 March at the Vier Jahreszeiten dinner, Eva may be using the word 'meeting' (Zusammenkunft, or 'rendezvous' in the original) to mean having sex. Several entries imply – only obliquely: she would never have risked putting anything explicit on paper – that they had sexual relations, but the euphoria afterwards is always brief. Soberly, she reflects, 'He only needs me for certain purposes, otherwise it is not possible [i.e. for me to spend time with him].' (11 March.) 'Certain purposes' must mean 'sexual relations'; no other interpretation makes sense. Occasionally

11. Emile Coué (1857–1926) was an early French psychotherapist who pioneered a belief in the power of positive thinking. He became the guru of autosuggestion in the 1920s, urging mental improvement through constant repetition: 'Every day in every way I am getting better and better.'

Hitler must have said he loved her: '*I am so infinitely happy that he loves me so much, and I pray that it will always be like this. It won't be my fault if he ever stops loving me.*' (10 March.) More realistically, '*He has so often told me he is madly in love with me, but what does that mean when I haven't had a good word from him in three months?*' (28 May.) Note her words: '*he loves me so much*' . . . '*he is madly in love with me*'. In private, perhaps when he was relaxed and gratified after sex, Hitler might tell Eva that he loved her but in public he treated her with indifference or, worse, contempt. Realistically, she describes his feelings for her as fond '*er hat mich gern*'.

On 23 May, Hitler had an operation to remove a polyp from his vocal chords, an operation that demands a week of near-silence afterwards from the patient, who may speak only occasionally and then only in a whisper. This could have explained Hitler's failure to telephone Eva that week, had she known about the operation, but her diary makes no mention of it. By late May she was exhausted, overwhelmed by months of emotional uncertainty. Like any woman obsessed with a man, she barely existed when they were apart. Hardly daring to go out in case he rang, hanging around his favourite haunts in case he should turn up, she spent most evenings at home, waiting. She could never plan ahead or look forward to a pre-arranged '*rendezvous*'. Aside from her monotonous job she scarcely had a life. '*If only I didn't go mad when he sees me so rarely.*' The despair became like a bad migraine. If it went on she preferred to die – she saw no alternative. She had been contemplating this for several weeks. '*There is only one thing I want. I would like to be seriously ill, and to hear nothing more about him for at least a week. Why doesn't something happen to me? Why do I have to go through all this? If only I had never set eyes on him! I am utterly miserable. I shall go out and buy some more sleeping powder and go into a half-dreamlike state, and then I won't think about it so much.*' (11 March.)

She tried to calm herself down, to hang on to reality, but the conviction grew that suicide was the only answer. She must have thought back to Geli, who had bled to death after shooting herself, and perhaps understood for the first time what drove her rival to such extreme measures. With the second suicide attempt Eva expected, and *wanted*, to die. '*Anyway, the uncertainty is more terrible than a sudden ending of it all.*' (28 May.) The diary ends abruptly halfway down the page. No guilt-inducing last words or melodramatic farewells to her lover or her family. The rest of the last page is blank. Below her final sentence the paper is stained – possibly by her tears but equally likely by some careless reader.

The twenty Vanodorm pills she swallowed were a milder sedative and a smaller dose than the thirty-five Veronals she originally planned to take. At the last moment she must have hesitated. Even so, she could not be sure that she would wake again. Had her sister not found her deeply unconscious, she probably wouldn't have done. Eva's diary, a record of hope and despair, proves beyond doubt that the attempted suicide was more than a cry for help. From the outset she had always known that she could not live without him.

In the eyes of the Catholic Church Eva had sold her soul for Hitler's love. Now she was ready to keep her side of the bargain. The idea of being hurled into hell was no fantasy to her but vividly real. She had written on 11 March 1935: *'Why doesn't the Devil take me with him? It would be much better with him than it is here.'*

Chapter Eleven

The Photograph Albums and Home Movies

Few people at the centre of a maelstrom in history can have left as little primary material as Hitler's mistress. Other than the diary, which is tantalisingly brief, there are scarcely any first-hand sources from Eva herself to provide posthumous insights into her character or reveal her secret feelings about her parents, her friends, her lover and the way he treated her. She was not a great letter writer and those she did write have mostly disappeared or are buried in unseen private collections. Few of her letters to Hitler survive, fewer still of his to her,[1] although during their frequent separations they wrote to each other regularly, almost daily. In April 1945 Eva asked Gretl to destroy 'an envelope addressed to the *Führer* and kept in the safe of the bunker', adding, 'Please do not read them! Please pack the *Führer*'s letters and my draft replies . . . in a watertight container and if possible bury them. Please do not destroy them.' (It is revealing that Eva specifically mentions the drafts of her letters to Hitler in the instructions to Gretl. Few women at the end of a long relationship would still feel they had to *draft* a love letter. Even on paper she always had to be on 'best behaviour'.)

The scarcity of primary sources is partly why Eva Braun has not

---

1. According to Werner Maser, *Hitler's Letters and Notes*, p. 137, Hitler wrote to her regularly, using a fountain pen and always in his own handwriting – presumably because the letters were too personal to dictate. In October 1972 Eva's sister Ilse told Maser that all the letters had been lost. Examples occasionally turn up in various Nazi auctions, memorabilia and collections, but the probability is that they are forgeries. The original buried cache of letters has never been found.

been the subject of an academic biography. A historian would be forced to reconstruct her life entirely from outside or secondary material – were it not for the fact that, from her earliest teens, Eva was a compulsive photographer. Her inner life has to be reconstructed from the pictures she took, not the words she left behind. Luckily, there are thousands of pictures.

Eva Braun had a particular need to be admired, implanted when she was a child by her father's disapproval and rejection. Later on, forced by Hitler to become invisible, she seemed to need photographs to prove that things really had happened; almost to prove to herself that she existed. She adored showing off the attributes she had cultivated to turn herself into a fitting partner for the *Führer*. She was a natural exhibitionist who longed to be a film star or public figure, applauded and loved by millions. If that was denied her, she wanted to be the woman at the side of the man who was.

Stored in the National Archives II building at College Park, Maryland, are thirty-three of Eva's private photograph albums with more than two thousand photographs documenting her life from babyhood until the summer of 1944, the year before she died. The frolicking pictures stop abruptly after the *Führer*'s fifty-fifth birthday in April 1944 (usual table spread with ingratiating presents from the usual attendant sycophants.)[2] Four of the albums, numbers 18–21, belonged to Eva's lifelong friend Herta (whose name since her marriage in November 1936 had become Schneider) and in late 1979 Frau Schneider requested their return. They were photocopied and, after some prevarication, the original albums were sent back to her.

The albums had originally been found in May 1945 when Soviet soldiers stormed the bunker after capturing Berlin. They had apparently been stored in a filing cabinet in Hitler's small study beneath the Reichs Chancellery. (The Allies joked that when the invading Russians looted Nazi offices they would empty top secret documents on to the floor and take away the filing cabinets, leaving the documents to the Americans. Four months after the death of Hitler, his engagement diary was found untouched on top of his desk in the bunker.)

Lady Williams, then Subaltern Gill Gambier-Parry, personal assis-

---

2. After this the war started going so badly that Hitler never returned to the Berghof.

tant to the brigadier for intelligence at General Eisenhower's HQ, was one of the first British servicewomen to enter Berlin after the war, in September 1945:

> When I got to Berlin in the autumn of 1945 it just was such an *extraordinary* world. By the time they'd finished allocating accommodation there was nowhere left for me so I slept on a sofa for a bit and was then assigned an Italianate villa at number 6 Grieg Street, beautifully furnished and kept, which had been where the Greek Ambassador kept his mistress. It had a huge double bed on a dais and a skeleton in the cellar. Because of the Russians' reputation for rape the Germans hid their daughters under furniture, in cupboards, cellars, God knows where. I saw long lines of women taking stones off bombed buildings and handing them along. I don't remember seeing many German men.
>
> One Sunday a Colonel – Hugh Boggis-Rolph was his name – said to me, 'Come on Gill, let's go and look at the Chancellery.'
>
> We found the entrance to the bunker and Eva Braun's room was off to the right. I picked up her nailfile. I took it and I used it too, until it was stolen from our hotel room in New York. In Hitler's medical cabinet there was this phial of vitamins.

She holds up a small glass phial brown with age, containing about 200ml of dark liquid.

> Apart from that there was almost nothing left. In his study I saw copies of Hitler's political testament and his Will, signed by him, with a carbon copy. I took a few of his headed note-cards and another card printed 'Berlin, Christmas 1942' signed by Hitler. There wasn't much else. It was a most extraordinary experience; very, somehow, *stark*. Like being in a fortress.

Gill Williams also remembers attending a meeting of the quadrapartite committee in Berlin, chaired by the four occupying countries in turn.

> On one occasion, when it was the Russians' turn to take the chair, they marched in, beaming like schoolboys, with a tall stack of books. These were Eva Braun's photo albums. We sat all afternoon handing them around, staring right back at Eva Braun:

*'Here's me in my party dress, me at my confirmation, me looking out
at the Berchtesgaden view, me at the Eagle's Nest' and so on . . .[3]*

Considering that she had not seen them for fifty years, Lady Williams'
recall of these photographs was extremely vivid and accurate. I asked
if she'd heard of Eva Braun before she found herself in Hitler's bunker.
'Oh yes – we knew about her even before she went to Berlin, probably just through gossip but when people talked about her it wouldn't
"stick", if you know what I mean. There was no evidence, just rumours.
No one would have used the term "mistress" in those days; we'd have
said "girlfriend".'

In November 1945, the Americans found the thirty-three NARA
albums in Eva's house in Wasserburgerstrasse. (These could have been
duplicates she'd had made of the ones in Berlin, since Eva sometimes
gave her friends copies of the albums.) An inventory was made of
them and other personal possessions that had escaped looting. The
albums and some reels of home movies were taken back to the United
States as spoils of war.[4] All these are available – not the originals but
full-sized facsimiles – to anyone with a NARA Researcher's Pass. (It
takes about ten minutes to obtain and costs nothing.) Clutching this
pass, I was told to leave behind everything from the outside world –
handbag, pencil (the silver propelling pencil from my mother that was
an exact replica of the one that had belonged to Eva), notebooks,
jacket – before presenting my pass for scrutiny by an armed security
officer. Once he was satisfied that I was empty-handed and could not
loot or bomb the nation's heritage the turnstile clicked open and
revolved. A lift to the fourth floor Research Room, my pass checked
again, white cotton gloves provided with which to handle the precious
material, and the rest of the day could be spent in a cocoon of concentration, searching, browsing, reading and annotating each page and
every image from the heavy black photograph albums shelved in one
corner.

3. Personal interview with Lady Williams, née Gill Gambier-Parry, 31 July 2003.
She is the widow of Edgar ('Bill') Williams, General Montgomery's intelligence
officer and former warden of Rhodes House, who was charged with responsibility
for escorting General Jodl when he signed the surrender of the *Wehrmacht* to the
Allies at Reims on 7 May 1945 that formally signalled the end of the war.
4. Jean-Michel Charlier and Jacques de Launay, *Eva Hitler née Braun* (Paris:
Editions de la Table Ronde, 1978), p. 261.

In March 2004 I spent a week poring over the most intimate evidence of Eva, her circle and their life in Obersalzberg. From a cavalcade of snapshots, photographs and film footage[5] I could deduce not only the rhythm and activities of her days but what she was trying to make of her life. The albums and films yield a mass of information, all the more valuable for being conveyed unconsciously. Thanks to them it's possible to reconstruct the pampered, poisonous hothouse where she was forever waiting for Hitler. Without him, the terrace and the echoing great reception rooms lacked their *raison d'être* and the emptiness of Eva's life becomes obvious. Without him she felt nothing and was nothing. When he was there, she was beautiful, effervescent and vivacious. She was the type of woman, often attached to older men, whose sole function is to please; who use charm and exaggeratedly childish behaviour to solicit male protection. In Eva's home movies her laughing, playful mock helplessness shows up clearly and looks more artificial than in photographs. This is where we see her as she wanted to be seen, projecting her carefully constructed image. Boredom and frustration lurked like an undercurrent and she had to work hard to conceal the truth from everyone including herself, calling from every photograph – look what *fun* we're all having!

Eva's attention span was too short to grapple with serious books (she never read anything except magazines or cheap romantic novels) or even the proper sticking in of photographs, but at some time between 1937 and 1941 – perhaps during one of Hitler's many absences, perhaps on a day when it was pelting with rain and they were forced to stay indoors – Eva and Gretl decided to deal with the mass of photographs they had accumulated. They dug out a pile of boxes and bulging envelopes full of unsorted photographs and settled down at the desk in her sitting room. The pictures they chose for the albums were picked at random – neither sister was the sort to organise them methodically first – and, far from being arranged chronologically, let alone neatly and helpfully captioned, they are assembled higgledy-piggledy, snapshots from babyhood or schooldays on the same page as studio portraits taken twenty years later. Eva was evidently pleased with the results, for she selected the best hundred photographs, had them copied and put into five leather-bound albums embossed with the initials EB, and gave them as presents to a few of her closest friends for Christmas 1941.

5. Part of the cache retrieved in Schloss Fischhorn, Austria, by CIC agent Robert A. Gutierrez.

One learns a lot about Eva's character from the way the pictures
are stuck in, especially her inability to concentrate or do things in an
orderly way. Given that she was obviously keen to chronicle her life
why did she do it so badly? Many photographs are duplicated, turning
up a dozen albums apart; some have been torn out (not necessarily
by Eva herself: the original albums have passed through many hands,
not all of them scrupulous); and the pictures are put together in a
slapdash way, as though she couldn't be bothered to sort them first
and arrange them in order. As a result they are a half-finished jigsaw
puzzle that the researcher struggles to complete.

The majority are also uncaptioned, a chore NARA has not attempted
either, so one has to deduce when they were taken from details like
Eva's hairstyle, its length or colour. The one in ten that do have captions
are typed on two different machines, one with an oversized font similar
to that used for official or military documents. The rest are handwritten
by three or four different people (her mother, perhaps, or her methodical friend Herta, may have insisted on adding some information) but
most are in Eva's looping, feminine hand. To make matters more difficult, many of the captions are written in white pencil so as to be more
legible against the black card to which the photographs were attached,
but the pencil has crumbled, leaving a soft, powdery imprint that is hard
to decipher. A few, printed in black ink (by Fanny?) are wonderfully
legible. Once or twice a strong masculine hand with slashing downward
strokes appears (could this have been Fritz? It's certainly not Hitler's
sclerotic handwriting). Hardest of all are a few written in the obsolete
Old German script that takes practice to decipher. Eva herself must
have written these: they are in the same hand as the diary.

A word in the archaic script that looked like *Bnilugrinb* stumped
me for a long time. It became clear when, a few months later, I spent
some days with Eva's cousin Gertraud. When I visited her in August
2004 I brought several photocopies from NARA to show her, since
she shared many of the people and places from Eva's childhood. One
picture from Album 31 of a large, solid, three-storey house was
captioned in the old script. Frau Weisker read it fluently: '*Grossvater's
Haus in Beilngries 1925*' – 'Grandfather's house in Beilngries.' 'I
remember this house,' she said; 'we often stayed here for family get-
togethers when I was little.' On the same page was a charming picture
of an old lady feeding chickens, again captioned in the difficult square
script: '*1925 – Grossmutter beim Hühner füttern*' – '1925: Grandmother
feeding the chickens.' This was Josefa Kronburger, Fanny's mother;

the patrician nose was identical. Frau Weisker had never seen the photograph before. (She would have been two years old when it was taken.) 'My *grandmother!*' she exclaimed, scrutinising it across three generations. Then eighty-one, she was older than her long-dead *Oma*. The seventy-four-year old woman in the photograph was the epitome of old age as it used to be – stout, grey-haired, dressed in black from head to foot. Gertraud, her descendant, looked decades younger. Behind Josefa stood one of her five daughters, but which one? '*Tante* Anni,' said Gertraud firmly. Gradually the script helped me to identify and date the pictures and the pictures sometimes gave a clue to the script. Progress was slow. No wonder NARA hadn't attempted to annotate and catalogue the albums in detail.

Eva's early interest in photography was sparked by vanity. From toddlerhood onwards, she adored the camera. No *Fasching* (Shrove Tuesday) or *Sylvester Abend* (New Year's Eve) party was complete without Eva Braun posing in yet another new outfit, recorded on black and white film and preserved for posterity. In other pictures her little sister Gretl nestles up to her wearing a miniature version of Eva's clothes. Family pets are presented in Eva's cupped hands: kittens, rabbits, pet birds. Not a single photograph shows her doing anything serious like homework or reading – except one, in which she poses with a book propped on her knees, displaying her legs. The ectoplasm of her character streams through these images. Vain, sentimental, self-centred and shallow, she is a typical pre-adolescent girl.

In her teens Eva acquired a camera of her own, probably a simple box Agfa. Now she need not always be the focus of other people's pictures; *she* could take them. She learned to pose in front of a mirror with the shutter mechanism set to auto. From 1925 to 1931, her adolescent years, she recorded herself, her family and her jostling, giggling schoolfriends. She makes sure she is the central figure in group photographs taken on hiking weekends with her father and his pupils and on outings with her parents and sisters. From these early snapshots one gets a strong sense of the Braun daughters' very different characters. Ilse seldom smiles. Even as a small girl she looks solemn, anxious and mildly disapproving. Eva flirts with the camera, Gretl is her admiring shadow. Whatever the hidden domestic tensions, in these snapshots the family seems close and affectionate, everyone's role clearly defined. Bullet-headed Fritz comes across as a tough father who would have done better with a trio of boys, Fanny as a proud mother, forever mollifying him and their daughters with a gentle maternal smile.

Photo Hoffmann, where Eva continued to work, sold cameras and photographic equipment as well as processing film and doing portraiture on commission, so she was familiar with the range of cameras available and, as an employee, probably got a reduction on anything she bought for herself. She quickly progressed from basic box cameras producing tiny, 4 x 5-centimetre pictures on 120 film to bigger, more elaborate ones taking 9-centimetre square prints and from that to a large-format camera producing rectangular images, 14 x 10.5-centimetres. Later, when Hitler rather than Eva was the buyer, Hoffmann advised him and supplied Eva's photographic equipment, making sure it was the best. The film she used was always of the highest quality, the latest Agfa intended for professional use, and because of this her pictures haven't faded or deteriorated as cheaper stock would have done. In the mid-thirties Hitler gave her a splendid twin-lens Rolleiflex, a camera that within a few years would be in demand all over the world for its advanced features and outstanding results. It weighed nearly 2 pounds – more with its sturdy leather case – and incorporated a shutter with speeds up to $\frac{1}{500}$th of a second and a Zeiss-Tessar f/3.5 lens. It was manufactured by Franke & Heidecke in Brunswick and each 120 or B 2 roll produced twelve small, square exposures (5½ x 5½ centimetres or 2¼ x 2¼ inches) that, when enlarged, gave exceptionally clear, sharp pictures. This Rollei, far more advanced than any previous camera she had owned, turned Eva from a happy-go-lucky amateur into an expert photographer. The fuzzy snapshots became strong, original images making creative use of light and shade. Her job in the studio and darkroom had taught her a lot of the technical stuff and she usually processed her own photographs. When she wanted to be 'artistic' she would photograph the scenes that meant most to her – pine-covered mountain slopes under snow, the shimmering waters of the Königssee, reflective lakeside and waterfall scenes and joyous pictures of Herta's little girls running through a meadow of wild flowers. If she'd wanted to, she could have made a career as a professional photographer.

Eva was not always behind the camera. If she wanted a studio portrait the best professionals were at her disposal – and not only Hoffmann. By the end of the thirties she had tired of his boorish behaviour and patronising manner (he continued to treat her as his junior apprentice[6]) and gone in search of other, better photographers who could compose a more flattering image. The most successful was Walter Frentz, leading cinematographer on Leni Riefenstahl's films and, unusually, a portrait photographer as well. He knew exactly what she was after, producing a series of tender and radiant pictures. He liked Eva very much, seeming to understand her difficult relationship with Hitler and the problems it caused, hence her desire to retreat into the fantasy world of the movies. She studied fashion magazines and controlled her image with great care, having her hair and make-up done before each portrait sitting and posing in a series of dazzling dresses. (A full-length evening gown in bias-cut white satin was a particular favourite, emphasising her slender body and flat stomach.) The pretext for these sessions was often that she needed a birthday present to give the *Führer*. His tastes were austere and he lacked nothing. What do you give such a man? Symbolically, over and over again, Eva gave herself, often dressed in white, with the obvious implication.

At the Berghof she was forever trying to catch a good picture of Hitler but he was wary of being photographed informally. He preferred a composed image that he could control, theatrically posed with flattering lighting. Alfons Schulz, a switchboard operator at the Berghof from the mid-1930s, noted that he rarely made a friendly face for Eva's camera. Traudl Junge, employed in 1942, at twenty-two the youngest and last of Hitler's secretaries, recalled in her memoirs:

> She'd often go outside with her camera or movie-camera and try to get the *Führer* to pose for her. She was the only person allowed to photograph him but it was very difficult to get spontaneous, unposed snaps. He wanted to be photographed unobtrusively, as if unconscious of the camera, but the moment the sun shone he'd put a hat on to shade his face and couldn't be persuaded to take it off because strong light blinded him; or he'd wear sunglasses. But Eva had such patience and cunning in pursuit of her passion for photography that in spite of him she often managed to get good shots . . . better than her former boss and teacher, Heinrich Hoffmann.[7]

6. Technically, she still was: she continued to do the odd day's work from time to time, partly to maintain her 'cover' and partly because, later on, wartime regulations required all unmarried women to work.
7. Junge, *Until the Final Hour*, p. 80.

Occasionally, in pictures taken by other people, Eva can be seen laughing, trying to coax him and sometimes, briefly, he relents. Even so, only a handful of photographs show the two of them together and these few have been reproduced over and over again, giving a false impression of their public closeness. In fact the distance he maintained and his behaviour towards her could seem chill to the point of insulting. On the terrace at the Berghof – which was *her* domain as well – Eva, in her sprigged dirndl dress, seems overawed by him. She folds her hands behind her back like a good little girl, her ankles twisted nervously. From their stance, one would never guess they were lovers. For the first six years of their relationship Hitler kept her under his thumb, a perpetually biddable seventeen-year-old. If by accident a picture did show them together it would be stamped NOT FOR PUBLI-CATION, a prohibition no German newspaper would dare disobey. Far from being a celebrity, Eva was completely anonymous. Beyond the immediate confines of the Berghof she could move about unrecognised. When she went shopping in Berchtesgaden or Munich she was just another pretty girl, rather better dressed than most. Her employer and her lover between them made sure she was a non-person, her very existence denied to the outside world.

Yet from the time Eva was in her twenties not a week passed without her being photographed. The faintest swelling of her flat stomach would have shown up and been seized upon by the gossips. Through a magnifying glass I studied pictures of her, especially those in which she is wearing a swimsuit, from the early thirties to 1942, the time when she was sleeping with Hitler regularly, and found no sign. The absence of any change in her figure is not *proof* but makes it much more likely that fanciful stories about a child turning up years after the war can be discounted.

Gradually one comes to recognise the *dramatis personae* who enlivened the dullness and repetition of her life. Gretl, of course (she looks very similar to Eva and the two are often confused in captions, but Gretl's hair was dark – she never dyed it – and her eyes rounder); their mother Fanny (pointed chin, piled-up greying hair, aquiline nose) and father Fritz: odd to find *him* at the Berghof when he disapproved so vehemently of Hitler's relationship with his daughter. The portly young man with a round face and dark Brylcreemed hair is Heinrich Hoffmann's son, Heini. He turns up in lots of pictures and one soft-focus portrait of him is inscribed '*Gretl, von Dein* . . . [illegible] *13.8 Grüss und Küss,*

Heini' – 'Gretl, love and kisses, from your Heini'. Did those two have a fling, perhaps? Gretl, very pretty with a good figure, was a bit of a simpleton but a dangerously flirtatious one. Heini would not have been her only admirer. In the spring of 1942, she and Martin Bormann seemed attracted to one another, though whether this turned into an affair is not known. It seems unlikely. Eva would have been dead against it and Bormann would have been wary of Hitler's reaction. Yet Anna Plaim, Eva's housemaid,[8] distinctly remembers the two of them dancing together at a party, drunkenly entwined. Tellingly, Eva wasn't present.[9]

The stout figure of Martin Bormann can often be seen in the photographs, hovering watchfully in the background whenever Hitler was in residence. The tall, patrician Albert Speer was a rare visitor who hardly ever appears in Eva's album, although he later became one of the few people at the Berghof whom she liked and trusted. He and his family had a comparatively modest house at the edge of Obersalzberg but Speer disliked the sycophantic crowd surrounding Hitler and stood fastidiously apart from the hangers-on and toadies. In pictures he never smirks, stoops or twists deferentially in Hitler's presence. Their body language could be that of equals.

Backing out of frame in one corner one may glimpse Josef Goebbels, a lizard-thin, club-footed mannikin, Minister of Propaganda and serial lecher. His wife Magda seldom features except as a role-model German mother with her blonde brood of immaculately dressed small children – the girls' hair tidily plaited, the boys' neatly combed – playing under the eye of uniformed nursemaids. As many as one in six of Eva's pictures was taken on the terrace and she began to photograph in colour – the blue-striped covers on the reclining chairs and cushions contrasting merrily with the red umbrellas that shaded the company in summer. Laid out on tables in the background is a perpetual supply of tea, coffee and cakes. Slim, blond adjutants proffer urgent papers, despatches, telegrams or summonses to the telephone, slipping in and out of the carefully contrived social comedy, a reminder that power lurked in the next room.

In the albums, Eva's captions are always followed by an exclamation mark and occasionally some ironic or wistful comment. Next to a

8. Anna Plaim came to the Berghof in 1941, aged twenty, to be the personal maid in charge of Hitler's and Eva's rooms. She was a cousin of Willi Mittlstrasse, manager of the household who was in charge of all the housemaids.
9. Plaim and Kuch, *Bei Hitlers: Zimmermädchen Annas Erinnerungen*, p. 95.

portrait in profile that pleased her she has written, '*So lass mich halt!*' – 'Let me stay this way!' Beside a rare shot of herself shaking hands with Hitler she notes ironically: '. . . *die kenn ich nämlich sehr gut!*' putting into his mouth the words, 'I know her very well!' There is a revealing sequence in Album 6. Several high-angle shots taken from Eva's bedroom window during the state visit of the dashing young Italian foreign minister Count Galeazzo Ciano[10] in August 1939 show a group of uniformed men. Beside them is the typed comment: '*Da oben gibt es verbotenes zu sehen – mich!*' – 'It's forbidden to look at what's up there – me!' A few shots later she adds another caption: '*Order: Fenster zu! und wass man daraus machen!*' Hitler must have noticed what she was doing and sent orders to shut the window and tell her to stop photographing. From such oblique and cautious comments one deduces the nature of their relationship. She was required to please Hitler ('she was always waiting for his orders,' Gertraud recalled), and he kept her submissive and dependent by alter-nately controlling and indulging her. In the hierarchy of relationships that really mattered to him she was much lower than Geli had been, lower than Speer, lower even than his dog Blondi, and she knew it.

As the years passed, Eva changed. One senses that instead of enjoying herself she became restless, bored, and ill at ease amid the venomous crew 'on the Berg', as the inmates called their enclave. Time was being wasted. The carefree energy became compulsive. Perched and singing in her 'gilded cage',[11] she grew more and more obsessed with her appear-ance. It was the only way she had of trying to make herself good enough for Hitler. She rarely appeared in the same dress twice and constantly experimented with new hairstyles and colours. She looked poised and sophisticated but in the few photographs that catch her unawares her face is often sad. She exercised until her body was magnificently fit, strong and supple. In an era that glorified health and athleticism, Hitler should have nothing but the best. Already an excellent swimmer, graceful diver and a fast, confident skier, she practised gymnastics for hours until she had almost reached competition standard. This is easier to see on moving film than frozen in still pictures. While the *Führer* was away in Berlin, using any equipment that came to hand – railings, the branch

10. The son-in-law of Mussolini, to whom no doubt he owed his office.
11. Eva, while ensconced in luxury at the Berghof, told Walter Frentz that 'she lived in a gilded cage'. See Anton Joachimsthaler, *The Last Days of Hitler* (London: Arms and Armour Press, 1986), p. 263.

of a tree – Eva honed her body and tried to sublimate her libido.

In June 1936 my parents married. Their wedding took place in England rather than Germany but none of the Schröder family came over for the occasion – perhaps because only her father could speak English, or perhaps they simply hadn't been invited. The latter is quite possible. My father's English side of the family took against my mother from the start because she was German. They must have been exceptionally bigoted to begrudge him his young bride, as madly in love with him as he was with her, but prejudice was not confined to Germans, nor was it directed only at Jews. After the war had broken out my mother's unworldliness and ignorance of politics – which matched if not exceeded Eva's – along with her inability to speak good English, led to five unhappy years as a victim of prejudice, loneliness and separation. Her chief satisfaction was that she had fulfilled her destiny as a German woman. She was married and before long she would become a mother.

In 1937, or possibly for her birthday in 1938, by which time Eva had been taking pictures of Hitler and the Berghof for seven years, she acquired a cine camera using 16mm colour film. It must have been given to her by Hitler: nobody else could have afforded or dared to buy her such a spectacular present. She began using it immediately and with great enthusiasm and soon became proficient, both at shooting and editing film, skills she had not learned at Hoffmann's.[12] Eight half-hour rolls of her home movies are lodged in NARA's vast Moving Images archive, and there are duplicates as well in Germany's Bundesarchiv.[13] They tell the same story as the photographs; sometimes *exactly* the same story, since Eva often took a series of photographs and then repeated the scenes on film. Their monotony is demonstrated by NARA's shot list for Reel 6:[14] '*Eva and others relaxing on terrace.*

12. Interviewed for *Adolf and Eva*, 3BMTV, roll 24.10, Frau Mittlstrasse, by then housekeeper at the Berghof, confirmed: 'She not only made films but edited them herself as well.'

13. The German National Archive where, for researchers who speak German, the shot lists are more detailed and accurate, giving, for instance, the names of all the people seen on film. NARA merely summarises the films shot by shot, usually stating the obvious.

14. Shot List for Item from Record Group 242: National Archives Collection of Foreign Records Seized.

Hitler comes out, shakes hands with the ladies, the men salute. Women sitting on edge of terrace. Group going off on a walk. Scenes of country-side. Children picking flowers.' Anodyne sequences like this are repeated over and over again, to be shown later in the Berghof cinema: Eva the film star in front of an audience of friends and enemies.

Many of her cine films date from the early 1940s, by which time she had mastered the camera and was becoming more ambitious. When not trying to be moody and artistic she filmed people making fools of themselves. In the midst of her gang Eva tumbles about, nestles up to her friends, puts her arms round them, bullies them into laughing groups so that she can sit in the middle and be crowded by their phys-ical proximity before leaping up to film them without her. She exag-gerates her gestures and expressions, mouth and eyes big round Os of surprise, or puts on a parody of flirtatiousness, teasing and pouting in mock disappointment. As time went on the participants had to work harder to prove they were having fun. Eva, drying herself after a swim, is approached by a young man who lunges at her, trying to pull her towel off. She shrieks and struggles yet the shoving and splashing and horseplay are oddly sexless. They play like children, like Chaplin, ungainly and frantic. At parties they drink too much champagne and wear silly hats; the men do simple conjuring tricks and the women cover their mouths, pretending to be amazed. These films show people performing life, not living it, like a spread from a celebrity magazine.

There is something unsettling about this compulsion to record every trivial occasion but if Eva was forbidden a public face she was deter-mined to make up for it in private. Cut off from everything that had previously grounded her, she struggled to find a solid foundation. The hapless object of jealousy, social ostracism and Hitler's refusal to acknowledge her publicly, she tried to compensate by making a pictor-ial fantasy of her life. The gulf between appearance and reality widened.

PART 3

MISTRESS-IN-WAITING

Chapter Twelve

Eva Leaves Home

When, after her second suicide attempt in May 1935, Hitler had accepted Eva as his official mistress, he decided she must be properly installed and well treated. Many older men took young mistresses, often with the knowledge of their male friends though not their wives, and were judged less on moral grounds than according to how generously they looked after them. 'Hitler attached great importance to keeping up appearances in respectable Munich,' comments uncle Alois drily.[1] Seven months later, Hoffmann acting as intermediary once more, Hitler bought a modest house at 12 Wasserburgerstrasse[2] for the two Fräulein Brauns, Eva and Gretl, in the elegant suburb of Bogenhausen and on 30 March 1936 the deeds were lodged in Eva's name.[3] Long afterwards, their cousin Gertraud rationalised:

> Hitler took notice of Eva's cry for help, either because he had a guilty conscience or because he had genuinely grown fond of her. He hastily provided her with a base of her own, away from her parents and the ties that bound her to them. This meant he could control her better, even if he was absent for much of the

---

1. Winbauer, *Eva Braun's Familiengeschichte*, p. 11.
2. As above. The street is now called Delpstrasse, perhaps in an attempt to deter visitors, though not very successfully, say the present owners. Forgivably, they are not prepared to open up their house to inquisitive tourists.
3. Source: Eva's official death certificate.

time, and as company and consolation he let her younger sister share this new home.[4]

The house was a typical suburban villa, an unimaginative stucco box like all the others in Bogenhausen, but it was close to Hitler's flat, discreet and anonymous. A maid came with it – he could afford to spoil his new mistress. The ground area of the little house was only 8 x 10 metres but it was pleasantly furnished and had some more than decent paintings appropriated from museums; she had a china dinner service for eight decorated with blue flowers and a well-equipped kitchen, all supplied at Hitler's expense. From the entrance hall a door opened into the living room, from which one door led into the garden and another to a tiny kitchen and even tinier maid's room. To the right of the front door was another sitting room with several pictures of Hitler affection-ately inscribed to both Eva and Gretl, and a dining room. Upstairs the girls each had their own bedroom and shared a bathroom. Eva's bedroom was in shades of blue, the double bed upholstered in ice-blue striped satin and laid with expensive linen bearing her initials EB. On the wall beside the bed was a telephone with lines out marked Berlin and Wachenfeld (the name of Hitler's original chalet at Obersalzberg).

She had, of course, plenty of wardrobe space and soft quilted satin boxes for her stockings and lingerie. A long, mirrored dressing table was dotted with her favourite Elizabeth Arden cosmetics and crystal bottles of expensive French scent. (Hitler may have disapproved of artifice for the average German woman but he indulged his mistress's fondness for luxury cosmetics.) Significantly, she kept a douche bag on the top shelf of her wardrobe, suggesting that she used a simple if not entirely reliable method of contraception: douching herself after sex with warm water and vinegar. The bathroom held a crowded medicine chest with all the usual remedies for colds and sore throats as well as a supply of sleeping pills and various treatments for 'women's problems' – Eva's periods were heavy and painful and she was forever trying to find an effective pallia-tive. In the cellar, until it was turned into an air raid shelter at Hitler's insistence, were cases of some very fine wines indeed.[5]

4. Weisker, *Wer War Eva Braun?* (translated by the author).
5. Antony Penrose (ed.), *Lee Miller's War* (London: Thames & Hudson, 19), pp. 197–9. Lee Miller was a war photographer and one of the first to enter Eva's house after peace had been signed on 8 May 1945. She had been preceded, however, by a number of looters, who helped themselves to Eva's clothes and wine and (more prosaically) her food stores: tins of sardines and tuna.

The rooms were small but Eva loved it, calling it 'my dear little Braunhaus'.[6] Its chief advantage where Hitler was concerned was the high wall that entirely surrounded an 800-square-metre garden, guaranteeing Eva (and, if necessary, him) complete privacy. He gave her a guard dog – a bull terrier called Blasko – but Blasko was surly and unpredictable, nobody liked him much and he didn't last long. He was followed by two Highland terriers. Negus came first. He was black, given to Eva by Hitler, probably in late 1935. She later bought a companion for him, a female named Stasi. They became her inseparable and devoted shadows. She loved them as much as Hitler loved Blondi, his Alsatian bitch. She groomed and petted them, took them for walks and was comforted by their faithful presence at her feet. She called them her 'little guys' and they provided a much needed emotional outlet, though it would be oversimplifying to think of them as surrogate children. Later they would become actors in the elaborate and revealing games that she and Hitler played. As a welcoming gift Hitler also gave her a smart black Mercedes, number IIA-525000, and a chauffeur, Herr Jung, to go with it. Best of all, Eva was able to get away from the daily tedium of the job at Photo Hoffmann, where she'd continued to work since October 1929. Hoffmann explained: 'For practical purposes she never left my employment but when Hitler was on the Obersalzberg she got leave for that time in order to be present at the Berghof. When the compulsory labour assignment for women started, she was assigned to my business.[7] Eva continued to put in occasional appearances right up to 1945.[8] Bormann doled out pocket money equivalent to the salary she would have been earning: 450 Reichsmarks a month.[9]

Their neighbours in this classy enclave soon worked out who the two young women had to be, although Eva made no attempt to get to know

6. Details from Gun, *Eva Braun: Hitler's Mistress*, p. 119 (who viewed it several times in the sixties) and from the author's observations.
7. From the interrogation of Heinrich Hoffmann at Nuremberg, 19 July 1948, in Vol. XI of the Musmanno Collection.
8. See her letter to Walter Ostermayr, brother of Herta née Ostermayr but by now Frau Schneider, dated 'München 24 XI 43': 'What with my job at Hoffmann's and the air-raid damage to my house, I have unfortunately not had time to write.' Quoted in Johannes Frank, *Eva Braun: ein ungewöhnliches Frauenschicksal in geschichtlich bewegter Zeit* (Coburg: Nation Europa Verlag, 1997).
9. In 1938 a pound sterling was the equivalent of just over RM 12.

them while Hitler, paranoid about being 'found out', visited the villa only after the most exhaustive security preparations. When he was in Munich and wanted to see her he would arrive – often without warning – jump out of the car and stride up the path to the front door, leaving a posse of bodyguards waiting round the corner. On these occasions Gretl would slip away so that they could be alone together. Eva would offer him tea, after which presumably they made love. He never stayed overnight.

Despite his generosity in setting her up with her own establishment, Hitler was too overworked and preoccupied to visit Eva more than a couple of times a month and weekends at the Berghof were more work than leisure. These were the crucial years during which he was directing – always *indirectly* – the subtle, day-by-day advance of the party's hidden agenda.[10] The Nuremberg Rally, due to be held in September, would unveil the Nuremberg Laws – the Nazi drive for 'racial purity' designed to 'cleanse' Germany of genetic and racial 'taints'. For the first time since feudalism, two degrees of humanity would be recognised.[11] A pure Aryan bloodline was all-important. (Hitler had had Eva's family background thoroughly scrutinised for any Jewish ancestors.)

When Hitler needed a break from his government duties he would retreat to the mountains of Obersalzberg, the inspiration for his vision of the sacred 'German-ness' of his people. In 1932 he had decided that, rather than continue to rent Haus Wachenfeld as he had done for the past four years, he would buy it outright.[12] Martin Bormann and Rudolf Hess, who together ran his private office, bullied its reluctant owner, Margarethe Winter, as well as the Schüster family who owned Gasthof zum Türken, the hotel above Haus Wachenfeld, into selling. After much heavy-handed persuasion these deals were finalised between September 1932 and November 1933.[13] Frau Schuster, more

10. In March 1933 Dachau, the first prison camp, had opened in a Munich suburb, to be followed by Sachsenhausen, Buchenwald and Mauthausen, custom-made camps built for hard labour and large numbers, all places of licensed brutality.
11. Gerald Reitlinger, *The Final Solution: The Attempt to Exterminate the Jews of Europe, 1939–1945* (London: Vallentine, Mitchell, 1968), p. 7.
12. In 1934 Hitler declared his 1933 income as DM1,232,355 in addition to his official salary of DM60,000 p.a. (*Der Spiegel*, 6 April 1970, pp. 92ff, cited by Werner Maser). On 15 March 1935 he disappeared from the list of taxpayers at his own request, probably because the royalties from *Mein Kampf* were now so high that he didn't care for the amount to be made public.
13. For details of all Bormann's transactions, see Helmut Schoner and Rosl Irlinger, *Der Alte Obersalzberg Bis 1937* (Munich: Verlag Berchtesgadner Anzeiger, 1989).

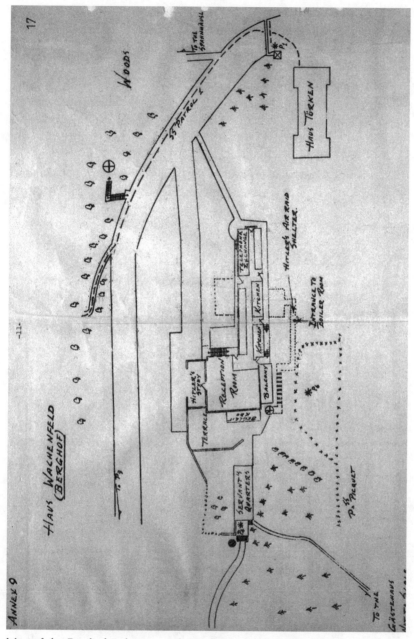

Map of the Berghof and its immediate surroundings prepared from secret information given to Operation Foxley, summer 1944.

than sixty years later, remembered with tears in her eyes how her mother had wept at leaving. Hitler paid a modest 48,000 Goldmarks (in the Weimar currency) for the chalet – not out of his own pocket, although royalties from Mein Kampf had made him rich. As usual, he left Bormann to take care of all that.

Bormann, like Heinrich Hoffmann, played a major role in Eva's life, especially once she came to live at the Berghof. Like most people in Hitler's circle, she disliked him intensely for his sly manipulativeness, his determination to monopolise Hitler and his iron control over the entire Obersalzberg complex, which he ran with robotic efficiency. A secret rivalry arose between them – secret, at any rate, from the Führer – but Eva always knew that in the last resort Hitler would back his 'most loyal party comrade', whom he trusted absolutely. She never risked an open confrontation.

Bormann was a complicated man from a simple background. His father, a former Prussian regimental sergeant major (hence, perhaps, his son's obsession with discipline and order) later became a post office employee; the young Bormann dropped out of school to work as an agricultural labourer. As with so many of Hitler's associates, the First World War – in which he served as a cannoneer in a field artillery regiment – created opportunities for him to rise above his provincial origins. In 1927 he joined the NSDAP and by 1928 was its business manager, controlling and dispensing much of its funds. That was the year he met Hitler for the first time, so he wasn't one of the 'Old Faithful' comrades who had been in the party from the very beginning. He became a Nazi delegate to the Reichstag and, in July 1933, head of Cabinet to the deputy Führer, Rudolf Hess (another of Hitler's earliest Nazi associates). Bormann's superlative abilities as an organiser and bureaucrat persuaded the Führer to give him immense responsibility over the party's finances as well as Hitler's own personal wealth, and to delegate to him the purchase and running of the Berghof. Putzi Hanfstängl, in a savagely accurate turn of phrase, described him 'licking the wishes off his master's lips and barking them out as orders'.

Bormann also doled out Eva's money and although, by order of Hitler, her allowance was generous she was always aware that it came, not directly from her lover but indirectly, from her hated rival. Bormann did his best to intimidate her, making her feel dependent since all her bills were paid by him. The humiliation of having to ask Bormann every time she needed money for her dressmaker or the manicurist must have been very great.

Bormann's rise within Hitler's inner circle to the point where he controlled the finances of the top party leaders went largely unnoticed. He was unimpressive to look at, squat, overweight and ugly. Because of his coarse manner and lack of culture he was underestimated by those like Göring who fancied themselves connoisseurs and lived like princes. Reticent and obsequious in the presence of his boss, arrogant and overbearing behind his back, Bormann manoeuvred himself into Hitler's favour until he was topmost of all the top dogs. He would behave ingratiatingly towards them in public – giving the impression that all was peace and harmony – while secretly manoeuvering behind their backs to undermine them. By the time they realised the full extent of his power it was too late to dislodge him. But he was the right-hand man who controlled access to the *Führer*; he had the power to inflate or blacken a newcomer's reputation. A formidable opponent, he resented Eva's role at the Berghof and was forever plotting to get the better of her. Not surprisingly, they hated each other – but in secret. Hitler would never have tolerated open enmity.

Having acquired Haus Wachenfeld, Hitler decided it should be enlarged and furnished in a style more suited to important guests and visiting heads of state, making the house much more than a weekend retreat: more a centre of government and military operations. This decision set off an avalanche of compulsory purchases by his associates, vying with each other for the biggest house and finest possessions. It was a contest that Göring won easily, amassing a vast fortune in plundered property and art. Hitler's establishment was much more modest, a fact he was well aware of and even joked about. When a visitor praised the Berghof he said, 'My Berghof of course can't compare with Carinhall [Göring's main residence in the Schorfheide, north of Berlin. Indeed, the Berghof hardly compared with his oversized and overstuffed residence on Obersalzberg.] Maybe it could serve as his gardener's house.' Like Stalin, Hitler's taste when it came to his own living quarters was for rooms that were plain and even ascetic. He permitted his henchmen to indulge in opulence but had no desire for it himself.

Bormann was the moving spirit behind the transformation of Obersalzberg, seizing the opportunity to enlarge his own sphere of influence and please the *Führer*. Between 1935 and 1940, in fifty-two separate transactions he requisitioned chalets, farms, land, forests, evicting the owners ruthlessly and buying up 600 acres of woodland

and 200 acres of farmland. Between 1935 and 1940 more than four hundred people, most of them peasant farmers who had lived there for generations, were forced out of their homes to accommodate the Nazi entourage. Those who refused to sell were threatened with – and sometimes sent to – nearby Dachau. Untroubled by moral scruples, Bormann took what he wanted, turning the old farming village into a fortress. The land and buildings of Obersalzberg were compulsorily purchased for slightly more than six million Reichsmarks,[14] paid out of Nazi Party coffers. Trees were felled and houses demolished to ensure that the *Führer* had the best possible view and in 1936 Bormann moved with his family to live in one of the better chalets, having worked out that Obersalzberg would soon be Hitler's second centre of operations, in which case Bormann wanted to be on hand. Ten years after Hitler had first rented Haus Wachenfeld in 1928, the little rural hamlet had been annexed as his private preserve. It is evidence of the *Führer*'s financial naiveté and the absolute trust he placed in his closest colleague that he almost certainly never realised that everything except the Berghof itself had been bought in Martin Bormann's name[15] so that by 1939 Bormann, personally, owned the entire village.

Surrounded by guards and high fences, set amid pine-scented walks below which lay Berchtesgaden and beyond it, to the west, the ice-cold Königssee, Obersalzberg was turned into a military encampment as well as a Nazi stronghold. It had barracks, a guardroom for the SS and accommodation for security personnel, a gym with boxing ring, a drilling ground and rifle range; a hospital for severely wounded members of the *Wehrmacht*, a wireless station, three telephone exchanges and a post office, as well as a tea house, kindergarten, school and theatre; even a model farm (the former Gutshof) that produced food for the inhabitants all year round from greenhouses growing fruit and vegetables.[16] Everything was there to serve the *Führer*, the dark spider at the centre of a web of army officers, *aides-de-camp*, soldiers, security guards, secretaries (Eva's 'cover' forced her to pretend to be one of them), cooks, housekeepers, housemaids and guests. Obersalzberg was

14. In 1938 one could get a decent meal in a restaurant for RM1.20, a litre of milk cost RM0.24 and an egg RM0.12.
15. See Helmut Schoner and Rosl Irlinger, *Der Alte Obersalzberg Bis 1937* (Munich: Verlag Berchtesgadner Anzeiger, 1989). (Rosl had lived at Obersalzberg as a child.)
16. Burleigh, *The Third Reich: A New History*, p. 274.

now Hitler's second centre of operations after Berlin. Besides all the usual accommodation the former hotel, Gasthof zum Türken, had been converted into sleeping quarters for the SS. For the next eight years the future of Germany and its forty-five million inhabitants and the fate of half Europe were planned in this monumental Hitler New Town, with the craggy Alpine landscape as a backdrop. Hitler told a visitor, 'My ideas mature here.'

Eva had been hoping for an intimate retreat for the two of them but she had no desire to live among tedious and intrusive politicians, let alone at the centre of a military headquarters. She had much preferred the cosy old Haus Wachenfeld but by the time Hitler had finished it was more than twice its original size and quite unrecognisable. He acted as his own architect on the redesign and when it was finished Speer commented coolly (out of earshot), 'it wasn't good but it wasn't bad either'.[17] The *Führer* may have intended to preserve the comfortable middle-class atmosphere of the original Bavarian chalet but the alterations made nonsense of that.[18] By the time the rebuilding and additions were finished the total cost of the newly christened Berghof was nearly 175,660 Reichsmarks, more than £700,000 in today's money.

As well as a new wing and basement garage on the east side of the house, in the main house a colossal reception area known as the Great Hall was created, looking like the hall of the Nibelungen and furnished like a commercial travellers' hotel. Huge upholstered sofas and giant armchairs covered in patterned moquette squatted with elephantine immobility. The hall was dominated by the largest window ever made from a single pane of glass, with a view of the Untersberg, Berchtesgaden down in the valley and, on good days, Salzburg. It was rendered yet more grandiose by a marble fireplace, Persian carpets and a Gobelin tapestry. This room summed up the contrast between Hitler's aesthetic aspirations and his private tastes. Behind the dull but valuable tapestry was a hidden screen that could be rolled into place by pressing a button, creating a private cinema. Here Hitler would watch his favourite films:

17. Sereny, *Albert Speer: His Battle with Truth*.
18. From Walden's website: http://thirdreichruins.com/berghof.htm. Plans were made to remodel Haus Wachenfeld in 1935. The work carried out in 1936 actually involved a total conversion, with large masonry additions of a main house and added wing, and an enlarged garage. Further work took place in 1938. Another site, posted by someone who denies any neo-Nazi connections, has many pictures of the Berghof/Haus Wachenfeld.

King Kong,[19] *Snow White and the Seven Dwarfs* – he was particularly fond of whistling 'Who's Afraid of the Big Bad Wolf?' – *The Lives of a Bengal Lancer* and, most improbably, *Metropolis*.[20] He was especially fond of Marlene Dietrich's films – apparently because he liked looking at her legs. Sometimes two films an evening would be shown, according to Herbert Döring, who later became manager (*Verwalter*) of the Berghof.

The dining room table seated sixteen. The living room was no longer a cosy *Stube*, or parlour; it was '. . . big, grand and monumental, like everything Hitler built, but cold. The room was too large and the people too small to fill it.'[21] Although he claimed to be a great connoisseur of music there were never chamber concerts in the Great Hall. Hitler preferred to listen to a selection of his favourite records: excerpts from Wagnerian operas, one or two movements from Bruckner's 7th Symphony and the bits of Mozart he liked best. For light opera he chose arias from *Die Lustige Witwe* (*The Merry Widow*), *Die Fledermaus* and his favourites from the weightier but still spirited *La Bohème*, *Madame Butterfly*, Verdi's *Aida* and Weber's *Der Freischütz*.

Hitler now had thirty rooms at his disposal (of which ten were bedrooms), opening off wide corridors lined with books – leather-bound editions of the classics, rarely opened – and a vast, imposing study with acres of desk space. The rooms were lit by hideous chandeliers and hung with hideous paintings from what can best be described as the Nazi Realist school. Unlike Göring, who 'requisitioned' – that is, stole – the pictures he wanted,[22] Hitler obtained most of his works of art relatively honestly. From 1941 onwards many were bought from Maria Almas-Dietrich, an art dealer who – not that he knew this – was a quarter Jewish.

By mid-1936 Eva had been accepted by the domestic staff at the

19. 'A frightful story, but it had Hitler absolutely spellbound. He talked about it for days,' scoffed Putzi Hanfstängl, *Hitler: The Missing Years* (London: Eyre and Spottiswood 1957), p. 221.
20. Improbable because this silent black and white film of 1927 showed workers pitted against their bosses.
21. Junge, *Bis Zur Letzten Stunde*.
22. These thefts were 'legalised' on 31 May 1938 by a law that stated: 'Products of "degenerate" art that have been secured in museums . . . can be appropriated by the Reich without compensation.' In this way important pictures by Braque, Chagall, Modigliani, van Gogh, Gauguin and Picasso could be 'appropriated' and, in some cases, sold on to museums outside Germany for high prices. (See Berthold Hinz, *Art in the Third Reich* (Oxford: Basil Blackwell, 1980), p. 43.)

Berghof although barred from all formal or official functions. Hitler encouraged her to invite her friends to stay – a concession not granted to anyone else at Obersalzberg – and she filled its chill, pompous spaces with young people, bringing lightness and entertainment to his life. She also decided it was high time he took some exercise. The *Führer* was beginning to look stolidly middle aged, even paunchy. This would not do for Germany's redeemer, its all-bestriding despot and figurehead. He must be persuaded to go for walks. Hitler had never climbed a mountain worthy of the name but he loved looking out on grand panoramas. Although the Nazi régime placed great emphasis on health and vigorous exercise, the *Führer* was extremely lazy – except in Hoffmann's propaganda photographs, which show him in manly poses, standing in front of a pile of logs, even sometimes sporting *Lederhosen* (leather shorts) and Bavarian peasant costume, though he is never actually seen chopping wood.

From 1933 onwards the Nazi Party, guided by the malign genius of Josef Goebbels steadily built its leader and his creed into an apocalyptic cult that demanded unwavering dedication from its adherents, a state 'counter-church' offering total explanations of the past, present and future.[23] They painted pictures in the clouds of a reborn Fatherland led by heroes and inspired by martyrs (the ruffians who had died in the Beer Hall Putsch of 1923 and young thugs like Horst Wessel, killed in 1930), giving the party faithful an iconography and images that shaped their dreams. Anyone who threatened their unity was disposed of. On 30 June 1934 the Nazis, led by Hitler in person, had carried out the Röhm putsch, a preventative measure to stop a planned revolt by Chief of Staff Ernst Röhm and his radical cronies.[24] Several leaders of the SA, including Röhm himself – a very early follower of the party and one of only four men with whom Hitler was on a first-name and '*Du*' basis – were executed. Hitler personally arrested him and tore off his decorations. The conspirators were shot on 1 July 1934.

Under cover of doctrines glorifying 'racial purity'[25] the Nazis perverted the language, using brilliantly chosen metaphors to justify sending the 'sub-humans' who 'polluted' the Aryan race to camps,

23. From a report for the ousted Social Democratic Party leadership, cited by Burleigh, *The Third Reich: A New History*, pp. 5–8.
24. Sereny, *Albert Speer: His Battle with Truth*, p. 115.
25. Known today by just as weaselly a euphemism, 'ethnic cleansing'.

asylums, hospitals, hard labour or worse. They orchestrated rituals in which all 'pure' Germans could take part, with torchlight processions and the mass glorification of a reborn *Übermensch* in the person of Hitler himself. Behind the spectacle, Nazi ministries and assiduous civil servants beavered to fulfil his promises. The nightmare was underway, gathering appalling momentum as each new horror passed with little public outcry, as though the latest atrocity were an exaggerated comic episode out of a Chaplin or Buster Keaton film, skinny, timid Jewish figures tumbling over each other to avoid the gleaming, black-booted SS. Ha ha ha – see how they run![26] This warped ideology was implemented from Berlin but it had its origins in Bavaria.

In the course of my research for this book I knew I had to visit the places where its narrative had happened, in an attempt to understand what drew Hitler to Berchtesgaden and why he had refined his schemes for annihilation *here*, of all places.[27] I went twice; first in the late summer of 2003. Each day was heralded by a cool, delicate sunrise. I would sit at the table outside my chalet in the fresh morning air, eating dark rye bread and a local egg for breakfast, drinking coffee (a taste for wickedly strong coffee is a legacy from my mother), reading or making notes, before taking the steep mountain path down towards Berchtesgaden. The little medieval town in the valley was packed with tourists and, like them, I wandered about, observing, eavesdropping, buying post-cards and noting traces of Nazi inscriptions and insignia, barely visible under several layers of whitewash. There was no reference anywhere to its most famous resident: no plaques reminding visitors that the station had been designed by Albert Speer or that the small pizza parlour beside the River Ach was once the first guard post on the road leading up to the Berghof. Berchtesgaden

26. German propaganda elided Jews with vermin, notoriously exemplified by the film *The Eternal Jew*, which has a famous sequence of rats pouring out of a hole, cross-cut with Jews pouring out of a ghetto. The film is no longer publicly screened and I haven't seen it, but the DVD is widely available on the Internet and a copy may be seen on request at the Imperial War Museum, London. I have taken the above description from Rainer Rother of the Deutsches Historisches Museum, Berlin, an expert on Third Reich archive film and pictures.
27. There is a good selection of photographs including one of Berchtesgaden station and many others from the thirties of Berchtesgaden and the Obersalzberg complex at www.thirdreichruins.com/bgaden.htm

today is an orderly theme park of all that's best in the German character. Everybody works hard and cheerfully, children obey their parents, wives obey their husbands and men obey authority. Even teenagers are respectful and trains always run on time. The town has suffered a collective amnesia since Hitler's day and its embarrassing past has almost been obliterated.

The one exception to this white-out is Dokumentation Obersalzberg, a recently opened historical centre sited almost directly above Hitler's wartime bunker. One day I took a coach trip up the lower slopes of the mountain to visit it. A long room divided into booths exhibited memorabilia and photographs from the Third Reich. I listened through headphones to Hitler's speeches and was surprised how moderate he sounded, his voice pitched low and slow until the gradual crescendo reached its screaming, orgasmic conclusion, speaker and audience hysterical with hatred. In the same section there was a display of news photographs taken when the extermination camps were liberated in May 1945. They showed flaccid, skeletal bodies, some dead, some alive, the two almost indistinguishable: the genocide in black and white. People studied them in silence before climbing to the next level to watch a video in which aged former residents from the once tiny hamlet of Obersalzberg described how their homes and farms were taken over, torn down and rebuilt as lavish country villas for the *Führer* and his entourage. One old man interviewed in 1989, choking back his tears at the memory of the family's eviction, said, 'My mother was born here and so was I and so were all my brothers and sisters: twelve or thirteen, I can't remember.' 'Of course life changed on the mountain,' said Rosa Irlinger, who had been a child when Hitler first arrived. 'It was very quiet when we were little. And then, after 1933, it became one vast construction site . . . Suddenly swarms of people started coming to tramp up the mountain and stand as close as they could get to Hitler's house until he came out. And then they would scream, applaud, sob, laugh hysterically, even fall to their knees.'

The coach carried on, passing without comment the peaceful, grassy site of the Berghof. Nothing remains. On the high bluff overlooking a panorama of mountains and neat fields, hidden among tall trees, is an overgrown area with shards of brick and rubble revealing the building's foundations. A few people wandered round, guidebook and camera in hand. They didn't look like Hitler devotees; they came in family groups, explaining to the children, fending off tricky questions by pointing through the dense pines to where Hitler's tea house once stood, its splendid view obliterated now by the height of the trees. Before leaving, a few slipped a lump of pinkish-red brick the size of a matchbox into a handbag or trouser pocket, to be taken home, labelled 'piece of brick from Hitler's Berghof' and displayed along with the holiday photographs. Did the fragments possess some sort of numinous charge, like the finger of Saint Foy or a splinter from the Holy Cross, as if they retained something of Hitler's aura? Or did people take them in the same spirit as they took stones from the Berlin Wall, to prove 'I Was There'? This was how the Nazi Party was founded, by people who weren't, on the whole, racist thugs. A brick here and there, starting in the early 1920s, and the foundations were laid.

Finally the coach reached the 1,834-metre[28] summit of the Kehlstein, on whose peak stands the fake medieval building called Kehlsteinhaus, later christened by the Americans the Eagle's Nest. It was constructed on Bormann's orders as a fiftieth birthday present to the Führer from his people. It came out of their taxes and cost 30 million Reichsmarks.[29] It is true that the views from up there are glorious.

In the evenings I went back to my little chalet, opened a cool bottle of wine and listened in the long, slow dusk to the trilling of the crickets, the shrieks of children playing before bedtime round the adjacent farm and the tetchy bleating of sheep. I gazed at the spectacular view – exactly the view that Eva and Hitler and their guests had overlooked from the Berghof terrace. Indoors, after supper (smoked meat and sausage, again with rye bread), I read Joseph Roth's The Radetsky March and Antony Beevor's Berlin, two books that bracket the history of the Third Reich.

28. 6,700 feet above sea level.
29. In 1938 RM34 was roughly equivalent to £100 or $170 today.

Chapter Thirteen

Mistress

Hitler's relationship with Eva was about coming home. He also wanted sex, probably; love, maybe; but he chose her mainly because she was the perfect woman to come home to. It goes without saying that Eva played no part in his political life in Berlin. All she knew was that it took him away from the Berghof for weeks on end. The *Führer* needed a loving, undemanding young woman to welcome him back and Eva fitted that description. Subtly, unobtrusively, she made herself indispensable and it seems that Hitler found himself growing genuinely fond of her. In spite of being concealed, denied and despised by the '*hohe Tiere*', the big beasts of Obersalzberg, Eva Braun had the secret satisfaction of having proved them wrong. She'd sworn to 'capture' Hitler and she'd succeeded. She was to spend the nine years from 1936 onwards as the invisible woman behind the *Führer*.

To understand the apparent paradox of their fourteen-year relationship it's essential to grasp – as Hitler's associates did not – that he wasn't looking for 'an alpha female' but for someone who would create the simple routine he liked best, who could get him to relax. Soon the Obersalzberg crowd had to admit, with some relief, that Eva *did* make Hitler relax. Her presence at the Berghof created a more comfortable atmosphere since if he relaxed, everyone else could relax too. She provided a refuge from the strain and pressures of his public role and the emotional marathons of his speeches. By now the *Führer* was a one-party dictator with the power of life and death over millions but another side of him craved the balm of affection for his own sake, not homage for his position. When his Munich housekeeper Anna Winter, who didn't like Eva and, like so many others, underestimated her intelligence, asked Hitler how, with his serious mind, he could put up with her chatter he answered, 'Eva keeps my mind off things I don't want to think about. She gives me a rest.'[1] Nor was his mind as unremittingly serious as he would have people believe. He loved kitsch and liked to watch the latest German and American films while holding her hand like a teenager. Eva loved all that too – movies and operettas, musicals, gossip and film stars. She fantasised about going to Hollywood: 'When the Chief [Hitler] has won the war,' she would tell her friends, 'he has promised that I can play my own part in the film of our life story.' Hitler indulged these harmless aspirations. Eva's real reward, said cousin Gertraud, was that 'She was important and necessary to him – she *meant* something, not just as a playmate but also as a person.'[2] She provided him with the one element in life that great men lack: not power, not esteem, not fame or wealth but *pleasure*.

What did his closest friends, the men he had known from the party's earliest days whose judgement he trusted, and equally if not more important, what did their venomous, competitive wives make of Eva Braun? She was twenty-three, an age at which she should have been without cares or responsibilities, but she had beautiful manners, looked nice, did her best to be friendly and was socially adroit; yet no one gave her credit for her efforts and she was unkindly, snobbishly treated. Few people bothered to disguise the fact that they thought her a fool, the men perhaps because they had been rebuffed, the women because they were jealous. Most of the élite wives disliked her, even the gentle and retiring Margret Speer, though in due course Margret changed her mind. She may have been jealous of Eva's friendship – *unthinkable* that it could have been an affair – with Albert, her charismatic and good-looking young husband.

Albert Speer had been appointed Hitler's chief architect in 1934 at the age of twenty-nine. Architecture is a potent yet subliminal way of expressing a nation's politics and ideology, a point that Hitler the frustrated architect understood better than most. He also knew that by the monuments he leaves behind a man's name and memory may be perpetuated for centuries, even millennia, and desired this immor-

1. Interview with Frau Winter, Munich, 3 September 1948, from the Musmanno Collection.
2. Gertraud Weisker in conversation with the author, 2001.

tality for himself. 'His version of the world he wanted to make to commemorate himself and his ideology was complete, overwhelming and Pharaonic.'[3] He chose the young and unknown Speer to build it for him, with giant buildings in concrete-clad marble and granite. Hitler spent hours poring over architectural plans and vast vistas with his new protégé, whom he thought of as his *alter ego*, the man he himself would have liked to be. Speer realised Hitler's vision in thousands of cubic metres of soulless monoliths, '*Führer* architecture', the defining art of the Third Reich, that reflected his patron's obsessional, unbending nature better than he ever realised.

Speer was one of the very few halfway decent human beings in Hitler's entourage[4] (though not quite as decent as he later tried to make out). He was always on Eva's side, describing her as 'very young, very shy and very modest'. He explained in more detail:

> She was very much a man's woman. That's borne out by the reac-tion of the secretaries and also by my wife, who was not enthusi-astic about Eva Braun at all. I myself and a number of the men around Hitler all liked her. It's curious because she was not a flirt, you know, that was not it. She was very much of a lightweight but with real feeling and a real capacity for *joie de vivre*. She was not anti-Semitic, she had no such feelings. She was a simple girl and simple people can be better than others.[5] [. . .] She was of course very feminine, incredibly undemanding for herself, helpful to many people behind the scenes – nobody ever knew that – and infinitely thoughtful of Hitler. She was a restful sort of girl. And her love for Hitler was beyond question.[6]

Speer believed 'she has been much maligned . . . she was a very nice girl'.[7] Restful . . . shy . . . modest . . . diffident . . . eager to please . . . undemanding . . . she doesn't sound like a vulgar, exploitative chit ready to offer sex in exchange for money, power or status. Gitta Sereny, no apologist for Hitler's hangers-on, concluded:

3. Robert Hughes, speaking in a long-lost 1978 interview with Speer, quoted in the *Guardian*, 1 February 2003.
4. Baron Freytag von Loringhoven was another; Dr Brandt perhaps another.
5. Interviewed in 2000 for *Adolf and Eva*, 3BMTV, roll 6.03.13.
6. Sereny, *Albert Speer: His Battle with Truth*, p. 193.
7. Ibid.

'She [Eva Braun] was gentle and gay, in the old sense of the word – and she maintained a lightness for him and that is why this simple young woman was so important to him. Hitler wanted somebody with whom he didn't have to *think*. She brought an element of life to Hitler which existed for him in the thirties but not after 1941, which must have been a very important thing for him.'[8]

Eva Braun had many sterling qualities. She was remarkably loyal, and not only to Hitler. The friends from her teens remained friends all her life. She kept in touch with a number of schoolfriends going right back to the days when she was only seven or eight and loved to visit them and talk about old times. She never took advantage of her position to lord it over the household staff, never lost her temper with them but talked to them as equals. Anna Plaim stressed that Eva 'didn't hold with being distant and I never heard her utter an insult or even a rebuke. She was not at all the typical employer who makes sure the staff know their place,'[10] while Traudl Junge noted at their first meeting, 'I was struck by her natural and unaffected manner.'

She tried to retain some independence for as long as possible. She continued to work intermittently at Hoffmann's shop during the times when she wasn't at the Berghof, which gave her the sense of having some money that was legitimately her own. Hitler called her 'proud', remembering how long it was before she would take money from him. He loved to ramble and reminisce with his secretaries in private and Traudl Junge recorded her boss's early impressions of his *Freundin*:[11]

'Above all she's proud. At the beginning she was working for Heinrich Hoffmann and really had to be careful with money, yet it took years before she'd even let me pay her taxi fare and for ages she slept in the office on a bench so that she'd always be

8. Gitta Sereny interviewed for *Adolf and Eva*, 3BMTV, roll 9.18.44.
9. Transcript of interview with Rochus Misch from *Adolf and Eva*, 3BMTV, roll 15.34.
10. Plaim and Kuch, *Bei Hitlers: Zimmermädchen Annas Erinnerungen*, p. 70.
11. *Freundin* is a neutral word that can simply mean 'girlfriend' but often has an added sexual connotation.

on hand if I rang, since their phone at home couldn't handle long-distance calls. It wasn't until a couple of years ago that I managed to get her to allow me to buy her that little house in Bogenhausen.'[12]

In wasn't just her good looks; Eva's good qualities also attracted Hitler to her in the first place. He knew he could trust her.

Hans Karl von Hasselbach, one of Hitler's surgeons between 1934 and 1944, commented:

That Eva Braun loved him with deep devotion is certain. Despite the external luxury her hopes were never completely fulfilled. *She hardly ever gave the impression of being happy.* [My italics.] Whether she wanted children I do not know; in any case they were denied her. But since Hitler would not make Eva openly his wife and since illegitimate children would have destroyed his greatness in the eyes of the German people he was forced to renounce them. It is absolutely certain that Hitler was faithful to Eva Braun and doubts about his fidelity were never expressed. Eva probably never had any influence on political affairs and always avoided political discussions. Hitler did not think much of the political and intellectual capabilities of women and his decision could never have been influenced by a woman.[13]

Throughout their relationship, Eva Braun was scrupulous in not exploiting her privileged position so close to Hitler, not a virtue found in every tyrant's companion. She never tried to influence him or accepted favours in return for seeking advancement for others.

Hitler gained from her vivacious presence but for Eva the new setting presented problems. She was cut off from everything that had sustained her for the first twenty-four years of her life. The places and people who had always grounded her – the network of aunts and cousins, her grandfather in Beilngries, her Catholic faith, the flat in Hohenzollernstrasse that had been her home for more than ten years

12. Junge, *Bis Zur Letzten Stunde*, p. 121 (translated by the author).
13. From NARA, HQ Military Intelligence Service: OI Special Report entitled *Adolf Hitler: A Composite Picture.*

– none of this counted at the Berghof. Her past was nothing, she herself a nobody. True, her sister was with her at the Berghof, but Gretl was a slender reed. Eva supported her, rather than the other way round. Later on her parents were persuaded to overcome their scruples and visit their daughters but for the time being her father was implacable. During this lonely time Eva paid several visits to Beilngries, although both her grandparents were now dead. On one occasion she drove to the little town on the Altmühl River in a Mercedes lent by Hitler, accompanied by two SS bodyguards. She visited her grandparents' grave regularly and when she couldn't go in person she sent flowers to adorn it: the observant Catholics of Beilngries noticed that there were always fresh carnations on the Kronburger family grave. Perhaps this persuaded them to overlook the Mercedes.

Fräulein Braun had apparently got what she wished for but it can't have been what she expected, surrounded as she was by sycophantic domestic staff, the *Führer*'s good-looking adjutants, his bloated top dogs and toadies and the high-ranking Nazi wives who made no secret of their contempt. Few friends in Hitler's camp, then. The only people she could trust were those she had known since her teenage years in Munich, whom she invited to stay, if their busy family lives could spare them, for days or even weeks at a time. Herta Schneider, her lifelong friend and confidante, spent so much time 'on the Berg' that in time she and her two young daughters were allotted a small flat of their own.

Henriette von Schirach observed: 'Eva lived discreetly in the Berghof but took no part in any discussions, asking no questions beyond which film they should watch that evening. She made no demands, so that buying presents was always a headache for Hitler until he left Bormann to cope with all that. Bormann chose moderately priced semi-precious jewellery and unremarkable paintings.'[14] Bormann would. There was a constant crowd of visitors to Obersalzberg but, if they were important or official guests, Eva had to leave or spend the day closeted in her room. 'He would not tolerate that she, this woman, could be seen.'[15] This ostracism annoyed Eva, who became 'angry, moody, truculent; she started complaining'.[16] Frau Mittlstrasse, the Berghof housekeeper during its later years, was more balanced in her judgement:

14. Henriette von Schirach, *Frauen um Hitler* (Munich: Herbig, 1983), p. 231.
15. Herbert Döring interviewed for *Adolf and Eva*, 3BMTV, roll 20.26.
16. Ibid., roll 15.20.26.

Eva was a likeable, charming Munich woman, but she kept her distance. If you accepted and liked her, then you'd get on very well with her. I was at her disposal in all kinds of ways: I was there when she ordered her clothes; I was there when she was buying hats. Not for shoes, though. She bought those in Italy, at Ferragamo in Florence.[17]

Surprisingly perhaps, Eva's shoes, like Hitler's, were repaired by the local master cobbler, Herr Kosian, who was a Catholic and therefore one of the local tradesmen whom people on the Berg were forbidden by Bormann to deal with. Eva ignored him.

In a memoir dictated decades after she had first joined the staff of the Berghof in 1941, Anna Plaim reflected on Eva's life 'on the Berg':

What was she supposed to *do* all day long? When he was away I had the impression that she and Hitler spoke on the phone very often. But nevertheless, her friends and her sister were all she had to make life moderately enjoyable, since actually she had nothing else to occupy her. She wasn't Hitler's wife so couldn't show herself openly; especially if he was at the Berghof when she had to retreat altogether, which for her certainly can't have been easy. And yet I believe she so idolised Hitler that she was prepared to sacrifice everything for him, above all the status of being his wife. All the same she praised him to the skies and took every opportunity to rave about his beautiful blue eyes. (They fascinated me, too.) Today I'm sure she never doubted that Hitler would marry her eventually. It's true that Eva Braun was imprisoned in a golden cage . . . definitely. On the one hand she could hardly ever leave the Berghof yet on the other, whatever she wanted was available there, to excess. Everything.[18]

Life as his mistress was not, on the face of it, arduous. It was intoxicating, for a while. Obersalzberg offered lakes, forests, mountain paths, a perfect background for the sporting activities she loved and excelled

17. Frau Mittlstrasse interviewed for *Adolf and Eva*, 3BMTV, roll 6.27.30.
18. Plaim and Kuch, *Bei Hitlers: Zimmermädchen Annas Erinnerungen*, pp. 87–8 (translated by the author).

at. She could spend hours sunbathing, go for long walks with her dogs, pick wild flowers; all pleasant enough ways of passing the time but not enough to keep her fully occupied. If she pined for the company of her own crowd she could go back to Munich to catch up on the gossip or go window shopping with her girlfriends. Only there could she let go, hold parties in her little house, go to the cinema or theatre, listen and dance to the latest records, study her own and her friends' and the stars' astrological charts, try on clothes and make-up. Eva could now buy anything she wanted, and as time went on she wanted a good deal.

In September 1936 a piece of unwelcome publicity threatened to end the Germans' trusting ignorance about their *Führer*'s private life. A French gutter press newspaper, *Paris Soir*, broke the story of Adolf and Eva under the headline 'Hitler's Women'. After touching on his relationships with Geli, the Mitford sisters and Leni Riefenstahl, it concluded: 'Right now the favourite is undoubtedly Eva Braun, daughter of a Munich teacher. Hitler has given up all other women in favour of her.' Her uncle Alois describes the effect this article had on him when he read it:

> I practically fell off my chair! Our little Eva! Impossible! Couldn't be true! The pretty child whom I had helped when she couldn't do her maths prep, for whom I'd done so many essays to save her from yet another disapproving report complaining that she hadn't done her homework; who – deeply imbued with her grandmother's piety – had said her prayers diligently every night? I hurled myself at the phone and rang her mother, my cousin Fanny. (My father and her mother, Josefa Kronburger, had been siblings.) Fanny was in a state of high indignation when I told her I'd just seen *Paris Soir* and I was astonished and delighted that she was evidently soon to be the *Führer*'s mother-in-law. 'Drop that nonsense!' she said; she was already in quite enough trouble over the story! She certainly wasn't going to discuss it over the phone. If I was that interested I'd have to get myself down to Munich and talk to her there.[19]

19. Winbauer, *Eva Braun's Familiengeschichte*, p. 3 (translated by the author).

He did so, finding Fritz and Fanny living in the apartment he'd visited as a hungry student, still the same unremarkable middle-class couple – 'nothing at all had changed in their solid bourgeois life'. Winbauer[20] goes on to give a detailed account of the affair between Eva his great-niece and Adolf Hitler his *Führer*, as divulged to him by cousin Fanny. At first she had been appalled when Eva confessed to the relationship but in time Fanny, ever the optimist, began to come round to the idea. She may have hoped that Hitler would eventually marry her daughter. She wasn't too upset; if anything, rather amused. Fritz, on the other hand was insulted, humiliated, exposed as an incompetent father. He was in a rage. Whatever impact the *Paris Soir* article may have had on the Braun family, it had no effect on German public opinion. As soon as its publication in France became known, the authorities removed all copies of the paper from the newsstands and played down the episode.

Fritz's world had fallen apart in 1934 (by which time Eva and the *Führer* had been lovers for more than two years) when he had learned – it's not known from whom but perhaps he finally put two and two together – about his daughter's 'sordid affair'. It made no difference that she was the mistress of Germany's idolised Chancellor; as far as he was concerned he had failed in his fatherly duty and Eva was a 'fallen woman'. Alois continued:

> He poured his heart out to me, not at home but in the Hofbräuhaus (a beer hall). There, in a quiet corner on the first floor, Fritz confessed that he'd long been suspicious and had eventually tried to persuade Eva to end this 'idiotic' friendship. He told me how enraged he'd been by the snide comments of his friends and colleagues and how this impudent 'fellow' was

20. Alois was by this time a successful journalist: editor-in-chief for the *Neue Mannheimer Zeitung* from 1933 until 1945 and then editor in chief for the *Heidelberger Tageblatt* after the war. He seems to have been comfortable working for the Nazis to have toed the party line in his work for the *Neue Mannheimer Zeitung*, with lots of propaganda articles under instruction from Goebbels, right to the end. Like so many of his colleagues, he continued with his career after the war and the transfer from one régime to another was very smooth. He is one of the journalists mentioned in a book about Nazi journalists in Mannheim, published in 1981, two years before his death. (I am grateful to Christiane Gehron for the information in this footnote, and for translating Alois's memoirs, all but a few pages.)

destroying their family life. He also told me about a letter he'd written to Hitler in September of the previous year, asking him to 'keep his hands off' Eva.[21]

What seemed to enrage him more than anything was that Hitler hadn't even had the grace to answer it. Instead, Fritz was summoned to the Rathaus in Munich and advised to join the party. He duly reported at Elisabethplatz, the local branch of the Nazi Party, but his application was rejected on grounds of political unreliability. Not until the following year was he deemed fit to join. He was rewarded with a low party number, implying that he'd been a member for years. His views had not changed but now he was entitled to wear a party uniform complete with high collar, Nazi eagle and oak leaves, which, although meaningless, eased his acceptance at the Berghof as well as in the increasingly one-track-minded Germany of 1936. Herr Braun shoved his scruples and his Bavarian patriotism into his knapsack and did as he was told.

Lodged at the very centre of the Nazi enclave, by 1937 Eva was in charge of Hitler's private life and his personal guests – an oddly assorted mixture of *his* early political cronies and *her* former school-friends, most of whom were thoroughly intimidated by their host.[22] In spite of this she gradually introduced new people from her own circle, young wives with delicious small children who helped to leaven the long-nosed formality of the grimly fecund Nazi women[23] and their place-seeking husbands. None of this can have been easy for a young woman with undeveloped social skills and little knowledge of rank and etiquette. She had to marshal people who were often twice her age, had no liking for her and less respect – yet by her natural warmth and her efforts not to have either favourites or enemies, Eva managed to lighten the atmosphere between the two sets at the Berghof.

From 1937 to 1940 it was Eva who drove this taxing social merry-go-round. Until she took up residence, Magda Goebbels – who idolised

21. Ibid., p. 15. For more details of this letter see also Chapter 9, pp. 145–147.
22. In Eva's home movies, people meeting Hitler for the first time, even frequent guests greeting him on arrival, display all the signs of obeisance and nerves. They smile too much, laugh too quickly at his jokes and their posture is humble and deferential. (NARA Moving Picture section, roll 1.242.2.)
23. Frau Bormann had ten children; Frau Goebbels seven; Frau Speer six.

Hitler and married her philandering husband Josef in 1931 partly to be close to the *Führer* – had performed the function of hostess. She continued to do so on formal or semi-official occasions when Eva was banished to her own quarters. Levity was not Magda Goebbels' strong point. She was a clever and beautiful woman and a dedicated Nazi but she had no idea how to amuse Hitler or enliven the company. Only Eva could playfully rebuke him when he talked too long in the evenings. When Hitler was on the point of sending everyone to sleep, Eva would say, 'Oh come on, Adolf, that's enough talk – let's watch a film!' or, 'Time we all went to bed!' The pair would retire discreetly, Eva following Hitler up the grand staircase to their adjacent rooms. The guests could only speculate on what happened next.

At the start of their relationship he had behaved towards her as he did towards any other woman: with impeccable politeness. Discretion was rigidly maintained and they were never demonstrative in public. Eva had to act like just another secretary. The precise relations between them continued to be a puzzle around which speculation whirled.[24] In front of servants he addressed her as 'Fräulein Braun'. When they were with members of the innermost circle, the only people he trusted, he would occasionally use her nickname, '*Tschapperl*',[25] a word that translates roughly as 'bumpkin' or, at best, 'wench'. It may not have been quite as disparaging as it sounds. In Austria – including the village of Spittal where his mother, Klara Pölzl, was born – it may also indicate affection, so it was equivalent perhaps to calling Eva a 'plump little partridge'. It was understood among Hitler's henchmen and their wives that she could not be referred to in public, ever, because she *didn't exist*. In private the Nazi wives looked down their noses and referred to her as 'EB' or '*die blöde Kuh*' – the silly cow, though not within earshot of the *Führer*. The unspoken convention on the Berg decreed that for much of the time everyone behaved as if Eva were simply not there. She alternated between being acknowledged as hostess and denied as mistress.

If the inner circle found Eva's position ambivalent, the domestic staff were clearly given to understand that Fräulein Braun headed the house-

---

24. Junge, *Bis Zur Letzten Stunde*, p. 115 (translated by the author).
25. Private communication from Gertraud Weisker to the author: 'I know from my aunt Fanny that Hitler nicknamed her "*Tschapperl*" which means "little idiot"' or in her original: '*Hitler hat ihr allerdings einen "KOSENAMEN" nämlich "TSCHAPPERL" gegeben. Das weiss ich von meiner Tante Fanny. Tschapperl bedeutet "kleines Dummerchen".*'

hold and would issue their daily orders. By the beginning of 1936 her role was established and Hitler instructed them to call her '*Chefin*', meaning Little Boss or The Lady in Charge; or '*gnädiges Fräulein*' (a respectful and courteous form of address that has no real equivalent in modern English). In private apparently, between themselves, the staff called her *die* Eva – 'The Eva' – or 'EB'. They were told never to refer to her by name to outsiders or in letters home; always as '*gnädiges Fräulein*'.[26] (Hitler was addressed with the formal '*Sie*' by everyone, even the highest Nazis, and not until they'd been together for years, did Eva call him '*Du*'. In referring to him, he was known as *der Führer* by everyone from Göring to the humblest housemaid, never as Herr Hitler, let alone, heaven forbid, Adolf.)

The Nazi families clustered on the Berg were serviced by a huge retinue of domestic and laundry staff, cooks and kitchen maids, waiters, nannies, messengers, telephonists, chauffeurs and security guards, at least as many as in a grand Victorian household. At Obersalzberg, 'upstairs, downstairs' was very much a reality. The Berghof and its attendant chalets lacked green baize doors with bells for every room marked on a board in the main servants' hall, but the hierarchy was as firmly in place. Every day scores of people had to be provided with food ranging from fresh cows' milk for the latest baby (though breast-feeding was preferred) to luxury banquets accompanied by fine wines for statesmen, royalty and other imposing visitors. The kitchens where these meals were prepared were ultra-modern in style and equipment, with huge white fridges, gleaming stainless steel sinks, rank upon rank of orderly cupboards painted white like the walls and hygienic tiled floors that were sluiced and scrubbed daily. Hitler had a separate kitchen to provide his vegetarian meals and two dieticians devising variations to tempt his appetite. There were platoons of nannies, aproned and uniformed, to care for the proliferating Nazi families, making sure that every child was quiet, obedient and spotlessly turned out, since at any moment the *Führer* might appear round the corner to pat a shining blonde head or lift a sweet-smelling toddler on to his lap. Then nanny would melt into the background and the mother stand beside Hitler for the inevitable photograph, framed and displayed as a cherished memento for generations to come. This was the smooth-running domestic unit that Eva supervised: not an easy position for a young woman in her early twenties, the same age as most of the undercooks and housemaids, and half as old as Frau Raubal, Hitler's formidable housekeeper.

26. Plaim and Kuch, *Bei Hitlers: Zimmermädchen Annas Erinnerungen* p. 71.

She was the main remaining obstacle. Geli's mother, while she remained there as housekeeper, was a constant reminder of the beloved girl she – and Hitler – had lost. For a year after Eva arrived at the Berghof, a secret struggle for power was played out between Hitler's fifty-year-old half-sister and his young mistress. It culminated in 1936 when Frau Raubal was dismissed at a moment's notice, partly for expressing too vehemently her resentment of Geli's successor. Herbert Döring, also part of the household, recalled: 'Frau Raubal didn't like Eva at all. They were like cat and dog. She told her brother off severely about Eva Braun being given one of the places of honour at the party conference [in 1936] and he became so angry that he banned his sister from Obersalzberg straightaway. The next day she had to pack her bags immediately and leave.'[27] Evidently he had never really liked Geli's mother, whom he described as 'robust and coarse', and was not sorry when she went. Surprisingly soon afterwards Frau Raubal met and married a high school head teacher, Professor Hammitsch, and went off to live with him in Dresden, after which she seldom saw her half-brother.[28] Perhaps Adolf felt guilty about letting Eva supplant her after nine hard-working years at the Berghof but, whatever the reason, he remembered her in his will, leaving her and his sister Paula RM1,000 each per month, for life.

A new housekeeper, Elsa, was hired from Munich, where she had been on the staff of the Osteria Bavaria. She and Eva had a good working relationship, despite the fact that Eva was much younger. In due course Elsa left and Döring, who had already been on the staff of the Berghof, was promoted. He in turn left in 1943 and was replaced by a married couple, Wilhelm and Margarete Mittlstrasse, who became and remained the Berghof's house managers. Frau Mittlstrasse liked and admired Eva: 'I would be summoned to her room in the morning after breakfast equipped with pen and paper and together we would go through the sequence of the day's events, what she had planned, and what my role was. She was a likeable, charming Munich woman but she kept a distance. She was not all over you.'[29] Eva's tact and

27. Herbert Döring interviewed for *Adolf and Eva*, 3BMTV, roll 16.20.
28. During the war, Herbert Döring claimed, Hitler offered his half-sister and her second husband safe haven at the Berghof and had them installed in a beautiful apartment on the second floor, with a view on to the Untersberg. If this is true it was an act of surprising generosity that can't have pleased Eva.
29. Frau Mittlstrasse interviewed for *Adolf and Eva*, 3BMTV, roll 6.22.31.

sensitivity towards the domestic team were diplomatic, bearing in mind her youth when her position was formalised and the fact that they had no idea how long she would stay. A son, Klaus, was born to the Mittlstrasses and a few years later a daughter, adding to the knee-high population that crawled, toddled or skipped across the terrace of the Berghof, stopping to cling fetchingly to Eva's hand or Hitler's knee. The *Führer* genuinely liked children and was gratified to watch the next generation being taught the essential German qualities of obedience, discipline and order, learning to respect their elders and love the Fatherland. They would be running it when he was an old man, driving forward his ideals, turning his plans for a higher, purer Europe into reality. These healthy little Speers and Görings and Goebbels and Mittlstrasses embodied the future.

Despite all her efforts, Eva remained Hitler's guilty secret. Uniquely among those at the Berghof, her name never appeared on the list of in-house telephone numbers while, to preserve her anonymity, her suite was listed as 'large guest room'.[30] Newcomers who asked about her were told 'She's part of the *Adjutantur* (private office), she's a secretary.'[31] This suited Hitler's purpose and it certainly worked – Eva remained completely unknown to the outside world. It must have been humiliating; a reminder that she was there for sexual and domestic purposes only, otherwise *persona non grata*. In this unequal relationship only one person counted: Adolf Hitler. Eva was his chattel and his dependant. As with Geli, she had no freedom of action. He was generous and liked to give her presents, but they were not always those she would have liked. His 1936 Christmas gift to her was a book about Egyptian tombs,[32] a reflection of his morbid and lifelong obsession with death but a bizarre present for a blooming twenty-five-year-old.

Henny von Schirach, a frequent guest at Obersalzberg since her childhood, said:

> Eva found her life as the invisible mistress depressing. In later years[33] she was often bad-tempered and ill because Hitler no longer took much notice of her. [. . .] She could have educated

---

30. Asserted by Rochus Misch in interview for *Adolf and Eva*, 3BMTV, roll 17.28.
31. Testimony by Herbert Döring for *Adolf and Eva*, 3BMTV, roll 15.17.28.
32. Beevor, *Berlin: The Downfall 1945*, p. 358.
33. She means the war years from 1941 to summer 1944, after which Hitler never returned to the Berghof.

herself, up there at the Berghof; she had every opportunity and every resource, but she just sat and waited while her life slipped by, so she had nothing to offer Hitler to interest him – anything that might have cut through his isolation. Her life was without effort or struggle; it was like a game, yet she wasn't happy. Outwardly she was perfect, changing her clothes and having her hair done, and apparently that's all Hitler wanted.[34]

Eva committed small illicit acts of defiance like smoking behind his back or wearing lipstick and nail varnish, both of which Hitler deplored, but they were only symbolic; she lacked Geli's spirit of rebellion. She seems to have tried hard to mould herself into his ideal woman, repressing her spontaneity and physical exuberance. She loved to dance but as Herbert Döring recalled:

> Eva had to do without everything with Hitler. You could see that when she was dancing. That turned her into a completely different person – you cannot imagine. She was a great dancer. Put on a gramophone record, wonderful, fast music, and all of a sudden Eva was as if transformed. She danced in a very elegant, racy way. Her favourite dance was the tango. The more sensual the dance, the more she gave herself up to it . . . I mean, she really got into the spirit of it. Hitler would only ever make fun of this dancing.[35]

Once Frau Raubal had gone, Eva no longer had to sleep at the Platterhof but moved to the inner sanctum of the Berghof itself. She was allocated three rooms directly adjoining Hitler's on the main first floor corridor and a room opposite for her personal maid. Her position at the Berghof and in his life could at last be recognised. It was not talked about, but the inner circle no longer had to guess at her role. A connecting door linked her rooms and Hitler's through a luggage cupboard which did not open on to the corridor, and then his private bathroom.

Eva's suite was light and feminine, a haven for her and her girlfriends and often for Hitler as well. She was luxuriously provided for, with her own sitting room, dressing room, bedroom and bathroom, decorated in

34. Henriette von Schirach, *Frauen um Hitler* (Munich: Herbig, 1983), p. 255.
35. Herbert Döring interviewed for *Adolf and Eva*, 3BMTV, 2000, roll 15.05.27.

a sophisticated but feminine style, with the white walls and white furniture made fashionable in London by Syrie Maugham. It could not have been more different from her parents' cluttered flat with its heavy provincial furniture and patterned wallpaper. The sitting room – overlooking the usual mountain panorama – had two comfortable armchairs and a sofa upholstered in pale linen chintz patterned with dark blue flowers. These were on a normal human scale, unlike the vast cushioned suites elsewhere. The sofa was flanked by two white side tables with reading lamps and the unlisted telephone stood on a shelf behind. Above it hung a painting of a reclining nude for which Eva herself was said to have posed. Two large net-curtained windows were framed by long turquoise curtains, stacks of movie and fashion magazines were piled up on tables and a heap of fluffy animals that she called 'Meine Menagerie' (my zoo) cuddled up in a corner of the sofa. On one wall in the place of honour hung Eva's favourite picture of her lover, a brooding, idealised portrait by Theodor Bohnenberger. At the other end stood a small desk at which she would spend hours writing letters or sticking in photographs. She kept a couple of bullfinches in a cage and would sometimes release them so that they could fly freely round the room.

Her bedroom next door was dominated by a capacious double bed covered by a thick duvet. Gretel Mittlstrasse, backed up by her husband Willi, said it was perfectly obvious that Hitler sometimes shared it with Eva. There was a white kneehole dressing table with three mirrors (large, small and magnifying), a set of engraved silver brushes, a crystal powder-puff holder, four glass scent bottles and yet another framed photograph of Hitler. A separate dressing room accommodated her growing collection of clothes; hats, handbags and the fine Italian shoes handmade for her in Florence, as well as drawers full of hand-embroidered silk lingerie, every piece bearing her personal monogram: an E and a B locked together to look like a four-leaf clover or perhaps, with a bit of imagination, a butterfly.[36] Eva did spend a lot of money on her clothes but vanity was almost her only solace and she needed it to

36. Some of these items eventually found their way into the stock of specialist dealers handling memorabilia from the Third Reich and from there on to the Internet. There is, for example, a transparent nightie said to have belonged to her, priced at $750 (it is in fact a bed jacket, but perhaps a purveyor of Third Reich items can't be expected to know that) and a silk embroidered slip described as 'lingerie' and priced at $600. (In July 2004 these could be purchased privately from Reichrelic@aol.com)

give her confidence amid a patronising crowd who looked down on her as their social and marital inferior. She had found a new dressmaker in Berlin, Fräulein Heise, who designed clothes specially for her. Hitler paid – dressmakers' bills were the least of his problems.

Over the years she bought hundreds of dresses, including a number of spectacular evening gowns, as well as coats and jackets (sometimes fur), skirts and blouses, all the height of chic. Clothes became her major interest and took up hours of her time – selecting and ordering them, having fittings. Like any woman who studies fashion and film star magazines keenly, she kept up with the latest trends and quickly adopted them, sometimes buying direct from couturiers but more often getting the Berlin dressmaker to modify their designs for her. Her clothes can be read like her diary for insights into her character and the new life she was leading.

A few garments became old favourites, turning up again and again in the photographs, and these are the most significant. There was one particular military-style coat – double-breasted, with eight brass buttons marching down the front – that she was especially fond of, perhaps because it resembled one of Hitler's uniform coats, and this she continued to wear for years. (It can be seen in the picture of her arm-in-arm with Albert Speer.) Out on the terrace on a cool spring or autumn day she often wore a trim little tweed coat and skirt over a short sweater, the very outfit an English country lady might have picked, which would have appealed to Hitler's admiration (until 1939) of all things English. Eva dressed for herself but always with him in mind. Her clothes were elegant but demure, revealing her pretty arms and legs but never a glimpse of cleavage. That Hitler would not have approved. His taste was extremely conventional. To please him she often wore traditional Bavarian dirndl dresses and frilly white blouses, not to mention the ribbed white socks and lace-up shoes that went with them, sometimes with a small feathered hat as well, every inch the demure Bavarian housewife. He also liked modest striped, sprigged or spotted fabrics and sleeves that ended in crisp white cuffs – almost like a uniform – and would have been happiest to see her wear his favourite dresses several times in succession, complaining that he never knew which woman to expect. When she'd finished with a garment (meaning, worn it two or three times) she would pass it on to her sister or friends or, if they rejected her cast-offs, to the domestic staff.

Eva changed her clothes several times a day so as to be modishly dressed for every occasion but also to kill time and give rein to her fantasies – and sometimes, Hitler's. Anyone who studies her wardrobe soon notices how much of it was *white* – not only outdoor wear like shirts, shorts and swimsuits but also her perfectly starched blouses and sleek, shimmering evening gowns. Consciously or not, she was in bridal dress.

Eva had always been vain but in the past her extravagance was restricted by her modest salary. Now she could indulge herself for the first time (Hitler must have instructed Bormann to give her a free hand[37]) and she spent enormous sums, buying only the best. Her clothes were never vulgar. To take one example, she had a brown silk dressing gown in a heavy brocade that flowed down to the ankles and wrists, but was fastened with a single mother-of-pearl button at the waist. Utterly modest, it was at the same time disturbingly sexy. Her exquisite lingerie was never scanty or blatantly provocative but its delicate silk and lace textures invited the touch.

Finally, she had her own film star bathroom with tiled white walls, the latest squared-off porcelain fittings, chrome taps and an enormous bevelled mirror. It can be seen clearly in one of her home movies in which a pet bird – it looks like a jackdaw – perches on the taps and drinks from a jet of running water. Every room was kept spotless by the housemaids and filled every second day with vases of fresh flowers. It lacked the taste and artistry of Madame de Pompadour's exquisite jewel box of an apartment at Versailles, but Eva was no Pompadour. For a young girl who'd been living at home until a year ago, these fresh, light-filled rooms were breathtakingly luxurious.

Alone among the Berghof's massively grandiose spaces Hitler's small bedroom was modest to the point of austerity.[38] His accommodation was always spartan, his taste frugal. A narrow study led to his bedroom with a single bed like a field soldier's and a small bedside

---

37. Frau Winter said, 'Although she did not see much of Hitler he made up for it by spoiling her terribly. She could have everything and she took advantage of it.' Interview from the Musmanno Collection, 3 September 1948.

38. In an odd parallel it very much resembles the reconstruction of Van Gogh's room in the mental asylum at St-Rémy, near Arles, to which he went in 1889 at the height of his mania. Both have the same narrow iron bed on the right of a window looking out over a glorious view – mountains, flowers and the convent vegetable garden respectively – the same small bedside table and one upright wooden chair.

table. Anna Plaim was surprised to find a stack of books by Karl May, Eva's favourite Wild West author. In 1933 Hitler had been delighted to discover that Karl Ludecke, an early Nazi enthusiast and financial backer, shared his love for these 'cowboy and Indian' stories. He still read them and got a thrill out of them, he told Ludecke.[39] Another bedside table book was not an official report, a newspaper or Carlyle's biography of Kaiser Frederick II or Napoleon (his two favourite role models): it was *Max und Moritz*, the very collection of comic stories by Wilhelm Busch[40] that Eva and her sisters had relished when they were children. (It can't have been a coincidence that Busch also drew political cartoons for a newspaper ridiculing Jews, giving them long hooked noses, straggling black beards and furtive expressions.) Next to his bedroom Hitler had an equally small private study, with pictures of both his parents – made posthumously, one assumes – hanging above a desk on which lay a blotter, piles of papers and a box of chocolates. Nothing else but a central table and a small bookcase. Hitler was not just tidy but, said the maid Anna Plaim, '*pedantically* tidy', and insisted that his rooms be kept in immaculate order.[41]

Eva's rooms adjoining Hitler's, which were out of bounds to everyone except her sister Gretl and their very closest friends, confirmed that Eva Braun was the official mistress of Hitler and the Berghof. Her status was reinforced when she began to be chauffeured in her own black, open-topped Mercedes Roadster bearing the number IIA-19130 20E.[42] This car, her second, must have been a gift from Hitler, though Bormann probably asked for, and got, it free from Mercedes as a compliment to the *Führer*. It was the most significant and public gift he had ever given her. All the signs indicated that Hitler was pleased with his young mistress and regarded her as a long-term fixture.

Eva was thrilled, of course, by her rise to favour and the pampered life that came with it, but all she ever really wanted was Hitler's company, his attention, approval and love. He was used to her, fond of her, but did he *love* her? In private they addressed one another informally as '*Du*' and she called him Adolf, occasionally Adi. No one

39. Kershaw, *Hitler, 1889–1936: Hubris*, p. 387.
40. *Bei Hitlers: Zimmermädchen Annas Erinnerungen*, p. 123.
41. Ibid., pp. 123–8; details of Eva's and Hitler's private rooms are taken from this book.
42. This car was auctioned at a Classic Car Auction in Phoenix, Arizona, in January 1982 and sold for an estimated $1.2 million.

ever heard her use any warmer endearment. Later on he started to call her *Kindl* (child) or occasionally *Patscherl* or *Schnacksi*, pet names for an infant or a child, but they all fell short of 'Princess', his pet name for Geli.

Nonetheless, by 1937 Eva had succeeded in making herself indispensable. 'Hitler needed her, he *did* need her,'[43] said Albert Speer. If she had known this at the time, or if Hitler had been able to acknowledge it, her life would have been a great deal happier.

43. Gitta Sereny interviewed for *Adolf and Eva*, 3BMTV, roll 6.09.06.

Chapter Fourteen

1936 – Germany on Display: The Olympics

Sport played a crucial part in Eva's life. It was the one thing she had always been really good at. As a teenager she had come first in a ski competition and if she'd concentrated on improving her prowess at winter sports or gymnastics she could have been, if not Olympic standard, at any rate a serious contender. However, when Hitler was at the Berghof the need to be at his beck and call precluded hours of practising and in any case it's doubtful whether she would have had the discipline or stamina to persist with rigorous daily training. The ubiquitous poster images of idealised Nazi womanhood – strong, supple and fit, a worthy mate and a healthy mother – influenced her as they did millions of young German women. The propaganda intention behind compulsory exercise was simple: it was designed to minimise the sense of self as an individual and replace it with the sense of being, above all, *German*, worthy of the Aryan race. Better the many than the one.

Leni Riefenstahl's[1] seductive images of athletes with sculpted muscles and gleaming skin are echoed by pictures of Eva in a swimsuit taken by her sister or a girlfriend as she practised gymnastics on her special beach beside the Königssee, above the painter's corner at the Rödler

1. Photographer and film-maker (1902–2003), ballet dancer, actress, film director and producer, she founded her own film company in 1931. The issue of whether *Triumph of the Will* and *Olympia* should be classified as 'documentaries' or as 'propaganda films' has been in constant dispute since they were made. Leni Riefenstahl always denied that she was a member of the Nazi Party and the records show that she was never a Nazi Party member and never came before a war crimes tribunal. Her complicity with Hitler's racist beliefs remains undeniable.

waterfalls: so secluded a spot that she could swim naked in the lake's icy waters.[2] Hitler's physical lethargy, coupled with a phobic reluctance to expose his body, ensured that he never joined Eva on these trips or came on picnics with her, as he used to with Geli when she was alive and he was still the leader-in-waiting. Even then he would never swim or even strip to the waist. At most he would wear a short-sleeved shirt with shorts or Lederhosen and braces decorated with the Alpine Edelweiss,[3] symbol of Bavaria. In the years since then he had become Reichs Chancellor, holding supreme power. He was no longer in the prime of life and it showed in his pallid, drawn skin, pouchy eyes and flabby body.

In 1936, then, Eva was twenty-four and physically superb, above all when naked or in a swimming costume. In one sequence, recorded both on film and in a set of still pictures, she performs feats of agility and suppleness that are remarkable for someone who was no longer an adolescent. Her body was toned, her limbs strong and slender. Herbert Döring commented: 'Eva had a good figure, she was chic, naturally slim,[4] not very tall,'[5] adding grumpily, 'She had the time to look after herself, didn't she? She had the money as well, and great clothes.' The plump, stocky girl who had walked away from the convent looking as though she had just that minute swallowed the very last of its rich cream cakes had honed herself into a mate fit for Hitler,

2. As recalled by Herbert Döring, manager at the Berghof: Adolf and Eva, 3BMTV, roll 15.21.30.
3. 'Botanical name Leontopodium alpinum, the Edelweiss is a small, white star-shaped flower of the Antennaria family, rare because it is only found on the highest mountain peaks. Its German name combines the two words 'noble' and 'white' and since the mid-nineteenth century it had been a symbol of Bavaria, along with blue gentian and red Alpenrose, used on endless Alpine postcards and souvenirs. Valued as a source of medicine for both men and animals, it was believed to be a powerful talisman with which to ward off evil.

Ironically, the plant also gave its name to the 'Edelweiss Pirates' (Edelweisspiraten), members of a loosely organised youth subculture that emerged in the late 1930s in opposition to the Hitler Youth movement, rejected the norms of Nazi society. And took great pride in fighting Hitler Youth supporters. See chapter 23, p 343 for details.
4. Not naturally at all: she could easily have run to plumpness had she not observed a strict diet.
5. (She stood at 5 foot 3 inches, the same height as Napoleon, as she once reminded Hitler. His height, according to Dr Morell, was 5 foot 7 inches and in 1936 he weighed a modest if not meagre 12 stone.)

but her fitness and vitality were denied their natural goal: mother-hood.

There's no firm evidence that she wanted children (though she would certainly have wanted his) or deeply regretted not having them. It was a sacrifice Hitler insisted upon and she accepted, although her tenderness towards anything young and helpless indi-cates that she might have welcomed a child. Her great friend Herta Schneider – to whom, as a married woman, Eva confided her gynae-cological problems – told biographer Nerin Gun that Eva never believed herself to be pregnant; never even had a late period. There are so many pictures of her with Herta's two little daughters, Brigitte (Gitta) and Ursula (Uschi), that it was often assumed Eva was their mother, which gave rise to a great many false rumours. She loved playing with toddlers, stooping indulgently to show how good she was with them. In March 1969 Ilse Braun assured Werner Maser, one of the first German historians to write a biography of Hitler: 'My sister was certainly never pregnant and if she had become preg-nant, she would in no circumstances have had her pregnancy termi-nated. It would have been contrary to her whole outlook on life . . .'[6] (referring to Eva's Catholic upbringing). It is possible that she used contraceptive suppositories as well as a douche and although this, too, is speculation it points to the same conclusion: Eva did not conceive. Hitler, although he encouraged millions of German women to be fecund, wasn't prepared to be a father and would not have tolerated a child. His image as an unattainable loner sacri-ficing his private happiness was, he believed, the key to his appeal to women. Regardless of his looks and his age (he was forty-seven in the year of the Olympics) he had the charismatic appeal of a modern-day pop star and evoked the same response from his female followers.

In 1931, well before Hitler became Chancellor, the International Olympics Committee had chosen Berlin as the setting for the XIth Olympic Games. It was a gesture intended to welcome Germany back into the world community after the shame of her defeat in the First World War. Then the Nazi Party came to power, and the International Committee could not ignore the increasingly anti-Semitic nature of the régime. A few countries made a token, feeble protest but the

6. Maser, *Hitler*, p. 204.

Committee was not prepared to intervene, let alone recommend that its members ostracise the Games. Hitler, under pressure, made concessions to world opinion by allowing a few Jewish athletes to compete and the Games went ahead as planned.

For the *Führer*, hosting the 1936 Olympic Games was a stroke of luck and good timing that he planned to exploit to the full; a chance to promote not just German youth and German sport but the new Germany itself and the ideal of Aryan supremacy. The Olympics were designed to present a bowdlerised vision of order and harmony to the world, underplaying and deliberately disguising the ugly realities of prejudice and persecution. Few among the hundreds of thousands of visitors to Berlin were aware that for the duration of the Games the régime had taken down anti-Jewish signs in the streets and banished Sinti and Roma people ('gypsies')[7] to a camp close to a sewage dump in the Berlin suburb of Marzahn, where many fell sick. *Der Stürmer*, a rabidly anti-Jewish newspaper, was temporarily removed from news kiosks, though it continued to publish.

Alois Winbauer[8] left an account of that triumphal year:

For National Socialism, 1936 was the year of display. The nations of the world were gathering in Berlin for the Olympic Games and the new Reich was making enormous efforts to present itself in a flattering light. The Party had been instructed to be on its best behaviour, the Gestapo and the SS were reined in and the press had regained a measure of freedom. As regards the race question, Göring's phrase 'I shall decide who is Jewish' was for a while given a new twist. In short, Hitler and Goebbels ordered a thorough spring cleaning. The thuggishness of the storm troopers [the SA] would be eclipsed by the glories of German culture and the world would be persuaded that the Third Reich was determined to become a respectable member of the international community.

7. The 1933 Law for Protection of German Blood and German Honour applied to Jews, Roma and Blacks – mulattos descended from American and French soldiers of the Rhineland occupation (1919–29). To the racists these peoples were of 'alien blood' and so genetically criminal. The 1935 Nuremberg Laws excluding Aryan intermarriage with non-Aryans included Roma. Like Jewish children, their children were excluded from public schools and public places. In 1938, Himmler ordered the sterilisation of Roma children.
8. For details of Alois's earlier career as a journalist, see Chapter 4, note 4.

He was, of course, speaking after the event. With hindsight it is always easy to discern the pattern or airbrush the past. Alois, the hungry student who used to cadge meals from his cousin Fanny, was now a forty-year-old journalist, editor-in-chief of the *Neue Mannheimer Zeitung*, a post he held from 1933 until the end of the war.

Few people and even fewer foreigners could have been fully aware of what was happening behind the scenes in the disinfected Germany that was on show to visitors, but it's salutary to examine what, with hindsight, is now known. From 1933 onwards, licensed looting of Jewish property – their homes and shops – had become increasingly shameless. 'Simple housewives were suddenly wearing fur coats, dealing in coffee and jewellery, had fine old furniture,' recalled Gertrud Seydelmann, a Hamburg librarian. It was 'one of the biggest changes of ownership in modern history, a massive robbery in which ever more sections of the German population participated'.[9] Attacks on Jews in the street were becoming a regular occurrence. Members of the SS or *Schutzstaffel* (literally, Protection Squad) chiefly responsible were often mindless thugs or simply inadequate, despised 'little' men driven by race hatred or a need to assert their superiority by violence. Anti-Semitism tapped into the obsession with ancient Teutonic mythology that underpinned the concentration camps and was used to validate the mass murder of Jews and other non-Aryan groups. Euphemisms such as 'disinfecting', 'cleansing' and 'mopping up' hid many individual acts of sadism behind a self-justifying façade of clinical necessity.[10] Once they had inculcated anti-Semitism in the majority of Germans and, by definition, all Nazis, the party was ready to test how successful the indoctrination had been.

On 1 January 1936 an apparently minor new law came into effect, banning Jews from employing women under thirty-five. At this stage it would still, just, have been possible for 'good' Germans to infer that this reflected the new focus on motherhood and the family. Millions more would have attributed it to the Jews' notorious predilection for raping young blonde women – a myth also promoted about black men in the American South during the period of slavery and still being

9. Adam Lebor and Roger Boyes, *Seduced by Hitler: The Choice of a Nation and the Ethics of Survival* (Naperville, IL: Sourcebooks, 2001), p. 24.
10. Norman F. Dixon, *On the Psychology of Military Incompetence* (London: Futura, 1979), p. 309.

used in the thirties as a pretext for l7ynching and judicial murder. At the same time Hitler sharply rebuked the League of Nations for complaining about Germany's increasingly racist treatment of Jews. As he and his zealots saw it, they were merely putting into practice the widely respected science of 'eugenics'.[11]

Hitler had first hinted at his eugenic beliefs in a speech at the Nuremberg Rally of 1929: 'As a result of our modern sentimental humanitarianism we are trying to maintain the weak at the expense of the healthy.' His arguments had powerful predecessors. Eugenics had not originated in Germany but among post-Darwinian scientists in England. The term was coined by Francis Galton,[12] a high-minded Victorian who believed that applying the principles of eugenics would lead to the long-term improvement of the human race, much as racing stables try to breed perfect horses. These ideas became immensely popular in Europe but Galton's theories took their firmest hold in America, a nation built upon ethnic mix, where people with severe mental or physical handicap or simply awkward behaviour were incarcerated or lobotomised. Many black women (often the victims of rape) were sterilised lest their genes, tainted by 'immorality' and spread by promiscuity, should infect the nation's healthy bloodstream. The idea of racial 'cleansing' or 'race hygiene' (*Rassenhygiene*) had been respectable and established among German academics and medical men when Hitler was a child. In England the idea was not taken up. George Bernard Shaw was an ardent supporter, with uncanny prescience, he predicted in 1910, 'A part of eugenic politics would finally land us in an extensive use of the lethal chambers.'[13]

In Germany, forced sterilisation was launched quietly in January 1934, practised on a few social outcasts suffering from diseases consid-

11. In America the new science was generously supported by such leading charitable foundations as the Rockefeller Foundation and the Carnegie Institute and used to justify the sterilisation of a mentally impaired young black woman on the grounds that 'her welfare and that of society will be promoted by her sterilisation . . . It is better for all the world if . . . society can prevent those who are manifestly unfit from continuing their kind.' The German targets included not only Jews (although they were by far the most numerous) but also gypsies, homosexuals, criminals and the mentally and physically imperfect.
12. Francis Galton (1822–1911) was an expert in the burgeoning science of heredity, a classifier and namer of types.
13. Lecturing to the London Eugenic Education Society.

ered hereditary – 'feeble-mindedness', mental handicap or illness, schizophrenia, physical deformity, epilepsy, blindness, deafness and severe alcoholism. Few people noticed or raised objections when the euthanasia programme got underway, except the parents of much-loved handicapped children, who protested vehemently but in vain. Once the authorities were assured of the public's passive acquiescence, the programme went a step further, legalising the killing of institutionalised handicapped persons. But the visitors from all over the world preparing to come to Germany for the Olympics knew nothing of this.

The 1936 Olympics are best remembered for the four gold medals won by the black American athlete Jesse Owens,[14] a modest and likeable twenty-three-year-old, although he was not alone – eighteen black Americans (sixteen men and two women) competed and won fourteen medals between them. Hitler hadn't reckoned with the possibility that the Games' outstanding athlete would not be one of Germany's great white hopes but black. He refused to give Owens a congratulatory handshake, which he was then obliged to deny to all other winners including those who were German. No doubt he congratulated them in private. In their own eyes the Germans 'won' the Berlin Olympics, but only by declining to count the medals won by 'sub-humans' – by which they meant the black Americans. Owens wore his victories modestly. Like Eulace Peacock and Ralph Metcalfe, he felt their medals repudiated Nazi racial theories.

The Games are brilliantly commemorated in the film *Olympia*, made by Leni Riefenstahl. More than forty cameramen were used, shooting 250 miles of film, which required Riefenstahl and her team of editors to spend eighteen months in the cutting room. She had been chosen as official recorder in the light of her earlier film, *Triumph des Willens* (*Triumph of the Will*), documenting the 1934 Nazi Party Congress in Nuremberg. Riefenstahl claimed that she had been approached by the International Olympic Committee coordinating the Games and asked to make *Olympia*, although its rules specifically forbade the use of material glorifying a single race or nation. In fact it was Hitler who suggested she film the Games and authorised the

14. Jesse Owens (1913–1980) won the 100 and 200 metres, the long jump, and led America to victory in the 400 metres relay.

funding of what was in effect a four-hour-long advertisement for the master race,[15] though to the end of her long life Riefenstahl never acknowledged this.[16] *Olympia*, the keystone of Third Reich propaganda, nonetheless remains an extraordinarily effective and disturbing work of art.

Triumph of the Will is rarely seen today[17] because of its dangerously persuasive power, but several years ago it was screened in Britain late one night on BBC2. I switched on because I was curious about the influences that had marked my mother's youth, and was shocked by its overwhelming allure. It tapped my most fundamental impulses, appealing to the spiritual (with the godlike arrival of the *Führer* in a state-of-the-art Junkers Ju-52,[18] breaking through the clouds in shafts of light above Nuremberg), emotional (ecstatic crowds lining the streets to welcome their leader), sensual (tanned, muscular farmhands in a sequence featuring the *Arbeiterdienst*, presenting arms with rakes and shovels instead of rifles) and, literally, hysterical (open-mouthed young women, eager bodies craning towards the *Führer*, shining eyes fixed on his face, hailing the bringer of happiness, duty and motherhood). I was appalled to find myself deeply stirred. The film ended in the small hours and such was its power that I sat in the dark for a while thinking *My God, he could have been right.*

15. . . . few of whose members were observant, or pedantic, enough to wonder why the car carrying Hitler from the airport to the Bayerische Hof had its windscreen up, then down, then up, then down, and why its number plates kept changing. (I am grateful to Jerry Kuehl for this and many other details.)
16. Leni Riefenstahl's claim to have been ideologically neutral seems unlikely, given her rapturous and erotic response to first hearing Hitler speak, in February 1932 when she was thirty: '. . . after the shouts of "*Heil Hitler!*" had died down I heard his voice. "Fellow Germans!" That very same instant I had an almost apocalyptic vision that I was never able to forget. It seemed as if the earth's surface were spreading out in front of me, like a hemisphere that suddenly splits apart in the middle, spewing out an enormous jet of water, so powerful that it touched the sky and shook the earth. I felt quite paralysed.' Leni Riefenstahl, *The Sieve of Time: Memoirs of Leni Riefenstahl* (London: Quartet, 1992), p. 101.
17. Although it can now be shown in the UK without paying royalties to Leni Riefenstahl's estate, the same is not true in the USA. The film is also widely available on DVD.
18. The equivalent of a modern-day Boeing 737.

Next morning I came to my senses, but that temporary reversal of all I believe in helped me to understand my mother and her lifelong attitudes towards health and hard work, though she denied ever having seen the film. Perhaps she hadn't. Like Eva, she preferred light, romantic stuff. Yet in 1935 Ditha Schröder was twenty-three, living in Germany, doing and seeing what her friends and contemporaries did and saw. She might well have seen *Triumph of the Will* and been affected by it. The unanswered puzzle gnaws at me.

Hitler had little interest in sport but he understood its appeal to the masses. Nothing moves the senses like young bodies glorying in their own prowess. *Olympia*, like the Games themselves, set out to celebrate the triumph of Aryan strength, power and physical perfection. Its director called the film 'a hymn to beauty and competitive endeavour'[19] and so it was, despite the underlying propaganda. It used imagery with a visceral appeal – like the flaming torch handed from athlete to athlete along a route from the site of the ancient Games in Olympia, Greece, to the stadium in Berlin, a ritual introduced for the first time in 1936. It exploited the subliminal power of flags, banners, swastikas, torches, fanfares and thousands parading to the stirring sound of music conducted by Richard Strauss. When a choir three thousand strong sang the 'Horst Wessel Song', not a German eye was dry.

The XIth Olympics opened with the Winter Games, held at Garmisch-Partenkirchen from 6 to 16 February 1936 and watched by Eva with particular interest. The main spectacle took place in Berlin five months later before a gathering of dignitaries, journalists and sports lovers from all over the world. Eva was hidden away anonymously several rows behind Hitler. The opening Games ceremony on 1 August was staged in a vast arena[20] with thousands of German athletes precisely synchronised to move as one, forming and dissolving the Olympic symbol of five linked rings. In a stunning finale, needles

19. Introduction by Leni Riefenstahl to *Schoenheit Im Olympischen Kampf*, a commemorative book of stills from the film published by Verlag Ullstein, Berlin, August 1937.
20. Designed by Albert Speer and, at Hitler's insistence, the biggest in the world, outstripping the one at Los Angeles built for the 1932 Olympics. Size mattered to Hitler.

of light pierced the night sky – Speer's 'cathedral of light' – as the Olympic flame was extinguished. Even the convinced anti-Fascist Robert Byron[21] was compelled to praise the display:

A wonderful sight – 34 lots of scarlet flags and in between them 33 bright searchlights going straight up into the sky but appearing to meet at a point and perform a dance. There were 100,000 men in the arena. Then 25,000 flags entered in one main stream and 14 little ones on either side, all shivering and twinkling scarlet and gold. The great tribune had its bowls of torchlight and all the flags lit up between its pillars.[22]

Impressive stuff, calculated to twang the strings of patriotism and hero-worship. Josef Goebbels, 'Minister for Popular Enlightenment and Propaganda' since 1933, knew that successful propaganda appeals to the heart rather than to reason. '*German sport has only one task: to strengthen the character of the German people, imbuing it with the fighting spirit and steadfast camaraderie necessary in the struggle for its existence.*'[23] Choreographed pageantry, record-breaking athletic feats and lavish hospitality made the Games a paean to the Germany the Nazis wanted to promote, exemplified by its athletes: living examples of physical beauty, discipline and teamwork.

The Games lasted sixteen days and during that time party leaders competed with one another to throw the most extravagant parties for their VIP guests. 'Chips' Channon – not a man easily impressed by wealth – wrote in his diary after one of Göring's banquets:

'There has never been anything like this since the days of Louis Quatorze,' somebody remarked.
'Not since Nero,' I retorted, but actually it was more like the Fêtes of Claudius, but with the cruelty left out . . .'[24]

With the cruelty left out. Channon, for all his social panache, was a gullible ass. The entry continues: 'Göring, wreathed in smiles and orders

21. English travel writer and journalist (1905–41).
22. Robert Byron, 'Nuremberg: The Final Rally', *Spectator*, n.d., 1938.
23. Goebbels said on 23 April 1933.
24. Robert Rhodes James (ed.), *Chips: The Diaries of Sir Henry Channon* (London: Weidenfeld & Nicolson, 1967), pp. 110–11.

and decorations, received us gaily, his wife at his side . . . There is about Göring a strong pagan streak, a touch of the arena, though people say he can be very hard and ruthless, as are all Nazis when occasion demands, but outwardly he seems all childish vanity and love of display.' Despite his forebodings, Chips and plenty of other English guests were happy to gorge themselves at Göring's table – and Goebbels', and Ribbentrop's.

When the Games had ended, the American journalist William Shirer – one of the few to have seen through the pomp and ceremony to the bleak future – wrote: 'I'm afraid the Nazis have succeeded with their propaganda. First, they have run the Games on a lavish scale never before experienced, and this has appealed to the athletes. Second, they put up a very good front for the general visitors, especially the big businessmen.'[25] Foreign spectators took back to their own countries the impression of a peace-loving, prosperous and friendly nation. The Games did much to reduce the apprehension many had hitherto felt about Nazi Germany.

The following year Hitler commissioned Albert Speer to design a new, even more colossal four-hundred-thousand-seat stadium at Nuremberg, confident that Germany would host the Olympics for all time. The huge spaces of Speer's architecture, culminating in a wide flight of steps and a podium flagged with red, black and white swastikas, put the *Führer* on a pedestal of infallibility. A remote, daemonic figure, he had said to the German people, 'You must submit to this over-whelming need to obey!' To deny Hitler's will had become tanta-mount to denying Germany, denying one's identity as a proud member of the German nation, the Aryan race. Very few had the indepen-dence or moral courage to stand back from this vision, ignore the mesmerising rhetoric and listen to the inner voice of conscience and sanity.

When the Games ended on 16 August, Eva had no chance to enthuse with her lover about their success, or congratulate him on the fact that Germany had taken more medals than any other country (if you ignored America's victorious black athletes). Hitler was polishing the final details of a four-year plan that would reshape Germany's economy. Little Fräulein Braun, anonymous as ever, slipped into one of the official cars returning to Munich or the Berghof and

---

25. Foreign correspondent William Shirer in his diary, Berlin, 16 August 1936.

was driven away with other members of his retinue. Had anyone bothered to ask 'Who's that pretty girl?' they would have been told she
was a secretary.

PART 4

THE BEST YEARS: IDLING AT THE BERGHOF

Chapter Fifteen

The Women on the Berg

The atmosphere at the Berghof, below its ordered surface, was intensely erotic. Given the plentiful supply of unmarried typists, telephonists, cooks and servant girls, Hitler's stout henchmen had virtual *droit de seigneur* and made full use of it. 'The Berghof was a veritable tumult of emotion. A great many love affairs went on there – at any rate affairs; *love*, I don't know – but it was very sensual. Hitler was not a sensual person, though as far as I understand it he had perfectly normal relationships with Eva Braun.'[1] Göring was a lecher who helped himself to any woman he wanted, and few dared to refuse. Nearly all the men kept mistresses, some with their wives' knowledge. Gerda Bormann, mother of ten, tolerated her husband's blatant affairs with his secretaries and with the actress Magda Behrens. The Goebbels had a relatively small house 'on the Berg' which they seldom used, preferring the splendour of their estate on a peninsula called Schwanensee, near the Wannsee. One reason could have been that Josef Goebbels preferred to keep his colourful private life well away from Hitler's censorious eye. He enjoyed a series of 'casting couch' liaisons – being in charge of propaganda films, would-be actresses seeking his favour knew it involved going to bed with him – and changed mistresses frequently in a merry-go-round of adultery. When the actress Lina Baarova became a fixture, his wife Magda was intensely jealous (despite the fact that she herself was having an affair with Karl Hanke, Goebbels' private secretary, at the time). The beautiful Baarova came close to breaking up the Goebbels marriage until Hitler banished her at twenty-four

1. Gitta Sereny interviewed for *Adolf and Eva*, 3BMTV, roll 9.

hours' notice and ordered Josef and Magda to get back together and make the best of it. Leading Nazis, especially if they had several children, could not be seen to flout the family ethos preached by the party.

Not every man on the Berg took advantage of his rank and status to indulge in serial promiscuity. Albert Speer didn't; despite his magnetic appeal for women and the fact that he was sixteen when he met his wife, he remained faithful to Margaret until the last years of his life. Dr Brandt, one of Hitler's personal physicians (introduced by Eva, who was rightly suspicious of Dr Morell, the quack who had insinuated himself into Hitler's confidence), didn't. Nicolaus von Below, the *Führer's* favourite adjutant, married to the beautiful Maria von Below, didn't either. Their proud young wives would have been highly indignant if their husbands had strayed and all the evidence is that these three, at least, were 'real' marriages and the couples genuinely devoted, despite the stifling atmosphere in which they lived. Maria von Below said:

> We were of course quite isolated. We depended entirely on each other, socially and emotionally. [. . .] You see, when you stayed at the Berghof, you didn't treat it like a hotel. You were always a community. Hitler's cook cooked for you, his maids took care of your clothes, your mending – you lived there and, like in many families, you were never really on your own except in your bedroom.[2]

The wives in Hitler's retinue were nearly as trapped as Eva but at least they had husbands and children to give them emotional ballast and the sense, however misguided, that beyond Hitler's pantomime they had ordinary, ongoing lives. Only a few, like Margret Speer, were frustrated by the absence of intellectual freedom let alone any cultural grit in their bland conversational diet: 'One just talked about people, gossip really, and about plays, films, concerts – and a lot of talk about artists. And one talked about one's children.'

The new Berghof had been completed in July 1936. In Hoffmann's photographs it was presented as the *Führer's* snug country house but in reality it had become the focus of a huge complex. The Berghof was the hub and centre of Obersalzberg but in due course the chalets dotted around it included many private homes belonging to top party officials. The old traditional farmhouses had been enlarged and converted into luxurious chalets for them and their families while

2. Sereny, *Albert Speer: His Battle with Truth*, p. 436.

others were demolished to make room for living space and facilities for the hundreds of guards, bureaucrats, estate workers and servants who waited on them. Göring's enormous chalet was more luxurious than the Berghof itself and stuffed with plundered art, as was Carinhall, named after his first wife, the even vaster country house near Berlin. He lived at Obersalzberg with his second wife Emmy and their only child, the revoltingly spoiled Edda for whom his workers tied apples to the trees in mid-winter. Only Goebbels, who took over the Bechsteins' former chalet but was seldom there, and Speer, whose house was on the very edge of the complex, had relatively modest accommodation. All these favoured associates, their families and their houses, were looked after by dozens of servants who cooked, cleaned, laundered and took care of their children, leaving the wives with too much time on their hands to speculate and gossip over coffee.

The women fell into three quite distinct groups. First there were the élite Nazi wives, who had often been young and beautiful when they married but had subsequently thickened from eating too much good food and bearing too many children. They were among the very few up on the Obersalzberg compound who were fully aware of Eva's role in his life yet Hitler forbade her to visit them, or them to invite her. Chief among them were Magda Goebbels (mother of seven), spiteful, status-conscious Emmy Göring and Gerda Bormann (mother of ten). The daughter of a Nazi judge, Gerda had been tall and beautiful when young but had been reduced almost to the status of a brood mare. Nervous and highly strung, she disliked life on the Berg, in part because Bormann treated her so badly. Speer described her as a 'modest and somewhat brow-beaten housewife'.[3] Yet she was such a fanatical Nazi that she wrote to her husband, with reference to his mistress, Magda Behrens: 'See to it that one year she has a child and next year I have a child, so that you will always have a wife who is serviceable.' Herbert Döring recalled, 'She was only there for the sake of having children. She had nothing to smile about. He would tell her off very badly sometimes and I would find out about it from the nanny, who would tell me what a terrible temper Bormann had.'[4] Coping with her multiple pregnancies was quite demanding enough. Heinrich Himmler's[5] wife Margaret was a pathetic creature who had suffered shell shock while nursing at the

3. p. 215, Albert Speer: *Inside the Third Reich* published Phoenix, 1995.
4. Interview for *Adolf and Eva*, 3BMTV, roll 15.25.10.
5. At that time Himmler was head of the Gestapo and *Reichsführer* of the SS.

front during the war and did her best to avoid socialising. Dr Morell's wife Hanni and Heinrich Hoffmann's second wife Erna were also banned from asking Eva to their homes and so too was Rudolf Hess's wife Ilse, although by 1936 she had become friendly with Eva. Ilse evidently felt some sympathy for Eva's ambiguous position, since she remembered: 'After 1933 she was his mistress but it must have been terribly hard for her, being kept out of sight. I tell you who she looked like: Geli. She was the *Führer's* type.'[6] Frau Hess fell from favour in May 1941 when her husband Rudolf took off on an unscheduled peace mission to Scotland and was promptly evicted from their home on the Berg. The other five – Magda, Gerda, Emmy, Hanni and Erna – condescended to Eva and fancied themselves her social superiors. To them, she was a little Munich nobody and they resented her position as Hitler's mistress. Magda Goebbels and Göring's wife Emmy vied to be top chicken in the pecking order and spent a lot of time denigrating her. Tiny details of precedence assumed vast significance, like the Duchesses' chairs at Versailles. The gardener would bring fresh flowers to the ladies on the Berg, and Frau Göring derived much satisfaction from the fact that *her* flowers were delivered daily, *Eva's* only every second day.[7]

The tensions and rivalries between members of this obnoxious group can be detected from a close study of Eva's photograph albums. Frau Himmler and Frau Göring rarely appear. One pities Eva, trying to navigate the reefs and tides of who's in, who's out; who can be trusted, who can't? As with any court revolving around an absolute ruler, everyone depended on Hitler's favour and people dared not express their true opinions.

The second group on the Berg was made up of Eva's sister Gretl, who rarely left her side, occupying a role midway between personal maid and closest confidante, and the friends of both sexes from Munich whom she invited for the weekend to keep her company and entertain Hitler, especially in the early days when she needed their support to ease her into the circle of envy and ambition in which she found herself. She had introduced Herta Ostermayr (as she then was) to Hitler back in 1933 and he liked her: she was just the sort of respectable, attractive Munich girl who appealed to him. After Herta married Erwin Schneider in 1936 she spent a great deal of time at the Berghof with her children during the long stretches when her husband was

6. Pryce-Jones, *Unity Mitford: A Quest*, p. 138.
7. Plaim and Kuch, *Bei Hitlers: Zimmermädchen Annas Erinnerungen*, p. 69.

away on military service. The Schneiders were eventually given their own suite of rooms in one of the adjacent houses normally reserved for distinguished visitors. Herta was a stabilising influence on Eva; a calm, level-headed woman whose sympathy and wisdom did much to compensate for the unreality of life at the Berghof. She didn't follow fashion, her hairstyle never changed and she chose not to wear make-up but her affection and support for her old schoolfriend were unwavering.

Another friend was Marion Schönmann, admired by Hitler for her intelligence and her connections with the artistic community. Viennese by origin, she had been involved with its opera house and for once he was prepared to listen to her views on music and not merely spout his own. Marion married Herr Theissen on 7 August 1937 and Eva took great pleasure in organising her wedding and a big glossy reception afterwards at the Berghof, the guests in formal evening wear. Eva sits in the front row of the group photograph looking, not sad, but decidedly wistful.

This second set mingled with the few Berghof wives who did like Eva: Anni Brandt,[8] the ravishing young Maria von Below and, later on, Margret Speer. (They were the best of the bunch and it speaks highly of Eva that they became her friends.) Younger and prettier than the top-notch wives, they were much the same age as Eva. The last member of the group was Fräulein Silberhorn, the flirtatious blonde telephone operator at the Gasthaus with whom Eva often went for walks around the Berghof and who later became one of Bormann's many mistresses.[9] It was essential for women to find allies at Hitler's treacherous court and these four, and Gretl, were Eva's defenders and supporters. Without them, the malice and ostracism of the other wives would have been unbearable. The two groups – the Nazi wives and Eva's friends – co-existed in mutual rivalry and disapproval and very few women were welcome in both; perhaps only Anni Brandt and Maria von Below, who were so lively and charming as to be irresistible.

Between them, occupying a neutral buffer state, was a third group

8. Brandt was only at the Berghof when Morell wasn't, since a fierce rivalry existed between the two doctors.
9. Fräulein Silberhorn was a slim, very attractive blonde who lived with Bormann during the war in his private bunker, according to another telephonist at the Berghof, Alfons Schulz.

consisting of Hitler's four private secretaries and his special diet cook, Constanze Manzialy. The secretaries, by no means all young or good-looking, were chosen not just for their supreme efficiency but because the *Führer* also enjoyed their company. One in particular – Gerda Christian (née Daranowski, hence her nickname, Dara) – was a 'stunner', *ein tolles Weib*, the object of many men's desire. Eva was jealous of her, too. A year younger than Eva, she joined the *Führer*'s private office in 1939. Frau Kempka, second wife of Hitler's chauffeur Erich, didn't like her a bit. She told an interrogator after the war: 'She was a hot girl. She slept with anybody if they paid her well enough.'[10] Traudl Junge gave a kinder description of her: 'She was charming to look at with dark brown hair, full of youthful temperament and the embodiment of life. Her glance was irresistible and her laugh like a silver bell. Apart from the fact that Hitler was aware of her sex appeal, she was an exceptionally good secretary. I've seldom seen anyone type so fast and accurately.' Christa Schröder, the senior secretary who had been with Hitler since 1933, disliked Eva and hinted to the *Führer* that she was unworthy of him but he took no notice of her barbed and side-long comments. On one occasion however, extolling the merits of another woman, she concluded, 'Let's face it, *mein Führer*, Eva isn't really right for you!' to which Hitler retorted sharply, 'She suits *me* well enough!'

Fräulein Schröder was a woman of character and intelligence who was not intimidated by her boss. She once dared to criticise Hitler when he objected to young soldiers smoking. For this *faux pas* she was ignored for weeks.[11]

Albert and Margret Speer tried to avoid being sucked into the *Führer*'s entourage. They were an unusual couple in many ways, not least in being nice to Eva, ignoring the edict about not socialising with her. Speer went his own way and did what he liked but Margret was intensely shy and more preoccupied with the care of her children than most wives on the Berg, who handed theirs over to nursemaids and nannies. It cannot have been easy for this rather aloof and straitlaced young mother to acknow-ledge Hitler's mistress. In the most old-fashioned sense, Eva wasn't respectable. In spite of her reservations, Margret befriended her, although she thought Eva sometimes put on airs: 'With us women, you know, she was quite aware of her position. On trips, she was very much the hostess.

10. Frau Kempka's interrogation from the Musmanno Collection, p. 2.
11. Sereny, *Albert Speer: His Battle with Truth*, p. 111.

If Anni Brandt said, "Let's go sightseeing", but Eva Braun wanted to go swimming, it's swimming we went and that was that.' To which Speer evidently riposted, 'Well, she *was* your hostess, wasn't she?'[12]

Hitler was very fond of his wife, whom he called 'my beautiful Frau Speer'. When he heard that Albert and Margret were childless he was appalled. Speer describes his response:

> He [Hitler] asked, 'How long have you been married?'
>
> I said, 'Six years, my *Führer*.'
>
> Then he asked how many children we had and I said, none. (Speer was reluctant to tell him that Margret was then five months pregnant.)
>
> 'Six years married, and no children?' he said. 'Why?'
>
> All I could think was that I'd like the floor to open so that I could disappear . . . Anyway, after that we had five children in fairly quick succession.
>
> It almost sounded as though he had the children for Hitler, I said.[13] He shrugged.
>
> 'One might say so. Ah, well . . .'[14]

The Speers' first-born child, Hilde, was born in July 1934; the sixth and last, Ernst, in September 1943. Hitler felt entitled to manipulate the private lives of the people around him and more than once propelled young women into hasty weddings they were not ready for, preferably to one of his personable and dedicated adjutants. He wanted his young Aryan heroes to beget children before they were killed. As the Speer story shows, he was quite prepared to interfere in their marriage – and even the proud and independent Speers did as they were told.

Speer was rarely at the Berghof after 1934, when he was appointed Hitler's personal architect at the age of twenty-nine. From then on he spent most of his time in Berlin, turning Hitler's grandiose schemes into architectural plans which when approved by the *Führer* (the two spent hours together poring over the plans) became colossal buildings designed to last as long as those of ancient Greece and Rome. An intense friendship was developing between Hitler and Speer – sixteen years his junior – that on both sides almost amounted to love, though

12. Ibid., p. 193.
13. The 'I' here is Gitta Sereny.
14. Sereny, *Albert Speer: His Battle with Truth*, p. 110.

quite without any sexual element. Speer confided to his biographer that Karl Hettlage, one of his senior employees who knew him well and an architect working with him on the Berlin project, had told him in the summer of 1938: '"You are Hitler's unhappy love." Speer added: "And you know what I felt? Happy. Joyful."'[15]

Albert Speer made a deep impression on everyone who met him. He seemed very different from most of the fawning Rottweilers and sycophants around Hitler. Speer won favour without apparently trying. He was almost the only person who didn't toady or lie to the *Führer*. Karl Hettlage described him: 'Here was this very young, extraordinarily powerful man, and there was nothing about him that showed awareness of his power. What one saw was someone exceptionally courteous, calm, friendly, humorous and modest.' Leni Riefenstahl, highly susceptible to handsome men, called him, 'Different. He had distinction; he was quiet; there was a kind of shyness too, not timidity – modesty. He was clean. It would have been unbelievable that he could do anything shifty.' She reckoned him 'the most important – and certainly the most interesting – man in Germany after Hitler'. Hugh Trevor-Roper was not so easily impressed. He reached the conclusion that it was precisely *because* Speer seemed so upright that he was one of the most dangerous people in Hitler's court, lending a spurious legitimacy to that evil crew.[16]

Eva instinctively liked Albert Speer but for a while she held back, not only because she wasn't supposed to associate with leading Nazis like the Speers but also perhaps because she felt it somehow improper to be Hitler's mistress *and* friendly with his young architect, at a time when the two men were so close. In fact Hitler doesn't seem to have minded. Perhaps, being strongly drawn to Speer himself, he found the attraction easy to understand and knew Speer well enough to know that any impropriety was out of the question. Later, he encouraged her to join the Speers on skiing holidays and in time Albert became her closest, indeed only, male confidant 'on the Berg'. She must have managed matters skilfully, and the friendship between the three main people in this emotional triangle remained warm and platonic.

15. Ibid., p. 157.
16. Hugh Trevor-Roper, *The Last Days of Hitler*, p. 215, wrote: 'For ten years he [Speer] sat at the very centre of political power; his keen intelligence diagnosed the nature and observed the mutations of Nazi government and policy; he saw and despised the personalities around him; he heard their outrageous orders and understood their fantastic ambitions; but he did nothing.'

Speer was the great exception at Hitler's court and one would expect him to have been bored by someone like Eva Braun but there was an element not of lightness only but of goodness in her that got to him. Eva Braun, strange as that may sound, was probably a good person. Curious, to find someone one refers to like that, so close to Hitler. Very curious. It's another proof of the non-existence of black and white.[17]

In addition to her old and new friends, Eva was slowly getting back in touch with her parents. By the time she had lived away from home for a couple of years the breach had begun to heal. Fanny was made miserable by the long separation from her younger daughters, especially since Ilse was now married and living in Berlin, and she won Fritz round to the idea that, as they couldn't change the situation, they might as well accept it. As early as the Whitsun weekend of 1935 (unless Eva has dated the photograph incorrectly, which is perfectly possible) Fanny visited her errant daughter at Obersalzberg. After this, neither the Brauns' non-political status nor their disapproval of Eva's relationship prevented them from accepting invitations to join her at the Berghof, where Hitler welcomed them almost effusively and treated them with marked respect, even deference. He sympathised with Fritz's outrage – it was what any good German father would feel – and while he wasn't prepared to marry their daughter he seemed to want them to know that she was in good hands: an ironic example of his petit bourgeois morality, the complete opposite of his unspeakable political ethic. Soon the whole family was taking holidays abroad at Hitler's expense. It was still just about possible for an ordinary German family, even the Brauns, to remain outside the Nazi Party without being penalised. Eva never joined and nor did any of the other Braun women. Fanny observed crisply to Nerin Gun: 'We didn't need to: we were *family*.'[18] Fritz – hitherto a convinced opponent of the Nazis and their ideology – finally became a member in May 1937, no doubt aware of pressure from Hitler's henchmen.

In spring 1936 Eva and Gretl, with their mother as chaperone, went to Italy for the first of many times with a group of young friends including Hoffmann's son Heini, with whom Gretl had a lengthy flirtation. A series of snaps shows the highlights of their trip. They

17. Gitta Sereny interviewed for *Adolf and Eva*, 3BMTV, roll 9.24.
18. In an interview with Nerin Gun, quoted in Gun, *Eva Braun: Hitler's Mistress*.

photographed themselves sunbathing beside Lake Garda, at the cathedral in Milan, beside the sea again at Viareggio, then in Florence, Bologna and Venice (the Piazza San Marco, with pigeons – impossible to photograph it without pigeons). They were probably unaware that the visit was sanctioned and discreetly supervised by the Italian foreign ministry. It wouldn't have made any difference if they had known. The Braun family were indefatigable tourists. Eva's fourth album contains several photographs showing them all on holiday together in Germany two years later, in 1938. They drove in convoy, Eva in the black Mercedes from Hitler with its IIA-51596 number plate, perched up in front beside the driver. (She had learned to drive herself but Hitler was afraid of her speeding and having an accident so on long trips he made her take a chauffeur.)[19]

In the summer of 1938, after laying the foundations of the new Volkswagen plant, Hitler arranged for Eva to receive one of the first prototypes of the 'People's Car', designed to match Henry Ford's Model T as a car everyone could afford, enabling ordinary Germans to travel and make use of the autobahns that were beginning to stream across the countryside. The car was another of his gifts to Eva, though it's unlikely that he paid for it himself – once again, Bormann would almost certainly have done a deal on his behalf. It can't have left the Berghof wives in any doubt that, whatever *they* thought of her, she pleased Hitler and he was generous in rewarding her.

19. In 1937 the BMW 327/8, a sports cabriolet, was also launched, a radical new design that Hitler may have thought was too racy or too risky for Eva, since its top speed was 87mph.

Chapter Sixteen

Three, Three, the Rivals . . .

Eva Braun was never First Lady of the Reich and never wanted to be. She cared nothing for politics and little for Hitler's official position, except that his duties too often kept them apart. Instead, on formal or state occasions when he needed a woman at his side Magda Goebbels presided. It was a role for which she was supremely well suited.

Frau Goebbels was a rare bird among Nazi wives. She was cultured and sophisticated, well-connected, highly intelligent and, in spite of all this, a dedicated Nazi who was fanatically devoted to Hitler. Contemporaries praised her cool blonde beauty, though her chiselled face and severe hairstyle look hard and condescending in photographs. Her clothes were elegant and expensive, but austere. She resembled a marble statue rather than a woman, let alone one who had borne several children, but behind the chill façade her nature was dramatic and passionate. For her history, and its potential to undermine Eva's, we shall have to abandon Eva for a moment and go back thirty-five years.

This formidable woman was born Maria-Magdalena Ritschel in 1901, the daughter of an engineer. Her parents divorced when she was four. Soon afterwards her mother married a wealthy Jewish businessman called Max Friedländer and took her small daughter with her to Brussels, where the child's surname was changed to that of her mother's new husband. The household was managed on Orthodox Jewish lines although her tolerant and doting stepfather allowed Magda, who had so far been brought up as a Catholic, to be educated in a school run by Ursuline nuns. In July 1914, alarmed by the assassination in Sarajevo, Magda, now aged thirteen, returned to Berlin with her mother. The young Magda's beauty must have been remarkable, for at the age of twenty she made a brilliant marriage to a millionaire industrialist twice her age, Günther Quandt. They first met on 18 February 1920 when she was returning to her finishing school at Goslar in Bavaria. Quandt saw her on the train and in the space of that journey was captivated by her. They married in January 1921 after less than a year's courtship and their only child, a son named Harald, was born ten months later. Over the next few years, despite her youth, Frau Quandt moved in the highest social circles and was much admired for her stylish apartment and the dazzling parties she gave there. The marriage was not happy, however, and in 1929 she petitioned her husband for a divorce. Devoted to Magda in spite of her many infidelities, Günther Quandt made a lavish settlement, which as well as a generous income included an apartment on Reichskanzlerplatz, in the most fashionable area of Berlin.

A year later Magda heard Goebbels at a party rally. Putzi Hanfstängl described him as a 'mocking, jealous, vicious, satanically gifted dwarf' and, in a deadly accurate phrase, 'the pilot-fish of the Hitler shark'.[1] The crowds listening to him soon forgot his diminutive stature and rodent-like features, for Josef Goebbels was a mesmerising orator. Hearing him speak changed Magda's life. Until then she had been a good Catholic but she was instantly converted and, with almost religious fervour, remained for the rest of her life an ardent Nazi. Ignoring the protests of her ex-husband and many friends she obtained a job at party headquarters where she was soon transferred to Goebbels' department: it was said, after he had passed her on the stairs. Highly sexed and highly susceptible, he fell madly in love with her and they embarked on an affair. Magda knew he was a philanderer and she could not expect him to be faithful but she too had had a varied sexual past – 'she has done a great deal of living in her life,' Goebbels noted cryptically in his diary on 30 May 1931.[2]

Proud of his latest conquest, in November 1931 he arranged for her to meet the *Führer* in the mundane setting of a hotel tea room, unaware that Hitler himself had already consoled himself following the death of Geli Raubal by seducing Eva Braun, probably that very

1. Putzi Hanfstängl, *Hitler: The Missing Years* (London: Eyre and Spottiswood, 1957), p. 224.
2. p. 246 *Die Tagebücher von Josef Goebbels: Samtliche Fragmente*, translated and edited by Fred Taylor, Introduction by John Keegan (London: Hamish Hamilton 1982).

month. Magda Quandt at thirty was at her most dazzling, before her face hardened and her self-confidence took on a cynical edge. With her patrician manners and worldly poise she was exactly the sort of woman Hitler's associates wanted for him. Goebbels had had many liaisons; if the *Führer* had wanted Magda he would have surrendered her; and if the leader-to-be were looking for an ideal marriage, here was a woman qualified to be First Lady of the Reich. Hitler was more tempted than he had been by any woman since Geli. Marriage to Magda would certainly be a challenge, but he was far from certain that a challenge was what he wanted and he remained quite sure that he didn't want marriage.

Back in Munich working eight hours a day in the Hoffmann studio and knowing nothing of this encounter was fresh-faced, uncomplicated, besotted Eva, years younger than her polished rival. She must have been fun in bed, innocent and willing, and, crucially, she was never likely to challenge him. Fräulein Braun, nineteen years old in 1931 and sweetly malleable, suited Hitler. He was, if not in love, already fond of her. The imperious Frau Quandt, on the other hand, would expect marriage and status. She was not the kind of woman a man could take as his mistress and then discard but she could definitely be useful to him. Quick to recognise Magda's potential, he confided to his friend Otto Wagener:[3] 'This woman could play an important role in my life, even without my being married to her. In all my work she could represent the feminine counterpart to my male instincts,' adding pointedly, 'What a pity she isn't already married.'

On a superficial level he may have been afraid that Magda would see through his pretensions and uncover the gauche provincial behind the strutting arriviste. But as always there was the more important, deeper reason: the secret, shameful Hitler, tainted by incest and feeble-mindedness. He knew, even if no one else did, the obstacles to marriage. He could find plenty of good reasons for rejecting the challenge offered by a brilliant woman of the world in favour of the undemanding Münchener girl. *Had* Magda Quandt been hoping Hitler would respond to her and if so, would she have transferred her allegiance from the serpentine, lascivious Goebbels? Many of the

---

3. Dr Otto Wagener, former Chief of Staff of the SA and now head of the Nazi Party's economic department (*Ekonomik Reichskommisar*) before being ousted by Göring.

Führer's associates[4] believed she was in love with him and only married Goebbels in order to stay close to the *Führer* but this is too glib. While she and Josef both had ulterior motives – each would gain from the other's status – their marriage was based on mutual love and sexual magnetism. On 19 December 1931 the wedding took place, with Hitler acting as a witness. From then on he took care to keep Magda Goebbels at a safe distance, enjoying her company as a platonic friend and accomplished hostess but well aware that her obsession with him could easily tip over into hysteria (and he knew a good deal about female hysteria).

For months afterwards the Goebbels behaved like doting newly-weds, to the irritation of their friends. Putzi Hanfstängl observed cuttingly: 'Magda calls out, "My angel!" but who should come round the corner but the black devil himself, right down to the goat's foot!'[5]

The splendid apartment at 3 Reichskanzlerplatz became Hitler's social base and in due course Magda Goebbels assumed the role of Hitler's official hostess and was almost accepted as Germany's First Lady as well, though that title properly belonged to Emmy Göring since her husband ranked above Josef Goebbels in the party hier-archy. Emmy, a statuesque former actress, lacked Magda's social skills although she shared her love of grandeur and was sometimes known to the women on the Berg as 'the Queen Mother'. The supposed rivalry between the two women was a source of much interest and speculation to the gossips around Hitler but neither Emmy nor anyone else seriously challenged Frau Goebbels. Bella Fromm, a Berlin gossip writer, wrote, 'Emmy is no feminine intriguer

---

4. I am told by David Irving that the wife of Otto Meissner, Hitler's praesidial secretary, told US interrogators after the war that Magda Goebbels had actually borne Hitler a child . . . possibly Hilde, born 13 April 1934 (who happened to be the daughter Goebbels liked least, having hoped for a son). She claimed to have been told this by Frau Goebbels herself. There is no foundation whatsoever for this myth other than post-war ingratiation and fantasy on the part of Frau Meissner. As far as one can tell from photographs (the poor child was only eleven when she was killed by her parents) Hilde bore no resemblance to Hitler but she did look very much like her younger sisters, especially Helga. Incidentally, none of the girls joined the BDM – the League of German Girls – although member-ship of a Nazi youth organisation was almost obligatory at that time.
5. Hans-Otto Meissner, *Magda Goebbels: Ein Lebensbild* (Munich: Bertelsmann Verlag; 1978), p. 116.

[but] a sympathetic, motherly woman . . . Her lovely blonde hair frames her brow in a large braid; her big blue eyes are soft and serene. She loves to wear floating gowns which make her look even plumper and rounder . . . the exact opposite of skinny, sour-tempered, mean Magda Goebbels.'[6]

Magda became an immense asset to the *Führer*, perhaps the only woman whose intelligence and judgement he took seriously. Over the years her loyalty and devotion never wavered, but she could be sarcastic and dismissive towards his associates and in particular their stolid wives. She also despised Hitler's mistress and snubbed her openly. On one occasion, as Putzi Hanfstängl recorded with glee:

Eva turned up unobtrusively at the Nuremberg Party Rally in 1935 in a very expensive fur coat. Magda Goebbels, who thought *she* was the one woman to whom Hitler ought to pay attention, was ill-advised enough to make a disparaging remark, which aroused Hitler to fury. Magda was forbidden to enter the Chancellery for months. Hitler repaid her [Eva Braun's] presence with his protection.[7]

Eva spent much of the summer of 1935 at the Berghof, fully aware by now of the threat posed by Magda Goebbels. She also went with her family and Herta to Baden Baden and Bad Schachen, where between 'cures' she also practised water-skiing. If sport was available, especially one new to her, Eva was up for it.

When at the Berghof, Eva was usually careful to show Magda Goebbels respect, knowing she would be a dangerous enemy. It must be significant, though, that in all her albums, containing some two thousand photographs, including even pictures of people she hated – like Bormann – there is not one of Frau Goebbels. On one occasion, however, according to a most satisfactory story, she got her own back. Eva and Frau Goebbels – who was heavily pregnant at the time – were alone together and at one point Magda said, 'Fräulein Eva, could you please do up my shoelaces? I can't bend over.' Eva rang the bell for a maid and when she appeared, murmured, 'Would you be so kind as to tie Madam's shoelaces?' before leaving the room. It's a rare instance

6. Klabunde, *Magda Goebbels*, p. 219.
7. Ernst Hanfstängl, *Hitler: The Missing Years* (London: Eyre and Spottiswood, 1957), p. 273.

of spite on Eva's part and was no doubt well-deserved.[8] She seems to have been touchy with pregnant women. Frau Winter recalled that by 1944: 'Eva was very high-handed, particularly with those she thought weak characters. Once Frau Bormann was at the Berghof shortly after having a new baby. She was not feeling well, but she had to stay up as long as the other guests. Eva asked for a coffee, then for milk. She didn't like the milk so Gerda Bormann had to go and get her another glass.'[9]

Hitler granted Eva more licence than anyone else. She was permitted to tease and even rebuke him in a way that would have had Magda Goebbels or Frau Göring ostracised if not banished from the Berghof, at least for a while. Traudl Junge records one occasion when Eva Braun was showing him her latest photographs. Hitler began whistling softly.

'You [she used the informal *Du*] are whistling it wrong,' she said; 'it goes like this,' and she whistled the right tune.

'No, that's not right, I had it first time,' said the *Führer*.

'I bet you I'm right,' Eva replied.

'You know I won't bet, since I have to pay either way,' Hitler pointed out.

'All right, let's play the record, then you'll see,' suggested Eva. The duty adjutant put the fragile record on the turntable and it proved Eva right. She was triumphant.

'Yes, you were right,' Hitler riposted '– but the composer was wrong. If he'd been as musical as I am he would have written it my way.'

We all laughed, but I think Hitler was being perfectly serious.[10]

The fact that she sometimes answered him back was proof not only of their intimacy but also of the secret power struggle that underlies many long-term partnerships. It's a tribute to her emotional intelligence that she was able to keep him interested and their relationship alive. In its closeness and intimacy, it was more complicated than

8. Gun, *Eva Braun: Hitler's Mistress*, p. 135.
9. Interview with Frau Winter, 3 September 1948, from the Musmanno Collection. Logically it has to be said that it seems unlikely that, in a house stuffed with servants at all hours, Frau Bormann would have had to make her own way down to the kitchen to fetch milk for Eva. Probably she hardly knew where it was.
10. Junge, *Bis Zur Letzten Stunde*, p. 92 (translated by the author).

anyone guessed, though Alois Winbauer came close when he wrote, in his memoir of the Braun family: 'There had been a large element of playfulness in Eva's relations with Hitler – an exciting, provocative game of the kind that a proud and inquisitive young woman could play with enjoyment.'[11] Eva sometimes used their dogs as cover for these games, part of the seesaw of power that adds spice to the relations between a man and a woman, even when the man is Hitler. The two conducted a semi-serious rivalry over whose animals had precedence. Their dogs didn't get on and would snarl and fight, so either Eva's pair of Highland terriers, Stasi and Negus, or Blondi, could be in the room but never both at once. Eva's two would sit like heraldic beasts on either side of her chair when she tucked up her legs under her while Hitler talked or slept. 'The dog-loving *Führer* was sometimes forced to plead on behalf of his beloved Blondi and would ask quite humbly, "Could I let Blondi in, just for a moment?" Eva Braun would take her dogs outside and Blondi was allowed to put in an appearance.'[12] Blondi was a one-man dog who never let Hitler down and whom he adored, yet he permitted Eva's two ill-tempered little black dogs to sit indoors while the mournful, puzzled Blondi was banished to the Berghof terrace. Seen in this light, the charade concealed a major concession and is further evidence of Eva's underrated power.

Hitler was fanatically devoted to his Alsatians, 'German shepherds'. Blondi, the favourite, was a beautiful and intelligent pedigree bitch. People at the Berghof were fond of saying he loved her better than Eva and certainly he was more publicly demonstrative to his dog, fondling and kissing her. He had taught Blondi a number of tricks and delighted in showing off her prowess. At times the dog's behaviour seemed almost human. A series of photographs shows Hitler and Blondi peering over a wooden fence in comically identical attitudes, she propping herself up on the railings with her paws, Hitler beside her leaning forward to look at the view. For Christmas 1939 he was given another Alsatian, a nine-month-old puppy whom he named 'Wolf', but although it grew up to be a dark, handsome dog, it never superseded Blondi in his affections and rarely appears in photographs.

11. Winbauer, *Eva Braun's Familiengeschichte*, p. 21. His speculations seem more than guesswork: could he have talked to Fanny, his close cousin, or did his niece Gretl confide in him? The description of Eva's erotic teasing seems uncannily precise.
12. Ibid., pp. 87–8.

Hitler insisted on slavish obedience from the dogs. If Blondi hesitated to obey his command even she would be punished with a severe
whipping. Then he would forgive and become foolishly, dotingly affectionate towards the fawning animal, showing the tender side of his
nature that the German people loved in each other and in him. His
relationship with his dogs betrays both his cruelty and his maudlin
sentimentality. Sentimentality, as Michael Burleigh points out, is 'that
most underrated, quintessential characteristic of Nazi Germany'.[13] The
German word for it – *rührselig* – means 'liable to move the emotions'.
It is entirely irrational, lacking mental or moral rigour as well as any
sense of proportion. A sobbing child, a neglected or beaten animal,
even a crushed flower, move the sentimental soul more than the fate
of people who have been starved, tortured or raped. Cruelty is its
Siamese twin. The two extremes co-existed in Hitler, who fastidiously
avoided watching the pain his racist policies inflicted. He would not
even visit soldiers wounded in the war he was to launch and deliberately prolong.

In a long-lasting partnership the balance between the two protag-
onists changes and develops. While Eva always remained suppliant,
there were some areas where, in a reversal of the norm, Hitler allowed
her the illusion of control (as with the dogs). It was a game that could
only have been played between two people who trusted one another,
whose private feelings could not be openly expressed but must be subli-
mated in pretence. Relations between the sexes are often an intricate
struggle for dominance, yet in the lover/mistress relationship the
balance of power is not necessarily what it seems. Much of its frisson
comes from the ambiguity of control, the power that youth and beauty
exert over older men and the thrill of secrecy. Secrecy cuts both ways.
A lover expects to buy his mistress's compliance and fidelity by paying
her bills, giving her money for clothes and buying her presents; but
what she does while he conducts the public business of his life remains
an intolerable mystery, as Hitler had discovered when he was Geli's
protector.

Their psychological interaction was a subtle interplay of emotional
– not sexual – control that would have astonished the stony, disapproving Nazi wives had they been acute enough to notice. Hitler was
always the dominant partner and could occasionally be coldly dismissive, especially in the early days, but when they were alone together

13. Burleigh, *The Third Reich: A New History*, p. 219.

Eva won concessions. Outwardly she seemed a paragon of submissiveness and devotion but behind the façade she was learning to use her hold over him. She too manipulated him: not much, but a bit. Hitler may have tolerated this, ascribing it to 'women's wiles', or he may not have been aware of it. His entourage – who always underrated her – certainly were not.

Psychiatrists call such behaviour 'passive/aggressive': an apparent docility concealing subversive manipulation. The bond between master and slave or lover and mistress is seldom a clear-cut case of the strong oppressing the weak. The dominant lover needs to be convinced that his mistress loves him single-mindedly and of her own free will. Even dictators can never have enough reassurance. At the same time he insists that she submit entirely to him. This paradox – these incompatible opposite needs – set the power play in motion. Subtly, without realising it, the master becomes dependent on her adoration until he pushes his dominance too far, at which point the subservient partner may either begin to assert herself or cease to love him. To maintain the submission he must either resort to compulsion, amounting sometimes to torture (in which case the mistress no longer loves freely) or he must make concessions. Gradually the fulcrum of power shifts, becoming more equal, even if to outsiders it seems unchanged.[14]

By her mid-twenties Eva had matured into a most beguiling woman. Many men coveted her, including the handsome and highly eligible Walter Hewel, Ribbentrop's liaison officer to Hitler, who was very popular with the Berghof crowd, but Eva remained faithful. There has been plenty of colourful speculation about the nature of Hitler's sex life, or lack of it, but little supporting evidence. Some historians have claimed that he was homosexual, the implication being that Eva was around simply as a decoy or cover. Why, in that case, should he have gone to such lengths to conceal her? The decoy theory seems as unlikely as the sado-masochism he was supposed to have enjoyed with Geli.

Heinz Linge, Hitler's loyal manservant, divulged that,

---

14. Similar 'passive/aggressive' behaviour sometimes surfaced among Hitler's colleagues, though without the element of play and with more dangerous consequences. Albert Speer wrote many years later, 'There is a special trap for every holder of power . . . His favour is so desirable to his subordinates that they will sue for it by every means possible. Servility becomes endemic; they compete among themselves in their show of devotion. This in due course exercises a sway upon the ruler, who becomes corrupted in his turn. Only a few individuals such as Fritz Todt [the architect who preceeded Speer] withstood the temptation to sycophancy.'

Hitler and Eva occasionally stayed alone in his study talking for a short while before retiring . . . Eva Braun, usually wearing nothing but a dressing gown,[15] would have some wine and Hitler a cup of tea. One evening I went in without knocking and saw Eva and Hitler standing embracing ardently in the middle of the room. Blushing, I turned, withdrew and closed the door.[16]

He may not have caught them *in flagrante* but this sounds very like the prelude to making love. When Frau Mittlstrasse, the *Führer*'s house-keeper at the Berghof, was asked about the relationship between Hitler and Eva she described it as 'a normal one between a man and a woman. Perfectly normal. [. . .] I am 100 per cent sure that they had a sexual relationship.'[17] With equal certainty, Herbert Döring pronounced, 'Hitler was incapable of it. [. . .] That might have been a large part of the reason why Eva Braun was always so unsatisfied.'[18] Anna Plaim, however, scoffed:

I know Döring claimed they never had an intimate relationship, but Döring later described her as a stupid dumpling, though at the time he called her '*gnädiges Fräulein*' all right! . . . As to whether they had a sexual relationship, all I can say is that Gretel Mittlstrasse's evidence contradicts him – and *she* was the one who used to go and get medications for Eva to postpone her period during times when Hitler was at the Berghof. Despite their evident closeness I can't remember one single occasion when they held hands let alone kissed . . . All I can say is this: during the day Hitler never went off to his own bed and at that time Eva Braun's bed was sacrosanct.[19]

15. The brown satin brocade dressing gown described earlier; a full-length garment lined in black silk, fastened at the waist with one covered button, was sold by the Munich auction house of Hermann-Historica in 1989. (Lot 4544, auctioned on 10/11 November.)
16. Heinz Linge, *Bis Zum Untergang, Als Chef des Persönlichen Dienstes bei Hitler* (Munich: Herbig, 1983).
17. Frau Mittlstrasse interviewed for *Adolf and Eva*, 3 BMTV, roll 21.12.
18. Herbert Döring interviewed for *Adolf and Eva*, 3BMTV, roll 15.24.
19. Plaim and Kuch, *Bei Hitlers: Zimmermädchen Annas Erinnerungen*, pp. 92–4 (translated by the author).

Despite the lack of proof, Eva's personal maid was positive that the two had full intercourse. After the war Dr Morell, Hitler's personal physician,[20] assured a team of investigators from the American Commission of Enquiry that 'the *Führer* had sexual relations with Eva Braun from time to time, although they slept in separate beds'.[21]

The clinching evidence is that of Frau Mittlstrasse, an honest and reliable witness. Asked whether Hitler and Eva had a complete sexual relationship she replied: '100 per cent. I know that because when she had her period and he arrived unexpectedly she would get something from Dr Brandt, our in-house doctor, to suppress the period. I collected it from his room. I don't know what it was, whether pills or liquid or whatever, but I am quite sure of that.'[22] Eva's concern about postponing her period and Hitler's insistence that she should use effective contraceptives point to the strong probability that in all the ordinary ways they enjoyed making love. *Proof* is too much to ask for and this is not the place to define 'ordinary'.

Hitler's pathological modesty and refusal to appear even semi-clothed in public were probably due to the fact that he suffered from two genital abnormalities: an undescended or possibly absent testicle and a rare condition called penile hypospadia,[23] in which the urethra opens on the underside of the penis or on the perineum, creating a hole that can lead to incontinence though not necessarily to impotence. Despite refusing to let his doctors carry out a full physical examination, this condition was observed and recorded in medical reports kept by Morell, who had been a venereal specialist before he met Hitler and was presumably expert in all sorts and conditions of men. On the other hand an independent army physician, Dr Erwin Giesing, who gave Hitler a complete physical check-up in June 1944 and again the following October, testified that the genitalia were normal. In any case, neither the single testicle nor hypospadia/hypoplasia need have prevented full intercourse. Hitler, it seems, was certainly *capable* of making love: the real question is, how often?

20. He had joined Hitler's household in 1937, in addition to Dr Brandt.
21. David Irving (ed.), *The Secret Diaries of Hitler's Doctor* (New York: Macmillan, 1983).
22. Marion Milne, the reporter/director of *Adolf and Eva*, was the first person to elicit this apparently clinching piece of evidence from Frau Mittlstrasse.
23. Information from David Irving, in conversation, 20 October 2004. He unearthed it in *The Secret Diaries of Hitler's Doctor*, published by Sidgwick & Jackson. I cannot trace this reference.

Hitler's libido was low, for reasons that a modern psychiatrist would suggest went far back into his childhood – disgust at his father's unbridled promiscuity; the unhealthy closeness to his adoring, self-sacrificing mother; the guilt provoked by the Catholic Church's stern teachings on sex and chastity in a lad who had briefly aspired to become a priest. His comparative lack of interest in lovemaking after the first few years with Eva may also have been due to the pressures on him: busy men often have less sex because they are too tired.

Yet they seem to have settled down with one another. Eva's uncle Alois – who must have got the information from Fanny or Gretl, since he himself was never a guest at Obersalzberg – wrote:

> It would be quite wrong to describe Eva's life on the Berghof as one of unalloyed sweetness and light. Hitler respected her and valued her friendship, not only because he needed her support amid the turmoil, absurdity and irrationality of his political life, but because he had really come to love her. [. . .] Surprising as it may seem, there was a great deal of teasing and banter between them but never a serious quarrel.[24]

Portraying Hitler as a man capable of playfulness or sentimentality or sexual passion – or its absence – may reveal his human side but it doesn't make him any less monstrous. To understand the origins and pathology of evil, it is more helpful to find out what the people who knew him as a human being said about him rather than portraying him as an incarnation of the Devil, a Mephistopheles who stole men's souls and burned their bodies. Maria von Below, for instance, the wife of Hitler's adjutant Nicolaus and a member of the innermost circle at the Berghof, admitted:

> When everything came to an end, people fell over each other to represent life at the Berghof as horribly boring, with Hitler spouting endless nothings. Of course, the repetitions became tedious but those first years particularly – how excited we all were! I don't know why so many people deny that extraordinary spark in him. [. . .] You know, it's easy to sneer, to criticise now. But my God, it was a different world then.[25]

24. Winbauer, *Eva Braun's Familiengeschichte*, p. 18 (translated by Christiane Gehron).
25. Sereny, *Albert Speer: His Battle with Truth*, pp. 113–14.

Albert Speer wrote in self-excusing tone in 1945: 'One thing is certain: all those who worked closely with him were to an extraordinary degree dependent on and servile to him. However powerful they appeared in their own domain, in his proximity they became small and timid.'[26] Speer was *never* 'small and timid'.

Many women described him as possessing a dual personality. There was the Hitler they never witnessed, a bully who could scream, shout, foam and terrify people by his eruptions of rage – but by all accounts women only saw the considerate, courteous, respectful Hitler, ever-thoughtful towards the wives and secretaries on the Berghof and his female staff, taking trouble to remember their problems and make solicitous enquiries after their health and that of their children or elderly parents.

Eva was *maîtresse de la maison* at Obersalzberg but this did not prevent her from being, at times, painfully and unnecessarily jealous. 'Eva Braun was very jealous of Unity Mitford. She was jealous of everyone,'[27] said Kukuli von Arent, whom Magda Goebbels had introduced into Hitler's social circle. Unity[28] had been introduced to Nazi ideology by her prospective brother-in-law, the British Fascist leader Oswald Mosley, and from the start she was fixated on the *Führer*. She came to Munich in 1934, supposedly to study art but in fact to be close to him. They had met for the first time on 9 February 1935, three days after Eva's twenty-third birthday, at Osteria Bavaria, where Unity had waited for days, hoping to accost him.

The Hon. Unity Mitford is invariably described as a stunning Nordic blonde although in photographs she looks heavy featured and lumpy, perhaps because of all the cream cakes that Hitler liked

26. Ibid., p. 287.
27. Pryce-Jones, *Unity Mitford: A Quest*, p. 168.
28. Selina Hastings writes perceptively about Unity in her biography of Nancy, eldest and most gifted of the six sisters: 'In many ways Unity was a child, emotionally and intellectually immature. Nazism appealed to her on a very simple level: she liked the marching and the songs and the good-looking young men in their uniforms; she liked the badges and the pamphlets and being able to dress up in her black shirt and gauntlets. Being with Hitler gave her for the first time in her life a sense of her own importance and she found no difficulty in swallowing his anti-Semitic propaganda; propaganda which she was only too willing to regurgitate on every possible occasion.' Selina Hastings, *Nancy Mitford* (London: Hamish Hamilton, 1985), p. 94.

to watch her eat. The Mitford sisters, Unity and Diana (who married Mosley in October 1936), took little notice of Eva Braun, snobbishly failing to realise that she was an important fixture in their hero's life. Diana remembered later: 'Unity and I had our film developed at Hoffmann's and I noticed Eva Braun's shoes, beautiful leather shoes which I knew she couldn't get in Munich. I pointed them out to Bobo [Unity]. She was just a little blonde girl behind the counter, always there.'[29] She was indeed, but she was much more than that.

In September 1935 Hitler teased Eva by inviting Unity and Diana to the *Parteitag* at Nuremberg and seating them next to her in his reserved stand, an oblique and unwanted introduction. Perhaps he thought they might become friends but after that one occasion they had no further contact. Eva did not hide her dislike and jealousy of Unity while the lofty Miss Mitford loftily ignored Eva, unaware as yet of the honour that had been bestowed upon her.

Diana Mosley viewed her sister's infatuation with a cool, disparaging eye and was convinced that Hitler and Unity never slept together. 'He enjoyed her company and it ended there, I think,' she said.[30] Leni Riefenstahl once asked him about Unity, and Hitler gave a different reply: '"She's a very attractive girl but I could never have an intimate relationship with a foreigner." I thought he was joking, but he assured me, "My feelings are so bound up with my patriotism that I could only love a German girl."'[31] Whether he said as much to Eva is not known, but if he had it might have spared her much misery. She mistook Unity for a serious rival although in fact Hitler, while flattered by the Valkyrie's attention, never contemplated replacing Eva.

The relationship, such as it was, between *Führer* and follower was probably opportunistic. Hitler was interested in Unity because of her connections but he would never have risked dallying with her; she was too unstable for that. However, he didn't scruple to use her for propaganda purposes, hoping to make contact with right-wing members of the influential English upper class. The Germans, with their passion for titles, referred to her as Lady Unity or even Lady Mitford but, as has been pointed out, she was merely the daughter

29. Pryce-Jones, *Unity Mitford: A Quest*, p. 105.
30. Mary S. Lovell, *The Mitford Girls* (London: Little, Brown, 2001), p. 250.
31. Ibid.

of a baron. 'If she'd been Miss Snooks,' observed her local vicar years later, 'Hitler would not have bothered with her.'[32] And if Hitler had been Herr Schicklgruber, she wouldn't have bothered with him, either.

The *Führer* assumed that the Mitfords were important and powerful English aristocrats and was proud of their conversion to the Nazi cause, a conversion he thought far more significant than it really was. There was never a chance that these two scatty young women would influence others of their own kind. Full-blown Fascism was rare in Britain, confined to disaffected working-class men and deluded upper-class mavericks like Lord Londonderry and his circle, and a few adherents of that most distasteful of all the extended Mitford tribe, Sir Oswald Mosley.[33] Unity made the mistake of thinking she had real political influence when in fact she was tolerated by both sides largely out of kindness. Nobody took her seriously. Her biographer David Pryce-Jones puts it brilliantly: 'she had always been lonely, uprooted, *the inner emptiness booming with Nazism* [my italics].'[34] To use the slang of the time, she was 'a bit dotty'.

The unbalanced Unity loved Hitler – whom she enthusiastically *Heil Hitler*ed when they met – because of his politics and charisma and because she was flattered that he seemed to take her seriously. Hitler liked her because he was still enough of a snob to be impressed: flattered by the fact that she was well-born. Princess Carmencita Wrede, a friend of Unity's, told her biographer:

Class differences were basic. Unity and Diana were too fine, really

32. Ibid.

33. By the early summer of 1934 Mosley's organisation, the British Union of Fascists, or BUF, known as 'the Blackshirts', was enjoying a period of respectability and had grown to approximately forty thousand members. (See D.S. Lewis; *Illusions of Grandeur: Mosley, Fascism and British Fascism, 1931–81.*) But the real face of Fascism was revealed at Mosley's monster rally at Olympia in June 1934. Thousands of people, including many from the upper echelons of British society, had gathered to hear him. As he began his oration, he was interrupted by hecklers. Mosley stopped speaking. A searchlight pinpointed the interrupter and Mosley directed blackshirted stewards to deal with them. This involved public, savage beatings. These acts of violence and the spirited opposition to Mosley both inside and outside the hall that night meant that thereafter the popularity of the BUF was suspect and began to wane.

34. Pryce-Jones, *Unity Mitford: A Quest*, p. 221.

too aristocratic[35] for him. Eva Braun was at his social level. My sister and I knew Eva and her sister, Gretl, well. Unity was always badgering me, Who is this Eva Braun? What does she have that I don't? How does she do it? She said to me, 'He never takes me to the Obersalzberg because Eva is always there.' Unity was thoroughly jealous.[36]

(It's true that Unity was seldom invited to the Berghof in tacit acknowledgement that it was Eva's domain. On the other hand she saw the *Führer* more often in Berlin.)

Unity's friend Mary St Clair-Erskine[37] often chaperoned her on visits to Hitler's flat, since he took care not to get into situations that might trigger gossip. Mary said: 'He was extremely nice and kind to us, a pleasant host. I can't think he was alone with Bobo [Unity] that wasn't the relationship. [. . .] With Bobo I never detected a shadow of flirtation. For her it was the highlight of the week. Her eyes would brighten and shine.'[38] Princess Carmencita Wrede said Unity had complained: 'I'm never alone with Hitler, or when I am, I sit at his feet and then Bruckner[39] butts in and stays there. When he wants to be alone with me, he sends his adjutants away, but they always come back.' The adjutants wouldn't have dared interrupt a *tête-à-tête* unless Hitler had given them orders to do so. Kukuli von Arent confirmed the platonic nature of the relationship: 'Unity was never Hitler's mistress. Absolute nonsense! She was never alone with Hitler that I was aware of . . . we had to invent pretexts to fetch him to the telephone, for some family matter or something, just to get him away.'[40] The most likely reason for this ungallant behaviour is that he wanted to avoid awkward questions, scenes or tears.

Yet although Unity's devotion to the *Führer* could not compensate for her inadequacies she remained part of his entourage until war was

35. The Mitford family, though long-established, belonged to the landed gentry rather than the aristocracy, with estates in Northumberland, Oxfordshire and Gloucestershire. The Redesdale baronetcy had lapsed but was recreated in 1902. Unity's father was the 2nd Baron Redesdale.
36. Pryce-Jones, *Unity Mitford: A Quest*, pp. 277–8.
37. [b. 1912; 1933 married Philip Dunn; later Lady Mary Dunn, mother of author Nell Dunn and former mother-in-law to the present Lord Rothschild].
38. Pryce-Jones, *Unity Mitford: A Quest*, p. 221.
39. Hitler's chief personal adjutant.
40. Pryce-Jones, *Unity Mitford: A Quest*, p. 170.

declared in 1939. His contacts with her – personal as well as social – took place more often in Berlin than Munich since she could be more useful in the city that housed the diplomatic community and foreign press, but by the end she had become an embarrassment. Even for Hitler, her racist bigotry was too blatantly obvious and she was incapable of discretion.

Coded anti-Semitic jargon is often used half-ironically to defuse the aggression behind it and mask underlying prejudices – which in Nazi Germany were almost unanimously in favour of 'the Aryan race'.[41] Americans categorise certain people as WASP, an acronym meaning White Anglo-Saxon Protestant, and nobody seems to object: it often crops up in the lonely hearts column of *The New York Review of Books*, a fortnightly magazine for liberal intellectuals. Deconstructed, these initials mean pale (ideally blonde, light-eyed and fair-skinned), of north European origin (not swarthy or dark-complexioned) and a follower, however loosely, of the Protestant faith. Not black, therefore; not Jewish, not Muslim – and by extension, not poor, either. The use of WASP as a collective noun is no less racist than classifying people as Aryan since it means exactly the same thing, with similar coded implications.

The belief that human beings can be graded on a scale of racial 'purity' – in practice, whiteness – makes one wonder if people are *taught* to mistrust and feel superior to those of other colours and races, or whether racism is universally embedded, an original sin that must be consciously routed, like envy, theft or rape. It is rare to find prejudice against Scandinavians, perhaps because their pale eyes, skin and hair embody what people secretly regard as the colouring of a superior race. Is this why gentlemen prefer blondes?

Despite her rivals, who were often better born, better looking and, in Magda Goebbels' case, much cleverer than she was, Eva had achieved

41. Gypsies as well as Jews were deported to ghettos such as Lodz, Lublin, Bialystok and Warsaw. Jews and gypsies were deported to Treblinka and Auschwitz in large numbers in 1943. At Auschwitz, a special section of Birkenau (built largely for Jews) was set aside for Roma (gypsies). The *Zigeunerlager* (gypsy camp) of twenty thousand lasted sixteen months; after which all its prisoners – men, women, and children – were gassed. The infamous Dr Josef Mengele served as medical officer at this camp, and, as with Jewish twins, performed horrible experiments on gypsy twins.

her position as semi-official mistress within seven years of meeting Hitler. She impressed her once-sceptical friends in Munich, when they came to visit her at Obersalzberg, by the luxury of her quarters and her familiarity with the top dogs of the party and their perpetually pregnant wives. The one thing she could not admit to anyone was that already she felt the first glimmerings of boredom. 'Be careful what you wish for in case you get it' says the old proverb. Eva was only in her mid-twenties and her life yawned into the future in a series of unchanging days. Endlessly, the same groups reclining on the terrace, endlessly admiring the mountains that rose before them in unchanging and reproachful grandeur. What possible fun was there in looking at a range of *mountains*?

Chapter Seventeen

1937–9 – Eva at the Berghof: 'A Golden Cage'

Eva's future had been wrenched off course when she met Hitler at the age of seventeen. Before then she had taken for granted that her life would be like her mother's and her grandmother's: she would encounter a series of young men, flirt, dance, fall in love and bring selected suitors home to meet her parents before being invited to a 'best behaviour' meeting with theirs. From this process a favourite would emerge, better loved and more eligible than all the rest. There would be a triumphant engagement, a solemn Catholic wedding and, as probably as birth follows bed, a baby – more babies – a family. It was the pattern ordained by the Church as well as the *Bund Deutscher Mädel*: a woman's role was to marry, bear children and sustain and adore her man.[1] In 1937 Eva was twenty-five and the only one among her girlfriends not engaged or married, yet she never considered becoming involved with another man. That truncated future was still waiting but, with Hitler implacably opposed to marriage and fatherhood, the natural course of events was stifled. Nothing was going to happen to change his mind or Eva's frustration, except that now she was at the Berghof where the windows were bigger and the view was better. Mountains.

By 1937 she had been *Chefin*[2] for two years, becoming more confi-

1. Far-fetched as it may seem, this is exactly the advice handed out today by organisations funded by the government of George W. Bush. One health programme called Wait Training, aimed at teenage girls, says, 'To admire a man is to regard him with wonder, delight and approval. A man feels admired when his unique talents and characteristics *happily amaze her* [my italics].' *Guardian*, 3 December 2004.
2. Little chief or the woman in charge.

dent and more firmly entrenched. Hitler's chauffeur Erich Kempka said that after 1932 there was never any other woman in the car with Hitler, yet he still thought Eva was 'the unhappiest woman in Germany'. Her cousin Gertraud likened her life to that of a pet dog '. . . on the end of a long, long rope, running round and round till it comes up against the point where the rope tightens on its throat . . .'.[3] Eva confessed to Leni Riefenstahl's cameraman Walter Frentz during a portrait session that living at the hermetically sealed Berghof was 'life in a golden cage' – and not merely a cage, but a cage high up on a mountainside. At times she must have felt like Rapunzel.

Had she been ten years older she might have taken to her boudoir and subsided into perfumed, plump, grumbling middle age. But she was still young, exuberant and longing to meet new people – in particular Hitler's glamorous guests from the worlds of film and theatre. Excluded from the receptions he gave in Berlin at which beautiful women shimmered through the mêlée holding glasses of *Sekt* (German champagne), Eva craved gossip, gaiety, compliments, noise; the latest records, movies, laughter . . . anything for diversion while *he* was doing his vague, important work. Despite sharing her bed, Hitler's behaviour could at times seem deliberately callous. Unity Mitford's friend Carmencita Wrede remembered, 'In 1937 I was with Nevile Henderson – "this idiot, Henderson", Hitler called him – at the Parteitag. Hitler was there, and Eva stood by herself, wearing a little raincoat. Hitler looked round, and his gaze fell on her without change of expression. No other woman would have put up with that.'[4]

Denied a public existence, Eva Braun frittered away her time, forever waiting. She may have been indulged and cosseted but she didn't have an enviable life. There was more to her than was generally assumed but her mental resources were few. She was very much a creature of impulse and feeling who needed attention and drama rather than a reader or a thinker; she could not be content with her own company. There was always Gretl, of course with whom she tried on nail varnish and lipstick, swapped dresses, flipped through movie magazines and played with the dogs. No wonder Eva changed her clothes several times a day: when *he* was away, what else was there

3. Interviewed for *Adolf and Eva*, 3BMTV, roll 03.15.16.
4. Pryce-Jones, *Unity Mitford: A Quest* pp. 227–8.

for her to do but primp and twirl in front of the mirror to Gretl's admiring squeaks?

In all the vast and pompous spaces of the redesigned Berghof, only Eva's suite had a welcoming, relaxing atmosphere. She spent hours in these pretty, feminine rooms, waiting for a phone call from Hitler or for the arrival of Herr Zechmeister, the postman, with a letter from him. On rainy days when she couldn't go out she practised her shooting skills in the underground rifle range, played bowls with the Dörings, groomed and petted her dogs, stuck photographs in her albums or hovered in the kitchen quarters, as much to gossip as to supervise. When he *was* there, the scented boudoir filled with cushions and flowers and foolish magazines was a haven of soft femininity after harsh days surrounded by men who barked and clicked and snapped, rigid yet servile, all *wanting* something, all scheming and jockeying for place. Eva wanted nothing, except to please him. Gradually he started to believe this, and to trust her.

She yearned for Hitler to spend more time with her. He came to the Berghof roughly every third or fourth week, no doubt attracted by her lively presence and the need to relax from the pressures of his work in Berlin. In between his visits Eva – marooned up 'on the Berg' – missed the crowded streets of Munich where she could stroll and window-shop; the pavement cafés from which drifted the smell of fresh coffee and the sound of fresh gossip, the noisy, smoke-filled bars where she met her friends to chat about anything except Hitler. She could take her chauffeur-driven Mercedes back to the little house in Wasserburgerstrasse, throw parties and catch up with the latest films – and she did, from time to time – but she worried that Hitler might turn up unexpectedly at the Berghof and be angry if she weren't there to greet him. (He was always reluctant to let her know his plans in advance and often left without saying where he was going or for how long, as if deliberately to keep her on tenterhooks.)

Although she had been given 'leave of absence' from Hoffmann's studio she continued to work there sometimes when she was in Munich, up to and during the war.[5] She could hardly have missed the tedious days behind the counter or in the darkroom at Hoffmann's

5. A letter she wrote to Walter Ostermayr, Herta's brother, in November 1943 says: 'What with my job at Hoffmann's and the air-raid damage to my house I have unfortunately not had time to write.' (Original reproduced in Johannes Frank, *Eva Braun: Ein ungewöhnliches Frauenschicksal in geschichtlich bewegter Zeit*, p. 261.)

studio but she did miss the companionship of her co-workers, the stories of their daily lives, boyfriends, husbands, their humdrum existence blessedly lacking the tension of her own. In October 1937 and again in 1939, by which time she had been doing the job only intermittently for four years, she still joined the annual works outing, setting off in high spirits with forty or so employees crammed into a coach emblazoned with *HEINRICH HOFFMANN* in large letters on the side.

Hitler's presence at the Berghof was indicated by a large swastika flying over his residence and the appearance of his bodyguards in the local hostelries. In the late 1930s he entertained many official guests. They would arrive at Berchtesgaden station beside the River Ach.[6] Disproportionately large for such a tiny town, the station looks very much as it did in the late thirties. It still has the special platform for trains bringing the *Führer* and his guests, from which distinguished visitors would emerge through a triple-arched exit to a thrilling view of the little town nestling in the valley amid an encircling bowl of mountains. Hitler's 5-ton armoured Mercedes would be waiting with a fleet of others to escort them up to Obersalzberg, past the first security post beside the burbling Ach where guards presented a knife-sharp *Hitlergruss*, or Hitler salute, at the convoy's approach.

Eva's boredom would have been alleviated if she'd been allowed some part in these visits. She could have stayed in the background and watched – she wouldn't have expected more – and it's hard to see why Hitler didn't let her. She would never have pushed herself forward or trespassed on Magda Goebbels' territory as official hostess. Perhaps Hitler feared – and perhaps he was right – that word of Eva's role in his life had reached the ears of his celebrated visitors via their ambassadors in Berlin, their security services, or plain gossip, and feared she might somehow embarrass him. At any rate 'Eva Braun (secretary)', as she was still listed in the Obersalzberg personnel directories, was forbidden to attend these functions and had to stay closeted in her rooms, bored and resentful, leaning out of the window to smoke, coming and going by the servants' entrance at the back lest anyone should see her. Herbert Döring remembers: 'Everybody else was left to roam freely, only Eva Braun had to stay in her room, which

6. For readers interested to see more of the town there is a good selection of photographs, including one of Berchtesgaden station and many others from the thirties of Berchtesgaden and the whole Obersalzberg complex, at www.third reichruins.com/bgaden.htm

of course annoyed her. She then became angry, moody, truculent, she started complaining. And rightly so.'[7] Henriette von Schirach also commented on Eva's moodiness. 'She found her life as the invisible mistress depressing. She was often bad-tempered and ill because Hitler no longer took much notice of her. She knew that the adulation of the crowds was more precious to him than her loving words and that his real beloved would always be power. She just sat and waited, while her life slipped by.'[8] She was never part of Hitler's public and political life and there were times when affairs of state became so pressing that, as Henriette observed, he took no notice of her. But for her, he *was* her life.

No one had taken *Paris Soir* very seriously in September 1936 when it broke the story of Eva's relationship with the *Führer* and the chatter and speculation soon passed. In those days the private lives of those in authority were regarded as their own business, both in Germany – thanks to Goebbels' iron control of the media – and in Britain. Hitler's Propaganda Ministry made sure that rumours about Eva were ridiculed and quashed. The same was true of the affair between the Prince of Wales and the twice-divorced Wallis Simpson, a scandal about which the British press maintained a prim, self-imposed reticence. (The French and American newspapers were less discreet. They lapped it up.) When George V died on 20 January 1936 the Prince came to the throne as Edward VIII. Shortly after the Hitler/Braun affair was leaked, Lord Beaverbrook, the proprietor of Express Newspapers, received a summons to Buckingham Palace. The new King asked him – and a royal request was a command – to ensure that the British press remained silent about his relationship with Mrs Simpson. It did.

Of all the *Führer*'s visitors, the Duchess of Windsor was the person Eva most wanted to meet. She had followed the romance with interest. The foreign press had published stories and pictures showing the Prince of Wales holidaying with Mrs Simpson in the South of France, he with furrowed brow, she as sleek as a Siamese cat. She looked as though she had swallowed the cream and so she had. Eleven months after his accession the little King abdicated and in June 1937, the moment her divorce was finalised, the ex-King, now the Duke of

---

7. Herbert Döring interview for *Adolf and Eva*, 3BMTV, roll 20.26.
8. Henriette von Schirach, *Frauen um Hitler* (Munich: Herbig, 1983), p. 232.

Windsor, became the third husband of Mrs Simpson, née Bessie Wallis Warfield of Baltimore.

Five months later the pair made a 'state' visit to Germany, prompted by Wallis's Nazi sympathies and the Duke's treacherous desire to retrieve the throne – this time with 'the support of the woman I love'. Eva longed to meet the new Duchess, curious to know what skilful manipulation had persuaded the King to the altar, in case it worked with Hitler. The *Führer*'s motive for meeting the former King, after a war that he never doubted Germany would win, was to install him as a puppet sovereign to win over the annexed British people. This dovetailed with the Duke's motive: to test the water for a possible return. Like all men who have once been flattered and then fallen from grace, he could never believe that he had been fawned upon because of his position, not because *he* was such an admirable fellow.

The climax to the Windsors' two-day visit was an afternoon in Obersalzberg on 23 October 1937. They took tea with Hitler, Magda Goebbels acting as hostess. The Germans made a gratifying fuss, the Duchess was treated like royalty – a status she was pointedly denied by the new King and Queen – but Eva, perhaps the one person who would have taken her seriously, was confined to her rooms and left to sulk. The visit ended with hand-kissing and whiplash salutes before they were escorted down the grand staircase by the *Führer*. Eva hadn't even glimpsed them.

In public, Hitler showed geniality and friendship towards all his foreign visitors – statesmen, ambassadors and minor European royals. From Anthony Eden, British Foreign Secretary, to Zakaria Faiz Muhammad Khan, Afghan Foreign Minister, the *Führer* was the magnet that drew them to Berlin or Berchtesgaden, hoping to ingratiate themselves and protect their countries or their thrones. The political reality behind the scenes was very different.

Eva was allowed to attend the September 1937 Nuremberg Rally (anonymously, it goes without saying) and once again Unity Mitford was there, too. A photograph shows Unity frowning, Anni Brandt sitting tactfully between her and Eva – who is smiling – and Erna Hoffmann. Four pretty women in a row, rising to their feet with the rest of the crowd, waving enthusiastically – nothing special about that. Nobody singled them out amid the orchestrated mass emotion. Did Eva *listen* to the speeches and grasp what they signified or was she more bothered by the presence of Unity than by the future genocide *der Führer*'s speech hinted at? Or none of these: just the girlfriend at a football match, proudly watching her man score?

Two weeks after the Windsors' visit, on 5 November 1937, at a crucial meeting with his foreign minister von Neurath and top military staff, Hitler outlined the Hossbach Protocol for the first time: an agreement to wage war if necessary, to colonise new territories that would provide living space – *Lebensraum* – for the Germans. The first casualties would be Austria and Czechoslovakia. His plans marched inexorably forward while the rest of Europe continued nervously to give him the benefit of the doubt. They had little choice: Hitler could not be deterred, contained or demolished. He scorned the idea of a negotiated compromise and would settle for nothing short of world domination – not that he had spelled *that* out to his distinguished foreign visitors.

In spring and summer the wide, flagged terrace of the Berghof was the hub and focus of all activity. Perhaps one in seven of Eva's thousands of photographs was taken here, showing her friends lounging on padded, reclining chairs, perching on the balustrade, playing with small children or with Eva's dogs. The terrace was her reception room, the mountain panorama her wallpaper. Despite all this space and beauty, she continued to be bored and inwardly dissatisfied. Hitler indulged her every whim, on condition she observed strict anonymity. She could have whatever she wanted, as long as she agreed to keep her existence secret and wore a cloak of invisibility over her fabulous clothes and perfect body. She was anonymous, a non-person. Eva Braun had given her life to Hitler and he had lost it.

Between 1932 and 1940 her unforced lightness and laughter slipped away and, although she still smiled for the camera, the smiles became artificial. The change must have seemed baffling to observers – she'd attained her longed-for role as the *Führer*'s mistress; what possible reason had she to be unhappy? The Berghof was a heavenly setting and she lived in luxury, yet her former joyfulness had gone. To divert herself, and because being attractive for Hitler was her job, she set out to create a new image. The *Führer* didn't like change and would have preferred to see her in starched dirndl dresses without any make-up. Eva thought differently. Denied her own identity, she could at least dress the doll. In 1935 she tried having her hair bobbed and curled and dyed ash blonde but it didn't suit her. She looked cheap, like an aspiring starlet. She learned from this and never tried anything so drastic again. She continued to vary its length and style, reverting eventually to her own natural mid-brown waves.

In the late 1920s and right up to the mid-1930s, my mother's hair was cropped short, the look adopted by post-war English 'flappers', though by 1930 it wasn't fashionable any longer. Ditha's hair was thick and it refused to form a neat cap round her head, in the manner of Louise Brooks (whom she may also have hoped to resemble) but sprang from her skull in an exuberant mass. My mother would never have dyed her hair, partly because she would have thought it vulgar but mainly because she simply didn't care enough about her appearance to go to so much trouble. Later she let it grow longer, fastening it off her forehead with a large satin bow crowning the top of her head – the very same look that Eva also adopted, briefly. The fashion idiom of the era that appears to perfection in Eva appears as a faint echo in pictures of my mother, too. They both preferred short skirts that showed off their legs and fluttery, flirty summer dresses, though by the mid-thirties Eva had dozens and my mother no more than two or three, which continued to appear in family photographs well into the war years.

By 1938 Eva Braun had become slimmer and more sophisticated, elegantly dressed with beautifully manicured hands. Young Traudl Humps (her maiden name) had first visited the Berghof in March 1943, a few months after joining his secretariat. Eva's role in Hitler's life came as a complete surprise to her. 'Hans Junge[9] explained to me that she (i.e. Eva Braun) was the hostess/mistress at the Berghof, tacitly accepted and recognised as such by guests there.' Traudl was naively impressed by Eva's sophistication:

She was very well-dressed and smartly turned out. Her well-groomed hair was tinted blonde and her attractive face was fairly heavily made up, but all in good taste. She wasn't tall but had an outstandingly good, well-developed figure and carried herself well. She understood perfectly what clothes suited her. She was never overdressed but always in good taste although she wore expensive jewellery.[10]

9. Hitler's long-time orderly, who married Traudl a year later and was killed within a few weeks, too soon to beget a little Aryan for posterity.
10. Here Traudl's memory played her false. Eva never had any expensive jewellery.

Eva worried about gaining weight and ate next to nothing, until Hitler complained that she was all skin and bone: 'I can't understand why it's supposed to be attractive for women to be as skinny as boys. We like women precisely because of their different shapes. It used not to be this way.'[11] Her thinness, like the constant smoking, drained her skin of its healthy outdoor glow and soft curves. Traudl Junge recalled that when she was seated opposite Hitler, 'He watched me help myself and said, "You don't eat nearly enough my child. You're far too thin as it is!"' She in turn watched Eva and observed how carefully she ate:

> Nothing could have persuaded her to try the *Führer*'s diet, although she herself claimed to have a weak stomach, ate very little, just light, easily digestible meals and very little fat and sometimes took medicine for her stomach after meals. As I got to know her better, however, I came to the conclusion that this restraint was mainly for the sake of her slim figure. She hated fat women and was proud of being slender and petite. Even so, the *Führer* used to tease her: 'When I first met you you were nicely plump and now you're practically skinny. Women always say they want to be attractive for their man and then they do all they can to rebel against his preference. They pretend they'd make any sacrifice to please him while at the same time following fashion slavishly . . . Women just want to be the envy of their friends.'
>
> Eva protested vigorously, while at the same time conceding that not for the world would she want to be any fatter.[12]

In fact they were both obsessed by what they ate. The *Führer* was a fastidious vegetarian who lived mainly on fresh vegetables, mashed potatoes and pasta, ending each meal with stewed fruit and mineral water. Since Geli's death in 1931 he had touched no meat or chicken or fish; not even eggs. He claimed to be extremely fussy, although one of his favourite dishes was mashed potato laced with linseed oil and topped with grilled cheese. Since his teens he had drunk no alcohol, apart from a very occasional glass of watered-down sweet white wine.

11. Junge, *Bis Zur Letzten Stunde*, pp. 83–4 (translated by the author).
12. Adapted and condensed from Traudl Junge, *Bis Zur Letzen Stunde* (translated by the author).

He employed dieticians[13] who were forever inventing new dishes in an effort to appeal to his querulous appetite. His favourite cook was the last, Constanze Manziarly, who joined Hitler's staff in 1944, aged twenty-four. Originally from Innsbruck, she had been trained in his favourite cuisine – Viennese/Bavarian – and made great efforts to accommodate his food fads and serve him nourishing and varied meals. She spent hours in the kitchen concocting mouth-watering desserts with immense care. Hitler greatly appreciated Fräulein Manziarly and although she was plain, humble and self-effacing this didn't stop Eva making a fuss on the frequent occasions when Hitler lunched alone with her. He constantly complained of suffering from a delicate stomach but this was not because of the food he ate but because of the number of dubious remedies he took, all prescribed by his favourite medical man.

Dr Theodore Morell, the *Führer's* personal physician after 1936, was essentially a charlatan[14] who administered all sorts of eccentric concoctions including several phials of vitamins daily.[15] Morell had initially gained his patient's confidence by curing his eczema, though not the meteorism (gas in the abdomen, which often leads to excessive farting) brought on, no doubt, by all those vegetables.[16] This he treated with Dr Koster's Antigas pills, which Hitler took after each meal for years. The fact that so many had to be taken for so long should have alerted Hitler to the fact that they were not doing him much good, but he always made decisions on the basis of instinct rather than common sense and he trusted this dubious and incompetent doctor blindly. Not until 1944 did an independent physician, the ENT specialist Dr Giesing – who tried them on himself and moni-

13. At the Berghof, Prof. Zabel and two his trained assistants, Fräulein Manziarly and Marlene von Exner, the latter whom Hitler reluctantly dismissed when he discovered that she had Jewish blood.
14. Although he had qualified as a doctor at Munich University in 1912 and held several orthodox medical posts, specialising in electrotherapy (ECT), diseases of the urinary system and venereal diseases.
15. I am grateful to Lady Williams for this detail (in conversation, January 2004).
16. Martin Bormann believed that the patent medicines Morell provided for Hitler's stomach problems were slowly poisoning the *Führer*. His doctor was dosing Hitler with his own make of 'anti-gas' pills (to combat Hitler's flatulence), sometimes giving him up to sixteen pills a day, pills which contained strychnine, moreover, and there is strong evidence to believe that Hitler was actually succumbing to persistent strychnine poisoning. (From a review of the film *The Downfall* (*Der Untergang*) by William Boyd in the *Guardian*, 19 March 2005.)

tored the consequences – discover that Hitler's agonising cramps were caused rather than alleviated by these pills, which contained almost the maximum dose of strychnine. The *Führer* was suffering from strychnine poisoning![17] When this was intimated Hitler refused to believe it, dismissed Giesing and continued to place his trust in the dangerously incompetent Morell. Eva Braun hated and mistrusted him and tried to replace him with her own nominee, the more reliable Dr Brandt, but although Brandt became part of Hitler's medical staff in Berlin, he never usurped Morell. The *Führer* had far better qualified physicians and surgeons but Morell – this fat, self-indulgent quack, his grey hair as stiff as a brush – remained Hitler's favourite provider of dodgy remedies and dietary advice.

According to Dr Morell's testimony, Hitler swallowed twenty-eight different medications, some every day, others only when the need arose, including camomile enemas which, says Morell, Hitler administered himself.[18] (This is the only shred of evidence that supports the rumours of Hitler's anal/sexual obsession and it's hardly conclusive. It is much more likely that he preferred to perform the enema himself rather than expose his malformed genitals, even to his personal doctor.) However, Morell failed to connect 'brown urine' of which Hitler complained with a possible diagnosis of gallstones that would also have fitted with other symptoms; nor did he identify the tremor in Hitler's left arm and leg as being – in all probability – the onset of Parkinson's. His diagnoses were largely guesswork and the medication he prescribed bizarre.[19] But once Hitler had settled on something – a person, a place, a routine – he never budged from it.

Hitler stayed at the Berghof for three weeks in June/July and nearly all of August 1937, which delighted Eva, even if he did spend most of the time working on state business rather than with her. Speer told one of the people charged with interrogating him in August 1945,

> Whenever he [Hitler] had to make big decisions, he went to Obersalzberg. Here his life was completely private. Fräulein Braun,

17. David Irving (ed.), *The Secret Diaries of Hitler's Doctor* (London: Sidgwick & Jackson, 1983).
18. The interrogation of Dr Morell from the Musmanno Collection, pp. 12–14.
19. I am grateful to my former liver consultant, Prof. Neil McIntyre, for this interpretation of Morell's medical report on Hitler given before Judge Michael Musmanno.

who up to the last year or two never appeared in Berlin, kept him company; and the circle was otherwise also completely un-political . . . There were walks in the vicinity of Obersalzberg which included visits to small inns and which brought him, so he said, the inner calm and assurance which he needed for his world-shattering decisions. There was more intensive occupation with artistic things, with architecture and viewing numerous films. In view of his extraordinary intake of two films daily, many had to be shown two or three times.[20]

Eva had as little clue of what he did when closeted for hours with the Nazi bigwigs or military men as does a small child who waves bye-bye to its father every morning when he leaves for work.

Hitler's regular daily round at the Berghof hardly ever changed. For those forced to observe it with him it must have been unbearably repetitive and boring. Mornings were empty and silent because nothing could happen until Hitler woke, usually at around noon (except for Bormann, who would have been toiling away in his office since 7 a.m., planning and preparing Hitler's schedule, sorting and censoring his papers and deciding which visitors he should see). After midday, when Hitler rose, the traffic would start up, people came and went and the telephone rang constantly. It seems astonishing that the *Führer* was able to make colossal plans affecting the lives (and deaths) of millions of people in just a few hours of work a day, unaided by the modern paraphernalia of e-mail, fax machines and numerous auxiliary staff (Hitler's office was run by comparatively few people) but there is a simple reason: he was idle, and, being idle, let his associates use their own initiative as long as he was confident that they were following his general, usually unstated, requirements. He preferred his henchmen to read his mind and act according to their own interpretation, after which yet more junior figures would put specific orders into practice. This idleness (which combined oddly with the *Führer*'s manic vocal energy) was the source of Martin Bormann's power. He understood that Hitler liked to be bothered as little as possible, and took it upon himself to interpret and filter Hitler's wishes as well as his visitors. No

20. Intelligence Report No. KF/Min/3, number 19, part III, p. 19, on Adolf Hitler, taken from the examination of Albert Speer by Mr O. Hoeffding, Economic and Financial Branch FIAT (US) on 1 August 1945, from the Musmanno Collection, Duquesne University, Pittsburgh, PA.

one gained access without Bormann's say-so and many were excluded, thus shortening Hitler's working day considerably.

Lunch might be at two or even three o'clock and was signalled by the *Führer*'s arrival with Eva, after which their guests were formally summoned:

> The meal is announced by Heinz Linge to Eva Braun with the words '*Gnädiges Fräulein, the Führer will lead you all in to lunch.*' Hitler, who already knew whom he would escort to the table, offered his arm; Eva Braun took that of Bormann – this *place-ment* never changed – followed by the remaining couples who walked along a wide corridor, round the corner and into the dining room. Hitler took his place on the long side of the table opposite the window; on his left sat Eva Braun and then Bormann. Opposite them sat the guest of honour, or the highest-ranking guest and his wife. Lunch usually lasted about an hour, after which the *Führer* took his afternoon walk.[21]

The food, especially when there were important guests present (in which case Eva would not, of course, have been included) would be fresh from the Berghof's vegetable garden or model farm, beautifully cooked and accompanied by fine German wines. The meal would end at 3 p.m., occasionally later still, after which he and Eva would either retire discreetly to their rooms for 'an afternoon nap'; or he would lead a group of friends and a few officials from his private office along the neatly gravelled paths unobtrusively lined with security guards that ringed the Berghof, down through the pines to the Teehaus (tea house) for coffee or, after four o'clock, afternoon tea. Hitler called this twenty-minute amble 'exercising the dogs' and on most days it was the only time he moved a step out of doors.

The Teehaus was built on an outcrop called the Mooslahnerkopf on the edge of a small rocky plateau, a natural viewing point. When the weather was good, Hitler and Blondi would sit on a bench over-looking the view. When the company was private, Eva could sit or stand nearby or take informal photographs of him. Far below the River Ach flowed in a series of loops, wooden houses strewn like match-

---

21. Junge, *Until the Final Hour*, pp. 73–4.

boxes along its banks, and on the opposite side rose the crags of the Wachensberg range.

The Teehaus was hideous from the outside and pretentious inside. The large circular room had marble walls inset with gold. Huge windows took up half of one wall. A long, low table almost filled the room, around which were a score of bloated armchairs with larger, deeper ones for the *Führer*. He would settle down with Eva Braun on his left and the main guests on his other side while the Teehaus filled with the aroma of fresh coffee. Hitler drank apple or caraway tea and urged his guests to eat freshly baked *Apfeltorte* and other small cakes.[22] They would spend an hour or two sipping, nibbling and chatting inconsequentially. Hitler would gradually fall asleep in his armchair, after which those around him had to conduct their conversation in whispers. When he woke, pretending (as afternoon sleepers always do) that he had not been dozing but thinking with his eyes shut, he would be driven back up the hill to the Berghof in an armoured Mercedes or in his specially designed black Volkswagen cabriolet. Eva preferred to go off on her own with the dogs, since if she stayed with the group as they strolled along the path she would be relegated to the very back like a lowly secretary or a telephone operator, despite the fact that an hour or two earlier she might have been making love with Hitler. Amazingly, most people outside their immediate circle continued to be taken in by this charade and until the end of the war very few from the lower party echelons at the Berghof had any idea who she really was.

Dinner – which might be eaten at midnight or even later, depending on how long Hitler's evening meetings had lasted – was much like lunch; usually cold meat with salad, roast potatoes with stewed meat or eggs, noodles with tomato sauce and cheese. Influenced perhaps by the Gayelord Hauser[23] diet that was all the rage in the thirties, he liked freshly squeezed fruit and vegetable drinks made from the produce picked all year round from the Obersalzberg greenhouses. Hitler ate quite a lot, rather fast, and even on his spartan diet he was putting on weight. (However frugal his main meals, between them he continued to gorge on cream cakes.) After dinner there might be a film show, with films selected in advance by Hilter and Eva from a list of new

22. Ibid.
23. Gayelord Hauser, *Look Younger, Live Longer* (London: Faber & Faber, 1951) had an entire chapter entitled 'Drink Your Vegetables'.

releases from Germany, America and Britain. (The film censor was ignored.)

Eva's job was to persuade the *Führer* to take time off and make sure he relaxed and enjoyed himself in his favourite company amid chatter and laughter. On thoroughly informal evenings when he was in a good mood he liked to have his court jesters around him, notably Heinrich Hoffmann and Max Amann (who had been his company sergeant and later became his personal banker), friends from way back, who were allowed any licence.

> 'I'm very fond of Hoffmann,' Hitler once said; 'When Hoffmann is away for a few days, I miss him.'[24]
>
> A guest exclaimed sycophantically: 'Oh *mein Führer*, if Professor Hoffmann knew that he'd be delighted!', to which Hitler replied: 'But he knows it very well. He's a man who always makes fun of me. He's a "dead-pan" humorist and he never fails to find a victim. Three people who, when they're together, never stop laughing, are Hoffmann, Amann and Goebbels.'

It is a surprise to find Goebbels included among the *Führer*'s favourite humorists.

Hitler loved telling the story of an outing he'd taken with Hoffmann in the 1920s:

> Hoffmann had bought a new car, a Ford, and he insisted that I must try the car out with him. I said, 'No, Hoffmann, I'm not going for any drive with you.'
>
> But he kept pestering me so finally I gave in and we set out from Schellingstrasse. It was already evening, it had been raining too, and Hoffmann went tearing round the corners like an idiot, almost ran into the corners of a building, ignored street junctions.
>
> 'Hoffmann,' I said, 'watch out, you're driving like a madman! This is terribly dangerous.'
>
> 'No, no, my *Führer*, it just seems like that to you because you haven't had a drink. If you'd put back a good glass or so of red wine like me you wouldn't notice a thing.'
>
> At that I got out and I never went for a drive with him again.

24. *Hitler's Table Talk, 1941–1944*, 24/25 February 1942, p. 165.

Hitler knew nothing of 'Professor' Hoffmann's orgies in Vienna and Munich or how revolting other people found him. Eva Braun was the only person who dared to criticise an associate from the old days. She told him:

> 'Hoffmann's behaving himself disgracefully; you should do something about it. He's permanently drunk and has great feasts at a time when people don't have enough to eat.'
>
> Hitler defended his old friend, saying, 'Hoffmann was a jolly fellow in the past when he was still slim and supple and worked tirelessly with his awkward old camera. He's a thoroughly loyal companion.'[25]

All the same, he did call Hoffmann to order. The temporary improvement didn't last long and Hoffmann's gargantuan eating, drinking and orgies soon resumed.

Albert Speer found the stifling boredom and predictability of this routine oppressive and yet, because of Hitler's charisma, unavoidable:

> He liked having those close to him around for lunch, for walks, for tea and then for his late suppers, the film shows and then long talks around the fire – these went on until late in the night, two o'clock or even later. [. . .] Even though the late evening sessions were exhausting and as time went on, increasingly boring, we were young and strong and always intensely aware of the honour of being one of the elect.[26]

Nobody was allowed to excuse themselves or withdraw to another room for more informal gossip, cards or dancing. Not even the perpetually pregnant wives could retire to bed before he did. Hitler imagined the members of the inner circle were his friends but there could be no easy flow of argument or banter. The only form of discussion Hitler permitted was the monologue . . . *his* monologue. He may have been a great orator but his thinking was banal and he was a rotten conversationalist. In private his charisma deserted him and, far from holding guests spellbound, he often bored them to tears, especially the habitués who'd heard it all dozens of times before. His secretary Christa Schröder said:

25. Junge, *Until the Final Hour*, pp. 86–98.
26. Sereny, *Albert Speer: His Battle with Truth*, p. 117.

I still wonder why he thus sacrificed his nightly rest in order to expound his theories to an audience most of whom would have preferred to be sleeping. Eva Braun, who was also sometimes present, took less trouble to conceal her boredom. She would occasionally cast a disapproving glance at Hitler or loudly ask the time. Then Hitler would cut short his monologue, make his excuses and the company could break up.

Otherwise they had no choice but to listen, playing the part of an attentive audience granted the privilege of his perorations on art, classical history and world religions. On the latter subject here he is, verbatim, holding forth about the downfall of the ancient world. 'The ruling class,' Hitler intoned:

> had become rich and urbanised. From then on it had been inspired by the wish to ensure for its heirs a life free from care . . . The power of each family depended to some extent on the number of slaves it possessed. Thus there grew up the plebs, who were driven to multiplication, faced by a patrician class which was shrinking . . . The Roman patriciate found itself submerged in the resulting mass. It's the fall in the birth-rate that's at the bottom of everything.[27]

– and much more along these lines. Out of interest, I sent this sample to a friend who is a classical scholar. His robust response was, 'Hitler's explanation is complete bollocks but a perfect comment on the sort of thing a person like him would like to believe.'[28] Hugh Trevor-Roper, after studying two years of Hitler's monologues, concluded:

> Much of it reflects the coarseness and credulity, the dogmatism, the hysteria, the triviality of Hitler's mind . . . But it is the mirror of his hideous genius . . . Hitler never meditated upon God, the human mind and the *summum bonum*. No word he ever uttered so much as touched the human spirit. He did not know the meaning of humanity. He despised weakness and pity and hated moral strength.[29]

27. *Hitler's Table Talk 1941–1944*, night of 28/29 January 1942.
28. From an e-mail from Dr Peter Jones of Newcastle, June 2003.
29. Introduction to *Hitler's Table Talk, 1941–1944*, by Hugh Trevor-Roper, p. xv.

Eventually Hitler would tire or Eva would coax him upstairs and as soon as he'd gone (another of his secretaries reported):

> the living room would be filled with the smell of tobacco and there was no more tiredness to be seen. The atmosphere was one of cheerfulness and good humour – which Hitler would have very much enjoyed, had he been there. The strong coffee we'd been drinking all evening in order to stay awake would not let us go to sleep straightaway but gradually guests and colleagues took their leave until at last the Berghof lay in deep slumber.

Chapter Eighteen

1938–9 – The Last Summers of Peace

On 29 April 1938 a party of about eight people, including Gretl Braun and Eva's mother Fanny, as well as the two doctors' wives, Anni Brandt and Hanni Morell, flew in one of the *Führer*'s private planes (he had three) to the north Italian lakes to indulge in another holiday of shopping, sightseeing and sunbathing in Italy. Eva herself left the Berghof a week later, on 3 May, travelling in Hitler's special train on the way to a state visit to the country. This was less of a concession than it seems: he had with him a retinue of nearly five hundred diplomats, military and party leaders and journalists, among whom Eva went unremarked. He arrived first in Rome on 3 May, where the German leader *der Führer* was to hold talks with the Italian leader *Il Duce* – Mussolini – to coordinate detailed plans for the coming of Nazi/Fascist Europe. Much less important, as a formality he would pay a courtesy call on the sidelined Italian king.

The state visit began with a splendid banquet at the Quirinale, the seat of the House of Savoy. Hitler exchanged empty compliments with King Victor Emmanuel III and the royal family, who returned them coolly. Hitler and his immediate entourage (but not Eva) stayed overnight at the Quirinale; Eva and her party were lodged incognito in the Hotel Continentale. She was received in audience by the Pope and, as a good Catholic, was impressed and moved. When Mussolini finally realised who she was he presented her with a wildly expensive crocodile case containing every kind of feminine accessory and Italian toiletries, which must have pleased her very much – both for itself and because it was a tacit acknowledgement of her role in Hitler's life.[1] She and the *Führer* contrived to meet occasionally, briefly and in secret, and his itinerary shows that they visited the same places – Rome, Florence and Naples – at the same time. No one seems to have guessed she was anything other than an anonymous onlooker filming the parades and the power and the glory. On 5 May, in Naples, she was threatened with a knife by an attacker who appeared to have no idea of her identity.[2] She was unharmed, and went on to witness a naval review and attend a glittering celebratory performance of Verdi's *Aida* in the evening, though not in Hitler's royal box. Eva was described by the Italians as '*la bella bionda*' – the beautiful blonde – which greatly pleased her. The *Führer* and his entourage didn't stay in Italy long. He left Rome on 9 May after five days, having secured Mussolini's agreement not to intervene in any action against Czechoslovakia, and was back at the Berghof by the 10th.

Eva and her party stayed on in Italy. She tottered in high heels across ancient cobbled squares, climbed the steps to the Ponte Vecchio in Florence with her mother, the two of them dressed in the height of Bavarian chic in grey felt suits and feathered Tyrolean hats. Eva, the Imelda Marcos of the Third Reich, ordered yet more shoes made on her own last from her favourite shoemaker, although she already had dozens, if not scores, of pairs.

Salvatore Ferragamo wrote in his autobiography[3] 'Queen Soraya of Persia, Mae West, Pavlova, and Eva Braun all took size 6B.' [This, in English terms, is a size 4–4$\frac{1}{2}$, Continental 36$\frac{1}{2}$–37, since Ferragamo shoes are sized differently from those of other manufacturers.] He goes on:

> . . . Eva Braun would wear nothing but Ferragamo shoes, of all sorts and styles. She had good, normal feet and anything would fit her. She first came to my salon before the war, always accompanied by a collection of goose-stepping Nazi guards who stomped about the room heiling Hitler at every opportunity. [This must be an invention, given Hitler's insistence on her anonymity.] I knew nothing of her intimate life at this time; to me she was

1. Henriette von Schirach, *Frauen um Hitler* (Munich; Herbig, 1983), p. 230.
2. Another version of this story states that it was Frau Dreesen – proprietor of a hotel in Godesberg, acting as Eva's companion for this visit – who was attacked, receiving a slight wound in the shoulder.
3. Salvatore Ferragamo, *Shoemaker of Dreams*, information supplied to the author 20 October 2004 by Paola Tabellini of the Ferragamo Museum in Florence.

only a German actress and another customer. It was not until years later that I fully understood the true connection between the demands from the German High Command that I make her shoes, and her appearance in my salon.

The inveterate tourists went on to Pompeii where Eva filmed the ruins, the statues, the wall paintings. They climbed Mount Vesuvius, peered over the crater into the volcano and filmed themselves doing so. In Capri they stayed at the Hotel Belvedere, in Ravenna she filmed again, and again in Venice: the Bridge of Sighs this time. Eva filmed voraciously: cafés, coffees, pools, rocks and boats, sun hats, begging children – everything. 'Now you'll see the *real* Italy!' Hitler would say as his guests sat down to watch Eva's home movies being screened in the private cinema at Obersalzberg. For Eva, these amateur films signified more than merely 'This is me on my holidays'. They were a symbol of her ambition to work in the world of the cinema one day . . . if not as an actress, then maybe as a director. Hope, and her illusions, sustained her.

When Eva and her group returned to the Berghof two weeks later someone filmed Hitler welcoming them back. It can't have been Eva, since he is seen shaking her hand impassively. She is wearing a new, three-quarter-length mink coat, Gretl an opulent fur jacket. After he has gone back inside the ladies of the party perch on the balustrade to show off their new handmade Italian shoes, skittishly swinging their ankles. These were luxury goods that they could never have afforded for themselves. Hitler's generosity laid everyone's conscience to rest.

He was generous to all the people who were close to him. His will, drawn up on 2 May 1938, recognised Eva's primary position in his life. Significantly, she was the first person named in his list of personal bequests – 'a) to Fräulein Eva Braun of Munich, the sum of 1,000 marks pm ie 12,000 marks a year for life'.[4] It is not the sum (which was fairly but not excessively generous) but her place at the top of the list that is telling. He left the same amount to his sisters Angela (now living in Dresden) and Paula (still in Vienna) and to his older stepbrother Alois Hitler a lump sum of 60,000 marks. Personal bequests to staff are interesting for his choice of the people to whom he left money. His housekeeper in Munich, Anna Winter, was bequeathed

4. From his handwritten 1938 will reproduced in facsimile in Maser, *Hitler's Letters and Notes*, pp. 152–3.

150 marks per month for life. His 'old friend Julius Schaub' – for many years his personal adjutant – got a lump sum of 10,000 marks as well as 500 marks per month for the rest of his life. Karl Krause, his valet at the time, received a monthly pension of 100 marks for life. There is no mention of the old cronies who fancied themselves his special comrades – men like Hoffmann or Amann – let alone manipulators like Bormann or Himmler, deemed well able to look after themselves. Most telling of all, in his final bequest Hitler left 'the contents of the room in my Munich apartment once occupied by my niece Geli Raubal to be forwarded to my sister Angela (her mother)'. That room had harrowing significance for him and he was not going to let its contents be casually dispersed. It's most unlikely that Eva saw the will but had she survived him the reference to Geli would have stung, as Hitler must have known. She may have been first on the list but his final thought was reserved for Geli.

Yet as time went on, Eva became increasingly necessary to him. One indication is that he worried about her a good deal, nagging her to drive slowly and ski carefully, which went against the grain of her reckless nature and her passion for vigorous exercise. 'When she was out skiing and it got dark and she wasn't back he'd get very nervous,' Speer recalled in his memoirs. It seems that, despite himself, Hitler had become deeply involved with 'the girl in Munich' about whom he'd been so disparaging: involved socially, sexually and even emotionally. This may have come as a surprise to the man who aspired to be a remote, untouchable, god-like figure, aloof from the blandishments of one woman so as to receive the adulation of all.

Three years after Eva's arrival at the Berghof, its routine and habitués were well established. A formal group photograph taken that New Year's Eve 1938/9 shows a line-up of the people closest to Hitler, the people he trusted, with whom he could relax. They are glamorously dressed yet despite their evening wear, or perhaps because of it, they are smiling uneasily, not at all as if they're having a riotous time. Hitler, in the centre, is the glummest of all. Given the concern for hierarchy and precedence with which – for instance – annual school photographs are assembled, it's pretty certain that the *placement* in this New Year's Eve photograph is significant. The group included, in the front row: Heinrich Hoffmann, Gretl Braun, Dr Theo Morell, Ilse Braun, Phillip Bouhler,[5] Gerda Bormann, Hitler; Eva Braun, Martin Bormann, Anni Brandt. In

5. Head of the Chancellery for party matters.

the row behind, Christa Schröder, Gerda Daranowski, Albert and Margret Speer, Hanni Morell and several unknowns; and in the back row Max Wünsche, someone who could be Albert Bormann, brother of the more notorious Hermann, Jacob Werlin (managing director of Daimler-Benz), Frau Esser (wife of Hermann Esser, a friend from the early Munich days), Herr Theissen, Gen. Rudolf Schmundt (Hitler's *Wehrmacht* adjutant), Marion Schönmann (Eva's friend and Theissen's wife), Dr Karl Brandt, and Christian Weber (*Kreisleiter*, or group leader of Munich).

Several things can be deduced from their positioning. The fact that Dr Morell is in the front row and Dr Brandt right at the back is further proof that Hitler preferred his quack doctor to a well-qualified and entirely professional one. It shows that the two leading Nazis to whom Hitler felt closest were Bormann and Speer. (Where was Göring? He must have been furious at his omission from the *Führer's* New Year's Eve party.) It proves that his secretaries really were part of the family. Both the lovely Gerda Daranowski and Christa Schröder, doyenne of his private office, feature, though they would surely have preferred to be at home with their real families. Four of the women closest to Eva are included, both her sisters prominent in the front row. (It is most unusual to find Ilse at the Berghof.) Neither of her parents was there, perhaps because she had spent the previous Christmas at home in Munich with them: another indication of the easing of family tensions. Marion Schönmann, now Frau Theissen, was there but not Herta Schneider, perhaps because she had an eight-month-old baby at home. Another friend, Sophie – known as 'Charly' – Stork manages a radiant smile amid the stolid faces in the back row. Above all, *Eva* takes precedence, placed firmly next to Hitler. Given the jockeying for position that went on, this was no small achievement. Her occupation of 'the Berg', after just over two years, was complete.

1938 was the year when the Nazis' steady progress towards European domination became unmistakably menacing. Hitler's plans were maturing and preparations for the annexation of Austria were followed within five months by the occupation of Czechoslovakia. Stamp, stamp. On 12 February Schuschnigg, the Austrian leader, visited Hitler at Berchtesgaden and was browbeaten into accepting, among other concessions, foreign dictation of his cabinet. It made no difference . . . on 11 March Schuschnigg was forced to resign anyway. Stamp, stamp, stamp. On 13 March 1938 the *Anschluss* (annexation) of Austria was announced. Hitler arrived in Vienna on the 14th, to be greeted with jubilant hysteria by huge crowds. Eva was there to witness his triumph. They spent the night together at the Hotel Imperial (not in the same room, though she was just across the corridor from him) chaperoned by her mother and Herta, and her presence was somehow kept secret from everyone including his advisers. Even so, the very fact that he wanted her there with him at this significant moment was a telling acknowledgement of her status.

By mid-September 1938 Neville Chamberlain was attempting to negotiate with Hitler. They met in Munich and posed for photographs in the drawing room in Hitler's Prinzregentenplatz flat, Chamberlain sitting on a long sofa covered in red velvet. When Eva saw the photographs she said archly to a friend: 'If only Chamberlain knew the history of that sofa . . .' Was she saying that she had surrendered her virginity to him there?

The two statesmen had several meetings and the gullible British Prime Minister was reassured when Hitler declared that 'the Czech problem was the last territorial demand he had to make in Europe'. Despite the *Führer*'s unequivocal statement that he would not stop until the Sudeten Germans were part of greater Germany, Chamberlain went back for a last meeting on 29 September 1938 and returned triumphant, certain that he had secured peace. He quoted Shakespeare. 'Out of this nettle, danger, we have plucked this flower, safety.' Hitler had signed the famous piece of paper (remarking in an aside to Ribbentrop, 'Ach, don't take it all so seriously. That piece of paper is of no further significance whatsoever.')[6] The *Guardian* reported the scene in Downing Street on Saturday 1 October 1938: 'Mr Chamberlain went to a first-floor window and leaned forward happily smiling on the people.

' "My good friends," he said – it took some time to still the clamour so that he might be heard – "this is the second time in our history that there has come back from Germany 'peace with honour'. I believe it is peace for our time." ' Not quite, although the Munich conference probably delayed the war by a year. More time to rearm, to train, to drill, to turn the teenage boys of *Hitler Jugend* into superbly fit young soldiers. *Links, links, links, links!*

The plans Hitler had laid were ripening to terrible fruit. By the

6. David Irving, *The War Path: Hitler's Germany 1933–1939* (New York, 1978), p. 151.

winter of 1938 he was in Prague. A photograph in Eva's album, probably taken by her and captioned in her handwriting 'Der Führer in Prag Winter 38', shows him surveying the city through a window. The forward march continued . . . the Nazi Party, invasive as a swarm of locusts, darkened Germany. The atrocities of the Holocaust and the Black Events were about to begin in deadly earnest.[7]

Christmas 1938 was not spent with Hitler at the Berghof: he was celebrating with a crowd of his favourite people, the old party workers, at Munich's Löwenbräukeller. For the first time, Eva entertained her parents and sisters in her own home, at the little house on Wasserburgerstrasse. It was victory of a sort. But although she must have known Hitler was in his apartment nearby, inviting him to join them for his first real family Christmas since childhood would have been a step too far for Fritz Braun.

In the summer of 1939 Eva escaped the growing international tension and Hitler's endless meetings with his generals from the *Wehrmacht* by going to Portofino, the beautiful little port on the north-western coast of Italy near Genoa. Its sparkling sea and golden climate offered a glorious contrast to the pressures of life on the Berg and there were many good hotels, restaurants, cafés and swimming pools. The usual holiday pictures in her albums show the usual images – Fanny, Herta and Gretl fooling about in rowing boats, diving off rocks, being pestered for coins by skinny urchins. (It seems odd that Herta was prepared to leave her children behind, when her second daughter, Brigitte, was only five months old. An invitation from Eva clearly had the force of a command.) In mid-August, having accepted an official invitation to the 1939 Film Festival, Eva went on to Venice – only to be summarily ordered to return home at once. She almost certainly had little comprehension of the significance of events but she knew that a storm was looming, dark and heavy. She cannot have dreamed how soon it would break over her head, and those of millions of hapless, helpless Europeans.

---

7. The first victims of the extermination programme were the mentally ill. By the autumn of 1941, ninety thousand had died and, while the extermination programme was formally ended then, in reality it continued to the war's end. The sick, the old and shell-shocked servicemen from the First World War were killed, often gassed by those who would go on to develop their 'skills' in Auschwitz and other death camps.

PART 5

THE WAR YEARS

Chapter Nineteen

1939 – War Approaches

Although she couldn't have known it at the time, Eva's best and happiest years with Hitler were 1938, 1939 and the first months of 1940. He spent much of his time at the Berghof where she was now fully accepted as his mistress, even by his most critical colleagues and friends. Her jealousy and insecurity had calmed down and she was no longer tortured by the fear that another woman might entice him away from her. Unity Mitford seemed to have been routed, although she still hung around in Berlin looking goofy and infatuated. The *Führer* enjoyed the company of pretty actresses and even occasionally summoned one for tea to the Reichs Chancellery, where he might stroke a willing little paw, but these encounters continued to be short-lived and platonic. Eva had resigned herself to the role Magda Goebbels played in his life, recognising that she herself would always lack that crystal poise, worldly sophistication and well-stocked mind. She also knew that, while the *Führer* might need a consort on formal occasions to impress his guests, intellectual qualities weren't what he looked for in the bedroom. When they were alone together she was a playful young woman with a taut and sexy body who knew that her first duty was to give him *pleasure*. Uncle Alois theorised: 'Hitler perhaps treated Eva as a little gift offered him by fate, a small private appendage to his turbulent political life.'[1] Over the last six years she had learned how to amuse him and look after him in the ways he liked – playing with him and the dogs, fussing about his diet, encouraging him to go for walks, making sure her Munich friends kept him in touch with the

1. Winbauer, *Eva Braun's Familiengeschichte*, p. 21 (translated by Christiane Gehron).

busy, humming city that had launched his career. Sometimes he would grumble that he could no longer move about like an ordinary citizen: 'If only you knew how much I'd like to be able to stroll down the streets by myself, unrecognised! I'd like to be able to go into department stores and buy my Christmas presents myself, or sit in a café and watch the people. But I can't.'[2] Eva would console him, saying it was because the German people loved him so.

By now their long intimacy and the *Führer*'s trust in her love and her perfect discretion had led – not to equality; that would never be possible – but to deep harmony between them.

Eva never complained to Hitler about being depressed or lonely. She once said to her mother, 'He has such great cares; how could I bother him with my little ones?' She acted silly and light-hearted because that was the best way to take the pressure off him: by teasing, letting him indulge his sentimental side, laughing at his jokes and listening to the old tales – by now almost pure fiction – of his childhood and youth: how solitary he'd been, how misunderstood, yet how cultured and well-read in the days when he had worked out his brilliant theories of how the world turned and the big ideas that mattered. Their true relationship will always be a mystery but at the heart of it may be this: only with Eva could he step down from his pedestal and allow himself to be dependent, childlike, attached. What did it matter if his vicious circle referred to her as '*die blöde Kuh*' — the silly cow? The *Führer* had quite enough clever people around him conspiring to reshape the world and its future. It was precisely her apparent 'silliness' that drew him to her. Albert Speer understood that Eva's demanding job – how demanding went unrecognised by everyone else – was to supply the relaxation that even dictators sometimes need.[3] 'She was really a very nice girl, young, shy and modest. I liked her right away and later we became good friends. She could use a friend.[4] She could indeed.

It is not my purpose to soften Hitler's image, let alone to find lovable traits or redeeming features. If such existed, they made up only a fraction of the man – but it was the part Eva saw. I don't doubt that he knew of the bloodthirsty events he was about to unleash. They lay at

2. Junge, *Until the Final Hour*.
3. Sereny, *Albert Speer: His Battle with Truth*, p. 193.
4. Ibid., p. 136.

the very heart of his politics and originated from his warped nature and his half-digested, half-scientific, half-mystic, wholly evil ideology. He initiated everything that happened during the twelve short but unbearably long years of his leadership, when he led the German people by the nose into moral chaos. But gullible women can love murderers, torturers, abusers and rapists – *and* religious fundamentalists *and* corrupt politicians – and Eva loved Hitler. In normal times she would have been simply a kind, generous, considerate, loyal woman. The fact that she shared Hitler's bed does not imply that she was well-informed about the hell and damnation enacted in the name of the *Führer* and the Third Reich. This is not to praise or condone her but to state a fact. The facts about the Holocaust must also be stated, however briefly, to set the intolerable scale of his wickedness against the cosy domesticity of the Berghof.

Hitler's anti-Semitic views had been firmly in place as early as 1920 and possibly even earlier, during the years in Vienna. Over dinner in the Berghof's stolid dining room he would reiterate them for the benefit of his like-minded Rottweilers. (No women can have been present on those occasions, *certainly* not Eva, or he would never have been so explicit.): 'I feel I am like Robert Koch[5] in politics. He discovered the bacillus and thereby ushered medical science on to new paths. I discovered the Jew as the bacillus and the fermenting agent of all social decomposition.' Josef Goebbels was of like mind: 'The procedure [for murdering the Jews *en masse*] is a pretty barbaric one and not to be described here more definitely. *Not much will remain of the Jews*. On the whole it can be said that about 60 per cent of them will have to be liquidated whereas only about 40 per cent can be used for forced labour.[6] The comparisons with disease and death, maggots, rats and vampires disseminated by Goebbels' propaganda machine had

---

5. Robert Koch (1843–1910) set out to prove scientifically that the anthrax bacillus was the cause of disease and did further important work on the study of diseases caused by bacterial infections of wounds, publishing his results in 1878. He provided a practical and scientific basis for the control of these infections. Koch discovered the tubercle bacillus and also the vibrio that causes cholera. On the basis of his knowledge of the biology and mode of distribution of the cholera vibrio, Koch formulated rules for the control of epidemics of cholera that formed the basis of the methods of control still used today. (Taken from *Nobel Lectures, Physiology or Medicine 1901–1921*, Amsterdam: Elsevier Publishing Company, 1967.)
6. On 27 March 1942.

led to the widespread perception of Jews as dark vermin polluting the German race. The first stages in the persecution of the 'racially unsound' or just plain different aroused little public outcry, though many people objected in private – some passionately, others with mild unease – and many Catholic priests and a few Protestants preached sermons castigating the Nazis.

Kristallnacht was not the first act of brutality perpetrated by the state against the Jews; indeed, it was the end of a period of hot street violence, to be followed by cold bureaucratic violence.[7] One young Jewess from Berlin recorded in her diary for 28 June 1938:

> New scenes of ferocity and misery are carved into my mind. [. . .] The renowned old linen house of Grunefeld was the first place we saw surrounded by a howling mob of SA men. They were 'working on' an old gentleman who insisted on entering the shop. We found the same thing going on everywhere, varying only in violence and ignominy. The entire Kurfürstendamm was plastered with scrawls and cartoons. 'Jew' was smeared all over the doors, there were revolting and bloodthirsty pictures of Jews beheaded, hanged, tortured and maimed, accompanied by obscene inscriptions. Windows were smashed and loot from the miserable little shops was strewn over the pavement and floating in the gutter.[8]

This was no organised outbreak; just another June day in Berlin, Jew-baiters having a bit of fun. *Kristallnacht*, however, was the first nationwide incident to take place openly, publicly, before the eyes of German citizens. It began on the night of 9/10 November 1938, and although the word *Kristallnacht* is often translated as 'the Night of Broken Glass', suggesting some smashing of Jewish-owned shop windows and a lot of looting, it was a hundred times worse than that. It loosed Hitler's street-fighting underdogs, now transformed into top dogs – and how hoarsely and menacingly they bristled and snarled.

For the last ten years the louts and hooligans of the Nazi Party and the SS had been panting for 'legitimate' outlets for brutality. Their

7. Burleigh, *The Third Reich: A New History*, pp. 322–8.
8. Bella Fromm, *Blood and Banquets: A Berlin Social Diary* (London, 1943), p. 236.

past actions would come to be seen as amateur infringements on the scale of humane behaviour. They were small fiends, underlings in a diabolic hierarchy that aspired to large, not yet imaginable acts of wickedness. *Kristallnacht* freed every Nazi – great Satan, minor devil and paltry collaborator – to do their worst. Orders passed down from Hitler and his fawning lieutenant, Himmler, were eagerly obeyed along a chain of command that might end with a local chief of police inter-preting his instructions from on high much as he pleased, barking commands to men straining at the leash. Some were simply ordered to kill Jewish men 'with as little noise as possible', others to destroy local synagogues. Throughout Germany they wreaked havoc. A later report from an SS group noted, 'All troops and leaders took great delight in the action. Such orders should be given more often.'[9] Bark, bark, bark. The pogrom – for that is what it was – lasted two, in some places three, days and nights. Scores of thousands of Jews were hounded, their homes and premises smashed, their possessions looted. Entire families were terrified, beaten, imprisoned and in some cases killed. The impact of these events can be judged from the fact that, in Vienna alone, 680 Jews committed suicide during *Kristallnacht*.[10]

Many people in Britain were appalled by the treatment meted out to the Jews. Oliver Lyttelton, later Lord Chandos, happened to be in Frankfurt on 9 November 1938, the first night of *Kristallnacht*, and witnessed scenes 'which can never be effaced from my memory'. From that moment he felt an 'obsessional' hatred for anti-Semitism and, spurred by this, arranged for three Jewish friends to be smuggled out of Germany and safely housed in England. His new-found convictions were seldom shared by his peers, as Lyttelton discovered when he proposed Isaiah Berlin for membership of his club. Berlin was blackballed. Viscount Cranborne – 'Bobbety' – later Marquess of Salisbury, rebuffed Lewis Namier's attempts to ease entry to Britain for Europe's Jews. Harold Macmillan made snide jokes about them. The upper classes took it for granted that anti-Semitism was one of their prerogatives.[11]

After *Kristallnacht* no one in Germany, including women, had any excuse for complete ignorance. Until then people might, *just*, have

9. Burleigh, *The Third Reich; A New History*, p. 350.
10. Ibid., p. 531.
11. Based on a review by R. W. Johnson in *The London Review of Books*, 7 October 2004, of Simon Ball, *The Guardsmen: Harold Macmillan, Three Friends and the World They Made* (London: HarperCollins, 2004).

interpreted the Reich's increasingly anti-Semitic decrees as a democratic response to a widely held prejudice. But the swastikas scrawled across Jewish shops and the increasingly draconian rules controlling their move-ments, to say nothing of the brutality directed against them, were now a matter of public knowledge. Eva – or her parents – might have had Jewish friends who were leaving the country, in fear of what might happen next. Even she would have known that *something* was going on, although she knew better than to ask questions and neither she nor, at this stage, anyone else could have envisaged the culmination of these ugly scenes. But the tacit acceptance and in many cases active involvement, of many – though, it must be stressed, not all – 'ordinary' German people in an ascending spiral of prejudice, ostracism and cruelty dates from these nights. This, although few people guessed it at the time, was the moment when the methodical production line that set out to kill German, Austrian, Polish and other European Jews became unstoppable.[12]

The extent of the Nazis' genocide was devastating. Ultimately at least one-third of Europe's Jews[13] were murdered, much the same percentage of the population as fell victim to the Black Death in the fourteenth century. When Hitler came to power in 1933 there were an estimated 561,000 people of the Jewish faith in Germany, 0.76 per cent of the population,[14] overwhelmingly concentrated in two cities: Berlin and Frankfurt. Munich, state capital of Bavaria, had four thou-sand Jewish citizens. In 1933 forty thousand Jews left Germany in the biggest exodus until 1938. By May 1939 Germany's residual Jewish population – those who had not yet fled, mainly to Britain or America

12. Stanley Milgram, the American academic who devised and oversaw the famous experiment with New Haven students in 1961, in which they were ordered to inflict up to 450 volts of electricity upon hapless volunteers (65 per cent complied, not knowing that the 'volunteers' were in fact actors, so their pain was not real, though it looked it), wrote afterwards: 'The results suggest that human nature [. . .] cannot be counted on to insulate its citizens from brutality and inhumane treatment at the direction of malevolent authority. [. . .] I once wondered whether in all of the United States a vicious government could meet the personnel requirements of a national system of death camps, of the sort that were main-tained in Germany. I now think that the full complement could be recruited in New Haven.' Quoted by Jenny Diski reviewing Thomas Blass, *The Man Who Shocked the World: The Life and Legacy of Stanley Milgram* (London: Perseus Books, 2004), in *The London Review of Books*, 18 November 2004.
13. With one notable exception: no Bulgarian Jews were sent to death camps from Bulgaria itself, and of Finland's 2000, only seven died.
14. Kershaw, *Hitler, 1889–1936: Hubris*, p. 410.

– numbered 330,892[15], about half of whom lived in Berlin or Vienna. Even so, it was not until autumn 1941 that the scale of the policy to murder *all* Europe's Jews (or as many as was inhumanly possible) became clear to the relevant underlings.[16] It did not arise out of any specific order from Hitler – at any rate, none has been traced, though his desire to eliminate the Jews had long been obvious.[17] Whatever the chain of command that led from fevered racism to death on a vast scale, by the end of the war some two hundred thousand German Jews had been gassed in the extermination camps.[18] The statistics for the whole of Europe were *thirty times* as high. The slaughter, seen from the point of view of the Nazi senior hierarchy, was never sadistic. It was certainly systematic but that's different; that's efficiency.

In the summer of 1939 Hitler proposed the logical conclusion to the euthanasia programme, telling Bormann and others, '[He] regarded it as right that the worthless lives of seriously ill mental patients should be eradicated. This would result in savings in terms of hospitals, doctors and nursing staff.'[19] *Eradicated.* No ambiguity there. The savings in cost could be channelled towards healthy,

15. The German historian Hans P. Fischer, writing in 1995, estimated the Jews left in Germany in 1939 at 234,000 – but such estimates can never be exact. A difference of 100,000 human beings, however, suggests that many such statistics cannot be much more than well-informed guesswork.

16. As few as six months earlier mass genocide was still not thought of, the intention – however mad and impractical – being to ship all Jews to Madagascar.

17. 'Hitler had certainly legitimised and prodded the ongoing search for final solutions. His obsession with the Jewish question ensured that the Nazi commitment would not slacken . . . No leading Nazi could prosper who did not appear to take the Jewish question as seriously as Hitler did himself.' And later, 'The perpetrators sensed what was expected of them . . . the extermination camp was a horrific monument to the perpetrators' problem-solving abilities.' Extracted from Christopher Browning, *The Origins of the Final Solution: The Evolution of Nazi Jewish Policy 1939–42* (London: Arrow, 2005).

18. Close to 6 million Jews were killed by the Nazis, about half in ways other than in the gas chambers of the four death camps of the Aktion Reinhard (which administered Chelmno, Belsec, Sobibor and Treblinka, and existed to murder European Jews by gassing), and also at Majdanek and Auschwitz in occupied Poland. Some two hundred thousand were *German* Jews. Please see appendix A for the number thought to have perished in other European countries from their initial population of Jews by the end of the war. Significantly, Hitler was never able to touch native Bulgarian Jews, showing that it was *possible* for a determined nation to resist his demands.

19. Burleigh; *The Third Reich: A New History*, p. 390.

productive recipients. A 'cull' was needed to purge the sacred German *Volk* of debilitating genetic weakness. To hammer home the message, guided tours of institutions for the mentally or physically handicapped were organised (harking back to the Christmas Fair freak shows of Eva's childhood) at which the public was encouraged to peer and laugh at the lunatics. Tens of thousands were ushered past the wards and laboratories and given pseudo-scientific lectures stressing the worthlessness and incurability of the crazies.[20] That should convince the undecided. See? They're not really human at all. Best got rid of.

That October Hitler gave assent to the innocuously code-named Operation T4 which allowed doctors to 'grant' a 'mercy death', in reality murder, to patients considered incurable. About seventy thousand were killed over the next two years but the final total was much greater. Hitler was later forced to suspend T4[21] but doctors got round that by effectively starving their patients, leaving them unattended in filthy beds until they wasted away. Under the euthanasia programme at least a quarter of a million, possibly as many as three hundred thousand, mentally and physically handicapped people died. All this happened quietly, carried out by white-coated doctors in hospitals and laboratories, testing how much killing public opinion would tolerate – or bother to know about.

On 15 March 1939 Hitler's troops entered Czechoslovakia. The *Führer* spent the day travelling in his private train from Berlin to Prague, arriving incognito and spending the night in Hradcany, the ancestral castle of Bohemian kings. Next day in Prague he issued a proclamation in which one can hear the very cadences of his voice: ('**For a thousand years** . . . the provinces of *Bohemia*, and *Moravia* . . . **belonged** . . . to the *Lebensraum* . . . of the **German people** . . .'.) That word again. *Lebensraum*: living space, the justification for every aggressive move. On to Brno to review the troops; then Vienna and back to Berlin, stopping for a nostalgic few hours in Linz. At last the British bulldog growled. Chamberlain warned that Britain would not tolerate further territorial aggression. Hitler took no notice. His designs on Poland were already far advanced. The smell of war filled his nostrils,

20. Michael Burleigh, *Death and Deliverance: Euthanasia in Germany 1900–1945* (London: Pan Books, 2002), p. 47.
21. In August 1941.

the vision of *Adolf, Kaiser Europas* – Adolf, Emperor of Europe – dazzled his eyes.

Eva, waiting impatiently at the Berghof, caught only faint and distant echoes of these momentous developments. Hitler had forbidden her to read newspapers or listen to the news on German radio and she had few sources of information. Her main concern was whether the *Führer* would be home in time for Easter. Good Friday fell on 7 April and they'd been busy making decorations for the children: *Osterhasen* (Easter bunnies) and fluffy yellow chicks, so sweet, and all the traditional Easter eggs and cakes and chocolates. She didn't want him to miss the fun.

Hitler hardly ever took holidays away from the Berghof – 'I can't afford to travel and enjoy myself, so I take my holidays in the hours that I spend with my guests around the fire'[22] – though he had once taken a trip with the Goebbels family to a North Sea resort. An exception was the beginning of April 1939 when he managed a few days off to join the maiden voyage of a brand new KdF[23] cruise ship. These voyages, with their slogan 'Strength through Joy' – *Kraft durch Freude*, or *KdF* – were provided free for German workers and their families, to give them a healthy break from their daily jobs and weld them more securely to the Nazi Party. Nourishing food was served and good accommodation provided. A photograph shows the *Führer* sitting glumly by the ship's rail with a young blonde woman: Inge Ley, the wife of Robert Ley[24] after whom the ship was named. She was an actress and singer, a beautiful blonde and, like Magda Goebbels, an ardent follower of Hitler, personally as well as politically. Frau Ley was his platonic companion on this voyage. The photograph is a rarity since he hardly ever allowed himself to be caught on camera next to a married woman. (Hitler deeply disapproved of adultery, above all because it sundered the family, the basic unit of Nazi power.) The weather was cold, the sea spray wet, his routine disrupted. He cut short the holiday and disembarked at Hamburg. A couple of weeks later he was back in Berlin for his fiftieth birthday on 20 April, hurling speeches at ecstatic crowds.

22. Junge, *Until the Final Hour*, pp. 90–91.
23. *Kraft durch Freude*.
24. Robert Ley was a much-disliked, foul-tempered drunk who was in charge of the *Arbeitsfront*, or German Workers' Front. His wife's deep unhappiness impelled her into a passionate admiration for Hitler.

Hitler made up for his absences by indulging Eva in every luxury. In February 1939 she spent a week skiing in Kitzbühel, practical and stylish in a cropped white ski jacket. The *Führer* was back at the Berghof in early May for ten days, recorded by Eva with yet more pictures of groups enjoying tea on the terrace, idling in the spring sunshine. One – perhaps taken by Hoffmann – shows her in the Bavarian costume Hitler preferred to the chic outfits that she sometimes ordered from Paris. He asked no questions about the cost and Bormann would not have risked querying the bills. Hitler's favour was the most important element in his life and, after all, the *Führer* had plenty of money. *Mein Kampf* continued to sell hundreds of thousands of copies every year and he received handsome royalties. However frugal his personal lifestyle, Hitler was rich.

Eva was becoming used to luxury but it had begun to have an effect on her, or so Ilse claimed. 'Sometimes I did not recognise my sister any more. Eva was arrogant, tyrannical, and insensitive towards us [the Braun family]. Associating with great men makes a person egotistical, even cruel.'[25] In the past Ilse Braun had not been invited to the Berghof because she worked as receptionist for a Jewish doctor and Hitler regarded her as tainted by this association. Finally, in 1936, by which time her employer's patients had dwindled to a mere handful, she left her job. Only then did she become *persona grata* on the Berg. Ilse, with whom Eva was always at odds, claimed after the war that her sister had passed down her once-worn clothes and shoes with an air of lofty graciousness; but those two had always had a difficult relationship and Eva's passion for clothes might well have irritated the cool, judgemental Ilse, who fancied herself above such worldly trivia. If Eva was high and mighty towards her parents and sister – and Ilse is the only one to assert this – she may have been retaliating for their coldness and disapproval in the early years when she was isolated by her passion for Hitler. Then, when she needed their understanding and support, it was lacking. Now, dispensing largesse, she could be forgiven for doing so in a lordly manner.

Relations between the Berghof and the Braun parents (still in the flat in Hohenzollernplatz, where they'd lived for nearly twenty years) had improved. Both sides behaved with mutual respect, in their own

---

25. Heinz Linge quotes this, although it seems highly improbable that Ilse would have confided in him. Perhaps he overheard the family talking among themselves.

best interests. Hitler gave them the occasional gift – a watch for Fritz, perfume for Fanny – but nothing spectacular. When they came to stay in Obersalzberg he treated them with impeccable politeness. In the summer of 1939 Fritz told Alois Winbauer a revealing story:

He and Fanny had been invited for tea and Hitler was almost pathologically affable as he played the part of their assiduous host. Fritz decided to seize the opportunity to appeal on behalf of the ageing president of the *Bavarian Heimat– und Königsbund*, a retired general who had been ousted by the Nazis in the usual brutal way. When Fritz asked Hitler to reinstate the general, his expression froze and all he would say was that it was a matter, not for him, but for his aides. As Fritz said bitterly afterwards: 'And this man is our *Führer!*'

It was brave of him to make this appeal, especially now that he had joined the Nazi Party. Support for a breakaway patriotic group would have signalled dissent if not actual treachery. To Fritz, however, the family's willingness to accept the *Führer*'s hospitality was a sign of capitulation, even humiliation.

Fritz Braun's fiftieth birthday fell on 17 September 1939 and to mark the occasion he was photographed wearing Nazi uniform with a swastika armband, flanked demurely by his womenfolk.[26] The picture is captioned, '*Vati's 50 Geburtstag*' – 'Daddy's 50th birthday'. Despite the reconciliation with his daughters Fritz looks dour and embittered. Fanny is smiling as usual. Her appreciation of the good things of life, her warm, pleasure-loving nature, above all her deep affection for her girls, meant she was genuinely happy at the way things had turned out. Peace had been made between parents and their daughters despite the fact that, as they saw it, Eva continued to 'live in sin' with Hitler. The inducement of holidays abroad paid for by the *Führer* and visits to the

26. A photograph sent to me by Frau Weisker shows the three Braun sisters wearing the same dresses as in the birthday portrait while she, their cousin Gertraud, features in the top right-hand corner of the group. When she stayed with her cousins in Munich at Easter 1940 she said it was the first time she had seen them since she was a child. In that case it doesn't seem very likely that they would have included her in this special birthday group. On close scrutiny it also becomes clear that the angle of light on her face is quite different from theirs. She has evidently had the picture 'doctored' – her covering note calls it a 'Photomontage' – adding herself, as though to demonstrate how close she was to her cousins.

Berghof with its excellent food and drink eventually outweighed the moral imperatives of the Catholic Church. Fanny, always the more easy-going of the two, was able to see Eva and Gretl without friction and her husband occasionally succumbed to the temptation of comfort and treats far above anything that he, a technical college lecturer, could have afforded himself. Eva knew this represented a concession rather than full acceptance of her status but her mother may even have been proud of her daughter's relationship. 'It's quite something, after all, to be the favourite of *der Führer*,' Fanny once said.[27] She felt perfectly 'at home' on the Berg and dozens of pictures show her lolling on the grass or laughing in the centre of a family group, happy to be with her daughters.

In late June 1939 Eva took her mother and sister on a KdF cruise round the Norwegian fjords aboard the MS *Milwaukee*.[28] Eva, Fanny and Gretl blended anonymously with the other holidaymakers. The advantage of being denied public recognition by Hitler was that, in public, nobody recognised her.

Bormann, always on the lookout for an opportunity to ingratiate himself, 'gave' Hitler for his fiftieth birthday in April 1939, on behalf of the Nazi Party (whose members were not consulted), a stupendous retreat

27. Interview with Gertraud Weisker, March 2004.
28. Its sister ship, the *Wilhelm Gustloff*, served as a hospital ship during the war and was torpedoed on the night of 30 January 1945 with the loss of 9,343 lives, the heaviest shipping casualty in history. Those who drowned were chiefly women and children being transported to the safety of Norway under the auspices of the Red Cross. Antony Beevor adds, in the on-line addenda to *Berlin: The Downfall 1945*: 'Sinking of the *Wilhelm Gustloff* on 30 January 1945 by the Soviet submarine S-13, commanded by Aleksandr Marinesko. A recent account (*SOS Wilhelm Gustloff – Die grösste Schiffekatastrophe der Geschichte* by Heinz Schön) has put the total of passengers far higher than the official figure of 6,050 people on board, with 1,300 rescued. According to Schön, a survivor and dedicated chronicler of the disaster, there were 10,582 people on the ship, of whom 8,956 were refugees, and the toll reached 9,343 dead. Clearly the official figure is too low, but Schön's figures seem extremely high. Günter Grass, in his novel *Im Krebsgang* based on the sinking of the ship, appears to put the true figure closer to 9,000 passengers. In any case, the extra passengers mean that this was the greatest disaster in marine history, just ahead of the sinking of the hospital ship *Goya* in the same area on 16 April when only 165 were saved out of a total of over 7,000 refugees. It is evidence of the contempt heaped upon the Germans since World War Two that the memory of this catatrophe was almost completely submerged until Günter Grass's novel restored it to public consciousness.

perched at 1,834 metres on the very top of the Kehlstein mountain, later called Eagle's Nest by the invading Americans. Constructed from huge blocks of stone that had had to be hauled up the steep mountainside (eight workers died during the building operations), it was designed to look like a medieval fortress, providing a conference centre in a legendary setting for the *Führer* and his latter-day Teutonic Knights. On a clear day endless views unfold over the glittering Königssee and across the Austrian border towards Salzburg. Huge black birds circle (they look like ravens) and a buzzard windsurfs the blue air. Vastly expensive to build, at a time when every *Pfennig* was being ploughed into manufacturing arms, aircraft and guns, Bormann's plan misfired. Hitler suffered from a fear of heights and hated to be confined in small spaces. The fake medieval eyrie could only be approached through a 124-metre-long narrow tunnel leading to a brass-lined lift that shot upwards through solid rock for another 124 metres. He found this such a nerve-racking experience that he went up to the summit no more than six or eight times, either to show it to foreign dignitaries or perhaps, coaxed by Eva on a cloudless day, to vary his routine by having lunch in this unusually spectacular setting. She, on the other hand, loved basking in the sun in a reclining chair on the Kehlstein's long glassed-in terrace, with its glorious view of the birds at eye level and the forest-clad mountain slopes beyond, and often went up there to escape the hermetically sealed monotony of the Berghof.

Salvatore Paolini, a young waiter, was the only Italian member of staff at the Eagle's Nest. He recalls: 'It was a convivial atmosphere in the dining room. Hitler sat at the centre of the table with his back to the wall, so that he could look out at the view. Eva Braun used to come to lunch, too, but he never let her sit next to him.' (He may be mistaken here since Eva Braun nearly always sat beside him at informal meals.) He confirms that Hitler was teetotal and vegetarian. 'He did like sausages and ham, but on the whole he never ate meat, preferring potatoes and green vegetables. They were always very highly spiced because he had lost his sense of taste after a mustard gas attack in the First World War.' Hitler was 'not much of a drinker', Signor Paolini said. 'The wine waiter opened the bottles, always vintage wine, but he scarcely drank anything. We always had to make sure there were plenty of water jugs on the table. He never complained about the food. He always said "very good" to us as he left.'[29]

29. *The Times*, 9 June 2003.

In April 1939 Hitler offered to requisition a flat in Berlin for Unity Mitford.[30] *Kristallnacht* had driven many prosperous Jews from the city, and staff from his private office showed her round a short list of four comfortable apartments. A month later she made her choice: Flat 4 at 26 Agnesstrasse, which had a drawing room, bedroom and a little spare room. Carmencita Wrede first saw it in August and recalled:

> Behind her bed two big flags with swastikas crossed over and their ends folded down on the pillows like drapes. On her bedside table stood Hitler's photograph, with the eyes and lips coloured in. In the sitting room she had a writing table and in one of its drawers a revolver, a little silvered revolver, and she took it out and waved it around, saying, 'When I'm obliged to leave Germany I will kill myself.'[31]

The flat should not be seen as evidence that he and Unity had sexual relations though if Eva had known about it she would have jumped to that conclusion, given the circumstances of his purchase of her own house in Wasserburgerstrasse three years earlier. There is absolutely no reliable evidence to suggest that the *Führer* was unfaithful to Eva at any time during their relationship – not even his scandal-mongering Nazi associates alleged that he was – and, of all the eager candidates, the statuesque Miss Mitford was the least plausible, but Eva was not to know this.

Unity spent the weekend of 6/7 May 1939 at the Berghof, confronting Eva face to face. It was the first time the two women had been in each other's company since the Nuremberg Rally of 1936 and Hitler may have wanted to demonstrate that Eva was well and truly in possession. At any rate it was Unity's only visit, although she continued to hang around him in Berlin. It would be surprising if the *Führer* had been able to pay much attention to either of them since his plans for the invasion of Poland were far advanced and his wider ambitions – more *Lebensraum* for the sacred German *Volk* – were well underway. The rest of the world could no longer deny that he planned to incorporate the vulnerable countries to the east of Germany into the Third Reich. The hounds of hell were massing. On 23 July Mahatma Gandhi

30. Pryce-Jones, *Unity Mitford: A Quest*, p. 212.
31. Ibid., p. 229.

wrote Hitler a personal letter, begging him not to start another war in Europe. Too late. The *Führer* was convinced his mission was a sacred obligation that history was waiting for him to fulfil.

On 7 August, after a row over Polish customs officials at the free port of Danzig, he declared that his patience had run out and summoned Carl Burckhardt, League of Nations High Commissioner in Danzig, to Berchtesgaden. Pulling out all the stops, Hitler had him conveyed in one of his personal planes and his own private car to Obersalzberg. From there Burckhardt was driven up the steep mountain road to the Eagle's Nest. Hitler had chosen this setting for their meeting to remind him that he, the *Führer*, and not the League of Nations was monarch of all he surveyed – and a good deal more besides. They discussed the Polish question, Hitler managing to lay the blame on their stubbornness, intransigence, etc. . . . Now if the West would only trust him, a peaceful solution could surely be found? The message was duly passed to Britain and France who duly urged restraint on the hapless Poles.

Mussolini's son-in-law, Count Galeazzo Ciano, the Italian foreign minister, had talks with Hitler and his foreign minister Joachim von Ribbentrop (who had succeeded von Neurath in February 1938) at the Berghof on 12/13 August 1939. Ciano had come to Obersalzberg in the hope of convincing Hitler and Ribbentrop that Italy was not ready for war. Mussolini wanted the Fascist countries to try for an advantageous settlement with the West but Hitler was adamant: the merciless defeat of Poland could not be delayed. If Britain and France intervened, they too would be defeated. Ciano reported back, 'There is no longer anything that can be done. He has decided to strike, and strike he will.'[32] Eva had no inkling of all this but she found the glamorous Count Galeazzo Ciano, who was only thirty-six, most attractive. Through a net-curtained upper window she photographed him with Hitler, who sat on the windowsill of the conference room smiling up at her as she leaned out to catch a glimpse of the Count.[33]

Eva's frustration at being hidden away may have prompted her only recorded 'feminist' comment. Beside a picture of a young man striding ahead of four women, she wrote: '*Even when out for a stroll, talking to women is banned!*'[34] The ignorance that resulted from this protective

32. Kershaw, *Hitler, 1936–1945: Nemesis*, p. 204.
33. See Chapter 11, p. 173.
34. Her original caption, in semi-Bavarian dialect, reads: '*Selbst auf die Spaziergangen sind Besprechungen während die Damen meist hindernd sind!*'

attitude towards women meant that, throughout the summer of 1939, Eva and her girlfriends had little idea that war was imminent, although away from their womenfolk the husbands talked of nothing else. In the stifling summer days of July and August the weather was oppressive, the atmosphere at the Berghof unbearably tense, the *Führer* grim and moody.

Not until the last days – hours, almost – did Eva Braun realise that war was about to begin. It had been inevitable since 19 August 1939 when Stalin agreed a non-aggression pact with Germany, drawn up and signed by the Russian dictator and Ribbentrop on 23 August. Believing that his arch-enemy had been neutralised, Hitler was triumphant. Despite the fact that Britain and France reiterated their pledge to stand by Poland, he issued the order to invade just after noon on 31 August. At dawn next day German troops began the assault, not waiting for a formal declaration of war.

According to Eva's biographer Nerin Gun, who interviewed Ilse in the fifties,

> Eva Braun and her sister were present at the Kroll Opera House when, on the morning of September 1, Hitler announced to the Reichstag and the nation that he had invaded Poland.
>
> 'That means war, Ilse,' Eva apparently said, 'and he'll leave . . . what will become of me?' When Hitler announced that he would wear his grey-green uniform unto death, Eva covered her face with her hands. In the fanatical excitement that reigned at that moment nobody except her sister noticed that she was crying.
>
> 'If something happens to him,' she said finally to her sister, 'I'll die too.' [. . .]
>
> As they left, Dr Brandt said, 'Don't worry, Fräulein Eva, the *Führer* told me that there will be peace again in three weeks' time.'
>
> Eva smiled, like someone who has just been offered a pain-killing dose of aspirin.[35]

Two days later, on 3 September 1939, Britain and France declared war on Germany. The Great War had ended twenty years earlier. Now a new war had begun. Werner von Fritsch, former head of the German

---

35. Gun: *Eva Braun: Hitler's Mistress*, p. 181.

army, had remarked a few months earlier: 'This man – Hitler – is Germany's fate, for good or evil. If it's now into the abyss, he'll drag us all with him. There's nothing to be done.' Fatalistic, pessimistic, realistic, he was right. There was nothing to be done. Hitler's mood was messianic, his mission unstoppable.

On the day war was declared, Unity Mitford, a misguided, unimportant cog in the mighty wheel of European conflict, shot herself hamfistedly in the temple. She survived for nine years, her brain more disordered than ever. She lost the power of speech and was partly paralysed. When Hitler was given the news, he seems to have worried most about what would happen to her dog. He visited her once in hospital, instructed his staff to make the necessary arrangements for her safe passage back to England and forgot about her. The gesture was futile, like all her rantings. She never realised how terribly little she mattered.

Chapter Twenty

Waiting for Hitler to Win the War

Beyond knowing that war had been declared, Eva had little idea what it would mean or how it would affect her; not very much, she hoped. Hitler's safety was her main concern. On 23 November 1939 he swore prophetically: 'As long as I live I shall think only of victory. [. . .] *I shall never survive the defeat of my people.*' He never discussed the war with Eva; for her it was all going on a long way away, happening to people about whom she knew little. 'War,' according to her uncle, 'was something entirely alien to her and she wanted nothing to do with it.'[1] She took it for granted that, sequestered at Obersalzberg with farms to provide fresh produce and luxury food and wine hidden away, those on the Berg would hardly be affected. What bothered her most was the fact that Hitler would be away more than ever and this meant she would see less of him. Everyone who came within Hitler's orbit, friends, colleagues or visitors, revolved around him, Eva most of all. When the fulcrum of her life was absent, Eva faltered, oscillating towards anxiety, depression and misery. Rochus Misch was one of the few staff members to notice. 'Eva, in a way that perhaps no one can imagine, suffered a great deal from her connection with Hitler.'[2] She did what she had always done – hid her private fears and carried on as usual.

Her first shock had nothing to do with the war, which in any case was slow to get underway (though not, of course, for the Poles). On

1. Winbauer, *Eva Braun's Familiengeschichte*, p. 20.
2. Transcript of interview with Rochus Misch for *Adolf and Eva*, 3BMTV, roll 16.13.

8 November 1939, the anniversary of the 1923 putsch, the Nazis' most sacred day, an attempt was made on Hitler's life at the Bürgerbräukeller in Munich – the party's original home ground – where he gave his annual oration in honour of its earliest 'martyrs'. The *Führer* had a miraculous escape. He had cut short his speech by half an hour so as to be sure of catching his special overnight train back to Berlin. (Hard to imagine it leaving without him.) At 9.20 p.m. a bomb went off directly behind the podium where he had been standing, killing seven people and wounding more than sixty – among them Eva's father. When Hitler heard the news he exclaimed, 'Now I am completely content! The fact that I left the Bürgerbräukeller earlier than usual proves that I shall achieve my destiny!' Eva, travelling in another section of his train, didn't hear about her father until the following day, when her sister phoned with the name of the hospital to which he'd been taken. In fact, although dramatically bloodied and dishevelled, Fritz Braun didn't suffer serious injury. This did nothing to diminish Eva's distress on behalf of her lover. She lived in perpetual terror of Hitler being assassinated although he told her – and firmly believed – that he possessed some special predictive sense that enabled him to intuit an imminent attack. This was no super-hero complex; he *did* survive as many as forty-six attempts, if one historian[3] is to be believed, although many came close to succeeding.

This is Eva's book, not a history of the Second World War or the Third Reich, and the progress of the war is relevant only to the extent that it was relevant to her. She knew nothing about the campaigns, the plans, the Operations code-named Yellow or Sickle Cut, because Hitler deliberately protected her from such knowledge. It was his firm belief that women and politics were poles apart – the less they knew the better – and Eva's ignorance made it easier for him to switch off. It is hard now to imagine that anyone could be completely unaware of what was going on. Information spews forth all day every day in the newspapers, on television, radio, the Internet – an ever-present and sometimes addictive background to daily life. Yet her cousin Gertraud confirmed that, sometimes to her frustration, Eva was kept in the dark: 'She was completely isolated on the Berg, without a radio or any newspapers to bring her the news. It made her very depressed to be so out of touch. Inside herself she was completely empty. She was anxious about the future. Sport and gymnastics and flirting and

3. Peter Hoffmann, *Hitler's Personal Security* (London: Macmillan, 1979).

changing her clothes were just a surrogate for the emptiness.' Someone
– perhaps Hoffmann but more likely an official war photographer;
Hoffmann was getting a bit old for war zones – took a series of propaganda shots of Hitler in a spartan field headquarters, surrounded by
officers, examining maps through a magnifying glass, and Eva stuck
these pictures into her album. She needed a mental image of where
he was, what his desk looked like, who were the people close to him.
She was afraid, she was lonely and, above all, she missed him.

More surprisingly, Hitler missed *her*. They exchanged letters almost
every day (she was the one person to whom he wrote with a pen in
his own costive handwriting – such an accurate reflection of the man
himself, forever costive –) but few if any of their letters are held in
public archives.[4] Frau Mittlstrasse, who was now the housekeeper at
the Berghof, remembered:

> We had a safe in the room between the two bedrooms to which
> I had a key and in this were all the letters between them. They
> were kept in a parchment box and I had access to it, I had the
> key. She [i.e. Eva] was not indiscreet, never, but my husband was
> determined to find out what Hitler called her – his nickname
> for her – so one day I pulled out a letter just far enough to read
> the opening line and it said, 'My *dear Tschapperl*.'

(This story sounds unlikely on several counts. Frau Mittlstrasse, or one
of the other personal servants close to Hitler and Eva, must surely
have heard him use her nickname; and in any case, why should Hitler
have given her a key to his private safe?) Frau Mittlstrasse claimed
that '*Tschapperl*' was a tender way of saying 'My loved one', commonly
used by local Bavarian working people, though it has a slightly condescending ring to it. Maybe; maybe not. At other times he called her
'Effie' or 'Evie' – diminutives of her name.

Paradoxically, the war brought Hitler and Eva closer. He was often
away in Berlin or conducting the eastern campaign from one of several

---

4. Johannes Göhler, Hermann Fegelein's adjutant, was with Hitler until a week
before the end. He was flown out of Berlin with secret orders, entrusted to him
by the *Führer* in person, to destroy all Hitler's and Eva Braun's papers, kept at
her house in Munich. For more detail about what happened to them after this,
see note 1, Chapter 10 pp. 148–149. A few may have been sold to private collectors – who have not opted to make them public – but most have disappeared,
to the deep regret of the historian.

military headquarters: usually the *Wolfsschanze*, the Wolf's Lair in Raustenberg, east Prussia, or at *Werwolf*, the Werewolf (Hitler was nothing if not consistent in his symbolism) near Vinnitsa in the Ukraine, where he could be closer to his southern front. The letters and phone calls to and from the Berghof were rare moments of tenderness in his life. His capacity for hysteria, which produced megalomaniac outbursts that boiled and foamed like a high sea, had to be controlled during meetings with his top brass and even then, if anyone crossed him, he could explode in tempers that appalled those who witnessed them. The other aspect of his nature – the sentimental side that craved affection and reassurance – needed all the more to be gratified. Eva, telling him about the small events of her day in the soft Bavarian accent that he loved, was the one person able to fulfil that need since his mother's death. Her constancy and love were genuine; everyone else merely fawned and pandered. Only in the final years of their relationship did he come to recognise and value her steadfastness. Her uncle Alois wrote:

> Now that war had come into their lives and taken them over these were difficult times for them both, driving them apart; but inwardly they also brought them closer together. [. . .] They had become companions in a common destiny and realised that they belonged together, for better or worse. The inner bond grew stronger and outer appearances were no longer so important.[5]

Hitler spent a few days before Christmas 1939 at the Berghof before setting off on a three-day morale-boosting tour of the troops. Christmas celebrations were brought forward so that the Speer and Bormann children, dressed up in their best party outfits, could make a pretty procession to watch the candles being lit on a tall Christmas tree, after which they accepted their presents from Hitler one by one, dropping a little curtsey or giving a tiny *Heil Hitler!* salute in return. Then the *Führer* left. As a final surprise, Eva had prepared a small Christmas tree for him to take on his official train as a reminder of her and a festive symbol of the *gemütliches* Christmas he was missing. In a telling anecdote, his valet Heinz Linge, interrogated by the Soviets after the war, recalled watching 'a completely drunk Martin Bormann trying to carry a small decorated Christmas tree, a gift from Eva Braun, to Hitler's

---

5. Winbauer, *Eva Braun's Familiengeschichte*, p. 16. Although he must be guessing, Alois Winbauer was probably right.

railway carriage and then dropping it amid a cascade of balls and stars'[6].

He came back in time for *Sylvester* – New Year's Eve. The formal line-up in 1939/40 is hardly any different from that of previous or later years – same secretaries, same doctors, same two Braun sisters – except that a naval adjutant and several SS aides have joined the group and Hitler looks much grimmer. He stayed at the Berghof for a week before returning to confront the unanimous opposition of his generals and his ally Mussolini to his planned attack on the Low Countries. Although Hitler argued fiercely that they were wrong, he did agree to postpone it till the early spring. The 'phoney war', as it was known in Britain, *Sitzkrieg* (sitting down war) in Germany, dragged on. Europe was technically at war yet eerily becalmed.

In February 1940 Eva went briefly to Berlin where she was cloistered in a comfortably furnished bedroom next to Hitler's in the Reichs Chancellery but, as at the Berghof, never appeared in public. Speer recalls, 'Here, even more than in Obersalzberg, she led a completely isolated life, stealing into the building through a side entrance and going up a rear staircase, never descending into the lower rooms even when there were only acquaintances in the apartment. She was overjoyed whenever I kept her company during the long hours of waiting.'[7] Hitler, more preoccupied than ever, had little time for her and knowing she was there, in the city that housed the centre of government and all the foreign embassies, made him uneasy. To him, she belonged in Obersalzberg and he would rather be consoled by the thought of her enjoying herself in the Utopia he carried in his head than bothered by her presence in the capital.

In April she spent some time in Munich, where she photographed a cheerful family group in front of her little house in Wasserburgerstrasse. The war was not yet in full swing, the city was undamaged and life carried on much as usual. Eva invited her seventeen-year-old cousin Gertraud Winckler (later Weisker), an only child who lived with her parents in Jena, to come and spend a month of the 1940 Easter holidays with her and Gretl.

To ensure that she got a proper classical education, Gertraud's father had arranged for his clever daughter to attend a boys' school. Here she was expected to look and behave as much like a boy as was physically possible. She wore a tight garment called a chest brace – presumably

6. From a review by Richard Overy of *Das Buch Hitler*, a secret dossier prepared for Stalin in 1946 by the MVD (Soviet Interior Ministry), edited by Eberle and Uhl, in the *Times Literary Supplement*, 14 October 2005.

7. Speer, *Inside the Third Reich* (Phoenix edn), p. 193.

on the lines of a liberty bodice – designed to flatten her breasts. Not surprisingly, the poor girl was confused about her gender, sexually ignorant and thoroughly inhibited. Looking back on that visit she wrote:

Life with Eva and Gretl in their little house at Wasserburger Strasse 12 in Bogenhausen was quiet, peaceful and idyllic. My classmates were still too young to volunteer for war.[8] All was well with my world and I was able to enjoy to the full the company of the cousins I had always greatly admired. There we were, three young girls who, like girls the world over, were interested in films, fashion, music and dancing; in Eva's case, especially tap-dancing, at which she was expert. We swapped clothes – by which I mean that they gave me some of theirs, in spite of my protests – and I really got to know and love them both, particularly Eva, who was deeply sensitive.

Gertraud, plainly, was delighted with her smart new things and didn't feel in the least patronised. She needed the worldly instruction the cousins were giving her.

When we were trying on some clothes, Eva suggested I try a particular dress, but I flatly refused.
'I don't need anything new,' I said; 'I don't want to try it on.'
My attitude was incomprehensible to them, and in the end I burst into tears. All three of us sat down on the bed and they took me in their arms. Still in tears I took off my dress. I was wearing a bra which was more like an instrument of torture than a garment for a teenager [*eine Halbwüchsige*] with a chest brace that made my female contours unrecognisable.
My two cousins were horrified. They understood my shame and tears, threw my instruments of torture into the bin, and took me straight to an Austrian lingerie store called Palmers to kit me out. Very gently they tried to find out why I was so constricted in the area where, as Gretl rightly said, I still had nothing but 'little buds'. The reason was that I had my sports lessons in the boys' school, and I could hardly take part with wobbly breasts [*wogenden Formen*]. When my mother collected me four weeks later Eva spoke firmly to her and saw to it that I got a whole new set of clothes.

8. By the end of the war, twenty-seven of the boys with whom Gertraud went to school had been killed.

She taught me to accept my femininity and take pleasure in it, especially in view of my pronounced and rather masculine interest in science, which as far I was concerned was really a man's world. I owe her a lot and I am grateful to her. She was there for me at an important point in my life and intuitively understood her little cousin's needs. She ushered me into a whole new world, far from the boisterousness I had been copying from the boys at school; a kinder and more tender world, and in four weeks transformed me into someone who was no longer ashamed of her womanhood. There was no hint of that hotbed of vice that my father had imagined – neither here in Munich, nor four years later on the Berghof.

She became Hitler's mistress to escape her family. In the end her parents were persuaded by foreign holidays and invitations to the Berghof to accept her situation. Her difficulties with him grew and grew but Eva generally managed to ignore or suppress her problems.[9]

The family that Franz-Paul and Josefa Kronburger had founded was imbued with Catholic convictions and bourgeois attitudes, many of which – bizarre as it seems – Eva brought with her to the Berghof. She and her mother continued to dream that Hitler might one day marry her and give her a child. When the war was over. It was the commonest illusion of all, essential if people were to get through months of mounting anxiety – everything will be all right *when the war is over*.

My mother nursed the same fragile conviction. When in 1940–41 the Blitz over London was delivering death and ruin every night,[10] my father arranged for her to be evacuated together with their first daughter, born the week Germany invaded Denmark and Norway. I was about a year old when we were sent to stay with an elderly relative who lived near Tadworth, south of London, in what was then green and leafy countryside, where my very *German* mother was an object of bafflement and prejudice to the aunt, her snobbish middle-class neighbours and even her cook.

9. Weisker, *Wer War Eva Braun?*, pp. 4–6.
10. The Blitz was launched in the autumn of 1940 and for the next consecutive fifty-seven days, London was bombed by day and night. The worst night was 10 May 1941 when three thousand Londoners were killed, although the bombing continued sporadically long after that, until almost the very end of the war.

Poor young Ditha Helps, transported to a foreign country and left to cope without the support of her husband or his family, unable to speak decent English, frantic with worry about her mother and sisters in Hamburg, must have suffered dreadfully. She was allowed to send and receive one letter of twenty-five words a month but no photographs. This forced her to choose between writing to her mother (crammed into a small flat with my aunt Trudl, her youngest and still unmarried daughter, and her own two surviving sisters, my great-aunts), or to her father. Predictably, she chose the former. Ignorant, isolated, shunned and lonely, she only had me for company. My mother cried a lot. So did Eva. She had plenty of people around her in the Berghof, but she was separated from Hitler. My mother, separated from her beloved husband, did at least have a toddler to console her.

On 10 May 1940, nine months after war had been declared, Germany delivered an all-out attack on Belgium and Holland. The long-delayed real war had begun. On the same day, Churchill took over as British Prime Minister. On 14 June German troops entered Paris and at dawn on the 23rd Hitler made a sightseeing tour of the city and was photographed standing by the Arc de Triomphe, posing in front of the Eiffel Tower with Albert Speer (who was there to pick up ideas for future Third Reich grandiosity) and a group of gleaming German officers; or looking grave and imperial at Les Invalides, which housed Napoleon's tomb. This was mainly for show. He was keen to visit the Paris Opera House but only his official life as the *Führer* was formally documented, always with the potential for good publicity in mind. He made a brief tour of newly conquered France, taking with him his old friend and former sergeant Max Amann – the joker who always made him laugh – and was photographed outside the house where he had been billeted as a soldier in 1916.

About sixty thousand civilians, most of them Londoners, were killed by enemy action in the war, many during the Battle of Britain between 8 August and 31 October 1940. The battle began when Hitler ordered the Luftwaffe to destroy the RAF and soften up Britain – Londoners in particular – as a preliminary to invasion. *Reichsmarschall* (Field Marshal) Göring, commander of the Luftwaffe, was entrusted with this task. His pilots fought well but, with the German fighter aircraft at the extreme limit of their range and without heavy bombers or accurate intelligence, they failed to establish air supremacy and the invasion was never attempted. The Luftwaffe lost hundreds of bombers and their crews. Göring sacrificed 697 aircraft between 8 and 18 August, 180 of them in a single day, the disastrous 15 August 1940. 'It was the finest shambles I've been in,' wrote a young RAF pilot jauntily in his report after one battle, adding, 'Enemy aircraft were a dirty-looking collection.' RAF Fighter Command led by Sir Hugh Dowding had many fewer young pilots, not nearly as well-trained as those of the Luftwaffe – some, in fact, hardly trained at all – and they died in droves. An RAF attack on Berlin on 25/26 August provoked retaliatory raids on London in September, first by day and then by night. Most people emerged from the rubble battered but defiant and after a few weeks intrepid Londoners had almost got used to the bombing and life went on much as usual. England's defences remained intact and apparently invulnerable while the morale and confidence of the 'unconquerable' Luftwaffe were shattered. But so, in the final reckoning, were the London Docks, the East End and part of Buckingham Palace, not to mention 23,000 people killed, 32,000 injured and many thousands of houses damaged or destroyed during eighty-four days of almost continuous attack, in spite of the defending Hurricanes and Spitfires. In the course of the Battle of Britain the RAF lost 1,023 fighter aircraft and at least 375 pilots, with 358 more injured, sometimes desperately, often maimed or disfigured for life.

The RAF's revenge was to come. Arthur 'Bomber' Harris,[11] the architect of British terror bombing, said 'They sowed the wind and now they are going to reap the whirlwind' – but it took time. The first British sorties, ill-equipped and imprecise, killed more than half the crews while barely one in five of the bombs they dropped at such cost fell anywhere near their targets. A climax came with the thousand-aircraft raid on Cologne in May 1942, which confirmed Harris in his

---

11. Air Marshal Sir Arthur 'Bomber' Harris (1892–1984), head of Bomber Command, was in charge of the massive Allied air campaign against Nazi Germany from 1942 to 1945. Sixty-one German cities with a combined population of twenty-five million inhabitants were attacked between 1939 and 1945; 3.6 million homes were destroyed (20 per cent of the total); and 7.5 million people made homeless. Three hundred thousand Germans are thought to have been killed as a result of the raids, and eight hundred thousand were wounded. Harris instigated the air raid that devastated Hamburg and was rewarded (among other tokens of the nation's gratitude) with a statue erected in the Strand, unveiled in 1992 by HM The Queen Mother, another who had earned the nation's affection by her wartime activities. From ctrueman@wsgfl.org.uk

conviction that Germany would be defeated by bombing its cities and destroying civilian morale, as the Luftwaffe had tried to do with the raids over London. That year, 1942, some 44,000 Germans died in air raids. Honours even, Göring and Harris might have thought, in the grim arithmetic of the time.

In the first years of the war, Eva, her mother and sisters and her close friends continued to enjoy the treats that Hitler provided. In the summer of 1941 Eva took a party in the privately piloted ORENZ-MARK and flew out for their usual summer break on the Italian Riviera at Portofino, where they revelled in the hot blue skies and limpid sea, pines, olives, cypresses and fields upon fields of roses, carnations and jasmine. The pursuit of pleasure ranked high in her life and she knew little enough about what was going on to seize any opportunity of indulging herself. Her chances of enjoyment were rapidly running out – not that she knew that, either. She expected Hitler to win the war any day now.

The *Führer* returned to Berlin in July to an ecstatic reception before going on to spend nearly three weeks at the Berghof, interrupted by a visit to Bayreuth for the annual Wagner festival, then back to Eva at Obersalzberg for much of August. The summer of 1940 was perhaps the last time she felt entirely confident and optimistic. Hitler told her the war was going well, his great plan unfolding as he had predicted. Everything would be all right. That year was the last in which he spent almost as long at the Berghof as before the war, though his time was monopolised by generals, admirals and their *aides-de-camp* pressing him for decisions rather than the generalised harangues and exhortations he preferred. On one occasion Eva burst into a conference, protesting that it had gone on far too long and their guests were waiting to eat. Hitler in a fury ordered her out of the room. Reinhard Spitzy, Ribbentrop's aide, recalled:

> Hitler and Ribbentrop were walking up, down, up, down, one hour, two hours, three hours. Then the door was opened and the small blonde face came in and she said to our *Führer*, 'Oh Adolf, please, we must go and have our luncheon!'
>
> I was shocked, how this person of no social quality was allowed to speak to him in that way. I went to the chief ADC and said to him, '*OberFührer*, who is that' – I didn't say lady – 'who is that woman?' And he said, 'Spitzy, listen [. . .] what you have

seen here you will forget [. . .] because our *Führer* has a right to a private life and she is his mistress.'[12]

Later, Spitzy rationalised:

Hitler wanted to be absolutely free, and that she should provide a small bourgeois home with cake and tea. He didn't want a socially high person. He could have had them but he didn't want a woman who could discuss political questions with him or who would try to influence him, and that Eva Braun never did. Eva Braun didn't interfere in politics.[13]

For Hitler, October 1940 was a month of meetings. A constant flow of European notables, from statesmen to minor princesses, visited the Berghof. He spent ten days at Obersalzberg but most of his time was taken up with discussions, conferences, formal dinners hosted by Magda Goebbels: who must have overheard what was said around the head of the table by the top brass sitting near Hitler and was therefore better informed than most of the women 'on the Berg'. She kept her counsel, however. On these official occasions Eva, as usual, was confined to her room and made to sneak in and out by the back entrance. It was humiliating for her and tantalising, too, knowing that Hitler was so close yet beyond her reach. Perhaps to compensate her, when he went to Florence at the end of October for talks with Mussolini and Ciano at the Palazzo Vecchio, he took her with him, strictly *incognito*. After this brief interlude he returned to Berlin, she to the Berghof.

Hitler did not come back to Obersalzberg for a month and when he did it was only for three days, to hold more talks with Ciano and hear the impotent pleas of Kings Boris III of Bulgaria and Leopold III of Belgium. Two weeks later it was the turn of the Queen Mother of Romania – threadbare royals who thought their ancestry entitled them to interfere with his grand plan. They were treated to a display of military pomp and knife-sharp salutes, then dismissed without concessions. Their time was over. His great scheme for the Aryanisation of half Europe under the eagle of the Third Reich was maturing.

He would take on Britain and Russia, if necessary both at once, whatever his pusillanimous generals and air marshals might say. Eva's

12. Haste, *Nazi Women: Hitler's Seduction of a Nation*, p. 56.
13. Ibid., p. 57.

consolation for a second Christmas without him was that the *Führer* arrived at the Berghof in time for New Year and stayed a whole month. 1941, she must have thought, had started well.

Meanwhile the greatest land invasion in modern warfare, Operation Barbarossa, was about to begin, its aim nothing less than the defeat of the mighty armies of the Soviet Union. It was launched at 3 a.m. on 21 June 1941 with a barrage from thousands of guns and waves of dive bombers. By late morning on the first day, the Luftwaffe had destroyed 890 Soviet aircraft, most of them still on the ground, and within three weeks 6,857 more had been put out of action and 550 planes lost. In the first euphoric days it looked as though victory was going to be easy. On 24 July the entire town centre of Minsk was destroyed. An eyewitness wrote: 'And when we came out [of the cellars] what did we see! Burning houses, ashes, ruins and corpses everywhere in the streets.' The terror and despair of that experience was common to millions of survivors of bomb attacks all over Europe. Having inflicted chaos and immolation like the flames engulfing Valhalla in *Götterdämmerung*, the German army, backed by the Luftwaffe, made triumphant progress, advancing rapidly along the western front of the Soviet Union. 'Stalin never had so great a shock in his life.'[14] Then came the beginning of winter, and the snow. The snow changed everything.

By September it was already holding up the *Wehrmacht's* advance in a terrible portent of the end. The harsh Russian winter known by the soldiers as 'General January' was an immense asset to the Red Army, well-equipped and well-used to it, and a murderous handicap to the German Army, ill-prepared in thin soft boots and skimpy uniforms. The hounds of hell were wolfhounds now, sleigh bells jangling merrily as they raced across the blood-stained snow. The fighting in Russia took a horrendous toll on German troops and by the beginning of 1942 it was obvious that Barbarossa had failed. Hitler was no match for Stalin's military leadership nor could his armies match the suicidal readiness of the Soviet forces to attack and die in the fight against the loathed *Reich*.[15]

14. Adapted from Burleigh, *The Third Reich: A New History*, p. 485.
15. Germany's invasion of the Soviet Union in 1941 failed because of the size, savagery, heroism and hardiness of the Soviet Army and because German troops were not equipped to deal with bitter winter conditions when the cold could reach minus 63 Fahrenheit. The war went on for four more years, resulting in 3.6 million German and 12 million Soviet battle deaths, and another 15–18 million civilians who died in massacres, diseases, and starvation.

In October 1941 the remaining Jewish population of Hamburg – much-depleted, living in perpetual fear but managing somehow to survive – was told at short notice that they were to be 'resettled in the east'. Hurriedly, they packed what they could carry and prepared to leave. Within days they were publicly turned out on to the streets in apprehensive, huddled queues and ordered to march to Hamburg's Ostbahnhof. Their destination and its purpose were unknown and none can have anticipated the horrors – separation, hard labour, starvation and death – awaiting them. Part of the reason for their eviction was that many people had been made homeless by bombs and 'resettlement' was an opportune and practical solution to the increasing housing shortage.[16] Although the Germans did nothing to conceal what was happening, my mother cannot have been told about this. In a monthly 25 word letter there was no room to spell out the disappearance of people who must once have been her friends and neighbours – and besides, it would only have upset Ditha.

These barbaric events did not concern Eva. *If* she heard anything about them, it was only as faint receding thunder from a distant storm. Where she was, the sun continued to shine, although the Sun God was absent.

16. Neal Ascherson pointed out in a review in the *Observer*, 16 January 2005, that: 'Often, these actions were improvised by local officials. It was the SS leaders on the spot as much as Hitler and Himmler who turned deportation into shooting, shooting into gassing, gassing into a programme of total extermination. The horrible truth is that Europe's Jews were murdered as much to solve problems of living space and food in occupied Poland as to fulfil Hitler's crazed anti-Semitism. In the end, the question for the Nazis was not: "Why must we kill all the Jews?" but a worse one – "Why not?" Their presence had become a problem, so abolishing them was the obvious radical solution. After all, they were not fully human.' The vast majority of Jews who died in the Holocaust (three million) were from Poland.

Chapter Twenty-one

Eva, Gretl and Fegelein

By 1942 the libido of the rapidly ageing *Führer* had dwindled considerably. As time went on he and Eva were almost bound to have made love less regularly than she would have liked. He was still, at fifty-four, comparatively young but he had never been a very libidinous man and the war made immense demands on his time, will and energy. By 1943, when the tide of war had turned against Germany, they no longer made love at all. The evidence comes from Speer, whose close friendship with Eva Braun made him her natural confidant:

> It was to Albert Speer that she came, in tears, to tell him that 'the *Führer* has just told me to find someone else, he can no longer fulfil me as a man!' There were no two ways of interpreting this, Speer went on: 'She made it quite clear that Hitler had told her he was too busy, too immersed, too tired – he could no longer satisfy her as a man.'[1]

The all-important words in this account are '*no longer*', making it perfectly clear that in the past Hitler *had* 'satisfied her as a man'. Eva, now thirty-one and entering her sexual prime, was sufficiently distressed by Hitler's inability to sustain their former sex life to seek advice from his personal physician, Dr Morell, whom she'd never liked or trusted. She probably knew he had formerly specialised in venereal diseases and thought he would be wise in matters of male sexuality – proof of how much she

---

1. Sereny, *The German Trauma*, p. 278. The story is told in almost identical terms in Sereny, *Albert Speer: His Battle with Truth*, p. 193.

wanted her lover restored to his former sexual powers, whatever they may have been. Morell later confirmed to an American Commission of Enquiry[2] that Eva had asked for something to stimulate Hitler's waning desire and that he had prescribed injections of a male sex hormone called Testoviron to the *Führer* (testosterone, more or less) thought to restore flagging sexual energy, but it failed to have any effect.[3]

In a magnanimous – or indifferent – gesture, the *Führer* gave Eva tacit permission to look for a more virile man to replace him. Hitler was not jealous – he had often said in the past that if she were to fall in love with a suitable young man, he would not stand in her way. He wanted her to be fulfilled, settled and happier than he could make her and if the urge for a husband and children became insistent she was free to look elsewhere. Many of the sycophants on the Berg alleged that she had affairs, spreading scurrilous gossip in an attempt to blacken her reputation and dislodge her as mistress of the Berghof. There isn't a shred of evidence that she ever did, in which case the sex life of this active and healthy young woman was over by her early thirties. Her sexual and biological frustration alone would have been a powerful reason for infidelity and she was surrounded by plenty of men only too glad to give her the opportunity to stray, yet when Speer was asked whether Eva Braun had ever thought of taking Hitler at his word, he replied, 'It was out of the question for her. Her love for him, her loyalty, were absolute – as indeed she proved unmistakably at the end.' On the other hand this same Speer, uncharacteristically, apparently told David Puttnam off the record – when they met during the making of a documentary film – that she *had* once had a holiday romance, pointing to a young adjutant in one of the winter sports scenes from her home movies as the man in question. Given Speer's tendency to tell people what they wanted to hear, this information should be treated with caution, particularly since it is not corroborated by anyone else.

If Obersalzberg was too claustrophobic to allow her a fling there was always Munich, where she had a wide circle of friends (though the young men were disappearing one by one). Failing that, she might have been picked up by a handsome Italian on one of her annual trips abroad. A pretty young woman in search of a lover seldom has very far to look and in wartime it is a natural, almost universal impulse for fighting men to

2. Page 1 of the interrogation of Dr Morell in the Musmanno Collection held in the Gumberg Library at Duquesne University, Pittsburgh, PA, to which I was given access with the invaluable help of its archivist, Mr Paul Demilio.
3. David Irving, *The Secret Diaries of Hitler's Doctor* (New York: Macmillan, 1983).

want to propagate their line and perpetuate their genes. The trouble was, Eva wasn't looking for a lover. She *could* have 'played away' but there is no evidence to show that she ever had a holiday romance – except, just possibly, once, early in the relationship with Hitler. Herta Schneider revealed to Nerin Gun, thirty years after the events she described, an encounter in 1935 between Eva and a stranger that might have led to an affair or even an engagement.[4] Gun claims to have checked its accuracy though how, or with whom, he does not say.[5] Yet somehow the minutiae of time and place and the fact that the story comes from a first-hand and reliable source, give it an air of truth. Here it is, just as Herta told it:

> Only once did Eva take an interest in another man. It was after the second suicide attempt [in May 1935 when Eva was twenty-three], that she went with her mother and her younger sister to Bad Schachen, a charming hotel castle on Lake Constance, near Lindau. A certain Peter Schilling, a businessman, younger than Hitler but nonetheless over thirty, started to court Eva. He was really smitten. They immediately became inseparable and they made a fine couple. Eva confided that she liked Schilling very much, that she found him perfect, and that in other circumstances she might have been able to love him. 'But there's already a man in my life and there will never be another. It's too late.' So she refused to see him again and would not even speak to him on the telephone. There is no way of knowing whether she told Hitler of this incident.

Indeed there isn't; nor of knowing whether she told Herta, or whether it even happened in the first place.[6] It's hard to imagine that Eva, entangled with a man of huge charisma who wielded national and international power, would have been content to live her life as Frau Schilling. Like an athlete or drug addict, she became hooked on the adrenalin

4. Gun, *Eva Braun: Hitler's Mistress*, p. 144.
5. John Taylor, intelligence doyen at NARA, who had known Gun, said scathingly of him, 'He wasn't a historian. He was a journalist, and journalists make things up to fill in the gaps.' As a former journalist myself I bridled at this, but I share his dismissal of Gun as a thoroughly unreliable source.
6. Significantly perhaps, Herta Schneider did not repeat the story when she talked to Johannes Frank, German biographer of Eva Braun, some thirty years later. Could Nerin Gun have invented the whole episode, had she regretted telling him about it, or was it simply that Herta – by then an old lady in her eighties – had forgotten this apparently trivial incident?

of her turbulent relationship with the *Führer*. Whether or not she knew it, plain ordinary happiness was no longer enough. By 1935 he already dominated her and by 1942 her life was utterly bound up with his.

Hitler's life was increasingly threatened by assassins.[7] Some attempts almost succeeded but all were frustrated, either by unforeseen circumstances or by the enhanced security measures taken by the paranoid dictator. But in the summer of 1942, Claus Schenk von Stauffenberg of the Kreisau Circle (about whom a great deal more will be said later) began to advocate the killing of Hitler. Von Stauffenberg first met Hitler at a staff briefing in June 1942 when, he noted, 'Göring appeared to be wearing make-up, Speer to be the only sane person present among psychopaths and Hitler's eyes were hooded, his hands palpitated. It was hard to breathe since the atmosphere was rank and rotten.' Eva, naturally, knew nothing about this, although she did worry constantly that some madman would try to kill the *Führer*.

The Braun family and friends continued to travel abroad under the protection of *Il Duce* – Italy being one of the few European countries where their presence was welcome – every year since the thirties. Well into the war, in July 1942, Eva took a holiday with a group of her friends on the Italian Riviera. It was their fifth visit since 1938, and it was to be the last. Within days of their leaving Italy, Mussolini was overthrown. Now their choice of holiday destinations had dwindled to – Greece, perhaps, or Norway? Neither was entirely safe. Eva and her friends had little choice but to stay at home and watch the sun set over Berchtesgaden.[8]

7. For example, in autumn 1941 Polish saboteurs attempted to blow up the *Führerzug*. The plan misfired when Hitler's train – on the way from Königsberg towards Schwarzwasse – unaccountably stopped at a small station to let another train go ahead. The explosion killed 430 Germans but left the *Führer* unharmed.
8. Local people point out a beautiful timber house set amid a grove of pine trees close to a sand spit, east of Gdansk towards the Kalinin border at a spot called Krysnica Norska. Here, they claim, Eva used to stay and from here she went down to the beach to swim. (I am grateful to Gerald Seymour for this information.) It seems unlikely, however. Hitler was far too preoccupied with war on the eastern front to have had time for a dalliance with Eva and would have been fearful of exposing her to danger from the 'bestial' Russians. Gertraud Weisker is certain she never lived there, so far away from the Berghof and Munich. It must be a legend dreamed up for the benefit of tourists. But if she *had* lived there, she would have had to pass the gates of a concentration camp called Statthof, or, in Polish, Szputowo, whose nearness may explain why Eva is said – accused, almost – of having stayed there. This peninsula saw the final stand of Königsberg (Kaliningrad) on 2–10 April 1945, where thousands of soldiers, and civilians, fought to the last bullet.

The good times, she must have lamented, were coming to an end.

By November 1942 the strain of the war – a war that he insisted on conducting almost single-handed – had begun to show on the *Führer*. Hitler's memory was starting to be fallible (his grasp of reality always had been). His megalomania when the war seemed to be going his way was unstoppable and getting worse. Count Ciano, in his account of meeting Hitler with Mussolini at Salzburg in April 1942, wrote: 'Hitler talks, talks, talks, talks. On the second day, after lunch, when everything had been said, Hitler talked uninterruptedly for an hour and 40 minutes'.[9] When he embarked on Operation Barbarossa against the Soviet Union, his former partner in their non-aggression pact, Hitler had believed that, '*We have only to kick in the door and the whole rotten structure will come crashing down.*'. It was proof of how prejudiced and ill-informed he was. Barbarossa was launched, and more than three million German soldiers and 3300 tanks crossed the Russian border, arms and men that could not be spared from the war against the Allies.[10] Hitler had refused to listen to advice, let alone warnings, and expected victory within a few months. He could not have been more wrong.

By early 1943 he was constantly on the move between his headquarters in Berlin and those at the *Wolfsschanze*, the Wolf's Lair on the East Prussian border, less often at his southern base, code-named *Werwolf*, near Vinnitsa in the Ukraine, where he spent a month in the late spring. By September the first snow was already holding up the *Wehrmacht*'s advance in a terrible portent of the end. Defeat by the Soviets had taken its toll. By March 1943 Hitler was, according to one biographer,

> 'a spent old man . . . He stared fixedly into space through bulging eyes, his cheeks were blotchy and his spine was twisted by kyphosis and a light scoliosis. His left arm and leg twitched and he dragged his feet. He became increasingly excitable, reacted violently to criticism and stuck obstinately to his own opinions, however ludicrous.

9. p. 732 from Ian Kershaw: Hitler 1936–1945: Nemesis Penguin Books edn 2001
10. Germany's invasion of the Soviet Union in 1941, which failed because of the size, savagery, heroism and hardiness of the Soviet Army and because German troops were not equipped to deal with bitter winter conditions, when the cold could reach minus 63 degrees Fahrenheit. The war went on for four more years, resulting in 3.6 million German and twelve million Soviet battle deaths, and another fifteen to eighteen million civilians who died in massacres, diseases and of starvation.

He spoke in a dull monotone, repeated himself, and liked to harp on his childhood and early career.'[11]

The *Führer* was ordered to take three months' rest. He arrived at the Berghof on 22 March, but having gone through the motions of Easter and birthday rituals (he was fifty-four on 20 April), he left again on 2 May, first for Munich, then Berlin, then on to the *Wolfsschanze*, where he was much cheered by a jubilant report from Albert Speer, now Minister for Armaments, on the increase in German arms productivity. On 21 May 1943 he was home again for five weeks but Eva could not persuade him to spend much private time with her since he was preoccupied with meetings, official visits, military conferences and vital if increasingly futile tactical decisions, in a war that was turning against him. More frenetically than ever, he talked, paced, sat up through the night with maps and generals, gobbled pills and could not be calmed. She snatched a few photographs of him on the terrace (every visit might be the last) but in all of them he looks tense and grim. On 29 June he flew back to the *Wolfsschanze*. Not for long. On 18 July he was back again at Obersalzberg and Eva spent two days with him but even this brief respite was interrupted by a visit from Mussolini, hoping for the *Führer*'s support in the rapidly disintegrating Italian situation. A week later *Il Duce* was overthrown and put under arrest.

His restless toing and froing continued. On 20 July the *Führer* returned to east Prussia for nearly four months, right through the autumn until 8 November, when he took a week's break at the Berghof. By the 16th he was back again at the *Wolfsschanze* for Christmas 1943 and the New Year, festivals which in the past he had nearly always managed to spend with Eva. In other words, between the end of June 1943 and 23 February 1944 – almost eight months – the two were apart for all but ten days. As Gertraud observed in her memoir of Eva, 'She suffered from Bormann's plots and intrigues against her and had to look on while Hitler was ruined by his doctors and their treatments, unable to do anything because she had no influence at all, not even on him.'

Given these long absences, coupled with the dramatic collapse in Hitler's health, it would have been forgivable if the constant stream of attractive young adjutants billeted at the Berghof (and they *were* attractive: Hitler made a point of surrounding himself with tall,

11. p 194 from Hitler's Notes and Letters by Werner Maser, published William Heinemann Ltd, 1974

blond, good-looking young men) had prompted Eva to infidelity. Asked what she was like with other men, Herbert Döring said: 'Certainly quite different from the way she was with Hitler. With him, she was all closed and artificial; bottled up. With other men she was immediately more relaxed, open, normal. She moved normally, looked normal, with her beautiful expressions and looks.' Vivacious, charming, fashionably turned out, Eva Braun was an obvious lure. She was kept out of sight when foreign delegations arrived at Obersalzberg but an observant young *aide-de-camp* might have glimpsed her returning from a walk or sunning herself on the terrace and followed up the glimpse with discreet enquiries. He would have been told she was a secretary. Had he pursued his curiosity further with a note asking for an assignation, how would Eva have responded? The fact is, we do not, and cannot, know. For the *Führer*'s mistress to take a lover would have been a dangerous move for both parties and, *had* it occurred, they would have had to take the utmost care to keep it secret. There are no verbatim reports of flirtatious approaches, no billets-doux, no love tokens, no blurred photographs of an illicit embrace – *nothing* to support the assertion that she had admirers to whom she might occasionally have succumbed. The Berghof lacked a supreme gossip or diarist from whom we might discover a hidden world of amorous frolic. No Nancy Mitford, James Lees-Milne or Duc de Saint Simon emerged from that philistine enclave. Eva has to be presumed innocent. It almost seems a pity.

Gretl on the other hand could do as she liked without word of her peccadilloes being repeated all over 'the Berg' next morning. Pretty Gretl with her crooked smile and velvet eyes was a great flirt who had enjoyed more than one affair, until she met the charming but widely disliked *Gruppenführer* Hermann Fegelein, SS general and liaison officer between Himmler and the *Führer*.[12] This handsome newcomer arrived at the Berg in March 1943 and cut quite a dash in the lives of both Braun sisters. Very soon he had wormed his way into the inner circle. Traudl Junge observed:

At first he was only to be seen in the surroundings of the Berghof but he befriended Bormann and soon became a leading

---

12. He was said to be responsible for the murder of twenty thousand Jews in Poland and the Soviet Union.

light. He was the classic dashing horseman type. Small wonder that he was used to having women flock to him. [. . .] He'd scarcely surfaced before he was sitting at the Berghof table. He toasted all the influential people, shared nightly feasts with Bormann, and soon had all the ladies at his feet. Fegelein, who was a good talker and excellent company, attracted the attention of Eva Braun and her sister Gretl. The latter especially became the object of handsome Hermann's display. As if he had no idea she was Eva Braun's sister, he declared, 'That one's a silly goose!'[13]

Was he camouflaging his true feelings? The gossipmongers and her enemies were quick to insinuate that Eva and Fegelein were lovers. Herbert Döring thought it quite possible. 'Fegelein was a great admirer of Eva Braun – oh, very much – and would have liked to have had her. Christa Schröder said Eva had loved Fegelein but I don't know about that. I could certainly imagine it.'[14] He fails to point out that while this supposed relationship was taking place he himself was no longer on the staff of the Berghof so his comments are hearsay; and further discredited by coming from the one secretary – Christa Schröder – who is known to have disliked Eva. In 1985, more than forty years later, Christa claimed in her memoirs that Eva had confided that when Fegelein first arrived at Obersalzberg he had made a great impression on her, adding, 'If I'd met him years ago I would have asked the boss to release me.'[15] Maybe. But more likely, not. Apart from anything, why should she confide in Fräulein Schröder, who was never an ally? Gitta Sereny believes such tales are nonsense. 'I've never seen any proof of this "affair" with Fegelein and I'm inclined to think it's a myth. Eva was not an immoral girl and this would have been a deeply immoral thing. I would rule out that they slept together. I just don't think it fits. I think she was Hitler's girl and that's it.'[16]

The malicious stories of a purported affair are based on hypothesis and surmise and do not take into account human considerations like loyalty and family affection. Eva loved Hitler with single-minded devotion. Infidelity would have been a terrible betrayal, even though

13. Junge, *Bis Zur Letzten Stunde*, p. 108 (translated by the author).
14. Ibid. – but then Christa Schröder had always belittled Eva.
15. Cited in Christa Schröder, *Er War Mein Chef* (Munich: Langen Müller, 1985).
16. Gitta Sereny interviewed for *Adolf and Eva* 3BMTV, roll 10.25.

he had indicated that he wouldn't blame her. As a good Catholic she had already sinned enough, without coveting her sister's husband-to-be as well. Perhaps the most powerful impediment was that it would have hurt Gretl deeply. She had lived all her life in Eva's shadow. If her big sister had stolen her lover or fiancé let alone her husband, the rift would have been irreparable. To override these considerations Eva would have had to be passionately in love with Fegelein, and she wasn't. From his point of view it would have been insanely risky to seduce the *Führer*'s mistress. Exposure – and in the hotbed of the Berghof *somebody* would have found out – would have meant demotion, banishment or even death. Fegelein certainly found Eva attractive but he knew better than to let matters go any further than dancing together in public with eye-catching abandon.

The loyal Gertraud, of course, remains convinced that Eva never took a lover:

> She was not interested in flirting with other men, she was entirely focused on Hitler. It was said that she had an affair with Fegelein but to me she spoke of him with great disapproval. I was sorry for Gretl, that she had this husband: rigid, proud, arrogant but also a ladies' man. He wanted to marry Gretl because it advanced him in the hierarchy.[17]

Eva too was well aware that Fegelein was pursuing Gretl not least because his status as Hitler's virtual brother-in-law would lodge him firmly at the heart of the charmed circle. She saw through the dashing horseman to the shameless social climber but, since Gretl was crazy about him, maybe it didn't matter. Gertraud points out:

> She [Eva] had been Hitler's girlfriend for ages [*seit fast Jahrzehnten*], but he had not married her; and now here was this man wanting to marry her sister. It is not clear whether Fegelein really wanted to marry Gretl, or whether he did it, as has been suspected, to please Hitler and Bormann. Hitler certainly provided financial and other support for the wedding.[18]

17. Gertraud Weisker in conversation with the author, 24 March 2004.
18. Always keen to see his coterie safely wed and bred, Hitler paid for many marriages, including that of Herbert Döring ('*ein widerlicher Kerl*' – a nasty piece of work – Gertraud thought him) and his wife Anna.

Eva put aside her own misgivings and backed her sister's unsuitable choice of husband.

Gretl herself, conscious of her age – she was now nearly thirty – and encouraged by Hitler's passion for matchmaking ('Eva and Gretl were always Hitler's marionettes,' said Gertraud), married Hermann Fegelein partly to please the *Führer*, partly to please her mother (pining for grandchildren), but above all to please herself. Her husband was a general, well placed in the SS hierarchy and highly attractive. Many women had pursued him ardently. Gretl must have thought she had made a good match.

On 3 June 1944 Eva arranged a lavish wedding for her sister – it's hard not to feel it was a substitute for her own. Gretl Braun and *Gruppenführer* Hermann Fegelein, SS, were married in Salzburg town hall; a civil wedding, it goes without saying. From there they drove back to the Berghof where a splendid lunch hosted by Hitler had been laid out for the bridal couple and their guests. Gretl looked dazzling in a white silk dress with a deep lace-covered décolletage, cut on the bias to emphasise her lissom figure and at the same time to show that she wasn't pregnant. She carried a trailing bouquet of white flowers and smiled rapturously at her pure-blooded, guaranteed 100 per cent Aryan husband. Photographs show the couple making a pretty show of newly-married devotion, Gretl's head laid trustingly on his shoulder, Fegelein looking strong and protective. In the official wedding photograph Hitler, for once in civilian dress (he had sworn to wear uniform, like his soldiers, until the war was over), smiles thinly through narrowed lips. Eva, most unusually, chose a rather unbecoming satin dress, stiffly draped across the bosom with a tight waist and flaring skirt, more fifties than forties and not at all her usual style. It can't have been deliberate, but it meant she didn't upstage her sister.

When lunch and the speeches were over the party (though not the *Führer*, who had weightier matters to attend to) was transported in several cars up the vertiginous mountain road to the Eagle's Nest on the Kehlstein summit. Here another feast was laid out with as much champagne as the guests could drink (overstimulated by the romantic and erotic atmosphere of the occasion, Göring drank so much that he was carried home insensible). The couple was serenaded by an accordionist and a violinist – not, of course, gypsy violinists; the Roma by now were stowed away in concentration camps where almost all of them died[19] – but by an uneasy pair from an SS band. Afterwards the happy party drank more champagne and everyone danced until three o'clock in the morning.

Three days later the Allied landings in Normandy began.

Traudl Junge noted:

> Amazingly, he [Fegelein] succeeded in making a friend of Eva – though perhaps not so astonishing, when you consider what fun and how amusing he could be. And Eva, young and full of life, who'd been forced to stay silent and in the background, was happy to have a brother-in-law with whom she could dance to her heart's content without any loss of face, disapproval or gossip.[20]

But Gretl's marriage changed Eva's relationship with her sister and changed her own status, too. Cousin Gertraud described the altered dynamic between the two, hitherto one another's closest companion and confidante:

> Eva's life entered a difficult phase following Gretl's marriage to Herr Fegelein [. . .] by which, as I see it, Eva's little hanger-on had been transformed into a married woman. It makes no difference whether Gretl loved her husband or not: she was married now, while Eva was still a mistress. Or perhaps not so much a mistress as the woman who 'stands by her man' out of loyalty and a certain sense of responsibility. Her sister's marriage created major psychological problems for Eva. The relationship between the two had always been very intense and now she had lost her sister, who had been her best friend, through her marriage to a man she didn't respect.[21]

Eva was more isolated than ever. Now that Gretl had gone – the person who had worshipped her and been at her side since the days when they were small and living in Isabellastrasse – Eva no longer came first

19. Of the eight hundred Roma (the name is thought to come from the Punjabi word 'Ramante', meaning moving or wandering) sent to Auschwitz, to be held in even worse condition than other inmates, seven hundred were eventually murdered. Between 80 and 90 per cent of gypsies died in the camps – about eight hundred thousand in all.

20. Junge, *Bis Zur Letzten Stunde*, p. 169 (translated by the author).

21. Weisker, *Wer War Eva Braun?*.

with anybody, certainly not with Hitler. Despite her established position, she suffered from the demeaning anonymity that he continued to force upon her. Like Fegelein, she had hoped her status would be enhanced by a legitimate family connection to the *Führer*. She was now officially '*gesellschaftsfähig*': fit for polite company. 'Now that I'm Fegelein's sister-in-law,' she said, 'I'm *somebody* at last!' It is a sad reflection that, having been mistress of Hitler and the Berghof for nearly ten years, Eva had such a low opinion of herself that she felt her claim to a legitimate position at Obersalzberg derived from her little sister's marriage to a social climber who had blagged his way into the inner circle.

Chapter Twenty-two

1941–3 – What Could Eva Have Known?

With hindsight, the frolicking seen in Eva's photographs and cine films from the late 1930s well into the war years looks macabre, the antics of people who were either mad or disconnected from the world outside. She and her companions hiked, picnicked and sunbathed in the pure mountain air, gathered armfuls of wild flowers, swam and showed off their acrobatics (well, Eva did) on the shores of the sapphire-blue Königssee. Millions of German women struggling to provide food for their families, improvising sanitary towels knitted from unravelled burlap sacks, washed and rewashed until they stank, would have been outraged had they known about these carefree pleasures.[1]

The racist, authoritarian Nazi movement was a specifically *masculine* movement and remains so for the few deluded neo-Nazis who strut their stuff, dreaming of an imaginary time and place when they would be important and respected. In the 1920s and 1930s German men were attracted by a dogma that elevated men above women, bullies above thinkers, obedience above intelligence, hierarchy above merit. They were aroused by mass rallies whose rituals – uniforms, marches, songs, flags, torchlight, fireworks and *Führer* – superseded those of religion. They responded to propaganda films and posters showing homoerotic images of young men – workers and soldiers – and were taken in by the simple, stirring slogans and false panoply of

---

1. However, comtemporary photographs – not taken by Eva – show that many families managed to contrive a day or two a year when they, too, could sit beside a lake or pool and let the children splash and have fun, almost as though no war were in progress.

nationalism. Women cared less about the creed; for them the attraction was the status they earned as good wives and mothers, nurturing their families and supporting their husbands. Nazism glorified them for carrying out their role – one which until then had been taken for granted. They flocked towards Hitler, an inspiring, chaste figure for whom they felt a mixture of awed hero-worship and schoolgirl infatuation. The ideal Nazi woman was the very reverse of everything the feminists came to stand for. She was a biological and domestic necessity, not an individual with her own mind, talents, needs and rights. In other words, women could be Nazis as long as they didn't think or ask questions. The easiest way to achieve this was if men never talked to them about politics.[2] During the war Hitler's meandering dinner-time pontifications were recorded verbatim. One evening in 1943 he said: 'I detest women who dabble in politics and if their dabbling extends to military matters it becomes utterly unendurable. [. . .] Gallantry forbids one to give women an opportunity of putting themselves in situations that do not suit them.'[3]

The different roles played by the two sexes were basic to the way Aryans defined themselves. Men and women were on a par only in one crucial function – procreation, if necessary without the formality of marriage. 'Better an unmarried but fulfilled mother than a dried-up spinster' summed up Hitler's view, not that he extended it to Eva. The Nazis believed in the ancient Teutonic distinction whereby men were warriors and women were family-makers. Men played almost all the leading roles in the Nazi state, with women excluded from political life.[4]

Women may be excluded from politics but that need not stop them seeing, and reacting to what they see; responding with their consciences and taking steps to resist what they cannot approve. The hard question at the crux of this book is this: were Eva Braun – and my mother and her two sisters, *their* mother and my dear, unworldly great-aunts, along with millions of other suffering German housewives – good women or wicked ones, albeit wicked by association? Were they tainted by the moral disfigurement that Nazism inflicted on their husbands, brothers and sons? Was Eva, in particular, guilty of complicity for

2. I am grateful to Jonathan Rée for the discussion that sparked these observations.
3. *Hitler's Table Talk, 1941–1944*, pp. 251–2.
4. Jill Stephenson, *Women in Nazi Society* (London: Croom Helm, 1975), p. 8.

remaining passive in the face of supreme evil; and *especially* guilty because of her relationship with Hitler? To judge her demands a realistic assessment of what she knew or, had she made an effort, *could* have known. Did she ever grasp that her lover initiated and master-minded twelve years of murderous violence, beginning with the euthanasia programme in the 1930s;[5] that he wanted the Jews of Europe wiped out[6] and willed every death and casualty in a war that killed tens of millions? There is frustratingly little first-hand evidence and the truth can only be surmised.

The respected Third Reich historian Richard Evans points out the danger of using retrospective knowledge to condemn those who could not read the future:

> Recounting the experiences of individuals brings home, as nothing else can, the sheer complexity of the choices they had to make and the difficult and often opaque nature of the situations they confronted. Contemporaries could not see things as clearly as we can, with the gift of hindsight: they could not know in 1930 what was to come in 1933, they could not know in 1933 what was to come in 1939 or 1942 or 1945. *If they had known, doubtless the choices they made would have been different . . .* [my italics].[7]

Right up to 1939 even the Jews themselves regarded rumours about the camps as exaggerated and chose to stay put – fatal optimism, fatal inertia – rather than leave home and country for an unknown future.

With all their unparalleled horrors, the black events of the Nazi

---

5. Under Hitler's euthanasia programme, at least 100,000 people and perhaps twice that number, many of them mentally or physically handicapped, were killed during the Third Reich. (Source: *Guardian*, 27 October 2003).
6. According to Franciszek Piper in an article entitled 'Auschwitz. How Many Perished – Jews, Poles, Gypsies', *Yad Vashem Studies*, 21 (1991), at least 1.3 million persons were deported to Auschwitz. They included approximately: 1.1 million Jews, 140,000–150,000 Poles, 23,000 Roma (gypsies), 25,000 Soviet POWs and 25,000 prisoners of other nationalities. Of these, about 1.1 million perished. The aggregate figures given by Piper are: 960,000 Jews, 70,000–75,000 Poles, 21,000 Roma, 15,000 Soviet POWs and 10,000–15,000 registered prisoners of other nationalities. These figures are probably about as close to the truth as we can approach. See also Chapter 19, p. 287, note 18.
7. Evans, *The Coming of the Third Reich*, Preface, p. xix.

era remain an area of moral ambiguity. The simplistic view has frozen the Nazi era into a cyclorama of horror, vilifying Hitler as a monster lacking all humanity and Eva as a complaisant bimbo. Truth has many nuances and crude black and white assertions aren't ever entirely true. The extent to which blame can be laid on those linked with the perpetrators – their wives, families and mistresses – is not easy to determine. The wives of other high-ranking Nazis were not punished. Did the women on the Berg know what was going on at the time and if so, how much did they know? Did they approve? Did they actively assist? Did they fail to do anything they might have done to help those being persecuted? Most of these questions must be answered with a 'yes' if people who were not directly implicated are to be held responsible or judged guilty. Even now, sixty years and two generations later, some critics of Germany assert that *all* Germans share an ancestral guilt for their country's wartime crimes, although today's young Germans weren't born when Hitler was in power and nor, in most cases, were their parents. Yet many Germans do admit to covert feelings of guilt and nearly all are defensive about the past. The Holocaust created a long darkness, longer than the aftermath of most wars, and the stigma remains today.

The glib response is that German women were guilty of going along with the Third Reich and not speaking out or rising up against it. Yet there is a difference between morality and heroism. People are expected to be morally virtuous, in an ordinary, decent, law-abiding sort of way, but they aren't *expected* to be heroic. (Heroism consists precisely in going beyond the call of ordinary civil and humanitarian duty.)[8] No one blamed the women of the Soviet Union for the crimes and camps under Stalin's equally evil régime. In both societies wicked women were encouraged and rewarded by the system – informers, rumourmongers and slanderers whose denunciations were responsible for the arrest and deaths of many innocents. Worst of all were the female camp guards, sadistic harridans as capable of brutality as their male counterparts. (Those at Ravensbrück, the concentration camp near Berlin, were former members of the *Bund Deutscher Mädel*, honed to unthinking obedience since their teens.) But they were exceptional; and, as Private Lynndie England has recently shown in Iraq, their type lives on. Cruelty is not gender linked. Younger German women had been programmed by the *Bund Deutscher Mädel*

8. See Chapter 6, p. 73, note 3.

(BDM) Their belief in the Nazi ideology had been hammered into them at an age when they had neither the information nor the moral judgement to argue. They were schooled to fulfil the aims of the party and in return given a pride in themselves that was unshakeable.[8] The great majority of German women under Hitler *were* decent, most of them would not in normal circumstances have been cruel, but very few were heroines, though one must not forget the huge resilience and courage that all German mothers needed in terrible times when simply keeping children and the old from freezing and starving demanded heroism.

In 1947, soon after the war ended, Traudl Junge wrote a detailed account of the indoctrination she had absorbed in her childhood and youth, in an attempt to understand her own compliance with the régime; a compliance that, like so many of the people around Hitler, she later repudiated. When she wrote it, Traudl Junge claims she had no thought of publication, but fifty-five years later the typescript was published as *Until the Final Hour: Hitler's Last Secretary*. To what extent it had been bowdlerised between 1947 and 2000, no one but Frau Junge can say with certainty. The book was hailed as the last true eye witness account of Hitler's circle and in the last months before her death on 10 February 2002 at the age of eighty-one it made her world-famous. The highly praised film *The Downfall (Der Untergang)*,[9] depicting the last weeks in Hitler's bunker, was partly based on her memories.

Born in Munich in 1920, at the age of fifteen Traudl enlisted in the *Bund Deutscher Mädel*, one of six girls from her class to join. They exercised and perfected their *Sieg Heils!* at the same time as they exercised and perfected their bodies. At school, her three Jewish classmates were treated as equals by both pupils and teachers, their Jewishness a different race and religion but hardly a stigma. Then after 1936 they began to disappear, one by one. Nobody knew where they went and nobody tried to find out. In 1938, when Traudl was eighteen, she joined 'Beauty and Belief', the organisation for young adults who had outgrown the BDM. It aimed to produce 'girls who believe unreservedly in Germany and the *Führer* and will instil that faith in the hearts of their children'.

The more infatuated Traudl became with the culture and aesthetic

9. Released December 2004 in Germany, January 2005 in the UK.

of her time, the more repellent she says she found the coarse aspects of street politics, which seemed lower class and philistine, suitable for the masses but not for people of her class. She could laugh at the jokes that circulated about Hitler or despise *Der Stürmer* and its anti-Semitic caricatures because that wasn't her kind of Nazism; it was *'none of her business'*. In any case, along with most of her contemporaries, Traudl thought men's politics had nothing to do with her. Like Eva and my mother Ditha, she had no idea how thoroughly she had been brainwashed. The persecution and disappearance of the Jews became routine, an everyday event, and *'in time she ceased even to be shocked'*. Could she, or any of the women on the Berg including Eva, have known about the ninety Jewish orphans under the age of six who were driven to a wood near Kiev in August 1941 and shot, one by one;[10] about the mothers who tried to protect their babies with their own bodies, only to have the infants' limbs broken as they were torn away to be butchered? If they *had* had the information – which they did not – and held Hitler responsible, *what could they have done*? Strong protest would have been punished by dismissal from the Berghof; continuing protest with exile to one of the camps; noisy, public protest, could have meant death.

Should women be blamed for their ignorance and acquiescence, which were imposed upon them? Their 'crime' was that they breathed a miasma of moral evil exemplified most clearly by the desperate plight of the Jews but also by the gradual disappearance of handicapped people, political dissidents, homosexuals and so on – all of whom must have had friends, colleagues and neighbours. They chose to ignore the signs, the rumours and the sudden absences, substituting a blind loyalty to Hitler and their menfolk for any attempt to face reality. Why weren't more German women interested in the fate of the despised minorities sent to the ghettos (whose existence *was* public knowledge)?[11] As for those deported to brutal camps in Poland, if people stopped to wonder where they had gone the easy reaction was . . . somewhere, anywhere, as long as it was out of sight. Jewish schoolfriends and neighbours became a dark smudge in the memory. German housewives knew that

10. Burleigh, *The Third Reich. A New History*, p. 619.
11. The developing dirt and squalor of the ghetto enabled German propaganda to elide Jews with vermin, as notoriously exemplified by the film *The Eternal Jew (Der Ewige Jude)*, directed by Fritz Hippler. It was first presented to the public on 18 November 1940.

fumigating an infested home can be very satisfying. Freed from the social and physical embarrassment of fleas, bedbugs, cockroaches or rodents, the home and family feel better, *cleaner*. These hygiene-loving *Hausfrauen* had been led, step by almost imperceptible step, to regard Jews and other minorities as just such an infestation, whose disappearance cleared the way for a purer, stronger Aryan race. They didn't feel blood lust but they *were* profoundly indifferent to their fate. It was *possible* to know a good deal about what was going on, though the existence of the extermination camps came as an appalling post-war revelation to almost everyone.

Apathy was not quite universal. Thousands of German women took huge risks by sheltering Jews underground, hidden in attics or cellars (they were known as 'U-boats' – submarines) sometimes even in cupboards, and protected – or, in other cases, betrayed – by their non-Jewish friends and neighbours. It was the women who bought and cooked food for these fugitives, sharing with them the family's precious food stamps; the women who washed and mended their clothes, although it meant living with the daily threat of denunciation. Had the hiding places been discovered, the whole family would have been sent to a concentration camp. By 1943 some 27,000 Jews remained in Berlin. No one knows exactly how many were protected by such women but each one was a heroine.

It may look, with hindsight, as though the *Führer* seduced the entire nation, yet not every German was corrupted by the Nazis. Eighty million people speak with many different voices. The notion that everyone under the Third Reich belonged to the Nazi Party and condoned, let alone supported, its racial policies and the methods by which they were implemented is over-simple. The whole nation cannot be lumped in with the Nazis, fanatics and psychopaths. The persecution of Jews and other minorities aroused some segments of society to opposition, especially people from old families with a long tradition of moral leadership and intellectual, creative or professional people, some priests (especially Catholics) and many university students – and as well, unknown and unrecorded people from every class, since moral goodness is not confined to the most prominent. Many people of extraordinary courage did what they could to oppose the seductive creed of *Führer, Volk und Vaterland*. However, as Burleigh points out, 'The only source of decency was human conscience . . . and the war's moral parameters were determined by Hitler. The *Führer* had decreed: "It is a war of extermination. The leaders must make the sacrifice of overcoming their scruples.'''[12] Morality had become synonymous with obedience to Hitler's grand plan and independent conscience was shrivelled by a decade of racial sadism that filtered right down to the family unit and its personal ethic. Yet even among the ordinary soldiery, conscience was sometimes outraged beyond bearing. Under Operation Barbarossa, four *Einsatzgruppen* A, B, C & D were formed, whose primary function was to kill or incite others to kill. They embarked on a higher order of slaughter which disturbed even their sensibilities: as proved by illness, requests for transfer to HQ or other duties. Others wept, drank too much, suffered nervous breakdowns or impotence. One man went berserk and shot several of his colleagues. Most had to be convinced of the necessity for what they were doing. But hardened soldiers become hardened to slaughter, and those who didn't were in a minority.[13]

Under the Third Reich the majority of Germans actively supported Hitler or, fearing for their families and their lives, did nothing to oppose the genocide. It was not easy for an ordinary citizen to speak out and doing so risked terrible punishment, but it was *possible*. Alexander Hohenstein, for example, a minor official – a district mayor in the Warthegau – kept diaries for 1941–2 that reveal a German nationalist struggling to maintain a normal life. He didn't want Poles or Jews to step aside or leave the pavement for him: '*You can't expect me to violate so grossly my concept of human dignity. If someone shows me respect then I owe him that, too. It is self-evident that I acknowledge people when they greet me. No authority can forbid me observing the most elementary manners.*' Hohenstein went out of his way to ease the situation of the ostracised Jews in the local ghetto, bringing them potatoes to fill their empty bellies and firewood to heat their bitterly cold rooms. He continued to discuss literature and exchange gifts with the dentist's wife: '*Yes indeed, she is a pure racial Jewess. But she has a heart of gold. What do differences of blood, race and skin colour matter in relation to the soul!*'[14] Such tensions between unthinking racism and instinctive human decency jostled in the minds of many Germans.

One bold and outspoken opponent of the Nazi régime was Count

12. Burleigh, *The Third Reich: A New History*, p. 520.
13. Ibid., pp. 603–4.
14. Ibid., pp. 452–3.

Helmet von Moltke.[15] On 10 September 1940 he wrote to his wife Freya, mother of his three small children: 'I am constantly surprised at the extent to which all these people have lost their orientation. It is just like a game of blind man's buff: they have been turned round and round blindfolded and no longer know what is left and right, front and back.'[16] Von Moltke was a founder member of the secret Kreisau Circle – a leading element in underground resistance to the Nazis – that met from time to time at his estate, Kreisau, in Silesia, to oppose Hitler on ethical and patriotic grounds and plan how to get rid of him. On 21 October 1941, after hearing of reprisals in Serbia and Greece (where in a single village almost two thousand people were shot in retaliation for an attack on three German soldiers) he asked Freya,

> May I know this and yet sit at my table in my heated flat and have tea? Don't I thereby become guilty too? What shall I say when I am asked: 'And what did you do during this time?' Since Saturday the Berlin Jews are being rounded up. Again and again one hears reports that in transports of prisoners or Jews only 20 per cent arrive, that there is starvation in the POW camps, that typhoid and all the other deficiency epidemics have broken out and that our own people are breaking down from exhaustion . . . How can anyone know these things and still walk around free?

Only a fraction – probably fewer than 10 per cent – of Germans knew about the secret atrocities in the transports and extermination

15. Count Helmut von Moltke (1907–45), descendant of one of Germany's most distinguished noble families. Trained as a lawyer, he became an international jurist, qualifying at the English bar, and was part of the government of the Third Reich, acting as legal adviser to the counterintelligence department of the German high command, while at the same time being a leading figure in the resistance to Hitler. In 1933 he founded the Kreisau Circle. Its chief concern was the creation of a new Christian Socialist morality that would restore the shattered Germany when the war was over, but, as Hitler became increasingly megalomaniac, the Circle accepted – Count Helmut von Moltke with some reluctance, since it ran counter to his Christian belief 'Thou shalt not kill' – that the quickest way to end the murderous war was by assassinating the *Führer*. This was the July plot of 1944, commonly known as the Stauffenberg Plot after another member who was to carry out the killing. After a farcical trial Count Helmut von Moltke was sentenced to die horribly in Plötzensee prison in Berlin on 23 January 1945.
16. Von Moltke, *Letters to Freya, 1939–1945*, p. 113.

camps, which were deliberately sited far away in Poland. This is not a generous estimate by a Nazi supporter but comes from Count Helmut von Moltke, who wrote to a friend in Stockholm in March 1943: 'At least nine-tenths of the population do not know that we have murdered hundreds of thousands of Jews. They still believe that the Jews have simply been segregated, that they are living in the east where they originated, perhaps somewhat poorer but without the worry of air raids.'[17] The sceptical 10 per cent would have suspected that this was far from being the case but full knowledge was confined to the minimum number of camp supervisors, officials and guards required to carry out the terrible work.[18] Count Helmut von Moltke's moral dilemma was, 'Since I know this, don't I therefore become guilty too for seeming to condone it, for knowing and yet doing nothing to stop it?' But note his proviso: *"Since I know this."* Does the same apply to people who *didn't* know – and was Eva Braun one of those who were ignorant? People like him, though very much the exception, concluded after hard soul-searching that they were, if not guilty, *complicit*; and being complicit, it was their moral duty to resist, even if they died for it – as did Count Helmut von Moltke, von Stauffenberg and two hundred people whose names were linked with theirs.[19]

In February 1942 Goebbels recorded Hitler's unequivocal statement of his plans for the Jewish race. He wrote in his diary for the 14th: 'The *Führer* once more expressed his determination to clean up the Jews in Europe pitilessly. There must be no squeamish sentimentalism about it. The Jews have deserved the catastrophe that has overtaken them. Their destruction will go hand in hand with the destruction of our enemies. We must hasten this process with cold ruthlessness.'[20] The logic of death was picking up speed. *'Pitiless'*, *'ruthless'* – incarceration, hard labour, disease and slow starvation were no longer enough. The proposed new measures remained a closely guarded secret and those who carried them out were fanatics, not just men obeying orders. Many were deeply committed to their task. One former

---

17. Adam Lebor and Roger Boyes, *Seduced by Hitler: The Choice of a Nation and the Ethics of Survival* (Naperville, IL: Sourcebooks, 2001), p. 99.
18. On 11 January 1940 a General Order No. 1 was issued, ordering that no member of a government or military agency was to be informed or try to know more about secret matters than was necessary for their duties.
19. The story of their courage and shameful deaths is told in Chapter 26.
20. L.P. Lochner (ed.), *The Goebbels Diaries, 1942–43* (New York, 1948), p. 86.

attendant at Auschwitz admitted forty years later that he still had 'very ambiguous' feelings about the killing of Jews:

> There's always behind you the fact that the Jews are enemies who come from inside Germany. The propaganda had for us the effect that you assumed that to exterminate them was basically something that happened in war. A feeling of sympathy or empathy didn't come into it. The children were not the enemy; the enemy was the blood in them. The enemy was their growing up to become a Jew who could be dangerous, and because of that the children were also affected.[21]

Most Germans knew little about the concentration camps beyond what Nazi propaganda told them – that they were places where Jews and other non-Aryans[22] were concentrated for the purposes of labour – *hard* labour, but then everyone was working hard for the war effort. They knew nothing of 'Aktion 14f13' authorising euthanasia for concentration camp inmates in Germany and Austria who could no longer work, although sermons by the Catholic Bishop Galen, fulminating against euthanasia and the murder of concentration camp inmates, were heard by many Catholics and widely discussed by those who dared. In December 1941 the Chelmno killing centre set in motion the first mass gassings, followed in spring 1942 by similar installations for murder on a vast scale at the extermination camps of Auschwitz, Sobibor, Belzec and Treblinka.

Another upright German who resisted the rising swell of mass murder, although it cost him his life, was Ulrich von Hassell, an old-school conservative diplomat who served as German ambassador to Rome from November 1932. Tall, urbane and multilingual, he too was a founder member of the Kreisau Circle. He and his like-minded friends took enormous risks in opposing Hitler, although from spring 1942 onwards he was well aware that Hitler's secret police were watching and following him. Von Hassell's diaries are punctuated with groans of disgust and shame at the treatment of Jews and the Soviets, which he described as 'devilish barbarity'. 'The whole war in the east is terrible; a return to savagery.' In November 1941 he wrote: 'There

21. Oskar Groening, former SS member, quoted in the *Observer*, 9 January 2005.
22. It's estimated that the male homosexual population of Germany in the thirties was about two million. Of these, at least fifty thousand were killed between 1939 and 1945, though the real figure is probably much higher.

is revulsion on the part of all decent people towards the shameless measures taken against the Jews . . .'[23]

Wilhelm Furtwängler remains a controversial figure. As Director of the Berlin Philharmonic and one of the finest conductors in Germany, if not the world, he was treated relatively well by the Nazis. His concerts were often broadcast to the troops to raise morale, but he was limited by the authorities in the music he was allowed to perform. Furtwängler's attitude towards Jews was ambivalent. On the one hand, he often praised and supported Jewish artists yet he also supported boycotts of Jewish goods and was critical of what he saw as Jewish domination of the newspapers. He has been damned on the evidence of, among other things, a photograph in which he appears beside a smiling Hitler. He was never a member of the Nazi Party[24] and tried on two occasions to persuade Hitler not to ban Jewish musicians. Hitler did not accede and Furtwängler's career suffered as a result of his plea.[25] In the end he accepted a mutually beneficial agreement with the Nazis, even though it compromised his conscience. There must have been many like him who, while able to live and work under the Nazis, had secret reservations and tried in a small way to resist.

Those who protested were not invariably men. In a famous demonstration on Berlin's Rosenstrasse on 27 February 1943, hundreds of 'pure-bred' German wives whose Jewish husbands were awaiting deportation and death packed the street outside the building where the men were being held. They stayed there day and night, holding hands, singing songs, and chanting 'Let our husbands go!' The authorities were helpless to retaliate since making martyrs of the wives would ruin the Nazis' carefully nurtured image as the protectors of motherhood. Until then the régime had managed to keep the genocide against the Jews and others largely secret, but, when it affected a group who weren't afraid to protest about the racist policies that threatened to kill their husbands, that secrecy was put at risk. The women, unarmed, unorganised and not linked to any resistance group, stood their ground for a week, demanding the return of their husbands so persistently and furiously that in the end Goebbels was forced to give way. On 6 March 1943 almost two thousand men were released, even the twenty-five who had already been transported to

23. Burleigh, *The Third Reich: A New History*, p. 694.
24. A list of people who *were* Nazis can be had from the Berlin Document Center at Finckenstein Allee 63, 12205 Berlin, tel. 01888 770 411.
25. Paxton, *The Anatomy of Fascism*, p. 139.

Auschwitz,[26] and nearly all survived the war. This was the *only* mass public protest against the Nazi régime in the whole twelve years of the Third Reich.

Gitta Sereny, a ruthless critic of German inertia in the face of evil, asked Margret Speer[27] long after the war whether the *Führer* had ever discussed anything serious with the women in his circle, let alone the concentration camps. Her answer was, 'We really did live very much on the outside [i.e. of world events]. Of course we knew *something* was going on, but if one thought about them at all, it was as prison camps, for criminals, I mean.' That phrase again: '*knew something.*'

Margret was a truthful woman, deeply troubled in retrospect by her own passivity at a time when she had surely suspected that all was not well. The meaning of her answer depends how the phrase 'Of course we knew' is interpreted. Does it mean 'we *knew*, of course' – that is, we knew everything; or, 'Of course we knew *something* . . .' implying that that *something* was so sinister as to be unmentionable. Sereny tried to clarify Margret's answer:

> Hitler's genius was to corrupt others, but with extraordinary skill he deliberately protected those closest to him from any awareness that could have disturbed the harmony of their relationship. What could anyone in Germany have known in the early 1930s about the eventual fate of the Jews? Aside from Hitler's and Goebbels' polemics, which few people – including Jews – took very seriously, the answer is: *very little*. Mass murder was not yet thought of, although persecution of the Jews developed slowly and steadily.[28]

Traudl Junge confirmed this: 'The word "Jew" was virtually never used. Nobody ever raised the subject.'[29]

Yet even on the Berg a few women found the courage to speak out. Göring's wife – the former actress Emmy Sonnemann, a woman of

---

26. Adam Lebor and Roger Boyes, *Seduced by Hitler: The Choice of a Nation and the Ethics of Survival* (Naperville, IL: Sourcebooks, 2001), pp. 76–9; see also Large, *Where Ghosts Walked*, p. 335.

27. Sereny, *Albert Speer: His Battle with Truth*, pp. 195–6.

28. Ibid, Introduction. p. 9.

29. Taken from an interview with André Heller in the DOR film *Blind Spot*, released in 2002.

remarkably strong character – interceded with Hitler on behalf of Jews, presumably with little success. If she interceded even once, it is nothing less than astounding. It meant defying both Hitler and her husband, an act of independent conscience forbidden to German wives. But Emmy was a special case and Hitler must have turned a blind eye to the fact that her previous husband had been Jewish and she continued to visit the children of her first marriage, who lived safely in Switzerland, once a year.

In 1943 Heinrich Hoffmann's daughter Henriette – Henny, the little ray of sunshine ('*mein Sonnenschein*') whom Hitler had adored when she was a child – was thirty and married to Baldur von Schirach, the former Hitler Youth leader who was by this time *Gauleiter*[30] of Vienna. A frequent guest at the Berghof throughout her life, she happened to spend a weekend there soon after passing through Holland. *She* acted on the evidence of her own, disbelieving eyes, describing to Hitler an incident at the main station in Amsterdam:

'I took a deep breath and said, "I want to speak to you about some terrible things I saw; I cannot believe you know about them." (In this she echoed millions of other Germans who, observing some public act of cruelty, would sigh and murmur: 'If only *der Führer* knew about this, he'd make sure something was done to stop it!') Henriette went on:

> 'Helpless women were being rounded up and driven together to be sent to a concentration camp and I think they will never return.'
> A painful stillness fell; all colour had left Hitler's face. It looked like a death mask in the light of the flames from the fire. He looked at me aghast and at the same time surprised and said:
> 'We are at war.'
> Then he stood up and screamed at me, 'You are sentimental, Frau von Schirach! You have to learn to hate!'[31]

Eva Braun must have heard this exchange – at informal dinners such as this with a trusted cadre of old friends she was always at Hitler's side – but, like the others, she said nothing. Traudl Junge, in her version of the episode, adds: 'A painful silence fell. Soon afterwards Hitler stood up, made his farewells and went back up. Next day Frau von Schirach returned to Vienna and the incident was never referred

---

30. Administrative head of a town or district.
31. In her autobiographical memoir, *Der Preis der Herrlichkeit* (Munich: Herbig, 1975).

to. She had evidently exceeded her privileges and not fulfilled her duty as a guest to entertain Hitler.'[32]

Henriette and her husband were at times a brave and outspoken pair. On another (or perhaps the same) occasion on 24 June 1943, according to Hitler's adjutant, the comparatively upright and decent Nicolaus von Below,[33] Baldur von Schirach insisted that a way had to be found to end the war soon. 'Hitler was very put out over this conversation with Schirach,' wrote von Below, 'and made it very plain that he wanted nothing more to do with him. And indeed it was their last encounter.'[34]

Speer, who wasn't present, noted that afterwards the atmosphere was very oppressive: 'Everybody was going around with dark faces because all of us felt very protective of Hitler. On the Berg one made it a rule not to bring up anything disagreeable, in order to protect his short periods of rest.'[35] The incident is significant, both for Henriette's astonishment when she saw for herself the tribulations of the Jews and for her assumption that Hitler knew nothing about it. He evidently banned her from the Berghof after this, since there is no mention of further visits. A guest who violated its carefully preserved illusion of sociable calm was unwelcome and those who breached the unspoken rules were not asked again.

For the women on the Berg their few dark suspicions were lit up by rare episodes like the von Schirachs' protest but then quickly extinguished. Eva, with little hard information on which to base her fears – if any – was not going to repudiate the man she had loved all her life for the sake of formless anxieties. She often complained: 'Everything is kept secret from me. I have no idea what's going on.'[36] She turned a blind eye to the phantasms that haunted her at night – premonitions of Hitler's death rather than visions of mass murder. I asked her cousin Gertraud Weisker whether it was true that Eva had no inkling about the persecution of Jews and she answered, 'Well, we did not know about the concentration camps. No. But we knew there was *something* because we had a lot of Jewish friends who were moving to America. And *Der Stürmer*, the extremist Nazi newspaper, was on every street corner.'[37] Everyone knew *something* but very few knew quite *what*. It does not mean

32. Junge, *Bis Zur Letzten Stunde*, p. 103.
33. Nicolaus von Below, *Als Hitler's Adjutant, 1937–1945* (Mainz, 1980), p. 340.
34. Ibid.
35. Sereny, *Albert Speer: His Battle with Truth*. p. 111.
36. Christa Schröder, *Er War Mein Chef* (Munich: Langen Müller, 1985).
37. From interview with Gertraud Weisker in *The Times*.

Eva knew the truth, let alone more of the truth than most people, but perhaps she *chose* not to know: a sin condemned as 'wilful ignorance' by the Catholic Church whose ethic and beliefs – rather than those of the BDM – had been instilled when she was an impressionable child. Eva was given information by a Nazi infrastructure that could be as strong in hiding the facts from one set of people (its women) as it was in destroying another (Europe's Jews). So called "willful" – meaning deliberate – ignorance or an imposed blindness in which its object acquiesces, can be a form of ruthlessness that is almost as responsible for evil as deliberate prejudice.

Gertraud Weisker thinks Eva Braun has been disgracefully slandered and remains convinced of her essential goodness. Speaking of Eva as she was in the last months of her life, Gertraud (biased in her favour) thought:

> Eva lived in a dream world. When the reality was not good she pushed it away. Politically, she was not aware of anything. . . . But she was true to herself and followed the path she had chosen. She largely succeeded in overcoming the pressures that cut her off from the outside world and by the end of the war had faced up to reality and was ready to die with dignity.[38]

But what *was* that reality? Gertraud continues to insist that Eva was not anti-Semitic and, like all her family except Fritz, never joined the Nazi Party.

In this, I finally discovered, she is right. Hard as it may be to accept, Eva was *not* a member – let alone an ardent member – of the party led by Hitler. I had suspected this (it simply didn't square with her character or his desire to steer her well clear of politics) but in February 2005, in Hermann-Historica, the respected Munich auction house specialising in military memorabilia,[39] I found proof that she was not. I had spent the morning at a borrowed desk surrounded by old swords, rust-spotted helmets, bayonets and uniforms, many from the Weimar years, as well as a vast array of objects from the Third Reich, all waiting their turn to be sold, as I searched through Hermann-Historica's catalogues, starting in 2004 and going back as far as 1980. After many hours and several cups of strong coffee drawn from the machine in a corner of the lobby when my concentration flagged, I found my evidence.

38. Quoted from interview for *Adolf and Eva*, 3BMTV, roll 05.17.29.
39. Its website is www.hermann-historica.de.

Lot 4549 of an auction held on 10/11 November 1989 read: '*Mit der Verleihung des Parteiabzeichens an Eva Braun, folgte Adolf Hitler seine Gepflogenheit, Persönlichkeiten die seine besondere Wertschätzen besassen, auch dann in dieser Form auszuzeichnen, wenn dies nicht Parteimitglieder waren.*' Roughly translated, this means: 'In awarding this Party badge to Eva Braun, Adolf Hitler followed his custom of indicating people who had the honour of his special esteem, even though they were not Party members, by singling them out in this way.'

The object was at first glance unremarkable – a round 18-carat gold medallion with her initials, EB, and the inscription engraved on the back – by whom, and when, it was impossible to tell. It had no date, but the inscription clearly meant the *Führer* accepted that his mistress was not a member of the Nazi Party, and implied that she was under no pressure to join. Despite living at the cold heart of Hitler's circle, Eva was *not* a Nazi. The medallion sold for DM3,200 – a good deal of money in 1989 – and has disappeared into some anonymous private collection.

No one can be accused of failing to act on a cause they do not espouse or facts they do not know. One cannot prove a negative and we shall never be sure how well informed Eva, Traudl Junge or the other women on the Berg were. If Eva knew nothing about the genocide, she can't be called guilty or even complicit, though she might be condemned for failing to notice or act on the growing evidence of persecution. On the assumption that she *did* know something – however little, however obliquely – what could she have done to signal her disapproval? Her only option was to leave Hitler, yet since 1931 her whole life had been founded upon him and it was impossible for her to walk away. It is easy to say what she *should* have done but for her, as (in Britain) for Sonia Sutcliffe, wife of the Yorkshire Ripper, or Prudence Shipman, wife of Dr Harold Shipman who deliberately murdered scores of his elderly patients, there was no choice.

Eva's proximity to the *Führer* is almost irrelevant to whether or not she was aware of the truth, although the chief reason she has been reviled by posterity is that few people can accept this. They have failed to understand the dynamics of public and private relationships between men and women under the Third Reich. Hitler strictly forbade anyone to talk to Eva – or any other woman on the Berg – about the torture, starvation and genocide perpetrated upon vast numbers of Jews, Roma, homosexuals, Jehovah's Witnesses, Bolsheviks, Slavs and dissident clerics, upon Catholics priests and Poles. Details of the horrors of the slave labour camps and their victims were kept from Nazi wives. Hitler would have imprisoned or even executed anyone who tried to tell Eva the unspeakable truth. The very fact that she was his mistress meant that she, of all people, had to know nothing. How could she be a warm and uncritical solace for him to come home to if she knew what he had done?

Once again, is it possible that Eva knew literally *nothing* about the Holocaust? She had always visited Munich regularly and continued to do so until almost the end of the war. In the 1930s she could hardly have avoided seeing anti-Jewish slogans, boarded-up shops, suitcases in the street; gaunt Jewish children and elderly, distinguished Jews being publicly humiliated by the SS. Jews wore the yellow Star of David on their coats, were allocated fewer rations than other Germans, banned from using the trams and only permitted to shop during restricted hours. Theatres, cinemas and concert halls were closed to them: a particular deprivation. All this she could have seen with her own eyes, had she cared to. After *Kristallnacht*, from 1939 onwards, there was more chilling evidence in the form of routine seizures ('requisitioning') of Jewish apartments, from which Munich's four thousand Jews – generous, cultured people, mostly professional men or thriving shopowners – out of the city's total population of 824,000 were forced into Jewish enclaves called *Judenhäuser*. This, too, she might have heard about. Other warning signs were more obscure. In early 1941 the Jews were sent to an overflowing ghetto at Milbertshofen, four miles outside the city. Then began the deportations, first to nearby Dachau and then to camps in the east. Only someone blind could have failed to notice at least some of these portents, which were widely debated and the subject of sermons in many churches.

Chapter Twenty-three

. . . What Could Eva Have Done?

The genocide continued its inexorable march. Heavy boots stamped and kicked, leather-gloved hands steadied and aimed as the order was issued: '*Feuer!*' Nothing less was at stake than the future of Europe for the next millennium and the ultimate survival of its Jews. Hermann Göring declared: 'This is the great racial war. It is about whether the German and Aryan prevails here, or whether the Jew rules the world.'[1] After visiting Lodz ghetto in Poland, Goebbels wrote: 'It is indescribable. These aren't human beings any more, these are animals. This is therefore not a humanitarian but rather a surgical task.'[2] On 16 July 1941, SS-*Sturmbannführer* Höppner in Posen wrote to his superior, Adolf Eichmann, Chief of the Jewish Office of the Gestapo – the headquarters for the implementation of the Final Solution: 'There is a danger of not being able to feed all the Jews this winter. Serious consideration is required on the question whether the most humanitarian solution would not be to finish off those Jews who are unfit for work by some expedient means. That would be less unpleasant than allowing them to die from hunger', adding, 'These things do sound somewhat fantastic but in my opinion they are entirely feasible.'[3] '*Some expedient means*' is a small masterpiece of evasion. This was incitement to general murder but the Nazi high command seldom cared to look facts in the face. On 12 December 1941, however, Hitler had declared with unusual directness that it was time to clear the decks on the Jewish question

1. Weisker, *Wer War Eva Braun?*.
2. Burleigh, *The Third Reich: A New History*, p. 574.
3. Ibid., p. 608

without pity or sentimentality – not that a call to 'clear the decks' unequivocally called for the extermination of European Jewry – which would have made it the smoking gun for which historians have searched in vain[4] – but it was an unusually explicit statement. Heinrich Himmler, ice-cold and impervious to suffering if it advanced the interests of the German race, was put in charge of the extermination camps. 'It's very upsetting to have to murder large numbers of people but nevertheless it must be done and we do it,' he said, with the pained air of a man doing the world a favour. Jews were murdered by firing squads and their corpses dumped in mass graves. In eastern Europe this happened at hundreds of sites.

The most efficient killing methods were scientifically refined and checked. In September 1941 the first experiments with Zyklon B gas took place at Auschwitz. Eight hundred and fifty Soviet prisoners of war and two hundred Poles were satisfactorily and hygienically murdered. In December 1941 (the hounds of hell loping and baying) the Chelmno killing centre launched its conveyor belt of destruction. A few months later, as spring bloomed, mass gassings were instituted at Sobibor, Belzec and Treblinka. Himmler's forward planning had paid off. By late 1943 one and a half million Jews had been killed, although few people apart from his deputy Adolf Eichmann knew the true extent of the slaughter. Eichmann (who, like Hitler, had spent his youth in Linz) was promoted to Lieutenant-Colonel of the SS in 1941 and put in charge of the extermination camps. A man without conscience but a bureaucrat of genius, he kept fastidious records, watching with quiet pride as the numbers mounted. Just over a million people died at Auschwitz, of whom 90 per cent were European Jews. By August 1944 Eichmann could report to his superiors that some four million Jews had died in the camps and another two million had been killed by 'mobile extermination units'. That was worth a click of the heels, a manly handshake and a shared *Heil Hitler!*

4. 'Hitler hated making clear, binding decisions, especially on sensitive matters. Preferring rule by inspiration, he signalled his preferences to subordinates in the form of vaguely expressed wishes. They then competed for his favour. Like other leading Nazis, he employed indirect or metaphorical language: to insiders, "special treatment" or "evacuation" meant "killing". There is scant evidence to indicate that Hitler was directly aware of the killing after it began.' From a review by John Connelly in *The London Review of Books*, 7 July 2005, of Christopher Browning's *The Origins of the Final Solution: The Evolution of Nazi Jewish Policy 1939–42* (London: Arrow, 2005).

Anna Plaim, Eva's loyal maid, was sure her mistress knew little or nothing about the ultimate fate of the Jews and insisted that most women at the Berghof didn't either. In 2002 she told Kurt Kuch, who questioned her about life at the Berghof:

> As for the Jews who were so brutally executed in Dachau, most people knew nothing about it. The extreme harassment of Jews before the war was obviously common knowledge; today nobody can deny that. Many were hounded out of their homes and neighbourhood. But I had absolutely no idea what was done to these people in the last resort. I believe that Eva Braun also was not privy to their fate and what really went on in the concentration camps although she, like everyone, must have known that Jews and opponents of the Nazis were being ill-treated. But the photographs of people being transported like cattle on their way to the extermination camps – these only surfaced after the war.[5]

Bearing in mind the tendency of those around Hitler to minimise or deny their racist beliefs, this seems a fair estimate of how well-informed Eva was, but it remains a guess. Gertraud Weisker is convinced that Eva knew none of the facts about the Holocaust. In an impassioned defence of herself as well as her cousin she said:

> We didn't know anything about Auschwitz. At that time it was really done so secretly that it's easy to believe most people knew nothing about it. The people who surrounded Eva knew much more than we knew but at that time it was so completely secret that ordinary German families didn't know about such things. I knew that Jews went, but I assumed they'd gone to America or elsewhere; I never thought they'd been killed by gas.[6]

The regimentation of youth culture by Hitler led to several underground protest movements. Their members were mostly male students aged between sixteen and twenty-five, or groups (*Meuten*) of working-class lads who had adopted the methods of Socialist and Communist dissenters. The latter became the targets of Nazi louts, along with groups like the *Edelweisspiraten* who attacked the Hitler Youth units who patrolled parks and other public areas. Confrontations between the two sometimes

5. Plaim and Kuch, *Bei Hitlers: Zimmermädchen Annas Erinnerungen*, p. 140.
6. *Adolf and Eva*, 3BMTV, roll 06.11.38.

resulted in an exchange of gunfire (one wonders where the dissidents got hold of guns). As the *Piraten* became more political they were harshly treated by the SS and a few were even executed. Some were sent to prison or to concentration camps. On 25 October 1944 Heinrich Himmler ordered a crackdown and in November of that year, thirteen *Edelweisspiraten* were publicly hanged in Cologne, including six boys aged sixteen.

Then, as now, the young used music to define themselves and their allegiances. A third group, consisting chiefly of middle-class young, used it as a sign of protest, rejecting the jolly *völkisch* (folksy) music promoted by the Nazi Party in favour of American jazz, especially the variety known as swing.[7] Its frantic rhythms to which people could dance more hectically than ever before made swing immensely popular. Fans called themselves *Swing Jugend*, 'Swing Youth',[8] in a mocking reference to *Hitler Jugend*. 'Swing kids' supported radical social, political and economic issues and, by rejecting racism, challenged the fundamental ideology of the Reich. Their easy-going behaviour was the opposite of the military ethos the régime was busy inculcating in German youth. Jazz had been banned around the time Hitler became Chancellor in 1933 as 'an ugly squeaking of instruments offensive to our ears' and was particularly repugnant to the Nazi hierarchy for its links with the 'inferior' black African race in the southern states of America. Jazz was disparagingly regarded as 'Negro music', no more than a primitive cacophony. Goebbels' propaganda machine tried unsuccessfully to counter swing with Charlie and his Orchestra, a big band playing a watered-down version of swing music and songs on the wireless, but without much success.

The swing movement was reluctantly tolerated until February 1940, when a Swing Festival held in Hamburg attracted more than five

7. The birth of swing took place in America during the years of the Great Depression, during a time of low wages and high unemployment. Starting in about 1931, black bands led by bandleaders such as Duke Ellington and Fletcher Henderson began to develop the swing style, which was well established by 1933. During the earlier part of the Depression, sentimental music had filled the airwaves. Now people were in search of something that would lift their spirits. Joy and excitement find their most spontaneous expression in music and dancing and Benny Goodman, with the music of big-band swing, led the way. (This and much of the information about swing in the main text is taken from www.anyswinggoes.com)

8. For more details about the resistance of the young to the rise of Nazism, see Detlev J.K. Peukert, *Inside Nazi Germany: Conformity, Opposition, and Racism in Everyday Life* (London: Yale University Press, 1987).

hundred youths – a tiny number compared with the tens, *hundreds* of thousands who turned out for party rallies, but enough to alarm the Nazi hierarchy. A report by agents from Hitler Youth described 'loose' dancing, adding, 'Several boys could be observed dancing together, always with two cigarettes in their mouth, one in each corner.' Such decadence! Nothing could have been better calculated to upset the Nazis.[9] Future gatherings were banned but defiant Swing Youth clubs quickly resurfaced. On 2 January 1942 Himmler instructed Reinhard Heydrich[10] to make scapegoats of the Swing leaders, who were sent to a concentration camp for two to three years and further punished with beatings and forced labour. A crackdown followed: the clubs were raided and more leading participants were hauled off to camps.[11]

It is hard to credit that Eva, who used to be such a keen dancer and clubber, could have known nothing about all this but she was never that kind of raucous, foot-stomping girl. Hectic jazz rhythms were a long way from the swoony, moony tunes she preferred, though she continued to go to nightclubs where jazz, swing and its followers could well have been talked about over beer or cocktails. She may not have heard of Swing Youth, very much a minority taste, and it's possible that her friends preferred not to discuss anti-Nazi movements in front of her. But *if* they had, she *could* have been aware that these groups were protesting about anti-Semitism, from which she *might* have deduced that there was something serious to protest about. Three hypotheticals don't enable one to say with certainty that Eva was well-informed about the *Edelweisspiraten* or Swing Youth and their liberal attitudes. Her policy, as ever, was not to ask awkward questions.

In 1942 a powerful propaganda film called *I Accuse*, which advocated euthanasia for the mentally and physically handicapped and the terminally ill, was seen by more than fifteen million Germans, more than quarter of a million of them in Munich alone. Its arguments were much debated and Eva – again, not must but *might* – have heard her friends talk about it. In the same year, 1942, a number of subversive Munich students led by Hans Scholl and his sister

9. Roger Lebor and Adam Boyes, *Seduced by Hitler: The Choice of a Nation and the Ethics of Survival* (Naperville, IL: Sourcebooks, 2001), p. 122.
10. Chief of Security Police and SD (Security Service).
11. This account is paraphrased from www.wikipedia.org

Sophie[12] formed a secret protest group called '*die Weisse Rose*' (the White Rose) to publicise and resist Nazi atrocities. They handed out three thousand leaflets revealing that three hundred thousand Jews had already been killed in Poland, which generated a good deal of controversy. On 18 February 1943 the Scholls and their friend Christoph Probst were tried for distributing leaflets around the university condemning the brutality in Stalingrad and the inhumanity of the Nazi régime. On 22 February they were found guilty of treason and guillotined.[13] This silenced the students of Munich and protest became rare.

Munich's citizens knew very little about what was happening in the east since the Nazis went to great lengths to keep the Holocaust secret and people could be jailed simply for passing on information about the camps.[14] It doesn't automatically follow from isolated acts of youthful rebellion that insurgent groups were widely discussed. Eva and her friends were neither students nor philosophers and didn't have much time for intellectual arguments. She came to Munich's nightclubs to get away from the oppressive mood of the Berghof and protest was the last thing on her mind.

Some of those close to Eva did know, or had *some* idea, of the increasing scale of horror. Her father, who had abandoned his scruples to enjoy the cushioned life of the Berghof – he knew. Hitler's sleek young adjutants, who often appear in her photograph album reclining on the grass in swimming trunks, displaying torsos honed for *Führer* and Fatherland – *they* knew, without question. Did she overhear whispered conversations, pick up hints? – all this is guesswork. Speer's daughter Hilde, who grew up in the family house on the Berg, insisted after the war: 'I am quite certain that she [Margret, her mother] remained entirely unaware of the horrors. Equally, however, although she never speaks of it, she fully believed what we learned afterwards,

12. Sophie Scholl (1921–43), sister of one of the White Rose ringleaders, was the subject of a widely praised film showing in Munich during my last visit in February 2005. Photographs show a vibrant and lovely young woman with defiantly boyish cropped hair. From 1942 she studied biology and philosophy at Munich University, also attended by her brother Hans, who was studying medicine. One of the ways in which the students of today, grandchildren of the old Nazis, are making sense of their past is to glorify those – especially the young – who *did* defy Hitler. Sophie Scholl was one such, and it cost her her life. (Source: www.jlrweb.com/whiterose/sophie.html)
13. Caption to photograph after p. 834 in Kershaw *Hitler, 1936–1945: Nemesis.*
14. Large, *Where Ghosts Walked*, p. 336.

and I think now she feels terribly guilty for having lived so close to this man, Hitler, for having so benefited from this proximity.'[15] Annemarie Kempf, who became Albert Speer's private secretary at the age of eighteen, said of her boss: 'In a way, I think he felt that *what he didn't know didn't exist* [my italics].'[16]

It is hard to credit that the women closest to Hitler, above all his secretaries, could have been so naive as to be unaware of what was going on. On 11 July 1943 Bormann issued a circular forbidding any mention of genocide, let alone of the numbers murdered. The word 'executed' must not be used; Jews had been 'evacuated'. Ignorance was not only possible but mandatory.

Traudl Junge, in an interview not long before she died, said:

We never saw him [i.e. Hitler] as the statesman; we didn't attend any of his conferences. We were summoned only when he wanted to dictate and he was as considerate then as he was in private. Our office, both in the Reichschancellery and in the bunkers, was so far removed from his command quarters that we never saw or even heard any of his rages that we heard whispers about. We knew his timetable, whom he received, but except for the few men he some-times had to meals we attended . . . we rarely saw any of them.[17]

It is certain that Eva, too, never sat in on ministerial meetings: *that* would have been unheard of. Those gatherings were strictly for men. Yet she was at the centre of Hitler's private life: she must have gleaned scraps of information, if not from him personally, from drinks or dinner-table conversations? Today it seems beyond belief that Nazi wives, married to the men perpetrating the worst excesses of the war, could really have remained ignorant of what was happening. Yet they had no access to the radio let alone BBC news broadcasts; no television; foreign newspapers were banned and the German press was full of exaggerations and lies. Everyone on the Berg knew the von Schirachs had been sent into the wilderness for questioning Hitler's policies, which in any case most of them enthusiastically supported.

For women, knowledge was confined to what they saw with their own eyes and few of the sheltered inhabitants of Obersalzberg ventured

15. Sereny, *Albert Speer: His Battle with Truth*, p. 132.
16. Ibid., p. 148.
17. Sereny, *The German Trauma*, p. 359.

far beyond its confines, preferring to sun themselves on the terrace during the '*Kaffeeklatsch*' – gossiping over coffee and cooing over each others' delightful children. A trip down the mountain to Berchtesgaden was a major outing, involving permission to borrow their husband's car and chauffeur, punctual timing and an armed security escort. Once there, they would have noticed few changes except that the shops, especially clothes shops, were emptier than usual and ration coupons were needed for every food purchase. Besides, Bormann had laid down strict rules about which establishments they were allowed to patronise – only those owned by loyal Nazis, which were not necessarily the best. Since Frau Goebbels and Eva, Frau Göring and Frau Himmler ordered their clothes from private dressmakers – the firm of Auracher in Munich was a special favourite – and their diet was generously supplemented from the model farm at Obersalzberg, these hardships didn't affect them too much. The Berghof was like a gated community. People deliberately cut themselves off from the unpleasantness of being made aware of others less fortunate.[18] Gitta Sereny recorded:

> One of the things I found out, thanks to Speer, was the extent to which Hitler protected the small circle of people among whom he lived socially. People like Eva Braun knew nothing of these things. He didn't really care what his generals knew – this was a matter of total indifference to him – what he didn't want was for those he depended on emotionally to know about them.[19]

Traudl Junge, who probably spent more time with Hitler during his last two years than Eva did, described the isolation she felt from the real world:

> Hitler would not have had the ladies of his household – his four secretaries, or the young wives of his aides, such as Below, and those of his closest associates, Speer and Brandt – disturbed with war horrors.[20] No rumours reached us, no enemy, no other point of view, no opposition. Just one view, one conviction; everyone used the same words to express the same opinion. I had to be in at the bitter end and it wasn't until I returned to ordinary life

18. From Martha Burke-Hennessy, by e-mail to the author.
19. Gitta Sereny interviewed for *Adolf and Eva*, 3BMTV, roll 9.10.
20. Sereny, *Albert Speer: His Battle with Truth*, p. 248.

that I understood all that clearly. *At the time I suffered an indefinable feeling of unease; a nameless sense of oppression and anxiety* [my itals] for as long as the daily encounter with Hitler prevented me from formulating these thoughts clearly.[21]

Did she really suffer this 'unease'? Claims to pangs of conscience by former Nazis must always be taken with a pinch of salt.

Forty years after the war ended Dr Theodor Hupfauer, a passionate National Socialist and Speer's right-hand man, said:

I want nothing to do with all those people who now claim they weren't Nazis; that indeed they were resisters. I really sometimes wonder who it was who elected Hitler and fought and won all those battles for him. All of Germany, it now appears, was nothing but anti-Nazi. [. . .] It was an incredibly exciting period. People of my age were given unprecedented opportunities and we came to feel there was nothing we couldn't achieve.[22]

In *Until the Final Hour*, Traudl described her first journey in his private train from the Wolf's Lair to Berlin after she had joined Hitler's private office in March 1943:

It made me think of all the other trains rolling through Germany at the same time, cold and unlit, carrying people who hadn't enough to eat and no comfortable place to sit and it made me feel uneasy. [She refers here to passenger trains, not those carrying Jews to extermination camps, of which she was unaware.] It's easy to run a war if you don't have to experience it personally, in your own body. I watched Hitler's personal staff smoking and drinking, relaxed and cheerful, satisfied with their lives, and hoped that the sole purpose of all this was to end the war as soon as possible.[23]

This sounds genuine enough and seems to show that even a young woman who had been subject to intensive Nazi propaganda could be troubled by the contrast between her own pampered life and those of millions of beleaguered Germans. Eva would have been incapable of

21. Junge, *Bis Zur Letzten Stunde*, p. 118 (translated by the author).
22. Sereny, *Albert Speer: His Battle with Truth*, p. 180.
23. Ibid., p. 51.

this response because to her it would have smacked of treason, but it enabled Traudl to reflect on the anomaly of her situation and the paradox of Hitler's dual personality:

> It is hard to recreate or imagine the mesmeric effect Hitler had on everyone he encountered. Even people bitterly opposed to him commented on the power he radiated, how they felt irresistibly drawn to him, even though it made them feel troubled and guilty afterwards. This phenomenon is often present in extremely powerful men when they choose to exert their charm – and *charm* or even more dangerously, *charisma*, rather than the emanation of evil, was Hitler's most obvious characteristic.[24] I myself have never understood the effect he had on all of us, including the generals. It was more than charisma, you know. Sometimes when he went off somewhere without us, the moment he was gone, it was almost as if the air around us had become deficient. Some essential element was missing: electricity, even oxygen, an awareness of being alive – there was a . . . vacuum.[25]

Another side to Hitler showed itself more often as the military situation worsened. Guderian, the Army Chief of Staff appointed on 20 July 1944, described one of the *Führer's* rages:

> His fists raised, his cheeks flushed with anger, his whole body trembling, the man stood in front of me beside himself with fury, having lost all self-control. After each outburst Hitler would stride up and down the carpet edge, then suddenly stop immediately in front of me and hurl his next accusation in my face. He was almost screaming, his eyes seemed about to pop out of his head and the veins stood out on his temples.

Hitler could seem self-pitying, vile-tempered, out of control, megalomaniac, even deranged, but very few of the people around him ever felt that he was *evil*. Albert Speer said: 'You simply cannot understand what it is to live in a dictatorship; you can't understand the game of danger

---

24. Dr Morell told his interrogator before the Nuremberg Trials, 'Hitler's facial expression had an intense quality that subdued and captivated most individuals who met the *Führer*.'
25. From www.fpp.co.uk/Hitler/doc/adjutants/SerenyTraudlJunge.html

but above all you cannot understand the fear on which the whole thing is based. Nor, I suppose, have you any concept of the charisma of a man such as Hitler.' Speer, one of the more objective and detached of the leading Nazis, couldn't distance himself from Hitler's magnetic field and the seductive 'game of danger' and, while denying much else, he admitted this. What hope was there for Eva, whose whole life was based on pleasing him? In his definitive account of the last days of Hitler, Hugh Trevor-Roper reached a provocative conclusion. 'Speer is the real criminal of Nazi Germany for he, more than any other, represented that fatal philosophy which has made havoc of Germany and nearly shipwrecked the world. For ten years he sat at the very centre of political power; his keen intelligence diagnosed the nature and observed the mutations of Nazi government and policy; he saw and despised the personalities around him; he heard their outrageous orders and understood their fantastic ambitions; *but he did nothing* [my italics].'[26]

Speer's secretary Annemarie was one of the few prepared to admit how much being in the presence of the *Führer* had thrilled her:

> The first time was the evening of the day Speer completed the new Chancellery. I was very proud that night. One has to imagine – well, it's almost impossible to imagine – the lights, the flowers everywhere, the excitement of it. I'd like to be critical in retrospect but I can't be. [. . .] Every day something happened that changed our future for us and it happened through this man. I'm trying to tell you not what I feel now, but what I felt *then*. I can't say whether I found him 'likeable' or not; the term has no relevance. It was just joy; he belonged to the joy of it.[27]

Maria von Below was another who did not try to pretend that she had known all along what a monster the *Führer* was, although after the war

26. *Hitler's Table Talk, 1941–1944*, p. 115.
27. Ibid., p. 151. My admiration for this writer's painstaking research and finely tuned moral antennae is very great, but while she may have been a ruthless critic of German inertia and Nazi racist politics, she was certainly fascinated by Albert Speer – as are many women, including myself. It is hard to believe that his handsome, upright bearing and post-war remorse cloak a man intent, albeit in different ways from most Nazis, on saving his skin at Nuremberg and rehabilitating his reputation. He certainly convinced Gitta Sereny but his evidence should be treated with caution and a dollop of scepticism.

she was devastated to learn what had been done in all their names. In 1988, when she was in her late seventies, she talked to Gitta Sereny:

> I have never understood how diminishing the gifts Hitler so clearly did have made it any easier for people to live with having been bewitched by him. After all, he didn't gain the loyalty of decent and intelligent men by telling them his plan was murder and allowing them to see that he was a moral monster. He persuaded them because he was fascinating.[28]

Nothing is more evanescent than charisma and today it is hard for anyone except neo-Nazis to believe that Hitler used it to paralyse the consciences of everyone around him. In the light of rapturous descriptions by his contemporaries it is not a simple matter, after seven decades, to pass judgement on Eva's behaviour, her surrender to the mesmerising power of the only man she ever loved. Eva's plight is reflected by that of thousands of women married to bullies and brutal men; alcoholics, drug addicts. They too sometimes plead that they love their man and cannot bring themselves to abandon him. Women who love evil men need not necessarily be evil themselves. Like them, Eva may have displayed, if you like, the banality of goodness . . . or just a victim's passiveness. *They* will understand Eva's dilemma where the rest of us cannot.

Was she even anti-Semitic? The strongest indication that she was not lies in her character. Given her open nature and her parents' tolerant views, as well as her own youthful rebellion against received ideas, it would be uncharacteristic. However, in the same way as it would be absurd to expect Eva to have been a feminist it may be unrealistic to expect her not to have had *any* such attitudes. Although she was not of an age to have been recruited and indoctrinated by the *Bund Deutscher Mädel*, she grew up in the twenties and came to adulthood in the thirties when propaganda was more sophisticated than the audience at whom it was directed and a degree of anti-Semitism was regarded as normal . . . and not only in Germany. It is hard to envisage the all-pervasive force of the drive towards Aryan purity that the Nazis instilled in the hearts and minds of credulous people, especially today when we are more aware of politicians' ploys to manipulate our thinking ('spin') and more resistant, too.

28. Ibid., pp. 113–14, 359.

History – insofar as it has taken any notice of Eva – has returned a damning verdict, one that can only partly be refuted by intuition and the balance of probability. Lacking conclusive evidence, there are many instances of her kindness, modesty, simplicity and concern for those around her; her generosity to the parents who had bullied and rejected her, her hospitality to the friends of her brief, pleasure-filled schooldays and youth; her utter fearlessness and unshakeable fidelity to Hitler. By the end of her life she had proved herself brave, resilient and invariably kind. Goodness is as banal as evil and may exist in the most unlikely people: even Hitler's mistress.

Try as one may to be objective, after following the ins and outs of her life, trying to peel back the layers, discern what drove her opinions, emotions and fantasies, after living with Eva Braun for nearly three years during which she became as real to me as my friends, I found no evidence whatever that she was racist or sadistic. As has been pointed out, none of the top Nazi wives was punished after the war, though it's possible that Magda Göbbels, had she survived, might at least have been harshly cross-questioned. If those women, also in Hitler's circle, were regarded as blameless at the time, the same verdict should be extended to Eva.

My conclusion, based on the circumstances and her character, is that she should not be condemned. She was not guilty or even implicated in the suffering that Hitler initiated; but not innocent either. She was – in the Catholic phrase – 'blameworthy'. Eva has often been called insipid, foolish, vain and self-indulgent and at times she was all these, but apart from the unreasoning hostility of the Nazi bigwigs, nobody ever accused her of more substantial faults. It is not a crime to be shallow and fun-loving, to try to bring pleasure and gaiety into stolid lives, having no idea they were dedicated to loathsome ends. All one can safely conclude is that Eva was not responsible for any *recorded* act of prejudice against Jews or of violence against anyone. Judged by the standards of her time, including those of my amiable mother, she was not anti-Semitic.

My mother's family – her sisters Ilse and Trudl, her two aunts Lidy and Anni and her mother *Oma* (Granny) – never joined the Nazi Party and certainly knew nothing of the fate of the Jews. *Tante* Ilse, being married to a doctor, might have known a bit, except that from 1942 her husband was attached to the German army in the Soviet Union, unable to communicate and presumed dead. Like nearly all German women, they inflicted no suffering but themselves suffered much.

My mother remained unthinkingly prejudiced against Jews all her life, though not rudely or poisonously so. She and the other Schröder women in Hamburg were incapable of a bold gesture like sheltering a Jewish family. Change, novelty and disorder always alarmed her. In south London in the fifties when we passed one of the newly arrived Afro-Caribbeans she would say, 'Hold your breath, darling, until he's gone by.' If I asked why, she answered, 'They're different from us. They eat different food. They smell different. And' (lowering her voice) 'they're a bit *sweaty*.'

She would have felt the same unconsidered distaste for Jews. Even after she had married my father in June 1936 and come to live in England, it wouldn't have crossed her mind to make room for a Jewish girl in their small south London flat, although every day *The Times* carried dozens of classified advertisements placed by German-Jewish or Austrian parents desperately seeking a safe haven for their daughters, urging their honesty and intelligence, their readiness to embroider, mend, teach a little French or do a little cooking. It wouldn't have occurred to my father either, who was always afraid of making himself conspicuous. My parents would have pleaded poverty as their excuse and in their young married days they *were* very hard up. They couldn't have afforded to feed a girl, let alone pay her. Yet other people managed . . . a few.

Throughout her life my mother referred to Jews as 'Jew-boys' and warned me that they were greedy and untrustworthy, especially about money. Knowing her generous nature, I try to excuse her by reflecting that these were standard attitudes and jargon at a time when words like 'Jew-boy' or 'nigger' were acceptable. Language that seems prejudiced now was not a problem then. Young Edith Schröder was not *personally* vengeful against the Jews and, after the war, Ditha Helps – British wife and mother – had complicated feelings when the truth about the killing camps was revealed.

Like Eva, my mother neither asked questions, nor did she want to know the answers, not even about the fellow pupils with whom she had grown up. My grandfather, on the other hand, who had daily professional contact with Jews in his work as a jeweller and diamond merchant, admired them and felt nothing but contempt for Hitler. When the *Führer* asked the Germans to donate their gold for the war effort to finance the manufacture of arms and aircraft, millions did. Women sacrificed their wedding rings for the communal defence. Not my grandfather. Gold was his livelihood. He buried it in the garden one dark night and dug it up intact when the war was over. I loved that flagrant disobedience.

The fate of the Jews was not a subject my mother was willing to discuss and I found it almost impossible to persuade her to talk about it. Once, when she was quite old and already becoming confused and forgetful, I asked, 'Mummy, were there any Jews in your family?'

Expression of shock, quickly veiled.

'What, darling?'

'Were there any *Jewish* members of the family?'

'No-o – because I suppose they must have been, tested, you know, to see if they were . . . pure. And they passed.' (She knew *that* much, then.)

Pause. Then, 'Were there in your family?'

'Mummy, my family *is* your family.'

'Oh, yes.' Pause. 'I had some very good Jewish friends.'

A presistent rumour has it that on at least two occasions Eva intervened on behalf of Jewish people in Munich and Hitler spared them. Since she had always attended Catholic schools they are unlikely to have been classmates; perhaps they were professional associates of her parents' – a doctor, maybe the Dr Marx for whom Ilse had worked as a receptionist for many years before her marriage. I have not been able to track down any reliable source to back up the stories.[29] However, Glenn Infield, that less than reliable chronicler of Eva and her circle, claims that a former neighbour of the Braun family – an elderly Jewish lady called Pearl Sklar – said of Eva: 'She was a very kind young girl and spent many hours with me because she knew I was lonely. This was before she met Hitler.' (In which case Eva would have been in her mid-teens: an unlikely age for a popular and sociable girl to spend hours visiting lonely old ladies.) Infield adds, 'She (Pearl Sklar) is convinced that her life was saved by Eva because most of her Jewish friends in Munich from that period died in the concentration camps.'[30] The evidence for this story is, unfortunately, no more than guesswork.

29. Even the Wiener Library, London's leading Jewish library, had never heard of them.
30. Infield, *Adolf and Eva: Eva Braun and Adolf Hitler*, p. 301. This book draws heavily on both the biography of Eva Braun by Nerin Gun and on quotations from the Musmanno Collection in Pittsburgh.

Gitta Sereny, a trustworthy source, is inclined to believe that Eva may occasionally have intervened. 'I vaguely remember,' she said, 'a Jewish doctor or some professional who received protection. In one case, Speer told me, she managed to get honorary Aryan citizenship for somebody and of course that was protection, total protection,'[31] adding, 'I say this almost unwillingly but just for the record, she did also help some Jews in Bavaria. She was in a position where she could do this and she did it. She didn't do anything extraordinary but you know, any little help was help.'[32]

Gertraud added: 'When it came to injustices suffered by others or infringements of their rights, she [Eva] was capable of taking a firm stand and insisting on getting what she wanted.'[33] Yet she also tells a story that puts Eva in a bad light, while proving that she had no desire to exert any influence over Hitler: 'We have an aunt, she was a nun, and at that time monasteries were occupied and my aunt asked Eva,

'Can you help us so that we can stay in the monastery?'

and do you know what Eva told her:

'Let your hair grow.'

That meant, if you have to leave the monastery nobody can see you are a nun. She had no influence and she didn't try to have influence.'[34]

On the other hand, when Fanny Braun was cross-questioned after the war she didn't mention this episode, although it affected her own sister Anni, but criticised her daughter for not having done more for the suffering Jews. 'After all, every woman has some influence if she is as close to a man as Eva was to Hitler and she should have influenced him about *the things that she knew were wrong* [my italics].'

People must be judged in the light of their own era and attitudes. It is, as Richard Evans has pointed out, all too easy to be wise after the event. Our consciences can tolerate and ignore the most excruciating suffering as long as it isn't happening in front of us. Racism has by no means disappeared and the desire for revenge remains strong. Moral attitudes and behaviour have changed less than we care to believe. Many people in today's world of suicide bombers regard it as permissible for British and American Muslims – most of whom are guilty of no crime except their unpopular beliefs – to be the objects of secret

---

31. As related by Gitta Sereny for *Adolf and Eva*, 3BMTV, roll 11.06.
32. Ibid.
33. Weisker, *Wer War Eva Braun?*, p. 5.
34. Interview by Linda Grant in The Guardian, Saturday April 27, 2002

surveillance and almost randomly confined in camps until the 'war against terrorism' is won. Many people believe it is acceptable to make them do hard labour, perhaps on limited rations and in none too comfortable accommodation. Many would go further and condone physical or mental punishment for those who resisted or tried to escape. What would be the proportion of political fanatics or religious bigots asserting that if such treatment did not teach the 'rag-heads' a lesson, they should be starved and tortured, humiliated, photographed and even executed, if this made the mother country safe for decent Christian citizens? 'When considering individuals, it must be within the context of the fallibilities and frailties of their lives . . . human beings and their actions cannot exist or be judged in isolation from the environment that nurtures them.'[35]

Any verdict on Eva is, in microcosm, a verdict on the German people. Must the entire nation – and its descendants, to the second, third and fourth generations – share a communal guilt, the ignorant as well as the all-knowing? Is the mere fact of being *German* a crime in itself? On 26 August 1941 Helmut von Moltke wrote presciently to his wife:

> What will happen when the nation as a whole realises that this war is lost, and lost differently from the last one? *With a blood-guilt that cannot be atoned for in our lifetime and can never be forgotten*, with an economy that is completely ruined? Will men arise capable of distilling contrition and penance from this punishment, and so, gradually, a new strength to live? Or will everything go under in chaos?[36]

The country has not 'gone under in chaos' but for many of its people the 'blood-guilt' remains.

When the Second World War ended in 1945, a great silence fell on Germany.[37] There were no angry tributes to the six hundred thousand killed in air raids, as there were in Britain (the new Coventry cathedral) or Spain (Picasso's *Guernica*). Germany's own aggression had provoked the annihilation of their cities and the Germans felt they themselves were to blame. The story of the Jews of the Holocaust and the manner of their deaths came to light almost at once – the

---

35. Sereny, *Albert Speer: His Battle with Truth*, p. 168.
36. Von Moltke, *Letters to Freya, 1939–1945*, pp. 155–6.
37. See Robert Muller's Afterword to *The World That Summer* (a novel set in Hamburg in 1936).

first eyewitness account of Dachau and Buchenwald[38] was published in 1943 – though not, of course, in Germany. An unspoken taboo long prevented authors and novelists from describing the war's devastating effects on ordinary Germans. The leading German novelist of that generation, Günter Grass, calls it 'a suppression complex'. His novel *Crabwalk*, published in 2002, stirred up a furore because after almost sixty years Grass was among the first German writers to reject the idea that he and his compatriots were forever and irredeemably tainted: 'Never should my generation have kept silent about such misery, merely because for years the need to accept responsibility and show remorse took precedence, with the result that we abandoned the topic to the right wing. This failure was staggering.'

Only now, sixty years later, are the Germans beginning to realise that they too were victims. A Luftwaffe pilot said after the war, 'Wars might be caused by weak or morally cretinous people but they are fought and endured by very decent ones.'[39] The questions that von Moltke posed are still being debated by many, from students and philosophers to politicians and racists, above all by the grand and great-grandchildren[40] of the German men and women who worked on the production lines of mass murder, whose lives continue to be darkened by the Holocaust.

38. 'Individual and Mass Behaviour in Extreme Situations', a paper by Bruno Bettelheim, published 1943.
39. Former fighter ace Günter Rall to Jonathan Glancey in an interview published by the *Guardian*, 20 December 2004.
40. One of the many young Germans I talked to in the course of writing this book (like most, he wished to remain anonymous) said: 'I have the same problem with my father who always forbade me to ask questions about his father, my grandfather. It's the biggest taboo in the family. I have done a bit of research on my grandfather who was a pretty devout Nazi. My family looks back on quite a bit of military history and I always thought it might be worth writing about the different kinds of soldiers it has bred. I often have the feeling that most Germans in today's Germany are still brainwashed fanatics, only in the extreme *opposite* sense, that they are brainwashed for denial. It's not so much shame. It's something else.'

Chapter Twenty-four

What Hitler Did

Obersalzberg was the one Utopia that Hitler could preserve intact; his ideal, his inspiration, the Potemkin village he had conjured for himself and his circle – above all for Eva. She in her turn kept it as a sanctuary for him, far from the rigours of conducting a war, although as the fighting progressed he came 'home' less and less often. By 1942 she was thirty, a poised young woman, wiser and more serious than the daffy shop girl Hitler had first met. She had been his companion for ten years and now that he was in his early fifties he had, almost despite himself, grown dependent on her love, though he still couldn't bring himself to show affection for her in public: that's to say, among his private coterie, perhaps because he was aware of their continuing disapproval. He was gallant towards her – as he was to all women, including his cook – but always circumspect.

Eva's attitude towards the fighting was naive in the extreme. Alois Winbauer said:

> She regarded the victories of the *Wehrmacht* as a personal triumph for Hitler, which sent her into ecstasies of joy; while any defeats were part of a malicious conspiracy against the man who was the love of her life. But the man who hurried to see her on the Obersalzberg had changed. She told her cousin Gertraud of their long lonely walks and the aimless conversations about the weather or the dogs, and how he would stop still for minutes on end, staring absent-mindedly into the distance; of oppressive

evenings watching films and sleepless nights racked with mounting anxiety.[1]

Hitler is often said to have given orders obliquely, leaving others to interpret them, preferring not to know the technical details or witness the consequences. (Albert Speer disagrees, however: 'I don't suppose he had much to do with the technical aspects but even the decision to proceed from shooting to gas chambers would have been his, for the simple reason, as I know only too well, that no major decisions could be made without his approval.'[2]) Christa Schröder, the *Führer's* senior secretary, stated in her memoirs, 'There will always be those who think that these acts of barbarism took place without the know-ledge of Hitler. I know for myself that Hitler was kept well-informed by Himmler as to what was happening in the camps. He regarded all these atrocities as necessary for his régime.'[3] Most extermination camps were in Poland, in part because the majority of murdered Jews – 3.5 million – were Polish but also to spare the local German population needless distress (from seeing lines of emaciated arrivals, we may assume, and smelling burning flesh). On the rare occasions when Hitler's official train had to pass a camp he would order the blinds to be drawn. Ignorance of unsavoury facts is a dictator's prerogative, one he considerately extended to the women around him.

Ordinary Germans also shrank from what was going on as rattling iron caterpillars made their way to 'work camps' from all over Europe. Jews, Bolsheviks, Roma,[4] Jehovah's Witnesses, homosexuals – they were all herded on to trains, the trucks bolted and barred (during the war two thousand railway trains out of a total of sixty thousand in Germany were earmarked for these transports) on their way to the genocide. Huge numbers had been gassed since spring 1942 and the concentration camps were filled with skeletal figures who were

---

1. Winbauer, *Eva Braun's Familiengeschichte*, p. 21.
2. Sereny, *Albert Speer: His Battle with Truth*, p. 362.
3. Christa Schröder, *Er War Mein Chef* (Munich: Langen Müller, 1985).
4. Dora Yates, secretary of the Gypsy Lore Society, noted: 'Nazi crimes against the Gypsies as well as the Jews bear witness to the fantastic dynamic of twentieth-century racial fanaticism, for these two people share the horror of martyrdom at the hands of the Nazis for no other reason than that they *were* – they existed.' In Europe, estimates of mortality of Sinti and Roma (major gypsy tribes) range from 220,000 to 500,000, about one-third of their population. Some even put the deaths as high as one and a half million.

literally being worked to death. Few civilians had any hard informa‑
tion and fewer still cared to investigate the *something* that pervaded
their consciousness with a new, unpleasant suggestion of – what?

The Jews themselves were not by any means all helpless victims,
shuffling to their fate. Some showed extraordinary courage and defi‑
ance. A rabbi arriving at Sobibor refused to believe the emollient talk
with which the Jews were greeted in an attempt to prevent mass
hysteria. Picking up a handful of sand, he declared, 'You see how I'm
scattering this sand slowly, grain by grain, and it's carried away by the
breeze? That's what will happen to you; this whole great Reich of yours
will vanish like flying dust and passing smoke.'[5] He was instantly shot.
Most moving of all are the words of a little Jewish girl of about five
when a brutal attendant seized her one-year-old baby brother: 'Don't
you lay your hands, dripping with blood, upon my lovely brother. I am
his good mother now and he will die in my arms, with me!'[6]

At the Wannsee Conference on 20 January 1942 – not, significantly,
held in the presence of the *Führer* – Reinhard Heydrich, charged by
Göring with making all necessary arrangements to rid Europe of its
Jews, announced that they would be worked or starved to death in
the east and any survivors killed 'by more direct means'. What had
to be done furtively, by night, in western Europe could be done in the
east without regard for local sensibilities.

By the summer of 1941 the war in the Soviet Union was being used
as an excuse for ethnic murder. The message from Hitler was: 'Whatever
succeeds is correct. Scruples are a crime against the German people
. . . No German participating in action is to be held responsible for acts
of violence, either from a disciplinary or judicial point of view.' Fighting
against an enemy that was itself barbaric, German soldiers behaved with
routine savagery. Civilians were hanged, raped, shot and tortured by
soldiers who were frequently drunk. Thousands of photographs record
mass executions by hanging or shooting of suspected partisans, their
bodies laid out like slaughtered game in aristocratic group photographs
taken as mementos at the end of a good day's shoot. Their executioners

5. Burleigh, *The Third Reich: A New History*, p. 642.
6. Reported from the final undressing room of a German extermination camp
and broadcast on 3 August 1995 in a TV programme commemorating VE Day.
I do not remember exactly what the documentary was called nor the source of
the story . . . a survivor? A camp guard? Its exact provenance doesn't seem to
matter; in that child's voice can be heard the anguish of millions of other inno‑
cents.

stare gormlessly at the camera, few seeming to register revulsion or shock. If anything, there is a prurient desire to record something that was not an everyday sight, capturing their moments of absolute power over other human beings.[7] Hitler refused to acknowledge the cruelty perpetrated by his soldiers, which grew worse the further east they went.

Starvation was hollowing bellies on another front. By September 1941, three million people were trapped inside Leningrad[8] in a siege that lasted nine hundred days. Bombs and shells rained down on the city. In November 11,000 people died; in December 52,000; in January 1942, 3–4,000 people a day, mostly from hunger. Many killed and ate their pet cats and dogs, using the fur to make gloves, until there were no animals left to eat, only a tiny daily ration of 'bread' made chiefly from flour and sawdust. Everyone starved and everyone froze. Corpses, if buried at all and not left in the street to harden into icy cadavers, were dumped in mass graves. Entire families, more than six hundred thousand people, died before the siege ended in January 1944. Europe was descending into Sodom and Gomorrah. German soldiers, sailors and airmen were dying in their hundreds of thousands, German civilians beginning to suffer from the lack of clothes, food and basic necessities like electricity and water. Things were about to get much worse.

Hitler turned his attention next to Stalingrad.[9] As with Operation Barbarossa, he greatly underestimated the Soviet Union's dogged powers of resistance as well as Stalin's skills as a military commander, which far exceeded his own.[10] In August 1942 Zhukov, Russia's only undefeated general, was put in charge of the defence of Stalingrad. On 14 October 1942 Hitler ordered the second 'final offensive' but heavy fighting failed to capture the city and on 17 November the Red

7. Adapted from Burleigh, *The Third Reich: A New History*, pp. 549–61.
8. The once and future St Petersburg.
9. Battle for Stalingrad, 19 August 1942–2 February 1943. A detailed account of this epic encounter has no place in a biography of Eva Braun but those seeking further details will find an excellent summary in http://en.wikipedia.org/wiki/Battle_of_Stalingrad or, of course, they may read Antony Beevor's *Stalingrad* (London: Viking, 1998).
10. From Max Hastings's review in the *Guardian* of *The Dictators: Hitler's Germany and Stalin's Russia*, by Richard Overy (London: Allen Lane, 2005): 'War made Stalin a realist, while Hitler remained a fantasist. Hitler was a disastrous war leader who learned nothing. Intelligence remained the weakest link in the Nazi war machine, not least because the *Führer* would not believe its findings unless they conformed with his own instincts. At every turn, the brilliant performance of the German Army was set at naught by Hitler's follies.'

Army counterattacked. A quarter of a million German soldiers were trapped in the city, cold and starving, by the end of November, surrounded by Soviet troops. As always, Hitler refused to recognise defeat. He ordered Paulus, commander of the German army, to stand his ground, promising reinforcements. They never came. Field Marshal Paulus said, 'We can't retake a position any more because the men are collapsing with exhaustion. The last horses have been eaten.' Within less than a week the German Sixth Army was encircled and, at the end of January 1943, Paulus – against Hitler's specific orders – was forced to surrender. Three hundred thousand German soldiers had died. It was the greatest Russian victory of the war and, with it, the blood-soaked Russian tide began to turn against Germany.[11]

On 20 September 1942 'Bomber Harris' launched the first serious air attack on Munich. Sixty-eight bombers killed 140 people and injured more than four hundred. This was the city's first experience of a raid and, while comparatively mild in contrast to those on cities further north, it was bad enough. Ludwig Rosenberger, a resident, wrote in his diary: 'The air pressure was terrible, our ears were half deaf, the British planes buzzed above our roofs like giant hornets. It was utter hell for an entire hour.'[12] Hitler was in his eastern headquarters at the *Werwolf* at the time, Eva at the Berghof, so although she worried about her friends in the city he had no reason to worry about *her*. But on the night of 9/10 March 1943 the city was hit by an enormous raid that killed 205 people, injured more than twice as many and left nearly 9,000 homeless and shocked, their household goods scattered amid the rubble, possessing nothing but their grimy, dust-covered clothes. Eva was again at the Berghof but even had she been in the city she would have been protected by a private bunker below her house constructed in 1938 – if she'd been prepared to go into it. Hitler lamented that she would not. Eva understood that his pride would not let him reveal his dependence upon her – he, the genius who occurred once in a thousand years (this was his firm belief) – dependent upon a *woman*? Yet his secretaries noticed how he feared for her life during raids on Munich.

Whenever München was threatened by an air attack he was as restless as a caged lion, waiting until he could speak to her on the phone. His agitation was nearly always unnecessary, although once

11. Source: www.history.acusd.edu/gen/WW2Timeline/BARBAROS.html
12. Large, *Where Ghosts Walked*, p. 325.

her house was damaged and some nearby ones caught fire. All day long he talked about Eva's courage:

'She refused to go into the shelter, even though I begged her over and over again. One day that little house will collapse like a house of cards. She also refuses to go round to my flat, although she'd be completely safe there. I've finally managed to persuade her to have a little shelter built inside the house, but she just invites all the neighbours in while she herself goes up on the roof to see if any incendiary bombs have fallen.'[13]

In March 1943 Hitler returned from his HQ near Vinnitsa in the Ukraine to the *Wolfsschanze*. The disaster at Stalingrad and defeat in North Africa had affected both his morale and his physical wellbeing. By the spring his health was failing rapidly and he was exhausted. The strain of conducting a war that to all except the *Führer* looked more and more unwinnable could no longer be disguised: 'His memory was going, his mental and physical state had deteriorated beyond all recognition . . . He was a spent old man, for whom doctors prescribed the stimulants Intelan and Tonophosphan and the antidepressant Procrastinum.'[14] Even on the telephone Eva could detect the change in him. She longed to have him back at Obersalzberg where she could nurture his energy with fresh food, clean air and exercise. At the *Wolfsschanze* he took none at all, Dr Morell remembered, often not stepping outside for days on end.

His nature, to be fully gratified, needed both the epic – be it Alpine scenes or colossal campaigns – and the trite. At one extreme he was conducting a military, naval and aerial campaign on several fronts, designed to ensure German domination of Europe for the next thousand years: yet this same megalomaniac craved home comforts, a doting woman and a birthday table laid out with cards, flowers and presents. Alone together in Eva's soft, cushioned rooms, Hitler could allow himself to be needy and sentimental. After a week or two of coaxing and cossetting he would begin to relax, chatting pleasantly with the women, strolling to the Teehaus, listening to records or telling stories round the fireplace in the evenings. Sometimes he would sit absent-mindedly in his chair, suddenly very old and tired. Eva Braun looked sad and troubled, going to greater lengths than ever to entertain

13. Junge, *Bis Zur Letzten Stunde*, p. 121 (translated by the author).
14. Maser, *Hitler's Letters and Notes*, p. 194.

Hitler and his guests, trying to cheer them up and involve them in gossip far removed from the war.

In April 1943, with Hitler somewhat rested and restored, preparations began for a major state visit, whose guest of honour was Mussolini, to take place in a nearby country house called Schloss Klessheim. (Traudl Junge remembers that, as they arrived, she was rushing down the corridor eating an apple and bumped into them. Hitler said, 'Doesn't matter, my child: a king is only human, too.')[15] In May he returned to the *Wolfsschanze*.

By 1943 Air Marshal Sir Arthur 'Bomber' Harris was attacking Germany with singular bloody-mindedness, having overridden any initial public disquiet and convinced himself and the Cabinet that bombing the civilian population into submission was a comparatively humane way to win the war.[16] At the end of July 1943, from 25 July to 2 August, for nine days and nights – the RAF attacking by night, the US Air Force by day – the ancient Hanseatic[17] port of Hamburg was all but demolished in the aptly named Operation Gomorrah. On the night of 28 July 1943 alone, forty thousand people were killed by the bombing, immolated by a man-made inferno.[18] A firestorm destroyed four square miles of the city centre, reducing it and the River Elbe to a lake of fire that consumed everything it touched. People, buildings, cars, animals; trees, statues, railings, lampposts, shops – nothing could survive such heat, or the spiralling wind that sucked oxygen from the air. Bodies turned to burning liquid or to ashes, leaving no corporeal trace to bury. Smoke and flames rose a mile into the sky. As many as two hundred thousand died and another million were made homeless.

So appalling was the devastation that even Goebbels was outraged by Hitler's refusal to visit the scene and hearten the survivors. He noted in his diary, 'it is very necessary that the *Führer* do this, despite the heavy burdens on the military sector; one cannot neglect the

15. Junge, *Bis Zur Letzten Stunde*, p. 104.
16. Burleigh, *The Third Reich: A New History*, p. 762.
17. See Chapter 3, note 2, p. 25.
18. 'People jumped into the canals and waterways and remained swimming or standing up to their necks for hours until the heat died down. Even then they suffered burns to the head. The firestorm swept over the water with its showers of sparks so that thick wooden posts burned down to the level of the water. Children were torn away from their parents' hands by the force of the hurricane and whirled into the fire.' (Hamburg's police chief, writing in 1943.)

people for too long.' But, of course, he dared not say anything to Hitler's face. Karl Otto Kaufmann, *Gauleiter* of Hamburg and one of the very earliest members of the Nazi Party, also begged the *Führer* to visit, as did Speer. 'Hitler's reaction when I asked him to go to Hamburg was surly. He was probably annoyed because he had already been pressed from another quarter [i.e. Kaufmann]. These approaches did not suit his concept of his elevated position. He gave no reason for his refusals.'[19] They should have known better than to ask. The *Führer*'s reluctance to see with his own eyes the suffering he was inflicting on the German people was well known.

My mother's aunts and at least one of her sisters, along with her sick elderly mother, shared a flat in Altona, one of the most heavily damaged areas of Hamburg, but I never heard them talk about the bombing – and seven-year-old girls listen carefully when grown-ups are telling horror stories. *Oma*, my German grand-mother, had been suffering from cancer for some time, but she had a deep-seated fear of doctors and hospitals and refused all but the crudest treatment at home for her pain. She died on 25 May 1943 at home in Hamburg, two months before the firestorm that engulfed her beloved city. My mother didn't receive the news of her death – which came in the monthly twenty-five-word letter sent through the Red Cross – until that August. She mourned her bitterly for forty years. Her remaining female rela-tives (sisters Ilse and Trudl and aunts Lidy and Anni) were at home on the night of 28 July 1943.

I cannot begin to imagine what they must have endured as the people of Hamburg were incinerated, calcified, roasted to nothing more than ashy black shapes, scalded, asphyxiated, crushed, buried and, in the heart of the firestorm, reduced to a pool of flaming oil which, like Hiroshima, left no human remains behind, no body to identify, mourn or bury. The women cowering indoors or crammed into an air-raid shelter – which could be more dangerous – survived nine nights of bombing; six major air raids (four by the RAF and two by American squadrons) which the citizens of Hamburg referred to, if at all, as *die Katastrophe*.

It must have been at exactly this time that *Opa*, my grand-father, for whom normal life had become a distant mirage, began

19. Ibid., p. 357.

to write his memoirs – before or after the bombing I don't know, since the original manuscript has vanished.[20] By 1943 he knew little more about me than my name but, prompted perhaps by the death of his former wife, he wanted to leave behind some record of his life for this three-year-old girl, his only grandchild, whom he never thought he'd survive long enough to meet. It is dedicated '*To my beloved granddaughter, Angela Maria, because I cannot hold her in my arms.*' He couldn't have imagined that he would live for another sixteen years, long enough to verify that his character and posterity were firmly imprinted on me.

Throughout the last two years of the war Hamburg remained a bomb site with scarcely any food or – at times – water. My youngest aunt, Trudl, being the strongest, would go out at night and walk beside the railway lines along which goods trains approached Hamburg, in the hope of finding potatoes or lumps of coal that had fallen (or been pushed) off the trucks on to the line. Anything she found would be hurriedly shovelled into a dark sack, heaved over her shoulder and humped back home to her mother, sister and the two great-aunts, Lidy and Anni. Without these nightly excursions they would have starved or frozen to death in their small, unheated flat.

I didn't visit Hamburg until the winter of February 1947, when I was six. My mother hadn't seen her family for at least eight years. A few months after we had arrived my mother's older sister Ilse – tall, clever and highly strung, not unlike Eva's elder sister, also named Ilse – who was my godmother, killed herself with an overdose. She was barely alive, comatose, lying on a sofa, when my mother happened to turn up at her flat. Ditha summoned a doctor immediately but when he came he said, 'Patience; she'll soon be gone.' There had been so many deaths; why try to prevent one more? My mother and Ilse's husband – one of the very few to return safely from the Russian front – apparently sat together, watching and waiting for her to die.

I have no idea what effect his eldest daughter's death had on my grandfather. I only heard the story much later; it wasn't the

20. My mother, probably at some point in the 1970s or 1980s after his death, made a heavily bowdlerised translation, inserting fulsome references to her adored mother in a style that makes it obvious she wrote them, before disposing of the original. The memoir may or may not have been dated to the month but, if so, she omitted this.

kind of thing you tell a child. Yet she was the most intellectual and sophisticated of all the Schröder girls, slim, blonde, elegant; surely her father's favourite. Although I was only seven when she died I have a clear picture of her in my mind's eye. Probably, like so many childhood memories, it comes from a photograph rather than life, but maybe not. I'm sure I would recognise her in a crowd. There was something distinctive and special about her – *apart* is the German word: unusual, striking

I was horribly precocious and already saw my family as individuals rather than as an amorphous, loving group and – if the truth be known – found *Opa* better company than my father. By 1948 my mother was his only remaining blood relative, such had been the devastation of the Hamburg bombing. Ilse had killed herself; round, jolly Trudl, weakened no doubt by the privations of the war years, had succumbed to an illness. My mother had little in common with her father and bitterly resented his plan to get married again: and to a younger woman. (He never did.) She modified her hostility as he got older but even during the years when we were living in Germany my grandfather remained a rare visitor to our household.

Bare dates and statistics convey little of the terrible truth or the monstrous roll call of the dead. *One* is a number anyone can grasp – half the world can go into paroxysms of grief over the death of one woman; ten is already stretching the bounds of the number who can be personally mourned. Perhaps the three thousand killed in the Twin Towers in September 2001 is the largest number the imagination can encompass and – given that they were mostly American – the number needed to spark a global response. But who can reconstruct the scenes or the sorrow caused when forty thousand citizens of Hamburg were immolated *in a single night*? The iconic number of six million murdered Jews is one from which imagination shies away. Some people can only cope by denying it altogether. Eva, gentle, naive, a fantasist, not someone with an active moral imagination, was spared the need to grapple with any number larger than one: her good friend the actor Heini Handschuhmacher was killed in an air raid on Munich in April 1944 and she was angry and grieved by his death. But Poles, Soviets, three-quarters of a million Roma, homosexuals, Catholic Priests and *six million Jews*? Unthinkable.

PART 6

CULMINATION

Chapter Twenty-five

February 1944–January 1945 –
Eva at the Berghof with Gertraud

Hitler based himself at the Wolf's Lair in east Prussia throughout the autumn and winter of 1943, with only a short break at the Berghof in mid-November. He was away for Christmas . . . no tree, no candles, no 'Tannenbaum, o Tannenbaum!' or cosy present-giving ceremonies centred on him, no Eva to lay on a glittering mid-winter festival. Instead he spent it at the *Wolfsschanze* and did not return to Obersalzberg until 23 February 1944, quite seriously ill and suffering from nervous exhaustion. In the cramped and oppressive atmosphere of his eastern headquarters constant overwork had once again affected both his physical and mental health. His doctors – no doubt backed up by Eva – insisted he remain at the Berghof for several months.

As winter dragged on, life on the Berg – as in the rest of Germany – became less and less predictable. The tension around Hitler was hard to bear. Discussions about the progress of the war went on endlessly, meals were late and lasted till ungodly hours. An endless stream of guests and Eva's gallant attempts at cheerfulness could not disguise the fact that everyone was deeply anxious. Hitler stayed in bed longer than usual and it was clear by now to all except the *Führer* that the war was going against him; yet the more his faculties declined, the more he insisted on his own infallibility. Despite growing evidence that he had become irrational and unfit to conduct a war on several fronts, Hitler ignored his generals' advice, convinced that only under *his* command would the Third Reich triumph. A staff officer later remembered: 'Meetings could last from two hours to infinity, depending on Hitler's mood. He thought himself a great strategist and despised professional officers. This had a debilitating effect on the military.'[1] He developed a tremor of the left arm and leg, 'possibly of a hysterical nature,' said Dr Morell dismissively.[2] It was more probably an early sign of Parkinson's disease. He still saw himself as the last and greatest Teutonic Knight, leading his warriors into Germany's thousand-year future. That belief never wavered, blinding him to the realities.

From February 1944, once they were together again, Eva noticed how lethargic he had become; how nervy and irritable. She implored Traudl Junge to tell her the truth.

Eva Braun sought out my company.

'How is the *Führer*, Frau Junge? I don't want to ask Morell: I hate him and I don't trust him. I was shocked when I saw the *Führer*. He's become so old and severe. Do you know what his worries are? He doesn't talk to me about these things but I suspect the situation isn't good.'

Close as she was to Hitler, Traudl could tell her nothing: 'You know the *Führer* better than I do.'

By April it was still snowing. Spring came at last and with it enemy planes, flying directly over Berchtesgaden. Hitler's huge air-raid shelter, carved sixty-five steps deep into the rock of the mountain beneath the Berghof, was reached from the main living room and contained everything necessary for him and his court. Hitler was terrified of being bombed, and awaited attack by the Americans every day. He was forever urging people, above all Eva, down into the concrete shelter, though very reluctant to descend himself, but despite his insistence few people took the idea of an attack on the Berghof seriously and they became more and more unwilling to go. Guests were woken almost every night to assemble in the dank, cave-like underground rooms. The planes passed over harmlessly, intent on attacking Vienna or Hungary. When Heini Handschuhmacher was killed in Munich Eva flouted Hitler's orders and insisted on attending his funeral with Herta and Gretl. She came back shattered by what she'd seen in the city.

1. *Observer*, 27 March 2005: interview by Alex Duval Smith with Baron Freytag von Loringhoven.
2. Report by Dr Morell to the Musmanno pre-trial commission at Nuremberg, *Hitler's State of Health and Medical Characteristics*; see Musmanno Collection at the Gumberg Library, Duquesne University, Pittsburgh, PA.

Hitler, with exaggerated gallantry, kisses Eva's hand;
she smiles joyously at him. (Bavarian State Library, Munich)

Away from the confines of the Berghof, Eva enjoyed herself uninhibitedly. Captioned in her own handwriting *'Auf dem Markusplatz'* – At St Mark's Square – she is in Venice, probably in 1938 or 1939, sporting a distinctly Bavarian costume and mobbed by the inevitable pigeons. (NARA)

Eva, accompanied by friends and relatives, visited Italy regularly between 1938 and 1941. This holiday snapshot shows Fanny Braun, Margret Speer, Anni Brandt, Eva Braun and Marion Schönmann on a bench in Rome, dressed in the height of Bavarian chic. War was by then in full swing but the happy quintet show no sign of letting that spoil their enjoyment. (NARA)

Another year (1939), another holiday. Eva – showing off a new white fur jacket – with one of her aunts, taking a break from the ski-slopes. (NARA)

va on holiday in Italy again, openly brandishing a cigarette at a café table. She could only smoke
 secret at the Berghof since Hitler disapproved. Away from him she could do what she wanted
– when he was around she had to trim her behaviour to his rules and whims. (Ullstein Bild)

Another kind of pleasure ... Eva (left), her mother (centre) and her sister Gretl noisily celebrate *Fasching* or Shrove Tuesday in 1939 at a Munich beer cellar. (NARA)

Hitler's good-looking young adjutants provided Eva with company and the opportunity for a little mild flirting, but nothing more than that. They knew better than to risk Hitler's anger and Eva remained devoted and faithful. Not even the highly eligible Walter Hewel (second left) could tempt her to stray. (NARA)

Much more boring were Hitler's lengthy monologues, delivered after dinner in the Great Hall at the Berghof. In this picture from 1944 Eva Braun faces the camera on the far left; beside her Hitler is talking to an unknown visitor. (Ullstein Bild)

Eva's parents, Fritz and Fanny, seduced by the luxury the Berghof offered, became regular visitors, although in the early days of the relationship with Hitler they had objected fiercely to her liaison. Eva's ties to her family remained strong and loving. (NARA)

This studio portrait, taken to mark Fritz's 60th birthday in 1939, shows (l. to r.) Ilse, Fritz, Fanny, Gretl and Eva. Their characters are evident in their faces: Ilse and Fritz grimly formal; Fanny smiling and proud, a hand on her husband's arm, Gretl somewhat vacant. Only Eva looks relaxed and happy. (NARA)

A rare snapshot showing Eva with a group of top Nazis: (l. to r.) Goebbels – arms protectively crossed, legs tightly together – still sinister despite the dapper suit and jolly laugh; Eva, Hans Haupner, architect of the Kehlsteinhaus, and Albert Speer: too detached to smile obligingly for Gretl's camera. (NARA)

Hitler wanted his Nazi henchmen 'on the Berg' to be model Aryan families and liked to watch their wives and children frolicking happily on the terrace. Here (second left) he looks into a cage (for rabbits and tortoises) or perhaps a playpen, while behind, adjutants await his attention. Eva (r. foreground) catches him on film. Close by as usual are her two black Scotties, Stasi and Negus.(NARA)

In winter sunshine, Eva dozes in one of the wicker chairs on the Berghof's terrace. By this time she had been with Hitler for about ten years and the strain is beginning to show in her face. (NARA)

Hitler sleeps after tea in the Teehaus, while Eva watches him tenderly. Not until he went back to the Berghof at about 5 p.m. did the *Führer* really get down to work. (Bavarian State Library, Munich)

Hitler and Eva with a posse of Bormann and Speer children, dressed in their best for 'Onk' Hitler. Margret Speer looks out of frame, (far r.). This picture was probably taken at Christmas 1939, which was brought forward a few days so that he could enjoy the celebrations before making a morale-boosting tour of his troops. After that year Hitler was usually too preoccupied with the war to come home. (NARA)

Hitler's birthday in 1943 or '44. By custom, his friends would gather at midnight to drink his health in the coming year. Next morning his birthday table would display flowers, personal gifts and a selection of presents from the German people. Hitler pretended to deprecate the fuss but Eva (extreme l., wearing his favourite dress) knew that secretly he loved to be cosseted. (NARA)

Even after 1940 and despite the suffering that was to engulf Europe, Eva continued to frolic in the idyllic meadows round Obersalzberg. Like most German women, she was not expected to know anything about politics or the war and its atrocities and Hitler insisted that nobody ever talked to her about the fate of the Jews and those deemed by the Nazis 'unfit to live'. (Bavarian State Library, Munich)

In full Bavarian costume, Eva poses winsomely on the terrace of the Berghof, the very image of Hitler's ideal woman – gentle, demure and guileless. Only the children she longed for are missing. Hitler, fearful of transmitting his own damaged genes, had always refused to father a child. (NARA)

This picture, taken in his private plane, became known as 'the handsome Hitler' because the clear light above the clouds flatters him by obliterating his sagging pouches and wrinkles, which makes it hard to date. Eva has captioned it '*Flug München – Berlin*' : flight from Munich to Berlin. (NARA)

Eva as a child of nature. This picture must have been taken some time in the early 1940s, as shown by her longer, more natural hairstyle. Hitler would have preferred her not to wear make-up or nail varnish but for once she took no notice. (NARA)

My grandfather, Wilhelm Schröder, aged about 70, in the spa town of Bad Salzuflen. He must have been visiting my parents, who lived there in the late 1940s. In this picture, probably by a street photographer, he stands outside the elegant club reserved for the British, dressed in his best suit and holding a smart grey Homburg in one hand and a glass of lemonade in the other. (Angela Lambert Collection)

Elizabeth ('Lidy') Neubert, my adored great-aunt. I took this picture in 1980 on my last visit to her in Hamburg. She lived by herself in a tiny flat but remained cheerful, loving and quite without self-pity. She never married but had a hard life and endured many wartime ordeals, including the bombing of Hamburg in July 1943. The youngest of more than a dozen siblings, she died alone in 1981, aged 86. (Angela Lambert Collection)

Eva arm-in-arm with Albert Speer. They shared a close but entirely platonic friendship and, after her sister Gretl, he was her chief confidant and supporter 'on the Berg'. On his last visit to the bunker he did his best to persuade her not to stay and die with Hitler and after the war he praised her goodness, courage and loyalty. (NARA)

Speer (r., nearest the camera) was Hitler's favourite among his acolytes for his patrician good looks, capacity for hard work, and the architectural projects designed to transform a victorious Berlin into a city to rival ancient Rome. (NARA)

At Speer's studio in Obersalzberg in the late Thirties, Hitler pores over grandiose plans. Speer became his chief architect in 1934 at the age of 29 and his vast, austere buildings embodied the Führer's vision of the Thousand Year Reich. The two men were very close but rumours of a homosexual relationship are nonsense. (NARA)

Eva fantasised about becoming a film star and loved to be photographed in glamorous poses wearing evening dress. She was keen that other photographers besides Hoffmann – whom she had come to dislike intensely – should take her portrait. This, from the early 1940s, is by Anton Sahm, a well-established Munich photographer. He shows her looking slim and classical in white – a colour she often chose for such portraits, perhaps in an unconscious desire to look bridal for Hitler. (NARA)

This image by Hoffmann shows Eva looking softer and more romantic, which may have been Hitler's preference. He humoured her passion for the cinema and promised that when the war was over she could star in a film about her life. (Bavarian State Library, Munich)

Eva and Herta Schneider (née Ostermayer) had been friends since the age of 12 or 13, when they met at the 'Lyzeum'. The deep affection between the two is obvious in this picnic snapshot. Herta's steadfast emotional support, and that of all her girlfriends, was a great comfort to Eva. Even after Herta married, she and her little girls – who became Eva's surrogate children – spent a great deal of time at the Berghof, especially when Herta's husband was away on military service. They and the two Scotties were vital to her, especially after Gretl had married and Eva was exposed to the spite and gossip of the Nazi wives. Herta's character was more serious yet they remained best friends for 20 years and Hitler thought she was a good influence on Eva. (NARA)

Eva Braun dances with her new brother-in-law, Hermann Fegelein, after his wedding to her sister Gretl. he was a fabulously good dancer but :ver in Hitler's presence. He forbade it, not from jealousy: more probably because he himself couldn't dance. (Bavarian State Library, Munich)

Three musicians from an SS band serenade Eva at the wedding. Her expression iggests embarrassment rather than joy. Formerly the musicians would have been gypsies but by 1944 the Romanies had been incarcerated in camps where between 500,000 and 800,000 were murdered – although we don't know whether Eva was aware of this. (Ullstein Bild)

Eva in a dirndl dress and Hitler wearing his uniform cap at the Berghof, perhaps on his last visit in July 1944. She looks a little thicker in the waist; he is more stooped than before, but their pose is relaxed and close. No longer lovers, they had become companions. Hitler finally trusted in her love and needed the comfort that only she could give him. (Bavarian State Library, Munich)

The sofa in the Berlin bunker on which Hitler and Eva Braun committed suicide on 30 April 1945, she by swallowing cyanide, he by shooting himself in the head. Witnesses before their death all agreed that she chose her fate willingly and spurned attempts to get her to leave the besieged city. In the final days, Hitler said bitterly, 'Only Fräulein Braun and Blondi have remained loyal to me.' (Getty Images)

For her, as for most Müncheners, it was the first time they'd seen death, destruction and suffering on a large scale and Eva was appalled. Hitler listened with a gloomy expression and swore revenge on the Allies.[3]

Yet there were still, occasionally, good times at the Berghof. The evening before Hitler's fifty-fifth birthday, Traudl Junge recalled:

We were all sitting round the fire, Hitler with his beloved Blondi. Hitler showed off her tricks. She did several but her star piece was when Hitler said: 'Blondi, sing!' and himself emitted a long howl. She joined in on a higher note and the more Hitler praised her the better she sang. Sometimes if she sang too high he would say, 'Lower, Blondi – sing like Zarah Leander!' [the popular singer known for her deep voice] and then she did a long drawn-out deep howl like a wolf. Almost the entire evening was spent talking about the dog, as though it were *its* birthday.

'She really is the cleverest dog I know,' Hitler said.

Punctually at midnight the doors opened and a procession of servants came in with trolleys laden with champagne and glasses. Everybody had a glass of champagne except Hitler who sipped very sweet white wine.[4] On the last stroke of twelve we all clinked glasses and everyone said, 'All the best, *Mein Führer*' or 'Happy Birthday, *Mein Führer*'. One or two made a little speech saying that the main thing was that his health and strength be preserved for the German people. Later all sorts of people came in to congratulate him from every part of the Berghof and alcohol was freely available all day long . . .[5]

His birthday was celebrated next day, 20 April 1944, as though nothing were happening – no hunger, no camps, no horror, no war. In the morning he came down earlier than usual, smiling and shaking his head at the sight of his presents. All this was Eva's doing. She knew how deeply he craved attention and spoiling. Pictures show him smiling indulgently at her and Gretl, Heinrich Hoffmann, Otto Dietrich and the hovering Bormann. A *Geburtstagstisch* (birthday table) covered

3. Much of this paragraph is loosely adapted from Junge, *Bis Zur Letzten Stunde*, p. 137.
4. This, if accurately reported, would have been an unusual exception and if he *did* have wine to mark some special occasion, he only ever took a sip or two.
5. Junge, *Bis Zur Letzten Stunde*, p. 104.

with flowers and presents had been prepared, as though he were the small boy of fifty years ago. Eva was wearing Hitler's favourite dress: navy blue silk, scattered with sequins. Her taste had matured and she could now carry off clothes that were chic rather than just pretty and youthful. He picked out one or two gifts, a lovely little statuette of a young girl, a wooden bowl that a fourteen-year-old boy had carved and some children's drawings to show Eva. There were many hand-embroidered and knitted offerings as well as home-made cakes, choco-lates and fruit sent by admirers who must have used their precious food coupons. Most of these simple gifts were sent to hospitals, chil-dren's and old folks' homes, such was his paranoia. The foodstuffs were destroyed in case they'd been poisoned. Hitler no longer trusted the German *Hausfrauen* whose adoration had buoyed him for so long.

Hamburg had already been pulverised; Dresden was yet to come. Munich was next. On 9 and 13 June, a few days after Gretl and Hermann Fegelein's wedding, Allied bombers delivered their heaviest blows yet on the exhausted and demoralised city, followed in mid-July by six colossal back-to-back raids. More than three thousand people died and two hundred thousand were made homeless. The beautiful Baroque city was being deliberately and ruthlessly punished for its role as 'the heart of Nazidom'. At the end of summer 1944, when dozens of buildings and churches had been flattened or gutted, art historian Wilhelm Hausenstein wrote, 'The city is more or less destroyed. Will the ruined core be left standing and [. . .] will generation after gener-ation live amid the ruins?'[6] It had become unthinkable that life could ever be normal again. Theatres, cinemas, nightclubs and concert halls were shut down; food rationing became ever more severe, new clothes almost unobtainable. Many people were thin and shabby, hungry, tired and in poor health. Only Hitler's retinue, along with his generals and air marshals, ministers and toadies and all ranks of the SS, lived in comfort. The battered German people, exhausted by grief and hard-ship, were losing patience. Retribution was closing in on functionaries and *Führer* alike.

By 1944 Eva and Hitler had matured and so had their relationship. She had become a wise if sometimes melancholy woman, lacking the exuberance of a young girl but kinder and more thoughtful, with a real concern for others.[7] In the Teehaus or at the end of the day Hitler

6. Large, *Where Ghosts Walked*, p. 342.
7. Adapted from Junge, *Bis Zur Letzten Stunde*, p. 141.

was less sociable and often sat slumped in his chair looking abstracted, old and tired. Worry about his condition took its toll: in June Eva herself had to be treated by Dr Morell with intravenous injections of Strophantin for a (presumably systolic) blood pressure of 110. This, if habitual, would have been cause for serious alarm because it would indicate low blood pressure, although a single reading can't reveal much. A consistent *diastolic* reading of over a hundred would indicate high blood pressure and be a cause for real anxiety. Fortunately her strong constitution soon restored her to health. Other than severe period pains, Eva had hardly known a day's illness in her life. But, then, she was only thirty-two.

Eva's unshakeable devotion and belief in Hitler – once shared by fifty million Germans – reinforced his need for her. Those closest to them observed that, although he continued to hide her away, he was much more than simply *fond* of Eva Braun. Like any couple, they missed each other when they were apart and comforted one another when they were together. Within the mysterious circle of their private relationship Eva depended on him for the comforts and necessities of life, but he relied quite as much on her unchanging devotion. Dictator, psychopath, mass murderer . . . Hitler was all these, but he also craved love. Only Eva and Blondi could be trusted to give it.

On 14 July 1944 Hitler left the Berghof for the last time. He seemed to sense that he would never return to Obersalzberg. On that final day he slowly toured its rooms, looking intently at his favourite paintings and possessions, waving away anybody who tried to accompany him. He said goodbye to Eva – secretly, they must both have feared it might be the last time they saw each other – and returned in his private plane to the Wolf's Lair.

Eva – as always when Hitler was not with her – was empty of purpose, listless, abandoned and depressed. Gretl, who had been her shadow for so long, was now a married woman and had left the Berghof to be with her husband. In 1938 Ilse had married a lawyer by the name of Hofstätter whom she'd met in Berlin. That relationship failed and they had divorced but Ilse remarried in 1944 and had gone to live in Breslau. Eva pined and worried, briefly consoled by her lover's cryptic phone calls. What could they talk about? Not the war, least of all when it was going so badly for Germany, and Hitler had never had any small talk. They exchanged soothing, affectionate clichés, he checked that she was safe, she asked about his health – night after night, the same stilted exchange. She worried about him; he worried about her, but it doesn't take long to say that. No doubt she told him that she loved and missed him.

Eva craved *his* presence above all but when he was away she needed a companion to offer attention and admiration; to admire her clothes and hair, to accompany her on long daily walks in the glorious summer landscape of the Berghof; a co-conspirator against the waspish wives; an ally to whom she could confide the machinations of Bormann and her mistrust of Morell and his perpetual pills. She still had her beloved dogs, Stasi and Negus, the black Highland terriers who for nearly ten years had shadowed her footsteps, accompanied her on long hikes and barked at the dressmaker, Fräulein Heise, when she came from Berlin bringing new clothes for Eva. But while their mistress could and did talk to the dogs, they couldn't talk back. Watched every moment of her day, her life subject to the caprices and commands of a man who denied her existence to the outside world while at the same time controlling her every move, Eva was aware how few people she could trust. Herta and her little girls were staying in their small flat nearby, having spent much of the summer walking in the mountains, swimming in the lake and enjoying better food than the spartan rations available in Munich, but at any moment Herta's husband Erwin might be granted leave and Herta would rush off to be with him. In any case, much of her time was now monopolised by the demands of her children. Yet again Eva found herself relegated to second place.

At this point she thought of the young cousin whom she had ushered into awareness of her femininity in July 1940, when sixteen-year-old Gertraud Winckler, the only child of Fanny's sister Paula, had spent part of the summer holidays with her and Gretl in their Wasserburgerstrasse house. The war had been going on for less than a year then, Munich had yet to be showered with bombs, theatres and cinemas were open (unless you happened to be Jewish) and the general mood was bright. By July 1944 things were very different but with luck Gertraud would have grown into a clever, lively young woman who would bring Eva news of the family and the outside world, while she in turn could groom her unsophisticated cousin, teach her more about clothes and make-up and turn her into a stylish young woman. She would be the ideal companion.

Gertraud Weisker, née Winckler, is now in her early eighties. (Eva, had she lived, would have been ninety-four in 2006.) Born in August 1923, Gertraud is the only child of Paula – one of the five Kronburger daughters – and Andreas Winckler; so she was Fanny's niece and Eva's cousin. Josefa was the grandmother she and Eva had in common, but while Eva knew and loved her *Oma* (Granny) Gertraud, who was only four when Josefa died, hardly remembers her. Gertraud and her three children, and theirs, are the last living descendants of the Kronburger family and she is the best-informed witness to the close-knit tribe in which she and Eva grew up. However, in the 1940s she had promised her then fiancé before their engagement, at a time when an association with Eva Braun was a disgrace, something to hide, to keep silent about the relationship – and did so, for fifty years. Once her husband had died, and after years of hearing Eva maligned and distorted, presented as an amoral, evil-hearted woman, her cousin was determined to tell the family story accurately.

In an account[8] of that summer written in 1998, Gertraud remembers:

> It was at this moment that Eva – following a suggestion from aunt Fanny – invited me to come and visit her. Shortly after Gretl's wedding in June 1944 she telephoned me at home and invited me to come and stay with her – even though I had hardly seen her since I was a little girl. We had not met for the past four years but we were still in touch with each other, so why not? Eva plucked up the courage to telephone us. She wanted to speak to my father about two matters. First she wanted to offer him her house at Wasserburger Strasse 12, for only 30,000 Reichsmarks – peanuts! My father would not even discuss it: 'I'm not going to buy a house off Hitler!' he said.[9]
>
> Eva tried to bring him round, telling him that the house was in her name, not Hitler's. I have always regretted it, but he was immovable. And then, in spite of his refusal, she asked him if I could come and visit her, which at first elicited a simple response:
>
> 'Out of the question!'
>
> It cost me plenty of tears and wiles, but in the end I was allowed to go.

8. Taken from Weisker, *Wer War Eva Braun?*.
9. Gertraud's father Andreas Winckler (1888–1946) had always opposed the Nazis, Hitler in particular, and would have been appalled by the idea that he might buy a house given by the *Führer* to his mistress; even more by the suggestion that his only child should stay as a guest at Hitler's secret retreat.

'Only to Munich, you're not to go to the Obersalzberg!' said
my mother.

The Winckler family held strong anti-Nazi views and Gertraud had
been brought up to take an interest in politics. To her, Hitler was
a deluded figure whom her father loathed and secretly resisted,
although that defiance put his own life at risk.[10] Why should she
accept the hospitality of this man, the instigator of all that was evil
in Germany?

> Like the rest of the family, my father regarded Eva's relationship
> with the dictator as monstrous [*ein Unding*]. Hitler was disap-
> proved of on principle, especially now that a member of the
> family had catapulted herself out of the ranks of rejection and
> resistance and entered into a relationship with him – an illegal
> and irregular one at that. And now I would be living in this polit-
> ical and moral swamp – an impressionable young girl, open to
> influences of all kinds![11]

Gertraud claims that when it came to it she had no choice but to
disobey the promise she had made her mother and travel from Munich
station to Obersalzberg under escort.

> When I got to Munich, however, it was obvious that I had to
> continue my journey, as there was no one there to meet me. An
> announcement over the public address system informed me that
> I should report to someone at the station exit in Holzkirchen.
> There I was met by a young soldier who saluted me – hand to
> his cap – and told me he was to take me to the Obersalzberg,
> where my cousin was expecting me. What was I supposed to do?
> Turn back, act the coward, and miss seeing Eva? I got into the
> car, but all the way from Munich to Berchtesgaden I kept wavering

10. Gertraud's investigations in the files of the Red Cross long after the war
showed that her father had indeed been a member of Admiral Canaris' group of
dissidents. Canaris' opposition to some of Hitler's policies and his links with other
Resistance groups did not apparently interfere with his duties as head of the
Abwehr, the military intelligence service of the High Command of the Armed
Services (OKW). Canaris was executed for treason only weeks before the war
ended, on 9 April 1945.
11. Source: Weisker, *Wer War Eva Braun?*.

between stopping the car and repressing my pangs of conscience. I chose repression.[12]

Six decades later, Gertraud confessed, 'I still have a very bad conscience about leaving my father.'[13]

Her visit to the Berghof started badly. Weekly passes were issued to all personnel in and around Obersalzberg, signed by Bormann or Rattenhuber. Special passes were required for the Führerstrasse – the street where Hitler's huge chalet stood – obtained at sentry post 8. This must have made for a chilling arrival. Gertraud describes the humiliation of having her luggage searched by 'lascivious' SS men before a kind woman took charge and led her up the steps to the Berghof. It turned out that Eva had gone for a swim in the Königssee. Gertraud waited and after a while a tanned and cheerful Eva appeared to greet her cousin and introduce her to Herta Schneider and her two little daughters. (So she was not alone at the Berghof after all.)

Gertraud hadn't changed much in the intervening four years since their last meeting. At twenty-one she remained so naive that, despite attending a boys' school, she had no idea of the facts of life. 'My life was completely devoted to my studies – there was nothing going on between the boys and me. I wasn't interested in such things – really, not even curious – and even if I had been, who could I have asked? I would have been ashamed.'[14] To this day she sometimes denies that Eva was Hitler's mistress, insisting, 'It was more of a father–daughter set-up.' By this stage sex played little or no part in the relationship, so she was almost right. Yet their adjoining suites of rooms and inter-connecting bathroom must have made it unmistakable, even to an innocent schoolgirl, that Eva was more than a platonic companion. Gertraud and her cousin didn't discuss sex or the troubling proximity of the couple's sleeping arrangements. They never talked about Hitler, said Gertraud, let alone the details of the relationship. 'It was a quite different time from now. There were many taboos, even between close relations. I would never have asked, do you love Hitler? Respect came even before intimacy. I knew she was in a relationship with him but I didn't believe it was sexual.'[15] Well-brought-up young women didn't

---

12. Ibid., p. 9.
13. Interview with the author at her home, 24 March 2004.
14. Ibid., 24 March 2004.
15. Gertraud Weisker in conversation with the author, March 2001.

talk about their sex lives in those days and Gertraud was, after all, very young.

Questioned about her impressions or memories of Hitler, she has nothing to offer. She never met him or even heard his voice on the telephone. He would usually ring between eight and ten o'clock in the evening to reassure Eva that he was safe and to hear news of the small, ordinary things that brought back the Alpine idyll he had created. Eva lived for these calls. If he were late in ringing she would be plunged into anxiety: 'He would telephone her every couple of days and that call was the most important thing in her life. I knew that inside herself she was completely empty. Her only thought was: "when will the phone ring?" I could have said anything at those times,' Gertraud believes, 'but I knew she was not listening. She just sat there waiting, straining for that call as if it were the most important thing in her life.'[16] It was, even though Eva, whose days were predictable and hardly varied, had nothing new to tell him. 'Eva sometimes asked *me* what she should say to him.' But, Gertraud went on: 'I never overheard these conversations – that was utterly taboo. Social conventions were very different in those days. If somebody got a phone call you left the room and closed the door. You wouldn't eavesdrop.'[17]

Alfons Schulz, on the other hand, the switchboard operator at Hitler's end, did sometimes listen in:

Every evening round about ten o'clock a number had to be called so that he could speak to Eva Braun. It was expressly forbidden for anybody to listen to these conversations with the *Führer* and they were mostly scrambled. On the telephone he [Hitler] never came across as a lover, more like a good friend, whereas on her part you could really sense that she was reciprocating with heart-felt love. She would mostly thank him for presents (which, I suspect, Bormann had bought) and Hitler would say, 'Right then, the main thing is that you're pleased. I'm glad you liked it. So, stay happy and calm. Till tomorrow, then . . .'[18]

16. A couple of sentences in Gertraud's account are taken from www.fpp.co.uk/Hitler/Eva_Braun/cousin.html
17. Gertraud Weisker in conversation with the author, 2 April 2001.
18. Transcript of interview with Alfons Schulz for *Adolf and Eva*, 3BMTV, rolls 22.20.48 and 22.25.36.

And that would be the end of their contact that day. It might have lasted ten minutes.

The two cousins soon fell into a pleasant, undemanding routine, helped by the Obersalzberg postman, *Herr Postboter* Zechmeister.

> We got up in the morning when the sun was up, perhaps at around seven or eight. After a breakfast of rolls, jam and coffee we waited for the post van which came four times a day. We took it so that the SS men wouldn't follow us. Otherwise, even if we were just picking strawberries, we always had two SS men behind us. I asked Eva, 'Are we being protected or controlled?' but she said, 'Don't worry . . . just be like me and don't take any notice.'

(Someone, perhaps Gertraud's mother Paula, must have talked to Alois Winbauer, since in his family memoir he wrote: 'When Hitler was absent from the Berghof, as happened increasingly during the war, Bormann and the SS assumed control, and were careful to remind Eva of their power.'[19])

Gertraud continues the recollection of her visit:

> We would wait with our bathing suits and provisions at the back of the house where the post van was unloaded, then get in the back and sit on the floor with our feet outstretched and he would take us down through Berchtesgaden to the Königssee. Not once was Eva recognised. We were dropped off at the lakeside, took a little boat and rowed out to a lonely, beautiful place near a water-fall that rushed down the mountain. From morning to late after-noon we were alone in that paradise. No human being anywhere near; just we two young women, our books and picnic, sun and water. We used to swim or climb up the waterfall and then let ourselves be swept down by the water.[20] If we wanted to swim across the lake, one of us would accompany the other in the little rowing boat, to make sure that she was strong enough to keep going.[21]

19. Winbauer, *Eva Braun's Familiengeschichte*, p. 18 (translated by Christiane Gehron).
20. This account is puzzling. Is it possible to 'swim' *up* a waterfall, or indeed to sweep down it wearing no more than a thin bathing costume? Gertraud Weisker's memory occasionally falters, or her imagination gets the better of her, and this may be one such occasion.
21. Weisker, *Wer War Eva Braun?*, p. 3.

They do sound culpably naive. All over Germany people were suffering and dying, hungry or homeless, living in ruined cities drawing water from standpipes, but Eva and her cousin splashed and prattled as if all were well with the world. Overlooking the cold blue waters of the lake, they enjoyed delicious picnics and talked: about home, parents and friends, but never about Hitler.[22]

In late August 2004 I visited the Königssee[23] (the King's lake) near Berchtesgaden, a long narrow stretch of water 200 metres deep. It lies in the well of a valley sliced as sharply as a fjord between two mountain ranges and is the deepest and cleanest lake in Germany. To the west are the peaks of the Watzmann (2,713 metres) and Kleine Watzmann (2,307 metres), overlooked by the Berghof, while to the east another range extends from the Grosses Teufelshorn (Great Horn of the Devil) to the Jenner and Hoher Göll. I took one of the tourist boats that ply to and fro along its 8 kilometres. It was a day of sun and cloud, light and shade constantly changing the colour of the water, making it iridescent or suddenly gloomy, and racing across the forested slopes and cliffs of the mountains. It was easy to see how these vistas with their jagged, wizened summits and the ice-cold, fathomless lake had inspired myths and legends; witches, devils, saints, kings, queens and their five daughters intermingling in the gullible peasant mind. Yet at the same time there were many signs of Christian piety, from the twelfth-century chapel of St Bartholomä on the western shore of the lake, to shrines and crucifixes bearing devout inscriptions, and carved stone memorials attached to the rocks at water level, commemorating monks and pilgrims drowned in some long-ago tempest. Odd, that this superstitious, haunted place could engender both the pitiless dictatorship of Hitler and Eva's home-loving *Gemütlichkeit*.

At the southern end of the Königssee is the Obersee, a smaller lake that was Eva's favourite bathing place. A fifteen-minute walk over a cool springy undergrowth of tumbled boulders and the roots of ancient trees leads to it and, for those who can find it, to the tumbling waterfall amid rocky slopes secluded enough

---

22. Ibid., pp. 11–12.
23. http://www.stadtplandienst.de/map.asp?sid=9d758f18ca7771f2f3befb1067e6ff5d&ix=1063&iy=136&grid=dedatlas10

for Eva to bathe in the nude. On the far side, no doubt, the SS
had their binoculars trained on her.

Gertraud continued with her account of her visit to the Berghof and
their routine –

> On days when the weather was bad we played cards, especially a
> game called *Bimbo* in which cards have letters and values (like in
> Scrabble). We'd sometimes play this game till late at night. We also
> played a Bavarian card game called *Tarock; Mensch Ärgere Dich
> Nicht* (a relic from Eva's childhood), *Mühle* (Nine Men's Morris)
> and another board game called *Halma*. We watched films every day,
> both current German ones and old silent films, because Eva enjoyed
> them. We never argued – no, wait, we did, just once. I had some
> wonderful high-heeled shoes but when I wore them for the first
> time, Eva said: 'Oh, you're so *tall!*[24] Don't you have any others?'
>
> All I had was a pair of cork-soled shoes, so a maid brought a
> basket from which Eva chose a pair of white ones that had almost
> no heel.
>
> '*These* are the right shoes for you!' she said. She didn't like
> being shorter than me.

They played games, they played with Eva's clothes like little girls
dressing up cardboard cut-out dolls, they played records. Marlene
Dietrich, whom Hitler had so admired, was now singing anti-Nazi songs
for the Americans, deriding the *Führer* and his corrupt court.[25] Each
day was much like every other, always under the eye of SS officers:

> For me that world was oppressive. And I felt oppressed by my
> challenge – to get her out of that lethargy. That is why I stayed.
> I wanted to get behind what it was that bound her to this man,
> I wanted to support her. But she was very depressed and I was

24. Eva told Hitler she measured 5 foot 4 inches. Gertraud is at least 5 foot 6.
25. The words of one were:
In the wonderful Fourth Reich there'll be
No more lying from Goebbels
No Funk to embezzle, no Hitler to bellow
No Himmler to murder, no Schirach to order
No Ribbentrop robbing, no Rosenberg rasping
And no more Ley getting drunk.

not a therapist – I realised that she was completely lost. She was the unhappiest woman I have ever met.

With Eva's encouragement, Gertraud continued to study, preparing for a physics degree at the University of Jena.[26]

Eva read fashion magazines but she was keen that I should revise for my exams. I think some people never grow up mentally, and Eva was one. My uncle Alois said: 'Eva is a very charming girl living in a fantasy world', but he never knew her as an adult; only as a child of about seven or eight. I think she's been much misunderstood. Of course she was bored to death – I was too – which is why she continued to change her clothes several times a day and endlessly restyle her hair. I learned a lot about fashion in those afternoons. Occasionally we had a visit from Eva's friends Mandi and Mitzi, or Georg and his sister Kathi. They would spend hours playing games. Eva showed me the jewellery she wanted me to have: implying that she had already decided to take her own life if the war were decisively lost. By the end of her life she *had* confronted reality; she was calm and I'm sure she chose how her life would end.".'[27]

One night when they were in Munich the city suffered a prolonged air-raid. They took refuge in the underground shelter beneath her house on Wasserburger Strasse. Eva opened one of two safes and showed her cousin some jewellery she wanted her to have – a very pretty diamond and pearl necklace. She said: "Traudl, [*the family nickname for Gertraud*] this necklace and bracelet are for you. I don't need them any more. Take care of it; don't let them steal it."

It is not certain quite how long Gertraud spent with Eva Braun at the Berghof. According to her own account she arrived in late July and left at the beginning of January 1945. She says of Christmas 1944, 'I can't remember whether I gave her a present – I had no opportunity to shop and never went to Berchtesgaden – so I must have given her something of my own.' Yet Gertraud could have shopped when she and Eva went to Munich on 16 December 1944. A conflicting account has Eva spending that Christmas either at her own house or

26. Gertraud obtained a place to read chemistry and physics at the University of Jena.
27. Interview with author, 24 March 2004.

the family home, after which she left Munich to be with Hitler in Berlin for New Year's Eve. Gertraud's version concluded, 'I stayed [where? At the Berghof? In Munich?] till about the second or third of January and was then summoned home by my mother because my father was critically ill. I wrote Eva a thank you letter but got no reply. I never saw or heard from her again.'[28]

Gertraud is the *only* close witness to those six months of Eva's life between the failed Stauffenberg Plot and New Year 1945, just as she is Eva's only living relative.[29] Is her account of their time together at the Berghof accurate, or is it a hotchpotch of snapshots from a genuine but much briefer visit, bodied out by hindsight, wishful thinking and post-war eyewitness accounts from denizens like Traudl Junge and Albert Speer? Eva's cousin is a clear-headed, honourable woman, not the sort to lie deliberately, but older people's recollections of their past are often embellished; they become a story of what they *wish* had happened rather than what actually happened. The German novelist Sibylle Knauss, whose book *Eva's Cousin* is set at the Berghof during those final months,[30] talked at length to Gertraud and got to know her well. She accepts her version of events, with this reservation: 'I think Gertrude Weisker has escaped from it [her past] in telling about it. It was a sort of coming free, but in my opinion she now very much enjoys being a person of interest and I try to think what I would do in her situation. I would have said, after a few interviews, this is it, but she never gets enough of it.'[31]

Frau Weisker's claim that she lived at the Berghof for six months is strongly disputed by Florian Beierl, a dedicated and knowledgeable local amateur historian who has made a detailed study of the Hitler years at Obersalzberg. He and I talked over dinner in one of Berchtesgaden's many *Bierstuben* one balmy August evening as

28. Ibid.

29. On 2 January 2004 she wrote to me in an e-mail: '*Nein, ich habe keine Verwandten mehr, weder in München noch sonstwo. Ich bin die letzte Überlebende der Familie.*' – 'No, I have no relatives left, neither in Munich nor anywhere else. I am the last survivor of the family.' She went on: '*Das ist für mich auch der Grund, weshalb ich gern mit Dir zusammen arbeite: Falsche Zeugnisse sind deren schon viele gegeben worden.*' – 'That's why I'm happy to work with you: there have been too many false reports [about Eva Braun].'

30. *Eva's Cousin*, published in an English translation by Doubleday (2002) and Black Swan in (2003).

31. Sibylle Knauss, interviewed by Linda Grant in the *Guardian* Saturday 27 April 2002.

tourists milled around the cobbled square outside. He was sure
Gertraud had exaggerated – or simply forgotten – the details of that
stay with her cousin. He had been emphatically assured by Frau
Mittlstrasse, (who took over as Hitler's housekeeper at the Berghof
after Döring had left and was there until the end of the war) that
she had no recollection of the visit, adding that Gertraud couldn't
possibly have been there for as long as six months or she would
definitely have remembered her. In fact, said Frau Mittlstrasse, she
could not recall any such person. She added that by 1944 everyone
at the Berghof, including Eva, required food stamps and although
the kitchen staff made deals with local farmers to obtain supple-
mentary rations, Frau Mittlstrasse claimed that the presence of an
extra person could not have been sustained for so long. Yet everyone
on the Berghof ate well – certainly by comparison with the rest of
Germany – their diet augmented by fresh fruit and vegetables from
the kitchen garden, eggs from hens on the model farm, milk from
its cows and fish from the lake. And couldn't Gertraud have brought
her own food stamps with her from Jena? Couldn't it have been
Frau Mittlstrasse whose memory was at fault, after fifty years?

Herr Beierl went on to suggest that, although Gertraud had said she
and Eva went there almost daily, Frau Weisker couldn't find her way
to the Teehaus. (Even if this were true, a certain vagueness would be
forgivable: the building itself has been almost razed and the hillside on
which it once stood is now so overgrown with tall trees, the path long
ago obliterated, that even a former habituée might find it hard to locate.)
On the other hand Marion Milne, director of the award-winning documentary *Adolf and Eva*, who spent hours with Gertraud, said:

> Certainly when we took her back to the Tea House, she was
> genuinely very moved by being there. It is hard to find as you
> know and a virtual ruin. Her reactions, a combination of clarity
> about where the Tea House was (she led us to it with the cameras
> rolling throughout), a sense of retracing steps previously trod but
> also a sense of being almost slightly let down when we got there,
> all rang very true to me. She was more moved by the memory
> and significance of what she recalled than by actually seeing a
> shabby old ruin in the cold light of day and she didn't seem to
> be inventing or falsifying her feelings and emotions.[32]

32. Marion Milne in an e-mail to the author, 2 August 2004.

Marion added, 'I always felt she was reliable but perhaps a little hazy in her recollections, a bit ambiguous on detail and facts; sometimes stretching the truth a little to put Eva in a better light?' She points out that archive footage exists[33] of the two cousins in swimwear beside the Königssee, indicating that she was definitely there at some point that summer, if not necessarily for the length of time she claims. A picture taken by her father of twenty-one-year-old Gertraud sitting at an outdoor café in Jena, is captioned '*Gertraud, Sommer 1944*'. Since neither is dated precisely, the puzzle remains.

Between 2001 and 2005, sixty years after she had kept Eva company at the Berghof, I visited Frau Weisker several times and questioned her in detail. At our first meeting I found her energy and vigour quite remarkable. In her early eighties, she was – and is – intelligent and articulate and, perhaps because her story was dammed up for so long, she remembered it in great detail. But she is dedicated to restoring the reputation of her much-maligned cousin and this may sometimes lead her to bend the truth. Her loathing for the man who destroyed Eva's life – and those of millions of others – is matched by devotion to her cousin. She is not consciously exaggerating when she claims to have spent six months at the Berghof but she was certainly there at some point and, whatever the exact duration of her stay, it was long enough for her to retain and convey a strong and convincing impression of Eva's privileged yet bleak existence. She has a vivid and angry recollection of her cousin, a healthy and vigorous young woman in her early thirties, yet without husband, children, lover, sex or a family home of her own; immured in a splendid setting and ostracised by the Obersalzberg coven. Gertraud rates these deprivations far higher than the pointless luxury that surrounded her.

To me, Frau Weisker's story rang broadly true. She may have overemphasised her closeness to Eva – bearing in mind that she was twelve years younger, a big difference when one woman is thirty-two and the other an unworldly twenty-one – but as her last living relative, this is forgivable. I believed the bulk of what she told me and she had plenty of evidence to back it. She dug out some trinkets Eva had given her – a cheap pot of bright orange-pink rouge (*Coryse Salomé*) that Hitler – or one of his underlings – apparently brought

---

33. I have not seen this film, or the picture of Gertraud in Jena, or indeed any photographs of Eva taken after April 1944.

from Paris for her (odd, since he detested women wearing make-up)
but it was an impossible colour and she had obviously never used it;
a dressing table set – not real silver but silver-plate, now tarnished
and worn in places – and her own family photograph album. In one
photograph taken at Gretl's wedding, Gertraud's mother Paula was
so enraged to see Hitler in the middle of the family group that she
had taken a pair of scissors and cut him out. The jagged outline
around his missing figure is proof of her fury. Gertraud adds that she
used to have many more pictures of Eva but disposed of them at a
Munich auction some time in the 1980s; she doesn't remember exactly
where or when. I searched the records of Munich's auction houses
including the most likely outlet – Hermann-Historica – but neither
they nor I could find any trace of such a sale.

A description of Eva dating from 1944 does not mention Gertraud.
It comes from *Operation Foxley*,[34] a dossier complied by SOE[35] in
preparation for an assassination attempt upon Hitler in 1945 and was
probably written by an intelligence officer, Major H. B. Court, some
time between May and early August 1944. Here is how the briefing
document describes Eva, based on observations passed to SOE (it is
not known precisely when) by a courageous foreign worker at
Obersalzberg:

EVA BRAUN: age about 24,[36] brunette, attractive and unconventional in her costume, sometimes wearing Bavarian leather
shorts. Walks around with two black dogs, generally in the company
of Fräulein Silberhorn, telephone operator at the Gasthaus, when
off-duty. Several RSD personnel always in the background when
she goes out. Unapproachable, no make-up (Hitler, it appears,
cannot tolerate the use of cosmetics). Until 1940, if not later, lived
at the Berghof. Relations with Hitler now appear to be of a platonic
nature.

The report's failure to mention Gertraud is not conclusive since the
information may have been gathered before her stay, but if it covered

---

34. *Operation Foxley: The Plan to Kill Hitler*, Introduction by Mark Seaman. The
original is in their collection (PRO HS 6/624).
35. Special Operations Executive – the subversive warfare agency and top British
spy network.
36. This was quite a compliment, since by now Eva was thirty-two.

the time when she was Eva's regular companion, her presence on these walks would surely have been noted.

As our conversation ended I asked Gertraud what she thought Eva wanted – was it celebrity, marriage, children, a life in film . . . ? '*Sie wollte geliebt werden, sonst nichts.*' 'She wanted to be loved; nothing else.'

Chapter Twenty-six

The Stauffenberg Plot and its Consequences

SOE, from whose report the description of Eva is taken, was the British Special Operations Executive. Its main job was to encourage and facilitate Resistance movements in occupied or enemy territory. There had been no significant plans to assassinate Hitler before midsummer 1944. Churchill was convinced that the *Führer* and Nazi Germany needed to be beaten on the battlefield rather than by a sniper's bullet. On 21 June 1944, Ismay (Churchill's chief of staff) wrote to the Prime Minister: 'From the strictly military point of view it is almost an advantage that Hitler should remain in control of German strategy, having regard to the blunders he has made; but on the wider point of view, the sooner he is got out of the way, the better.' The following week, on 28 June, the senior staff of SOE sat down to debate the issue. It was agreed that, despite some resistance on high, an attempt should be made. Detailed planning for Operation Foxley began, predicated on Hitler being either at Obersalzberg or on his special train. In fact Hitler left the Berghof two weeks later, on 14 July, never to return. Foxley never stood a chance. In any case, it was forestalled by another assassination attempt, one that came closer to success than any of the preceding forty or more.

Not every German was indifferent to the growing rumours of bestial atrocities committed on the field of battle, in the camps and upon civilians. The Kreisau Circle, some of whose members came from the old nobility – distinguished men like von Moltke, von Stauffenberg and Adam von Trott – was founded in 1933. It became 'a coherent, long-standing, widespread and well-organised resistance movement'[1]

1. Michael Baigent and Richard Leigh, *Secret Germany: Claus von Stauffenberg and the Mystical Crusade Against Hitler*, p. 16.

that included some of the most powerful and influential names in Germany. Its members, ranging from aristocrats to leading economists, clergy, theologians and military men, met regularly to formulate a plot against Hitler, possibly his assassination. They were forced to operate in great secrecy and to censor or code their letters and phone calls, never forgetting that exposure would be followed by a terrible retribution. Many in the circle had known one another all their lives, which made it easier for them to hold meetings disguised as weekend house parties at von Moltke's estate in Silesia to discuss and plan their strategy. Their purpose – to put an end to the Nazis, the camps and the war – became more focused in the autumn of 1941. The Circle spent hours debating the ethical aspects of killing Hitler. 'Why are we opposed to the Third Reich?' asked von Moltke. 'Isn't it precisely because it is a lawless system? We cannot set about creating something new . . . by committing a lawless act ourselves. And murder is always unlawful.'[2] This was sophistry, however admirable. Claus von Stauffenberg had been seriously wounded while serving with the 6th Panzer Division during Operation Barbarossa, losing one eye and his right hand.[3] He was appalled by the barbarities committed by the SS. 'This man,' he said, 'is evil incarnate.' Knowing very well that, whatever the outcome, an attempt on Hitler's life amounted to a suicide mission, he insisted: 'Now it is not the *Führer* or the country or my wife and four children that are at stake; it is the entire German people.'[4] The meetings, the discussions and the planning continued.

The Kreisau Circle finally resolved to assassinate the *Führer* at the Berghof on 2 July 1944 but the carefully devised operation was called off because neither Göring nor Himmler, whom they also intended to kill, was there. It was postponed for three weeks, until a day when Hitler and many of the military top brass would be gathered at the

2. Von Moltke, *Letters to Freya, 1939–1945*.
3. Germany's invasion of the Soviet Union in 1941, which failed because of the size, savagery, heroism and hardiness of the Soviet army and because German troops were not equipped to deal with bitter winter conditions when the cold could reach minus 63 degrees Fahrenheit. The war went on for four more years, resulting in 3.6 million German and 12 million Soviet battle deaths, and another 15–18 million civilians who died in massacres and of disease and starvation.
4. Peter Hoffmann, *The History of the German Resistance, 1933–45* (Cambridge, MA: 1988), p. 374.

Wolfsschanze. Unaware of the impending danger, Hitler and his retinue travelled back to Raustenberg.

Hitler spent more than eight hundred days at the Wolf's Lair during the war. He felt secure deep in the woods in his concrete fortress, guarded by an SS battalion. Eva would cheerfully have joined him, had he allowed it, but the *Wolfsschanze* was a purely military base and Hitler had no time for relaxation, let alone pleasure. The bunker had tiny airless rooms, 1944 was a very hot summer and the *Führer* and his entourage spent much of their time immured underground. His four secretaries were working flat out. Traudl Junge was assigned a cubicle in the secretaries' bunker: 'I was given a pass and lived about 100 metres away from the *Führer*. I wasn't at all happy about my new accommodation: I like light and air, not living like a rat underground, sleeping in an uncomfortable windowless cabin.'[5] The atmosphere was stale and foetid from the breath of nearly fifty people eating indifferent food and not getting enough fresh air. Even above ground there was little fresh air to be had – the temperature was nearly 90 degrees with high humidity. Hitler and his staff surfaced for occasional walks in the dense pine forest but the mosquitoes were a torment and Hitler had to wear a special protective helmet like a bee-keeper's to ward them off. 'To this day I can feel the oppressive closeness of those days,' wrote Traudl Junge, 'preventing us from sleeping and making the air shimmer with heat.' Hitler took hardly any exercise but pored over maps at a huge, solid oak conference table, big enough for two dozen people to gather round.

20 July 1944 was a day of sultry weather, the kind that makes people cross and prone to headaches. For once Hitler's intuitive ability to sense approaching danger gave no warning of the event that was to shatter the invulnerability of the Wolf's Lair. Colonel Graf von Stauffenberg had succeeded in smuggling a ready primed 2-pound bomb into the daily conference attended by Hitler and many top *Wehrmacht* officers. The Kreisau Circle had chosen him as the assassin since he was the only one of their members who could gain access to Hitler without being challenged, although his war injuries meant he couldn't use a pistol, hence the need for a bomb: a clumsier and more obvious weapon. Hidden in a briefcase, he carried it in to the meeting room and placed it under the table, close to where Hitler would stand. Then von Stauffenberg, with the excuse that he had to make an urgent tele-

5. Junge, *Bis Zur Letzten Stunde*, p. 43 (translated by the author).

phone call, left the room. At 12.42 p.m. the bomb exploded, with devastating results.

Traudl Junge recalled:

> Frau Christian and I had been for a cool swim in the afternoon and when we got back I began to write a letter. Suddenly a loud volley of shots rang out – which was not all that unusual – but then a panic-stricken voice shouted for a doctor. It wasn't the bang that made my heart stand still – we were used to hearing shots fired; people were forever testing their weapons and there was flak practice too, all of which we took for granted. But what had happened just now threw me into unease and terror.

The plot failed, but only just. At the last moment the location had been changed so that the conference was not held underground as originally intended (in which case the room would have contained the blast, making it more deadly) but in a hut above ground with three large windows. The explosives detonated successfully, but moments beforehand a helpful colonel had moved the briefcase away from the *Führer* and put it behind one of the heavy table supports, greatly reducing the impact of the blast on him. Even so, four people were killed instantly and twenty wounded but Hitler survived. His trousers were ripped to shreds but other than concussion, burns and more than a hundred splinters of oak deeply embedded in his right leg, his injuries seemed at first to be relatively minor. His right arm was temporarily paralysed, his eardrums punctured and for a while he suffered hearing loss. The long-term effects only became evident later. For the rest of his life he had a persistent and noticeable tremor in the left hand. This is visible in photographs where he either clasps it in the right hand or holds it behind his back. The *Führer* was heard to repeat afterwards, 'I am invulnerable, I am immortal.'[6] Had he died on 20 July 1944, the total casualties of the Second World War would have been halved.[7]

Claus von Stauffenberg watched the explosion from a safe distance and was convinced Hitler must have been killed. Within half an hour he was on his way back to Berlin to activate the coup intended to set

6. Peter Hoffmann, *Hitler's Personal Security* (London: Macmillan, 1979), p. 252.
7. Michael Baigent and Richard Leigh, *Secret Germany: Claus von Stauffenberg and the Mystical Crusade Against Hitler*, p. 66.

up a new government – Operation Valkyrie. He and three of his co-conspirators were arrested that evening and shot soon after midnight, almost exactly twelve hours after the bomb had gone off.[8] They were lucky. For them, death was quick and painless. Later, in a farcical 'People's Court' trial, another two hundred people were sentenced to death in reprisal for the coup that failed. They were taken to Plötzensee prison to be hanged and their slow death agonies were filmed. It was said that Hitler enjoyed watching this footage in the company of his cronies and guffawing SS officers. Albert Speer – who declined to attend – reports seeing photographs of their strangulation on Hitler's desk. If so, it was a departure from normal practice: the *Führer* was squeamish and disliked being confronted with the results of his sanguinary orders.

After July 1944, like every European Jew and a great many ordinary Germans, Eva Braun spent the rest of her life expecting and preparing to die. During the nine months before the end of the war 13,500 civilians were killed by bombs every month, hundreds of thousands more dying from hunger, cold and disease. In the extermination camps in occupied Poland – Auschwitz, Treblinka, Belzec, Majdanek, Sobibor and Chelmno – the Holocaust moved with ever-greater speed as the SS hastened to complete its diabolical task.

At the Berghof, von Stauffenberg's assassination attempt was the topic of every conversation. In a letter to Eva written directly afterwards Hitler tried to reassure her:

> My dear Tschapperl,
> Don't worry, I'm fine, just a bit tired perhaps. I hope to be home soon and then to be able to relax in your arms. I have a great need of rest but my duty towards the German people must come first . . . I am sending you the uniform that I was wearing on that unfortunate day. It is proof that Providence protected

8. Not only Claus von Stauffenberg himself died. A fortnight after the attempted assassination and coup, Himmler reintroduced the medieval custom of *Sippenhaft*, or 'blood guilt', whereby treachery was a manifestation of diseased blood, and thus the entire family must be extinguished. In the end most contrived to escape, although many children – including Claus's four – were separated from their parents and placed in the care of the state. Not only were they in need of re-educating; they would provide ideal future breeding material.

me and we have nothing to fear from our enemies. My hand is still trembling from the attempt on my life, [ending] I am full of hope for our coming victory.[9]

The trousers, ripped to shreds and covered in his blood, were all too vivid proof of how close he had come to death. This upset her terribly and she replied with a distraught letter:

> My love, I am beside myself. Desperate, miserable, unhappy. I am half dead now that I know you are in danger. Come back as soon as possible. I feel slightly crazy. Here the weather is fine and everything seems so calm that I feel ashamed. [. . .] You know, I've always said so, that I shan't go on living if anything happens to you. From the time of our first meetings, I promised myself to follow you everywhere, even in death. You know that my whole life is loving you.
> Your Eva

Hitler was deeply moved by this evidence of her devotion.[10] He replied tenderly in a letter that ended, '*With all my heart, your AH*'.

With all his heart.

Two things are especially interesting about her letter, apart from its unmistakable anguish. The first is that it has exactly the same tone as her diary written nearly ten years earlier, emphasised by the similarity of '*The weather here is so lovely . . .*' to a despairing comment made in 1935: '*The weather is so wonderful, and I, the mistress of the greatest man in Germany and in the world, am sitting here and gazing at the sun through a window.*' Eva never confused comfort or status or even sunshine with personal happiness. Second is the new-found certainty that Hitler loved her. His letter, brief as it is, reveals a depth of affection and mutual need that he was at last compelled to acknowledge.

A day or two later – at the end of July 1944 – Eva sent Gertraud to stay at Schloss Fischhorn near Fuschl, a castle where dozens of SS men were billeted: a dubious refuge, one might think, for such a young girl. When she got there she was reunited with her cousin Gretl and her aunt Fanny. 'Fegelein was present too – he was on leave, having

9. NARA records, RG 319, Box 31A.
10. Junge, *Bis Zur Letzten Stunde*, p. 151.

been injured during the attempted assassination. Everybody was running around, exchanging photos of the executed conspirators, all laughing. They were passed from hand to hand but when they came to me, *Tante* Fanny said: "This is not for you!"'[11] [Could the photographs really have reached a remote Bavarian castle within days of the conspirators being shot?] It is uncertain what happened to Gertraud next. According to *her* she returned to the Berghof for the next five months; however, none of the domestic staff mentions her presence and, as already described, Frau Mittlstrasse claims she cannot have stayed for more than a week or two. In her own version, she says:

> Meanwhile I had gone back to be with Eva. She seemed very composed; there was no mention of the assassination attempt, and tears – like so much else in those days – were taboo. Apart from occasional secret outings to Munich, we followed much the same routine every day: watching films, drinking sparkling wine, and eating fruit and biscuits.[12]

This report of Eva's apparent equanimity after 20 July is very much at odds with other people's accounts of her reaction to the attempt on Hitler's life. As her anguished letter shows, she was more worried about him than ever.

In early September, with the Russians fast approaching his field headquarters at Raustenberg, Hitler moved his entourage to *Werwolf*, near Vinnitsa, and in November he returned to Berlin.

By now Eva Braun knew that her death was not only inevitable but would not be long delayed. She began to make preparations. She drew up a will on 26 October 1944 although her possessions were far from lavish. An inventory of the contents found in her Wasserburgerstrasse house by the invading Americans in November 1945 lists £10 in sterling, US $1,000 and more than 100,000 in German Reichsmarks. Hitler's torn jacket and bloodied trousers were hanging in her wardrobe. Besides this there were a few bits of jewellery, too modest to itemise, and a gold and diamond watch and diamond brooch – nowhere near the largesse that most mistresses accumulate. Everything, including a set of her photograph albums, was seized as 'spoils of war'.

In November an imminent operation to remove a polyp on Hitler's

11. Weisker, *Wer War Eva Braun?*, p. 13.
12. Ibid.

vocal chords and an abscess on his upper jaw meant they wouldn't even be able to talk on the phone. Alarmed at the prospect of his surgery and the resultant break in their daily conversations, Eva travelled to Berlin on 20 November and they had lunch together before the operation next day. She stayed on for some days afterwards. (This trip casts further doubt on Gertraud's claim. Eva would never have left her cousin by herself at the Berghof. Perhaps Herta was staying there, or Gretl – who would have been five months pregnant and needed fresh, nourishing food for herself and her child.) Hitler got through the medical procedure safely but for days after the harmless polyp had been removed he was forbidden to speak and could only whisper. Soon everyone at the Reichskanzlei was whispering too.

Once the crisis had passed, Eva found time to order a new dress for Christmas from her dressmaker before returning to Obersalzberg. (Eva always felt guilty about Fräulein Heise's bills, fearing that if the German people heard about them she would be vilified for her extravagance, although Magda Goebbels was ordering handmade leather shoes and a trio of hats as late as January 1945.) She implored the *Führer* to take a few days' break and celebrate with her at the Berghof, but he told Traudl Junge, 'Yes, one ought to spend Christmas with one's family. Eva writes me urgent pleas to go to the Berghof this year. She says I must be badly in need of recuperation after the assassination attempt and my illness. But I know it's mostly Gretl behind all this, wanting her Hermann [Fegelein] with her.'[13] Hitler was adamant; because of the Ardennes offensive he planned to be at his western front headquarters, *Adlerhorst*, near Bad Nauheim in the wooded hills of the Taunus.

Eva went back to Munich and on 16 December she seems to have met up with Gertraud at Wasserburgerstrasse. When an air raid drove them into the shelter below the house where the strong boxes were kept, Eva offered her cousin a necklace and bracelet. It was only then, from her cousin's remark – *I don't need them any more* – that Gertraud realised for the first time that Eva was determined to carry out her plan to die with Hitler.

Eva spent Christmas in Munich with her family and Gertraud may have joined them. This was brave, when they all could have retreated to the safety of the Berghof, since the city that had been badly bombed on 17 December 1944 was to be bombed again on the night of 7/8

---

13. Junge, *Until the Final Hour*, p. 152.

January 1945.[14] After the second raid Eva – who had gone back to the Berghof – begged Hitler to let her check that her little house was unharmed but he was fearful for her safety and she had to resort to badgering everyone she knew for information. After two years of air attacks Munich was now one of the most devastated cities in Germany, the Allies taking revenge on the place where Nazism had first taken root. The population had shrunk to almost half its pre-war size and fewer than half a million people remained, many living in the bombed ruins of their homes. Almost 90 per cent of the beautiful, historic centre had been destroyed. Eva knew now, if she hadn't before, the devastation wreaked by Hitler's war on her country and her birth-place.

Gertraud is convinced that 'had I not left her in the January, maybe she wouldn't have gone to Berlin. That's something that's in my mind now. There was no one to keep her at the Berghof. She had no other way than going to him. I can't say that's true but that is what I feel now.' A much more likely reason is that Eva had now accepted – though she would never have said so publicly – that the end must be near. Hitler needed her and she wanted to be with him. Eva returned briefly to Berlin on 19 January 1945 and there, for the last time, had a meeting with her elder sister Ilse, now Frau Fucke-Michels. She and her husband had been living in Breslau in east Germany, which had just suffered and lost an appalling battle against the invading Russians from which thousands of refugees fled in panic and chaos, Ilse making her way towards Eva in Berlin. By this stage of the war German troops were so depleted that Breslau had to be defended by veterans from the *Volkssturm* (the Home Guard) and by teenagers, twelve to sixteen years old, from *Hitler Jugend*. By the time the war ended in May, half the young recruits had died in the pointless battle for the city, the boys crying out for their mothers.

Nerin Gun interviewed Ilse in the early 1960s for his biography of Eva and reports the following conversation between the two sisters. Allowing for dramatic licence, it rings more or less true:

Ilse, in a state of some distress, said 'I've no clothes left to wear . . . and my beautiful furniture . . . and my books . . .'

14. Altogether some 6,632 Müncheners were killed and another 15,000 wounded in the bombing of the Second World War. Large, *Where Ghosts Walked*, p. 346.

Eva comforted her: 'Don't worry, in a fortnight's time you'll be back home in Breslau, I have this from reliable sources. Did you lock up your house well? Then you have nothing to fear.'

Ilse, infuriated by her sister's wilful blindness, burst out: 'You wretched creature, wake up, open your eyes to reality. Breslau is lost, Silesia is lost, Germany is lost. Do you realise that hundreds of thousands of people are choking the snowy roads, fleeing from the enemy, who is ravaging and carrying off everything? Your *Führer* is a fiend; he's dragging you into the abyss with him and all of us along with you.'

Eva now raged in turn: 'You're mad, crazy! How can you say such things about the *Führer*, who's so generous and who told me to invite you to his house in the Obersalzberg until you return to Breslau. You deserve to be lined up against the wall and shot!'[15]

If Ilse and Gun recorded her words accurately, without vengefulness or melodrama, Eva's last comment is her most aggressive on record, echoing Hitler's rants about former acolytes who had lost faith. Ilse had told her the truth, but did Eva know it was the truth or did she still believe that what *she* said was the truth, given what she had just seen in the cities and streets of Munich and Berlin? Or was her angry retort the culmination of years of coolness between the two? After this conversation she seems, at any rate, to have accepted that the enemy was approaching fast.

By the winter of 1945 the Germans were cold, hungry and disillusioned, their cities smashed and armed forces drastically depleted. Only the extermination camps functioned with ever-greater efficiency. Jews continued to arrive from all over Europe in long, agonisingly slow trains, victims of Himmler's orders to the SS: gas them quickly, kill them all, no matter how, kill till not a Jew is left.

On 13 February 1945 Dresden was bombed; the priceless city of Dresden that had thought itself protected by its cultural heritage. It was not quite razed to the ground but the city was as devastated as Hamburg had been in July 1943. The following night Bomber Command attacked again. At least 35,000 Dresdeners died in these raids, perhaps five times as many – some estimates put the number at two hundred

15. Gun, *Eva Braun: Hitler's Mistress*, p. 238.

thousand.[16] Two nights later, on 16 February 1945, the tiny town of Pforzheim – of no strategic value whatsoever – was attacked by British bombers, killing one-third of its 63,000 inhabitants. Eva Braun, if the news reached her, must have thought the war was reaching a terrible culmination.

At the beginning of the war Henriette von Schirach had asked Eva what she would do if the war was lost.

'Then I'll die with him,' she said.

I said that since her face was unknown she could go abroad.

'You think I'd let him die alone? I'll be with him right up to the final moment; I've thought about it and decided. Nobody can stop me.'[17]

If Eva were to be with Hitler for the final conflagration, she must wind up her affairs in Munich and join him as soon as possible.

16. Some 3,907 tons of bombs were dropped. Out of 28,410 houses in the inner city of Dresden, 24,866 were destroyed. An area of 15 square kilometres was totally destroyed, including 14,000 homes, 72 schools, 22 hospitals, 19 churches, 5 theatres, 50 banks and insurance companies, 31 department stores, 31 large hotels and 62 administration buildings. The number of people killed in February 1945 was estimated at 35,000–45,000 but may have been many more.

17. Henriette von Schirach, *Frauen um Hitler* (Munich: Herbig, 1983), pp. 235–6.

Chapter Twenty-seven

In the Bunker

In four and a half years of agony that had left scarcely a corner of Europe untouched and many devastated, Eva had largely been spared the horror of war. She had never been injured or cold or hungry and hardly ever frightened; but she had grown used to seeing its aftermath. The cities were grey, cold heaps of brick and stone with gaping chasms where houses once stood; the streets, when not towering canyons, were cratered and potholed. Most cars were wrecks and petrol was almost impossible to obtain. German people in these cities were often wraiths in tattered clothing dragging thin, pale children to standpipes for water or in search of food. Food had become everyone's first concern; then a roof over their heads; and rarest of all, warmth. Few had all three and Hitler rather than the RAF was increasingly blamed for these calamities. By now, German women were deeply disillusioned, not only with their *Führer* but with their own menfolk. 'These days I keep noticing how my feelings are changing,' wrote an anonymous Berlin journalist as Hitler's régime collapsed. 'We feel sorry for them; they seem so miserable and power-less. [. . .] The Nazi world – ruled by men, glorifying the strong man – is beginning to crumble, and with it the myth of "Man". [. . .] Among the many defeats at the end of this war is the defeat of the male sex.' It was a far cry from the glory days of the BDM.[1]

Of Eva's close friends, only one had been killed. Her family was alive, safe and reasonably well fed. Gretl would soon bear the first child of the next generation. But Eva suffered, as all Germans suffered, to see her country brought low.

Martin Bormann accompanied her from the Berghof to Berlin on

1. Anonymous, *A Woman in Berlin* (London: Virago, 2005), p. 11.

19 January 1945. It must have been a tricky journey since, although both maintained a civil façade in front of Hitler, they disliked one another intensely. Eva stayed for three weeks in the rooms she had occasionally used at the Chancellery, until her thirty-third birthday on 6 February. Hitler gave her a diamond bracelet and topaz pendant – apart from the Mercedes, his most generous present ever – which she later bequeathed to her sister. (They never reached Gretl.) A party was held in one of the marble reception rooms of the Reichskanzlei, after which the *Führer* persuaded Eva to go back to the Berghof. He may well have thought this was their final parting but Eva knew she would soon be back. The prospect of life in a world without him was unendurable and she would never take another man. Hitler had still not fully grasped her strength of character or her genuine devotion. He trusted in his fawning, incompetent yes men but not until the very end did he trust the rock-solid Eva.

She agreed to leave Berlin after her birthday but only for a couple of weeks. She needed to pack up ten years of her life for what she felt would be a final departure. She didn't want anyone to find and read her personal letters from Hitler or the diary she had resumed after 1935 and kept intermittently thereafter. She had to make sure her beloved dogs would be well cared for, say goodbye to her family and friends, give away her clothes and share out her jewellery. The railways were still operating fairly reliably and on 7 or 8 February Eva caught the midnight train from Berlin. She lay in the darkness, incongruously comfortable in a womb-like couchette with clean white sheets, as the train passed through Germany's devastated towns and wintry countryside, waking amid the ruins of Munich to change trains, and finally alighting at Speer's snow-covered station to be met by an armoured Mercedes and an SS driver.

It is impossible to be sure exactly when she returned to Berlin but the best evidence points to a date three weeks later. In the meantime on 17 February she and Herta Schneider had met up in Munich – Herta, the staunch friend from her girlhood and youth whose unmade-up olive skin and piercing gaze had never changed; Herta who knew all her secrets; Herta, who had always given her sound advice, shared her marriage and children with Eva and who, in twenty years of friendship and loyalty, had never let her down. They can't have known for sure that it was the last time they would see each other, although Herta, always the more down to earth, must have had a pretty good idea while Eva, with her usual tendency to look on the bright side, still believed they'd meet again.

For the last time, Eva slept in her own double bed, opened her wardrobe and selected clothes to wear in the bunker, luxuriated in her large mirrored bathroom and gazed out of her windows on the view she loved. How – given all this – could she bring herself to leave? Herbert Döring probably got it right when he said:

> Well, first of all her life was over. It had come to a full stop, ever since it was clear that the war was lost. She had no future here any more. She would have been . . . who knows what would have happened to her? Perhaps she would have been imprisoned. And that was all she was thinking: life is over, whether I end it here on the Obersalzberg or whether I see him . . . after all, it has been many years. And so she ended her life together with him.[2]

Turning her back on the Berghof for the last time to gaze across the snow-capped mountains and dark green forests that had enfolded her for the past ten years, she may have thought of lines from Goethe's poem *Wandrers Nachtlied*, memorised by every German schoolchild:

Wandrers Nachtlied

Über allen Gipfeln
Ist Ruh,
In allen Wipfeln
Spürest du
Kaum einen Hauch;
Die Vögelein schweigen im Walde.
Warte nur, balde
Ruhest du auch.[3]

2. Interview with Herbert Döring for *Adolf and Eva*, 3BMTV, roll 15.29.30.
3. Like all the best poetry, this brief evocative poem can only be rendered bluntly and approximately into English. Here is my rough version:
Nightfall for the Wanderer
Silence drops
Over mountain tops;
No breath of wind sways
The high treetops.
The twittering of birds
Dwindles and stops.
Just wait; soon that peace
Will drop like a pall
And shroud us all.

She climbed into the waiting car and was driven down the mountainside to Berchtesgaden station. She couldn't leave Hitler to celebrate his fifty-sixth birthday without her. After the months spent in
dank concrete rooms underground amid grey and black uniforms,
boots with treacherously clicking heels and insincere 'Sieg Heils', he
would be heartened by her pretty face and fresh, colourful clothes.

Frau Mittlstrasse, who accompanied Eva from Munich, recalled:
'On 7 March 1945 she travelled of her own free will by special train
to Berlin, which was now under siege. And there she stayed, though
Hitler was appalled and tried to send her back straightaway. But there
was no shifting her.'[4] This fits with an entry in Bormann's diary for
that same date: 'In the evening Eva Braun left for Berlin with a courier
train. 20.14. o'clock.'[5] Other accounts, including that of Albert Speer,
Henriette von Schirach and Hugh Trevor-Roper, put her return a good
month later, to 15 April, but by that they probably meant the day
when she and Hitler abandoned their shattered – and now perilous –
rooms in the Reichskanzlei to take refuge underground, in the bunker.
Eva was returning to a city in its death throes, knowing that she would
soon die there, prepared, for once, to defy Hitler. She had chosen to
come to Berlin and there she would stay.

Although Hitler had forbidden her to return, when she turned up
at the Reichskanzlei on 7 March, having been in Munich and
Berchtesgaden for a month, his first reaction to her unexpected arrival
was joy. Yet within a few days he was pressing her to go back to the
Berghof, promising that he'd be there soon himself.[6] Calmly, almost
light-heartedly, she ignored him. If proof were needed of her devotion,
this was it: she had come to Berlin to be with him *in extremis*, as she
had always sworn she would. Death held few terrors for her. She had
contemplated it so often now that it had become familiar, almost
welcome. Her uncle Alois surmised: 'Life was over as far as Eva was
concerned and she freely resigned herself to her fate. Of all those who
found themselves trapped in the cells of the bunker, she was perhaps

4. Interview with German journalist and film-maker Guido Knopp, quoted in
Knopp, *Hitler's Women*, p. 46.
5. Quoted by Frank, *Eva Braun: Ein ungewöhnliches Frauenschicksal in geschichtlich
bewegter Zeit*, p. 279, and by Antony Beevor, *Berlin: The Downfall 1945*.
6. Hitler had in fact planned to go to the Berghof on 15 April and conduct the
rest of the war from there, but mumbo-jumbo from Göring about the stars being
in good alignment for a sudden breakthrough victory in late April distracted him
and he stayed on in Berlin.

the only one who was able to accept death with dignity and bid a calm farewell to life.'[7] Only the method and the moment must have haunted her – would dying be painful or long-drawn-out; would she be horribly disfigured, would her body be mauled by strangers? She was plagued by these fears, yet Fräulein Braun, whom long ago Henny Hoffmann had likened to a little soubrette from comic opera, was determined to stay to the last. Eva and Adolf had seven weeks to live.

Even Heinrich Hoffmann, who had denigrated her for so long, was forced to admit that the teenager whom he had dismissed as 'an ordinary, pretty little shop girl, with all the frivolity and vanity of her kind' had matured into a very different woman:

> Under the influence of the tremendous events through which she lived and as the war years marched towards their grim conclusion, Eva's mental stature grew and her character broadened and deepened; and by her final gesture and decision to remain at the side of her protector to the end, she attained heights which more than atoned for the frivolity and vanity of the past.[8]

Eva may have been given a tour of the bunker on previous visits – it had been under construction since 1943 and was still not entirely finished when the war ended – but now it was crammed with military and medical personnel, nearly all complete strangers to her, as well as Hitler's usual entourage. What did she find when she descended into this ashen labyrinth?

The word 'bunker' conjures up a dark, damp air-raid shelter rather than a centre of operations capable, at its overcrowded capacity, of accommodating nearly a thousand people. There was, of course, no natural light; the public spaces were illuminated by cold neon rods. Night and day looked the same. The underground complex consisted of not one but several separate bunkers connected by stairs or corridors. The deepest, safest and best-furnished section was Hitler's, known as the *Führerbunker*. Imagine a concrete box, some 20 metres or 65 feet square, divided down the middle by a wide corridor, with several small concrete cells leading off on either side. This main area was about 50 feet wide and housed sixteen rooms, each roughly

7. Winbauer, *Eva Braun's Familiengeschichte*, p. 23 (translated by Christiane Gehron).
8. Hoffmann, *Hitler Was My Friend*, pp. 163–4.

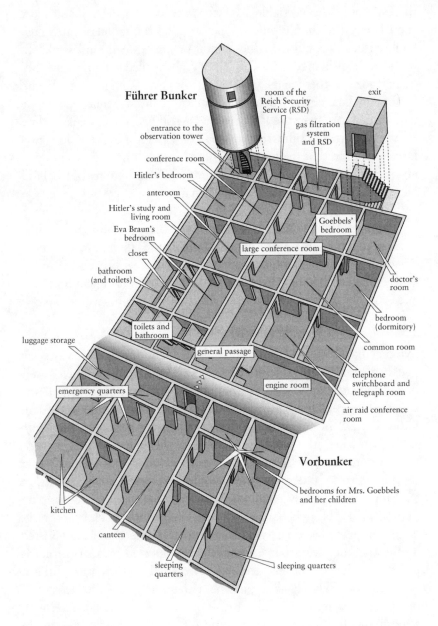

Führer Bunker

exit

room of the
Reich Security
Service (RSD)

entrance to the
observation tower

gas filtration
system
and RSD

conference room

Hitler's bedroom

anteroom

Hitler's study and
living room

Eva Braun's
bedroom

Goebbels'
bedroom

closet

large conference room

bathroom
(and toilets)

doctor's
room

toilets and
bathroom

bedroom
(dormitory)

luggage storage

general passage

common room

emergency quarters

engine room

telephone
switchboard and
telegraph room

air raid conference
room

Vorbunker

bedrooms for Mrs. Goebbels
and her children

kitchen

canteen

sleeping
quarters

sleeping quarters

Map of Hitler's bunker

11 x 10 feet. On one side of the corridor were the *Führer's* bedroom, study – its sole decoration a portrait of his hero, Frederick the Great – and bathroom. Next to these was a small map room; then Eva's miniature suite with a 'dressing room' hardly bigger than a wardrobe. Even Blondi had a cupboard of her own where she suckled her new-born pups. From the other end of Hitler's suite an anteroom led via a short flight of steps up to the garden.

On the opposite side of the main central corridor was a sitting room where people could relax, except that true relaxation had become a thing of the past, and several utility rooms. Halfway along it a partition separated the end nearest Hitler, used for official conferences, from the other end where more informal meetings were held. Although nominally private, the passage through the *Führerbunker* was criss-crossed all day long by visitors, messengers, adjutants, officers, ministers and servants bringing despatches, telegrams, memoranda, coffee and cakes, letters and orders for Hitler to sign. When the bombardment was at its worst people slept and dressed and lived all hours of the day and night in this concrete cave. Privacy was impossible. Eva spent the last month of her life under the constant scrutiny of scores of uniformed men, most of whom had no idea who she was. Only Hitler, Eva and top-ranking military men were looked after by their usual staff and shared the occasional luxury of a proper bathroom with a bath, for which they would have to go upstairs to the Reichskanzlei. Everyone else in the bunker managed as best they could with inadequate washing facilities and erratic laundering, which sometimes meant none at all. Despite air conditioning of a sort, all those hurrying, unwashed male bodies must have become unpleasantly smelly.

A few metres above and behind the *Führerbunker*, linked by a curving stairway, was another bunker, a concrete box about half the size of Hitler's, containing a dozen small rooms: the kitchen, servants' quarters, four bedrooms and a separate section with a surgery, dispensary and bedroom for Dr Morell. The passageway running down the middle served as a communal dining room or canteen.

These two areas were the centre of operations but there were many other bunkers below the monumental Chancellery. For people used to the grandiose spaces and panoramic views of the Berghof, being confined down there must have been physically and psychologically claustrophobic. The rest of the complex included the bunker of the Party Chancellery – Bormann's domain – and Mohnke's bunker, where he lived with his SS brigade as Commandant of the Chancellery and conducted the defence of 'the Citadel'. Goebbels and his staff were living in the cellars of the Propaganda Ministry. Here, in varying degrees of discomfort, the '*hohe Tiere*' and their functionaries scurried to and fro to assist *der Führer* in the dying days of a war that had long been hopeless. By the end of March 1945 nearly everybody had accepted the inevitable and moved out of the vast, ravaged rooms of the Reichs Chancellery to shelter below ground, making the best they could of it.

In addition to all this there was a crowded field hospital where casualties of the fighting – sometimes hundreds at a time – were operated on, nursed, recovered or died. Six months after the war had ended, Erna Flegel, a surgical nurse attached to this hospital, described it to her US interrogators:

> When the ring around Berlin kept drawing closer and closer . . . we had to keep the injured there [i.e. in the bunker below the Reichskanzlei] and it grew to be a large hospital with up to five hundred wounded. By the time parts of Berlin were already occupied and the Russians were coming close to the centre of the city one could feel, almost physically, that the Third Reich was approaching its end.[9]

The bunker continued to function more or less perfectly to the last. Thanks to the efficiency with which it had been designed and constructed and its services installed, hot water was always available and the electricity and air conditioning rarely failed, even under the heaviest bombardment. A large staff of technicians stayed behind to supervise this equipment. Designed to supply heat, light, food and fresh water, sanitation, contact with the outside world and medical treatment, perhaps for months on end, it did so admirably. And it was indestructible.

By April 1945 Germany had become an inferno by day and night, like the visions of hell depicted by Hieronymus Bosch; but Hitler, holed up in the Reichs Chancellery, refused to acknowledge that the war could no longer be won, least of all by the miracle aircraft and miracle

9. Testimony of Erna Flegel, interrogated 30 November 1945 by Frederick Stalder under the command of Richard Helms Lt.-Commander USNR, APO 742. Detailed transcripts are at NARA, RG 226, Box 465.

bombs that only he believed would soon be delivered. He never visited a concentration camp or saw anyone being tortured, murdered or gassed and, while he had viewed the death agonies of the Kreisau plotters on film with apparent pleasure, it was because they had tried to assassinate him.

Ever more dissociated from the outside world, he continued to issue impossible orders to armies that no longer existed, and had officers appointed, sacked and executed as the whim took him. He roamed about his nether kingdom, gorging himself on chocolate cake. According to one of his secretaries, 'his craving for cake had become pathological. Before, he used to eat three pieces of cake at most, but now he had them fill his plate three times.' He became increasingly attached to Blondi and her five puppies, who lived in one of the bunker's bathrooms.[10]

His health continued to deteriorate; he walked with increasing feebleness, especially on the left side, often needing to lean on walls or tables to support himself. His moods were violent and irrational.[11] Morell, who was himself a morphine addict, regularly injected Hitler with some stimulant and his behaviour, the sudden mood swings, moments of intense dynamism followed by somnolence and inertia, exhibit all the signs of morphine dependency. No one knew what it was exactly that Morell gave Hitler and he did not confide the details to the other doctors who attended the *Führer*.

Hitler and Eva still indulged in the fantasy of a future together. It was their way of protecting each other, he with pretended optimism, she with pretended gaiety. They talked of retiring to Linz after the war, where Hitler had spent part of his youth, and living quietly in Bavarian domesticity. Secretly, Eva dreamed of starring in a film based on her life. Hitler dreamed of displaying German culture and civilisation to the world. Hermann Giesler, the architect who replaced Speer when the latter was made Minister for Armaments in 1942, had constructed a model of the great new city planned for Linz, with a splendid opera house, the biggest and best in Europe; colossal museums

10. Fest, *Inside Hitler's Bunker: The Last Days of the Third Reich*, first published in Germany in 2002 as *Der Untergang: Hitler und das Ende des Dritten Reiches*.
11. Information from a review of *Inside Hitler's Bunker* by William Boyd, *Guardian*, 19 March 2005.

and galleries filled with the idealised Teutonic art the *Führer* admired as well as muscle-bound Old Masters allegories, plundered from German Jews and collections all over Europe. To the contemporary eye Hitler's city of the future is dictator architecture at its worst: vast granite buildings approached by wide marble staircases flanked by tall marble columns dominated by angular marble eagles and rank upon rank of high flagpoles with swastikas; a truly soulless vision. Hitler loved it. He had the model installed on a table in the Reichskanzlei and would study it for hours.

Hitler surfaced only occasionally to go to his half-empty office in the half-ruined Chancellery. On 15 April Eva gave up her first floor set of rooms and moved all her things to the three narrow cells next door to his, declaring that she was there to stay. Albert Speer, who made a number of visits to the bunker, found the admiration and friendship he had always felt for Eva warming to deep respect. 'I tried repeatedly to persuade her to get out of Berlin. I liked her so much; I wanted her to be safe.' On three separate occasions he offered her a seat in one of the ever-more infrequent planes leaving Berlin. 'She persistently refused and finally told me, with a big smile, to stop pestering her.'[12]

Few survive today from the inner circle to describe those stygian weeks. Those who did get out mostly went out of their way to praise Eva's courage, buoyancy and thoughtfulness. Speer said afterwards how much he had admired 'her dignity: almost a kind of gay serenity' in the final days. Nicolaus von Below, Hitler's adjutant from the Luftwaffe and one of the few people around him who was not loathsome, was also struck by Eva's calm good humour. 'She adapted herself entirely to life in the bunker. She was always neat, beautifully dressed, invariably warm and helpful to everyone. She never wavered to the end, showing no weakness right up to the last moment.' What is this, if not grace under pressure? Hans-Karl von Hasselbach,[13] a military surgeon in the bunker during some of those final days, offers a more barbed description: 'She was rather intelligent and quick in repartee. She could be arrogant, moody, selfish and over-opinionated.' 'Quick

12. Sereny, *Albert Speer: His Battle with Truth*, p. 505.
13. From NARA: OI Special Report in Box 392, RG 319, Box 2 of 2 entitled *Adolf Hitler: A Composite Picture*, dated 2 April 1947. -Karl von Hasselbach was Chief Surgeon in the Army Field Hospital 2/562 and one of Hitler's regular physicians from 1934 to October 1944. He would often have seen Eva Braun and got to know her quite well.

in repartee', 'over-opinionated' – this was not at all what was expected from a woman, let alone one supposed to be invisible – but he was describing her in the years before the bunker. Her ordeal allowed her to reveal the strength of character, stamina and fortitude that she had always possessed but dared not show before. No wonder Bormann and Himmler didn't care for the new Eva. Hasselbach went on, 'Hitler treated her as a lady at all times and expected the rest of his entourage to do likewise. The "*Sie*" and "*Mein Führer*" they used in the beginning was replaced in later years by "*Du*".' Dr Brandt, Hitler's Berlin-based doctor for more than a decade, made a similar comment: 'Her character was stern rather than pliable and feminine. During her years with Hitler she developed from an average middle-class girl into a lady of style. She tried to do everything in her power to be to Hitler what he needed.'[14]

Only in the last weeks of her life did Eva use any influence with Hitler. Gottlob Berger, a general in the Waffen SS, met her on 22 April 1945 after a meeting with the *Führer*:

> Then came the much-maligned Eva Braun. I must stand up for this woman in one thing . . . [She] always made it possible for one to approach Hitler from the back, so to speak . . . When I needed help I asked her, and she could be convinced if the reason was good and always got me an interview with Hitler. At that time she definitely had an influence on him [but otherwise] it was a purely personal relationship.

By this stage those powers of persuasion, if any, could have had no impact on the fate of the Jews; all Eva did was make it possible for Berger to gain access to the *Führer* and present the latest doomed strategic initiative.

The final weeks in the bunker have been recorded in detail by many historians[15] but none of the men (and they are nearly all men[16]) who have excavated every inch and hour of Hitler's claustrophobic hiding

14. Taken from the same intelligence report, Box 392, RG 319, Box 2 of 2.
15. First and most brilliantly by Hugh Trevor-Roper in *The Last Days of Hitler*, published in 1947 by Macmillan Press, and more recently by Joachim C. Fest with a masterly summary, *Inside Hitler's Bunker: The Last Days of the Third Reich*.
16. Gitta Sereny and Traudl Junge are notable exceptions. Both write about her approvingly. The few women around Hitler – Nazi wives or domestic servants – interviewed by the Americans before the Nuremberg Trials were mostly catty about her.

place has paid much attention to Eva Braun. They disagree about the date of her arrival and how the other subterraneans treated her, dismissing her sacrifice as little more than melodrama.[17] They condemn her for being vain and shallow and she was, at times – she had always been confined to female trivia. On 18 April she fulminated in a letter to her sister, *'Just imagine: the dressmaker is demanding thirty marks for my blue blouse! She's out of her mind; how can she have the nerve to charge thirty marks for such a trifle?'* Now she tried to cheer everyone up by changing her outfits and her make-up, filing and polishing and repolishing her nails. What else could she have done? She had no nursing or practical skills. The point of her being down there was to comfort Hitler as best she could. For the past fifteen years her creativity and talents had been stifled. Dressing up was what she did best and so, in the gloomiest circumstances, that's what she did. If she had been a singer, she would have sung; if a dancer, she'd have danced. However absurd the idea that changing her clothes might cheer people up (though who knows – maybe it did) it shows her optimistic, indomitable nature. She was one of the very few who preserved their self-respect till the last day. Alfons Schulz, the switchboard operator whose job it was to keep open the telephone lines to the outside world, said when he was asked how she behaved in the bunker, 'Everyone agreed that Eva and Magda Goebbels were the only ones who talked to people in a quiet, friendly and balanced way. They calmed the waves of excitement down there. They didn't seem desperate – on the contrary, they remained amazingly composed, right up to the end. *Unlike the men*'. [my italics].[18]

What Eva and the other bunker-dwellers endured was a thousand times better than the fate of ordinary Berlin citizens who, in these last days, were similarly immured. By April they had little light and water, almost no heat, were short of food and sanitary conditions were indescribable. An unnamed Berlin woman wrote bleakly in her diary:

17. For example, from yet another book about Hitler's last days in the bunker by Anton Joachimsthaler, *The Last Days of Hitler* (London: Arms and Armour Press, 1996): 'She [i.e. Eva Braun] never cared a fig about Hitler, the state of his health or his worries. She even criticised his conduct in front of his secretaries and preferred to dance while in the bunker. Eva Braun had no intention of going under with Hitler . . . etc. etc.' This is pure masculine spite with no evidence whatsoever to support it.

18. Interview with Alfons Schulz for *Adolf and Eva*, 3BMTV, roll 23.29.43.

My last ration cards for bread. No new cards in sight. No decrees and no news, either. Nothing. Not a soul cares about us any more. We're suddenly individuals, no longer members of the German Nation. Old ties are broken; friendship don't extend further than three buildings away. There's only the group of us, huddled in the cave, a clan, just like in prehistoric times. The horizon has shrunk to three hundred paces.[19]

Worst of all, the women would soon take the brunt of the invading Russian soldiers, so long dreaded, who proved to be as bestial as the rumours had predicted.

The men in the bunker, except for a few from the top ranks of the army, were spineless and scared in the expectation of imminent death. The knowledge that they were cornered rats revealed their true nature. Discipline had gone by the board; litter, disorder and moral and physical squalor had invaded the *Führer*'s former obsessively clean environment, though not his personal quarters. Without servants or wives to keep them immaculate, people's clothes were often food-stained, crumpled, reeking of sweat. In the final days, when Hitler and his aides were depressed and suicidal, many of his henchmen became unwashed, drunken and lecherous. The '*hohe Tiere*', the strutting, preening top dogs, generals and parasites overblown with arrogance, swigging champagne, mouths stuffed with caviar – decadent, deluded Göring with his jewellery and his varnished fingernails who had amassed a king's ransom in stolen goods; the equally predatory Goebbels, who for fifteen years had enjoyed exercising his *droit de seigneur* over pretty young women too scared to resist; Bormann, Hitler's toady and keeper of the purse; Himmler, *der treue Heinrich*,[20] hungry for power, coldly overseeing the murder of millions and scuttling from death himself – all were seen for what they really were – men bloated with power, seeking their own aggrandisement. The so-called last and greatest of the Teutonic Knights faced their approaching immolation less than heroically.[21] Erna Flegel commented: 'In the last weeks so much treachery, cowardice and meanness had revealed itself in Hitler's immediate entourage and this treachery affected Eva Braun very deeply.'[22] And

19. Anonymous, *A Woman in Berlin* (London: Virago, 2005), p. 40.
20. Faithful Heinrich.
21. With the possible exception of Bormann, Goebbels and Robert Ley, who did stick it out with Hitler to the last.
22. As note 9, p. 407.

still the *Führer* deluded himself that 'at my last hour, my officers would gather around me in unshakeable loyalty, their daggers drawn . . .'[23] As nemesis approached, Eva was heard to say, 'Poor, poor Adolf, deserted by everyone, betrayed by everyone. Better that ten thousand others die than that *he* should be lost to Germany.' It is not an attractive remark. Perhaps only the mothers or lovers of men facing death in a war the women do not understand would be capable of saying the same thing. Yet all her life, Eva had put Hitler above everything. He was, literally, her god on earth.

In mid-April the Russians crossed the River Oder, 70 kilometres away, to begin their final, unstoppable push towards Berlin. Little more than the exhausted remnants of the German army – hastily conscripted veterans of the First World War, poorly trained civilians in *Volkssturm* battalions and skinny boys in their mid-teens (some were even younger, terrified children who were shot if they tried to escape) from Hitler Youth – had been pressed into battle. The anonymous diarist described them: 'You see very young boys, baby faces peeping out beneath over-sized steel helmets; it's frightening to hear their high-pitched voices. They're fifteen years old at the most, standing there looking so skinny and small in their billowing uniform tunics.'[24] This ragtag and bobtail was all that stood between the enemy heading for Berlin and the all-conquering Nazis cowering in the bunker. On 16 April 1945, the 1st Belorussian Front commanded by Marshal Zhukov launched the Soviet offensive against Berlin with three-quarters of a million men, nearly 4,000 tanks and 17,000 guns and mortars. The bombardment and bomb attacks could be heard 70 kilometres – nearly 50 miles – away. On 18 April the Russians broke through the German army defences and advanced to within 30 kilometres of the capital, planning to encircle it on two fronts and cut it off. The end could only be a matter of days.

By this time Eva could hear the distant artillery and observe the breakdown of order in the bunker. Most people thought only of escape – or suicide. There was a valedictory note in her letter to Herta Schneider dated 19 April 1945.[25] She began by apologising for not being in touch by phone:

23. Junge, *Bis Zur Letzten Stunde*, p. 139.
24. Anonymous, *A Woman in Berlin* (London: Virago, 2005), p. 40.
25. This letter was shown to Johannes Frank by Frau Schneider not long before she died and quoted in his biography *Eva Braun: Ein ungewöhnliches Frauenschicksal in geschichtlich bewegter Zeit*, pp. 281–3 (translated by Christiane Gehron).

Dear little Herta,

Thank you so much for your two lovely letters. Please accept all my best wishes for your birthday in writing. The poor connections have made it impossible for me to speak to you on the telephone. I do hope you'll soon have a happy reunion with your Erwin [Herta's husband]. I hope his birthday letter will still get through to you. It cannot have gone missing!

In the midst of cacophony and destruction, Eva clung to the customs by which friends celebrated each other's birthdays.

Germans pay a great deal of attention to birthdays. Well into her eighties my mother continued to be as playful and excited as a child at the prospect of marking another year, although she never stopped lying about her age, remaining stuck at thirty-nine for a decade and thereafter subtracting a year or two; five; ten, confident that she would be believed. She met my partner for the first time when she was seventy-four and whispered conspiratorially, '*Don't tell him how old I am!*' Yet heaven help the daughter who forgot her birthday and failed to send a card and flowers. She certainly never forgot ours. For days beforehand she would ring – it made no difference whether I was about to be twenty-five or fifty-five – and ask, 'Are you *excited* darling? I won't tell you what you're getting . . . it's a *secret!*' Wild horses on their bended knees wouldn't have got her to divulge, though the present usually turned out to be what I had asked for.

After offering birthday greetings to her friend, Eva expressed concern for those she loved who were still at the Berghof, which although safer than Munich could still not be guaranteed safe:

I'm so glad you've decided to keep Gretl company at the Berghof. Since Traunstein was bombed, I'm no longer so sure that you're safe at Garmisch. Thank God my mother is joining you tomorrow. Now I needn't worry any more . . . We can already hear the gunfire from the eastern front and of course we suffer from air raids every day . . . I spend all my time in the bunker now and as you can imagine I'm terribly short of sleep. But I'm so happy to be near HIM at this time. Not a day passes without my being begged to take refuge at the Berghof but so far I've always won. In any case, from today there's not any more the slightest chance of getting through by car. Even if everything fails I'm sure we'll find a way of seeing each other again . . .

The secretaries and I are doing pistol target practice and have mastered it so well that the men daren't compete with us.

Given her situation, Eva sounds extraordinarily light-hearted, and not just to reassure Herta. All that mattered was being near HIM. Yet she must have been concerned by accounts of Soviet bestiality towards women. Appalling tales of the atrocities committed by their conquering soldiers were rife – and accurate – and many women in the bunker preferred to kill themselves rather than face multiple rape.[26] Eva, already an expert shot, knowing that her friend would be upset if she explained the true reason for her sudden interest in target practice, made a joke of it.

She continued:

Yesterday I telephoned Gretl, probably for the last time. From today on, there'll be no hope of getting through on the phone. But I am absolutely convinced that everything will turn out well in the end and HE is unusually optimistic. [She is keen to have news of her sisters and all her old friends.] How are things with Gretl and where has Ilse got to? Where is Käthl? And Georg, and Bepo? Please write a long letter soon! I'm sorry if mine lacks its usual style but I'm in a hurry, as usual. With all my very best wishes[27] to you all, Your Eva, always.[28]

26. Their fears were not exaggerated. Here, for those who can bring themselves to read it, is an account by the anonymous German woman of her first encounter with a Russian soldier: 'The one shoving me is an older man with grey stubble, reeking of alcohol and horses. He carefully closes the door behind him and, not finding any key, slides the wing chair against the door. He seems not even to see his prey, so that when he strikes she is all the more startled as he knocks her onto the bedstead. Eyes closed, teeth clenched. No sound. Only an involuntary grinding of teeth when my underclothes are ripped apart. The last untorn ones I had.

Suddenly his finger is in my mouth, stinking of horse and tobacco. A stranger's hands expertly pulling apart my jaw. Eye to eye. Then with great deliberation he drops a gob of gathered spit into my mouth. [. . .] The stranger's lips open, yellow teeth, one in front half broken off. The corners of the mouth lift, tiny wrinkles radiate from the corners of his eyes. The man is smiling.' Anonymous, *A Woman in Berlin* (London: Virago, 2005), p. 84.

27. This expression at the end of a letter is not as cool as it sounds in translation. In German, 'Alle herzlichsten Glückwünsche' is an affectionate, even effusive, way to conclude a personal letter.

28. Beevor, *Berlin: The Downfall 1945*, p. 254.

Eleven metres – 35 feet – above her head the earth rumbled and the bunker's reinforced concrete walls trembled as Soviet grenades exploded and their tanks moved closer, but Eva's bravado was undimmed.

She ended the letter with a touching PS: 'The photograph is for Gretl. One of the little sausages [Blondi's five puppies] is going to be hers. Please tell Frau Mittlstrasse to grant the Austrian maids leave to go home – orders from on high. But only for a limited period – fourteen days or so, I reckon. Please send her my best wishes too.' Thoughtful and generous to the last, Eva expects to be back at the Berghof within two weeks and makes plans for the maids accordingly. By now she and Magda Goebbels must have been among the last people in the bunker to have faith in Hitler. Almost everyone else thought he was deranged, irrational, deluded, suicidal. But for Eva, everything would soon be all right, she and her loved ones would be reunited, all would be well. Hitler had said so.

Her cousin Gertraud – having read Traudl Junge's account of life in the bunker – commented to me,

> It's very interesting how in those last days people threw off all the shackles, smoking and drinking in Hitler's presence as if to say 'What the hell, it doesn't make any difference now . . . Hitler can't stop us.' Eva seemed genuinely calm and composed. As Traudl Junge puts it, 'Her fate was understandable but deeply moving all the same. There's a German expression, "*Imprisoned together, hanged together.*" That's how it was for Eva who, as she'd always promised, remained true to herself.'[29]

On 19 April Eva took a last stroll through the Tiergarten, the spacious gardens laid out around the Reichskanzlei. The weather was beautiful but fire bombs had almost stripped the trees of their young leaves.

29. E-mail dated 29 September 2004 from Gertraud Weisker to the author. In German, the original, translated by the author, reads: '*Es ist sehr interessant, dass die Menschen in den letzten Tagen alle "Fesseln" von sich geworfen haben, sie haben in Gegenwart Hitlers geraucht und getrunken, so als wollten sie sagen, es ist jetzt alles egal. Hitler hat uns nichts mehr zu verbieten. Eva schien echt ruhig und gelassen zu sein. Das sagt Traudl Junge, die Sekretärin von Hitler. "Eva's Schicksal ist schon sehr unverständlich aber auch tief berührend. Wir haben ein deutsches Sprichwort 'Mitgefangen – mitgehangen.' Das trifft für Eva zu. Sie ist sich, wie ich schon immer sagte, selbst treu geblieben."*'

Even nature was being annihilated. Traudl Junge came with her on that final excursion:

> Eva Braun emerged from her room. Outside it had gone quiet. We had no idea what the weather was like. We wanted to go up to the park so that we and the dogs could get a bit of fresh air and daylight. A heavy cloud of dust and smoke hung over Berlin. The air was mild with a hint of spring. Eva Braun, Frau Christian and I wandered silently through the park. There were deep craters everywhere in the well-kept lawns yet we couldn't believe the burned-out tanks were the very last of the German defences. Tomorrow, surely, the troops would arrive and drive out the enemy. The trees were coming into bloom, the grass grew and everything in nature was being renewed. [. . .] We were almost happy that it all went on, that you could clear the stuffiness from your head and breathe freely. The dogs romped about; we sat on a stone and smoked a cigarette. Even Eva Braun lit up and when she saw our surprise, she said, 'Oh, come on, let me have a smoke. With such exceptional problems I'm allowed to do something exceptional.'
>
> All the same, she had a tin of peppermints in her bag and put one in her mouth as we made our way back to the sound of the first siren and retreated into the bunker again.[30]

After this she occasionally climbed to the top of the steps leading from the bunker to breathe fresh air – not in fact fresh at all but gritty with dust and smoke – for a few moments, but she never stepped into the outside world again.

That evening, Traudl Junge reminisced:

> Hitler asked us to come and sit by him – it had all become quite unconventional since the circle had shrunk so much – and Eva Braun sat beside him and without a second glance at the others began talking to him: '*Du*, do you know that statue by the Minister of Foreign Affairs? It's a glorious piece of sculpture! It would fit perfectly in my garden, by the bowl. Please buy it for me, if all goes well and we get out of Berlin!' – and she looked at him pleadingly. Hitler took her hand:

30. Junge, *Bis Zur Letzten Stunde*, p. 164 (translated by the author).

'But I've no idea who owns it. Perhaps it belongs to the city, in which case I can't just buy it and install it in a private garden.' 'Oh,' she said. 'If you succeed in beating back the Russians and freeing Berlin, then you can make this one exception!' Hitler laughed at female logic.[31]

Next day, 20 April, was Hitler's birthday. It had been the custom for members of the inner circle to greet him at midnight and offer good wishes on his birthday. Hitler had forbidden any celebrations at such an inopportune moment as this but Eva Braun overruled him and – still seeking favour at the eleventh hour – they gathered anyway. Speer recalled: 'They all came to congratulate Hitler, the same people who had come every year.' Their greetings must have sounded hollow. Pale spelunkians who had spent too long in their artificial cave below the tortured earth, Göring (porcine as ever despite war shortages), Speer, Ribbentrop, Bormann and half a dozen leaders of the *Wehrmacht* congratulated their crumbling *Führer* on having attained the age of fifty-six and wished him well for the future before swilling *Sekt* and guzzling caviar. It is ironic that by this time the bunker's stores of food had dwindled to little more than luxury items, long hoarded and available in abundance, while supplies of milk, butter, eggs, bread and above all fresh vegetables were scarcely to be found. For Hitler this was particularly hard to stomach.

The birthday table was a glum affair. The mood was grave, the bonhomie false, the gifts sparse and superfluous. Eva had commissioned a special portrait of herself in an ornate silver frame. (What can Hitler have done with all the pictures she gave him? He couldn't display them openly on his desk let alone on the wall, although Geli's portrait had hung in his bedroom in the Reichskanzlei. She could be shown but Eva had to be hidden.) Despite Eva's attempts at gaiety the mood was heavy, Hitler himself dispirited and exhausted. The failed assassination attempt of July 1944 had permanently weakened his limbs while overwork, disappointment, anger at the superiority of the Allied forces – which could no longer be denied, since they were battering at his very gates – made him look far older than the fifty-six years he was meant to be celebrating. The rest of the party soon moved upstairs to larger rooms in the new Reichskanzlei, making merry against the ceaseless howl and whine of air-raid warnings. Eva left them to their revelry and returned

31. Ibid., pp. 179–80.

to the bunker to drink tea alone with Hitler in his small study and reminisce about former, happier, birthdays.

The *Führer* finally went to bed at 5 a.m. and rose next morning later than usual, at 2 p.m. Shaved and dressed in his habitual uniform he slowly mounted the steps that led to the Reichskanzlei park. He was photographed for the last time in his life, greeting some war-weary soldiers and twenty Hitler Youth recruits assembled to receive the Iron Cross for exceptional bravery – young teenagers white faced with tiredness. Hitler, his left hand trembling convulsively behind his back but making an effort to smile, is seen pinching the cheek of one blond lad who gazes back at him with an enigmatic expression – awe, terror, accusation?[32] These boys honed in battle were very different from the sturdy, triumphal blockheads from Hitler Youth who'd raised their arms in a mass *Heil Hitler!* salute at Nuremberg seven years earlier. Now they were fighting to defend Berlin against Russian tanks and in place of the glory they had dreamed of their reward was bitter and often deadly. They died in their tens of thousands at the hands of the Soviets, before they ever had a chance to grow up. The men from the *Volkssturm* and boys from *Hitler Jugend* who answered the call to defend their *Führer* in the final days had believed General Wenck was on his way to relieve them. Another lie. Their commanders knew the truth; but still the exhausted boys – some as young as twelve – had continued to build makeshift barricades. Yet they fought bravely and their courage should be recognised, although their loyalty was to an evil cause.

It was at this exact time – same day, early afternoon – that a column of trucks from Neuengamme, the concentration camp outside Hamburg, delivered a consignment of Jews to an empty school building in the north of the city – twenty-two children aged between four and twelve, two women and twenty-six men. They had all been used in medical experiments and provided ghastly evidence of the atrocities the régime perpetrated on those it did not kill. Because of this they could not be allowed to live. All fifty were taken to the school's gymnasium and one by one they were hanged; the children, the adults, and four medical personnel who had accompanied them.[33] Mercy and compassion had died long ago.

---

32. This scene was filmed for the *Deutsche Wochenschau* – newsreel – providing most Germans with a last glimpse of their *Führer*.
33. Sereny, *Albert Speer: His Battle with Truth*, p. 515. Gitta Sereny learned about it from a TV documentary made in 1988 by the German film-maker Lea Rosh.

Hitler and his small group returned to the Reichskanzlei, where he lunched with the two older secretaries, Johanna Wolf and Christa Schröder. Christa had been his secretary for as long as he had been Chancellor – twelve years – while the steady, unflappable Johanna had been working for him ever since 1929. He knew, and they must have known, that they would never sit round a table together again.

Now there could be no more pretence. The defining moment had come. Everyone including the *Führer* knew the Soviet army was about to encircle the city, leaving only two escape routes which might be closed at any moment. Everyone was summoned to hear Hitler and people crowded into the so-called 'large conference room' in the *Führerbunker*: Göring, Dönitz, Keitel, Ribbentrop, Speer, Jodl, Himmler, Kaltenbrunner and Krebs, most of his personal staff, about a hundred other officials and denizens of the bunker – and Eva. Hitler made a speech that began by sketching a futile plan for the city's defence and ended by acknowledging that those who wanted to go should do so while there was still time. He hoped they would all reassemble at Obersalzberg and continue to conduct the war from there. He himself was still undecided about whether to leave Berlin, or stay. Speer recorded the moment: 'Hitler told them he wanted them to go, and go west. He recommended them all to go to southern Germany where they would be safe and many trips were organised – flights, car trips. The only thing Hitler did not contemplate was leaving himself. And of course most people wanted to save themselves and came to say goodbye.'[34]

On the evening of 20 April 1945, Speer, Himmler, Göring and Ley, along with dozens of others, left the bunker.

By now it was mid-afternoon. This was the release they had been waiting for – notably Göring, though his possessions and his wife and child had been safely stashed away in the Bavarian mountains for the past two months. He could hardly disguise his eagerness to get moving. Hitler announced that he would remain in Berlin to hearten his soldiers and when all hope was lost he would kill himself. Everyone urged him to come to Bavaria. Ribbentrop turned to Eva, begging her to get Hitler to abandon Berlin. It is significant that he thought her the one person who might succeed in persuading him. Eva refused. Traudl Junge records:

34. Interview with Gitta Sereny from *Adolf and Eva*, 3BMTV, roll 11.19.30.

He had a conversation with Eva Braun that she told me about later.

'Tell him you want to leave Berlin with him. That way you'd do Germany a great service.'

But Eva replied: 'I won't mention your suggestion to the *Führer*. He alone must decide. If he thinks it's right to stay in Berlin then I'll stay with him. If he goes, I'll go too.'[35]

Only a couple of hours were left for the troglodytes in the bunker before the route to the south was cut. Hurriedly, eighty or more people packed their bags and came to take leave of Hitler. He stared at each one in silence or mumbled something inarticulate. His very first supporters from the early twenties, men with three-digit party numbers, the old comrades-in-arms he had trusted and enriched, were deserting him. Although he had given them permission to go, secretly Hitler had believed they would stay. His adjutant Julius Schaub testified: 'Hitler was deeply disappointed – in fact shattered – that his Palatinate wanted to abandon him now. He simply nodded his head and left the men he had elevated to such power without saying a word.'[36]

Like rats emerging from a hole, furtively but with feverish haste, with bulging cases and sketchy goodbyes, Hitler's praetorian guard scuttled off to save their skins. A procession of cars and aircraft headed south, many men disguised in civilian clothes, hoping to evade arrest. Others had stripped the decorations from their jackets in case the invaders realised how important, how *very* important, their wearers had been. The popinjay Göring exchanged his dove-grey uniform encrusted with thick gold epaulettes for a less conspicuous one in plain khaki – 'like an American general' someone remarked sourly. In the course of the next three days, twenty planes left the two remaining Berlin airports that were still open, having been commandeered to fly the refugees to safety. Many chose to go to Berchtesgaden.

Johanna Wolf and Christa Schröder had been ordered by Hitler to leave. Fräulein Wolf had tears in her eyes, knowing she would never again see the man who had been her kindly, considerate boss for sixteen years. Albert Speer, once the beloved protégé, left at 4 a.m. next morning without saying goodbye and drove north to join his

35. Junge, *Bis Zur Letzten Stunde*, p. 178.
36. Testimony to Nuremberg, 27 October 1947, quoted in Anton Joachimsthaler, *The Last Days of Hitler* (London: Arms and Armour Press, 1996), p. 97.

family who had been evacuated to relative safety at Kappeln, near Hamburg, on an isolated peninsula extending into the Baltic. On his way through fog-bound Berlin, moved by a sudden impulse, he got out of the car and wrote on a wall: *Albert Speer 21 April 1945*.[37] The desire to leave one's mark or simply a record for history: the universal egoism that says, '*I was here*'?

Hitler was deeply disillusioned by the departure of the very people who, less than twenty-four hours earlier, had uttered vows of loyalty which, blinded by their flattery, he had believed. A few of his intimates – faithful adjutants, the two younger secretaries, his cook Fräulein Manziarly – joined him and Eva for a *schnapps* before he took an early supper, after which he retired alone to bed.

What happened next was typical of Eva's unconquerable spirit – or her essential shallowness, depending how you care to interpret it. Traudl Junge recalls that after Hitler had retired Eva organised, of all things, an impromptu party.

Eva Braun wanted to numb the fear that had awoken in her heart. She wanted to celebrate once again, even when there was nothing left to celebrate, she wanted to dance, to drink, to forget . . . She carried off anyone she met, all who crossed her path, sweeping them away with her up to Hitler's old living room on the first floor, which was still intact although by now the good furniture was down in the bunker. Even Bormann and fat Dr Morell came along. Someone produced an old gramophone from somewhere with a single record: 'Blood Red Roses Speak to You of Happiness'.[38] Eva Braun wanted to dance! Suddenly she dragged us all, no matter whom, after her into a giddy whirl, like someone who's already felt the first chilly draught of death. We drank champagne and laughed shrilly and I laughed too, because I'd rather that than cry. In the middle of all this the company was briefly silenced by an explosion, a phone call, another desperate message, but nobody spoke of war or battle or death. This was a party given by ghosts. And throughout, roses promised happiness.[39]

37. Sereny, *Albert Speer: His Battle with Truth*, p. 514.
38. *Blutrote Rosen erzählen Dir vom Glück*.
39. Junge, *Bis Zur Letzten Stunde*, p. 160.

Traudl found it horrible and took herself off to bed but the others danced far into the night, the ever-repeated 'Blood Red Roses' blaring from a gramophone placed on a table that Speer had designed, the only decent piece of furniture left.

Of all the extraordinary scenes in Eva Braun's life, this was among the most extraordinary. A few miles away the Russians were advancing, looting, raping and killing without scruple. By 20 April the army was on the outskirts of Berlin itself. And at the heart of this ravaged and besieged city the very people whose ideology had created the Third Reich were *celebrating*, drinking champagne, shouting, singing and laughing with hysterical abandon. If ever there were a *danse macabre* this was it. As in all bacchanalia, the singing and dancing degenerated into orgy. Women – not, of course, Eva, who was horrified by the scene – were shoved up against the walls, their skirts yanked above their thighs, some kissing and groping, a few copulating on the floor. The moral degeneracy of old lechers like Morell, Hoffmann and Bormann was exposed for all to see. Eva Braun too slipped away. The party raged into the small hours until the sound of artillery fire drove everyone down below to shelter in the bunker.

At 9.30 on the morning of 21 April an even more intensive artillery bombardment of Berlin was launched just a few hours after the night-time air raid had ended. Otto Günsche,[40] Hitler's SS adjutant, reported that Hitler emerged angrily from his bedroom shouting, 'What's going on? Where's this firing coming from?'

It had to be explained to him by General Burgdorf that the centre of the city was under enemy fire.

'Are the Russians so near?'[41] Hitler asked incredulously.

On the evening of 22 April the Goebbels family arrived in the bunker.[42]

22 April was a Sunday. The sun shone radiantly, that clear spring sunshine that coaxes forth new life and growth, but few Berliners ventured out of doors to parade along the Kurfürstendamm[43] or play

---

40. As personal adjutant and SS captain, Günsche was near Hitler at the assassination attempt in the *Wolfsschanze*, 20 July 1944. After this he was an adjutant constantly assigned to the *Führer*'s headquarters.
41. Beevor, *Berlin: The Downfall 1945*, p. 262.
42. Erna Flegel, interviewed by US officer Richard Helms, puts the date at 20 April.
43. Berlin's main boulevard.

with their children in what had once been the parks. Such activities had become unimaginable. In the bunker there was no sense of time, season or weather. People burrowed as if through tunnels from room to claustrophobic room, knowing the end could come at any moment, the brutish soldiery crashing in with guns and yells, to rape and kill. The bunker was emptying. The essential support staff, including the women closest to Hitler, remained, sleepwalking towards the inevitable. Only once did Eva disclose her true state of mind. Traudl Junge records:

> We had no normal feelings any more; we thought of nothing except death. Hitler and Eva, when they would die . . . when and how we would die. Outwardly Eva Braun displayed the same calm, almost cheerful demeanour. But once she came to me, took my hands and said in a hoarse, trembling voice:
> 'Frau Junge, I am so dreadfully afraid! If only it were all over!'
> Her eyes showed all the inner suffering that she had concealed until now.[44]

She wrote a last letter to her beloved friend Herta, in a very different tone from the one three days earlier:

> Dearest Hertalein,
> These are going to be my final lines and therefore the last sign of life from me. I cannot bring myself to write to Gretl so you will have to break it to her gently. I am going to send you my jewellery and ask you to share it out in accordance with my will, which is kept at Wasserburger Strasse. I hope it will help to keep you afloat for a while. Please leave the Berghof if you possibly can. If everything is coming to an end the place will be too dangerous for you.
> Here we are going to carry on fighting to the last, but I fear that the end is drawing nearer and nearer. I cannot tell you what I myself am suffering for the *Führer's* sake. Please forgive me if this letter is rather confused but I am surrounded by G's[45] six children and they are far from quiet. What more can I say? I

44. Junge, *Bis Zur Letzten Stunde*, p. 178.
45. i.e. Goebbels'.

cannot understand how it has all come to pass but it is impossible to continue believing in God!

The man is waiting to take the letter – all my love and best wishes to you, my faithful friend! Send my greetings to my parents – greet all my friends: I shall die as I have lived.

It is not hard for me. As you know.

Love and kisses to you all from

your

Eva.

Maybe everything will come good again but <u>he</u> has lost his faith and I am afraid we hope in vain.[46]

Eva had lost faith in God and Hitler had lost faith in victory. But she remained steadfast: '*I shall die as I have lived. It is not hard for me. As you know.*' What else was left to say, beyond vain hope and loving platitudes?

My mother hardly even had the consolation of letters. I remember her showing me one of *Tante* Lidy's notes, written on the inside of a smoothed-out paper bag. '*Gibt's kein Papier!*' my aunt had scribbled – there's no paper.

My mother was distracted with worry about her family in Hamburg, victims of a war she had never understood, but she clung to the familiarity of her daily chores – 'my routine' as she called it – cooking, setting out and washing up meals, polishing the furniture (including a baby Bechstein piano: almost the only thing she had brought from the Schröder home in Hamburg as a reminder of her youthful ambition to be a singer); making beds, doing the laundry by hand, darning and re-darning the opaque lisle stockings that did not flatter her elegant legs, eking out meals concocted from dried egg, potatoes, turnips and Spam,[47] giving me her milk and butter ration so that I'd grow up to be a big, strong girl (I did). But these privations were small compared with what her family endured as they scavenged the ruined streets of Hamburg in search of food, firewood, even paper.

---

46. Previously unpublished letter from Frank, *Eva Braun: Ein ungewöhnliches Frauenschicksal in geschichtlich bewegter Zeit*, pp. 286–7.
47. In those days Spam was a sort of compressed 'ham' made of otherwise unusable cuts of meat and used in sandwiches or pies; about as unpalatable as the commercial effluent that gushes through today's computers.

Details of the larger events in Germany, the troop movements, the advance on Berlin by the Russian army, were hazy to my mother, who could hardly make sense of a map. She knew little about what was going on – taking for granted that the news reports in the papers and on the BBC Home Service were biased and over-optimistic – and I knew nothing. Far more important to me, this was the week of my fifth birthday. I got one present from my parents: a miniature table about 3 inches long, for my doll's house, with two matching wooden chairs. I was not much of a child for dolls but I can see those three small objects as clearly as if they were here on the desk in front of me.

Later that Sunday 22 April at 3.30 in the afternoon Hitler held a final situation conference with the chiefs of the three armed services. He became agitated and then hysterical. He lost control, cursed, denounced his commanders (Keitel, Jodl, Krebs and Burgdorf) as unworthy incompetents, cowards and traitors, raved and screamed until he was exhausted; and finally conceded – on being told that the Russians were already within the city's northern perimeter – that it was futile to prolong the fighting. The tantrum over, he collapsed into his chair sobbing feebly and authorised a general exodus before retreating to his own quarters, leaving his audience dazed and shattered.

Next, the culminating incident of Eva's years with Hitler took place; a moment that, after years of pretence and concealment, proved he had come to love and value her. He summoned the two remaining secretaries, Traudl Junge and Gerda Christian, his personal diet cook, Constanze Manziarly, and Eva Braun. Frau Junge records what happened next:

Hitler's face had lost all expression, his eyes were blank. He looked like a death mask. He said: 'Go and get ready at once. In an hour's time a plane will leave to take you south. All is lost, hopelessly lost.' ['*Es ist alles verloren, hoffnungslos verloren.*']

Eva Braun was the first to shake off her paralysis. She went over to Hitler – whose hand was already on the handle of the door – took both his hands in hers and said with a comforting smile as if talking to a sad child, 'Come on, you know I'm staying with you. I won't let you send me away.'

Then Hitler's eyes began to light up and he did something that no one, not even his most trusted friends and staff, had ever seen: he kissed Eva Braun on the mouth.

He kissed Eva Braun on the mouth. Not the usual formal kiss on her hand, his lips hovering just above the skin; not a token kiss or a social kiss but a real kiss, full on the mouth. He declared his love by showing the women – before whom he had kept up the façade for ten years – that she was his chosen partner, his mistress, his *Geliebte* (beloved). He overcame his deepest inhibitions with an unambiguous public gesture that acknowledged and honoured her. *This* was her triumph; the crowning event of her life.

> Then Hitler said, 'I can hardly bear to say it but it comes of its own accord: I don't want to stay and die here but I have no choice.'
> Frau Christian and I said almost simultaneously, 'We're staying too!'
> Hitler looked at us for a moment: 'I beg of you, go!' but we shook our heads. He gave us his hand: 'I wish my generals were as brave as you are!'
> Even Fräulein Manziarly, who had no more duties to perform, didn't want to leave Berlin.[48]

The four women left the room to write to their friends and families, assign their possessions, make their wills and leave their clothes and anything they couldn't dispose of neat and tidy for the barbarians. Hitler gave most of the remaining women in the bunker permission to leave and promised them transport out of Berlin, an offer that many accepted. With nothing left to do, he turned his attention to the dogs. He sat in the corridor, one of Blondi's puppies squirming in his lap, watching people come and go. The staff got on with their duties, calmly and silently carrying out his instructions. The feasting and the bawdy were over.

That evening the first of the élite Russian tank brigades reached the southern edge of the city. By now the cityscape through which they fought their way street by street was tumbled, blackened and scarred. Buildings had been reduced to rubble, some intact as far as the first or second floor, gaping rooms tottering above them, or pillars of brick. Burned-out cars like dead black beetles lined the streets. A thick cloud of ash and dust deposited a grey bloom over everything. By day the sound of intermittent gunfire menaced those who crept out in search of food or to collect water from the standpipes; by night the sinister whizz, thump

48. Junge, *Until the Final Hour*, p. 163. Fräulein Manziarly killed herself by taking cyanide on 2 May 1945. She was twenty-five.

and fireburst of bombs dropping out of the sky menaced everybody.

The artillery was now very near – only 8 miles away and closing in fast – and the shelling practically continuous. The *Führerbunker* seemed a safer haven than the Goebbels family's quarters above ground in the Reichskanzlei. Hitler ordered Josef and Magda Goebbels to move underground with their six children aged between twelve and five. On the evening of 22 April they took over the suite of four rooms formerly used by Dr Morell in the smaller bunker on the upper level. Helga, Hilde, Helmut, Holde, Hedda and Heide were unaware of their fate and everyone did their best to make sure they remained so, though Helga, the eldest at twelve, obviously suspected something and was disturbed and unhappy. To the smaller ones it meant that *Mutti* and *Vati*, dear *Onkel* Adolf and *Tante* Eva were always on hand to play with them. They were thrilled with Blondi's three-week-old puppies – 'the sausages', as Eva called them. 'The Goebbels children were the one bright spot in the shadowy life of the bunker. They talked about "being in the cave" with *Onkel Führer* and everyone entered into the game of making the time as pleasant as possible for them.'[49] The six beautiful and beautifully mannered children moved in orderly procession through the crowded passageways, bringing delight and pity to everyone who saw them. Their parents had ordained that they should not live on in a defeated Germany, robbed of the destiny their blondness conferred. Magda, still a fanatical Nazi, declared, 'I would rather have my children die than live in disgrace, jeered at. They have no place in Germany as it will be after the war.'

The hardest thing left for Eva to do, apart from dying, was to compose a final letter to her heavily pregnant sister. She had told Herta the previous day that she could not bring herself to write, yet she knew it had to be done. She expressed herself carefully, not understating the gravity of the situation but trying not to alarm the vulnerable Gretl. (This letter did arrive, remarkably promptly, four days later on 27 April.)

Berlin 23 IV 45

My darling little sister,

I am sorry for you, to be getting a letter like this from me! But there is no other way. Any day now, any hour, it may all be over, so I have to take this final opportunity to tell you what still needs to be done. In the first place: Hermann [Gretl's husband] is not here

---

49. Testimony of Hanna Reitsch (see below, note 8, p. 437).

any longer! He went off to Nauen in order to organise his battalion or something like that. I am absolutely convinced that you will see him again: he is sure to fight his way through, perhaps to carry on the resistance in Bavaria at least for a little while. The *Führer* himself has lost all faith in a successful outcome. <u>All of us here, including myself, will carry on hoping as long as we live.</u> Hold your heads up high and do not despair! There is still hope. <u>But it also goes without saying that we will not allow ourselves to be captured alive.</u>

My faithful Liesl [Anneliese, her personal maid] will not leave me. I have suggested it so many times. I would really like to give her my gold watch. Unfortunately I left it to Miezi [a friend] in my will. Perhaps you could give Miezi some other equally valuable piece of my jewellery instead. I am sure you will do the right thing. Apart from that I would like to carry on wearing the gold bracelet with the green stone right to the end. I will ask for it to be removed after that, and then you must always wear it just as I always have. It too has been left to Miezi in my will. So please deal with it as above. Unfortunately my diamond watch is being repaired – I will give you the address at the end of this letter. With any luck you should still be able to get it back. It's for you: you have always wanted one for yourself. The diamond bracelet and topaz pendant are yours as well – they were the Führer's present for my last birthday. I do hope that these wishes of mine will be observed.

In addition I must beg you to do the following: destroy all my private correspondence, especially the business stuff. I do not want any bills from that Heise woman [Eva's dressmaker] to be found under any circumstances. Also please destroy the enve-lope addressed to the *Führer*,[50] which is in the safe in the bunker. Please do not read it! As for the *Führer*'s letters and the drafts of my answers (in a blue leather notebook): please wrap them in a waterproof package and bury them. Do not destroy them please![51] There are some outstanding bills from the Heise

50. Presumably a farewell note she had written in case something happened to her and she died before him; or maybe a declaration of love; we cannot know, except that it was obviously deeply private.
51. Werner Maser, an assiduous collector of written memorabilia from Hitler and those closest to him, confirms that Ilse Braun told him on 31 October 1972 that all the letters between Eva and Hitler had been 'lost'. Perhaps they found their way with Gutierrez to New Mexico, as David Irving has claimed, but, if they did, he died without revealing their whereabouts.

company, and it is just possible that some more invoices are on their way, but they will not come to more than RM 1,500. I have no idea what you should do with the films and photograph albums. In any case, please wait till the last moment before destroying everything, except for the business and private letters and the envelope to the Führer, which you can burn at once. I am also sending along some food and tobacco with this letter. Please give some of the coffee to Linders and Kathl; also please give them some of the tinned food from my cellar. The cigarettes in Munich belong to Mandi, and so do those in the suitcase. The tobacco is for Papa, the chocolate for *Mutti*. There's some more chocolate and tobacco on the Berghof: help yourselves to all of it. I cannot think of anything else. They have just started saying that things are improving. Yesterday General Burgdorf put our chances at 10 per cent but now he has gone up to 50 per cent. There! Perhaps everything will turn out well in the end!

Did Arndt arrive with the letter and the suitcase? [Wilhelm Arndt had taken a plane on 22 April but it was shot down and there were no survivors.] The word here was that the plane did not get through on time. Let's hope that Morell landed safely at your place with my jewellery. It would be awful if something had happened. I shall write to *Mutti* and Herta and Georg first thing tomorrow if I can.

But enough for today.

Now my dear little sister I wish you lots and lots of happiness. And don't forget, you're sure to see Hermann again!

With my fondest good wishes and a kiss,

I am

Your sister,

Eva

PS I have just spoken with the *Führer*. He seems to have a more optimistic view of the future than he did yesterday. The address of the watchmaker is: SS-Unterscharführer Stegemann, SS Lager Oranienburg, evacuated to Kyritz.[52]

---

52. Translated by Christiane Gehron and taken from Johannes Frank, *Eva Braun: Ein ungewöhnliches Frauenshicksal in geschichtlich bewegter Zeit*, pp. 288–9. NARA has a slightly different version quoted by the Special Investigation Squad CIC Detachment 970, discovered by their agents and circulated by 2nd Lieutenant Henry P. Hoffshot, Jr from APO 757.

This was Eva's last recorded communication with the outside world. The phone lines were cut, the roads blocked, and no sane pilot would risk flying in or out of Berlin. The letter contains not a word of regret or self-pity. Eva's thoughts were entirely for her sister, her parents, her friends and her faithful maid.

On 22 April, as the Goebbels were installing themselves, Baron Freytag von Loringhoven – *aide-de-camp* to General Krebs and one of only three survivors from the last days in the bunker still alive at the time of writing[53] – arrived in the bunker as Russian troops were beginning their final assault on Berlin. The *Führer*, knowing that all was lost but determined to fight to the very end, asked Krebs to stay on in Berlin as his chief military adviser. Von Loringhoven admits, 'I thought, "This is my death sentence."' Arrangements were being made for the last of the women to leave the bunker and he recalled: 'I shall never forget how Morell begged, on 22 and 23 April. He sat there like a fat sack of potatoes and begged to fly out. And he did.'[54] In answer to Morell's request, Hitler evidently snapped at him, 'Take off that uniform and go back to being the doctor of the Kurfürstendamm!'[55]

On 23 April Dr Morell left the bunker, as did Julius Schaub, who had been Hitler's senior adjutant for twenty years; nearly all the remaining women, several stenographers, and many others.

Morell, grunting with relief on the road south, must have congratulated himself on his escape. Like all con men, he was a natural survivor.[56]

53. May 2005. The other two are Rochus Misch, the telephone operator, and the nurse, Erna Flegel.
54. From the *Observer*, 27 March 2005: interview by Alex Duval Smith with Baron Freytag von Loringhoven about his newly published book *Dans le Bunker de Hitler* published in France.
55. According to David Irving (see Introduction to *The Secret Diaries of Hitler's Doctor*). Hitler was referring to Morell's previous career as a venereal specialist, since in the Kurfürstendamm, Berlin's main boulevard, men could pick up prostitutes.
56. Not for much longer. Morell was cross-examined, found guilty and hanged after the Nuremberg Trials in 1948.

Chapter Twenty-eight

Hitler's Last Stand

On 23 April an insolent telegram was despatched from Berchtesgaden. It came from Göring, now safely ensconced beyond Hitler's orbit, proposing that since the *Führer* was unable, in the circumstances, to conduct the war from Berlin, he himself should 'take over the leadership of the Reich with all powers immediately. [. . .] If no reply is received by ten o'clock tonight, I shall take it for granted that you have lost your freedom of action and shall consider the conditions of your decree [an agreement of April 1941 to hand over to Göring under certain circumstances] as fulfilled.' When it emerged that Göring had also made secret approaches to the enemy, Hitler's rage was terrible. He railed against his deputy – the swine whose sty he had stuffed with luxury – stripped him of all his decorations and official responsibilities and ordered his arrest. He announced that Göring was no longer *Oberfehlshaber* in charge of the Luftwaffe and appointed Lt-General Ritter von Greim to the post. It was a bitter disillusionment to find that his chief henchman had not, as he believed, revered his genius and leadership but had merely craved the bombast of power and the magnificent possessions that came with it.

On 24 April Speer came back to the bunker, leaving again after eight hours.

Eva Braun clung to her belief that Albert Speer, Hitler's favourite and her good friend, would join them in the bunker. 'I know him; I'm sure he'll come,' she reassured Hitler. 'He's your friend, a real friend; he wouldn't stay away.'[1] On 24 April he did return. Speer was flown to Gatow – the

1. This quotation, and the following five, is taken from Sereny, *Albert Speer: His Battle with Truth*, pp. 523–32.

only Berlin aerodrome still open for traffic – and made his way to the bunker, where he was met with astonishment and joy. More than forty years later he said, 'Although I had announced my imminent arrival by phone, Hitler's adjutants, whom I found drinking upstairs in his Chancellery apartment, appeared quite startled to see me.' Traudl Junge confirmed:

> We were amazed to see Speer. There didn't seem to be any reason for his coming back but we thought it was wonderful of him. And Eva Braun, with whom I had by that time become rather friendly, was really over the moon that he came, just as she had predicted. Everybody knew how much she liked him; he'd really been her only friend among the high-ups for years. But more than that, she was so happy for Hitler.

That evening Speer and Hitler talked for hours and Speer admitted for the first time that he had deliberately flouted Hitler's orders to destroy Germany, leaving nothing but 'scorched earth' in case of an Allied victory, but Hitler evidently forgave him this defiance. His one-time protégé later recalled:

> The *Führer* looked very old, very tired but actually very calm, resigned it seemed to me, ready for the end. [. . .] Because now, everything he said was imbued with that feeling, his planned suicide, and he assured me that he felt no fear of it but was glad to die. [. . .] He went into all the details: that Eva Braun had decided to die with him, that he would shoot his dog Blondi before he died.

(In fact it was Dr Stumpfegger who killed Blondi by poisoning her. Hitler was worried that the suicide pills Himmler had given him might be out of date and therefore ineffectual. He used Blondi as his 'poison-taster' to make sure they would work. The man who was prepared to let Eva Braun die with him – perhaps even to put the cyanide pill between her lips himself – could not bring himself to kill his dog. 'Hitler was very fond of the dog and took her death very much to heart,' Erna Flegel noted. Sentimentality, the Germans' besetting vice, enabled him to isolate his feelings from moral scruples.)

Speer stayed in the bunker for eight hours attending a situation conference. When it was over he wanted to say a last goodbye to

Magda Goebbels. He had always admired her intelligence and stead-fastness and hoped to persuade her not to die, let alone kill her six children for Hitler's sake, but to get out of Berlin while she still could. His secretary recalled after the war, 'Speer had got to know her very well; [. . .] he was her confidant then, as he was and would be to the end for Eva Braun.'[2] She was prostrate in bed with an angina attack, pale, weeping. Speer was furious when her husband intruded, allowing them no privacy for their final parting. 'It was he, that monster,' he exploded, 'who, for the sake of appearing heroic to posterity, had forced this appalling decision [to kill their children] upon her. And then he wouldn't even allow her a few moments alone with me. Disgusting.' There had never been anything in the least improper between them but Speer respected Magda's intellect and her outward dignity in the face of her husband's flagrant infidelities. She was one of the very few up at the Berghof whom he would have considered his equal.

Later that evening at around midnight an orderly came to tell Speer that he was invited to visit Eva. For more than two hours they chatted and gossiped, recalling the good times, the skiing holidays, long walks through the mountains and forests around Obersalzberg. They talked without recriminations or sentimentality; two old friends who trusted and admired one another, chatting affectionately for the last time. It says a good deal for her intelligence as well as her integrity that Speer should have liked her so much. He must have recognised – as clowns and lechers like Bormann and Göring did not – that she was entirely sincere in her love for Hitler. Speer, who in his own way had also been infatuated with the *Führer*, if not entirely disinterestedly, recognised and respected this. In his memoirs he wrote: 'She was the only candidate for death in the bunker who displayed an admirable and superior composure.'[3]

Eva ordered Moët et Chandon and cakes for them both. (She was the only person, Speer commented, who realised that, having eaten nothing all day, he must be hungry, and this thoughtfulness was typical of her.) She told him yet again how glad she was that he had come: *der Führer* had begun to think that he too was against him. She evidently assumed that Speer was planning to stay and die with Hitler.

She said to me, [Speer remembered thirty years on], 'You came. I told him you would. And that proved that you are with him.'

2. Ibid., p. 508.
3. Speer, *Inside the Third Reich*, p. 646.

I didn't know what to say, to her of all people, but I did tell her that I was not staying but leaving a bit later that night. She said, very calmly, that of course I must.

This young woman, he told his biographer, was the only person in the bunker to show dignity, what he called 'almost a kind of gay serenity. And then she put her hand on my arm, just for a moment, and said she was really happy to be where she was and that she was not afraid. Oh, that girl . . .'

At about 3 a.m. an orderly came to report that Hitler was up again and Speer and Eva said goodbye. 'She wished me luck and sent greetings to my wife. It was extraordinary. On the face of it, a simple Munich girl, a nobody . . . and yet she was a most remarkable woman. And Hitler had known this. He never said it; I don't think he often made her feel it, but he had sensed it . . .'

Hitler offered Speer a briefer, colder farewell. 'Oh, you are leaving. Good. Well, goodbye.' No good wishes, no thanks, no greetings. This was the man whose beloved friend and confidant Speer had been for the past eleven years, for whom he would spend the next twenty in Spandau prison, to be released in 1966 at the age of sixty-one, the best years of his working life wasted.[4] Asked why he'd returned to visit Hitler that last time, Speer told the Nuremberg Trial, 'I felt that it was an obligation not to run away like a coward but to face up to it once more.'[5] He told Gitta Sereny a rather different story, explaining that when the others took their leave of Hitler on the 21st, he himself had not said goodbye. 'I could never explain this to myself later,' he said. 'It must be that I knew – though certainly not consciously, that I would see him again. Though it could of course also have been that

4. Note that David Irving claims 'It was symptomatic of Speer's truthfulness to history that while he was in Spandau he paid for the entire wartime diaries of his office (*Dienststelle*) to be retyped omitting the more unfortunate passages, and donated these faked documents to the Bundesarchiv in Koblenz. My comparison of the 1943 volume, housed in the original in British Cabinet Office archives, with the Bundesarchiv copy made this plain, and Matthias Schmidt also reveals the forgery.' Speer outlived all his colleagues and told the story of his relationship with Hitler with missionary zeal, never failing to express remorse and penitence for having been so misled. His sincerity has recently come into question. Close as he was to Hitler, he could not have failed to know exactly what was going on and, had he exercised his usual subtlety, might in some small way have moderated Hitler's obsessional determination to destroy the Jews.
5. Interrogation of Albert Speer at Nuremberg on 21 June 1946.

I couldn't bear to say goodbye to him . . . like that' – meaning publicly. Their bond had not been like the relationship Hitler had with any other colleague. It was stronger, more intense, more private. Rather than a father/son relationship, it had almost been a platonic love affair.

All his staff except those who were indispensable were told by Hitler to escape by any means they could find. He urged Magda Goebbels to leave with her children while it was still possible but she refused. Helga must have understood what was happening – the younger children, thankfully, did not – and begged to be allowed to go, saying she didn't want to die.

In the last few days Hitler's right eye had begun to hurt intensely and Günsche had to administer cocaine drops to numb the pain. Hitler compared himself to Frederick the Great, who lost his teeth because of the stress of fighting the Seven Years War. Erna Flegel, having listed the signs of his physical decline, added: 'When he was in the room he filled it entirely with his personality – you saw only him. The fascinating thing about him was his eyes: up to the end, it was impossible to turn away from his eyes.' Despite his marked disintegration, Hitler's charisma could still exert a pull. However unreasonable, *impossible*, his commands the most loyal of his supporters would still obey.

On 25 April, unnoticed at the time, Fegelein left the bunker. On 26 April, Lt.-Gen Ritter von Greim and Hanna Reitsch arrived, having been summoned by Hitler in spite of the near-impossibility of flying into Berlin.

On 24 April he summoned Ritter von Greim from Munich to receive in person his promotion to head of the Luftwaffe. The skies above Germany were buzzing with enemy aircraft like a swarm of hornets. The Feldwebel pilot who had also flown Speer to Hitler's side was at the controls for most of the way. The attempt was suicidally dangerous and the plane was attacked by heavy fire as it approached Berlin, disabling the pilot and badly wounding von Greim in the foot. Yet on the afternoon of 26 April Hanna Reitsch, steering from behind over von Greim's shoulders and coming in at the level of the treetops, contrived to land safely within a few hundred yards of the Reichskanzlei. Von Greim said later: 'She was my good angel. She piloted me in marvellously.'[6]

6. Testimony of Erna Flegel, interrogated 30 November 1945 by Richard Helms Lt.-Commander USNR, APO 742, now held at NARA, RG 226, Box 465.

Von Greim, the new commander-in-chief, had been seriously wounded in the foot by the enemy attack. The wound turned septic and he was obliged to wait for three days while Hanna took care of him, helped by the nurse, Erna Flegel, before he was fit to encounter the *Führer*. Hitler's morale was greatly lifted by this demonstration of loyalty and courage and when von Greim was eventually brought to his side on a stretcher the *Führer* expressed deep gratitude.

Later that same evening, 26 April, the *Führer* summoned Reitsch to his room. Hanna – the world's first female test pilot[7] – had always hero-worshipped Hitler. Now she watched him with pity and despair.

It was pathetic to watch a man's complete mental and physical deterioration, a tragi-comedy of frustration, futility and uselessness, a man running blindly from wall to wall in his last retreat, waving papers that fluttered like leaves in his trembling hands or moving buttons across a table to represent armies that no longer existed, impotently playing at his table-top war.

He had no more to offer her, except the death she had so often risked for his sake.

He said in a feeble voice,

'Hanna, you belong to those who will die with me. Each one has a phial of poison.'

He handed her two; one for herself and one for von Greim.

'I do not wish one of us to fall to the Russians alive, nor do I wish them to find our bodies. Eva and I will be burned.'

Hanna sank to her chair in tears, realising for the first time that the Nazi cause was lost and Hitler knew it.

7. Hanna Reitsch was born in Hirschberg, Silesia, on 29 March 1912 (seven weeks after Eva and three weeks after my mother), and abandoned a medical career to become a test pilot. She flew many of Germany's latest aircraft designs and eventually became Adolf Hitler's favourite pilot. She had many accidents and was badly injured several times, but survived the war. She was held for eighteen months by the American military after the war, interrogated and then released. She died aged sixty-seven of a massive heart attack. (Source: http://en.wikipedia.org/wiki/Hanna_Reitsch)

After the war Hanna Reitsch was questioned by the Americans. Her testimony, stored in NARA Archives, has been cited by few historians, despite its sober and convincing detail. Her account of those final days was described by her interrogator as 'probably as accurate as will be obtained. She was one of the last, if not *the* last, of the people to get out of the bunker alive and her information is evaluated as reliable.'[8] In reading her verdict on Eva it should also be borne in mind that Hanna, as well as being a most loyal Nazi, had long been in love with Hitler and could hardly fail to have been jealous of his – as she would have seen it – unworthy partner. The two women could not have been more different.

Hanna said of Eva:

> She remained true to her role as the 'showpiece' in the *Führer*'s circle. Most of her time was occupied in changing her clothes, doing her nails and so on. In Hitler's presence she was always charming and thought only of his comfort but the moment he was out of earshot she would rave about the ungrateful swine who had deserted him and accepted the prospect of dying with the *Führer* quite matter-of-factly.

At the same time she described Eva's mentality as shallow and thought she had no control or influence over Adolf Hitler, dismissing as fantastic the claim that they had ever had children. She gives a scathing vignette of Josef Goebbels, self-deluding to the last:

> He was insanely angry about Göring's treachery and strode about his small but luxurious quarters uttering vile accusations against him. This ranting and raving was made even more grotesque by Goebbels' jerky up-and-down hobbling walk. 'We are teaching the world how men die for their honour. We shall be an eternal example to all Germans that will blaze as a holy thing from the pages of history.'

Hanna, a young woman whose own courage and fidelity needed no trumpeting, was contemptuous of Josef Goebbels and admired his wife

8. From Hanna Reitsch's interrogation on 8 October 1945 by the Air Division at headquarters, US Forces in Austria; Air Interrogation Unit (USDIC) in the files at NARA, Box 332.

far more: 'She was a very brave woman whose control, while mostly strong, broke down from time to time into spasms of pitiful weeping. Her main concern was her children, with whom she was always cheerful. She represented the epitome of Nazi indoctrination. It was in recognition of this that Hitler presented her with his personal gold Party insignia.' Frau Goebbels was deeply moved by this gesture and wore the brooch constantly in the days before her death. Afterwards it was found still pinned to her dress. For the time being she lay on her bed in a state of nervous collapse, letting the cooks and secretaries take care of her children, making sure they ate at regular hours and got enough rest. When she did leave her bed she burst into tears at the sight of them. Traudl Junge preserved a small, touching moment: 'That evening Hanna Reitsch and Eva Braun put the Goebbels children to bed. Hanna sang a three-part round with them, the children covering their ears [this is the detail that brings the scene to life] so as not to lose their own part. Then they all wished each other a cheerful good night and fell asleep at last.'[9]

Death was now the subject of every briefing and every conversation, a sickly miasma in the air around them. More than ever, death was all they talked about, weighing up the best (fastest, least painful) way to commit suicide. Their favourite pastime and the sole topic of conversation in the bunker was discussing methods of suicide.

> They would get together for a smoke and argue whether you should shoot into the mouth or the temple. Somebody else would suggest a new poison that killed instantly. The Reichs Chancellery had one of the best wine cellars in the country, in order to provide for receptions. Everybody was drinking these exquisite wines and cognacs. Few people paid attention to the *Führer*, who rarely left his rooms. He was cruel and egocentric, but not mad. He saw himself as a Wagnerian hero, straight out of *Ring of the Nibelung*.

The chances of making it to freedom grew slimmer every day. Nobody said, 'Just like the Jews.' No one down there could have considered it, although even at this late hour thousands, *tens* of thousands, of Jews were still being hurried to extermination camps to be murdered. Within days, perhaps hours, the bunker-dwellers too would die, some

9. Junge, *Bis Zur Letzten Stunde*, pp. 174–5 (translated by the author).

of them horribly. Anyone whose instinct for survival drove them to attempt an escape above ground would be branded a traitor by their own side and shot, or captured by the enemy, tortured or raped and then shot. Yet hope is the last comfort of the doomed, and most people – especially the young and strong and fit – secretly hoped to get home again. They discovered the deep camaraderie that hostages develop in extreme situations. According to Erna Flegel:

> In the end we were like a big family experiencing a common fate in an atmosphere of truly comradely association. The terrific dynamics of fate which were unrolling held sway over us. We were Germany; we were living through the end of the Third Reich and of the war, having hoped to the end for a favourable and tolerable outcome. Everything petty and external had fallen away.[10]

Why were so many people prepared to die for Hitler? Not only those close to him – some of whom seemed, bizarrely, to prefer death to hurting his feelings, as shown by the number who changed their minds once he himself was dead[11] – but also the seven million Germans, military and civilian, who were killed in battle, in air raids, or died of wounds, cold and near-starvation. That *Hitler* – the down-and-out from Vienna who had tried to evade conscription – should become the driving force that inspired these and many more deaths, anaesthetising the Germans' moral sense so that they ignored, condoned or denied the deaths of six million Jews and millions more 'racial undesirables' is a puzzle that has baffled historians for sixty years. Yes, he took the chaos of Weimar and the shame of the Treaty of Versailles

---

10. See footnote 8.

11. A number, however, were unable to continue life without him. At the end, very many of his closest associates committed suicide: the Goebbels family, Göring (just before he was to be hanged), Himmler, when caught by the Allies; the two generals in the bunker, Burgdorf – who conducted the surrender negotiations with the US – and Krebs; SS Captain Schedle and *BrigadFührer* Albrecht, one of his young officers, 24-year old SS Lieutenant Stehr, all shot themselves after the escapees from the bunker had left. General Ritter von Greim killed himself a month later, as did Hanna Reitsch's whole family immediately after Hitler's death. Ambassador Hewel, newly married, managed to get out of Berlin but then killed himself. Hitler's valet, Linge, tried to but was stopped by Rochus Misch; General Mohnke tried but Otto Günsche stopped him.

and transformed Germany into a country run according to its own tenets of order and efficiency. Yes, he came to power at a time of economic disaster that his policies did much to alleviate; yes, he was without question a mesmerising orator who could hold an audience in thrall; he understood the madness of crowds and how to orchestrate spectacles that would rouse them to a frenzy. But although he basked in mass adulation he was emotionally cold and hated touching strangers or being touched by them. He saw the German people as a mass, never as individuals. A hopeless judge of character, he put his trust in self-serving charlatans like Dr Morell or Göring, with his ludicrous racial theories and shameless greed, and allowed the Berghof to be administered by the fawning, scheming Bormann. Undemonstrative with his friends, only Blondi prompted his uninhibited, hands-on affection. Apart from the famous blue eyes he was unprepossessing – stocky and swarthy rather than tall, blond and Aryan in appearance. His intelligence was that of the auto-didact, elaborately detailed but without any sense of proportion or knowledge of countries, cultures or philosophy except those that interested *him*. His inner circle found him trite, his monologues tediously repetitive. In spite of all this he was adored by millions as the inspired prophet and leader of the new Germany. And Eva loved him from the day they met.

Adolf Hitler possessed charisma, which is charm multiplied by a hundred, unmistakable when you meet it; a combination of intense energy and a seemingly approving, single-minded attention focused on the speaker. Although the vast majority of Germans never met him in person, he somehow managed to embody their dreams and fantasies. He could justify and sanitise his creed with apparently reasonable facts and figures, bolstered by the brilliance of Goebbels' propaganda machine. He spoke to their deepest, unexpressed emotions and prejudices – and *how* he spoke! That was his diabolic genius.

None of this explains why Eva fell for him, still less why she died for him, since she knew and cared nothing for politics. At seventeen, as she was when they first met, she was vain, gullible and easily impressed. The flattery of an older man, especially to a girl who could never seem to please her father, turned her head. His charm and gallantry, the little gifts and favours he offered, seemed in her naïveté to show that he was sincerely interested in her. The seducer's tactic of blowing hot and cold kept her fixated on him – emotional pain has never deterred young girls. But why – assuming that their physical affair began in 1932 when she was twenty – should she have remained in thrall to him for the next thirteen years? It must have been in response to his morbid obsession with death. Dracula, the ultimate romantic anti-hero, has always had a strong erotic attraction for young girls. Brainwashing a young woman to shoot herself through the neck or crunch a poison ampoule between her teeth are the methods used by the modern vampire.

Eva was much possessed by death.[12] Her first childhood impressions, absorbed in the crucial years before her seventh birthday, were simple songs and fearful stories about cruelty and dying; hideous old women from Grimm's fairy tales, derived from the original witches of *Walpurgisnacht*, who plotted with wolves (wolves!) to kill little girls – like the witch in *Hansel and Gretel*, who is pushed into a boiling cauldron. Her girlhood was darkened by the mass slaughter of the First World War that put maimed and crippled men on show on the streets of Munich exposing their deformities at the children's event of the year, the Christmas Fair. She was fifteen when her beloved grandmother Josefa Kronburger, died: the *Oma* who had been the guiding spirit of her tangled early years. The convent filled her mind with lurid scenes of punishment, death and hellfire. Wagner – how many times had Hitler taken her to see *Götterdämmerung*? – promised the same immolation, death as a reward this time. Throughout her life, the threat of death was as real and ever-present to Eva Braun as sexual abuse or abduction has become for children today. It was a prospect she lived with and believed to be her fate. Hitler was the Mephistopheles who promised it, wooing her (as he had wooed other young girls) towards suicide. That too was his diabolic genius.

On the night of 26 April a heavy barrage fell on the Reichskanzlei, filling the bunker with the thump of shells and the crash of falling

12. With a bow to T.S. Eliot for his *Whispers of Immortality*:
Webster was much possessed by death
And saw the skull beneath the skin;
And breastless creatures under ground
Leaned backward with a lipless grin.
This seems to me to sum up Eva's expectation of death in her final days. She may have hoped that her immortal soul would survive but she knew her beautiful body would not.

masonry. Next morning Hanna Reitsch met the old faithfuls, the people who were staying to die with Hitler,[13] including of course, the last two secretaries, Traudl and Gerda, and Eva and her maid Annaliese. Up to a hundred people remained, sleeping badly on camp beds if they were lucky – most had to lie on the floor – eating poor food, breathing recycled air, writing farewell letters, drinking, smoking and playing cards. Hitler's fresh vegetables no longer arrived – they were the one luxury he had allowed himself all through the war – but his meals were well-prepared and delicate. Even so, he continued to be plagued by agonising stomach pains.

Eva, who did not share Hitler's meals and rarely ate with him, continued to behave with grace and consideration towards everyone – which must have been made easier by the use of Hitler's bathroom and her faithful maid, Liesl, to keep her outfits fresh and ironed so that she could still change several times a day. In an extraordinary situation where every outcome was worse than the last, she carried on doing ordinary things. She wasn't heroic but she was steady. She didn't complain, weep, or make scenes, though she had definitely become more assertive. She did what she had always done: attending to Hitler; trying, in this grey concrete underworld, to offer feminine lightness and brief moments of pleasure. It is impossible to exaggerate the strain she endured, along with the other women incarcerated down there, most of whom were in their twenties. Devotion to the *Führer* and belief in his promises had found its dead end in a hellhole jammed with injured, moaning, filthy and often drunken soldiers, crammed cheek by jowl with Hitler's staff and associates, military chiefs and their orderlies, deprived of almost all privacy, comfort, hygiene, sunlight, fresh air and exercise. The lack of exercise in particular must have been torture for Eva, who was used to swimming, walking and climbing in the open air until her healthy young body was exhausted.

13. These included the Goebbels family; Martin Bormann; former Ambassador Hewel, the liaison officer from Ribbentrop's office; Hermann Fegelein, Himmler's liaison officer; his adjutants Nicolaus von Below and Otto Günsche; Chief Surgeon Haase, along with the nurse Erna Flegel and others caring for wounded men too sick to be moved; Doctor Stumpfegger, Hitler's personal doctor, his dentist Dr Kunz, a score of officers and their support staff; the telephone operator Rochus Misch, the cooks and cleaners, various orderlies, chauffeurs and messengers. Many of these escaped from the bunker after Hitler's suicide and were later tried at Nuremberg or wrote their memoirs; sometimes both.

On the afternoon of 27 April the bunker was thrown into consternation. Hitler summoned *Gruppenführer* Hermann Fegelein, liaison officer for the Waffen-SS. Fegelein could not be found.[14] His wife Gretl – Eva's sister – was due to give birth within days. Had he gone to join her in Munich? An officer despatched to look for him discovered Fegelein in civilian clothes in the comfortable apartment in Charlottenburg to which he used to bring his girlfriends – having remained as much a philanderer as before his marriage. He was taking it easy on his bed, with or without his Hungarian mistress, who did or did not have flaming red hair, depending on whose story is believed. According to Traudl Junge he telephoned Eva from there, saying that everyone who stayed with Hitler was doomed. There was no need and no time to think it over; she must join him and escape while she still could.

'Eva, you must leave the *Führer*. Don't be stupid. It's a matter of life or death!'

She replied, 'Hermann, where the hell are you? Come back here at once; the *Führer* has already been asking about you, he wants to talk to you.'

Then the connection was broken.[15]

14. From testimony given by Judge Michael Angelo Musmanno (1897–1968). Musmanno was a naval aide to General Mark W. Clark at the end of the Second World War who recommended to his navy superiors that Hitler's death should be fully investigated. Musmanno himself was given the assignment, with the authority to interrogate anyone he believed might have information about Hitler. Later, as an official navy observer at the International Military Tribunal trials at Nuremberg, he had access to many people involved with the Third Reich. He was appointed a judge at the Nuremberg War Crimes trials and served as presiding judge at the Intenational War Crimes Tribunal for the *Einsatzgruppen* case where twenty men in charge of concentration camp and labour supply administration were tried for the murder of one million civilians. He retired from active duty with the rank of rear admiral. Between May 1945 and summer 1948, in an attempt to establish that Hitler had really died, he interviewed more than two hundred people who had known Adolf Hitler and Eva Braun, either in the setting of a private chat at their home or in the full interrogation of German prisoners. According to Judge Musmanno, 'Fegelein left the bunker and went to his home. Then when news of the Himmler betrayal came to Hitler, he inquired about Fegelein and he sent out soldiers to get Fegelein, brought him back and in a matter of hours had him shot. He had Fegelein executed only because at one time Fegelein had been Himmler's adjutant, had been close to him. Eva Braun had made protestations because he was, of course, her brother-in-law.'

15. Junge, *Until the Final Hour*, pp. 178–80.

Eva, whose loyalty to Hitler was even greater than to her sister, refused to go.

Hanna Reitsch has a different version. According to her, Fegelein, still defiant, had been captured on the outskirts of Berlin and brought back to the bunker. Overnight, on 28/29 April, the *Führer* was shown a Reuters report alleging that Himmler and his sidekick, the flamboyant, confident Fegelein, were involved in peace negotiations with Count Folke Bernadotte, the Swedish Red Cross representative acting as go-between for the Allies. (These overtures were refused, the Allies insisting on unconditional surrender.) Hitler, naturally, was furious; but perhaps bearing in mind Fegelein's position in the Braun family as well as Himmler's long and devoted service, he waited for the first report to be confirmed.

On 28 April the doomed veterans underground heard a report on Stockholm Radio confirming the rumour that Himmler had been talking to the Allies.[16] This was the last and sharpest betrayal. Himmler had been one of Hitler's earliest comrades, a veteran of the Beer Hall Putsch of 1923. Now he – *even he* – had joined the list of traitors. Hitler raged like a madman, his face so suffused with blood as to be unrecognisable, beside himself with fury and, strange as it sounds, grief. Almost all the top dogs had loathed Heinrich Himmler, the sadistic *Reichsführer* (head) of the SS and minister for cruelty who was in charge of the concentration and death camps, but Hitler had held stubbornly to the belief that he was loyal and trustworthy. Once more he had been proved wrong. The Nazi court upon whom he had lavished rewards was a sham – hollow, lying, self-serving. Göring, Fegelein, even Himmler . . . his *fidus Achates*[17] or '*treue Heinrich*' . . . faithful Heinrich.

Beside himself with fury and faced with the possibility of further treachery, the *Führer* did the only thing he could: he ordered Fegelein to be court-martialled. At this point Eva intervened, begging him to spare her brother-in-law for the sake of her sister and their unborn child, who would otherwise come into the world fatherless. Hitler refused and Eva, in tears, answered meekly, 'You are the *Führer*.' Fegelein was held in the bunker under lock and key. At 11 p.m. on 28 April, when Fegelein's complicity in the peace overtures

16. In fact Himmler met Bernadotte four times to negotiate a surrender.
17. *Fidus Achates*, loyal Achates, was Aeneas' companion in Virgil's *Aeneid*, accompanying him on the long journey from Troy to Rome, always at his beck and call.

had been confirmed, he was taken up to the Reichskanzlei garden and shot.

At midnight on 29 April Lt-General Ritter von Greim and Hanna Reitsch left the bunker with orders to arrest Himmler. They reached safety and Hanna managed to get Magda's last letter delivered to her twenty-four-year-old son Harald, held in a British POW camp.[18]

On 29 April Major von Loringhoven and two other officers were ordered by General Krebs to escape from Berlin and join Wenck's forces, still vainly trying to relieve the city. They went to Hitler to get their orders signed and take their leave. 'Hitler was very calm. For a brief moment I seemed to discern a trace of envy in his voice. We were young and healthy and had a chance to survive. He was doomed.'[19]

On the same day came news that the Russians would overrun the Reichskanzlei the following morning and were even now approaching Potzdamer Platz with thousands of men. Nemesis was on its way, not with a steady tramp but pounding, shelling, ducking, taking cover and fighting through the pock-marked chasms that had once been streets, through the last pathetic resistance of the shreds and tatters of the *Wehrmacht* and the children and old men of the *Volkssturm* as they struggled to defend their leader and the creed he had taught them. Hitler had failed in his ambition to bequeath Europe a régime founded on racial superiority; failed to crush the Communist hordes from the east; failed to wipe out the Jews and all the other 'defectives', undesirables and those he defined as 'unfit to live' – Catholics, gypsies, homosexuals, damaged people who were physically or, worse still, mentally defective. The Third Reich should not waste resources that could be better spent on Aryan baby farms, or allow their fine genes to be sullied. The madness of the man had become the madness of a nation,[20] almost an entire continent, but it was nearly over.

During the twelve years of the Third Reich many Germans had retained an underlying sense of honour, order and patriotism towards what von Stauffenberg and his followers called 'the Secret Germany'

18. Hanna's biographer, Judy Lomax, tells me that Harald Quandt remained in touch with Hanna Reitsch after the war and the two became good friends. Hanna regularly borrowed a summer house on Harald's land. She died in 1979 aged sixty-seven.
19. I am grateful to my daughter, Carolyn Butler for drawing my attention to this interview in *The Tablet*, May 2005, given by Baron von Loringhoven to Konstantin Eggert, editor-in-chief of the BBC Russian Service's Moscow bureau.
20. Langer, *Inside the Mind of Adolf Hitler*, p. 154.

and some had courageously resisted the Nazis – but not enough. Many more had been seduced by the *Führer*. To them his dream seemed not only possible but *right*. The outcome was the defeat they now faced. The war had taken the lives of 13.6 million Russian soldiers, 3.25 million German troops, half a million from Britain and the Commonwealth, nearly 300,000 Americans and 120,000 Polish fighting men, every one of them mourned and missed.

The only initiative left for Hitler was to choose the time and manner of his own death and those of his loyal entourage. It could not be worse than the vengeance the Russians would wreak on his exposed corpse. Hitler had always hated to be seen naked and dreaded the idea that the world would mock his pale, flabby body. On 28 April the corpses of Mussolini and his mistress Clara Petacci had been strung upside down from scaffolding in the Piazza Loreto in Milan and derided by a gleeful mob.[21] Poison or a pistol were better than that, followed by a funeral pyre that would leave nothing behind but a heap of ashes.

On 29 April in the evening [recorded the nurse, Erna Flegel] we were told we were all to be received by Hitler. It was 10.30 when we were instructed to hold ourselves in readiness. We went over at 12.30 a.m. [i.e. just after midnight]. About 25–30 people were already gathered there . . . the secretaries, the cleaning women and a few strangers who had taken refuge in the shelter. They were all standing in a row. Hitler was told the names of the people he didn't know and shook hands with each one as he walked down the line. 'Each one,' said Hitler, 'must stand in his place and if fate requires it, there he must fall!' I had the feeling that for him we were the forum of the German people, to whom he was presenting himself since he had no more extensive one. [. . .] Each one of us had the feeling that this was farewell and it affected us all deeply because of course we all believed that we too would not come out of this hell alive.

Hitler had decided that as soon as the Soviet onslaught reached the gardens of the Reichskanzlei the mass suicide of those who remained should begin. That moment was now imminent. Farcically, he appointed a new government, naming Goebbels as Chancellor. On 28 April he called the last few of his colleagues together and told them that he

21. Hitler may not have known this, however.

intended to kill himself. He had always been obsessed with suicide and now it had become the final test of loyalty. When they had finished listening he handed round potassium cyanide capsules like sweeties, seeming morbidly gratified that so many who had shared his life were now about to share his death. (Hanna's capsule was later examined by her interrogator. It was a little brass tube with a removable top, inside which was a tiny, fragile glass ampoule containing about half a teaspoonful of dark brown liquid.) The *Führer* gave instructions on how to use the poison – the ampoule to be broken between the teeth and its contents swallowed quickly. (But what about the glass shards? Death will be instantaneous; you won't feel a scratch.) They listened, hypnotised. In the dying hours of the Reich Hitler's grip had not lessened. Everyone present resolved to share his fate by eating the poisoned apples Hitler handed out.

Later he told the secretaries and Eva that the best way to die was by shooting yourself through the mouth. Characteristically, Eva said she couldn't put a gun to her head – she wanted to be a beautiful corpse. She'd prefer the poison method.

> 'I wonder if it hurts very much? I'm so frightened of suffering for a long time. I'm ready to die heroically but at least I want it to be painless.'
>
> Hearing this, Traudl and Frau Christian asked for a cyanide pill and Hitler handed them one each, saying he was sorry he couldn't offer us a better farewell present.

Eva's nerve did not fail. Hitler finally discovered which of his followers was truly loyal. Only a few stalwarts, men like Günsche and Heinz Linge, his personal valets, and the women, above all Eva. It was time to grant her public recognition, adding her name to his in the scroll of history. They were about to die together. It might as well be as man and wife.

Afterwards some of the women retired to Eva's room. Traudl Junge recalls:

> Eva said to Frau Christian and me. 'I bet you'll be weeping again by this evening.' We looked at her in horror.
>
> 'Is it so soon?'
>
> 'No, no, this is different. We'll be moved by what happens, but I can't tell you more just yet.'

On 30 April a number of Hitler's adjutants, including Nicolaus von Below, left the bunker.

During these apocalyptic days Eva's kindness and consideration were unchanged, if sometimes impractical. On 30 April she invited Traudl Junge into her dressing room and opening the wardrobe, unhooked a magnificent fox fur cape: a film-star garment to go with her film-star dreams. She pushed it into Traudl's arms. 'Take it,' she said. 'Wear it and enjoy it.'

A German popular song of the time, much played over the wireless to encourage the troops and cheer their families, went like this: '*Es geht alles vorüber, es geht alles vorbei, / Nach jedem Dezember kommt wieder ein Mai.*' – 'Everything ends, all the pain goes away, / After each December comes another May.' For Eva, there would be no May.

Chapter Twenty-nine

Frau Hitler for Thirty-six Hours

The situation in the bunker was surreal, a concrete hell populated by the undead. Above ground the very earth shook; below ground death preoccupied everyone. Imagination shuddered under the imminence of a fate no one could have predicted. Yet even in the extraordinary circumstances of the bunker ordinary humanity kept breaking through. On the night of 27 April a modest wedding presaged the greater, briefer marriage that was to come. It took place in a once grand room of the bombed-out Chancellery, its ruined walls now sliding into heaps of rubble, windows gaping into the troubled darkness beyond. Traudl Junge described it:

> One of the kitchen maids married her sweetheart, a driver from the motor escort. The courageous driver even managed to negotiate the ruined streets of Berlin to fetch the bride's mother and family so that they could see their daughter married. A city official gave an address but as the pair clasped hands the walls and windows shook and rattled so loudly that one could hardly follow the solemn words. Everyone congratulated the young couple and went back to the bunker of death.[1]

When the formalities were over the guests celebrated, one with a harmonica, another with a fiddle, and the bridal pair danced together like country folk from their home villages. It is not known if the newly-

1. Junge, *Until the Final Hour*, p. 180.

weds managed to escape from Berlin, lived an ordinary life together, had children and disappeared into blessed obscurity.

Eva Braun knew this was not an option for her. Forced to be anonymous for most of her life, she appeared like magic in Hitler's circle at the very end. For twelve years her name was not mentioned; now, suddenly, she was everywhere. More is known about her during the last two months of her life than throughout the previous thirty-three years. Survivors from the final days in the bunker have praised or belittled her for the benefit of journalists or historians and as a result one can reconstruct her last days with hour-by-hour accuracy.

Around midnight on 28/29 April Hitler retired with Traudl Junge to dictate his Personal and Political Testaments. Traudl recalled the occasion clearly: '"How are you, my dear?" he asked me. "Have you had a bit of rest? I want to dictate to you. Do you think you are up to it?"'

She realised what he wanted to dictate only when he said the title, 'My Testament'.[2] It began awkwardly with the words:

> Since I did not think I should take the responsibility of entering into marriage during the years of combat, I have decided now, before the termination of life on this earth, to marry the woman who, after many years of true friendship, entered voluntarily the city which was already besieged, to share my fate. She goes to death with me as my wife, according to her desire.

The wording sounds as though designed to absolve him of any wish or responsibility for marriage, in keeping with his previously expressed views, and even at this late stage he could only describe their years together as 'friendship'. His will ended: 'Myself and my wife choose death to escape the disgrace of being forced to resign or surrender. It is our wish to be cremated immediately at the place where I have done the greatest part of my work during the twelve years of service to my people.' An illegible scrawl serves as his signature.

Next, Hitler dictated his Political Testament,[3] a longer and more incoherent document, leaving Fräulein Junge to type it up (a task that,

2. Taken from an interview with Traudl Junge by Gitta Sereny in the *Sunday Times*, 25 September 2000.
3. Hitler's Will and Marriage Certificate are in Munich's Photoarchiv Hoffmann, T474 10861, 10863 and (with his signature) 13502.

with the necessary copies, took her till about six o'clock in the morning). 'I typed as fast as I could,' she said. 'My fingers worked mechanically and I was surprised that I made hardly any typing mistakes.' Long afterwards she explained her response to what she had typed:

I thought that now I would be the first person on earth to know why all this had happened. He would say something that explained it all, that would teach us something, leave us with something. But then, as he dictated, my God, that long list of ministers he so grotesquely appointed to succeed his Government [a list that, oddly, did not include Albert Speer] I thought – yes, I did then think – how undignified it all was. Just the same phrases, in the same quiet tone, and then, at the end of it, those terrible words about the Jews. After all the despair, all the suffering, not one word of sorrow, of compassion. I remember thinking, he has left us with nothing. A nothing.[4]

Hitler's final words to his country and the world, inflated by bombast and delusion, driven by racial fanaticism to the last, concluded: '*Above all I enjoin the government and the people to uphold the race laws to the limit and to resist mercilessly the poisoner of all nations, international Jewry.*' The document was signed and dated: *29 April 1945, 4.00 a.m.* The mystery remained: how did he fool tens of millions of Germans into acquiescing in the unconscionable murder of millions of Jews?

Four copies of this testament were entrusted to Major Johannmeier, Hitler's last army adjutant, and Lorenz, his press chief, who were to deposit them in Munich to be kept safe for posterity. This done, his work was over – not completed but finished. Hitler could no longer procrastinate. The time had come to get married.

The wedding of Fräulein Braun and Adolf Hitler took place in the bunker's cramped map room in the small hours of 29 April 1945,[5] in keeping with the nocturnal hours they had always kept. The problem of finding some official who could legally conduct the marriage was solved by Goebbels, who was *Gauleiter* of Berlin and knew of a registrar fighting

4. Interview with Gitta Sereny, *Sunday Times*, 25 September 2000.
5. It is difficult to be certain of these times since they all depend on whose account is believed. Even the normally reliable Traudl Junge said different things at different times. I have chosen to follow Ian Kershaw's sequence of events as set out at the end of Vol. II of his magisterial biography of Hitler, *Hitler, 1936–1945: Nemesis*, pp. 821ff.

with the depleted *Volkssturm*. Walter Wagner, one of Berlin's municipal councillors, was hastily summoned to conduct the civil ceremony and arrived to find the *Führer* standing before him; not the *Führer* he knew, the leader before whom all Germany and half Europe had quailed, but a stooped, frail man with trembling hands and greying hair. Everything about him had diminished; even his voice seemed to have shrunk. Beside him, smiling rapturously, was a beautiful young woman whom Wagner didn't recognise, wearing an elegant navy blue dress embroidered with sequins and black suede shoes from Ferragamo, her hand slipped through the arm of the *Führer*. Was this some plot, a deception, the prelude to an escape? Walter Wagner must have felt nervous and thoroughly bewildered.

The document from US Intelligence[6] recording the precise form of their marriage sets it out almost as though the participants were singing in a trio, or perhaps reading from a play by Samuel Beckett, short lines alternating on opposite sides of the page. It begins:

Before Walter Wagner, City Councillor, as appointed Registrar for the purpose of joining in marriage
1. Adolf Hitler, b. 20 April 1889 at Braunau, residing in Berlin, Reichskanzlei [Hitler omitted to fill in the blanks for the names of his parents]
2. Frl. Eva Braun, born 6 February 1912 in Munich, present address Wasserburger Strasse 8, residing at Wasserburger Strasse 12 [some unsolved confusion over house numbers?]
    Father: Friedrich BRAUN
    Mother: Franziska BRAUN née [a mistyping] DRON-BURGER
3. Witness: *Reichsminister* GOEBBELS Dr Joseph [he spelled his name 'Josef']
    b. 26 October 1897 Rheydt, residing at Berlin, Hermann Göring str. 20
4. Witness: *Reichsleiter* Martin BORMANN
    b. 17 June 1900 in Halberstadt, residing Obersalzberg

The persons named under 1. and 2. state that they are of pure Aryan descent and that they are not affected by incurable diseases that would exclude them from marriage. Considering the war

---

6. NARA at College Park, RG 319, Box 393, HITLER XE oo 36 55, Vol. III, Folder 2.

situation and the special circumstances they apply for marriage under special wartime laws. They also ask to accept an oral publication of the banns and to disregard all legal delays.
Accepted and in order.

'Now' – says Wagner, his voice unsteady,

I am coming to the ceremonial of marriage.
In the presence of the witnesses mentioned under 3 and 4, I ask you . . .

Mein Führer, Adolf Hitler,
Are you willing to take Frl. Eva Braun as your wife?
If you are, answer, 'I do.'

[There is a blank space for Hitler's affirmation.]
Now I ask you,

Frl. Eva Braun,
Are you willing to take
our *Führer*, Adolf Hitler,
as your husband?
If you are, answer, 'I do.'

After both newly-weds stated their intentions I declare this marriage legal before the law.
Berlin, 29 April 1945

Read and signed,
Adolf Hitler

1. Husband
2. Wife   Eva –
[She began her surname with a B, crossed it out and signed] –

Eva Hitler, née Braun

3. Witness 1.   Joseph Goebbels
4. Witness 2.   Martin Bormann

Signed Waagner (in his excitement the official misspelled his own name) as Registrar

And that, in its entirety, was Eva's wedding ceremony. No family in attendance, parents mollified at last, no friends, no flowers, no music, and the wrong Wagner.

A few people gathered for a brief reception and, although it was by now 3.30 a.m., the bottomless well of champagne was dipped into again. Hitler sipped from a small glass of Tokay.

And that was it. Hardly the romantic wedding she had dreamed of, yet many small details epitomised the past fifteen years. Hitler's shame about his parents, who were not even mentioned; his lifelong secrecy about his flawed genes – he declared himself fit to marry ('*not affected by incurable diseases*') knowing very well that under Nazi eugenic laws he was not.[7] The omnipresence of his two evil geniuses, Goebbels and Bormann, roped in as witnesses although neither of them cared for Eva and thought the 'marriage' a farce. The absurdly punctilious observance of the regulations governing civil marriages, which obliged the *Führer* to request leave to *make a verbal declaration of the intended marriage* – rather than what? Posting the banns at Berlin's town hall? The attempt to stick to protocol and be married by a properly qualified functionary was typical of the Nazis' scrupulous adherence to the formalities, no matter how bizarre or horrific the circumstances. And finally, the bride's touching slip-up when signing her name. In haste, out of habit or nerves or maybe joy at having achieved her life's ambition, she began to write Eva *Braun*; realised her mistake, crossed out the B, and replaced it with the name *Hitler*.

He had recognised her virtues and her devotion at last. For thirty-six hours she had the deep satisfaction of being addressed as '*Frau Hitler*'. (Except by her husband, who, according to some observers, continued to refer to her as 'Fräulein Braun'.)

Traudl Junge remembers the end in crystal-clear detail. On the wedding night everyone went to bed late – Hitler not till 5 a.m., Traudl herself at least an hour after that. They woke later than usual, despite the hammering and sizzling of monstrous fireworks above ground. The morning was spent between tension and trivia. At about three o'clock in the afternoon of 30 April, Traudl recalled:

---

7. 'A series of laws enacted by the Nazi Party had made marriage subject to intense eugenic vetting. Ideology rather than human affection determined who could marry whom or who had the right to reproduce. All benefits for married couples were subject to racial criteria.' Under the Law for the Protection of German Blood and Honour of September 1935, marriage and sexual intercourse between Aryans and Jews were prohibited. The Law for the Prevention of Hereditarily Diseased Progeny had come in with effect from 1 January 1934. See Burleigh, *The Third Reich: A New History*, p. 236.

We'd had lunch with Hitler. Afterwards I'd gone out for a cigarette when Linge came and said, 'The *Führer* would like to say goodbye.'

He emerged from his room looking more stooped than ever and held out his hand to each of us. I felt its warmth but his gaze was blank. He seemed a long way away. He said something that I couldn't understand. This was the moment we'd all been waiting for and now it had come I was numb and could hardly observe what was happening. Only when Eva Braun came up to me did the spell lift. She smiled and hugged me.

'Please, do try to get out; you may still be able to get through. And if you do, give my love to Bavaria,' she said, smiling but with a sob in her voice.

She was wearing the *Führer*'s favourite dress, the black one with appliquéd roses, and her hair was freshly-washed and beautifully coiffed.[8]

The two of them entered the small sitting room and closed the heavy door. The oldest of the old guard – Goebbels, Bormann, Axmann, Ambassador Hewel, Otto Günsche, Heinz Linge, Hitler's valet, and Erich Kempka, his chauffeur – clustered outside in the corridor and waited. The women kept their distance, staying in their own quarters. Traudl Junge had slipped away to distract the Goebbels children by playing a game with them. Their mother Magda, still prostrate on her bed, could not look at them without tears.

Herr and Frau Hitler sat down side by side on the sofa in their favourite positions, she on his right, her legs folded under her so that she could snuggle up close to him in the position she had always favoured in the evenings at the Berghof, curled up in a deep armchair, the two black dogs mounting guard at her feet. None of the people outside the door could hear what was said in those last minutes. The door shut off all sound. They heard no sobbing or yells, not pleas nor prayers; not sighs, not even the last scream they were all secretly waiting for. Their own heavy breathing filled everyone's ears, the acrid stink of sweat filled their nostrils as they crowded round, waiting. A long silence, broken only by the noise from the diesel ventilator. One or two glanced covertly at their watches. Five minutes, six . . .

Alone together, Eva and Adolf would have talked, as they always had, in banalities.

8. Junge, *Bis Zur Letzten Stunde*, p. 187 (translated by the author).

There was a sudden sound of feet clattering. Everyone turned, aghast. Magda Goebbels was running helter-skelter down the corridor, wide-eyed and dishevelled, her icy composure abandoned. She stopped and drummed her fist on the closed door. Otto Günsche, standing guard, tried to stop her but she pushed him away. The door opened and she stumbled inside, babbling incoherently . . .

Hitler half-rose from the sofa and pointed at the door.

'Raus!'[9]

Frau Goebbels tried to utter a few frantic words –

'Raus!' he shouted.

Magda backed away, retching and sobbing, elbowed through the semi-circle round the door and tottered back down the corridor. In the breathy silence her retreating footsteps could be heard all the way. Hitler's door was pulled to by an unseen hand.

Inside the room, charged with tension like an execution chamber, Eva would surely have wanted to know – to reassure herself as much as him – 'Do you believe in God, Adi? You used to.'

And the once-omnipotent Hitler might have answered bitterly, 'God doesn't believe in me.'

And then she must have said, for the thousand, thousandth time, 'I love you.'

Her breathing quickened in the final minutes. To calm herself she put a hand to the racing pulse in her throat, then splayed her fingers to admire the new wedding ring. There hadn't been time for it to be engraved with their initials and the date. She could have that done later on, once they were out of here. Except of course that there wasn't going to be a 'later on'.

Did her courage hold firm or might she have asked, 'Will it hurt?' Would he have had the kindness to reply, 'No'?

Perhaps, not wanting him to think for a moment that she was unwilling to die, she added, 'I'm not afraid, really.'

The listeners on the other side of the door waited, almost impatiently. Ten minutes they'd been in there now, longer, and still nothing. It was half past three in the afternoon.

Eva would have needed one last kiss, would have tipped her face trustingly towards his grey lips. They were dry, the contact brief. At last she unfolded her other hand to show the brass pellet nestled in her palm and extracted the slim glass ampoule. Her heart was beating,

9. Get out!

as though somehow that deaf and dumb organ knew its end was imminent and beat harder to fend it off. Whatever the mind had decided,
the body was young and strong and eager to live.

Death seemed quite painless. It took less than a minute. She bit
down upon the glass bullet, her breathing quickened and rasped; slowed,
stopped. Her head slumped sideways on to his shoulder. When she
was quite still, Hitler put an ampoule between his teeth, pointed the
7.65mm Walther pistol into his mouth, bit the capsule and fired. The
deafening gunshot reverberated through the bunker.

Helmut Goebbels, playing with Traudl and his sisters just a few cells
away, looked up and said happily, 'Bull's eye!'[10]

Linge and Bormann waited ten more minutes before pushing open
the heavy door. The smell of bitter almonds hung in the air. Hitler's
body had slumped over one end of the sofa, blood oozing from a crater
in his temple. There was blood on his jacket, an explosive splatter of
blood on the wall behind him, blood trickling down the side of the
sofa and a coagulating pool of blood on the floor. The pistol lay at his
feet. Eva's face was calm, her lips blue. Her legs were still tucked under,
her head lolled against his collapsed body. The small brass tube that
had held the poison had rolled off her lap on to the floor. It looked
for all the world like a discarded lipstick.

10. Source: Traudl Junge.

Aftermath

Immediately after the suicide of Hitler and his wife, before the bodies had cooled or rigor mortis set in, they were lifted off the sofa by Hitler's adjutant Otto Günsche and his valet Heinz Linge, helped by Bormann, who carried Eva's body in his arms to the foot of the stairs from where Erich Kempka took her up the twenty-five steps to the outside world. Günsche carried her from there into the garden. The *Führer* was enveloped in a blanket to conceal the horrific state of his head. Eva was not, and her body and face were clearly recognisable. Several feet from the bunker's emergency exit was a shallow crater and here they were laid side by side. Otto Günsche doused them with gallons of petrol and threw matches at the corpses, but they would not ignite. Finally Linge improvised a paper torch and a huge ball of fire rose from the bodies, which began to burn convulsively. The whole area was under constant bombardment, Soviet shells falling in the garden, and the funeral party was in real danger. After sketching a hasty *Sieg Heil!* and watching for a few moments, they retreated down the steps back into the bunker. Only Günsche kept coming back for the next half-hour to add petrol to the flames, until the charred and blackened corpses were unrecognisable though not entirely consumed. In the end, quite a modest *Götterdämmerung*.

The following day, before sunrise, their bodies were removed by the Russians, wrapped in sheets, placed in wooden crates and taken to the Counter Intelligence headquarters of the Soviet 3rd Shock Army. From there they were transferred to a field hospital, where an autopsy was performed on Hitler and Eva three days later. Identification was made on the basis of their dental records, supplied by his dentist's assistant, and Hitler's bridgework. The conclusion was firm and positive: these were without question the bodies of the *Führer* and the woman known as Eva Braun. That conclusion, however, continues to be disputed, chiefly by rabid neo-Nazis. Adolf Hitler, were he alive today, would be 117; Eva ninety-four.

In the evening of the following day, 1 May, the Goebbels children were poisoned with cyanide by their mother,[1] after which Josef Goebbels shot his wife and then himself.[2] All eight were buried together in a hastily scooped-out grave. Blondi, who had also had a cyanide capsule forced between her jaws, was buried nearby, her body almost intact. On 5 May the ashy remains of ten corpses – Hitler and Eva and the Goebbels family, whose bodies had scarcely been incinerated and were clearly recognisable – were found by a Red Army soldier.[3]

Fifty years later a new witness emerged. Elena Rzhevskaya, a young interpreter from Russian military reconnaissance, claimed that on 8 May 1945, the day the Germans finally surrendered, she was entrusted with a small, satin-lined box. Inside was the jawbone of Adolf Hitler, wrenched from his skull a few hours earlier by a Russian pathologist, fragments of flesh still adhering to it. The assistant to the former *Führer*'s dentist confirmed that the jaw corresponded with Hitler's dental records. Rzhevskaya was carrying the box on orders from Colonel Vassily Gorbushin, head of a small, secret

---

1. According to Erna Flegel, 'Frau Goebbels was far superior to an average human being. It took a resolute spirit to decide to sacrifice her own children. But, she said, "Where shall my children go? The shame of being Goebbels children will always rest upon them." The six children died in the afternoon. They had been told they were to be inoculated.' Fräulein Flegel claimed it was Hitler's dentist, Dr Kunz, who actually poisoned the children. This has never been proved nor indeed disputed since Erna Flegel's evidence is virtually unknown. See NARA NND 974345, RG 226, Box 465, testimony given to Frederick Stalder under the command of Richard Helms, Lt. Commander USNR, Berlin Detachment/SSU; APO 742 on 23 November 1945.
2. In her last letter to her son Harald, written in the *Führerbunker* three days before she killed herself, Magda Goebbels said: 'Our magnificent idea is finished – and with it everything beautiful, admirable, noble and good that I have known in my life. The world that will come after the *Führer* and National Socialism is not worth living in, and for that reason I have brought the children here as well.'
3. Heavy bruising on Helga's face, observed in the post-mortem, suggests that she fought her poisoner and had to be violently restrained while the capsule was pushed down her throat and her jaws clamped shut.

Russian team given the job of identifying Hitler's corpse in order to quash rumours that he and Eva his wife had survived and escaped from Berlin. The box eventually made its way to Moscow, where the jaw remains today.[4]

An interrogator from the American CIC (Counter Intelligence Corps), Team Commander 970–45, one Robert A. Gutierrez – a significant name in this saga – established that Eva's personal possessions were entrusted to two of Fegelein's former staff. The first was SS *Oberführer* Wilhelm Spacil of the *Reichsbesicherheitshauptamt*, who arranged for their transport from Berlin to Austria. There they passed to SS *Hauptsturmführer* Franz Konrad, who was captured and interrogated at Kirchberg, Austria, on 21 August 1945[5] by agents of the US CIC.[6] Eva's diary and photograph albums – but no letters – were found at Konrad's mother's house in Schladming on 24 August 1945 and ended up at NARA's huge archive in College Park, Maryland. The subsequent history of the trunks containing the rest of her private papers is a tangled chain of events around the names of men now long dead. Whatever the truth may be, it seems fairly

4. Details from an article by Tom Parfitt in the *Observer*, 8 May 2005.

5. These private possessions were said in various reports to consist of one chest of silverware bearing emblems of the Polish crown; silverware bearing the monogram of Eva Braun; four gold men's watches and a woman's gold watch set in fifty diamonds (presumably the one Eva had promised to Gretl in her last letter) and two pairs of gold cufflinks; a diamond brooch and a medallion on a chain; a Leica camera and thirty to forty unexposed films, a gramophone, part of a postage stamp collection stolen by Konrad from the Warsaw ghetto, worth an estimated RM30,000; Hitler's damaged suit from the Stauffenberg assassination attempt; finally, RM104,625 and in foreign currency, $1,000 and £10. It is quite a haul but nowhere near a king's ransom. The trunkful of personal papers said to include about fifty personal notes from Hitler to Eva written between 1938 and 1945, the letters that Eva had worried so much about, is also mentioned, together with names of the various people through whose hands it passed. They were last heard of in Schloss Fischhorn but there they disappeared before allegedly turning up in Schladming, Austria. From there, on 4 February 1946, they were received into the custody of Robert A. Gutierrez, SA, CIC. After his death it was claimed that they had been buried; it was never revealed where. From the oddments that steal into the lists of auction rooms or eBay it seems likely that he gradually sold some of them. The bulk of the letters have still not surfaced. Their eventual discovery is the Holy Grail of serious historians as well as Hitler groupies and other neo-Nazis.

6. Konrad was most reluctant to reveal any significant information and his account of how the papers came into his possession and where they had been is riddled with contradictions and factual impossibilities.

safe to conclude that, as she had so ardently hoped, the love letters exchanged between Eva Braun and Adolf Hitler will never be made public.

On 5 May 1945, at a hospital in Garmisch-Partenkirchen, Gretl Fegelein gave birth to a daughter, Eva, always known in the family as 'little Eva', the only grandchild of Fritz and Fanny Braun. Gretl later married a businessman, Kurt Berlinghoff. On 28 June 1971 'little' Eva, then twenty-seven, committed suicide by poisoning herself with E605, a toxic substance used in weedkiller and insecticide,[7] after her boyfriend, driving her new car – a Kharmann Ghia – had been killed in a head-on collision with a lorry near Lake Garda. After the war Gretl Braun severed all contact with her cousin Gertraud, cousin Alois [Winbauer] and another cousin, Willy. By the time Gertraud tracked her down in the 1970s she had developed Alzheimer's disease, from which she died, aged seventy-three, in 1987.

Soon after her divorce from Hofstätter in 1941 Ilse Braun married for the second time: a solicitor again, Dr Fucke-Michaels, and moved with him to Breslau. After the war they lived anonymously at Klingenteichweg 21 in Heidelberg but again the marriage was not a success and the couple had no children. She left him and returned to Munich for her second divorce, dying there of cancer in 1979, aged seventy. Ilse was buried in Munich's Waldfriedhof, in a plot shared with her sister Gretl Berlinghoff and her niece Eva Fegelein. The name Braun does not appear on the tombstone.

Before the war was over Franziska and Friedrich (Frite and Fanny) Braun, fleeing the bombing of Munich, bought a house in the village of Ruhpolding in the Chiemgau, at Wiesenstrasse 13. In May 1945 they were imprisoned for interrogation by the Americans but quickly released when it became clear that they had nothing to disclose about Hitler and had gained nothing by their association with him. They continued to live in Ruhpolding for the next twenty and – in Fanny's case – thirty years, not least because most local people stood by them. Fritz Braun would state to all enquirers his firm conviction that Eva had died with the *Führer*. Until the late fifties, 'Fritz often returned to the Altmühl valley to go trout fishing in Beilngries and Biberbach or chase butterflies in Kinding,' said the local doctor, Wolfgang Brand, recalling their excursions together as boys. Fritz Braun died in 1964 when he was eighty-five, Fanny in 1976 at the great age of ninety-

7. Information from Gertraud Weisker.

one. They are buried side by side in the cemetery close to the yellow Baroque church of St George, above the peaceful Bavarian village where they spent their last years.

Gertraud Weisker's father, a chartered engineer at the Zeiss works in Jena, was arrested by the Russians towards the end of the war and transported to the Soviet Union. Word later reached her mother that he had died of starvation in March 1946. Another version says he was executed by Soviets for having collaborated with the Americans. Long after the war, in response to enquiries from his daughter, the Red Cross certified that he had indeed been in the Resistance. Frau Weisker and her daughter were evicted from their home and Gertraud says that for two years after the war she wandered her derelict country with a knapsack. Once she nearly got engaged but when her fiancé found out who she was he changed his mind, being unwilling to father children who would, by marriage at least, be related to Adolf Hitler. When she met her future husband in 1948, he agreed to marry her only if she kept quiet about her family association. Gertraud kept the secret for more than forty years and her three children only learned about the relationship after their father's death in 1986. She worked for many years as a translator of patents for the Zeiss optical company in Jena and her spoken English is still excellent. Her link to Eva Braun did not become public until the late 1990s when Gertraud finally broke her silence after first telling her children, all adults by then. She did so, she says, because she wanted to restore the reputation of her beloved cousin. In the years since she has faithfully tried to rehabilitate Eva, if sometimes through rose-tinted spectacles.

Alois Winbauer, Eva's uncle and author of the memoir of the Braun family, became a successful journalist and died on 17 October 1983 at the age of eighty-seven.

Traudl Junge was captured as she tried to escape from Berlin – *without* the grey fox fur. 'I had no use for it. I didn't need anything except the pistol and poison . . . I had no money, provisions, clothes – just lots of cigarettes and a couple of pictures that I couldn't bear to part with.' She was imprisoned for six months by the Russians. Later she became a journalist, first on *Quick* magazine, then as a freelance writer. In 1947–8 she wrote down her memories of two and a half years as Hitler's secretary, based on notes she had made during the time she was working for him, but they were not published until 2002 in a book, *Bis Zur Letzten Stunde* (*To the Final Hour*). In 1972 she gave a long interview to *The World at War*. A half-hour condensation of her remarks was later part of a series produced by Jerry Kuehl entitled *Hitler's Secretary*. Hans Junge, Hitler's aide whom she had married in 1943, was killed during a British air raid on Normandy. Traudl never remarried.

Speer was found by the Americans in Glücksburg, the Duke of Mecklenburg and Holstein's castle a few miles from Flensburg, near the Danish border, where Dönitz's brief government had its head-quarters. He was first interviewed in early May 1945, within days of Hitler's suicide. At the Nuremberg Trials he was spared the death penalty meted out to many of his Nazi associates but was sentenced to twenty years in Spandau prison, where he spent the time gardening, writing letters and making copious notes for his subsequent memoirs, *Inside the Third Reich*. He was released from Spandau at midnight on 1 October 1966 into the care of his devoted wife Margret and their six children – all now adults – and spent the rest of his life trying to rehabilitate himself by writing books and giving interviews. He died in the Waldorf Hotel in London on 1 September 1981 after a stroke, rumour has it in the arms of his young English mistress.[8]

On 27 April Göring, who had fled to Obersalzberg from Berlin, was captured along with members of his staff and eventually taken to Nuremberg, where the war crimes trial sentenced him to death. He avoided the gallows by swallowing a hidden cyanide capsule on 15 October 1945. Himmler, after his capture, also swallowed a poison capsule and died on 23 May 1945 before he could be brought to trial. Bormann left the bunker after Hitler's suicide and travelled along an underground railway tunnel to Friedrichstrasse station, where he disappeared. He was probably killed while trying to escape when a shell hit the tank in which he had been hoping to get across the Russian lines. At the Nuremberg Trials he was sentenced to death *in absentia*. His skull was found by chance in 1972 by workers excavating a building site and was identified from his dental records, and again many years later by DNA, after which his ashes were scattered at sea. His wife Gerda died of cancer in 1945 but all ten of their children survived the war. His eldest son Martin became a Catholic priest. He later said, 'You can't choose your parents or get rid of them. There's nothing I can do about that. Nor can I judge him . . . I must leave that to God.'[9]

8. Sereny, *Albert Speer: His Battle with Truth*, pp. 715–16.
9. This quotation is taken from *Hitler's Fixer*, a documentary by 3BMTV, written and directed by Marion Milne and first shown on ITV 13 May 2001.

Otto Günsche, together with Hitler's chief private secretary Gerda Christian, was able to escape from the bombed-out Chancellery, under fire from the Soviet soldiers fighting in Berlin, through the underground metro all the way to the station on the Friedrichstrasse.

Many of the buildings on Obersalzberg were severely damaged and substantially destroyed by 318 RAF Lancasters and 700 aircraft in a bomb attack on 25 April 1945, while its refugees sheltered fearfully in the complex of tunnels and poky concrete rooms beneath. The Berghof was finally obliterated seven years later, on 30 April 1952, and today virtually no trace of it remains. Hitler's private property and all his assets, as well as the Wasserburgerstrasse house in Munich that he gave to Eva Braun, were handed over to the state of Bavaria by the Allied Control Commission of Germany, or CCG, the organisation for which my father worked in the late 1940s.

Acknowledgements

All sorts of people, friends and strangers, professional historians and in one case a passerby, have helped me with this book. There are too many to mention each one in detail – endless, fulsome thanks, however deeply-felt by the author, are tedious for the reader. Some, however, deserve more than just their name on a list.

First and foremost is my agent, Caradoc King, whose idea it was in the first place that I should write a biography of Eva Braun. I thank him for that, and for his rock-steady support throughout nearly three years of hard but fascinating research and writing.

I am also deeply grateful to Frau Gertraud Weisker, Eva Braun's younger cousin, who trusted me, talked for hours on several occasions about Eva and their shared family background, and showed me much unknown and invaluable material, including the hitherto unpublished memoirs of her uncle, Alois Winbauer, which gave a fresh slant on the lives and characters of the Braun family. I could not have written this book without her cooperation.

Many thanks to Peter Palm for his generosity in letting me reproduce the map of Hitler's bunker (on page 406).

Overwhelmingly, I must thank my friend Marion Milne, who directed the award-winning 3BMTV documentary *Adolf and Eva* and freely offered me access to her research, including transcripts of all her interviews, as well as reading the final typescript.

Next, my thanks to Professors David Cannadine and Linda Colley, for encouraging me at the very outset and offering invaluable suggestions. Their generosity and enthusiasm were boundless.

Jerry Kuehl, an expert historian of the Third Reich, was an endless source of information and an assiduous fact-checker who saved me from many mistakes. My thanks to him and the Office Cat.

Fran Yorke, whose ear is perfectly tuned to English prose, read and commented on the typescript and gave invaluable criticism and support. I can't thank her enough.

There would have been no book without the joint efforts of all these, and of my professional helpers: Christiane Gehron, who did much translating with verve and accuracy; Ann Williams, who supplemented my own picture research with some original photographs that I would never have found; and Beth Emanuel, who typed up some intractable notes. Richard Collins was the copy editor every author dreams of, with his minuscule attention to detail and unfailing ability to spot repetitions. My three alpha computer doctors, Adam, Adis and Adrian, and Chris Jones in Suffolk, kept me up and running on the many occasions when the machine tried to crash.

In addition, for services large and small, I owe thanks to:

Florian Beierl; Martha Burke-Hennessy, for her brilliant and sustaining e-mails; Nancy Durham; Anton Grad, deputy mayor of Beilngries (especially for giving me the umbrella); Herr Grohle and Herr Volk from the Institute for Contemporary History in Munich; Mr Paul Demilio, curator of the Musmanno Collection at the Gumberg Library, Duquesne University, Pittsburgh, PA; Joachim von Halasz; Dr David Irving; George Jonas; Dr Peter Jones; Sadakat Kadri; Herr Künzel, archivist of Beilngries; Judy Lomax; the patient and efficient staff of the London Library; Prof. Neil McIntyre; Christopher Morgan; Frau Obermaier at the Bayerische Staatsbibliothek in Munich, which holds the Hoffmann Picture Archive (Bildarchiv Hoffmann); Dr Jonathan Rée; Herr Josef Riedl, editor of the Bavarian newspaper *Donaukurier*; Peter Scott; Gitta Sereny; Gerald Seymour; Rupert Graf Strachwitz, and Graham C. Greene for introducing me to him; Paola Tabellini, curator of the Salvatore Ferragamo Museo in Florence; John Taylor from NARA; Mrs Monica Unwin; Lady Williams, née Gill Gambier-Parry; Wolfgang Hermann, Ernst Wagner, and Frau Barbara Geresbeck of the Hermann-Historica auction house, Munich; Stephen Wright.

Every biographer offers guilty gratitude to their much-neglected family. All three of my children, Carolyn Butler (and her husband, Malcolm), Jonathan Lambert and Marianne Lambert read the book at various stages and responded with abrasive and helpful comments. They had a lot to put up with while I was obsessed with Eva and I thank them with all my heart. To their names I should add that of my

Acknowledgements

late mother, Mrs Ditha Helps, née Edith Schröder, who taught me her language and by reading, singing, reciting poetry and reminiscing in German about the first twenty-five years of her youth, gave me the cultural background that brought the subject of this book alive.

Finally, the biggest thanks of all to my beloved partner, Tony Price, who drove me round Bavaria, tolerated my absences, read and criticised and improved every page and hardly ever sounded sick of Eva and Hitler. Without him, above all, this book would simply not have been written. Darling, it's finished, at last.

Angela Lambert
London, Groléjac, Orford
March 2003–October 2005

Select Bibliography

Non-fiction

Air Ministry; *The Battle of Britain 8th August–31st October 1940* (London: HMSO, 19410)

Baigent, Michael, and Richard Leigh, *Secret Germany: Claus von Stauffenberg and the Mystical Crusade Against Hitler* (London: Jonathan Cape, 1944)

Beevor, Antony, *Berlin: The Downfall 1945* (London: Viking, 2002)

Bullock, Alan, *Hitler, A Study in Tyranny* (London: Odhams, 1952)

Burleigh, Michael, *The Third Reich: A New History* (London: Macmillan, 2000)

Dalley, Jan, *Diana Mosley: A Life* (London: Faber & Faber, 1999)

Evans, Richard J., *Telling Lies About Hitler* (London: Virago, 2002)

—*The Coming of the Third Reich* (London: Allen Lane, 2003)

Fest, Joachim C., *Hitler* (London: Weidenfeld & Nicolson, 1974)

—*Inside Hitler's Bunker: The Last Days of the Third Reich* (London: Macmillan, 2004)

Frank, Johannes, *Eva Braun: Ein ungewöhnliches Frauenschicksal in geschichtlich bewegter Zeit* (Coburg: Nation Europa Verlag, 1997) (no English translation available)

Gilbert, Martin, *The Holocaust* (London: William Collins, 1986)

Gun, Nerin E., *Eva Braun: Hitler's Mistress* (New York: Meredith Press, 1968; London: Leslie Frewin, 1969)

Hanfstängl, Ernst ('Putzi'), *Unheard Witness* (New York: J. Lippincott Company, 1957; republished with a new Appendix, Concord, NH: Gibson Press, 2005)

Haste, Cate, *Nazi Women: Hitler's Seduction of a Nation* (London: Channel 4 Books, 2001)

Haunder, Milan, *Hitler: A Chronology of His Life and Times* (New York: The Macmillan Press, 1983)

Hoffmann, Heinrich, *Hitler Was My Friend* (London: Burke, 1955)

Infield, Glenn, *Adolf and Eva: Eva Braun and Adolf Hitler* (London: New English Library, 1975)

Junge, Traudl, edited by Melissa Müller, *Bis Zur Letzten Stunde* (Berlin: Claassen Verlag, 2002); translated as *Until the Final Hour* (London: Weidenfeld & Nicolson, 2003)

Kershaw, Ian, *Hitler, 1889–1936: Hubris* (London: Allen Lane, 1998)

—*Hitler, 1936–1945: Nemesis* (London: Allen Lane, 2000)

Klabunde, Anja, *Magda Goebbels* (Munich: Bertelsmann Verlag, 1999; London: Little, Brown, 2001)

Knopp, Guido, *Hitler's Women* (Munich: Bertelsmann Verlag, 2000; New York: Routledge, 2003)

Langer, Walter, *Inside the Mind of Adolf Hitler* (London: Plume Books, 1988)

Large, David Clay, *Where Ghosts Walked: Munich's Road to the Third Reich* (New York: W. W. Norton and Co., 1997)

Maser, Werner, *Hitler*, translated by Peter and Betty Ross (London: Allen Lane, 1973)

Select Bibliography

—*Hitler's Letters and Notes* (London; Heinemann, 1974)

Middlebrook, Martin, *The Battle of Hamburg: The Firestorm Raid* (London: Allen Lane, 1980)

Moltke, Helmut James von, *Letters to Freya, 1939–1945* (London: Collins Harvill, 1991)

Morell, Dr Theodore, *The Secret Diaries of Hitler's Doctor* (London: Sidgwick & Jackson, 1983; New York: Macmillan, 1983)

Paxton, Robert O., *The Anatomy of Fascism* (New York: Knopf, 2004)

Plaim, Anna, and Kurt Kuch, *Bei Hitlers: Zimmermädchen Annas Erinnerungen* (Kleindienst Verlag, 2003)

Pryce-Jones, David, *Unity Mitford: A Quest* (London: Weidenfeld & Nicolson, 1976)

Read, Anthony, *The Devil's Disciples: Hitler's Inner Circle* (New York: W. W. Norton and Co., 2003)

Roper, Lyndall, *Witch Craze: Terror and Fantasy in Baroque Germany* (London: Yale University Press, 2004)

Seaman, Mark, Introduction to *Operation Foxley: The British Plot to Kill Hitler* (Belfast: The Blackstaff Press in Association with the Public Record Office (PRO), 1998)

Sereny, Gitta, *Albert Speer: His Battle with Truth* (London: Vintage, 1996)

—*The German Trauma* (London: Allen Lane, 2000)

Speer, Albert, *Inside the Third Reich* (London: Weidenfeld & Nicolson, 1970; Phoenix edn, 1995)

Trevor-Roper, Hugh, *The Last Days of Hitler* (London: Macmillan, 1947)

—Introduction to English translation of *Hitler's Table Talk, 1941–1944* (London: Weidenfeld & Nicolson, 1953)

Wistrich, Robert L., *Who's Who in Nazi Germany* (London: Weidenfeld & Nicolson, 1982; London: Routledge, 1995)

Fiction

Hundreds, perhaps thousands, of novels have been set in the period of the Third Reich and tens of thousands of books written in an attempt to understand or come to terms with the Holocaust, but until recently comparatively few were about the experience of ordinary Germans before, during and after the Second World War. Some of the best are:

Grass, Günter, *Im Krebsgang* (Göttingen: Steidl Verlag, 2002); translated as *Crabwalk* (London: Faber & Faber, 2003)

Kertész, Imre, *Sorstalanság* (1975); translated as *Fateless* (London: Vintage, 2006)

Knauss, Sibylle, *Eva's Cousine* (Berlin: Claassen Verlag, 2002); translated as *Eva's Cousin* (New York: Doubleday, 2002; London: Black Swan, 2003)

Ledig, Gert, *Vergeltung* (Frankfurt: S. Fischer Verlag, 1956); translated as *Payback* (London: Granta Books, 2003)

Muller, Robert, *The World That Summer* (London: Sceptre, 1994)

Schlink, Bernard, *The Reader* (London: Phoenix House, 1997)

Sebald, W. G., *Austerlitz* (London: Penguin, 2002)

—*The Emigrants* (London: Vintage, 2002)

Memoirs and diaries

First and foremost are the twenty-two remaining pages from her private diary that Eva wrote between February and May 1935, now preserved in the US National Archives and Records Administration (NARA), 8601 Adelphi Road, College Park, Maryland. There are also thirty-three photograph albums, c. 1913–c. 1944 (Record Group 242: National

Archives Collection of Foreign Records Seized), and some eight hours of her home movies, '*Eva Braun and Adolf Hitler*', '*Berchtesgaden*', '*Germany, pre-World War Two*', ARC identifier: 24134 (Still Pictures Moving Images archive department) are all held here.

Anonymous, *A Woman of Berlin* (London: Virago, 2005) is one of the best accounts of Berlin in the weeks before and after it fell to the Soviets, detailing the experiences of women at the hands of the Russians.

Unpublished material

Eva Braun's Familiengeschichte (Eva Braun's Family History), a personal account by Dr Alois Winbauer written in 1976 at the request of his niece Gertraud Weisker and typed up by her in October 1992.

Wer War Eva Braun? Bericht von Gertraud Weisker (Who Was Eva Braun? A Report by Gertraud Weisker), written in 1998, translated for the author by Christiane Gehron (with individual passages, as stated, also translated by the author).

Memoirs of Wilhelm Schröder, this author's grandfather, written c. 1943, translated into English (heavily edited, unfortunately, by the author's mother, Ditha Helps) in 1976. Original German MS now lost.

Archive material

Bayerische Staatsbibliothek, Ludwigstrasse 16, DE-80539 Munich (picture curator: Frau Obermaier): holds many photographs of Eva Braun and her circle from the extensive Hoffmann Picture Archive (Bildarchiv Hoffmann)

Ferragamo Museo, Palazzo Spini Feroni, Via Tuornaboni, Florence: for material relating to Eva Braun's love of Ferragamo shoes
Hermann-Historica, Linprunstrasse 16, D-80335 Munich: for back catalogues of auctions of Hitler, Eva Braun and Third Reich memorabilia

Institut für Zeitgeschichte, Bibliothek, Leonrodstrasse 46 b, 80636 Munich: for rare or unpublished material on Eva Braun

Modern Military Records, Textual Archives Services Division, Archives II at NARA, College Park, Maryland, for post-war American army records and interviews

Musmanno Collection (archivist: Mr Paul Demilio), Gumberg Library, Duquesne University, Pittsburgh, Pennsylvannia 15282 for pre- and post-Nuremburg Trials interviews by US Judge Michael Musmanno with many of Hitler's circle, from which I used the following:

Series I: The Interrogations
Arthur Axmann
Dr Karl Brandt
Hugo Blaschke (Hitler's dentist)
Gerda Christian
Margaret Himmler
Erich Kempka
Hanna Reitsch
Traundl Junge (statement of events of April 1945 only)

Box 2
Dr Morell
Julius Schaub
Baldur von Schirach
Christa Schröder
Albert Speer

Box 3
Nicolaus von Below
Frau Anna Winter
Joanna Wolf

Appendix A

Country	Pre-war Jewish Population	Minimum Loss	Maximum Loss
Austria	185,000	50,000	50,000
Belgium	65,700	28,900	28,900
Bohemia and Moravia	118,310	78,150	78,150
Bulgaria	50,000	0	0
Denmark	7,800	60	60
Estonia	4,500	1,500	2,000
Finland	2,000	7	7
France	350,000	77,320	77,320
Germany	566,000	134,500	141,500
Greece	77,380	60,000	67,000
Hungary	825,000	550,000	569,000
Italy	44,500	7,680	7,680
Latvia	91,500	70,000	71,500
Lithuania	168,000	140,000	143,000
Luxembourg	3,500	1,950	1,950
Netherlands	140,000	100,000	100,000
Norway	1,700	762	762
Poland	3,300,000	2,900,000	3,000,000
Romania	609,000	271,000	287,000
Slovakia	88,950	68,000	71,000
Soviet Union	3,020,000	1,000,000	1,100,000

Index

Adolf and Eva (TV programme)
xii, 9(n)
Adlerhorst, the 397
Allied Control Commission 466
Alliluyeva, Nadezhda 12(n)
Almas-Dietrich, Maria 186
Altmühl River 23
Amann, Max 105, 305
Amsterdam 336–7
Anderson's Fairy Tales (Anderson)
31–2
anti-Semitism 9, 43, 66, 77–8,
215–16, 251, 283–4, 351–4;
see also Jews
apathy 329
Ardennes offensive 397
Arent, Kukuli von 247, 250
Arndt, Wilhelm 431
art, appropriation legalised
186(n)
Aryan norm, the 95
Ascherson, Neal 310(n)
assassination 133
Auschwitz 139(n), 251(n), 277(n),
321, 325(n), 333, 342
Austria, annexation of 275–6
autobahns 140

Baarova, Lina 225–6
Bad Schachen 313
Baden-Powell, Robert 55(n)
Bambi (Salten) 33
Bavaria 91–9

Bayerischer Heimat und Königsbund
36
Bayreuth 97
BDF (*Bund Deutscher
Frauenvereine*) 71–2
BDM (*Bund Deutscher Mädel*,
League of German Girls) 72–3,
74(n), 326
Bechstein, Helene 84, 85
Beer Hall Putsch, the 87–8, 187
Behrens, Magda 225, 227
Beierl, Florian 85(n), 385–6
Beilngries 18, 21, 24, 44–6, 91,
195, 196
Belgium 305
'Belief and Beauty' 73, 327
Below, Maria von 226, 229, 246,
351
Below, Nicholaus von 226, 410,
450
Belzec 333, 342
Benedict XVI, Pope 24
Berchtesgaden 188–9, 255, 347
Berger, Gottlob 411
Berghof 97
Berghof, the
photographs 169–70
comparison with Carinhall 183
layout 184–7
Eva's lifestyle 197–8
Eva's role 200–4
Eva's suite 205–8, 255–6
Hitler's accommodation 208–9

affairs 225–6
Nazi wives 226, 227–8, 229,
    346–7
chalets 226–7
Eva's friends 228–9
secretaries 230, 275
atmosphere 246
official guests 256–7
life at 259–61
Hitler's routine 263–70
meals 265, 266, 386
the Teehaus 265–6, 386
New Year's Eve 1938/9 274–5
the Braun's visit 291
Unity Mitford's visit 294
Christmas and New Year, 1939
    301–2
summer, 1940 307–8
ignorance of horrors 335–7,
    346–7
isolation 347–8
air raid shelter 372–3
Hitler's fifty-fifth birthday
    373–4
Hitler's final departure 375
Gertraud Weisker's visit 376–89
and the Stauffenberg Plot
    394–5
Eva's final visit 401–4
obliterated 189–90, 466
Berlin
    comparison with Munich 111
    Grieg Street 163
    Olympic Games, 1936 213–15,
        217–22
    Marzahn 214
    Jewish population 284, 287, 329
    Kurfürstendamm 284, 431
    Kristallnacht 284–6
    Agnesstrasse 294
    bombing raids 306

    Rosenstrasse demonstration
        334–5
    Hitler's return 396
    Eva's January 1945 visit 401–2
    conditions, 1945 412–13
    defenders 414, 420
    assault on 414, 424–5, 428–9,
        443–4, 447
    the Tiergarten 417–18
    Potzdamer Platz 447
Berlin, Isaiah 94(n), 285–6
Berlinghoff, Kurt 463
Bernadotte, Count Folke 446
Birkett, Norman 82
Blasko (dog) 179
Bloch, Dr 65–6
Blondi (dog) 241–2, 374, 434, 461
blondness 95
blood-guilt 356, 394(n)
Boggis-Rolph, Colonel Hugh 163
Bolsheviks 9(n)
Bolshevism from Moses to Lenin
    (Hitler and Eckart) 93(n)
Boomtown Rats 76(n)
Bormann, Gerda 200(n), 225, 227,
    228, 240, 465
Bormann, Martin 106–7, 146–7,
    171, 179, 180, 182–4, 196, 225,
    229, 262(n), 264–5, 274–5,
    293, 346, 347, 381, 401, 404,
    413, 423, 454, 459, 460, 465
Boy Scouts 55(n)
Brand, Wolfgang 45, 46
Brandt, Anni 271
Brandt, Dr 226, 263, 275, 411
Braun, Eva
    appearance 7, 55, 212, 259–60,
        388
    background x
    biographies x–xii
    riddle of xi

context xii–xiii
birth 16
family background 16–25, 84
religious background 17, 50–1
stubbornness 19
and the First World War 25
literary influences 26–33
childhood 36, 37–44, 46–9
education 37, 44–6, 49–50
confrontations with father 50,
    52
and boys 50, 55
at convent/finishing school
    51–4
adolescent freedom 55–6
employment at Photo Hoffmann
    3–5, 56, 158, 168–9, 179,
    194–5, 255–6
early photography 4
introduced to Hitler 5–7
political background 8–9
attraction to Hitler 10
pursuit of Hitler 11–12, 109–12,
    115, 117, 125
starts relationship with Hitler
    13–15
age gap with Hitler 56–7, 68
devotion to Hitler 57
and Bavaria 91–2
and Geli Raubal 111, 115
comparison with Geli Raubal
    117–20
relationship with Hitler 118,
    129, 154–5, 191–210, 240–1,
    242–6, 274, 281–3, 300–2,
    311–12, 374–6, 379–81, 395,
    442–3
deflowering 126
early relationship with Hitler
    126–32
becomes Hitler's mistress 128–9

suicide attempt 133–4
Hitler declares love for 135–6
depression 141
role 141, 267
second suicide attempt 142–3,
    149, 159–60
accepted as Hitler's companion
    and mistress 143–7
leaves family home 144
anonymity 147, 155, 170, 201,
    204–5, 221–2, 259, 452
diary 148–60
loneliness 154, 195–6, 375–6
money received from Hitler
    154–5
generosity 155
material expectations 155–6
optimism 156, 158
jealousy 156–8, 247
love letters 161, 430
scarcity of primary sources
    161–2
natural exhibitionist 162
photograph albums 162–7,
    171–2
need for Hitler 165
lack of concentration 165–6
photograph captions 166–7,
    171–2
interest in photography 167–71
Hitler buys camera for 168
control of image 169
submissiveness 172
sport and exercise 172–3,
    197–8, 211–13
cine films 173–4, 200(n), 273
installed in Wasserburgerstrasse
    177–80
allowance 179, 182
cars 179, 209, 234
dogs 179, 241, 376, 401

relationship with Bormann 182–3
at the Berghof 186–7, 197–8, 200–9
Speer on 193, 282–3, 312
loyalty 194
shoes 197, 272–3
role as hostess 200–1
nicknamed *Tschapperl* 201
role as housekeeper 201–4
suite at the Berghof 205–8, 255–6
clothes 206–8, 244, 290, 374, 397, 412
height 212(n), 383(n)
and children 213
and the 1936 Olympic Games 219, 221–2
and the Nazi wives 228, 229
Berghof friends 228–9
and Speer 232–3
reconciliation with parents 233
Italian tour 233–4
and Magda Goebbels 239–40, 281
allowed to use the informal *Du* 240
psychological interaction with Hitler 242–3
and Unity Mitford 247, 248, 258–9
achievement 251–2
boredom 252, 254–5, 259, 384
exclusion 253–5
life at the Berghof 256–7, 259–61, 265
moodiness 257
weight 261
attempt to replace Dr Morell 263
on Hoffmann 268
Italian tour, 1938 271–3
provisions in Hitler's will 273

New Year's Eve 1938/9 274–5
and the annexation of Austria 276
visit to Portofino 277
forbidden information 289
luxury and 290–1
and the beginning of the war 296–7
lack of knowledge of the war 298, 299, 337
Christmas, 1939 301–2
isolation 302, 322
Gertraud Weisker stays with 302–4
summer, 1940 307–8
confides in Speer 311
affairs 312–13
fidelity 316–17, 319–20
alleged affair with Fegelein 318–19
and Gretl's marriage 320–2
question of guilt 324–5, 339
non-membership of Nazi Party 338–9
knowledge of Jewish genocide 342–3
avoidance of awkward questions 345
and anti-Semitism 351–2
'blameworthy' 352
goodness 352
interventions on behalf of Jews 354–5
at thirty 358
attitude to the war 358–9
Hitler's dependence on 362–3
Hitler's fifty-fifth birthday 373–4
blood pressure 375
Gertraud Weisker's visit to the Berghof 376–89

Hitler's telephone calls 380–1
desire to be loved 389
and the Stauffenberg Plot
    394–5
will 396, 430
Christmas, 1944 397
and Hitler's polyp operation 397
preparations for death 397, 400,
    404–5, 426
conversation with Ilse, 1945
    398–9
January 1945 visit to Berlin
    401–2
final visit to the Berghof 401–4
return to Berlin 404
Hoffmann on 405
in the bunker 409–12, 413–14,
    422, 427–8, 429
strength of character 410–11
role in the bunker 412
letter to Herta Schneider, April
    1945 414–17
last stroll through the
    Tiergarten 417–18
and Hitler's birthday in the
    bunker 419–20
organises party in the bunker
    423–4
last letter to Herta Schneider
    425–6
Hitler kisses 427–8
and the Goebbels children 429,
    440
final letter to Gretl 429–32
and Hanna Reitsch 439–40
and death 443
final days in the bunker 444,
    449–50
and Fegelein's execution 446
suicide plans 449
marriage to Hitler 453–6

suicide 456–9
body 460–1
personal effects 462–3
Braun, Franziska (née Kronburger)
    16–17, 18, 19, 21, 38, 43–4, 47,
    51, 111, 130, 170, 198–9, 233–4,
    271, 292–3, 355, 395, 463–4
Braun, Fritz
    opinion of Hitler 9
    disapproval of cosmetics 14
    Eva's birth 16
    marriage 16, 18
    background 17–18
    teaching 23
    pastimes 23–4
    First World War service 35
    effect of First World War on 36–7
    relationship with Eva 37–8, 50,
        52
    separation from Fanny 43–4
    reunites with Fanny 47
    daughter's marriage prospects
        50–1
    and Eva's adolescent freedom
        55–6
    and Hitler's relationship with
        Eva 130–1
    attempts to intercede with
        Hitler 144–6
    at the Berghof 170
    learns of Eva's 'sordid affair'
        199–200
    joins Nazi party 200
    visits to the Berghof 233, 291
    fiftieth birthday 291–2
    and the Bürgerbräukeller
        assassination attempt 299
    post-war 463–4
    grave 47
Braun, Gretl: see Fegelein, Gretl
    (née Braun)

Braun, Ilse 18, 37, 38, 52, 56, 132,
    149, 213, 290–1, 375, 398–9,
    463
Braunau am Inn 52–4
Brecht, Bertolt 75, xi(n)
Breslau 398
Britain, Battle of 305–6
British Union of Fascists 249(n)
Bruckmann, Elsa 84–5
Buchenwald 357
Bulgaria 286(n)
bunker, the
    layout 405, 407–8
    Hitler's accommodation 405,
        407
    lack of privacy 407
    hospital 408
    technicians 408
    life in 408–14
    Eva's role 412
    lack of discipline 413–14, 417
    Hitler's birthday 419–20
    departures 421–3
    party 423–4
    final situation conference 427
    Speer's final visit 433–7
    Hanna Reitsch in 437–40
    suicide discussions 440–1
    camaraderie 441
    final days 443–50, 451–6
    suicide plans 448–9
    surreal atmosphere 451
    Hitler and Eva's wedding 453–6
    Hitler's suicide 456–9
    the end 460–1
Burckhardt, Carl 295
Burgdorf, General Wilhelm 441(n)
Busch, Wilhelm 32–3, 209
Byatt, A.S. 30(n)
Byron, Robert 220

Canaris, Admiral Wilhelm Franz
    378(n)
Carinhall 183, 227
casualties 448
CCG (Control Commission of
    Germany) 96(n)
Chamberlain, Neville 276, 289
Channon, Sir Henry 'Chips'
    220–1
Charles, Emperor-King of Austria
    35(n)
Chelmno 333, 342
childhood games 39–40
children's songs 27–9
children's stories 29–34
Christian, Gerda (née Daranowski)
    230
Christmas 41–2, 301–2
Churchill, Winston 305, 390
Ciano, Count Galeazzo 172, 295,
    315
cine films 173–4, 200(n), 273
Cologne, bombing raid 307
Communism 138
concentration camps 42(n),
    139–40, 180(n), 326, 332–3
Convent of the English Sisters
    52–4
cosmetics 14, 178
Coué, Emile 158(n)
Court, Major H. B. 388
Crabwalk (Grass) 357
Czechoslovakia, occupation of
    288–9

Dachau 6(n), 42(n), 139–40,
    180(n), 342, 357
Danzig 295
declaration of war 297
depression, the 58(n)
Deutelmoser, Ernst 112

die Weisse Rose (the White Rose) 345
Dietrich, Marlene 75, 186, 383
divorce 46–7
Dokumentation Obersalzberg 189
Döring, Herbert 10(n), 11–12, 117(n), 123, 128, 186, 203, 205, 212, 227, 244, 256–7, 317, 318, 402
Dresden, bombing raids 399–400

Eagle's Nest, the 190, 293–4, 321
Eckart, Dietrich 66, 82, 93
Edelweiss 212
Edelweiss Pirates 212(n), 343
Eichmann, Adolf 341, 342
Einsatzgruppen 330
elections, 1932 and 33 138
Eppelheim xii
Eternal Jew, The (film) 188(n), 328(n)
eugenics 216–17
Europe, Jewish population 287
Eva's Cousin (Knauss) 385
Evans, Richard 325(n), 355
exercise 211, 220
Exner, Marlene von 262(n)
extermination camps 139(n), 333, 341–2, 359–60, 394(n), 399
extermination programme 277(n), 288, 325–6, 332–3, 345, 359–60

fairs 26(n), 29, 41–2
family attitudes 48
Fegelein, Gretl (née Braun)
  birth 18
  employment at Photo Hoffmann 5(n)
  fragility 132
  leaves family home 144
  appearance 170
  admirers 171
  in Wasserburgerstrasse 177
  at the Berghof 228
  Italian tours 233–4, 271–3
  Fegelein's pursuit of 317–20
  marriage 320–2
  at Schloss Fischhorn 395
  Eva's final letter 429–32
  post-war 463
Fegelein, Hermann 317–22, 395–6, 445–7
feminists 71–2
Ferdinand, Archduke, assassination of 25
Ferragamo, Salvatore 272–3
film stars 75, 76
Finland 286(n)
First World War 25, 35–6, 67–8
Fitzgerald, William George 98
Flegel, Erna 408, 413, 431(n), 434, 437, 438, 441, 448, 461(n)
Florence 308
flu epidemic of 1919 43
food prices 80
Four Elements (painting) 114(n)
France 297, 305
Frankfurt, Jewish population 287
Freikorps Oberland 36
Frentz, Walter 169, 254
Freud, Sigmund 38
Freytag von Loringhoven, Baron Bernd 431
Fritsch, Werner von 297
Fromm, Bella 238–9
Fuchs, Du hast die Gans gestohlen (song) 28
Furtwängler, Wilhelm 333–4

Galton, Francis 216
Gandhi, Mahatma 295

Garmisch-Partenkirchen 96, 219
gas chambers 42(n)
Gatow aerodrome 433–4
Gdansk 314(n)
Gehron, Christiane 3(n)
genocide 9, 141, 189, 258, 286–8,
     325, 330, 332–3, 339, 340, 346,
     359: *see also* Jews
German Blood and German
     Honour, Law for the Protection
     of 214(n), 456(n)
German character 29, 30(n)
German Civil Code 63
German National Archive 173(n)
German Worker's Party (DAP) 77
Germany
     unification of 17
     effect of First World War on
          35–6
     shame 58(n)
     class system 83
     Jewish population 287
     RAF bombing campaign begins
          306–7
     arms production 316
     morality 329–30, 331(n)
     guilt 356–7
     suffering 401
     defeat 447–8
Gestapo, report on the
     Schicklgrubers 85(n)
ghettos 251(n), 328, 341
Giesing, Dr Erwin 245, 262–3
Giesler, Hermann 409
Gilbert, John 76
Gilligan, James 58(n)
Glassl, Anna 60
Goebbels, Helga 461(n)
Goebbels, Hilde 238(n)
Goebbels, Josef
     and the rise of Hitler 187

on propaganda 220
adultery 225–6
meets Magda 236–7
anti-Semitism 284
on Jews 341
and the bombing of Hamburg
     364–5
in the cellars of the Propaganda
     Ministry 408
in the bunker 413, 439
Speer on 435
and Hitler's marriage 453–4,
     454
suicide 461
Goebbels, Magda
     clothes 140, 397
     children 200(n)
     and Hitler 200–1, 235, 236–8
     marriage 225–6, 238
     at the Berghof 227, 228
     background 235–40
     and the Windsor's visit 258
     and Eva Braun 281
     guilt 352
     in the bunker 412, 435, 440
     and Hitler's suicide 457, 458
     poisons children 461
     suicide 461
Göhler, Johannes 300(n)
Göring, Emmy 140, 227, 228,
     238–9, 335–6
Göring, Hermann
     on Hitler's early disciples 86
     appetite 114
     introduces Hitler to suitable
          women 127
     Carinhall 183, 227
     art collection 186
     pagan streak 220–1
     as lecher 225
     Berghof chalet 227

and the Battle of Britain 305
at Gretl's wedding 321
on racial war 341
mumbo-jumbo 404(n)
in the bunker 413
escape from the bunker 421,
422
arrest ordered 433
suicide 441(n), 465
Grass, Günter 357
Great Britain
fascism 249
anti-Semitism 285–6
declaration of war 297
the Blitz 304, 306
the Battle of Britain 305–6
Greim, Lt-General Robert Ritter
von 433, 437–8, 441(n), 447
Grimm's Fairy Tales (Grimm)
29–32, 443
Guderian, General Heinz 349–50
Gun, Nerin xi, 6(n), 146, 296–7,
313, 398–9
Günsche, Otto 424, 437, 441(n),
458, 460, 466
Guten Abend, gute Nacht (song) 27
Gutierrez, Colonel Robert A.
148–9(n), 165(n), 462
gypsies 9(n), 216(n), 251(n), 321,
325(n), 359

Hamburg 306(n), 310, 344,
364–7
handicapped, the 42, 140, 216(n),
217, 277(n), 288, 345
Handschuhmacher, Heini 368,
372–3
Hanfstängl, Ernst ('Putzi') 81–3,
84, 85, 102, 103, 107–8, 114,
121(n), 123(n), 126–7, 182,
236, 238, 239

Hanfstängl, Helene 81(n), 84
Harris, Air Marshal Sir Arthur
'Bomber' 306–7, 362, 364
Hasselbach, Hans Karl von 195,
410–11
Hassell, Ulrich von 333
Hastings, Selina 247(n)
Haus Wachenfeld 97–9, 101, 117,
125, 180, 182, 185
Hausenstein, Wilhelm 374
Hauser, Gayelord 266
Hébuterne, Jeanne 12(n)
Heidenaber, Fräulein von 49–50
Heidi (Spyri) 33
Heimat (TV programme) 26(n)
Heise, Fräulein 207
Helps, Ditha (née Edith Schröder)
x, xiii, 14, 29, 41, 46–7, 72, 96,
173, 304–5, 353–4, 353–4,
365–6, 426–7
Henderson, Neville 254
Hess, Ilse 228
Hess, Rudolf 89, 93, 228
Hettlage, Karl 232
Hewel, Walter 243, 441(n)
Heydrich, Reinhard 344, 360
Hiedler, Johann Georg 59
Himmler, Heinrich
and Geli Raubal's death 121
and *Kristallnacht* 285
put in charge of extermination
camps 341
reintroduces 'blood guilt' 394(n)
in the bunker 413
suicide 441(n), 465
peace negotiations 446
Himmler, Margaret 227–8
Hitler, Adolf
secret xii
family background 59–61, 83–4
birth 61

siblings 61, 64
childhood 62–4
religious background 62
ascetic tastes 63–4, 183
attitude towards women 63, 247
education 63, 64
relationship with mother 63,
65–6
life in Vienna 65–7
physical abnormalities 65, 245
First World War service 67
control of image 5, 169–70
introduced to Eva Braun 5–7
'Herr Wolf' alias 6, 31, 78
and Hoffmann 8
ideology 9(n), 77–8, 93
anti-Semitism 9, 66, 77–8,
283–4, 287
appearance 9–10, 65, 79
eyes 10, 63, 79, 437
at the Hoffmanns 11
Eva's pursuit of 11–12, 109–12,
115, 117, 125
comparison to Stalin 12(n)
girlfriends 12–13
starts relationship with Eva
13–15
age gap with Eva 56–7, 68
taste in women 56–7, 119,
143
motivation 58(n)
support for 58(n), 329–30
and the Hitler Youth 74
return to Munich 76–7
first political speech 77
learns political skills 77–9
entry into upper middle classes
81–6
speech giving style 82, 83
relationship with Paula Hitler
83–4, 203

fear of fathering imperfect children 85–6, 103, 131
wounded in the Beer Hall
Putsch 87–8
prison term 88–9
personal fortune 89, 290
and Bavaria 92–5
passion for Wagner 97
relationship with Geli Raubal
100–1, 102–7, 108(n), 109,
118, 120
and Geli Raubal 101–2, 121–4
love of Geli 103–4
frugality 106
fixed habits 112
and art 114–15
on marriage 118
relationship with Eva 118, 129,
154–5, 191–210, 240–1,
242–6, 274, 281–3, 300–2,
311–12, 374–6, 379–81, 395,
442–3
early relationship with Eva
126–32
and suicide 132–3
assassination attempts 133, 299,
314, 331(n), 390–5
October 1932 tour 133–4
appointed Chancellor 135,
136–7, 137–8
declares love for Eva 135–6
gifts to Eva 136
adulation 137
'married to Germany' 137
proclaimed *Führer* of the
German Reich 140–1
mood swings 141, 301
and Eva's second suicide
attempt 142–3
Eva accepted as companion and
mistress 143–7

indifference to Eva 154
payments to Eva 154–5
dislike of dachshunds 156(n)
and Unity Mitford 157, 248–51,
    294–5, 297
polyp operation 159
letters 161(n)
gives Eva a camera 168
control 172
installs Eva in
    Wasserburgerstrasse 177–8
visits to Wasserburgerstrasse
    179, 180
directs race laws 180
purchase of Haus Wachenfeld
    180, 182
taste in films 185–6
redesigns the Berghof 185
musical taste 186
and the Röhm putsch 187
architectural vision 192–3
and Magda Goebbels 200–1,
    235, 236–8, 440
meals 202
will 203, 273–4
and children 204, 231
accommodation at the Berghof
    208–9
literary influences 209
height 212(n)
charisma 213, 349, 350–1, 437,
    441–3
and the 1936 Olympic Games
    214, 217
eugenic beliefs 216
relationship with Speer
    231–2
and Fritz Braun's visit to the
    Berghof 233
dogs 241–2, 374, 434
sentimentality 242

psychological interaction with
    Eva 242–3
and the Windsors' visit 258
outlines the Hossbach Protocol
    259
diet 261–2, 266, 293–4
medication 262–3, 363
routine at the Berghof 263–70
cars 266
table talk 267–9, 324
Speer on 268, 350, 359
on the ruling class 269
state visit to Italy 271–2
annexation of Austria 275–6
and the Munich agreement
    276
and *Kristallnacht* 285
euthanasia programme 288
and occupation of
    Czechoslovakia 288–9
holidays 289–90
and the Brauns 291
fiftieth birthday 293–4
invasion of Poland 295–6
Germany's fate 297
Bürgerbräukeller assassination
    attempt 299
Christmas, 1939 301–2
in Paris 305
summer, 1940 307–8
and Operation Barbarossa
    315–16
strain 315–16
at Gretl's wedding 320
on women 324
resistance to 330–2, 333–5,
    343–6, 378(n), 390–5
plans for Jewish extermination
    332
Henriette von Schirach's visit to
    Amsterdam 336–7

forbids anyone talking about
  genocide to Eva 339
and the Jewish question 341
protection of social circle 347–8
dual personality 349–50
rages 349–50
orders 359
knowledge of Jewish genocide
  359–60
and the Battle of Stalingrad 362
dependence on Eva 362–3
exhaustion 363–4, 371–2
refusal to visit Hamburg 365
fifty-fifth birthday 373–4
telephone calls to Eva 380–1
Stauffenberg Plot 331(n), 390–5
Stauffenberg Plot injuries 393
returns to Berlin 396
polyp operation 396–7
Eva's January 1945 vast 401
plan to return to the Berghof
  404(n)
dissociation from outside world
  408–9
in the bunker 408–14, 421, 423
mood swings 409
physical deterioration 409, 419,
  437
birthday in the bunker 419–20
last photographs 420
and the Russian assault on
  Berlin 424
kisses Eva 427–8
final situation conference 427
orders Göring's arrest 433
Speer's final visit 433–7
and Hanna Reitsch 438–40
suicide plans 438, 448–9
achievement 441–2
meals in the bunker 444
and Fegelein's execution 445–7

and Himmler's betrayal 446
Personal and Political
  Testaments 452–3
marriage to Eva 453–6
suicide 456–9
body 460–1
jawbone 461–2
property handed over to state
  466
sexuality passim
Hitler, Alois 53, 59–61, 62, 63–4
Hitler, Brigid 121(n)
Hitler, Klara (née Pölzl) 60–6
Hitler, Paula 61, 64, 83–4, 88,
  203, 273
Hitler Jugend (Hitler Youth) 74–5
Hitler Was My Friend (Hoffman)
  5(n)
Hitler's Children (TV programme)
  73(n)
Hoffmann, Erna 228
Hoffmann, Heini 170–1, 233–4
Hoffmann, Heinrich
  as Nazi official photographer 4
  employment of Gretl Braun 5(n)
  introduces Hitler to Eva Braun
    5–6
  on Eva Braun 7, 115
  background 8
  family home 10–11
  pushes Eva on Hitler 12
  on Eva's impression on Hitler
    13
  hires Eva 56
  at Hitler's release from prison 89
  on Geli Raubal 102, 105
  drinking 113–14
  and Geli Raubal's death 123,
    123(n)
  on Hitler and Eva's early rela-
    tionship 128

buys house in
Wasserburgerstrasse 177
Eva's continued employment by
179
Hitler on 267–8
on the mature Eva 405
Hoffmann, Henriette: *see* Schirach,
Henriette von (née Hoffmann)
Hohenstein, Alexander 330
Holland 305, 336
Holocaust 9, 87, 283, 326, 340,
343, 345, 357, 394
Holocaust-denial 6(n), 148(n)
Holocaust, the 9, 188; *see also*
Jews
Homes and Gardens (magazine)
97–8
homosexuals 9(n), 141, 216(n),
332(n)
Höppner, SS-*Sturmbannführer* 341
Hossbach Protocol 259
Hupfauer, Dr Theodor 348

I Accuse (film) 345
Infield, Glenn 354–5
inflation 43, 80–1
Irving, David 6(n), 148–9(n),
238(n), 436
Italy 233–4, 271–3, 314

jazz 344
Jehovah's Witnesses 141
Jews
disappearance of xiii, 327, 328
extermination 9(n), 440
toleration of 17
seen as financially manipulative
parasites 43
threat of 58(n)
attitudes towards 73
Hitler's views on 77–8

as secret power 93(n)
boycott on 138, 140
excluded from government
employment 140
anti-Jewish laws issued 141
propaganda view of 188(n)
fear of 215–16
attacks on 215
compared with disease 283–4
Kristallnacht 284–6
genocide 286–8, 325–6, 332–3,
359–60
German population 287
'resettlement' 310
murder of 328
fugitives 329
normal treatment of 330
resistance to deportations 333–5
knowledge in the Berghof
335–7
deportations 340
property seizures 340
executions 340–3
Eva's attitudes 351–2
prejudice 353–4
Eva's interventions 354–5
defiance 360
Joachimsthaler, Anton 412(n)
Johannmeier, Major 453
Junge, Hans 260
Junge, Traudl 169, 194–5, 230,
260, 261, 318, 321, 327–8, 335,
336, 346, 348, 348–9, 372, 374,
392, 393, 411(n), 418–19,
421–2, 427–8, 434, 445, 449,
450, 451, 452–3, 456–7, 464–5

Kaufmann, Karl Otto 365
Kehlstein, the 190
Kehlsteinhaus (the Eagle's Nest)
190, 293–4, 321

Kempf, Annemarie 346, 350–1
Kempka, Erich 116, 117, 254, 460
Kempka, Frau 230
Klein, Ada 12–13
Knauss, Sibylle 385
Koch, Robert 283–4
Königssee, the 381–3
Konrad, SS *Hauptsturmführer* Franz 462
Kosian, Herr 197
Kraft durch Freude 289
Krause, Karl 274
Krauss, Maria 45
Krebs, General Hans 441(n)
Kreisau Circle, the 314, 331, 333, 390–4
Kristallnacht 284–6
Kronburger, Bertha 23
Kronburger, Franz-Paul 19–23
Kronburger, Josefa (née Winbauer) 16, 20–1, 44, 166–7, 443
Krysnica Norska 314(n)
Kubizek, August 66–7, 105
Kunz, Dr 461(n)
Künzel, Max 45, 46

Landsberg prison 88–9
Langer, Dr Walter C. 108
Last Days of Hitler, The (Joachimsthaler) 412(n)
Lebensraum 259, 289
Lenya, Lotte 75
Leonding 63
Ley, Inge 133, 289–90
Ley, Robert 289(n)
Lili Marlene (song) 75
Linge, Heinz 243–4, 265, 290(n), 441(n), 459, 460
Linz 64, 65, 409–10
Lipstadt, Deborah 148(n)

Lodz ghetto 341
London, the Blitz 304, 306
Londonderry, Lord 249
Ludecke, Karl 209
Ludwig III, King of Bavaria 35(n)
Luftwaffe 305–6, 309
Lyttelton, Oliver (later Lord Chandos) 285–6

MacMillan, Harold 286
Mann, Thomas 136
Manziarly, Constanze 262, 428
Marie-Magdalena, Sister 53–4
Markt am Inn 24
marriage 46, 61–2, 118, 456(n)
Matzelsberger, Franziska 60
Maser, Werner 161(n), 430(n)
Maugham, Syrie 206
Maurice, Emil 89, 99, 115–16
Max and Moritz (Busch) 32–3, 209
May, Karl 33, 62, 209
Mein Kampf (Hitler) 9, 57, 62, 89, 93, 97
Meissner, Otto 238(n)
Mengele, Dr Josef 251(n)
'mercy death' 42(n)
Metcalfe, Ralph 217
Miesbacher Anzeiger (newspaper) 86
Milgram, Stanley 286(n)
Miller, Alice 58
Miller, Lee 178(n)
Milne, Marion xi–xii, 386–7
ministerial meetings 346–7
Misch, Rochus 298, 431(n), 441(n)
Mitford, Unity 13(n), 133, 143, 157, 247–51, 258–9, 281, 294–5, 297
Mittlstrasse, Margarete 173(n), 196–7, 203–4, 244, 245, 300, 386, 404

Mittlstrasse, Wilhelm 203–4
Mohnke, General 441(n)
Moltke, Count Helmut von 331–2, 333, 356, 390, 391
Morell, Hanni 271, 228
Morell, Theodore 65(n), 226, 245, 262–3, 274–5, 311–12, 349(n), 372, 409, 423, 431
Mosley, Diana (née Mitford) 248
Mosley, Sir Oswald 157, 247, 249
Müller, Renate 133
Münchener Post (newspaper) 122–3
Munich
    Schellingstrasse 3, 8
    Schnorrstrasse 10–11
    and the First World War 25
    Schwabing-West 49
    celebrations and holidays 76
    Kindl Keller beer hall 81–2
    Residenzstrasse 87
    Thierschstrasse 104
    Shrovetide Ball 105
    Prinzregentenplatz 106–7
    comparison with Berlin 111
    Osteria Bavaria 112
    Osteria Italiana 112–13
    Nazi connections 113
    Wiedenmayerstrasse 144
    Wasserburgerstrasse (Delpstrasse) 144, 177–80, 377(n), 384, 396
    Jewish population 287
    Bürgerbräukeller assassination attempt 299
    resistance 345–6
    bombing raids 362–3, 374, 384, 397–8
Munich agreement 276
Musmanno, Michael 145, 445(n)
Mussolini, Benito 271, 314, 315, 448

Naples 272
NARA (National Archives and Records Administration) 150–1, 162, 164–5, 173, 439, 462
nature, communing with 92–3
Nazi Party
    and women 72–4
    symbols and iconography 78–9
    class profile broadened 86
    militancy 86–7
    growth of 89, 137
    Reichstag seats 138
    ideology 187–8
    journalists 199(n)
    and the 1936 Olympic Games 214
    and *Kristallnacht* 285
    masculinity 323–4
    role of women 324–5
Negus (dog) 179, 241
Neubert, Lidy 152
Neuengamme 420
Night of the Long Knives 108
Normandy, Allied landings 321
North German Confederation 26(n)
Nuremberg 96–7, 221
Nuremberg Rally 180, 216, 258–9
Nuremberg Trial 436, 465
Nuremberg Laws 180, 214(n)
nursery songs and stories 26–33

Obersalzberg 92–4, 96–9, 104, 106, 135, 180, 182–5, 189, 202, 358, 466
Olympia (film) 217–19
Olympic Games, 1936 213–15, 217–22
Operation Barbarossa 309–10, 315–16, 330
Operation Foxley 388, 390

Operation Valkyrie 394
Ostermayr, Walter 255(n)
Owens, Jesse 217

Paolini, Salvatore 293–4
Paris, fall of 305
Paris Soir (newspaper) 198, 257
patriotic organisations 72–5
patriotic songs 74–5
Peacock, Eulace 217
Pforzheim 400
Phayre, Ignatius 98
photographs
    Weisker family collection xii
    official 5, 8
    childhood 40
    stereoscopic slides 40
    Eva's albums 162–7, 171–2
    at the Berghof 169–70
    New Year's Eve 1938/9 274–5
Picasso, Jacqueline 12(n)
Plaim, Anna 194, 197, 209, 244,
    342
Plaim, Anna 171
Plankstetten 23
Poland, invasion of 295–6
Pölzl, Johanna 64, 83
Popp, Joseph 67
popular songs 75
Portofino 277, 307
Prague 277, 288–9
Prevention of Hereditarily
    Diseased Progeny, Law for the
    42(n)
prisoners of war 325(n)
propaganda, successful 220
Pryce-Jones, David 249
punk rockers 76(n)

Quandt, Günther 236
Quandt, Harald 447(n)

race hygiene 216
race laws 180, 214(n), 215–16
racial awareness 73
racial policies 215–17
racial prejudice 251, 353
racial theories 180, 187–8
racial undesirables 140
racism 356
Rall, Günter 357
rallies 74–5
Raubal, Angela 12(n), 66, 83–4, 88,
    98–9, 104, 106, 203, 273, 274
Raubal, Elfriede 99
Raubal, Geli
    childhood 88
    education 99, 100–1
    relationship with Hitler 100–1,
        102–7, 108(n), 109, 118, 120
    charm 101
    calls Hitler 'Onk' 101–2
    as Hitler's social consort 102
    moves to Thierschstrasse 104
    sex drive 106
    moves into Prinzregentenplatz
        106
    and Eva 111, 115
    affair with Emil Maurice
        115–16
    lovers 116–17, 119, 120–1
    comparison with Eva Braun
        117–20
    appearance 119
    death of 121–4
    grave 122(n)
Raubal, Leo 88
Ravensbrück 326
Red Army
    advance 396
    assault on Berlin 414, 424–5,
        428–9, 443–4, 447
    soldiers assaults 416(n)

Reichsmarks, value of 80–1
Reiter, Maria 12, 132
Reitsch, Hanna 437–40, 441(n), 444, 446, 447
resistance 330–2, 333–5, 343–6, 378(n), 390–5
Ribbentrop, Joachim von 295, 421
Riefenstahl, Leni 89, 143, 211, 217–19, 232
Röhm, Ernst 187
Roman Catholicism 24
Rosenberger, Ludwig 362
Roth, Joseph 95
Royal Air Force 306–7, 364, 399–400, 466
Ruhpolding 24, 463–4
Ryback, Timothy 85(n)
Rzhevskaya, Elena 461–2

SA, the 73(n), 187
Salome (Wilde) 34
Salten, Felix 33
Schattenhofer, Franz 45
Schaub, Julius 119, 274, 422, 431
Schelling, Friedrich 3
Schicklgruber, Maria 59
Schicklgruber family, Gestapo report on 85(n)
Schilling, Peter 313
Schirach, Baldur von 74, 102, 337
Schirach, Henriette von (née Hoffmann) 12, 51, 98, 101(n), 105, 117, 122, 126, 132, 144–5, 196, 204–5, 257, 336–7, 376, 404
Schlafe, mein Prinzchen, schlaf ein (song) 27
Schloss Fischhorn 165(n), 395–6
Schneider, Erwin 228–9

Schneider, Herta (née Ostermayr) 37, 50, 162, 196, 213, 228–9, 313, 401, 414–17, 425–6
Scholl, Hans 345
Scholl, Sophie 345
Schönmann, Marion 229
Schreber, Dr Daniel Gottlieb 58
Schreck, Julius 116
Schröder, Christa 230, 268–9, 318, 359, 421, 422
Schröder, Edith *see* Helps, Ditha (née Edith Schröder)
Schröder, Manfred von 136–7
Schulz, Alfons 169, 380, 412
Schwabia 17–18
Schwanensee 225
Sereny, Gitta 9(n), 10, 150, 153(n), 193–4, 318–19, 335, 347, 351, 355, 411(n)
Seydelmann, Gertrud 215
Shaw, George Bernard 216
Shirer, William 221
Silberhorn, Fräulein 229, 388
Simbach 52–4
Sklar, Pearl 354–5
Slezak, Gretl 127
Sobibor 333, 342
SOE 388, 390
Soviet-German Non-aggression Pact 296
Soviet Union
    Communist iconography 79(n)
    invasion of 309–10, 315–16, 330, 391(n)
    winter conditions 310(n)
    atrocities 360–1
    siege of Leningrad 361
    Battle of Stalingrad 361–2
Spam 426
Speer, Albert
    on the Hoffmanns 11

on Haus Wachenfeld 97
and Hitler 109
on Hitler's relationship with
    Eva 129, 154–5
on Hitler's relationship with
    women 143
at the Berghof 171
on the Berghof 185
and Hitler's vision 192–3
and Eva Braun 193, 210,
    232–3, 282–3, 312
design for Olympic Stadium 219
Nuremberg stadium 221
fidelity 226
marriage 230–1
children 231
relationship with Hitler 231–2
on power 243(n)
on dependence on Hitler 247
on Hitler's visits to the Berghof
    263–4
on Hitler 268, 350, 359
New Year's Eve 1938/9 274–5
on Eva's isolation 302
Eva confides in 311
Minister of Armaments 316
Trevor-Roper on 350
Eva's return to Berlin 404
attempt to persuade Eva to
    leave the bunker 410
leaves the bunker 422–3
final visit to the bunker 433–7
Speer, Hilde 346
Speer, Margret 192, 226, 229,
    230–1, 335, 346
Spitzy, Reinhard 307–8
SS, the 74, 215, 285
St Clair-Erskine, Mary 250
St-Rémy, Arles 208(n)
Stalin, Josef 12(n), 296, 361
Stasi (dog) 179, 241

Stauffenberg, Claus von 79(n),
    314, 390–4
Stauffenberg Plot 331(n), 390–5
Stempfle, Bernhardt 86, 116
sterilisation 42(n), 140, 216–17
Stocker, Wilhelm 115, 117
Strasser, Otto 108
Streicher, Julius 114(n)
Stuttgart 18
Struwwelpeter (Hoffmann) 32
swastika, the 78–9
Swing Jugend (Swing Youth) 343–5
symbols and iconography 78–9

T4 42(n), 288
Taylor, John 151, 313(n)
Treblinka 333, 342
Trenker, Luis 153(n)
Trevor-Roper, Hugh 232, 269, 350,
    404, 411(n)
Triumph of the Will (Film) 217,
    218–19
Trott, Adam von 390

unemployment 137
Ungerer, Tomi 74–5
*Until the Final Hour: Hitler's Last
    Secretary* (Junge) 327

Van Gogh, Vincent 208(n)
Versailles, Treaty of 35
Vienna 65–7, 287
Veit, Aloisia 85(n)
Volkswagen 234

Wachenfeld 178
Wagener, Otto 237
Wagner, Richard 94–5, 97, 443
Wagner, Walter 454–5
Wagner, Winifred 13, 97, 124, 157
Wait Training 253(n)

walking 92–3, 96
Walthierer, Max 45
Wandervögel 96
Wannsee Conference 360
Warsaw ghetto 6(n)
Weill, Kurt 75
Weisker, Gertraud xi–xii, 6(n), 7,
    12(n), 14, 15, 19, 21, 23(n), 43,
    44, 45, 47, 51, 110–11, 150,
    166–7, 177–8, 192, 291(n),
    302–4, 319, 321–2, 337–8, 343,
    355, 376–89, 395–6, 398, 417,
    464
Wessel, Horst 187
Wiedemann, Fritz 136
Wilde, Oscar 34
Wilhelm II, Kaiser 17, 35
Wilhelm Gustloff (ship) 292(n)
Williams, Lady (née Gill Gambier-
    Parry) 162–4
Winbauer, Alois 5(n), 6(n), 21,
    22–3, 37, 127, 129–30, 131–2,
    134–5, 136, 146, 177,
    198–200, 214–15, 241, 246,
    281, 282, 301, 358–9, 404–5,
    464
Winbauer, Alois (the elder) 20
Winckler, Andreas 377(n)
Windsor, Duchess of 257–8
Windsor, Duke of 257–8

Winter, Anna 12, 121, 123, 129,
    191–2, 208, 273–4
Winter, Margarethe 180
Wolf (dog) 241
Wolf, Johanna 421, 422
Wolf's Lair, the 301, 316, 371,
    392–3, 396
wolves 30–1
women
    stereotype of young 14
    attitudes towards 62, 63, 71–2
    role in Nazi Party 72–4
    lifestyle of young 75–6
    role 253, 323–4
    exclusion from politics 324
    question of guilt 324–9
    camp guards 326
    indoctrination 327
    the Rosenstrasse demonstration
        334–5
    disillusionment 401
Wrede, Princess Carmencita
    249–50, 250, 254, 294

Yates, Dora 359(n)
youth culture 343–5
Ypres, Battle of 67

Zabel, Prof. 262(n)
Ziegler, Adolf 114(n)
Zugspitze 154

EVA BRAUN FAMILY TREE

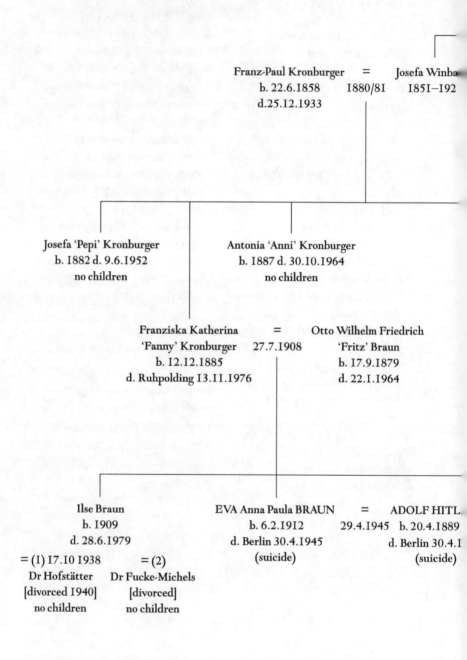

Franz-Paul Kronburger　　=　　Josefa Winba
b. 22.6.1858　　　1880/81　　1851–192
d.25.12.1933

Josefa 'Pepi' Kronburger
b. 1882 d. 9.6.1952
no children

Antonia 'Anni' Kronburger
b. 1887 d. 30.10.1964
no children

Franziska Katherina　　=　　Otto Wilhelm Friedrich
'Fanny' Kronburger　　27.7.1908　　'Fritz' Braun
b. 12.12.1885　　　　　　　b. 17.9.1879
d. Ruhpolding 13.11.1976　　　d. 22.1.1964

Ilse Braun
b. 1909
d. 28.6.1979

= (I) 17.10 1938　　　= (2)
Dr Hofstätter　　Dr Fucke-Michels
[divorced 1940]　　[divorced]
no children　　　no children

EVA Anna Paula BRAUN　　=　　ADOLF HITL.
b. 6.2.1912　　29.4.1945　　b. 20.4.1889
d. Berlin 30.4.1945　　　　　d. Berlin 30.4.1
(suicide)　　　　　　　　　(suicide)

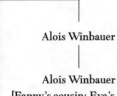

Alois Winbauer

Alois Winbauer
[Fanny's cousin; Eva's uncle]
b. 1896 d. 17.10.1983
3 children

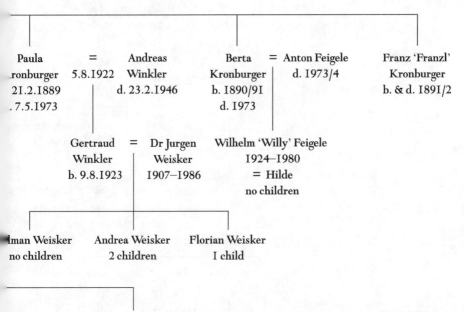

Paula   =   Andreas   Berta   = Anton Feigele   Franz 'Franzl'
ronburger   5.8.1922   Winkler   Kronburger   d. 1973/4   Kronburger
21.2.1889   d. 23.2.1946   b. 1890/91   b. & d. 1891/2
. 7.5.1973   d. 1973

              Gertraud   =   Dr Jurgen   Wilhelm 'Willy' Feigele
              Winkler   Weisker   1924–1980
              b. 9.8.1923   1907–1986   = Hilde
                                                 no children

lman Weisker   Andrea Weisker   Florian Weisker
no children   2 children   I child

              Margarethe 'Gretl' Braun
                    b. 30.8.1915
                    d. 10.10.1987

         = (I) 3.6.1944   = (2)
         Hermann Fegelein   Kurt Berlinghoff
           d. 23.4.1945   no children

              'Evi' or 'Little Eva' Fegelein
                     b. 5.5.1945
                     d. 28.6.1971
                      [suicide]

HITLER/RAUBAL FAMILY TREE

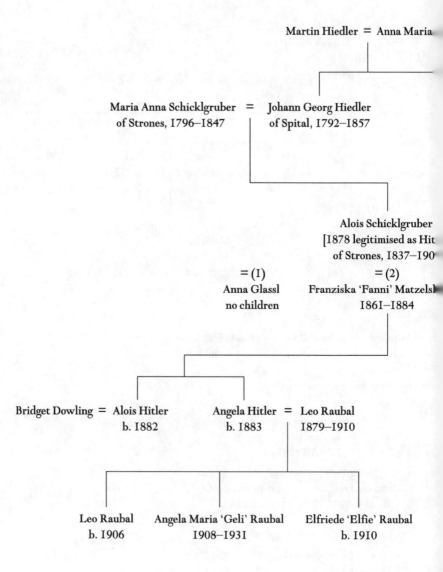

Martin Hiedler = Anna Maria

Maria Anna Schicklgruber = Johann Georg Hiedler
of Strones, 1796–1847   of Spital, 1792–1857

Alois Schicklgruber
[1878 legitimised as Hit
of Strones, 1837–190

= (I)   = (2)
Anna Glassl   Franziska 'Fanni' Matzels
no children   1861–1884

Bridget Dowling = Alois Hitler   Angela Hitler = Leo Raubal
b. 1882   b. 1883   1879–1910

Leo Raubal   Angela Maria 'Geli' Raubal   Elfriede 'Elfie' Raubal
b. 1906   1908–1931   b. 1910

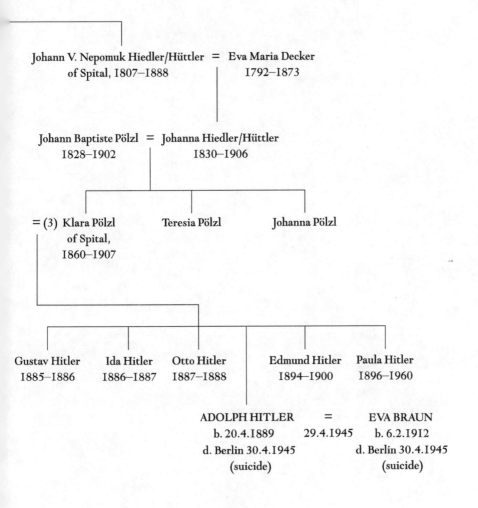

Johann V. Nepomuk Hiedler/Hüttler = Eva Maria Decker
of Spital, 1807–1888   1792–1873

Johann Baptiste Pölzl = Johanna Hiedler/Hüttler
1828–1902   1830–1906

= (3) Klara Pölzl   Teresia Pölzl   Johanna Pölzl
      of Spital,
      1860–1907

Gustav Hitler   Ida Hitler   Otto Hitler   Edmund Hitler   Paula Hitler
1885–1886   1886–1887   1887–1888   1894–1900   1896–1960

ADOLPH HITLER   =   EVA BRAUN
b. 20.4.1889   29.4.1945   b. 6.2.1912
d. Berlin 30.4.1945   d. Berlin 30.4.1945
(suicide)   (suicide)